Computer Communications and Networks

Series editor

A.J. Sammes
Centre for Forensic Computing
Cranfield University, Shrivenham Campus
Swindon, UK

The **Computer Communications and Networks** series is a range of textbooks, monographs and handbooks. It sets out to provide students, researchers, and nonspecialists alike with a sure grounding in current knowledge, together with comprehensible access to the latest developments in computer communications and networking.

Emphasis is placed on clear and explanatory styles that support a tutorial approach, so that even the most complex of topics is presented in a lucid and intelligible manner.

More information about this series at http://www.springer.com/series/4198

Sherali Zeadally · Mohamad Badra
Editors

Privacy in a Digital, Networked World

Technologies, Implications and Solutions

Editors
Sherali Zeadally
University of Kentucky
Lexington, KY
USA

Mohamad Badra
Zayed University
Dubai
United Arab Emirates

ISSN 1617-7975   ISSN 2197-8433 (electronic)
Computer Communications and Networks
ISBN 978-3-319-35631-0   ISBN 978-3-319-08470-1 (eBook)
DOI 10.1007/978-3-319-08470-1

Springer Cham Heidelberg New York Dordrecht London
© Springer International Publishing Switzerland 2015
Softcover re-print of the Hardcover 1st edition 2015

Printed on acid-free paper

Springer International Publishing AG Switzerland is part of Springer Science+Business Media
(www.springer.com)

To my wife Borrara and my daughters
Zobia and Zofia
                                    —Sherali Zeadally

To my wife Rouba and my parents
                                    —Mohamad Badra

Contents

List of Reviewers

Each chapter in this book has received at least three reviews during the peer-review process. We thank the following list of reviewers for their hard work and support in providing timely feedback.

Habtamu Abie, Norwegian Computing Center, Norway
Carlisle Adams, University of Ottawa, Canada
Hossam Afifi, Institut Telecom, France
Claudio Ardagna, Università degli Studi di Milano, Italy
Man Ho Au, The Hong Kong Polytechnic University, Hong Kong
Dorsaf Azzabi, Canadian University of Dubai, UAE
Ahmed Badi, Florida Atlantic University, USA
Elyes Ben Hamida, Qatar Mobility Innovations Center (QMIC), Qatar
Michael Brenner, Leibniz Universität Hannover, Germany
Tat Wing Chim, The University of Hong Kong, Hong Kong
Isabelle Chrisment, LORIA-TELECOM Nancy Université de Lorraine, France
Prokopios Drogkaris, University of the Aegean, Greece
Bertrand Du Castel, SLB, USA
Maurizio Dusi, NEC Laboratories Europe, Germany
Atilla Elçi, Aksaray University, Turkey
Ahmad Fadlallah, Arab Open University, Lebanon
Eduardo Fernandez, Florida Atlantic University, USA
Kanwalinderjit Gagneja, Southern Oregon University, USA
Sebastien Gambs, Universite de Rennes INRIA, France
Alexandre Guitton, Clermont University, France
Jun He, University of New Brunswick, Canada
Benoit Hudzia, SAP Research, UK
Nafaa Jabeur, German University of Technology in Oman GUtech, Oman
Zhanlin Ji, University of Limerick, Ireland
Bo Jiang, Intel, USA
Achilles Kameas, Hellenic Open University, Greece
Stamatis Karnouskos, SAP Research, Germany

Sokratis Katsikas, University of Piraeus, Greece
Rida Khatoun, Telecom ParisTech, France
Sherif Khattab, Cairo University, Egypt
Marek Klonowski, TU Wrocław, Poland
Jerzy Konorski, Gdańsk University of Technology, Poland
Stefan Köpsell, TU Dresden, Germany
Hristo Koshutanski, University of Malaga, Spain
Romain Laborde, Université Paul Sabatier, France
Maryline Laurent, Institut Mines-Télécom Télécom SudParis, France
Vijay Laxmi, Malaviya National Institute of Technology, Jaipur, India
Albert Levi, Sabanci University, Turkey
Bisheng Liu, University of Waterloo, Canada
Luigi Logrippo, Université du Québec en Outaouais, Canada
Gregorio Martinez Perez, University of Murcia, Spain
Azzam Mourad, Lebanese American University (LAU), Lebanon
Hassnaa Moustafa, Intel, USA
Al-Sakib Khan, Pathan International Islamic University, Malaysia (IIUM),
Malaysia
Jonathan Petit, University College Cork, Ireland
Stefan Rass, Alpen-Adria Universitaet Klagenfurt, Austria
Ricardo Rodriguez, Technologic University of Ciudad, Juarez, Mexico
Nabil Sahli, GUTech, Oman
Abed Ellatif Samhat, Lebanese University, Lebanon
Altair Santin, Pontifical Catholic University of Parana (PUCPR), Brazil
Zhefu Shi, University of Missouri—Kansas City, USA
Nicolas Sklavos, University of Patras, Greece
Piotr Syga, Wrocław University of Technology, Poland
Juan Pablo, Timpanaro Universite de Lorraine, France
Artemios Voyiatzis, SBA Research, Austria
Alexander Wiesmaier, AGT International, Germany
Alexander Wijesinha, Towson University, USA
Yanjiang Yang, Institute for Infocomm Research, Singapore
Marcin Zawada, Wrocław University of Technology, Poland

Chapter 1
Introduction

Sherali Zeadally and Mohamad Badra

1.1 Overview

Over the last decade, we have witnessed a growing interest and increasing investments in technologies, applications, and system communications around the world. Almost every component in our entourage is being completely networked. With so much sensitive data being generated in the digital world, security and privacy continue to be seen as impediments refraining users from widely using these recent technologies and applications. While privacy is relatively easy to manage within simple client/server architecture, it becomes a significant challenge to ensure privacy in the era of Big Data, cloud computing, and smart applications.

Privacy in a Digital, Networked World—Technologies, Implications and Solutions presents state-of-the-art research results from recognized experts on technical, legal, and ethical privacy issues in various technological areas and emerging paradigms. We expect this book to be a valuable, authoritative reference for students, educators, faculty members, researchers, and engineers currently working or interested in the area of privacy spanning various areas including smart cities, smart grids, Big Data, databases, social networks, healthcare, and so on.

S. Zeadally (✉)
University of Kentucky, Lexington, USA
e-mail: szeadally@uky.edu

M. Badra
Zayed University, Dubai, United Arab Emirates
e-mail: mohamad.badra@zu.ac.ae

© Springer International Publishing Switzerland 2015
S. Zeadally and M. Badra (eds.), *Privacy in a Digital, Networked World*,
Computer Communications and Networks,
DOI 10.1007/978-3-319-08470-1_1

1.2 Database Privacy

Chapter 2 on database privacy presents several privacy techniques (such as statistical disclosure control (SDC) methods, anonymization methods, or sanitization methods) that can be applied to databases. The authors present an overview of the issues in database privacy, a survey of the best-known SDC methods, a discussion on the related data privacy/utility trade-offs and a description of privacy models proposed by the computer science community in recent years. Some relevant freeware packages are also identified. A priori and a posteriori approaches to disclosure control in database privacy sanitization have been reviewed. This chapter looks at sanitization methods, which are common to both approaches, through the discussions on tabular data, queryable databases, and microdata, with a special focus on the latter. Finally, research challenges and opportunities have been identified in the area of statistical disclosure control.

1.3 Privacy and Big Data

Chapter 3 presents a brief review of Big Data technologies, describes the benefits, and outlines how Big Data has come to harm privacy in subtle new forms. The chapter investigates privacy issues that have come up due to technological advancements leading to mostly huge amounts of personal data being stored and communicated. The chapter then reviews the legal and technological issues and describes some possible solutions. It further discusses many open research problems and challenges related to privacy and Big Data. Moreover, this chapter also covers technology, law, and ethics aspects of Big Data analytics from a non-technical perspective.

1.4 Privacy in Crowdsourced Platforms

An overview of privacy in crowdsourcing platforms is given in Chap. 4, with a focus on platforms (such as the Amazon Mechanical Turk (AMT) platform) that specifically deal with the collection and aggregation of information. This chapter emphasizes the privacy risks in online systems and discusses how these risks apply to crowdsourcing platforms, focusing on the potential for exposing Personally Identifiable Information (PII). These risks are illustrated with an example of a real world attack conducted through a series of survey tasks in AMT. In addition, the chapter provides an overview of solutions that can provide privacy protection in online services in general, and identifies those that could also be applied to crowdsourcing platforms. Furthermore, the chapter includes a specific proposal for a privacy-preserving crowdsourcing platform that relies on obfuscation, and describes the design choices surrounding obfuscation techniques, privacy levels, privacy loss quantification, privacy depletion, cost settings, and utility estimation of workers in crowdsourcing platforms. The chapter describes the implementation details for a prototype of the system and summarizes the challenges that still need to be addressed to enhance the privacy of workers in crowdsourcing platforms.

1.5 Privacy in Healthcare

Privacy of healthcare records has been a major concern for a very long time now. Various legislations have been put in place to ensure the privacy of patients. Chapter 5 discusses a few electronic healthcare systems that can be classified into a variety of systems with their own features and faults. The chapter also presents several privacy concerns related to the storage and transmission of health information, the use of mobile devices and social media, and the use of cloud storage systems in healthcare. Moreover, the chapter discusses the privacy challenges that exist in all of the electronic health systems and solutions to address these challenges in those systems. Finally, the chapter highlights future privacy challenges and opportunities related to the development and deployment of electronic health systems.

1.6 Privacy in Peer-to-Peer Networks

Peer-to-peer (P2P) networks are designed to take advantage of dispersed network resources and enable participants to act as servers or clients; their main characteristics include the direct sharing of resources among users, their self-organization, stability, and autonomy. As with other systems, privacy is a major concern in P2P networks. Chapter 6 on privacy in P2P networks starts with an introduction to P2P networks, their classification, and their characteristics. After presenting a brief overview of P2P networks, the chapter identifies and analyzes the existing privacy issues when using P2P networks and the current privacy solutions that can be used. These solutions include anonymous systems, routing modifications, protection of contents when stored and during transmission, private and split credentials, hidden services, and application configuration and hardening. The chapter further explores the challenges that must be addressed in the future. It also discusses future research directions.

1.7 Privacy in the Cloud

Cloud computing technologies are being deployed and used by many businesses, governments, and organizations and are becoming increasingly popular as they offer access to a wide range of infrastructure resources, very convenient pay-as-you-go service, and low cost computing and storage. However, the advantages of clouds come with increased security and privacy risks. Chapter 7 discusses the need for privacy protection and the confidentiality of data and applications outsourced to the cloud. The authors present an overview of multi-tenancy and other inherent properties of the cloud computing model, as well as the novel attack surfaces and threats to cloud users' privacy. The chapter also discusses existing approaches for protecting privacy, and analyzes the pros and cons of these solutions. Finally, it outlines a list of open problems and issues which need to be further investigated and addressed by researchers in the future.

1.8   Privacy in Vehicular Ad Hoc Networks

Chapter 8 discusses various privacy issues in vehicular ad hoc networks (VANETs). The chapter starts by presenting VANET as a new and promising technology that can enhance road safety and provide the foundation for many possible added value applications and services. The chapter then investigates the various security and privacy concerns associated with this technology. The authors present several approaches aimed at protecting user and vehicle privacy in VANET communications and also include a discussion of current solutions and their limitations. Finally, the chapter discusses a broad range of critical security and privacy challenges currently present in VANETs which should be investigated in future research works.

1.9   Privacy Law and Regulation

Chapter 9 deals with the regulation of personal information disclosure and the privacy of individuals. It provides an overview of the laws and regulations used to regulate privacy in the digital age. This chapter examines the current state of US laws that have a direct or indirect impact on the privacy of individuals. The authors of this chapter consider government surveillance and both the laws that allow it and those aimed at placing restraints on law enforcement activities. This is followed by an analysis of privacy regulation in the European Union. The chapter concludes by examining opportunities for change with respect to privacy laws and regulations.

1.10   Privacy in Mobile Devices

The ubiquitous use of mobile devices for personal communications, and subsequently for almost all types of data transactions, has introduced the next level of privacy problems. Chapter 10 includes a review of on-going efforts aimed at retaining the privacy of users constantly interacting with mobile devices for most of their daily activities. It presents an overview of mobile devices and their related technologies. It also highlights the privacy issues associated with the use of a mobile device and discusses the type of personal data that may be collected by a mobile application and the methods by which this data may leak to third parties that are not directly authorized by the user. The chapter discusses the solutions that can be deployed to mitigate mobile device privacy concerns. Finally, the chapter ends with a discussion on the challenges we currently face in making a mobile device a more privacy-aware sensitive platform.

1.11 Privacy with Biometrics

Chapter 11 discusses the topic of privacy in biometric systems. Biometrics can be a very effective tool to keep us safe and secure, prevent individuals from applying for multiple passports or diving licenses, and keep the bad guys out or under control. However, the fact that we are surrounded by so many biometric sensors does limit our privacy in one way or another. This chapter is mainly concerned with privacy issues and solutions surrounding the use of biometrics for recognizing individuals. It provides an adequate background on biometrics and discusses several privacy concerns and solutions about biometrics. The chapter ends with a discussion of some of the outstanding challenges and opportunities in the area of privacy with biometrics.

1.12 Privacy in Social Networks

Social networks such as Facebook and LinkedIn have gained a lot of popularity in recent years. These networks use a large amount of data that are highly valuable for different purposes. Hence, social networks become a potential vector for attackers to exploit. Chapter 12 focuses on the security attacks and countermeasures used by social networks. Privacy issues and solutions in social networks are discussed and the chapter ends with an outline of some of the privacy challenges in the social networks.

1.13 The Right to Privacy in the Age of Digital Technology

Chapter 13 reviews some of the privacy issues that have arisen as a result of the emergence and proliferation of digital information networks. It presents a brief overview of the threats posed to personal privacy, especially for vulnerable groups such as the consumer or users of social media to better understand the nature and scope of the challenges presented by evolving information technologies such as social networking platforms. The author then analyzes several theories of privacy and justifications for privacy, the right to privacy, and how to protect this right. The chapter concludes by describing both the law and technological tools to secure the privacy rights.

1.14   How to Explore Consumers' Privacy Choices with Behavioral Economics

Chapter 14 describes the tools and the evidence to better understand consumers' privacy behaviors. The tools discussed will be useful to researchers, practitioners, and policy makers in the area of consumer privacy. The author presents interesting results about surveying/testing privacy-related behavior of individuals during electronic communications with a particular focus on e-services. The chapter also outlines the principles of conducting empirical research on consumers' privacy consumption behaviors. Explanation is given as to why experiments rather than surveys or hypothetical choices are needed for delivering valid insights to decision makers. After reviewing the existing empirical evidence about the importance that consumers attach to their privacy, the chapter explains the methodological requirements of valid privacy experiments and offers practical advice for conducting privacy choice experiments. This chapter provides a good insight into privacy-enhancing solutions and policies that meet consumers' needs.

1.15   Techniques, Taxonomy, and Challenges of Privacy Protection in Smart Grid

The deployment of Smart Grid technologies has also raised considerable concerns in data privacy issues of Smart Grid users. Privacy concerns in the Smart Grid environment are mostly related to the collection and use of energy consumption data of Smart Grid users. In this context, Chapter 15 discusses various Smart Grid privacy issues and presents Smart Grid privacy protection architectures and approaches. The authors provide a unique taxonomy of the different privacy protection mechanisms that have been recently proposed in the literature. Various strengths and weaknesses of these privacy solutions are also identified. Finally, the chapter discusses some outstanding challenges that need to be addressed to provide robust and scalable privacy protection solutions to Smart Grid users.

1.16 Location-Based Privacy, Protection, Safety, and Security

One of the major benefits of location-based services (LBS) is their ability to maintain safety and security. But LBS can also result in risks such as the use of LBS for cyber stalking others. To establish the need for LBS regulation, we need to understand that there will always be a trade-off between LBS's benefits and the risks associated with their implementation and adoption. Chapter 16 examines privacy and security issues with respect to LBS and recognizes the need for technological solutions, in addition to commitments and adequate assessments/considerations at the social and regulatory levels. The authors discuss various solutions that have been recently proposed in the area of location-based privacy and identify the various strengths and weaknesses of these solutions. The chapter concludes with a list of interesting challenges relevant to privacy in LBS and the need for further investigation on issues associated with mobility and location technologies.

We hope you will enjoy reading this book as much as we did!

Chapter 2
Database Privacy

Josep Domingo-Ferrer, David Sánchez and Sara Hajian

2.1 Introduction

There is a growing social and economic demand for open data to improve planning, scientific research, market research, and so on. In particular, the public sector is under pressure to release as much information as it can in the name of transparency. Organizations releasing data include national statistical institutes, healthcare authorities (epidemiology), or even private organizations (e.g., consumer surveys).

When published data refer to individual respondents, care must be taken that the privacy of the latter is not violated. It should be de facto impossible to relate the published data to specific individuals. Indeed, supplying data to national statistical institutes is compulsory in most countries but, in return, those institutes commit to preserving the privacy of respondents. Hence, rather than publishing exactly accurate information for each individual, the aim should be to provide useful *statistical* information, that is, to preserve as much as possible in the released data the statistical properties of the original data. This is why privacy-preserving databases on individuals are called *statistical databases*.

Statistical databases come in three main formats:

1. **Tabular data**. That is, tables with counts or magnitudes, which are the classical output of official statistics.

J. Domingo-Ferrer (✉) · D. Sánchez · S. Hajian
Department of Computer Engineering and Mathematics, Universitat Rovira i Virgili,
UNESCO Chair in Data Privacy, Av. Països Catalans 26, 43007 Tarragona,
Catalonia, Spain
e-mail: josep.domingo@urv.cat

D. Sánchez
e-mail: david.sanchez@urv.cat

S. Hajian
e-mail: sara.hajian@urv.cat

© Springer International Publishing Switzerland 2015
S. Zeadally and M. Badra (eds.), *Privacy in a Digital, Networked World*,
Computer Communications and Networks,
DOI 10.1007/978-3-319-08470-1_2

9

2. **Queryable databases**. That is, on-line databases to which the user can submit statistical queries (sums, averages, etc.).
3. **Microdata**. That is, files where each record contains information on an individual (a citizen or a company).

Inference control in statistical databases, also known as *Statistical Disclosure Control (SDC), Statistical Disclosure Limitation (SDL), database anonymization* or *database sanitization*, is a discipline that seeks to protect data in statistical databases so that they can be published without revealing confidential information that can be linked to specific individuals among those to whom the data correspond. SDC is applied to protect *respondent privacy* in areas such as official statistics, health statistics, e-commerce (sharing of consumer data), etc. Since data protection ultimately means data modification, the challenge for SDC is to achieve protection with minimum loss of the accuracy sought by database users.

In [16], a distinction is made between SDC and other technologies for database privacy, like privacy-preserving data mining (PPDM) or private information retrieval (PIR): what makes the difference between those technologies is whose privacy they seek. While SDC is aimed at respondent privacy, the primary goal of PPDM is to protect owner privacy when several database owners wish to co-operate in joint analyses across their databases without giving away their original data to each other. On its side, the primary goal of PIR is user privacy, that is, to allow the user of a database to retrieve some information item without the database exactly knowing which item was recovered.

The literature on SDC started in the 1970s, with the seminal contribution by Dalenius [12] in the statistical community and the works by Schlörer and Denning [14, 62] in the database community. The 1980s saw moderate activity in this field. An excellent survey of the state of the art at the end of the 1980s is [1]. In the 1990s, there was renewed interest in the statistical community and the discipline was further developed under the names of statistical disclosure control in Europe and statistical disclosure limitation in America. Towards the turn of the century, with the flourish of data mining, there was renewed activity in the database community, where the field was called data anonymization or data sanitization and was often confused with privacy-preserving data mining. Subsequent evolution has resulted in at least three clearly differentiated subdisciplines:

- **Tabular data protection**. The goal here is to publish *static* aggregate information, that is, tables, in such a way that no confidential information on specific individuals among those to whom the table refers can be inferred. See [72] for a conceptual survey.
- **Queryable databases**. The aggregate information obtained by a user as a result of successive queries should not allow him or her to infer information on specific individuals. Since the late 1970s, this has been known to be a difficult problem, subject to the tracker attack [14, 63]. SDC strategies here include perturbation, query restriction, and camouflage (providing interval answers rather than exact answers).

- **Microdata protection**. It is only recently that data collectors (statistical agencies and the like) have been persuaded to publish microdata. Therefore, microdata protection is the youngest subdiscipline and is experiencing continuous evolution in the last years. Its purpose is to mask the original microdata so that the masked microdata are still analytically useful but cannot be linked to the original respondents.

The rest of this chapter is organized as follows. Section 2.2 introduces the basic concepts used throughout the chapter. In Sect. 2.3, we detail algorithms and mechanisms for sanitizing (i.e., anonymizing) the records in a database. These algorithms seek to output a sanitized version of data that satisfies a privacy definition (prevents disclosure risks) and has high utility. Section 2.4 is devoted to ways of measuring disclosure risk and the utility of sanitized data while the formal definitions of privacy models are presented in Sect. 2.5. Section 2.6 explores outstanding challenges that must be addressed in the future and opportunities for new research directions. The final section concludes the chapter and lists relevant software.

2.2   Background

In this section, we introduce some basic definitions and concepts that are used throughout this chapter related to data formats (Sect. 2.1) and sanitization of each format (Sect. 2.2).

2.2.1   Formal Definition of Data Formats

A *microdata* file $\mathbf{X}$ with s respondents and t attributes is an $s \times t$ matrix where X_{ij} is the value of attribute j for respondent i. Attributes can be numerical (e.g., age, salary) or categorical (e.g., gender, job). The attributes in a microdata set can be classified in four categories that are not necessarily disjoint:

- **Identifiers**. These are attributes that *unambiguously* identify the respondent. Examples are the passport number, social security number, name-surname, and so on.
- **Quasi-identifiers or key attributes**. These are attributes that identify the respondent with some degree of ambiguity. (Nonetheless, a combination of key attributes may provide unambiguous identification.) Examples are address, gender, age, telephone number, and so on.
- **Confidential (a.k.a. sensitive) attributes**. These are attributes which contain sensitive information on the respondent. Examples are salary, religion, political affiliation, health condition, and so on.
- **Non-confidential (a.k.a. non-sensitive) attributes**. Other attributes which contain non-sensitive information on the respondent.

From microdata, *tabular data* can be generated by crossing one or more categorical attributes. Formally, a table is a function

$$T : D(X_{i1}) \times D(X_{i2}) \times \cdots \times D(X_{il}) \to \mathbb{R} \text{ or } \mathbb{N}$$

where $l \leq t$ is the number of crossed categorical attributes and $D(X_{ij})$ is the domain where attribute X_{ij} takes its values.

There are two kinds of tables: *frequency tables* that display the count of respondents at the crossing of the categorical attributes (in $\mathbb{N}$) and *magnitude tables* that display information on a numerical attribute at the crossing of the categorical attributes (in $\mathbb{R}$). For example, given some census microdata containing attributes "Job" and "Town", one can generate a *frequency table* displaying the count of respondents doing each job type in each town. If the census microdata also contain the "Salary" attribute, one can generate a magnitude table displaying the average salary for each job type in each town. The number n of cells in a table is normally much less than the number s of respondent records in a microdata file. However, tables must satisfy several linear constraints: marginal row and column totals. Additionally, a set of tables is called *linked* if they share some of the crossed categorical attributes: for example "Job" × "Town" is linked to "Job" × "Gender".

2.2.2 Basic Sanitization Concepts

We will review sanitization/anonymization concepts used for each data format: tabular data, queryable databases, and microdata.

2.2.2.1 Sanitization of Tabular Data

In spite of tables displaying aggregate information, there is risk of disclosure in tabular data release. Several attacks are conceivable:

- **External attack.** For example, let a frequency table "Job" × "Town" be released where there is a single respondent for job J_i and town T_j. Then if a magnitude table is released with the average salary for each job type and each town, the exact salary of the only respondent with job J_i working in town T_j is publicly disclosed.
- **Internal attack.** Even if there are two respondents for job J_i and town T_j, the salary of each of them is disclosed to each other.
- **Dominance attack.** If one (or a few) respondents dominate in the contribution to a cell of a magnitude table, the dominant respondent(s) can upper-bound the contributions of the rest (e.g., if the table displays the total salary for each job type and town and one individual contributes 90 % of that salary, the dominant respondent knows that his or her colleagues in the town are not doing very well).

Sanitization methods for tables fall into two classes: non-perturbative and perturbative. *Non-perturbative methods* do not modify the values in the tables; the best known method in this class is *cell suppression* (CS). *Perturbative methods* output a table with some modified values; well-known methods in this class include *controlled rounding* (CR) and the recent *controlled tabular adjustment* (CTA).

2.2.2.2 Sanitization of Queryable Databases

In SDC of queryable databases, there are three main approaches to protect a confidential vector of numerical data from disclosure through answers to user queries:

- **Data perturbation**. Perturbing the data is a simple and effective approach whenever the users do not require deterministically correct answers to queries that are functions of the confidential vector. Perturbation can be applied to the records on which queries are computed (input perturbation) or to the query result after computing it on the original data (output perturbation). Perturbation methods can be found in [24, 55, 71].
- **Query restriction**. This is the right approach if the user does require deterministically correct answers and these answers have to be exact (i.e., a number). Since exact answers to queries provide the user with very powerful information, it may become necessary to refuse to answer certain queries at some stage to avoid disclosure of a confidential datum. There are several criteria to decide whether a query can be answered; one of them is query set size control, that is, to refuse answers to queries which affect a set of records which is too small. An example of the query restriction approach can be found in [11].
- **Camouflage**. If deterministically correct non-exact answers (i.e., small interval answers) suffice, confidentiality via camouflage (CVC, [30]) is a good option. With this approach, unlimited answers to any conceivable query types are allowed. The idea of CVC is to "camouflage" the confidential vector a by making it part of the relative interior of a compact set Π of vectors. Then each query $q = f(a)$ is answered with an inverval $[q^-, q^+]$ containing $[f^-, f^+]$, where f^- and f^+ are, respectively, the minimum and the maximum of f over Π.

2.2.2.3 Sanitization of Microdata

Microdata protection methods can generate the protected microdata set $\mathbf{X}'$ either by *masking original data*, i.e., generating $\mathbf{X}'$ a modified version of the original microdata set $\mathbf{X}'$, or by *generating synthetic data* $\mathbf{X}'$ that preserve some statistical properties of the original data $\mathbf{X}$.

Masking methods can in turn be divided in two categories depending on their effect on the original data [72]:

- **Perturbative**. The microdata set is distorted before publication. In this way, unique combinations of scores in the original data set may disappear and new unique combinations may appear in the perturbed data set; such confusion is beneficial for preserving statistical confidentiality. The perturbation method used should be such that statistics computed on the perturbed data set do not differ significantly from the statistics that would be obtained on the original data set. *Noise addition, microaggregation, data/rank swapping, microdata rounding, resampling and PRAM* are examples of perturbative masking methods (see the next Section and [42] for details).
- **Non-perturbative**. Non-perturbative methods do not alter data; rather, they produce partial suppressions or reductions of detail in the original data set. Sampling, global recoding, top and bottom coding, and local suppression are examples of non-perturbative masking methods.

2.3 Database Sanitization Methods

Data publishing organizations usually face a fundamental trade-off between privacy and utility.

The two extreme policies are the following:

- To release no data in order to maintain total privacy.
- To release original data without any modification to maximize data utility, without regard to privacy protection.

In this section, we detail methods based on the concepts introduced in Sect. 2.2 that offer good trade-offs between the two above extreme policies. We focus on *microdata sanitization methods*, because microdata are the most detailed type of data. In fact, based on protected microdata, one can also obtain protected tables and protected query answers: just build tables and compute query answers based on the protected microdata records.

Each sanitization method consists of an algorithm instantiating in a specific way a generic sanitization mechanism. We first discuss methods based on deterministic sanitization mechanisms, and then methods based on randomized sanitization mechanisms.

2.3.1 Deterministic Sanitization Mechanisms

2.3.1.1 Microaggregation

Microaggregation is a family of SDC techniques for continous microdata. The rationale behind microaggregation is that confidentiality rules in use allow publication of microdata sets if records correspond to groups of k or more individuals, where no individual dominates (i.e., contributes too much to) the group and k is a threshold value. Strict application of such confidentiality rules leads to replacing individual values with values computed on small aggregates (microaggregates) prior to publication. This is the basic principle of microaggregation.

To obtain microaggregates in a microdata set with n records, these are combined to form g groups of size at least k. For each attribute, the average value over each group is computed and is used to replace each of the original averaged values. Groups are formed using a criterion of maximal similarity. Once the procedure has been completed, the resulting (modified) records can be published.

The optimal k-partition (from the information loss point of view) is defined to be the one that maximizes within-group homogeneity; the higher the within-group homogeneity, the lower the information loss, since microaggregation replaces values in a group by the group centroid. The sum of squares criterion is common to measure homogeneity in clustering. The within-groups sum of squares SSE is defined as

$$SSE = \sum_{i=1}^{g} \sum_{j=1}^{n_i} (x_{ij} - \bar{x}_i)'(x_{ij} - \bar{x}_i)$$

where x_{ij} indicates the microaggregated version of the attribute value. The lower SSE, the higher the within group homogeneity. Thus, in terms of sums of squares, the optimal k-partition is the one that minimizes SSE.

Given a microdata set consisting of p attributes, these can be microaggregated together or partitioned into several groups of attributes. Also the way to form groups may vary. Several taxonomies are possible to classify the microaggregation algorithms in the literature: (i) fixed group size [13, 21, 40] vs variable group size [19, 44]; (ii) exact optimal (only for the univariate case, [37]) vs heuristic micro-aggregation (the rest of the microaggregation literature); (iii) categorical [21] vs continuous (the rest of references cited in this paragraph).

To illustrate, we next give a heuristic algorithm called MDAV (Maximum Distance to Average Vector [18, 21]) for multivariate fixed group size microag-gregation on unprojected continuous data. We designed and implemented MDAV for the μ-Argus package [40]. In the algorithm below we assume $n \geq k$.

1. Compute the average record $\bar{x}$ of all records in the data set. Consider the most distant record x_r to the average record $\bar{x}$ (using the squared Euclidean distance).
2. Find the most distant record x_s from the record x_r considered in the previous step.
3. Form two groups around x_r and x_s, respectively. One group contains x_r and the $k-1$ records closest to x_r. The other group contains x_s and the $k-1$ records closest to x_s.
4. If there are at least $3k$ records which do not belong to any of the two groups formed in Step 3, go to Step 1 taking as new data set the previous data set minus the groups formed in the last instance of Step 3.

5. If there are between $3k - 1$ and $2k$ records which do not belong to any of the two groups formed in Step 3: (a) compute the average record $\bar{x}$ of the remaining records; (b) find the most distant record x_r from $\bar{x}$; (c) form a group containing x_r and the $k - 1$ records closest to x_r; (d) form another group containing the rest of records. Exit the algorithm.
6. If there are less than $2k$ records which do not belong to the groups formed in Step 3, form a new group with those records and exit the Algorithm.

The above algorithm can be applied independently to each group of attributes resulting from partitioning the set of attributes in the data set.

2.3.1.2 Bucketization

Like microaggregation, bucketization (also known as Anatomy, [75]) partitions the input data into non-overlapping buckets. However, rather than summarizing records in each bucket into one average record, the bucketization approach simply breaks the connection between quasi-identifier and confidential attributes. The bucketization mechanism produces a sanitized data set by first partitioning the original data set into non-overlapping groups (or buckets) and then, for each group, releasing its projection on the quasi-identifier attributes and also its projection on the confidential attributes. The idea is that, after bucketization, the confidential attribute values of an individual are indistinguishable from those of any other individual in the same bucket.

2.3.1.3 Data Swapping and Rank Swapping

Data swapping was originally presented as a perturbative SDC method for databases containing only categorical attributes. The basic idea behind the method is to transform a database by exchanging values of confidential attributes among individual records. Records are exchanged in such a way that low-order frequency counts or marginals are maintained.

Even though the original procedure was not very used in practice, its basic idea had a clear influence in subsequent methods. A variant of data swapping for microdata is *rank swapping*, which will be described next in some detail. Although originally described only for ordinal attributes [32], rank swapping can also be used for any numerical attribute. First, values of an attribute X_i are ranked in ascending order, then each ranked value of X_i is swapped with another ranked value randomly chosen within a restricted range (e.g., the rank of two swapped values cannot differ by more than $p\%$ of the total number of records, where p is an input parameter). This algorithm is independently used on each original attribute in the original data set. It is reasonable to expect that multivariate statistics computed from data swapped with this algorithm will be less distorted than those computed after an unconstrained swap.

2.3.1.4 Global Recoding

This is a non-perturbative masking method, also known sometimes as generalization. For a categorical attribute X_i, several categories are combined to form new (less specific) categories, thus resulting in a new X_i' with $|D(X_i')| < |D(X_i)|$ where $|\cdot|$ is the cardinality operator. For a continuous attribute, global recoding means replacing X_i by another attribute X_i' which is a discretized version of X_i. In other words, a potentially infinite range $D(X_i)$ is mapped onto a finite range $D(X_i')$. This is the technique used in the μ-Argus SDC package [40]. This technique is more appropriate for categorical microdata, where it helps disguise records with strange combinations of categorical attributes. Global recoding is used heavily by statistical offices.

Example. If there is a record with "Marital status = Widow/er" and "Age = 17", global recoding could be applied to "Marital status" to create a broader category "Widow/er or divorced", so that the probability of the above record being unique would diminish.

Global recoding can also be used on a continuous attribute, but the inherent discretization leads very often to an unaffordable loss of information. Also, arithmetical operations that were straightforward on the original X_i are no longer easy or intuitive on the discretized X_i'.

2.3.1.5 Top and Bottom Coding

Top and bottom coding are special cases of global recoding which can be used on attributes that can be ranked, that is, continuous or categorical ordinal. The idea is that top values (those above a certain threshold) are lumped together to form a new category. The same is done for bottom values (those below a certain threshold). See [40].

2.3.1.6 Local Suppression

This is a non-perturbative masking method in which certain values of individual attributes are suppressed with the aim of increasing the set of records agreeing on a combination of key values. Ways to combine local suppression and global recoding are implemented in the μ-Argus SDC package [40].

If a continuous attribute X_i is part of a set of key attributes, then each combination of key values is probably unique. Since it does not make sense to systematically suppress the values of X_i, we conclude that local suppression is rather oriented to categorical attributes.

2.3.2 Randomized Sanitization Mechanisms

2.3.2.1 Additive Noise

Additive noise is a family of perturbative masking methods. The noise addition algorithms in the literature are:

- **Masking by uncorrelated noise addition**. The vector of observations x_j for the j-th attribute of the original data set X_j is replaced by a vector

$$z_j = x_j + \varepsilon_j$$

  where ε_j is a vector of normally distributed errors drawn from a random variable $\varepsilon_j \sim N(0, \sigma_{\varepsilon_j}^2)$, such that $Cov(\varepsilon_t, \varepsilon_l) = 0$ for all $t \neq l$. This does neither preserve variances nor correlations.
- **Masking by correlated noise addition**. Correlated noise addition also preserves means and additionally allows preservation of correlation coefficients. The difference with the previous method is that the covariance matrix of the errors is now proportional to the covariance matrix of the original data, i.e., $\varepsilon \sim N(0, \Sigma_\varepsilon)$, where $\Sigma_\varepsilon = \alpha \Sigma$ with Σ being the covariance matrix of the original data.
- **Masking by noise addition and linear transformation**. In [43], a method is proposed that ensures by additional transformations that the sample covariance matrix of the masked attributes is an unbiased estimator for the covariance matrix of the original attributes.
- **Masking by noise addition and nonlinear transformation**. Combining simple additive noise and nonlinear transformation has also been proposed, in such a way that application to discrete attributes is possible and univariate distributions are preserved. Unfortunately, the application of this method is very time-consuming and requires expert knowledge on the data set and the algorithm. See [42] for more details.

2.3.2.2 PRAM

The Post-RAndomization Method (PRAM, [31]) is a probabilistic, perturbative method for disclosure protection of categorical attributes in microdata files. In the masked file, the scores on some categorical attributes for certain records in the original file are changed to a different score according to a prescribed probability mechanism, namely a Markov matrix called the PRAM matrix. The Markov approach makes PRAM very general, because it encompasses noise addition, data suppression, and data recoding. Since the PRAM matrix must contain a row for each possible value of each attribute to be protected, PRAM cannot be used for continuous data.

2.3.2.3 Sampling

This is a non-perturbative masking method. Instead of publishing the original microdata file, what is published is a sample S of the original set of records [72]. Sampling methods are suitable for categorical microdata, but for continuous microdata they should probably be combined with other masking methods. The reason is that sampling alone leaves a continuous attribute X_i unperturbed for all records in S. Thus, if attribute X_i is present in an external administrative public file, unique matches with the published sample are very likely: indeed, given a continuous attribute X_i and two respondents o_1 and o_2, it is highly unlikely that X_i will take the same value for both o_1 and o_2 unless $o_1 = o_2$ (this is true even if X_i has been truncated to represent it digitally). If, for a continuous identifying attribute, the score of a respondent is only approximately known by an attacker, it might still make sense to use sampling methods to protect that attribute. However, assumptions on restricted attacker resources are perilous and may prove definitely too optimistic if good quality external administrative files are at hand.

2.3.2.4 Synthetic Microdata Generation

Publication of synthetic, that is, simulated data was proposed long ago as a way to guard against statistical disclosure. The idea is to randomly generate data with the constraint that certain statistics or internal relationships of the original data set should be preserved. More than 20 years ago, Rubin suggested in [57] to create an entirely synthetic data set based on the original survey data and multiple imputation. A simulation study of this approach was given in [56].

Synthetic data are appealing in that, at a first glance, they seem to circumvent the re-identification problem: since published records are invented and do not derive from any original record, it might be concluded that no individual can complain of having been re-identified. At a closer look this advantage is less clear. If, by chance, a published synthetic record matches a particular citizen's non-confidential attributes (age, marital status, place of residence, etc.) and confidential attributes (salary, mortgage, etc.), re-identification using the non-confidential attributes is easy and that citizen may feel that his or her confidential attributes have been unduly revealed. In that case, the citizen is unlikely to be happy with or even understand the explanation that the record was synthetically generated.

On the other hand, limited data utility is another problem of synthetic data. Only the statistical properties explicitly captured by the model used by the data protector are preserved. A logical question at this point is: why not directly publish the statistics one wants to preserve rather than release a synthetic microdata set? One possible justification for synthetic microdata would be if valid analyses could be obtained on a number of subdomains, that is, similar results were obtained in a number of subsets of the original data set and the corresponding subsets of the synthetic data set. Partially synthetic or hybrid microdata are more likely to succeed in staying useful for subdomain analysis. However, when using partially synthetic or hybrid microdata, we lose the attractive feature of purely synthetic data that the number of records in the protected (synthetic) data set is independent from the number of records in the original data set.

2.4 Evaluation

Evaluation of sanitization methods must be carried out in terms of data utility and disclosure risk.

2.4.1 Measuring Data Utility

Defining what a generic utility loss measure is can be a tricky issue [39]. Roughly speaking, such a definition should capture the amount of information loss for a reasonable range of data uses. We will attempt a definition on the data with maximum granularity, that is, microdata. Similar definitions apply to rounded tabular data; for tables with cell suppressions, utility is normally measured as the reciprocal of the number of suppressed cells or their pooled magnitude. As to queryable databases, they can be logically viewed as tables as far as data utility is concerned: a denied query answer is equivalent to a cell suppression and a perturbed answer is equivalent to a perturbed cell. We will say there is little information loss if the protected data set is analytically valid and interesting according to the following definitions by [73]:

- A protected microdata set is *analytically valid* if it approximately preserves the following with respect to the original data (some conditions apply only to continuous attributes):

  1. Means and covariances on a small set of subdomains (subsets of records and/or attributes).
  2. Marginal values for a few tabulations of the data.
  3. At least one distributional characteristic.

- A microdata set is *analytically interesting* if a significant number of attributes (say half a dozen) on important subdomains are provided that can be validly analyzed.

More precise conditions of analytical validity and analytical interest cannot be stated without taking specific data uses into account. As imprecise as they may be, the above definitions suggest some possible measures:

- Compare raw records in the original and the protected data set. The more similar the SDC method to the identity function, the less the impact (but the higher the disclosure risk!). This requires pairing records in the original data set and

records in the protected data set. For masking methods, each record in the protected data set is naturally paired to the record in the original data set it originates from. For synthetic protected data sets, pairing is less obvious.
- Compare some statistics computed on the original and the protected data sets. The above definitions list some statistics which should be preserved as much as possible by an SDC method.

A strict evaluation of information loss must be based on the data uses to be supported by the protected data. The greater the differences between the results obtained on original and protected data for those uses, the higher the loss of information. However, very often microdata protection cannot be performed in a data use specific manner, for the following reasons:

- Potential data uses are very diverse and it may be even hard to identify them all at the moment of data release by the data protector.
- Even if all data uses could be identified, releasing several versions of the same original data set so that the i-th version has an information loss optimized for the i-th data use may result in unexpected disclosure.

Since that data often must be protected with no specific data use in mind, generic information loss measures are desirable to guide the data protector in assessing how much harm is being inflicted to the data by a particular SDC technique.

Information loss measures for numerical data. Assume a microdata set with n individuals (records) $I_1, I_2, \ldots, I_n$, and p continuous attributes $Z_1, Z_2, \ldots, Z_p$. Let X be the matrix representing the original microdata set (rows are records and columns are attributes). Let X' be the matrix representing the protected microdata set. The following tools are useful to characterize the information contained in the data set:

- Covariance matrices V (on X) and V' (on X').
- Correlation matrices R and R'.
- Correlation matrices RF and RF' between the p attributes and the p factors $PC_1, \ldots, PC_p$ obtained through principal components analysis.
- Communality between each of the p attributes and the first principal component PC_1 (or other principal components PC_i's). Communality is the percent of each attribute that is explained by PC_1 (or PC_i). Let C be the vector of communalities for X and C' the corresponding vector for X'.
- Factor score coefficient matrices F and F'. Matrix F contains the factors that should multiply each attribute in X to obtain its projection on each principal component. F' is the corresponding matrix for X'.

There does not seem to be a single quantitative measure which completely reflects those structural differences. Therefore, we proposed in [20, 66] to measure information loss through the discrepancies between matrices X, V, R, RF, C, and F obtained on the original data and the corresponding X', V', R', RF', C', and F' obtained on the protected data set. In particular, discrepancy between correlations is related to the information loss for data uses such as regressions and cross tabulations. Matrix discrepancy can be measured in at least three ways:

- **Mean square error**. Sum of squared componentwise differences between pairs of matrices, divided by the number of cells in either matrix.
- **Mean absolute error**. Sum of absolute componentwise differences between pairs of matrices, divided by the number of cells in either matrix.
- **Mean variation**. Sum of absolute percent variation of components in the matrix computed on protected data with respect to components in the matrix computed on original data, divided by the number of cells in either matrix. This approach has the advantage of not being affected by scale changes of attributes.

Information loss measures for categorical data. These have been usually based on direct comparison of categorical values, comparison of contingency tables, or on Shannon's entropy [20]. More recently, the importance of the semantics underlying categorical data for data utility has been realized [51]. As a result, semantically-grounded information loss measures have been proposed both to measure the practical utility and guide the sanitization algorithms [23]. Since this is an ongoing research line, it is further discussed in Sect. 2.6 on Challenges and Opportunities.

Bounded information loss measures. The information loss measures discussed above are unbounded, that is, they do not take values in a predefined interval. On the other hand, as discussed in Sect. 2.4.2, disclosure risk measures are naturally bounded (the risk of disclosure is naturally bounded between 0 and 1). Defining bounded information loss measures may be convenient to enable the data protector to trade off information loss against disclosure risk. In [52], probabilistic information loss measures bounded between 0 and 1 are proposed for continuous data.

2.4.2 Measuring Disclosure Risk

In the context of statistical disclosure control, disclosure risk can be defined as the risk that a user or an intruder can use the protected data set $\mathbf{X}'$ to derive confidential information on an individual among those in the original data set $\mathbf{X}$ [15]. Disclosure risk can be regarded from two different perspectives:

1. **Attribute disclosure**. This approach to disclosure is defined as follows. Disclosure takes place when an attribute of an individual can be determined more accurately with access to the released statistic than it is possible without access to that statistic.
2. **Identity disclosure**. Attribute disclosure does not imply a disclosure of the identity of any individual. Identity disclosure takes place when a record in the protected data set can be linked with a respondent's identity. Two main approaches are usually employed for measuring identity disclosure risk: uniqueness and re-identification.

2.1. *Uniqueness.* Roughly. speaking, the risk of identity disclosure is measured as the probability that rare combinations of attribute values in the released protected data are indeed rare in the original population the data come from. This approach is used typically with non-perturbative statistical disclosure control methods and, more specifically, sampling. The reason that uniqueness is not used with perturbative methods is that, when protected attribute values are perturbed versions of original attribute values, it makes no sense to investigate the probability that a rare combination of protected values is rare in the original data set, because *that* combination is most probably *not found* in the original data set.

2.2. *Record linkage.* This is an empirical approach to evaluate the risk of disclosure. In this case, record linkage software is constructed to estimate the number of re-identifications that might be obtained by a specialized intruder. Re-identification through record linkage provides a more unified approach than uniqueness methods because the former can be applied to any kind of masking and not just to non-perturbative masking. Moreover, record linkage can also be applied to synthetic data.

In the specific setting of tabular data protection, Bayesian methods for disclosure risk assessment have been proposed [15].

2.4.3   Trading off Information Loss and Disclosure Risk

The mission of SDC to modify data in such a way that sufficient protection is provided at minimum information loss suggests that a good sanitization method is one achieving a good trade-off between disclosure risk and information loss. Several approaches have been proposed to handle this trade-off. We discuss *SDC scores*, *R-U maps* and *k-anonymity*.

2.4.3.1   Score Construction

Following this idea, [20] proposed a score for method performance rating based on the average of information loss and disclosure risk measures. For each method M and parameterization P, the following score is computed:

$$Score(\mathbf{X}, \mathbf{X}') = \frac{IL(\mathbf{X}, \mathbf{X}') + DR(\mathbf{X}, \mathbf{X}')}{2}$$

where *IL* is an information loss measure, *DR* is a disclosure risk measure and $\mathbf{X}'$ is the protected data set obtained after applying method M with parameterization P to an original data set $\mathbf{X}$. In [20] *IL* and *DR* were computed using a weighted combination of several information loss and disclosure risk measures. With the resulting score, a ranking of masking methods (and their parameterizations) was obtained.

Using a score permits regarding the selection of a masking method and its parameters as an optimization problem. A masking method can be applied to the original data file and then a post-masking optimization procedure can be applied to decrease the score obtained. On the negative side, no specific score weighting can do justice to all methods. Thus, when ranking methods, the values of all measures of information loss and disclosure risk should be supplied along with the overall score.

2.4.3.2 R-U Maps

A tool which may be enlightening when trying to construct a score or, more generally, optimize the trade-off between information loss and disclosure risk is a graphical representation of pairs of measures (disclosure risk, information loss) or their equivalents (disclosure risk, data utility). Such maps are called R-U confidentiality maps [26].

Here, R stands for disclosure risk and U for data utility. In its most basic form, an R-U confidentiality map is the set of paired values (R, U) of disclosure risk and data utility that correspond to various strategies for data release (e.g., variations on a parameter). Such (R, U) pairs are typically plotted in a two-dimensional graph, so that the user can easily grasp the influence of a particular method and/or parameter choice.

2.5 Privacy Models

The computer science community has also contributed to sanitization for disclosure control under the names *Privacy Preserving Data Publishing* (PPDP) [2, 3, 9] and *Privacy Preserving Data Mining* (PPDM) [28, 29]. The former focuses on privacy-preserving publication of microdata, whereas the latter focuses on bringing privacy protection to traditional data mining tasks (for example, data classification or clustering).

There is a substantial difference between the sanitization approaches by the statistical and the computer science communities:

- A posteriori **disclosure risk control**. The statistical community is mainly concerned with analytical validity, so it first applies a sanitization method that incurs tolerable information loss and then measures the disclosure risk that publishing the sanitized data would incur (a posteriori control). If the extant disclosure risk is too high, then sanitization is re-applied to the original data with higher information loss. The process is iterated until tolerable disclosure risk is obtained.

- A priori **disclosure risk control**. In the computer science community, the primary focus in on disclosure risk. A *privacy model* is used to select the tolerable disclosure risk level from the outset (a priori control). Then a sanitization method is applied which guarantees by design that the selected disclosure risk level is not exceeded. The incurred information loss is measured after sanitization has been completed.

We next review the two main privacy models used in the literature.

2.5.1   k-Anonymity

A common approach to prevent disclosure via record linkage attacks is to hide each individual record within a group. This is the approach that k-anonymity [58, 59, 68] takes:

Definition 1. (k-Anonymity) A data set is said to satisfy k-anonymity for an integer $k > 1$ if, for each combination of values of quasi-identifier attributes, at least k records exist in the data set sharing that combination.

To achieve k-anonymity, identifying attributes are removed and quasi-identifiers are masked so that they become indistinguishable within each group of k records. Confidential attributes remain in clear form so that they preserve their analytical utility. In this way, an intruder with access to an external non-anonymous data set that contains the quasi-identifiers in the related data set will be unable to perform an exact re-identification.

Table 2.1 shows a sample medical data set containing one identifying attribute (SS number), three quasi-identifier attributes (age, zip code and nationality) and one

Table 2.1 Sample input data set

	Identifier	Quasi-identifiers			Confidential
	SS number	Age	Zip code	Nationality	Condition
1	1234-12-1234	25	23053	Russian	Heart disease
2	2345-23-2345	26	23068	Catalan	Heart disease
3	3456-34-3456	21	23068	French	Viral infection
4	4567-45-4567	27	23053	Italian	Viral infection
5	5678-56-5678	49	44853	Indian	AIDS
6	6789-67-6789	43	44853	Chinese	Heart disease
7	7890-78-7890	47	44850	Japanese	Viral infection
8	8901-89-8901	49	44850	Indian	Viral infection
9	9012-90-9012	32	33153	Spanish	AIDS
10	0123-12-0123	38	33153	French	AIDS
11	4321-43-4321	34	33168	Greek	AIDS
12	5432-54-5432	35	33168	French	AIDS

Table 2.2 4-anonymous output

	Identifier	Quasi-identifiers			Confidential
	SS number	Age	Zip code	Nationality	Condition
1	*	[20–30)	230**	European	Heart disease
2	*	[20–30)	230**	European	Heart disease
3	*	[20–30)	230**	European	Viral infection
4	*	[20–30)	230**	European	Viral infection
5	*	[40–50)	448**	Asian	AIDS
6	*	[40–50)	448**	Asian	Heart disease
7	*	[40–50)	448**	Asian	Viral infection
8	*	[40–50)	448**	Asian	Viral infection
9	*	[30–40)	331**	European	AIDS
10	*	[30–40)	331**	European	AIDS
11	*	[30–40)	331**	European	AIDS
12	*	[30–40)	331**	European	AIDS

confidential attribute (condition). Table 2.2 shows a possible sanitized version of the data set after 4-anonymization.

The sanitization method originally proposed to generate a k-anonymous data set was based on generalization and suppression [60].

Generalization reduces the granularity of the information contained in the quasi-identifier attributes, thereby increasing the chance of several records sharing the values of the attributes. A generalization hierarchy should be defined for each attribute. On the other hand, suppression removes records from the original data set that present outlying values. Suppression is usually performed prior to generalization to reduce the amount of generalization required to generate the k-anonymous data set.

An important goal of k-anonymity sanitization proposals is to obtain a protected data set where the information loss is as small as possible. Optimal k-anonymity was shown to be NP-hard in [53]. To render k-anonymity practical, a large number of heuristic generalization algorithms have been proposed [4, 7, 46, 47, 59] that reduce the search space or look for sub-optimal solutions.

A different approach towards k-anonymity is based on the microaggregation method discussed in Sect. 2.3.1.1. k-Anonymity via microaggregation was introduced in [21]. First, records are clustered so that each cluster contains at least k records and then these records are replaced by a representative value from the cluster to which they belong (typically the centroid record), thus producing a k-anonymous data set. Different heuristics and comparison functions have been proposed to group similar records together, so that the information loss resulting from the replacement by the representative record can be minimized (see [22, 45]).

Despite being one of the most commonly used privacy models, k-anonymity suffers from certain limitations. The most common criticism refers to the lack of protection against attribute disclosure [17, 48, 49, 74]: if all the individuals within a group of k-indistinguishable records share the same value for a confidential attribute, then the intruder will learn that value for all the members of the group without requiring an unequivocal re-identification.

For example, take the 4-anonymized output from Table 2. The last group of four records sharing a combination of quasi-identifier attribute values also shares the confidential attribute value condition (AIDS). In this case, if the intruder can establish that her target respondent's record is within that group (because it is the only group with compatible age, zipcode and nationality), the intruder learns that the target respondent suffers from AIDS without requiring an unequivocal re-identification.

To tackle this problem, some refinements to the basic k-anonymity model have been proposed. First l-diversity [49] requires the presence of l different well-represented values for the confidential attribute in every group of records sharing the same quasi-identifier attribute values. The stricter t-closeness [48] defines a tighter requirement, stating that the distribution of the confidential attributes within any group of records sharing the same quasi-identifier values should be close to (at distance no more than t from) the distribution of the confidential attributes in the whole data set.

2.5.2 ε-Differential Privacy

Disclosure limitation via k-anonymity is based on guessing the information that is available to potential intruders, that is, which attributes in the data set should be considered as quasi-identifiers. As long as this guessing is accurate, the disclosure limitation method accomplishes its duty, but a privacy breach may happen if more information is available to intruders.

A different approach to anonymization is ε-differential privacy [27]. This approach was designed for sanitization in queryable databases and it makes no assumptions on the intruder's knowledge. The goal is to transform the answers to queries so that the effect of the presence or absence of any single individual record on the returned answers is minimized.

To achieve this goal, the influence of each individual on the query answer needs to be limited. More concretely, the model imposes that the presence or absence of any single individual changes the query answer by at most a factor depending on ε. The smaller ε, the more difficult it is for an intruder to use the query answer to infer the contribution of any specific individual. A formal definition of the ε-differential privacy model follows:

Definition 2.(ε-Differential privacy) A randomized function κ gives ε-differential privacy if, for all data sets X_1, X_2 such that one can be obtained from the other by modifying a single record, and all $S \subset Range(\kappa)$, it holds

$$P(\kappa(X_1) \in S) \leq \exp(\varepsilon) \times P(\kappa(X_2) \in S). \tag{1}$$

Differential privacy was introduced as an interactive mechanism, where the data set is held by a trusted party that provides masked answers to queries made by data users. To do so, the trusted party computes the real response $f(X)$ to the user query f (e.g., the average of an attribute value, the number of records with a specific attribute value, etc.), perturbs the result and sends the output to the user. The usual way to compute the perturbed result is to add a random amount of noise, say $Y(X)$, to the answer $f(X)$ that depends on the ε and the variability of the query response; thus the perturbed response can be obtained as $\kappa(X) = f(X) + Y(X)$.

To generate $Y(X)$ according to ε-differential privacy, a common choice is to use a Laplace distribution with zero mean and $\Delta(f)/\varepsilon$ scale parameter, where:

- ε is the differential privacy parameter;
- $\Delta(f)$ is the L_1-sensitivity of f, that is, the maximum variation of the query function between neighbor data sets, that is, sets differing in at most one record.

Specifically, the density function of the Laplace noise is

$$p(x) = \frac{\varepsilon}{2\Delta(f)} e^{-|x|\varepsilon/\Delta(f)}.$$

Notice that, for fixed ε, the higher the sensitivity $\Delta(f)$ of the query function f, the more Laplace noise is added: indeed, satisfying the ε-differential privacy definition (Definition 5.2) requires more noise when the query function f can vary strongly between neighbor data sets. Also, for fixed $\Delta(f)$, the smaller ε, the more Laplace noise is added: when ε is very small, Definition 5.2 almost requires that the probabilities on both sides of Eq. (1) be equal, which requires the randomized function $\kappa(\cdot) = f(\cdot) + Y(\cdot)$ to yield very similar results for all pairs of neighbor data sets; adding a lot of noise is a way to achieve this. In the interactive setting, however, the type and number of queries that can be performed over the data are limited, in order to avoid an attacker to reconstruct the original data by performing consecutive queries.

Differential privacy was also extended for the non-interactive setting, that is, for sanitization of microdata sets [8, 10, 25, 38]. Even though a non-interactive data release can be used to answer an arbitrarily large number of queries, in all these proposals, this is obtained at the cost of offering utility guarantees only for a restricted class of queries [8], typically count queries. This contrasts with the general-purpose utility-preserving data release offered by the k-anonymity model.

In fact, it must be said that, while ε-differential privacy offers very high disclosure protection, it causes a huge information loss unless ε is quite high. But taking a high ε somehow seems to contradict the basic requirement of the model, namely that the influence of any single record on the returned output must be small.

2.6 Research Challenges and Opportunities

Most privacy-preserving methods have been designed to deal with numerical attributes. Numbers are easy to treat because arithmetical functions can be applied on them to perform the comparison and transformation operations required for data anonymization. However, categorical attributes (such as diagnoses, preferences, etc.), which take values from a finite set of categories and for which arithmetical operations do not make sense, are very common in available data sets.

Applying existing data anonymization methods to categorical attributes is not straightforward:

- Several anonymization techniques replace each categorical attribute by as many binary 0–1 attributes as the number of possible attribute categories; such is the case of multiply-imputed synthetic data [57] and data shuffling [54]. This approach soon yields unmanageable data sets.
- PRAM [31] is an anonymization technique designed for nominal attributes. It certainly does not need binary attributes, but it requires as a control parameter a Markov transition matrix, whose size grows quadratically in the number of nominal categories.
- In [70] and [21], extensions of microaggregation algorithms for categorical attributes were proposed: the former paper addressed only categorical ordinal attributes and proposed the median as an aggregation operator; the latter paper also considered categorical attributes using the equality/inequality predicate and proposed the modal value as an aggregation operator for them. However, the modal value is a very coarse aggregation operator which may not even be uniquely defined, especially over a small group of values.

In summary, the above-mentioned methods incur a high complexity for anonymizing categorical data or they are coarse and cause substantial information loss. This is because they treat categorical data as flat categorical values, for which the only possible operator is the binary comparison for equality [21]. This simplistic approach omits data semantics. Overlooking semantics decreases the utility of the anonymized data set since it fails to preserve the meaning of the original data. Semantically-grounded analyses would be desirable to better preserve data utility.

Since categorical attributes are usually words or noun phrases referring to concepts (e.g., disease names) which capture their semantics, and semantics is a human-inherited feature, a semantic analysis requires a human-tailored knowledge base that captures and structures the conceptualization of nominal attributes. For this purpose, structured thesauri, taxonomies, or ontologies [33] can be used.

Recently, some ongoing works have been proposed exploiting available knowledge bases to anonymize categorical data sets. In [23] a knowledge-based numerical mapping for categorical attributes that captures and quantifies their underlying semantics is presented. By means of this mapping, the authors show that it is possible to compute semantically and mathematically coherent *mean*, *variance* and *covariance* functions for nominal data, which can be used to compare and manage categorical data sets in existing anonymization methods. In [51], the notion of semantic similarity [61], that is, the semantic resemblance between categorical attribute values, is extensively exploited to define *comparison*, *aggregation* and *sorting* operators. Those are then used to create semantically-grounded versions of existing anonymization methods based on recoding, microaggregation and resampling. In [6], similar principles are applied to anonymize multi-valued categorical attributes (i.e., set-valued data like query-logs) by defining a set of aggregation functions that allows comparing multi-valued attributes with different cardinalities. Most of the above semantic methods have been applied to microaggregation algorithms. Future lines of research may apply semantic technologies to other anonymity mechanisms such as those based on noise addition.

Regarding privacy models, it is not uncommon in the data anonymization literature to oppose the "old" k-anonymity model to the "new" differential privacy model, which offers more robust privacy guarantees. However, compared to the general-purpose data publication offered by k-anonymity, which makes no assumptions on the uses of published data, ε-differential privacy offers quite limited utility. Combining the strengths of k-anonymity (flexible utility) and ε-differential privacy (strong privacy) remains a challenge.

The usual approach to release differentially private microdata sets is based on histogram queries [76, 77]; that is, on approximating the data distribution by partitioning the data domain and counting the number of records in each partition set. To prevent the counts from leaking too much information they are computed in a differentially private manner. Apart from the counts, partitioning can also reveal information. One way to prevent partitioning from leaking information consists in using a predefined partition that is independent of the actual data under consideration (e.g., by using a grid [50]). The accuracy of the approximation obtained via histogram queries depends on the number of records contained in each of the histogram bins: the more records, the less relative error. For data sets with sparsely populated regions, using a predefined partition may be problematic.

In a recent approach [67] the authors show that a synergy between k-anonymity and ε-differential privacy can be found in order to achieve more accurate and general-purpose ε-differential privacy. Specifically, they show that the amount of noise required to fulfill ε-differential privacy can be greatly reduced if the query is run on a k-anonymous version of the data set obtained through microaggregation of all attributes (instead of running it on the raw input data). The rationale is that the microaggregation performed to achieve k-anonymity helps reduce the sensitivity of the input versus modifications of individual records; hence, it helps reduce the amount of noise to be added to achieve ε-differential privacy.

In any case, there is still room for improvement because, as it has been empirically shown in [67], the practical utility of general-purpose differentially private data sets is still significantly lower than the one of k-anonymous data sets.

On the legal side, parallel to the development of privacy legislation, anti-discrimination legislation has undergone a remarkable expansion, and in some countries it now prohibits discrimination against protected groups on the grounds of race, color, religion, nationality, sex, marital status, age, and pregnancy, and in a number of settings, like credit and insurance, personnel selection and wages, and access to public services. On the technology side, efforts at fighting discrimination have led to developing anti-discrimination techniques in data mining. Some proposals are oriented to the discovery and measurement of discrimination, while others aim at discrimination-protected data mining (DPDM), that is, at data mining which does not become itself a source of discrimination, due to automated decision making based on discriminatory models extracted from inherently biased data sets.

Another challenge in this area is the relationship between PPDM and DPDM. Is it sufficient to guarantee data privacy while allowing automated discovery of discriminatory profiles/models? In [34–36], the authors argue that the answer is no. If there is a chance to create a trustworthy technology for knowledge discovery and deployment, it is with a holistic approach which faces both privacy and discrimination threats (risks).

2.7 Conclusions and Relevant Software

In this chapter, we have reviewed a priori and a posteriori approaches to disclosure control in database privacy sanitization. The a posteriori approach is adopted in the statistical community, which prioritizes publishing analytically valid data and, once the sanitized data have been obtained, measures disclosure risk. The a priori approach is followed in the computer science community, which focuses on selecting the maximum tolerable disclosure risk from the outset via a privacy model; after data are protected according to the privacy model, their extant utility is evaluated.

Common to both approaches is the use of sanitization methods, which we have also reviewed for tabular data, queryable databases and microdata, with a special focus on the latter. Finally, we have identified research challenges and opportunities in the area of statistical disclosure control.

Freeware packages that implement the sanitization methods and the risk estimation needed by the a posteriori approach include the following:

- The Argus software: τ-Argus for tabular data [41] and μ-Argus for microdata, see [40].
- The *sdc* software: *sdcTable* [65] for tabular data and *sdcMicro* for microdata [64, 69].

Regarding the a priori approach, a software package that implements k-anonymity, l-diversity and t-closeness is ARX [5].

Acknowledgments and Disclaimer This work was partly supported by the Government of Catalonia under grant 2014 SGR 537, by the Spanish Government through projects TIN2011-27076-C03-01 "CO-PRIVACY" and TIN2014-57364-C2-R "SmartGlacis", and by the European Commission under H2020 project "CLARUS". J. Domingo-Ferrer is partially supported as an ICREA Acadèmia researcher by the Government of Catalonia. The authors are with the UNESCO Chair in Data Privacy, but they are solely responsible for the views expressed in this chapter, which do not necessarily reflect the position of UNESCO nor commit that organization.

References

1. Adam NR, Wortmann JC (1989) Security-control for statistical databases: a comparative study. ACM Comput Surv 21(4):515–556
2. Agrawal R, Srikant R (2000) Privacy-preserving data mining. Proceedings of the 2000 ACM SIGMOD International conference on management of data, SIGMOD'00ACM, New York, USA, pp 439–450
3. Aggarwal CC, Yu PS (eds) (2008) Privacy-preserving data mining: models and algorithms, vol 34 of Advances in database systems. Springer, Heidelberg (2008)
4. Aggarwal G, Feder T, Kenthapadi K, Motwani R, Panigraphy R, Thomas D, Zhu A (2005) Anonymizing tables. In: Proceedings of the 10th International conference on database theory, ICDT 2005, pp 246–258
5. ARX—Powerful data anonymization (2014). http://arx.deidentifier.org
6. Batet M, Erola A, Sánchez D, Castellá-Roca J (2013) Utility preserving query log anonymization via semantic microaggregation. Inf Sci 242:110–123
7. Bayardo RJ, Agrawal R (2005) Data privacy through optimal k-anonymization. Proceedings of the 21st International conference on data engineering ICDE'05. IEEE Computer Society, Washington, DC, USA, pp 217–228
8. Blum A, Ligett K, Roth A (2008) A learning theory approach to non-interactive database privacy. In: Proceedings of the 40th Annual symposium on the theory of computing-STOC 2008, pp 609–618
9. Chen B-C, Kifer D, LeFevre K, Machanavajjhala A (2009) Privacy-preserving data publishing. Found Trends Databases 2(1–2):1–167
10. Chen R, Mohammed N, Fung BCM, Desai BC, Xiong L (2011) Publishing set-valued data via differential privacy. In: 37th International conference on very large data bases-VLDB 2011/Proceedings of the VLDB endowment, vol 4, issue no 11, 1087–1098
11. Chin FY, Ozsoyoglu G (1982) Auditing and inference control in statistical databases. IEEE Trans Softw Eng SE-8:574–582
12. Dalenius T (1974) The invasion of privacy problem and statistics production. An overview. Statistik Tidskrift 12:213–225
13. Defays D, Nanopoulos P (1993) Panels of enterprises and confidentiality: the small aggregates method. In: Proceedings of 92 Symposium on design and analysis of longitudinal surveys, Ottawa, Canada, pp 195–204
14. Denning DE, Denning PJ, Schwartz MD (1979) The tracker: a threat to statistical database security. ACM Trans Database Syst 4(1):76–96
15. Dobra A, Fienberg SE, Trottini M (2003) Assessing the risk of disclosure of confidential categorical data. In: Bernardo J et al (eds) Bayesian statistics 7, Proceedings of the Seventh Valencia International meeting on Bayesian statistics. Oxford University Press, Oxford, pp 125–139
16. Domingo-Ferrer J (2007) A three-dimensional conceptual framework for database privacy. In: Secure data management-4th VLDB workshop SDM'2007, vol 4721. Lecture notes in computer science, pp 193–202
17. Domingo-Ferrer J (2008) A critique of k-anonymity and some of its enhancements. In: Proceedings of ARES/PSAI 2008. IEEE Computer Society, pp 990–993
18. Domingo-Ferrer J, Martnez-Ballesté A, Mateo-Sanz JM, Sebé F (2006) Efficient multivariate data-oriented microaggregation. VLDB J 15:355–369

19. Domingo-Ferrer J, Mateo-Sanz JM (2002) Practical data-oriented microaggregation for statistical disclosure control. IEEE Trans Knowl Data Eng 14(1):189–201
20. Domingo-Ferrer J, Torra V (2001) A quantitative comparison of disclosure control methods for microdata. Confidentiality. Disclosure and data access: theory and practical applications for statistical agencies, North-Holland, Amsterdam, pp 111–134
21. Domingo-Ferrer J, Torra V (2005) Ordinal, continuous and heterogenous k-anonymity through microaggregation. Data Min Knowl Disc 11(2):195–212
22. Domingo-Ferrer J, Sebé F, Solanas A (2008) A polynomial-time approximation to optimal multivariate microaggregation. Comput Math Appl 55(4):714–732
23. Domingo-Ferrer J, Sánchez D, Rufian-Torrell G (2013) Anonymization of nominal data based on semantic marginality. Inf Sci 242:35–48
24. Duncan GT, Mukherjee S (2000) Optimal disclosure limitation strategy in statistical databases: deterring tracker attacks through additive noise. J Am Stat Assoc 45:720–729
25. Dwork C, Naor M, Reingold O, Rothblum GN, Vadhan S (2009) On the complexity of differentially private data release: efficient algorithms and hardness results. In: Proceedings of the 41st Annual symposium on the theory of computing-STOC 2009, pp 381–390
26. Duncan GT, Fienberg SE, Krishnan R, Padman R, Roehrig SF (2001) Disclosure limitation methods and information loss for tabular data. In: Confidentiality, disclosure and data access: theory and practical applications for statistical agencies. North-Holland, Amsterdam, pp 135–166
27. Dwork C (2006) Differential privacy. In: Proceedings of 33rd International colloquium on automata, languages and programming, ICALP 2006. Springer, pp 1–12
28. Fung BCM, Wang K, Yu PS (2005) Top-down specialization for information and privacy preservation. Proceedings of the 21st International conference on data engineering, ICDE'05. IEEE Computer Society, Washington, DC, USA, pp 205–216
29. Fung BCM, Wang K, Chen R, Yu PS (2010) Privacy-preserving data publishing: a survey of recent developments. ACM Comput Surv 42(4)
30. Gopal R, Garfinkel R, Goes P (2002) Confidentiality via camouflage: the CVC approach to disclosure limitation when answering queries to databases. Oper Res 50:501–516
31. Gouweleeuw JM, Kooiman P, Willenborg LCRJ, DeWolf P-P (1997) Post randomisation for statistical disclosure control: theory and implementation. Research paper no. 9731. Statistics Netherlands, Voorburg
32. Greenberg B (1987) Rank swapping for ordinal data. U. S. Bureau of the Census, Washington, DC (unpublished manuscript)
33. Guarino N (1998) Formal ontology in information systems, In: Proceedings of the 1st International conference on formal ontology in information systems, Trento, Italy, pp 3–15
34. Hajian S, Domingo-Ferrer J (2013) A methodology for direct and indirect discrimination prevention in data mining. IEEE Trans Knowl Data Eng 25(7):1445–1459
35. Hajian S, Monreale A, Pedreschi D, Domingo-Ferrer J, Giannotti F (2012) Injecting discrimination and privacy awareness into pattern discovery. In: Proceedings of the IEEE 12th International conference on data mining workshops, pp 360–369. IEEE Computer Society
36. Hajian S, Domingo-Ferrer J, Farràs O (to appear) Generalization-based privacy preservation and discrimination prevention in data publishing and mining. Data Mining Knowl Discov
37. Hansen SL, Mukherjee S (2003) Polynomial algorithm for optimal univariate microaggregation. IEEE Trans Knowl Data Eng 15(4):1043–1044
38. Hardt M, Ligett K, McSherry F (2010) A simple and practical algorithm for differentially private data release. Preprint arXiv:1012.4763v1
39. Karr AF, Kohnen CN, Oganian A, Reiter JP, Sanil AP (2006) A framework for evaluating the utility of data altered to protect confidentiality. Am Stat 60(3)
40. Hundepool A, Van de Wetering A, Ramaswamy R, Franconi L, Polettini S, Capobianchi A, DeWolf P-P, Domingo-Ferrer J, Torra V, Brand R, Giessing S (2008) μ-ARGUS version 4.2 Software and user's manual. statistics Netherlands, Voorburg NL. http://neon.vb.cbs.nl/casc/mu.htm. Accessed 22 Dec 2008

41. Hundepool A, Van de Wetering A, Ramaswamy R, de Wolf P-P, Giessing S, Fischetti M, Salazar J-J, Castro J, Lowthian P (2011) τ-ARGUS v. 3.5 Software and user's manual. CENEX SDC Project Deliverable. http://neon.vb.cbs.nl/casc/tau.htm
42. Hundepool A, Domingo-Ferrer J, Franconi L, Giessing S, Schulte-Nordholt E, Spicer K, De Wolf PP (2012) Statistical disclosure control. Wiley, New York
43. Kim JJ (1986) A method for limiting disclosure in microdata based on random noise and transformation. In: Proceedings of the section on survey research methods. American Statistical Association, Alexandria VA, pp 303–308
44. Laszlo M, Mukherjee S (2005) Minimum spanning tree partitioning algorithm for microaggregation. IEEE Trans Knowl Data Eng 17(7):902–911
45. Laszlo M, Mukherjee S (2009) Approximation bounds for minimum information loss microaggregation. IEEE Trans Knowl Data Eng 21(11):1643–1647
46. LeFevre K, DeWitt DJ, Ramakrishnan R (2005) Incognito: Efficient full-domain k-anonymity. Proceedings of the 2005 ACM SIGMOD international conference on management of data, SIGMOD'05ACM, New York, USA, pp 49–60
47. LeFevre K, DeWitt DJ, Ramakrishnan R (2006) Mondrian multidimensional k-anonymity. In: Proceedings of the 22nd International conference on data engineering, ICDE'06. IEEE Computer Society, Washington, DC, USA, p 25
48. Li N, Li T, Venkatasubramanian S (2007) t-Closeness: privacy beyond k-anonymity and l-diversity. In: Proceedings of the IEEE International conference on data engineering, ICDE 2007, pp 106–115
49. Machanavajjhala A, Gehrke J, Kifer, D, Venkitasubramaniam M (2006) l-Diversity: privacy beyond k-anonymity. In: Proceedings of the IEEE International conference on data engineering, ICDE 2006, p 24
50. Machanavajjhala A, Kifer D, Abowd J, Gehrke J, Vilhuber L (2008) Privacy: theory meets practice on the map. In: Proceedings of the IEEE international conference on data engineering, ICDE 2008, pp 277–286
51. Martínez S, Sánchez D, Valls A (2013) A semantic framework to protect the privacy of electronic health records with non-numerical attributes. J Biomed Inf 46(2):294–303
52. Mateo-Sanz JM, Domingo-Ferrer J, Sebé F (2005) Probabilistic information loss measures in confidentiality protection of continuous microdata. Data Min Knowl Disc 11(2):181–193
53. Meyerson A, Williams R (2004) On the complexity of optimal k-anonymity. Proceedings of the 23th ACM SIGMOD-SIGACT-SIGART symposium on principles of database systems PODS'04. ACM, New York, USA, pp 223–228
54. Muralidhar D, Sarathy R (2006) Data shuffling—a new masking approach for numerical data. Manage Sci 52(5):658–670
55. Muralidhar K, Batra D, Kirs PJ (1995) Accessibility, security and accuracy in statistical databases: the case for the multiplicative fixed data perturbation approach. Manage Sci 41:1549–1564
56. Reiter JP (2002) Satisfying disclosure restrictions with synthetic data sets. J Off Stat 18 (4):531–544
57. Rubin DB (1993) Discussion of statistical disclosure limitation. J Off Stat 9(2):461–468
58. Samarati P (2001) Protecting respondents' identities in microdata release. IEEE Trans Knowl Data Eng 13(6):1010–1027
59. Samarati P, Sweeney L (1998) Protecting privacy when disclosing information: k-anonymity and its enforcement through generalization and suppression. Technical report, SRI International
60. Samarati P, Sweeney L (1998) Generalizing data to provide anonymity when disclosing information. In: Proceedings of the 17th ACM SIGACT-SIGMOD-SIGART symposium on principles of database systems, PODS'98, p 188. ACM, New York, USA (1998)
61. Sánchez D, Batet M, Isern D, Valls A (2012) Ontology-based semantic similarity: a new feature-based approach. Expert Syst Appl 39(9):7718–7728
62. Schlörer J (1975) Identification and retrieval of personal records from a statistical data bank. Methods Inf Med 14(1):7–13

63. Schlörer J (1980) Disclosure from statistical databases: quantitative aspects of trackers. ACM Trans Database Syst 5:467–492
64. sdcMicro: statistical disclosure control methods for anonymization of microdata and risk estimation, v. 4.2.0. http://cran.r-project.org/web/packages/sdcMicro/index.html. Accessed 10 Jan 2014
65. sdcTable: Methods for statistical disclosure control in tabular data, v. 0.10.3. http://cran.r-project.org/package=sdcTable. Accessed 4 Nov 2014
66. Sebé F, Domingo-Ferrer J, Mateo-Sanz JM, Torra V (2002) Post-masking optimization of the tradeoff between information loss and disclosure risk in masked microdata sets. In: Inference control in statistical databases. Lecture notes in computer science, vol 2316. Springer, Berlin, pp 163–171
67. Soria-Comas J, Domingo-Ferrer J, Sánchez D, Martnez S (to appear) Enhancing data utility in differential privacy via microaggregation-based k-anonymity. VLDB J
68. Sweeney L (2002) k-Anonymity: a model for protecting privacy. Int J Uncertain Fuzziness Knowl-Based Syst 10(5):557–570
69. Templ M (2008) Statistical disclosure control for microdata using the R-package sdcMicro. Trans Data Priv 1(2):67–85
70. Torra V (2004) Microaggregation for categorical variables: a median based approach. In: Privacy in statistical databases-PSD 2004, LNCS, vol 3050. Springer, Heidelberg, pp 162–174
71. Traub JF, Yemini Y, Wozniakowski H (1984) The statistical security of a statistical database. ACM Trans Database Syst 9:672–679
72. Willenborg L, DeWaal T (2001) Elements of statistical disclosure control. Springer, New York
73. Winkler WE (1998) Re-identification methods for evaluating the confidentiality of analytically valid microdata. Res Off Stat 1(2):50–69
74. Wong R, Li J, Fu A, Wang K (2006) (α, k)-anonymity: an enhanced k-anonymity model for privacy preserving data publishing. In: Proceedings of the ACM SIGKDD International conference on knowledge discovery and data mining, KDD 2016, pp 754–759
75. Xiao X, Tao Y (2006) Anatomy: simple and effective privacy preservation. In: Proceedings of the 32nd International conference on very large data bases-VLDB 2006, pp 139–150
76. Xiao Y, Xiong L, Yuan C (2010) Differentially private data release through multidimensional partitioning. In: Proceedings of the 7th VLDB conference on secure data management, SDM'10, pp 150–168
77. Xu J, Zhang Z, Xiao X, Yang Y, Yu G (2012) Differentially private histogram publication. In: Proceedings of the IEEE International conference on data engineering, ICDE 2012, pp 32–43

Chapter 3
Privacy and Big Data

Masood Mortazavi and Khaled Salah

I've not been an eavesdropper.
Papyrus of Ani (1250 BCE).

3.1 Introduction

In order to better understand how the "Big Data" phenomena affects our private lives and social personality, we need to gain a better grasp of the concepts involved. Legalism and technological positivism misapprehend either the radical changes in privacy-violating systems or the historical context of rules of civility or both. As a result, legislatures extend and apply bandages to the cracks in existing privacy laws in a confused frenzy [1] and technological naïveté entraps our minds in non-solutions that confuse the scope of the privacy-related issues with access control in inter-personal data exchanges [2, 3].

Communications technologies and Big Data analysis have facilitated the intrusion of privacy by devising and strengthening audio-visual surveillance and "dataveilance" [4]. Governments have used these technologies for continuous and massive collection and collation of data from our private spaces. Big Data phenomena are a constellation of data storage and processing extensions to modern communications technologies that have given rise to further, new modes of privacy intrusions that were not anticipated when much more primitive communications and eavesdropping technologies gave rise to the existing privacy laws [1]. Not only do we need new laws that can anticipate technological changes in their formulation but we also need new technologies to counter various forms of privacy intrusions.

M. Mortazavi
Innovation Center, Huawei Technologies, Santa Clara, CA, USA

K. Salah (✉)
Khaled University of Science, Technology and Research (KUSTAR), Abu Dhabi, UAE
e-mail: khaled.salah@kustar.ac.ae

© Springer International Publishing Switzerland 2015
S. Zeadally and M. Badra (eds.), *Privacy in a Digital, Networked World*,
Computer Communications and Networks,
DOI 10.1007/978-3-319-08470-1_3

This chapter will first present a brief review of Big Data technologies, describe its benefits, and outline how it has come to harm privacy in subtle new forms. Next, it will review the legal and technological issues and describe some possible solutions. It will conclude by suggesting and anticipating some future development.

3.2 Big Data

"Big Data" has come to refer to a constellation of phenomena having to do with the production, consumption, amassing, and analysis of large data sets produced by a vast variety of sources in a very large number of formats, in unprecedented volumes and data flow velocities. Figure below shows the main functions and entities participating in a typical Big Data application. The phrase "Big Data" has been mentioned in formal literature since the 1990s and the associated techniques were first utilized in scientific applications such as CERN's large Hadron collider, Search for Extra-Terrestrial Intelligence (SETI), and genome projects [4]. Later, these techniques found applications in computational social sciences, whether it is movie recommendation systems, consumer marketing, advertising, or data mining on social networks. So, while volume, variety, and velocity are the three "V"'s that have been commonly associated with the Big Data phenomena [5], we believe a fourth "V," i.e. value, should also be understood in the context of Big Data, and is perhaps, the easiest to miss.

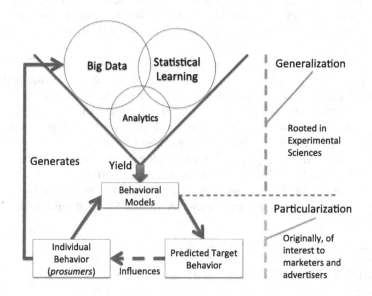

Big Data information pipeline: modeling and targeting "prosumers" behavior

3.2.1 Benefits and Limitations

In any early example of what we may call "indirect" Big Data, Ancient Babylonians had no doctors and crowd-sourced medicine. "When a man is ill, they lay him in the public square, and passers-by come up to him, and if they [or someone they knew] ever had his disease ... they give him advice" [6]. So, it is not surprising that of the most recent benefits cited for Big Data, one can refer to several examples from the medical field: research through Big Data analytics (including analytics on web search queries) led to the discovery that the combined use of Paxil and Parvachol would lead to increased blood glucose to diabetic levels. Dr. David Graham studied medical records of some 1.5 million of Kaiser Permanent's 6 million patients (California residents). This study led to the conclusion that over the previous five years, Vioxx had caused 88,000–139,000 heart attacks 30–40 % of which were fatal [7]. It is worth noting that Graham had to go to the Government Accounting Office as a whistleblower because his FDA superiors prevented him from publishing his findings. Graham's study saved thousands of lives. Analytics on Twitter, it has been claimed, detected the spread of cholera epidemic in Haiti faster than conventional methods did later.

Google Flu Trends (GFT), which estimates flu trends based on analytics on web search, location, and other data [8], is frequently cited as another benefit of Big Data [9]. More detailed recent studies pointed to "substantial errors" in GFT estimates of influenza timing and intensity. GFT over-estimated the threat in the 2012–2013 season and badly under-estimated it during the 2009 pandemic. This analysis also shows that the error in GFT (when compared to ground facts given in the official US sentinel for excess in flu percentages) grows as we reduce the scope of the data from the entire United States to its Atlantic Coast and finally to New York City [10]. This should be a warning against over-estimating the power of Big Data to actually predict anything although it might still be good enough to provide insights.

One can imagine even more interesting applications with the proliferation of mobile medical devices working independently or through tight integration with smart phones. With such tools, it will be possible to prevent and contain epidemics and catastrophic and costly health issues of the sort Graham discovered [7]. Recent industry analysis shows that Big Data applications in health-care are fast accelerating and it is estimated that Big Data can save $300–$400 billion in US health care costs alone [11]. Much of this saving will be due to deployment of smart devices on the periphery of health networks for sensing, notification, and control. However, this McKinsey & Company study seems to overestimate the power of Big Data to be able to discover what the population needs for "right living," "right care," "right provider," "right value," and "right innovation." The concept of "right" is never defined.

Sensor and mobile collection of data have been cited to lead to better inventory and traffic management, dynamic pricing, drought and migration prediction, crime wave prediction, monitoring education to discover effective techniques, and a slew of other benefits. Smart power grids, self-organizing networks of sensors, devices, and people will lead Big Data and information and communications technology advances [12]. Perhaps, the most interesting application of Big Data will be in social networking of users enabled by modern information and communications technologies (ICT), including ad hoc social networking. The theory of emergent and self-organizing social institutions as expounded in the works of Nobel Laureate Eleanor Ostrom [13] is finding direct application to ICT-enabled social networks. More transparent use of Big Data knowledge commons, at the periphery of networks, can raise ICT users' collective awareness towards economic use of common resources [12].

There are other, somewhat dangerous "benefits" that have given rise to serious privacy and civil rights concerns. Here, we will only name one: "Predictive Policing." (For a more detailed critique of these dubious "benefits," refer to Crawford [14].) "Predictive Policing" gets us very close to the realm of Kafka's Trial ("Der Process") because it can easily lead to unclear accusations, unknown accusers, inversion of onus of proof, and denial of due process [4, 14].

Indeed, massive businesses operate and are founded on the premise of extracting value from data that flows in large volumes in a variety of formats at high velocities. In fact, in order to extract value from masses of largely undifferentiated data, we need specialized tools for pre-processing, filtering, and clustering.

3.2.2 Curse of Dimensionality

When discussing Big Data analytics, it is worth noting the curse of dimensionality. In high-dimensional analysis or complex modeling techniques where a large number of adjustment parameters are used, statistical learning theory has pointed out the curse of dimensionality [15]. Most statistical learning techniques refer to a set of sample data to produce a model and subsequently test the model with test data. It turns out that sample density is proportional to $N^{1/n}$, where N represents the sample size and n represents the number of dimensions involved. If for a statistical analysis or statistical learning of a single-dimensional model, 100 "learning" data points can provide adequate accuracy, as much as 100^{10} data points would be required for a similar accuracy in learning a 10-dimensional model. One possible explanation for growing inaccuracy of an increasingly complex model is always the inclusion of additional dimensions of analysis in the more complex model. This may have some relevance to the earlier noted study of GFT [10].

3.2.3 Scale and Technology

Big Data phenomena has always been associated with massive scale and daunting complexity. The spread of the Web and Internet services gave rise to companies such as Yahoo, Google, (modern) Apple, Amazon, YouTube, Twitter, and Facebook.

These Big Data companies extract value from the large datasets under their control for the purposes of service definition and refinements, trend analysis, product discovery, marketing and advertising, in all their varieties.

Big Data companies have had to develop special tools for transporting, processing, storing, and analyzing the "Data." The general techniques used in the classical data management systems have proven to be inadequate at best. Physical constraints of data centers have led to other technological innovations. For example, Yahoo was one of the earliest companies that ran into the Big Data problems. It has some of the most interesting early architectures as well as more recent developments, including many of the early NoSQL databases [16] and more recently PNUTS or Sherpa [17]. To create a platform that was suitable for massive data centers and web-scale applications, Google created a rather complete framework for web-scale big data processing. GFS [18] handled the requirements of a large-scale, highly available file storage. Chubby [19] provided for a distributed lock manager for purposes of coordinating and managing clusters. MapReduce [20] provided a base programming model. Pregel [21], a graph processing system complemented MapReduce. Megastore [22] provided for the web-scale serving of data to a variety of applications, with ease, and Dremel [23] extended the platform to the Structured Query Language (SQL), which is generally used in traditional databases and with which data programmers and scientists are quite familiar.

Web companies have freely published and released open-source code of high quality and value. The Apache Hadoop family of open-source projects are a powerful analytics platform with some important recent advances [24]. The Hadoop platform has found great currency including support from Amazon Web Services [25], and Google Cloud Platform [26], and in its upper tiers, Hadoop has found a formidable competition in the Berkeley AmpLab's Data Analytics Stack (BDAS) [27]. Open-source publication of software and availability of AWS-like services have been a bonanza for smaller companies in the field of distributed computing and Big Data.

Through a combination of machine learning, distributed computing, and highly optimized nodes, services are created on the data fabrics in massive data centers. Some of these companies have created virtual services for Big Data analytics where data scientists can load and query large data volumes (e.g., Google's Big Query).

To support Big Data businesses, new distributed file systems have been created to handle unavoidable and noticeably frequent failures of storage media at large-scale data centers. Resilient distributed systems such as MapReduce have been created to support multi-tenant data processing and data analytics through a simple processing paradigm. Massive indexing systems have been constructed over time to minimize the user-experienced latencies and to maximize relevant results in web search queries. Non-SQL databases have been revived over the last few decades in order to address the problems related to transaction processing at the web-scale. Column stores have been created to address analytics at high throughput and to take advantage of new computer architecture in order to break the memory barrier. Relational models, which seem to be fundamental to applications of logic in data exploration, have been brought to bear on Big Data through a re-purposing, retooling, and extension of the existing SQL-based distributed query processing strategies.

User experience and massive data processing systems are the two poles that define the business of web-scale companies.

Notwithstanding the intended or unintended allowance for governmental data leaching and intrusions or the limited collaborations with social and data scientists, Big Data or web-scale companies have generally gone to pains to ensure security mechanisms to protect the bulk of their internal and transactional data streams. Not doing so would be costly and will have deep impact on existing business models.

Both "Big Data" and "cloud computing" are euphemisms used to refer to the computing, storage and search models that re-emerged from the ashes of "personal computing" and which rearranged the assignment of data storage and computing tasks on the network. Cloud computing is that very aspect of Big Data which introduces privacy concerns. It is contemporaneous with the rise of the Web and the data center as a computer [28].

In cloud computing users utilize the "cloud provider's" computing, storage, and networking infrastructure primarily due to the offered resource elasticity [29, 30]. Infrastructure as a service is complemented with software as a service where the provider offers specific applications both of the desktop variety (e.g., Google Apps, Microsoft Office Live) and of the non-desktop variety (e.g., Facebook, Twitter).

The conveniences of cloud computing has come with a cost: loss of effective control over users' data. Business and legal requirements force providers to have policies and safeguards to protect users' data. However, these protections are generally inadequate, can hardly be a guarantee against provider equivocation, and have led to privacy concerns and ensuing research and innovation [31]. On the other hand, Big Data analytics has given rise to a slew of new applications and services. However, provision of data to unauthorized users (in secret or through open transactions) can lead to unexpected results, privacy violations and the consequent chilling of users' liberties, not to mention direct and physical harm, and mis-classification. We say more regarding these problems later in this chapter.

3.3   Privacy Issues

Earlier research indicates a plethora of the privacy issues that Big Data analytics and storage needs to address.

Users have an inadequate understanding of how privacy violations impact individuals as well as social behavior [1, 32–34]. There is a lack of transparency regarding privacy policies or predictive analytics applied to users [14, 35]. There is a lack of data due process of law [14]. There can be unplanned disclosures of data [31]. False data or false analytics results may be shared (often automatically) across data centers, making it difficult for users to make amends through a data due process [32]. It is possible to predict private traits, originally meant to be private, using Big Data analytics [36]. There is a mismatch of provider's claimed policies and the actual controls made available to users [2] and providers often have an economic incentive to equivocate [31]. There is an economic incentive to disclose users' data [31] and there exists a similar policing incentive to use advanced surveillance techniques to gather continuous data including all digital impressions [32]. There are technical limitations to some of the most advanced techniques devised to allow analytics on private data [37]. Centralization of information tilts the gain–loss trade-off in favor of potential attackers and intruders [31, 32]. There currently exist information privacy laws that are entirely out of pace with current technology and which no longer conform to the spirit of original laws (e.g., the 4th Amendment of the US Constitution) in preventing breaches of privacy and civility [1, 32]. Government investigative agencies have a tendency to violate reasonable expectation of privacy if there are no barriers to unfettered intrusion, and Big Data brings a new level of scale and capability not foreseen by earlier laws [1, 32].

3.4 Ethics and Law

Privacy has a tangible and physical as well as a more intangible informational aspect. From "womb" to "tomb," we need private spaces within which our personality and social relationships develop and find definition. The Arabic word meaning one's private surroundings (*Hareem*) relates to the word meaning womb or one's private relations (*Reham*). As such, the significance of privacy and its moral dimension was recognized far earlier than the US Constitution and its Amendment. Ancient Egyptians had 42 negative confessions to the god of the dead, Osiris. The 17th of these confessions reads: "I've not been an eavesdropper" [38]. Besides the ancient Egyptian, Chinese, Greek, and Persian beliefs, all later Abrahamic religions also condoned violation of privacy and personal integrity [39]. More recent socio-legal and philosophical accounts view privacy as arising from the exercise of demeanor and deference [40]. They suggest that violation of privacy not only harms individual integrity but also degrades social health and cohesion. Privacy as the underpinning of many rules of civility and social norms is intrinsically valuable [33]. Modern legal scholars, inspired by the 4th Amendment to the US Constitution, have advanced the philosophical account of privacy based on the notion that the proper development of social personality and identity as well as citizenship depend, critically, on the protection of privacy including one's digital and informational effects [32].

Big Data deployments greatly enhanced the risks of privacy violations but more subtly. Even before 9/11, the US' Patriot Act, or the Edward Snowden revelation brought Big Data's privacy harms into full public view, there was gathering concern regarding violations that large databases of mostly private information made possible [1, 35]. Although, in the US, leading scholars have continuously re-evaluated and reassessed philosophical and socio-legal foundations of data privacy, 2013 saw an amazing increase in scholarly publications and open conferences regarding Big Data's privacy harms.

When considering privacy within modern communications systems, the following taxonomy has been proposed [41]:

- **Information collection**. Information collection refers to surveillance and interrogation.
- **Information processing**. Processing refers to aggregation, identification, insecurity (loss of identity to theft), secondary use, and exclusion (through erroneous "facts" or analytics).
- **Information dissemination**. Dissemination refers to breaches of confidentiality, disclosure, exposure, increased accessibility (for the users or by the potential intruders), blackmail (by powerful institutions or individuals), appropriation, and distortion.
- **Intrusion and decisional interference**. Invasion of privacy has two essential components: intrusion and decisional interference. The latter aspect is perhaps the most difficult to grasp, and we will discuss it further in what follows.

Some technologists have pointed out a distinction between the scientists' use of Big Data, which focuses primarily on generalization, and the business and governmental use of Big Data, which focuses primarily on particularization [4]. To refer to this particularization, legal scholars have used the acronym PII, personal information identification [14]. We can identify two general classes of problems, one more insidious than the other: the "Orwellian Problems," which arise from data collection and surveillance, and the "Kafkaesque Problems," which arise from non-transparent decision making beyond one's control and in the absence of any due processi [2].

Given this analysis, researchers, including leading privacy researchers from technology firms and academic centers, have an array of proposals and systems for the following [1, 9, 14, 32]:

1. Accounting and auditing for Big Data analysis and decision making.
2. Transparency and procedural data due process for all involved including the "prosumers" of Big Data. [1]
3. As part of 1 and 2, technologies, processes, and policies that make it possible for users to challenge classifications and automated decisions prior to their making or implementation.
4. New derived interpretations of original privacy laws that intended to protect privacy as a rule of civility.

Proposal 4 above seeks to address the new power differentials caused by technological advances that have removed physical barriers to privacy intrusion by governments either directly or indirectly through powerful third party Big Data service providers.

---

[1]The invented word "prosumer" has recently been used in industry circles to highlight that the consumers of Big Data services are also the original producers of the Big Data digital repositories.

The issues are complex and subtle but it is clear that we will either be moving towards systems that reflect social norms and rules of civility or to a "Big Brother" environment that chills behavior and destroys independent thought and action.

However, when it comes to automated decision making, false data, false algorithmic classifications, and subsequently, false automated decisions can lead to all sorts of problems. For example, "predictive policing" lauded and used by some precincts can seriously harm citizens' rights and can also lead to vicious cycles of violence. Some "credit rating" techniques can cause behavior by other shoppers in a location to lead to a lower credit rating of another shopper in the same location—in other words, a case of guilt-by-association. A popular example of analytics intrusion in private life is Target's pregnancy prediction. It led to a teenager's parents find out about their daughter's pregnancy through product marketing material sent to their home by Target [42].

An ACLU researcher in privacy and technology has identified several problems that arise with the advent of Big Data [34]:

1. It incentivizes the broader and deeper collection of data and the longer retention of the collected data.
2. It is easier to identify private personal information when combined with information from others.
3. Most people are unaware how much information is being collected about them.
4. It can tilt the playing field toward big institutions and away from the individual due to the ensuing information asymmetries, which economists and social scientists take to be a cause for much opportunism. (The Target story is a good example of this potential problem as is the NSA/Snowden affair.)
5. It can accentuate power differential among individuals by amplifying existing advantage and disadvantage. Those who are better educated or richer get improved treatment while others get poorer treatment by service providers, leading to a vicious oppressive cycle that stifles general social growth and advancement.
6. In the absence of due process, automatic decision making based on algorithmic data mining can lead to capricious classification and economic guilt-by-association.
7. Citizens can be tagged and suffer consequences due to governmental use in administrative automation.
8. Over time, there can be a chilling effect on independent thought and action. This "chilling," where agents' behaviors are automatically shaped, is probably the gravest harm of all to society at large, its well-being, and proper development.

It is highly unlikely that we can rely, purely, on legal and market-based approaches to resolve the risks posed to users' privacy [31].

Users' generally lack enough information about providers' privacy policies and practices to allow them to measure the price and cost of one provider as opposed to another. With the ability to price having suffered, pure reliance on the current market's forces to drive to better privacy policies becomes impractical [43].

Legal approaches have suffered in the past because of difficulties to measure harm and economic damage [1].

As such, many computer scientists have called for a complete redesigning of cloud services and for a fresh look at various techniques to protect privacy.

3.5 Privacy Protection and Big Data

Big Data analytics applies statistical learning on what one might say is mostly private data "prosumers" produce, and uses this learning for purposes of prediction. As some have observed, therefore, there are "natural tensions between learning and privacy that arise whenever a learner must aggregate data across multiple individuals" [44].

There exist a variety of technical measures to protect privacy but not all have the same level of effectiveness or address the same set of problems. Here, we will present a larger list and will then address a subset in some greater detail: f^*-branch consistency, sampling (e.g., polls), aggregation, suppression, data swapping, obfuscation, data synthesis, multi-party computation, simple anonymization, k-anonymization, l-diversity, and differential privacy. Anonymization allows scientific generalization (through Big Data value extraction) to proceed but is intended to make particularization difficult.

Technical measures can be categorized according to their emphasis (see the Table 3.1): (1) intentional limitations, (2) transformations (with intention to preserve statistics), (3) ownership controls and rights, and (4) process-based safeguards. Techniques such as polling and aggregation (used traditional census) intentionally limit the scope of learning to anonymous polls or aggregate values. Transformation techniques include suppression, swapping, randomization, synthesis, k-anonymity, and differential privacy. Techniques that emphasize preservation of data ownership and expand the domain of privacy include, among other techniques, multi-party secure computation (useful for financial aggregate metric calculation without revealing individual bank assets) and f^*-consistency (which reduces the task of the provider to that of consistent ordering of encrypted changes to documents). More recently, with revelations of the US government's mass intrusion into data privacy, methods that emphasize process have found some renewed currency: audit logs, and accountability systems.

3.5.1 Anonymization

One of the most common methods of protecting privacy in analytics is the anonymization of personal records by which the subject identity of the data records are removed, concealed, or hidden. Such an action can be taken by either the users or providers of data. Users may perform anonymization before doing analytics on the

Table 3.1 Categories of privacy-preserving techniques

Category	Example techniques	Description
(1) Intentional limitations		Analytics intentionally limited
	• polls,	
	• aggregation (as used in census),	
	• etc.	
(2) Perturbations or transformations		Transformations selected to preserve as much of the statistics as possible
	• suppression,	
	• swapping,	
	• randomization,	
	• synthesis,	
	• k-anonymity	
	• differential privacy,	
	• etc.	
(3) Ownership guarantees		Strict ownership and control by prosumers of data
	• multi-party secure computation,	
	• $f*$-consistency	
	• enterprise security	
	• etc.	
(4) Process guarantees		Reliance on voluntary or regulatory safeguards honored by service providers and data "custodians"
	• audit logs,	
	• accountability systems,	
	• etc.	

big datasets. Providers may perform anonymization before storing the datasets which then can be used, sold, or shared by others. Sometimes, health data providers in the US and UK provide only limited anonymity by removing direct identification such as personal details which include names or home address, but leaving out other indirect identification such as personal details which include age, gender, or town. The providers may aggregate and classify datasets by age group before the health records are published, shared, rented, sold, or traded [45].

The common basic techniques for anonymization is to combine one or more of the following techniques:

- Removal or omission of personal details such names, DOB, age, gender, marital status, and address.

- Pseudonymization which is the process of amending the data records by substitution some code numbers (possibly by the use of encryption or hashing) for personal details.
- Grouping, aggregation, or classification of datasets by age, gender, marital status, postcode, and town.

The removal or omission of direct identification is often considered adequate to prevent identifiability. In [46], the author proposed guidelines to ensure patient privacy when sharing health research datasets. The guidelines recommend deleting direct identifiers including names, email addresses, IP addresses, biometric information, and medical device identifiers. For the remaining indirect identifiers such as age or gender, the guidelines recommend independent review if more than three indirect identifiers exist in the data sets. The author considers more than three indirect identifiers present sufficient risk of identification.

According to [47], pseudonymization is the process of disguising identifiers to facilitate the collection of key information on the same individual without revealing his or her identity. Two types exist for this purpose [45]: reversible pseudonymization and irreversible pseudonymization. In reversible pseudonymization, direct identifiers such as names are replaced with encrypted code numbers usually by applying symmetric or asymmetric encryption with an encryption key that enables obtaining the plaintext identifier from the encrypted code and vice versa. This is particularly needed for research, statistics, auditing, and pharmaceutical trials. However, irreversible pseudonymization works only in one direction where it takes the plaintext identifier and generates a fixed size encrypted or ciphered code number. The original plaintext identifier can not be obtained from the generated ciphered code number.

3.5.2   Re-Identification Attacks

A major concern to anonymization or de-identification is re-identification attacks in which correlations among various datasets are conducted in order to lead a unique finger print of a single individual. When performing automated data mining techniques on combined and linkable large datasets from multiple sources, individuals can be identifiable. That is, by linking different types of datasets, the uniqueness of each record is increased, up to a point that a link back to an individual's identity is accurately established [48]. It is worth noting that re-identification is an intentional and not accidental act with the end purpose of identifying individuals and revealing personal details. A number of studies had been published on re-identification. Computer scientist Latanya Sweeney demonstrated in her Ph.D. thesis at MIT that 69 % of the names of publicly available records for voter registration in Cambridge, Massachusetts, can be identified using birth date and the ZIP postal code [49]. With birth date and ZIP code, 97 % of the voter names can be identified. She was able to also identify the name of Governor William Weld in an anonymized medical dataset [50]. As shown in the figure on re-identification, medical data with anonymized names and addresses can be linked and matched with voter lists containing names and addresses. Matched records with overlapping zip, birth date and sex can be shortlisted to identify names and addresses of medical records with high degree of certainty.

Another example about re-identification was carried out by Arvind Narayanan and Vitaly Shmatikov [51]. The authors had developed a robust algorithm to identify several Netflix subscribers by linking and matching the anonymized data on movie ratings of 500,000 Netflix subscribers. Netflix (the world's largest online DVD rental service) had published this dataset to support the Netflix Prize data mining contest. The authors in [51] had demonstrated in their study that an attacker who knows a slight background knowledge about a particular subscriber can easily identify with high probability the subscriber's record if it is present in the dataset, or, at the very least, may be able to identify a small set of records which include the subscriber's record. The attacker's background knowledge need not be precise, e.g., the dates may only be known to the adversary with a 14-day error, the ratings may be known only approximately, and some of the ratings and dates may even be completely wrong.

However, the most popular re-identification breach occurred in 2006 [48] with America Online (AOL) releasing 20 million user search queries over a three-month period with the purpose of facilitating research in the area of information retrieval. Prior to releasing the dataset, AOL had anonymized all queries containing personal and sensitive information such as social security and credit card numbers. Anonymization was done by replacing user identifiers with random numbers [52]. However, within two hours after the release, two reporters from the New York Times were able to reveal the identity of user No. 4417749 based on just her search history. The user was identified as "Thelma Arnold." Consequently, this breach had resulted in firing several AOL high ranking employees. This incident had prevented many search engine companies from releasing their search logs, and also many researchers are reluctant to use the released AOL queries to conduct retrieval research [48].

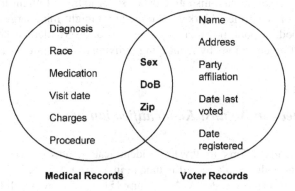

Re-identification by linking and matching lists [50].

The author in [48] has classified the re-identification attacks into three types: (1) correlation attacks, (2) arbitrary attacks, and (3) targeted identification attacks.

1. **Correlation attacks.** This attack involves linking a dataset to other sources in order to create more fine-grained and unique database entries. The example given in [48] links pseudonymized customer data of pharmacies to equivalently pseudonymized data of medications obtained from a hospital. It may lead to more fine-grained data per entry. That is, if one database lists user IDs with visited pharmacies, and the other lists the same user IDs with medication prescriptions, then it is possible to correlate and deduce relationships to show the hospital patients who bought medications from what pharmacy. In general, a correlation attack may consists in linking additional datasets from different sources to yield a finer-grained database such that there is either at least one entry that is unique in its combination of data fields, or no two entries in the database would have all data fields identical.

2. **Arbitrary attacks.** This re-identification attack attempts to link with high probability at least one entry in an aggregated dataset to the identity of a particular individual. The AOL breach is a good example which illustrates that the anonymized dataset when analyzed in correlation with other datasets can potentially identify individuals by name. This type of attack may not be able to find an entry in the correlated dataset that can clearly be linked with sufficient probability to an individual identity.

3. **Target identification attacks.** Unlike target identification attacks, this approach involves an intentional attack and more threatening to individual's privacy. The attack targets a specific person and succeeds only if it can link with high probability some entries in the database to the individual's identity. Using this attack, an employer with a priori of personal details about the prospect or current employees can search various pharmacy customer datasets for occurrences of its employees. An insurance company can use the same technique to search for prior existing conditions in the history of prospective applicants. Other examples of people who may carry out an attack may include a nosy neighbor or relative who can learn sensitive information about someone they knew participated in a survey or administrative database. A journalist might try to identify politicians or celebrities. Marketers or creditors might mine large databases to identify good, or poor, potential customers. And, disgruntled hackers might try to discredit organizations by identifying individuals in public datasets.

3.5.3 Protection Against Re-identification

Some of the early efforts to thwart re-identification attacks were focused on ensuring that no individual's record is unique in a given dataset. This motivated a popular notion of privacy called K-Anonymity [51, 53, 54] by which the dataset is released such that no individual's record is distinguishable from at least $K - 1$ other records. K-anonymity does provide a level of protection against correlation and arbitrary attacks. However, for target identification attacks in which an adversary has prior knowledge or background about an individual, K-anonymity may not provide a suitable level of protection. For example, if a hospital releases a dataset with K-anonymous records about patients who either have diabetes or cancer, and adversary knows that patient X is in this dataset but does not have cancer, then an adversary would be certain that patient X has diabetes.

L-diversity is an enhanced version of K-anonymity to mainly address K-anonymity shortcoming [55] of not being able to protect against target identification attacks. L-diversity requires that each group of individuals who are indistinguishable by means of quasi-identifiers (such as age, gender, town, postcode, etc.) not share the same value for the sensitive attribute (such as illness or medication), but rather has L distinct well represented values. The authors in [56] have described adequately a critique of k-anonymity and some of its enhanced versions like p-sensitive, l-diversity, and t-closeness.

The current state of the art anonymity technique and protection against re-identification attacks is called differential privacy [57]. It eliminates most of the notable shortcomings in K-anonymity, L-diversity, and their extensions. In [58], differential privacy was explained using an opt-in/opt-out example in which an individual can have a say to opt-in or opt-out when releasing the dataset to the public. An individual can opt-out to have their privacy protected, or opt-in and hope that an informed attacker will not be able to infer sensitive information using the released dataset. Then, the release mechanism satisfies a particular e-differential privacy if for every pair of inputs D1 and D2 that differ in one individual's record, and for every data release M, the probability that the mechanism outputs M with input D1 should be close and within some exp(e) of the probability that the mechanism outputs M with input D2. This way the data release is insensitive to an individual's presence (opt-in) or absence (opt-out) in the data.

We next summarize the popular types of privacy protection methods which can be utilized. Our summary is based on the work reported in [58]. The protection methods include Data Aggregation, Suppression, Swapping, Randomization, and Synthesis.

1. **Data aggregation.** With aggregation, privacy is protected by aggregating individual records within a report-based and summarized format before release. Aggregation reduces disclosure risks by turning records at risk into less-risky records. Aggregation is similar to K-anonymity in many ways. However, aggregation makes analysis at finer levels difficult, and it also may create problems of ecological inferences whereby relations deduced by aggregation are not seen without aggregation.
2. **Data suppression.** In suppression, not all the data values are released. Some values are removed, withheld, or disclosed. Typically, data agencies remove sensitive values from the released dataset. They may select to suppress entire variables or just at-risk data values. However, suppression may lead to inaccurate data mining and analysis as important data values are suppressed and

missing. For example, if large income values in the dataset are removed and small incomes are left out, income distribution analysis of the released data will be inaccurate and skewed to low incomes.

3. **Data swapping.** In swapping, data values of selected records are swapped to hide the true owner of the records, thereby making the matching inaccurate. Agencies may choose to select to have high rate of data swapping in which a large percentage of records are selected for swapping, or low rate in which only a small percentage of records are selected for swapping. Swapping at high rate destroys relationships involving the swapped and unswapped variables. Because of this, it is generally perceived that swapping usually involves a small fraction of data records.

4. **Data randomization.** This technique involves adding noise of randomly generated numerical values to data variables to distort the values of sensitive variables and make it difficult to deduce accurate matching. This technique is also similar to barnadization that involves randomly adding or subtracting 1 from data variables [45]. The level of privacy protection depends on the nature of the noise distribution. Greater protection is achieved when using a noise distribution with large variance. However, large-variance noise distribution may introduce measurement errors and inaccurate regression coefficients. It was found that long-tailed distribution like Pareto and Laplace may provide stronger protection [58].

5. **Data synthesis.** With synthetic data, the values of sensitive variables are replaced with synthetic values generated by simulation. In a way, the synthetic values are basically a random value generated by a probability distribution function simulator. These distributions are selected to reproduce as many of the relationships in the original data as possible. Sometimes, the synthetic values are the representation of values after transforming them into a different space, e.g., Fourier.

3.6 Challenges

In general, as human beings we will most probably aspire to live freely and will inadvertently, consciously or subconsciously fight the chilling impact of any oppressive automated decision making based on Big Data analytics used by systems and institutions. This kind of conflict can give rise to "an arms race" between the individual and institutions that rely on Big Data analytics either for generalizations or particularizations. If we are cognizant of the problem, we should be able to devise tools and technologies for privacy protection and transparent engagement of users with Big Data systems.

It is a fact that many individuals, researchers, data service and communications operators, and technology providers are thinking about these problems, and the subtleties are bound to continue that process of exploration until we have a new system of laws, practices and technologies that prevent us from destroying rules of civility while allowing the benefits of cloud computing and Big Data to flow to enrich our individual but also social life and personality.

The privacy of personal data still poses many open research problems and challenges which remain to be investigated. The research thus far has focused on data records with the assumptions that the records are unique and independent. In reality, records in social networks can be related and linked. In social networks, data records are often linked to other people whereby different types of entities and relations do exist. Protection against privacy in such linked records becomes challenging as information about one individual record can be leaked though other linked records to that individual record. Another challenging research problem is the sequential releases of the same dataset over time. The privacy can be jeopardized as attackers might be able to infer and deduce additional information from the subsequent releases that could not be inferred from one single release. A third challenge is related to devising sound mechanisms and solutions to maximize the utility of the data while guaranteeing the maximum privacy and protection. This may involve developing mathematical formulas and models that can be used to understand the trade-off between privacy and utility.

References

1. Solove DJ (2011) Nothing to hide. Yale University Press, New Haven
2. Anthonysamy P, Greenwood P, Rashid A (2013) Social networking privacy: understanding the disconnect from policy to controls. IEEE Comput 46(6):60–67
3. Johnson M, Egelman S, Bellovin SM (2012) Facebook and privacy: it's complicated. In: Symposium on usable privacy and security (SOUPS)
4. Wigan M, Clarke R (2013) Big data's big unintended consequences. IEEE Comput 46 (6):46–53
5. Zikopoulos P et al (2012) Understanding big data: analytics for enterprise class Hadoop and streaming data. McGraw Hill, New York
6. Herodotus (c. 430 BCE) The histories of Persian wars. Via http://goo.gl/sjU0um
7. Graham D et al (2004) Risk of acute myocardial infarction and sudden cardiac death in patients treated with COX-2 selective and non-selective NSAIDs. Memorandum issued at the Office of Drug Safety, Federal Drug Administration (FDA). Available via FDA. http://goo.gl/ScGpQI Accessed 6 Jan 2014
8. Ginsberg, et al (2009) Detecting influenza epidemics using search engine query data. Nature 457:1012–1014
9. Tene O, Polonetsky J (2013) Big data for all: privacy and user control in the age of analytics. Nw J Tech Intell Prop 11(5): 239–273
10. Olson D et al (2013) Reassessing Google flu trends data for detection of seasonal and pandemic influenza: a comparative epidemiological study at three geographic scales. PLoS Comput Biol 9(10)
11. Groves P, Kayyali B, Knott D, Van Kuiken S (2013) The "big data" revolution in healthcare: accelerating value and innovation. Center for US Health System Reform, Business Technology Office, McKinsey & Company
12. Pitt W et al (2013) Transforming big data into collective awareness. IEEE Comput 46 (6):40–45

13. Ostrom E (1990) Governing the commons: the evolution of institutions for collective action. Cambridge University Press, Cambridge
14. Crawford K, Schultz J (2013) Big data and due process. B Col L Rev 5(1). SSRN http://papers.ssrn.com/sol3/papers.cfm?abstract_id=2325784. Accessed 6 Jan 2014
15. Hastie T, Tibshirani R, Friedman J (2009) The Elements of statistical learning, 2nd edn. Springer Series in Statistics, New York
16. Cattell R (2010) Scalable SQL and NoSQL data stores. ACM SIGMOD Record 39(4):12–27
17. Silberstein A et al (2012) PNUTS in flight: webs-scale data serving at Yahoo. IEEE Int Comp 19(1):13–23
18. Ghemawat S, Gobioff H, Leung S (2003) ACM Symposium on operating systems principles (SOSP) 37(5):29–43
19. Burrows M (2006) Chubby lock service for loosely-coupled distributed systems. Proceedings Operating Systems Design and Implementation (OSDI). pp 335–350
20. Dean J, Ghemawat S (2008) MapReduce: simplified data processing on large clusters. Commun ACM 51(1):107–113
21. Malewicz G et al (2010) Pregel: a system for large-scale graph processing. Proceedings of the 2010 ACM SIGMOD International conference on management of data. ACM, New York, pp 135–146
22. Baker J, et al (2011) Megastore: providing scalable, highly available storage for interactive services. In: Conference on innovative data systems research (CIDR), pp 223–234
23. Melnik S et al (2011) Dremel: interactive analysis of web-scale datasets. Commun ACM 54 (6):114–123
24. Radia S, Srinivas S (2014) HADOOP 2: what's new. USENIX;login: magazine 39(1) 12–15
25. Amazon (2014) Overview of Amazon web services. Available via Amazon. http://media.amazonwebservices.com/AWS_Overview.pdf. Accessed 17 Jan 2014
26. Google (2014) Google cloud platform. Available via Google. http://cloud.google.com. Accessed 17 Jan 2014
27. AmpLab (2014) BDAS, the Berkeley data analytics stack. https://amplab.cs.berkeley.edu/software/. Accessed 10 March 2014
28. Barroso LA, Holzle U (2009) The datacenter as a computer: an introduction to the design of warehouse-scale machines. Morgan & Claypool Publishers, San Francisco
29. Armbrust M et al (2009) Above the clouds: a Berkeley view of cloud computing. Technical report UCB/EECS-2009-28, University of California, Berkeley
30. Mell P, Grance T (2011) The NIST definition of cloud computing. NIST Special Publication, pp 800–145
31. Feldman AJ (2012) Privacy and integrity in the untrusted cloud. PhD dissertation, Princeton University
32. Gray D, Citron D (2013) The right to quantitative privacy. Minnesota Law Rev 98:62–144
33. Post R (1989) The social foundation of privacy: community and self in the common law tort. Cal L Rev 77(5):957–1010
34. Stanley J (2012) Eight problems with big data. Available via ACLU. http://www.aclu.org/print/blog/technology-and-liberty/eight-problems-big-data. Accessed 6 Jan 2014
35. Garfinkel S (2000) Database nation: the death of privacy in the 21st century. O'Reilly Media, Sebastopol
36. Kosinski M, Stillwell D, Graepel T (2013) Private traits and attributes are predictable from digital records of human behavior. Proc Natl Acad Sci 110(15):5802–5805
37. Chaudhuri K, Hsu D (2010) Sample complexity bounds for differentially private learning. In: 24th Annual conference on learning theory. J Mach Learn Res: Workshop and conference proceedings
38. Budge EAW (1967) The Egyptian book of the dead: the papyrus of Ani in the British Museum. Dover Publications, New York
39. Jafari MT (2000) Religion and moral ethics. Institute for the Publication of MT Jafari's Works, Tehran
40. Goffman E (1967) Interaction ritual. Anchor Books, New York

41. Solove DJ (2006) A taxonomy of privacy. Univ Pennsylvania Law Rev 154(3):477–560
42. Duhig C (2012) How companies learn your secrets. New York Times Mag
43. Vila T, Greenstadt R, Molnar D (2003) Why we cannot be bothered to read privacy policies: privacy as a lemons market. In: Proceedings of the international conference on electronic commerce (ICEC)
44. Duchi J, Jordan M, Wainwright M (2013) Privacy aware learning. AmpLab technical report, UC Berkeley
45. Hon WK, Millard C, Walden I (2011) The problem of "personal data" in cloud computing— what Information is regulated? Cloud Unknow Int Data Privacy Law 211–228
46. Hrynaszkiewicz I (2010) Preparing raw clinical data for publication: guidance for journal editors, authors, and peer reviewers. Br Med J c181
47. EC (2007) European Commission, Directorate general justice, freedom and security, Article 29 Data protection working party, opinion 4/2007 on the Concept of Personal Data, Available via EC. http://ec.europa.eu/justice/data-protection/index_en.htm. Accessed 15 Jan 15 2014
48. Jensen M (2013) Challenges of privacy protection in big data analytics. In: Proceedings of the 2013 IEEE 2nd International congress on big data, June 27–July 2, Santa Clara, pp 235–238
49. Sweeney L (2001) Computational disclosure control: a primer on data privacy protection. Thesis draft, MIT
50. Sweeney L (2000) Uniqueness of simple demographics in the U.S. population, LIDAPWP4. Carnegie Mellon University, Laboratory for International Data Privacy, Pittsburgh, PA
51. Narayanan A, Shmatikov V (2008) Robust de-anonymization of large datasets (how to break anonymity of the Netflix Prize dataset). Proceedings of 29th IEEE symposium on security and privacy, Oakland, CA, May 2008, pp 111–125
52. Barbaro M, Zeller T (2006) A face is exposed for AOL searcher no. 4417749. NewYork Times. http://goo.gl/Et4N92. Accessed 17 Jan 2014
53. Ciriani V et al (2007) k-anonymity in secure data nanagement in decentralized systems. Springer, New York, pp 323–354
54. Sweeney L (2002) k-anonymity: a model for protecting privacy. Int J Uncertain Fuzziness Knowl-Based Syst 10(5):557–570
55. Machanavajjhala A et al (2007) L-diversity: privacy beyond k-anonymity. ACM Trans Knowl Discov Data (TKDD) 1(1)
56. Domingo-Ferrer J, Torra V (2008) A critique of k-anonymity and some of its enhancements. In: The 3rd International conference of availability, reliability, and security
57. Dwork C (2008) Differential privacy: a survey of results. In: Proceedings of TAMC'08, the 5th international conference on theory and applications of models of computation
58. Machanavajjhala A, Reiter J (2012) Big privacy: protecting confidentiality in big data. ACM Crossroads Mag 19(1):20–23

Chapter 4
Privacy in Crowdsourced Platforms

Thivya Kandappu, Arik Friedman, Vijay Sivaraman
and Roksana Boreli

4.1 Introduction

Crowdsourcing has emerged, in recent years, as a means of outsourcing various tasks to groups of individuals that are recruited online. As defined in [23]:

> Crowdsourcing is the act of taking a job traditionally performed by a designated agent (usually an employee) and outsourcing it to an undefined, generally large group of people in the form of an open call.

Crowdsourcing is increasingly used in a large number of application areas, from user opinion surveys and other information collection (including, e.g., testing of new designs) to contribution of content, for example, photos or other media, and even funding of new ventures via crowdfunding. A list of crowdsourcing companies and their classification includes over 20 task categories and around 170 companies that provide crowdsourcing activities.[1] These services have been used widely—both academic and market researchers have been increasingly relying on crowdsourcing platforms for conducting surveys, to gain new insights about customers and populations.

---

[1] http://www.resultsfromcrowds.com/features/crowdsourcing-services/.

T. Kandappu (✉) · V. Sivaraman
University of New South Wales, Sydney, Australia
e-mail: t.kandappu@unsw.edu.au

V. Sivaraman
e-mail: vijay@unsw.edu.au

A. Friedman · R. Boreli
National ICT Australia, Sydney, Australia
e-mail: arik.friedman@nicta.com.au

R. Boreli
e-mail: roksana.boreli@nicta.com.au

© Springer International Publishing Switzerland 2015
S. Zeadally and M. Badra (eds.), *Privacy in a Digital, Networked World*,
Computer Communications and Networks,
DOI 10.1007/978-3-319-08470-1_4

57

In this chapter, we focus on a narrower set of platforms that deal with collection and aggregation of information, like the Amazon Mechanical Turk[2] (AMT) platform that enables completion of human intelligence tasks or the Google Consumer Surveys platform[3] that enables large-scale market surveys.

In the vast majority of platforms, workers provide the information in a quasi-anonymous way, as there is no direct relationship between the requester (the company that requires completion of specific tasks) and the workers. Although the majority of such platforms use a payment (or micropayment) system, all direct interactions with the requesters are done thorough pseudonyms (worker IDs). Nevertheless, the release of personal information and opinions, albeit in small increments, can over time be accumulated (by the requesters or by the platform) to identify and profile individuals. This gradual loss in privacy may be undesirable for many workers, and even harmful (in social, financial, or legal ways) for some. Furthermore, the threat comes not only from requesters, but also from the platform itself, which can exploit the profiling for its own ends, or cede the information gained about the workers to another entity for monetary gain.

In this chapter we concentrate on the privacy issues of workers in crowdsourcing platforms. After a short overview of crowdsourcing platforms in Sect. 4.2, we start in Sect. 4.3 with a brief review of privacy risks in online systems. We then discuss how these risks apply to crowdsourcing platforms, focusing on the potential for personally identifying information (PII) exposure. These risks are illustrated through an example of a real world attack, conducted through a series of survey tasks in AMT. Following this, we present in Sect. 4.4 an overview of solutions that enhance privacy in online services in general, and which could also be applicable to crowdsourcing platforms.

In Sect. 4.5 we focus on a specific proposal for a privacy-preserving crowdsourcing platform [27] that relies on obfuscation, and describe the design choices surrounding obfuscation techniques, worker privacy levels, privacy loss quantification, worker privacy depletion, cost settings, and worker utility estimation. We also present the implementation details for a prototype of the system. We summarize in Sect. 4.6 the challenges that still need to be addressed to enhance worker privacy in crowdsourcing platforms and conclude the chapter in Sect. 4.7.

4.2 Crowdsourcing Platforms

Crowdsourcing platforms are leveraged to obtain feedback on goods and services, and to collect content or ideas, by soliciting contributions from an online community, rather than from more traditional sources like company employees or suppliers. A classification of crowdsourcing was presented in [47], distinguishing

---

[2]https://www.mturk.com/mturk/welcome.

[3]http://www.google.com/insights/consumersurveys/home.

between *integrative* crowdsourcing, where clients seeks to build databases or information bases (like data collection or translation of simple texts) and *selective* crowdsourcing, where a problem may be solved by relying on competencies of the crowd-based contributors.

Platforms like AMT, Crowdflower,[4] and oDesk[5] are used to crowdsource from online workers tasks like deciphering images, ranking websites, and answering surveys. AMT, launched in 2005, is extensively used by researchers in experimental psychology to conduct low-cost large-scale behavioral studies by obtaining opinion survey data from paid volunteer populations. Today AMT engages over 500,000 workers from 190 countries.[6] The Google Consumer Surveys platform utilizes a "surveywall" approach, where access to premium content is gated and enabled for users upon completion of survey questions. The Consumer Surveys platform customers include over 130 publishers (online newspapers and magazines) only in the US based market.[7] Crowdsourcing has also gained popularity in the research community. As of March 2014, Google Scholar counts more than 10,000 academic publications that involve crowdsourced experiments via AMT.

Given that mobile devices have become an integral part of people's daily lives, mobile crowdsourcing has also gained high popularity, especially in the area of environmental monitoring. For example, mCrowd [56] is an iPhone-based mobile crowdsourcing platform that enables mobile workers to contribute to geolocation-aware image collection, road traffic monitoring, and so on, which exploit the sensors available on iPhones. Txteagle [14] is a mobile crowdsourcing marketplace used in Kenya and Rwanda for translations, polls, and transcriptions. Waze[8] is a mapping app that relies on users' contributions to provide real-time traffic information. It has 15 million active users who upload their live driving data by default, so others can benefit by seeing the speed at which the contributors are moving. OpenSignal[9] allows its users to map cellular coverage, find Wi-Fi hotspots, test and improve their mobile reception, and obtain faster data rates. OpenSignal has been downloaded 3.7 million times and has about 700,000 active users (at the time of writing).

A crowdsourcing system typically comprises the following actors: *workers* (users, or contributors), who are the individuals forming the crowd that provides the data, or accomplishes selected tasks; *requesters*, who are the companies or individuals that need a set of tasks to be completed; and the *crowdsourcing platform*, which manages the crowdsourcing process, including matching workers to requesters and handling worker compensation.

---

[4]https://crowdflower.com/.

[5]https://www.odesk.com/.

[6]https://www.requester.mturk.com/tour, accessed March 27, 2014.

[7]http://www.forbes.com/sites/stevecooper/2013/03/29/qa-with-paul-mcdonald-co-creator-of-google-consumer-surveys/.

[8]https://www.waze.com/.

[9]http://opensignal.com/.

4.3 Privacy Issues in Online Services

In recent years, a number of real-world attacks have shown the importance of taking privacy into consideration when contributing data in online services. In this section, we discuss the main risks to worker privacy in online services and then focus on specific risks in crowdsourcing services, with a detailed description of an example attack.

We note that privacy issues may exist not only for the workers, but also for the requesters. For example, a company that requires a set of tasks to be accomplished by the crowd, may wish to keep such tasks, or the content of the data it shares, private. This problem can be encountered, for example, in services related to image classification and text translation [53]. However, as the vast majority of studies and real-world breach examples address worker privacy, in this chapter we consequently focus on worker privacy issues.

4.3.1 Risks of Re-Identification

Privacy risks related to public release of anonymized data sets have been demonstrated by a number of real-world events. As a prominent example, in 2006, AOL[10] released a 2 GB file containing 21 million web search queries from 650,000 users, conducted over a period of three months [4]. The consequences of the data release were devastating from the privacy perspective. AOL took down the data within days of publication due to public outcry, but the data has already been downloaded, reposted,[11] and made searchable by a number of sites. In a matter of days, the identity of user 4417749 had been unmasked by *New York Times* reporters [1]. Besides harm to the users whose names and social security numbers were published,[12] the AOL search log release may have had other harmful consequences the extent of which is difficult to assess, such as: loss of user trust in AOL, as well as, possibly, in other search engines; increased anxiety regarding the privacy of online activities for users; and hesitation of other companies to share their data to enable broader innovation [21]. Following the release of this private data set, the CTO of AOL resigned, two employees were dismissed [24], and a class action lawsuit was filed.

Similarly, in 2006, DVD rental company Netflix announced a contest with a $1 million prize for the best movie recommendation algorithm, and made an anonymized dataset of user ratings available to all interested participants [5]. The Netflix prize data release included over 100 million ratings given by over 480,000 users to 17,700 movies. Despite the anonymization of the dataset, Narayanan and

---

[10]http://www.aol.com/.

[11]See, for example, http://www.gregsadetsky.com/aol-data/.

[12]http://superjiju.wordpress.com/2009/01/18/aol-search-query-database/.

Shmatikov [39] have shown how to de-anonymize several users in the published dataset by cross-correlating anonymized Netflix ratings with non-anonymous movie ratings on the Internet Movie Database (IMDb) website. While the ratings of movies users made on IMDb did not pose privacy risks, as they were made public deliberately by the users, the re-identification of these users in the Netflix dataset exposed also their private ratings on Netflix. The study demonstrated how little auxiliary information is needed for reliable cross-correlation: for example, with eight known movie ratings, 99 % of the records could be uniquely identified; two ratings and their dates are sufficient for re-identification of 68 % of the records.

Overall, prior research, including [39], has shown analytically that even a relatively small amount of background information about an individual can facilitate a fairly reliable de-identification of that individual, in a seemingly well-anonymized dataset.

4.3.2   Risks of Profiling and Data Misuse

The growing amount of information collected about individuals is increasingly utilized for profiling and subsequent targeting of users. For example, the popular loyalty and rewards cards enable retailers to collect details of users' consumption patterns, track their shopping habits, and mine the data to determine users' interests and needs. Australian retailer Woolworths recently stated in an industry publication that it has managed to "overlay" its insurance company's car crash database and its Everyday Rewards statistics, to reveal which consumers were best to target for insurance purchases [54]. Woolworths also shares its anonymous data with Quantium, a company that sells this data to its clients for direct marketing [54].

As a specific example of customer data use, it was shown in [22] how Target can successfully predict whether a female customer is expecting a child. Target assigns every customer a Guest ID number, tied to her credit card, name, or email address, and becomes a depository for her history of purchases and any demographic information collected from her, or bought from other sources. Using this data, Target assigns a score to every female customer to indicate the likelihood that she may be pregnant. More importantly, it can also estimate the due date, so that coupons can be timed to very specific stages of a customer's pregnancy.

In a second example, the US based political media firm, Engage,[13] is able to predict who users will vote for, how likely users are to go to the polls, and the potential for them to change their vote. They have reported, during the previous US elections, that if users use Spotify to listen to music, Tumblr to consume content, or Buzzfeed to keep up on the latest in social media, there is a high likelihood that they will vote for President Obama. On the other hand, if they buy things on eBay, play

---

[13]http://enga.ge/.

FarmVille, or search the Web with Bing, they are more likely to favor Mitt Romney.

Finally, a team of British researchers have developed an algorithm that uses tracking data from people's phones to predict where they will be in 24 h [40], with an average error of just 20 meters. The researchers combined tracking data from individual participants' phones with similar data from their friends, that is, other people in their contact list.

While these examples represent a small fraction of the ways in which companies are using data to predict user behavior, the proliferation of personal data is likely to drive a rapid increase in the business of prediction. As more of user movements, browsing patterns, purchase history, and social media interactions become recorded, more companies will find ways to use this data to profile users and exploit this knowledge for profit. These capabilities incentivize a multi-billion dollar industry of data brokers to collect and sell personal user data, with little or no transparency, and often without the knowledge and consent of the individuals to whom the data pertains [43].

4.3.3 Privacy Issues in Crowdsourcing Platforms

The examples outlined in the previous sections relate to online services in general. In this section, we consider specific risks in crowdsourcing platforms and provide an example of how a requester can attain knowledge about the personal details of workers in an anonymous crowdsourcing system.

4.3.3.1 The Lack of Worker Anonymity Guarantees

In a technical report, Lease et al. [32] have identified a direct loss of worker anonymity on AMT. In AMT, requesters and workers are identified with a 14-character alphanumeric string. However, Lease et al. have observed that the same string that identifies a worker in AMT is also the unique identifier of that account across all Amazon services. Therefore, any public information associated with an Amazon account, such as name and picture on the public Amazon profile, product reviews and ratings, or a wish list, will be easily accessible via that account's Web URL.[14] The use of the same account to access both AMT and other Amazon services allows workers to use the proceeds for their AMT work towards purchases on Amazon's website. Moreover, Lease et al. pointed out that the term "anonymous" has never been used on AMT's website and policies, and while these policies express Amazon's concern for workers' privacy, they do not state explicit guarantees of worker anonymity. However, it is unclear whether workers are aware

---

[14]www.amazon.com/gp/pdp/profile/<WorkerID>.

of the tight connection between their alphanumeric identifier on AMT and their public information on other Amazon services. In fact, a thread on Turker Nation (a forum dedicated to AMT discussions), predating Lease et al.'s work, reflects the surprise of workers who learned about this relation.[15]

4.3.3.2 De-Anonymization and Privacy Loss via Inference Attacks

Lease et al. [32] suggested that having worker IDs that are not linked to other (Amazon) services may mitigate the current direct anonymity loss issue for workers. However, such measures may not be sufficient to eliminate all threats to worker anonymity and privacy. Kandappu et al. [26] have shown how privacy risks like those explored in Sect. 4.3.1, could easily apply to existing crowdsourcing platforms to de-anonymize workers and obtain sensitive private information, in a short time period and at very low cost, by correlating responses across multiple surveys.

The inference attack in [26] comprised of launching a series of survey tasks in AMT (through the third-party aggregator CrowdFlower[16]). The first survey queried workers for their opinions on astrology services, and in the process obtained their star-sign and day/month of birth. The second survey purportedly conducted market research of online match-making services, and thereby obtained the workers' gender and year of birth. With the third survey, on mobile phone coverage, the researchers obtained workers' zip code information.

The surveys were designed with sufficient redundancy to help identify and filter out workers who gave random responses. Further, these surveys were posted independently over several days, and workers were unlikely to have known that they were conducted by the same entity. The researchers used the unique IDs (constant across all surveys) to link workers who took all the three surveys above and to obtain a combination of their personal details, that is, their date of birth, gender, and zip code. We note that previous studies [20, 51] have shown the effectiveness of using these attributes in re-identification of individuals.

A fourth survey was then launched, asking workers about their smoking habits and coughing frequency. Overall, of the 400 unique workers who took the surveys, 72 could be linked from the first three surveys, and the respiratory health (and likelihood of tuberculosis) for 18 of these individuals could be inferred from the fourth survey using their unique ID, resulting in a potentially serious breach of privacy. This experiment took only a few days and cost less than $30; one can only imagine what the scale of privacy loss could be, were this experiment to be conducted by entities with larger resources.

Finally, the above experiment was followed up with another survey, where workers were asked if they would participate in a survey, if they knew they could be

---

[15]http://turkernation.com/archive/index.php/t-6065.html.

[16]https://crowdflower.com/.

de-anonymized and profiled. Out of 100 workers who took this survey, 73 (including 15 of the 18 workers above, whose respiratory health could potentially be made public) responded that they were not aware that they could be profiled, and indicated that they would not have participated otherwise. These experiments illustrate that workers can be profiled easily and at low cost, despite their disapproval of such practices.

The release of personal facts and opinions, albeit in small increments, can over time be accumulated (by the requesters or by the platform) to profile individuals (e.g., the work carried out in [30] shows that a wide variety of people's attributes can be accurately inferred using their Facebook likes). This gradual loss of privacy may be undesirable for workers, and even harmful (in social, financial, or legal ways) for some. Furthermore, the threat comes not only from requesters, but also from the platform itself, which can exploit the profiling for its own ends, or cede it to another entity for gain.

We note that AMT's policies[17] explicitly forbid using the platform to collect personally identifiable information, or requiring workers to disclose their identity, directly or indirectly. However, partial information (e.g., gender or age), which is not sufficient for identifying an individual on its own, may be legitimately acquired for the purpose of a specific survey. Despite the policy restrictions, it may be difficult to track and enforce limitations on subsequent combining and (mis)use of this information.

4.4   Overview of Existing Solutions

We now present an overview of recent technological advances in defining and protecting individuals' privacy and data confidentiality (visibility of the data values used for aggregation) in data publishing and aggregation. We note that in crowd-sourcing, as in most services that rely on users' data, there is a need to balance the privacy of individual participants with the greater good for which the aggregate data can be used.

4.4.1   Anonymization

Early research works on data anonymization proposed sanitizing user data by masking or removing PII such as name and address, and quasi-identifiers such as gender and zip code. k-anonymity [46, 52] takes a "blend into the crowd" approach to privacy, and requires that every combination of quasi-identifiers appears in at least k data instances. This is achieved by generalization of such identifiers, for

---

[17]https://www.mturk.com/mturk/help?helpPage=policies, accessed March 27, 2014.

example, by limiting the zip code to four or fewer, rather than five, recorded digits. Further refinements of k-anonymity include l-diversity [37], t-closeness [33], and other variants, which introduce additional restrictions on the released data values. It was demonstrated, however, that such intuitive anonymization techniques are not effective in protecting user privacy, as individual users can be re-identified via the use of background information [10, 39, 44, 51], as shown by the AOL and Netflix data release examples from Sect. 4.3.1. To date, safe release of anonymized data for analysis purposes is still an open research problem. In addition, using such techniques in crowdsourcing scenarios may not be practical, as users need to be identifiable so that they can be compensated for contributing their data.

4.4.2 Data Obfuscation

Data obfuscation techniques protect user privacy by perturbing the data contributed by individuals.

4.4.2.1 Randomized Response

A traditional method to obfuscate data is by randomization—this can be done by adding noise sampled from a selected distribution, by multiplying with noise or by projecting the data, to alter the individual values of the records. This method relies on the ability to recover the probability distribution of the aggregate (non-noisy) data, which can subsequently be used for data analysis. The earliest work on randomization was presented in [34, 55], where it was used to eliminate the untruthful answer bias. A generic approach proposed in [2, 3] is to add random distortion values drawn independently from a known distribution, for example, the uniform distribution. A number of improvements to this technique were subsequently proposed [15, 16].

We note that randomization methods apply noise to the records in a *data-independent way*, thereby this technique can be utilized at the *source* of data collection. Thus, perturbation of the records does not require a trusted server. However, it was shown that an adversary may analyze the data and filter out some of the noise, effectively reducing the bounds of uncertainty introduced by the noise and compromising the privacy guarantees [29].

4.4.2.2 Differential Privacy

Differential privacy [13] is a privacy model based on the principle that the output of a computation should not allow inference about any record in the input, irrespective of an adversary's computational power or the available background knowledge. This guarantee is obtained by constraining the effect that any single record could have on the outcome of the computation. Consequently, the promise of differential privacy is that the probability of a "bad" outcome resulting from a computation on the data will be almost unaffected by the specific value of any particular record in the dataset. Yet in aggregate, these records would still provide useful information. Formally, a mechanism K provides (ε, δ)-differential privacy [12] (or simply ε-differential privacy for $\delta = 0$) if for any two datasets A and B differing in a single record, and for all outcomes S:

$$\Pr[K(A) \in S] \leq exp(\varepsilon) \times \Pr[K(B) \in S] + \delta. \tag{4.1}$$

The parameter ε controls the level of privacy, where smaller values of ε provide stricter bounds on the influence of any particular input record on the outcome, and therefore provide better privacy—adding or removing any particular record would hardly change the probability of obtaining a given outcome, so the outcome would not reveal much about any underlying record. The parameter δ allows the condition in Eq. (4.1) to be relaxed for unlikely events, allowing ε-differential privacy to be breached in some rare cases. One of the prevalent methods to achieve differential privacy is by adding noise to the outcome of a computation. The noise is calibrated according to the influence that any record may have on this outcome such that Eq. 4.1 holds, as further described in Sect. 4.5.2.2. Differential privacy maintains composability, that is, if two computations maintain $(\varepsilon_1, \delta_1)$ and $(\varepsilon_2, \delta_2)$ differential privacy respectively, then executing both would amount to $(\varepsilon_1 + \varepsilon_2, \delta_1 + \delta_2)$ differential privacy.

The practical implications of differentially private analysis were studied in many application domains, including network trace analysis [38], intelligent transportation systems [28], collaborative security mechanisms [42], and distributed stream monitoring [17]. Most applicable to the *crowdsourcing* scenarios are the distributed differential privacy mechanisms [12, 41], that provide strong privacy guarantees in distributed settings. Rastogi and Nath in [41] designed a two-round protocol based on the threshold homomorphic cryptosystem, and Shi et al. in [48] applied cryptographic techniques to allow an untrusted aggregator to compute sums without learning anything about the user inputs. Both designs presented in [41, 48] achieve distributed differential privacy while reducing the computational load per user. These systems leverage cryptographic techniques to generate differentially private noise in a distributed manner, but unfortunately do not scale well. In Sect. 4.5 we describe in greater detail a system that relies on differential privacy to track privacy loss in a crowdsourcing scenario.

4.4.3 Cryptographic Mechanisms

Cryptographic mechanisms are commonly used in conjunction with obfuscation to achieve both data confidentiality and privacy [41, 48]. Chen et al. [8] proposed a system that performs statistical queries over private client data (distributed on local databases, e.g., on client devices), where the analyst communicates with clients via an honest-but-curious proxy. On first connection, a proxy assigns a unique ID to a client. Answers are provided as binary values corresponding to a set of buckets, that is, the potential values that a query may result in. Each binary value is encrypted using the Goldwasser-Micali (GM) cryptosystem [19], a probabilistic public-key cryptosystem that ensures each encrypted value is represented by a different cyphertext. The analyst combines the decrypted client answers (that are also obfuscated using a differentially private mechanism) to produce the result. The authors extended these concepts in [7] to propose the SplitX system. This again includes an analyst, a set of clients who locally store their data and a set of intermediate entities: an aggregator and two mixes. However, SplitX uses a simple XOR-based crypto-mechanism and a series of split messages (each message is split into two, which are sent in parallel to any of the two intermediate nodes). This provides the additional properties of anonymity and unlinkability and enables considerably improved system performance.

A different approach to enabling confidentiality is to apply a secret sharing cryptographic mechanism to the distributed private data, and perform Secure Multi-Party Computation (MPC). However, this approach is only resilient to a specific proportion of honest-but-curious attackers who collude to learn the private data and/or the result of aggregation. MPC has been applied to crowdsourcing platforms using the Sharemind implementation, as described in [6].

4.4.4   Compensating Users for Privacy Loss

Rather than limiting privacy loss when collecting and using personal information, an alternative approach is to accept this loss and compensate the users accordingly, so that they are incentivized to share information. Laudon [31] proposed a market for personal data, which relies on individual ownership of this information. In fact, several start-ups, such as Reputation.com [50], Handshake [36], and Datacoup [49], are endeavoring to make such markets a reality.

Further to this, Ghosh and Roth [18] initiated a study of markets for private data, where the privacy of users, as measured by differential privacy, is the sold commodity. Specifically, they consider a setting where the data is binary, and the aggregator wishes to estimate the sum of bits. They proposed the *FairQuery* mechanism, which achieves the optimal accuracy given a budget B, among the set of all truthful, individually rational envy-free fixed purchase mechanisms. Dandekar et al. [11] generalized these results to linear predictors (with inputs in $\mathbb{R}^n$), and observed that while these settings are similar to the knapsack auction mechanism, they also pose the challenge that privacy costs exhibit externalities. That is, the privacy cost of an individual depends also on which other individuals are being compensated.

One of the challenges highlighted by Gosh and Roth [18] is that the data collector will only get the information of individuals who value their privacy at a lower cost than that offered by the buyer. This introduces a selection bias, which could lead to inaccurate results. Another challenge is that an individual's cost for privacy may be correlated to private information, and therefore might be itself private information. In fact, they showed that, in general, it is not possible for any individually rational direct revelation mechanism to compensate individuals for their privacy loss due to unknown correlations between their cost functions and their private data. Ligett and Roth [35] proposed to circumvent this impossibility result by considering a "take-it-or-leave-it" framework, where a surveyor randomly samples members of the underlying population, and offers them the same price in return for participating in the survey. These offers are repeated with fresh population samples and with increasing prices, until a sufficient rate of participation is obtained. This model captures that individuals may also experience a cost when information about their cost function (i.e., the cost they associate with privacy loss) is revealed. The model also captures that individuals can suffer negative utility even when they choose not to participate in surveys, as this choice may be correlated with their private information.

All the aforementioned works [11, 18, 35] assumed that users cannot lie about their private information, but can lie about their costs. The truthful mechanisms ensure that individuals do not mis-report their cost functions in an attempt to maximize their payment. In contrast, Chen et al. [9] did not assume that players provide truthful answers. Instead, they considered settings where users may choose to lie, but also have a direct interest in the outcome of the mechanisms. They explicitly modeled privacy in the participants' utility functions, and designed truthful mechanisms with respect to it. The mechanisms leverage the users' interest in the outcome, such that the payoff overcomes the users' value for privacy. Essentially, the privacy parameter should only be set to be small enough such that the privacy costs are outweighted by the participants' preferences for outcomes.

Finally, Riederer et al. [45] introduced a mechanism of transactional privacy, which enables end-users to sell or lease portions of their personal information (on a strictly opt-in basis) in exchange for monetary compensation. This compensation is determined in an auction, where data aggregators place bids based on their valuation of the user's information. The users can then decide what and how much information will be disclosed to the aggregators, and the data can be sold multiple times.

4.5   Loki: Privacy Preserving Crowdsourcing Platform

In Sect. 4.4 we surveyed general techniques for protecting user privacy in data analysis, which are also applicable to crowdsourcing platforms. In this section we consider in depth "Loki," a system proposed by Kandappu et al. [26, 27], which focuses on facilitating the crowdsourcing applications in a privacy preserving way.

4.5.1   Architecture and Entities

The proposed system (Fig. 4.1) comprises three entities: requesters, workers, and the broker platform.

Requesters acquire data from workers using a set of questions in a survey form (the work largely focuses on ratings-based questions and multiple-choice questions). The requester pays the broker to run the survey, specifying an upper bound on total cost. The requester aims for high accuracy (utility) in the aggregated response for any survey, so that it closely represents the feedback of the entire population.

Workers respond to questions in the surveys, using a supplied application (app) installed on their personal device (smart phone/tablet). The app allows workers to obfuscate their responses at source. The workers' monetary compensation may in general depend on their choice of privacy level—higher privacy levels entail higher obfuscation and hence lower payment. Loki does not deal with intentional lying (or cheating) by workers to get higher compensation; however, lying may make the worker a worse predictor of the population average, reducing the chances that the algorithm (described in Sect. 4.5.3.4) will select this worker for subsequent surveys, thereby offsetting the monetary gains from cheating.

The **broker** provides a platform for launching surveys. It receives payment from requesters, and passes it on to workers (less a commission). The broker has a dual

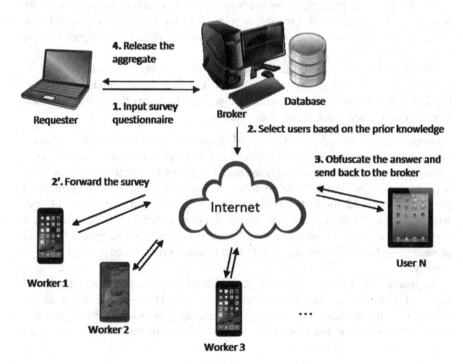

Fig. 4.1 Loki: System components and the basic protocol

objective: to provide accurate population estimates to requesters, and to extend the lifetime of workers in the system. The broker keeps track of workers' performance (i.e., how good a predictor of population behavior each worker has been in the past) and privacy (cumulative depletion of a privacy "budget" due to participation in surveys), so it can balance the trade-off within the cost budget.

4.5.2 Design Choices

4.5.2.1 Obfuscation and Worker Privacy Levels

In Loki, the worker client locally obfuscates the answer before reporting it to the broker. For *ratings-based* questions, Gaussian noise $\mathcal{N}(0, \gamma^2)$ is locally added to the worker response. Gaussian distribution was chosen over uniform as it has unbounded range, and hence does not compromise worker privacy in boundary cases. It was preferred over Laplace noise since it is additive, that is, the sum of Gaussian noise terms is still Gaussian. Further, note that the mean of the noise is chosen to be zero for convenience, so as not to introduce any bias one way or the other. The standard deviation γ is adjusted based on the worker's privacy chosen privacy level. For *multiple-choice* questions, Loki relies on the randomized response technique [55], whereby the worker's true selection is preserved with probability $1 - p$, and with probability p $(p < 0.5)$ the response is changed uniformly randomly to one of the other choices. Again, the value of p is dictated by the worker's chosen privacy level, described next.

For the sake of simplicity, Loki uses a set of four privacy levels: *none*, *low*, *medium*, and *high*. The chosen privacy level determines the amplitude of the noise that is added to obfuscate the true worker response. The higher the privacy level, the larger the obfuscation parameter (γ or p above).

Example 1 Consider a 5-point Likert scale commonly used in psychology studies, with the possible response values including: 1 (strongly disagree), 2 (disagree), 3 (neutral), 4 (agree), and 5 (strongly agree). A reasonable selection of obfuscation parameter might be: $\gamma = 0$ for no privacy, $\gamma = 3$ for low privacy, $\gamma = 6$ for medium privacy, and $\gamma = 12$ for high privacy (note that the reported responses will consequently be real-valued rather than integers). For a multiple choice question with five options, a reasonable selection of obfuscation parameter might be: $p = 0$ for no privacy, $p = 0.1$ for low privacy, $p = 0.3$ for medium privacy, and $p = 0.4$ for high privacy.

In general, the worker can set the desired level of privacy for each conducted survey. For simplicity, we assume that the worker's choice is consistent across surveys (i.e., the worker tends to choose the same level of privacy for each survey), but our selection algorithm (described in Sect. 4.5.3) can be easily modified to adapt based on different user choices.

4.5.2.2 Quantification and Tracking of Privacy Loss

Loki quantifies the privacy loss for a worker who answers a particular survey at a particular privacy level, so it can be accumulated and tracked across multiple surveys. For this purpose, Loki relies on differential privacy, where the differential privacy constraint is applied to each survey answer. That is, the parameters ε and δ capture how easy or difficult it is to infer the original user response given the noisy survey response. For *rating-based* questions, the privacy guarantees of Gaussian noise $\mathcal{N}(0, \gamma^2)$ can be mapped to (ε, δ)-differential privacy measures through the relation [12]:

$$\frac{\varepsilon\gamma^2}{2R^2} + \ln(\varepsilon\gamma^2) \geq \ln\frac{1}{\delta}, \tag{4.2}$$

where R is the range of the user's possible answers. To illustrate by an example:

Example 2 Following from the previous example, the 5-point Likert scale based ratings with privacy levels {no, low, medium, high} respectively used $\gamma = \{0, 3, 6, 12\}$. Since $R = 4$, and fixing $\delta = 0.01$, the privacy settings correspond to differential privacy guarantees of $\varepsilon = \{\infty, 3.42, 0.85, 0.21\}$ respectively.

For *multiple choice* questions (with n options) obfuscated using the randomized response technique, the mapping from the probability measure p to (ε, δ) can be derived from (4.1) as:

$$\varepsilon \geq \ln(1 - p - \delta) - \ln(p) + \ln(n - 1). \tag{4.3}$$

Example 3 Following from the previous example of a multiple choice question with five options, the privacy settings {no, low, medium, high} respectively used $p = \{0, 0.1, 0.3, 0.4\}$. Fixing $\delta = 0.01$, the privacy settings correspond to differential privacy guarantees of $\varepsilon = \{\infty, 3.57, 2.22, 1.77\}$ respectively.

The differential privacy metrics are composable (i.e., additive), and the worker's privacy loss over successive surveys can therefore easily be upper bounded by accumulating these metrics over the worker's lifetime. These upper bounds capture the relative privacy loss for each of the workers, which the broker can rely on to ensure a fair distribution of the privacy loss across workers. In the rest of this chapter, we will fix the value of δ at 0.01, and use ε for comparing privacy loss across workers. Further, for cases where workers choose privacy level "none," ε is set to 0 (rather than the theoretically correct value of ∞), since the workers are explicitly indicating that they do not value privacy for that survey, and the effect of this survey on their cumulative privacy loss should not be accounted for.

4.5.2.3   Cost Settings

A worker i, who contributes data in response to a survey questionnaire, receives a compensation c_i. Workers who choose a higher privacy level (and consequently add more noise to their responses) may receive lower compensation than those who choose a lower level of privacy.

Example 4 Following from the previous example that uses a 5-point Likert scale, the privacy levels none, low, medium, and high could correspond to worker payments c_i of \$0.8, \$0.4, \$0.2, and \$0.1 respectively. The unit of cost is arbitrary and can be scaled appropriate to the complexity or value of the survey.

4.5.2.4   Worker History and Utility

Despite noise addition by workers to obfuscate individual answers, some characteristics of worker behavior can be discerned by the broker over time. As an example, noise added by a worker to n successive ratings-based questions, each with iid noise $\mathcal{N}(0, \gamma^2)$, can be averaged by the broker to estimate the worker's mean noise $\mathcal{N}(0, \gamma^2/n)$ that has lower variance. This fact can be leveraged by the broker to estimate metrics such as the "error" of the worker's ratings, that is, to determine on average how close the worker's ratings in the past have been to the population averages. This in turn indicates how representative this worker is of the general population, and helps the broker estimate the "value" of the worker towards obtaining an accurate population estimate. In Sect. 4.5.3, this notion of worker "value" is leveraged to select workers for each survey, in a balanced way.

4.5.3   Privacy-Preserving User Selection Mechanism

This section describes a practical method for the broker to select workers to participate in each survey so as to balance cost, accuracy, and privacy. We outline the approach for ratings-based questions (continuous-valued); the analysis for multiple-choice questions (discrete-valued) is presented in the authors' full version [25].

4.5.3.1   Quantifying Estimation Error

The broker is tasked with estimating the population average of a statistic (e.g., movie rating, product popularity, disease prevalence). Due to the cost constraint set by the requester, the broker can query only a subset of workers S from the universal set of workers U, and this selection is based on accuracy, cost, and privacy depletion.

Denote by $x_i \in \mathbb{R}$ the input of worker $i \in U$. The desired population average θ is given by $\theta = \sum_U x_i / |U|$. The broker estimates this statistic by sampling a subset of workers S. Further, each worker i sends obfuscated input $\hat{x}_i = x_i + n_i$ to the broker, whereby the true input x_i is combined with noise n_i taken from $\mathcal{N}(0, \gamma_i^2)$, where γ_i depends on the worker's chosen privacy level. The broker's estimate $\hat{\theta}$ of the population average is then given by

$$\hat{\theta} = \sum_S \hat{x}_i / |S| = \sum_S (x_i + n_i) / |S|. \tag{4.4}$$

The mean squared error in the estimator is given by:

$$RMSE^2 = (\hat{\theta} - \theta)^2 = \left[\frac{\sum_S n_i}{|S|} + \left(\frac{\sum_S x_i}{|S|} - \theta \right) \right]^2. \tag{4.5}$$

When selecting S, the broker therefore accounts for two influencing factors: the level of privacy required by each worker, which determines the error due to privacy-related noise (first term above), and the expected sampling error (second term above).

The "value" of a worker depends on how accurately the worker's responses reflect those of the population at large. To quantify this, consider the worker error, i.e., the difference Δ_i between the worker's response and the true population average, given by $\Delta_i = x_i - \theta$. Treating the worker error Δ_i as a random variable, we can estimate its mean μ_i and variance σ_i^2 from the history of prior responses $H_i = \{\hat{x}_{ij}\}$ of the worker using:

$$\mu_i = \mathbb{E}[\Delta_i] = \sum_{j : x_{ij} \in H_i} (x_{ij} - \theta_j) / |H_i|, \tag{4.6}$$

$$\sigma_i^2 = Var[\Delta_i] = \sum_{j : x_{ij} \in H_i} (x_{ij} - \theta_j - \mu_i)^2 / |H_i|, \tag{4.7}$$

where θ_j denotes the true population average in a past survey question q_j. New workers can be assigned a default value of worker error.

Similarly, we can define the value of a group of workers S. The average rating by the group is defined as $x_S = \sum_S x_i / |S|$. Denoting by Δ_S the group error, which quantifies the difference between this group's average rating and the population average, we have $\Delta_S = x_S - \theta$. The mean and variance of the group error can be deduced from the prior history $H_S = \{\hat{x}_{Sj}\}$ of this group using:

$$\mu_S = \mathbb{E}[\Delta_S] = \sum_{j : x_{Sj} \in H_S} (x_{Sj} - \theta_j) / |H_S|, \tag{4.8}$$

$$\sigma_S^2 = Var[\Delta_S] = \sum_{j : x_{Sj} \in H_S} (x_{Sj} - \theta_j - \mu_S)^2 / |H_S|. \tag{4.9}$$

The estimation of the worker and group errors above assumes perfect knowledge of the true worker responses x_i and the population averages θ_j. In reality the broker only has the noisy worker/group responses ($\hat{x}_i$ or $\hat{x}_S$), as well as noisy population estimate $\hat{\theta}_j$ for prior survey questions. The mean (μ_S) and variance (σ_S^2) of the true group error can be approximated with the mean ($\hat{\mu}_S$) and variance ($\hat{\sigma}_S^2$) of the computed errors, using the fact that the noise is independent of worker responses and has zero mean:

$$\hat{\mu}_S \approx \mu_S, \tag{4.10}$$

$$\hat{\sigma}_S^2 \approx \sigma_S^2 + \frac{\sum_S \gamma_i^2}{|S|^2} + \frac{\sum_U \gamma_i^2}{|U|^2}. \tag{4.11}$$

The expectation of the error in Eq. (4.5) is then derived as:

$$\mathbb{E}(RMSE^2) = \mathbb{E}\left[\left(\frac{\sum_S n_i}{|S|}\right)^2\right] + \mathbb{E}\left[(x_S - \theta)^2\right] =$$

$$= \frac{\sum_S \gamma_i^2}{|S|^2} + \sigma_S^2 + \mu_S^2 \approx \hat{\mu}_S^2 + \hat{\sigma}_S^2 - \frac{\sum_U \gamma_i^2}{|U|^2}. \tag{4.12}$$

4.5.3.2 Balancing Cost and Accuracy in a Single Survey

As described in Sect. 4.5.2.3, each worker chooses a privacy setting, which incurs a privacy cost (ε_i, δ_i). The privacy protection is obtained by adding noise with variance γ_i^2. The privacy setting is also associated with monetary compensation c_i. Given the worker choices, the broker proceeds to select a group of workers to be included in the survey, based on two constraints:

Monetary cost constraint. A requester sets an overall cost C for a survey. The broker selects n_j workers who picked the j-th privacy setting associated with cost c_j. To stay within the overall cost bound, the broker ensures $\sum_j n_j c_j \leq C$.

Privacy constraint. For each worker, the cumulative privacy loss throughout the system lifetime is capped at ($\varepsilon_{max}, \delta_{max}$). Each worker i in survey j incurs a known privacy cost ($\varepsilon_{ij}, \delta_{ij}$). The accumulated privacy loss for worker i is therefore ($\sum_j \varepsilon_{ij}, \sum_j \delta_{ij}$) where the summation is over all the past surveys taken by this worker. The residual privacy budget for the worker is consequently ($R_i^{(\varepsilon)}, R_i^{(\delta)}$), where $R_i^{(\varepsilon)} = \varepsilon_{max} - \sum_j \varepsilon_{ij}$ and $R_i^{(\delta)} = \delta_{max} - \sum_j \delta_{ij}$. To guarantee that the worker's cumulative privacy loss stays within the lifetime privacy budget, the broker must ensure that for the new survey, $\varepsilon_i \leq R_i^{(\varepsilon)}$ and $\delta_i \leq R_i^{(\delta)}$.

For a new survey, we can therefore pose the selection of a set S of workers to survey as an optimization problem:

$$\arg \min_{S \subseteq U} RMSE$$

$$\text{s.t.} \sum_j n_j c_j \leq C \text{ and } \forall i \in S : \varepsilon_i \leq R_i^{(\varepsilon)} \wedge \delta_i \leq R_i^{(\delta)}, \qquad (4.13)$$

where the RMS error is obtained from Eq. (4.12). For the special case when a worker chooses a "no privacy" setting, which in theory translates to an unconstrained loss in privacy ($\varepsilon \to \infty$), we make the practical choice of using $\varepsilon = 0$, $\delta = 0$, reflecting that the worker is not concerned about the privacy implications in this case.

Note that the upper bounds ε_{max} and δ_{max} are used to capture the relative privacy loss for each of the workers, which the broker relies on to ensure a fair distribution of the privacy loss across workers. Workers whose privacy budget is exhausted can be given a new identity which is unlinked to the previous one, and a new privacy budget, allowing them participation in future surveys. Another possible option is to increase all the workers' privacy budgets once a significant portion of the workers deplete their budget. Regardless of the broker's policy, workers can always choose to quit the system when they deem their cumulative privacy loss too high.

4.5.3.3 Balancing Cost, Accuracy, and Privacy Fairness Across Multiple Surveys

When considering a series of surveys, additional factors may influence the broker's choices, beyond the cost and privacy constraints. In particular, *Quality of Service (QoS)* across surveys aims to keep an (ideally) constant *RMS* error over successive surveys that can be maintained and guaranteed to the requesters, while *fairness* aims to balance the residual level of privacy across workers, since privacy can be seen as a non-renewable resource, which should be equally depleted across workers. QoS considerations may motivate the broker to select for a survey workers with low error, but this may deplete such workers' privacy budget rapidly. Consequently, those workers may be excluded from participation in subsequent surveys, resulting in deterioration of QoS over time.

To control the influence of QoS and fairness considerations, a "fairness parameter" $\alpha \in [0, 1]$ is set by the broker. The monetary and privacy cost of worker i are then combined into an overall cost F_i, given by:

$$F_i = (1 - \alpha) \frac{c_i}{C} + \alpha \cdot \max \left[\frac{\varepsilon_i}{R_i^{(\varepsilon)}}, \frac{\delta_i}{R_i^{(\delta)}} \right]. \qquad (4.14)$$

The first term considers the monetary cost of the worker for this survey, as a fraction of the budget available for the survey. The second term considers the privacy depleted by this worker's participation in the survey, as a fraction of the worker's residual privacy budget. When $\alpha \rightarrow 0$, monetary cost is of primary concern and fairness in privacy depletion is ignored. Conversely, when $\alpha \rightarrow 1$, monetary cost is ignored and workers with a low residual privacy budget are assigned high cost, disfavoring them for selection so as to maintain fairness in privacy depletion. The next section presents the selection algorithm that uses this combined cost metric.

4.5.3.4   Algorithm for Worker Selection

For a new survey, Algorithm 4.1 is executed to select the set of workers who yield the best accuracy within the given cost constraint, while also maintaining fairness in privacy depletion among workers. The initial construction of this set assumes that (a) all selected workers will actually take the survey, and (b) Loki can correctly predict the privacy level choice of each worker according to their past history. In reality, these assumptions may not hold, but the algorithm can be easily modified to refine the set based on actual worker feedback.

Evaluating all possible subsets $S \subseteq U$ of workers to determine the optimum would be intractable. Instead, Loki uses a greedy heuristic approach, by which the broker constructs the set S incrementally, each time adding the worker who would be most cost effective, while taking into account the QoS and fairness considerations. Given a set of workers $S \subseteq U$, Eq. (4.12) evaluates the expected error $RMSE^{(S)}$ of the set, based on past performance. Adding the worker i to the set would result in the set $S \cup \{i\}$, for which the expected error $RMSE^{(S \cup \{i\})}$ can be evaluated as well. The difference $\Delta RMSE(S, i) = RMSE^{(S)} - RMSE^{(S \cup \{i\})}$ encapsulates the reduction in error by inclusion of the worker i in the set. We can then compute β_i, the improvement in RMS error per unit of cost, for the worker i:

$$\beta_i(S) = \frac{\Delta RMSE(S, i)}{F_i}, \tag{4.15}$$

where the worker cost F_i is given by Eq. (4.14) and includes both monetary and privacy costs. The broker bootstraps the algorithm by choosing the worker with the highest accuracy gain per unit of cost. Then in the greedy selection process, the broker picks the worker with the highest β_i at each step. By starting with an empty set of workers, and iteratively adding workers one by one, the broker can construct the target set S, until the monetary cost limit C is reached. Note that workers who have depleted their lifetime privacy budget are not eligible for selection. Algorithm 5.3.4 has complexity $O(KN^2)$, where K is the number of items that constitute prior history and N is the number of workers.

Algorithm 4.1 Greedy Worker Selection Mechanism

1: **Input:** U: a set of workers, each with cost c_u; C: overall cost bound.
2: **Output:** $S \subseteq U$: a set of survey participants.
3: $S \leftarrow \emptyset$.
4: $P \leftarrow \{i \in U : c_i \leq C \wedge \varepsilon_i \leq R_i^{(\varepsilon)} \wedge \delta_i \leq R_i^{(\delta)}\}$.   ▷ candidate workers within budget
5: **while** $P \neq \emptyset$ **do**
6:     $u \leftarrow \arg\max\limits_{i \in P} \beta_i(S)$.
7:     $S \leftarrow S \cup \{u\}$.
8:     $P \leftarrow P \setminus \{u\}$.
9:     $C \leftarrow C - c_u$.   ▷ remaining budget
10:    $P \leftarrow \{i \in P : c_i \leq C\}$.
11: **end while**
12: **return** S.

4.5.4 Evaluation

To study the trade-offs between cost, utility, and fairness, and the long-term system performance, the algorithm was evaluated using the Netflix dataset,[18] a large dataset of movie ratings, as a survey answer set [27]. The dataset contains over 100 million movie ratings (on a 5-point scale) from 480,000 anonymized Netflix customers over 17,000 movie titles, collected between October 1998 and December 2005. The movies released in 2004 (1,436 in number) were used as historical information, and the objective was to estimate the population-wide average rating of movies released in 2005 within a specified cost budget C.

The experiments assumed a simple model of privacy choice, in which each worker was permanently assigned into one of four privacy bins {none, low, medium, high} at random, with probabilities 13.8, 24.4, 38.9, and 22.9 % respectively. The probabilities were derived from the experimental study with real users, described in Sect. 4.5.4.1. While this experimental setup is different from the one discussed in Sect. 4.5.4.1, this allows us to evaluate performance on the basis of a privacy preference breakdown observed in real-world settings. In general, different settings can induce different preference distributions. The bins were associated with zero-mean Gaussian noise with standard deviations $\gamma = 0, 3, 6, 12$ respectively (corresponding to $\varepsilon = 0$, $\varepsilon = 3.42$, $\varepsilon = 0.85$, and $\varepsilon = 0.21$), and respective payments of $0.8, $0.4, $0.2, and $0.1 for each worker. Noise sampled from $\mathcal{N}(0, \gamma^2)$ was added to each of the workers' movie ratings.

Within these settings, Loki's selection mechanism was evaluated for different values of the fairness control parameter α. Figure 4.2(a) shows the estimation error $\mathbb{E}(RMSE)$ for varying values of the available budget C and for various selection

---

[18]http://www.netflixprize.com/.

policies. For different α values, both the true error (i.e., difference between the estimate and the ground truth available in the dataset), depicted with solid lines, as well as the corresponding estimated error (computed using Eq. 4.12), depicted with dashed lines, are shown in Fig. 4.2(a). The estimated error closely reflects the true error, and is hence of sufficient accuracy to be useful in the selection decision. The figure shows also two baseline selection strategies: random selection, in which a random set of workers is selected subject to the cost constraint, and a "best predictors" selection, in which the subset of the population that has the highest historical accuracy (i.e., is most representative of the population) is selected subject to the cost constraint. As can be expected, random selection of workers resulted in the lowest accuracy (users who are "bad predictors" or who provide very noisy answers to protect their privacy are just as likely to be chosen as more "valuable" users), and the selection of "best predictors" consistently yielded near-perfect estimates, even by surveying as low as 37 % of the population. Setting α = 0 yields accuracy identical to the "best predictors" selection algorithm, but as α progressively increases, the error increases.

The loss in accuracy is compensated for in privacy fairness. To evaluate the performance in a series of surveys, the selection algorithm was applied, sequentially, to a set of 500 movies released in 2005, again using the movies from 2004 as prior history. Figure 4.2 shows the privacy depletion, for various α settings. When α

Fig. 4.2 Impact of the selection policy on (a) accuracy versus cost in a single survey, and (b) the estimation error over multiple surveys

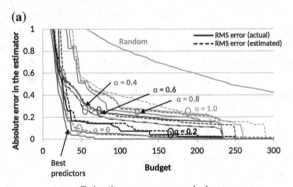

Estimation error versus cost budget

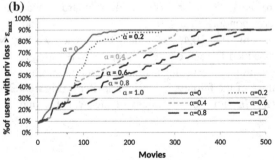

Privacy loss over time

is low, the error is initially low, but rises rapidly with successive movies. This happens because the best performing workers are selected for the initial movies (yielding low error), but deplete their privacy rapidly. Conversely, a choice of high α results in fairer depletion of privacy, prolonging the lifetime of workers in the system and giving more consistent quality of estimates over time. In the long run, the broker therefore has an incentive to choose a larger α setting to ensure fairness and consistency in the quality of the results. Note that the algorithm allows this parameter to be chosen by the surveyor on a per-survey basis.

4.5.4.1 Prototype Implementation

Loki was also implemented as a prototype to evaluate the system with real users, in an experiment involving 131 volunteers [27].

The prototype[19] consists of a front-end application for workers to participate in surveys (screenshots of the iPhone app are shown in Fig. 4.3), and a back-end database/server that stores worker data and communicates with the app. Gaussian noise is generated locally by the app using the Box-Muller method, and obfuscated responses are uploaded to the server. The *no, low, medium,* and *high* privacy settings correspond to $\gamma = 0, 3, 6,$ and 12 and $\varepsilon = 0, 3.42, 0.85$ and 0.21 respectively. The server was built using the Django (Python) Web Framework and uses a MySQL database to store worker details and surveys.

The system was trialed with 131 volunteers, all 3rd and 4th year undergraduate students studying Electrical Engineering at UNSW. Of the 131 students who took a lecturer assessment survey, 18 (13.7 %) chose no privacy, 32 (24.4 %) chose low privacy, 51 (38.9 %) chose medium privacy, and 30 (22.9 %) chose high privacy. Medium was chosen by most since users perceived it as a "safer" option than any of the extreme values.

The accuracy of the responses was validated by comparing them to the university-run rating mechanism, and by comparing the ratings across the privacy bins in the system. In general, the standard deviation of the mean lecturer rating falls with the square root of the number of samples constituting the mean. The evaluation showed that even with a relatively small sample size of 131 participants, the error in estimates was still reasonably small.

4.6 Challenges and Opportunities

Crowdsourcing is an emerging and promising model for information gathering and problem solving that is already transforming industry and scientific practices, allowing researchers access to human resources in a scope that was not possible

---

[19]Available at https://itunes.apple.com/au/app/loki/id767077965?mt=8.

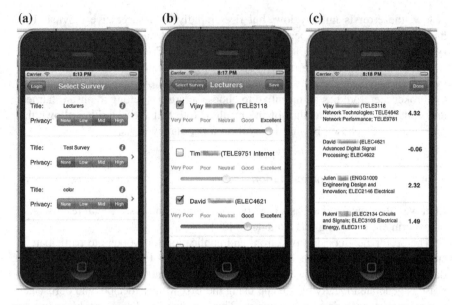

Fig. 4.3 Screenshots of iPhone app showing (**a**) list of surveys and privacy levels available to the workers, (**b**) the questions and ratings entered by the worker, and (**c**) the worker responses uploaded after noise addition

before. Unfortunately, while the opportunities of crowdsourcing are still being explored, little attention has been given to the privacy implications that crowdsourcing platforms may impose for their workers. The topic of privacy in online systems has earned much research attention in recent years, but the study of privacy in the context of crowdsourcing systems is still in its infancy. We outline below some of the challenges that are yet to be addressed in this area.

Understanding privacy risks in crowdsourcing platforms. The research community has come a long way in the last few years in understanding the implications of the "Big Data" revolution on users' privacy in online services, and the power of data mining tools to uncover information in ways that may break users' expectations of privacy. Crowdsourcing platforms, which provide the ability to solicit information from a large community of workers, are not devoid of these risks, yet only little work has been conducted to understand how such risks apply to crowdsourcing. Exploration of existing crowdsourcing platforms and the privacy risks involved in using them would be vital for educating both workers and requesters on these risks and for designing proper privacy-enhancing mechanisms in crowdsourcing platforms.

Understanding the role of anonymity in crowdsourcing platforms. Among the privacy risks involved in the use of crowdsourcing platforms, anonymity plays a unique role. On one hand, some instances of crowdsourcing, like academic studies that are vetted by Institutional Review Boards, include an integral requirement to minimize the privacy risks that the human subjects are exposed to, including safeguarding their anonymity. On the other hand, establishing a link between virtual worker accounts and real people could play a vital role in establishing the reliability of the gathered information and in mitigating worker fraud. Finding the right balance between these conflicting goals is one of the challenges that existing crowdsourcing platforms will need to face as this area keeps evolving. This conflict also presents an opportunity for specialized crowdsourcing services that emphasize one aspect over another, depending on the specific subject area, for example, crowdsourcing services that impose harsh restrictions to guarantee worker anonymity in (highly sensitive) human studies, versus services that forgo worker privacy to provide better matching between requesters and skilled workers.

Designing privacy-preserving crowdsourcing mechanisms. Participation in surveys and disclosure of information in crowdsourcing platforms exposes workers to risks of privacy loss, and these risks increase as workers participate in an increasing number of surveys and give away more information over time. While any particular piece of information may seem insignificant, the aggregated data, linked to the same worker, may be collected over time and may reveal significant amounts of information about the worker. While regulations and legally-binding terms of use may be sufficient to prevent privacy-invading data misuse by honest parties, they may not be effective in preventing privacy loss in the face of data theft or human error. Therefore, proposing and evaluating mechanisms for enhancing privacy in crowdsourcing applications is vital for protecting worker privacy in such platforms, or at least for educating workers and giving them more control over the rate of privacy loss. Such research could draw from existing works on privacy-preserving computations, and adapt them to the distributed nature of crowdsourcing applications.

Worker compensation for privacy loss. Existing crowdsourcing platforms tend to ignore the impact of privacy concerns on worker participation, and set a fixed price per task. This policy may consequently drive away workers who value their privacy above the suggested compensation, and introduce a bias towards workers who place a lower value on their privacy. Compensating workers for their privacy loss may somewhat mitigate this problem, but it introduces many other challenges: the workers' privacy choices may become a source of privacy leak even before participation in the survey; workers may not be truthful about their privacy costs and may provide false answers in surveys, to protect their privacy while maximizing compensation; and participation in multiple surveys over time may call for different mechanisms than those studied so far in single-query settings. While several works have started investigating such problems, many of these questions are still open.

4.7 Conclusion

We provided in this chapter an overview of the state-of-the-art of privacy in crowdsourcing platforms, including existing frameworks that can be leveraged to enhance user privacy in these platforms, and the challenges that are yet to be addressed. The research community has made great strides in recent years developing new semantic definitions of privacy, given various realistic characterizations of adversarial knowledge and reasoning. However, while research and technology play a critical role in privacy protection for personal data, they do not solve the problem in its entirety. In the future, technological advances must dovetail with public policy, government regulations, and developing social norms. Many challenges still remain, and we believe that this will be an active and important research area for many years to come.

References

1. A face is exposed for AOL searcher No. 4417749. http://www.nytimes.com/2006/08/09/technology/09aol.html
2. Agrawal D, Aggarwal CC (2001) On the design and quantification of privacy preserving data mining algorithms. In: PODS
3. Agrawal R, Srikant R (2000) Privacy-preserving data mining. In: SIGMOD
4. Arrington M (2006) AOL proudly releases massive amounts of private data. In: TechCrunch
5. Bennett J, Lanning S (2007) The Netflix prize. In: KDD Cup and workshop
6. Bogdanov D (2013) Sharemind: programmable secure computations with practical applications. PhD thesis, University of Tartu
7. Chen R, Akkus I, Francis P (2013) SplitX: high-performance private analytics. In: ACM SIGCOMM
8. Chen R, Reznichenko A, Francis P, Gehrke J (2012) Towards statistical queries over distributed private user data. In: NSDI
9. Chen Y, Chong S, Kash IA, Moran T, Vadhan SP (2013) Truthful mechanisms for agents that value privacy. In: EC, pp 215–232
10. Coull SE, Right CV, Monrose F, Collins MP, Reiter MK (2007) Playing Devil's advocate: inferring sensitive information from anonymized network traces. In: NDSS
11. Dandekar P, Fawaz N, Ioannidis S (2012) Privacy auctions for recommender systems. In: WINE
12. Dwork C, Kenthapadi K, Mcsherry F, Mironov I, Naor M (2006) Our data, ourselves: privacy via distributed noise generation. In: *EUROCRYPT*
13. Dwork C, McSherry F, Nissim K, Smith A (2006) Calibrating noise to sensitivity in private data analysis. In: TCC, pp 265–284
14. Eagle N (2009) txteagle: Mobile crowdsourcing. In: Internationalization, design and global development. Springer
15. Evfimievski AV, Gehrke J, Srikant R (2003) Limiting privacy breaches in privacy preserving data mining. In: PODS
16. Evfimievski AV, Srikant R, Agarwal R, Gehrke J (2002) Privacy preserving data mining of association rules. Knowl Discov Data Mining
17. Friedman A, Sharfman I, Keren D, Schuster A (2014) Privacy-preserving distributed stream monitoring. In NDSS, San Diego, USA
18. Ghosh A, Roth A (2011) Selling privacy at auction. In: 12th ACM Conference on electronic commerce
19. Goldreich O, Micali S, Wigderson A (1987) How to play any mental game. In: 19th Annual ACM symposium on theory of computing, STOC '87, pp 218–229. ACM
20. Golle P (2006) Revisiting the uniqueness of simple demographics in the US population. In: ACM Workshop on privacy in the electronic society
21. Hafner K (2006) Researchers yearn to use AOL logs, but they hesitate. The New York Times
22. Hill K (2012) How target figured out a teen girl was pregnant before her father did. Forbes

23. Howe J (2008) Crowdsourcing: why the power of the crowd is driving the future of business, 1st edn. Crown Publishing Group, New York
24. TZ Jr. AOL technology chief quits after data release. The New York Times
25. Kandappu T, Sivaraman V, Friedman A, Boreli R (2013) Controlling privacy loss in crowdsourced platforms. Technical Report, NICTA
26. Kandappu T, Sivaraman V, Friedman A, Boreli R (2013) Exposing and mitigating privacy loss in crowdsourced survey platforms. In: ACM CoNEXT student workshop
27. Kandappu T, Sivaraman V, Friedman A, Boreli R (2014) Loki: a privacy-conscious platform for crowdsourced surveys. In: COMSNETS
28. Kargl F, Friedman A, Boreli R (2013) Differential privacy in intelligent transportation systems. In: WiSec, pp 107–112, New York, NY, USA, 2013. ACM
29. Kargupta H, Datta S, Wang Q, Sivakumar K (2003) On the privacy preserving properties of random data perturbation techniques. In: International conference on data mining
30. Kosinski M, Stillwell D, Graepel T (2013) Private traits and attributes are predictable from digital records of human behavior. In: National Academy of Sciences
31. Laudon KC (1993) Markets and privacy. In: ICIS, pp 65–75
32. Lease M, Hullman J, Bigham JP, Bernstein MS, Kim J, Lasecki W, Bakhshi S, Mitra T, Miller RC (2013) Mechanical turk is not anonymous. SSRN
33. Li N, Li T, Venkatasubramanian S (2007) t-closeness: privacy beyond k-anonymity and l-diversity. In: International conference on data engineering
34. Liew CK, Choi UJ, Liew CJ (1985) A data distortion by probability distribution. In: ACM TODS
35. Ligett K, Roth A (2012) Take it or leave it: running a survey when privacy comes at a cost. In: 8th International workshop of internet and network economics
36. Lomas N (2013) Handshake is a personal data marketplace where users get paid to sell their own data. Techcrunch, 2 September 2013. Accessed 27 March 2014
37. Machanavajjhala A, Gehrke J, Kifer D, Venkatasubramaniam M (2006) l-Diversity: privacy beyond k-anonymity. In: International conference on data engineering
38. McSherry F, Mahajan R (2010) Differentially-private network trace analysis. SIGCOMM Comput Commun Rev 40(4):123–134
39. Narayanan M, Shmatikov V (2008) Robust De-anonymization of large sparse datasets. In: IEEE symposium on security and privacy
40. Oremus W (2012) What happens when our cellphones can predict our every move? Slate
41. Rastogi V, Nath S (2010) Differentially private aggregation of distributed time-series with transformation and encryption. In: SIGMOD
42. Reed J, Aviv AJ, Wagner D, Haeberlen A, Pierce BC, Smith JM (2010) Differential privacy for collaborative security. In: EUROSEC, ACM, pp 1–7
43. S. report for chairman Rockefeller. A review of the data broker industry: Collection, use, and sale of consumer data for marketing purposes. Committee on Commerce, Science, and Transportation, United States Senate, 18 December 2013. Accessed 27 March 2014
44. Ribeiro BF, Chen W, Miklau G, Towsley DF (2008) Analyzing privacy in enterprise packet trace anonymization. In: Network and distributed system security symposium
45. Riederer C, Erramilli V, Chaintreau A, Krishnamurthy B, Rodriguez P (2011) For sale: your data, by: you. In: ACM Workshop on Hotnets
46. Samarati P, Sweeney L (1998) Generalizing data to provide anonymity when disclosing information (abstract). In: PODS, p 188
47. Schenk E, Guittard C (2011) Towards a characterization of crowdsourcing practices. J Innov Econ (1):93–107
48. Shi E, Chan THH, Riefel EG, Chow R, Song D (2011) Privacy-preserving aggregation of time series data. In: Network and distributed system security symposium
49. Simonite T (2014) Sell your personal data for 8$ a month. MIT Technol Rev. Accessed 27 March 2014
50. Simonite T (2013) If facebook can profit from your data, why can't you? MIT Technol Rev. Accessed 27 March 2014

51. Sweeney L (2000) Simple demographics often identify people uniquely, laboratory for internation data privacy. Carnegie Mellon University, Pittsburgh
52. Sweeney L (2002) k-Anonynity: a model for protecting privacy. Int J Uncertain Fuzziness Knowl-Based Syst 2002
53. Varshney LR (2012) Privacy and reliability in crowdsourcing service delivery. In: SRII global conference, pp 55–60
54. Wallace N, Whyte S (2013) Supermarket spies: big retail has you in its sights. In: The Sydney Morning Herald
55. Warner SL (1965) Randomized response: a survey technique for eliminating evasive answer bias. J Am Stat Assoc
56. Yan T, Marzilli M, Holmes R, Ganesan D, Corner M (2009) mCrowd: a platform for mobile crowdsourcing. In: ACM SenSys

Chapter 5
Privacy in Healthcare

Drew Williams, Ivor Addo, Golam Mushih Tanimul Ahsan,
Farzana Rahman, Chandana Tamma and Sheikh Iqbal Ahamed

5.1 Introduction

Upholding a promise of patient privacy has long been a standard for healthcare
providers. The Hippocratic Oath, devised by the ancient Greeks, requires takers to
vow to keep patient information private. The World Medical Association's
Declaration of Geneva also asks physicians to promise not to divulge secrets told to
them, even after a patient's death [1]. Even in the gravest emergency, protecting
patient privacy remains a high priority: the Principles of Ethics for Emergency
Physicians asks doctors to disclose confidential information only with the patient's
consent, or due to an overriding duty, such as that to obey the law [1].

D. Williams (✉) · S.I. Ahamed
Department of Mathematics, Statistics and Computer Science, Marquette University,
Milwaukee, WI 53201, USA
e-mail: drew.williams@marquette.edu

S.I. Ahamed
e-mail: sheikh.ahamed@marquette.edu

I. Addo · G.M.T. Ahsan · C. Tamma
Marquette University, Milwaukee, WI, USA
e-mail: ivor.addo@marquette.edu

G.M.T. Ahsan
e-mail: golammushihtanimul.ahsan@marquette.edu

C. Tamma
e-mail: chandana.tamma@marquette.edu

F. Rahman
Department of Computer Science, James Madison University, Harrisonburg,
VA 22807, USA
e-mail: farzana.rahman@mu.edu

© Springer International Publishing Switzerland 2015
S. Zeadally and M. Badra (eds.), *Privacy in a Digital, Networked World*,
Computer Communications and Networks,
DOI 10.1007/978-3-319-08470-1_5

However, advancements in technology have only complicated the process of keeping up these promises. In the 19th century, we were able to send data from electrocardiographs over telephone wires. By the 1960s, consultations using current communications technology could be facilitated between hospitals and psychiatric institutes using then-current telecommunications technology. By the 1970s, the term "Telemedicine" was coined, defined by the World Health Organization (WHO) as "The delivery of health care services, where distance is a critical factor, by all health care professionals using information and communication technologies for the exchange of valid information for diagnosis, treatment and preventions of disease and injuries, research and evaluation, and for the continuing education of health care providers, all in the interests of advancing the health of individuals and their communities" [2]. In more recent years, the advent of the computer brought with it the ability to store healthcare information in an electronic format, adding to the number of ways doctors and patients can access healthcare information. In response to this, the Health Insurance Portability and Accountability Act (HIPAA) of 1996 was passed, regulating access to health information and medical records of individuals in order to ensure their privacy [3]. However, new technologies such as cloud computing and mobile health mean that privacy requirements for healthcare related applications will only continue to evolve. After all, the use of personal computer and mobile devices is still growing. In 2011, 75.6 % of households in the United States reported owning at least one computer and 71.7 % reported using the Internet [4]. Current smart phone service subscriptions are set to outnumber the number of people that exist in the world [5]. This changing device scene, among other emerging technologies, has led to a huge number of concerns regarding patient privacy in healthcare.

As an example of how advances in technology can affect our efforts to protect patient privacy, take a theoretical application designed to capture information about a patient's mood and activity levels. The application can gather data related to a patient's everyday habits via phone sensors over the course of a day, tracking how much exercise they get and their travel habits. The application can then ask the patient how they felt that day, logging the results each evening. From here, the application might transmit the data to a cloud storage, where healthcare providers can access that data. By charting the data received, doctors can find trends in activity and mood over weeks of logs, which can determine the impact of treatments the patient might be undergoing.

This is useful and convenient for doctor and patient. However, an application such as this has many user privacy considerations to take into account. For one, application developers must ensure secure transmission of patient data to the cloud. Both in the cloud and on the phone, one must make certain health data is also stored in a secure fashion. There is also the problem of device theft, often solved by implementing a device lock. If a malicious party steals an unlocked phone, it might compromise data stored on the device. Finally, if the website is accessible by doctors through a web application, the design of this application must also ensure that the data remains private and inaccessible by outsiders. It is easy to see that privacy in healthcare is a challenging and complicated subject. Despite the positive impact of transitioning to electronic healthcare systems, securing these systems against privacy leaks is a complex task, and deserves careful thought.

In this chapter, we consider a number of the existing electronic healthcare systems in the field—from personal health records (PHRs) to the use of radio-frequency identification (RFID) chips in storing patient data. We also consider technology not directly related to healthcare but used in healthcare systems, such as cloud computing and mobile computing. We then discuss the privacy implications of these different systems and technologies. After all, each comes with its own unique privacy challenges. Finally, we look at methods of protecting the privacy of the information contained by these systems, followed by case studies of privacy protection for a few examples of up and coming technology as well. In doing this, we present both a summary of privacy challenges in a healthcare environment, and methods of ameliorating healthcare systems.

The remainder of this chapter is set out as follows. In Sect. 5.2, we provide some background regarding different systems actively used in healthcare. Section 5.3 discusses different privacy challenges of each of these systems. In Sect. 5.4 we go into potential solutions for protecting patient privacy. Section 5.5 gives particular case studies related to up and coming technology in healthcare, and finally, Sect. 5.6 concludes the chapter.

5.2 Background

The Occupational Safety and Health Administration of the United States defines healthcare as the "provision of health services to individuals [indirectly or directly]," and acknowledges that it can occur in hospitals, clinics, dental offices, nursing homes, emergency rooms, and other such locations [6]. As in most other areas of work, there has been a persistent demand to switch from paper documentation to electronic records for a number of reasons: health provider accuracy, the use of data mining in healthcare, and instantaneous record access from different parts of the world. Unfortunately, this transition from paper to electronic patient records has been progressing with caution, due to the aforementioned privacy considerations inherent with healthcare data. There have already been some cases of compromised private electronic health data [7]. However, in spite of this fact that the advancement of the electronic world into healthcare is plagued with privacy woes, it also offers superlative benefits, thus making the problem of ensuring patient data privacy a hot topic in the computing world.

Before one looks into the particular privacy problems that healthcare is encountering, it would be good to discuss different sorts of healthcare systems. Some of the more prominent systems in electronic healthcare are briefly discussed in the following subsections.

5.2.1 Management of Patient Data

For a long time, paper records were used to keep track of patient medical history. Transmission of medical records often involved faxing or mailing record copies manually. Recently, there has been a push towards using electronic means for managing patient data. Electronic medical records (EMRs) and electronic health records (EHRs) are two of the more prevalent outcomes of this push. EMRS contain the history of a patient's data, replacing the outdated paper charts of old [8]. Although these data are only gathered from a singular practice, the records include a wealth of information about that practice, such as quality of care and notes regarding how a patient measures up to particular parameters (such as an ideal blood pressure). However, these data are not easily shared outside of a single practice.

EHRs, on the other hand, are designed to contain a patient's medical history that can be shared outside of a practice, including information about all medical practitioners that have been involved in caring for a particular patient [9]. By bringing together medical information about a particular patient in one place, EHRs can assist doctors to access helpful information from other doctors in an instant, such as emergency medical situations that a patient's primary care physician was not involved in. This can be very useful in diagnosis and treatment of a patient in a timely fashion.

Electronic prescription (e-prescription) systems do not deal with the wealth of information that EHRs and EMRs do, but they are no less useful. They allow doctors to enter information about a user's prescriptions into a computing device, and send this information to a pharmacy that can prepare the order for pickup by the patient [9]. It has been suggested that these systems will have a positive impact on the process of prescription and dispensation, improving a variety of aspects of the process; including safety, quality, efficiency, and cost-effectiveness [10]. Data gathered in e-prescription systems might also be more easily added to the patient's electronic health record, if it exists.

E-prescriptions, EMRs, and EHRs are all designed with clinicians in mind. However, patient-managed PHRs are also an option for the user wishing to keep track of their health records themselves. PHRs are records of medical information, such as allergies and immunizations, which a patient edits and adds to themselves. These can be tethered to a portal managed by hospitals, or stored on a user's own computer [9].

However, it should be noted that these systems are not the only paperless methods doctors can use to keep track of patient data. A variety of up-and-coming systems are in the works that would further enhance the privacy of medical records. RFID chips would end the need for patients with chronic illnesses to wear bracelets identifying their condition. Implantation of the tiny chip could allow doctors to scan for the chip in an emergency situation, access the chip's data and access an EHR with the patient's background and history included in it. There are also systems that use the data gathered by patient data management systems such as barcode tracking systems, clinical decision support systems, and enhanced reporting [11].

5.2.2 Telemedicine

Electronic healthcare systems do not just manage the collection of patient data for physicians, they can assist a physician in gathering said data too. As mentioned earlier in the chapter, telemedicine involves using information and communication technology to deliver healthcare services across great distances [2]. In telemedicine, a variety of technologies are used in treating, diagnosing, or otherwise providing assistance to patients requiring medical care. In the past, radios or telephones were used in telemedicine to transmit medical details: for example, a patient living in a rural area could call a doctor and discuss their symptoms rather than making a long trip to visit a surgery. However, telemedicine now also involves web-based applications such as email and videoconferencing—patients can communicate concerns in real time with a doctor via video. In some cases, doctors can even diagnose a patient over video, sending along a prescription for the patient following the meeting. As telemedicine can allow for the remote diagnosis, management, and monitoring of patients, low-income countries and regions with limited resources are poised to benefit greatly from the expansion of telemedicine [2].

5.2.3 Managing Health Knowledge

As shown already, we can use different systems to gather a great deal of knowledge from a particular patient and store it. However, we also have the opportunity to gather a lot of information in general about healthcare, and keep it in a single place for easy access. This is something that can benefit both practitioner and patient.

Health knowledge management deals with the organization of healthcare knowledge in order to use it for clinical decision making. Formally defined, it can be characterized as the systematic creation, modeling, sharing, operationalization, and translation of healthcare knowledge to improve the quality of patient care [12]. This healthcare knowledge can be specific to a hospital or city (i.e., operations knowledge) or more related to patient care, and can come from a wide variety of sources. Use of health knowledge management systems can assist clinicians in improving hospital workflows, patient care, and making decisions both related to operations and next procedures. Having this knowledge in one place can also potentially assist in training new physicians.

While health knowledge management systems are practitioner oriented, the field of consumer health informatics is targeted at involving the patient as well. In 2009, Or and Karsh defined Consumer Health Informatics Technologies, or CHITs, as "computer-based systems that are designed to facilitate information access and exchange, enhance decision making, provide social and emotional support, and help behavior changes that promote health and well being" [13].These systems help inspire patients to take charge of their own medical records, and communicate with practitioners regarding their care, combining access to patient records with a method of electronic communication with their care provider. The majority of CHITs involve health-related websites for patient use, but crossovers with other areas of healthcare, including telemedicine, are common as well.

However, while CHITs involve patient–doctor communication, cybermedicine involves applying Internet and global networking technologies to the area of medicine in a global exchange of open, non-clinical information, mostly from patient-to-patient [14]. In doing this, patients can discuss symptoms and solutions that they have encountered, thus improving their understanding of what physicians can offer them. In this way, patients and doctors can work together to find the best solution for an ailment. As access to the Internet evolves and becomes more widespread, cybermedicine is expected to in turn have an increased impact.

5.2.4 Mobile Computing and Healthcare

mHealth refers to the idea of mobile healthcare, where mobile devices and computers are involved in patient care and monitoring. Unlike telemedicine, mHealth can carry on without a physician's direct involvement, as apps can collect data from a user's habits for an extended period of time. This allows for a user to be monitored without needing to stay in a hospital.

Various types of mobile technologies can be utilized for mHealth interventions. A few examples are low-end cell phones, smart phones, laptops, tablets, mobile-enabled diagnostic identification and monitoring devices, and devices with mobile alert systems. There are also a variety of small, wire-free devices such as pedometers that interface with web applications and sleep monitoring systems. Mobile devices in particular offer promise for extending healthcare opportunities across a wide variety of people. It is estimated that there are currently more wireless devices than there are people in the United States. In addition to monitoring patients and providing on-demand information for physicians, applications in mHealth can also replace equipment previously thought to be large or cumbersome using the sensors inherent in the mobile devices by interfacing with existing equipment such that results of measurements may be instantly recorded and analyzed electronically [15].

5.2.5 Technology Used in Healthcare

Finally, we can use a number of systems in healthcare that were not developed with healthcare use specifically in mind. For example, the use of systems designed to manage "Big Data" allows for detailed analytics about a person based on information from a variety of data sources. This could assist doctors in predicting disease or recognizing a patient who was managing a chronic illness incorrectly [16]. Data about a patient from their last doctors' visit could be combined with data from mobile applications and social networking websites to provide a more complete diagnosis system for a person.

Cloud computing is another popular technology, often combined with mobile healthcare. Cloud computing involves the storage of information in an off-site data center, and the on-demand availability of that information to a variety of connected users and devices. From this description alone, it is easy to see how it could greatly benefit the medical community. For example, the on-demand availability of patient records anywhere in the United States would be incredibly useful in times of emergency. mHealth can use cloud storage for saving the data gathered by mobile devices; however, major concerns exist regarding user trust in cloud computing. Providers often cannot ensure the control of security and privacy related to user data, and individual cloud providers offer different rules related to client auditing procedure (and even the ability of the client to audit its own data) [17]. A variety of security problems also exist in cloud computing that could result in privacy breaches for the user. For this reason, along with the legal liability that legislation such as HIPAA imparts on a provider, cloud storage implementation in healthcare is still quite challenging.

5.3 Privacy Concerns in Modern Healthcare

Several systems involved with electronic healthcare have been discussed in Sect. 5.2, and we can now narrow our focus to privacy concerns. This section will focus on the storage and transmission of health information, use of mobile devices and social media in healthcare, and the use of cloud storage—all prominent privacy problems. Details of the particular privacy concerns for each of these areas will be addressed in the following subsections.

5.3.1 Storage of Electronic Healthcare Records

As already mentioned, an EHR is a collection of patients' information. Like with any other data storage, the storage of EHR has some privacy concerns as well. There is always a worry about breach of the data. There have been several incidents reported of hackers getting access to sensitive data. Such incidents can have some extreme repercussions as hacked information can lead to identity theft. It can even destroy a person socially and economically as well. For all these reasons, a very high quality security measure is needed to overcome the threat of potential loss of data.

The Health Resources and Services Administration (HRSA) has discussed the privacy and security risks in electronic health records [18]. HRSA identified three types of risks: (1) risk of inappropriate access, (2) risk of record tampering, and

(3) risk of record loss due to natural catastrophes. Among these risks, the first two are directly related to privacy issues and therefore will be discussed further.

Inappropriate access can be of two types. First, a user without the necessary authority or authentication might get access to data due to some flaw in the system or by using some kind of illegal measure like hacking, for example. Secondly, a user with appropriate access can violate the rules by using the authorized data in an inappropriate way, that is, by sharing the data with someone without the authentication or authority. These types of violations affect a user's privacy. On the other hand, if the data is tampered with, it not only violates the patient's privacy, but can also lead to fatal consequences for that patient.

Data integrity can be compromised if the architecture of the system is not also well designed. Malwares and different bots can attack the server, which can corrupt the information and also jeopardize the privacy of the patients.

Rahim et al. conducted a study in 2013 about the privacy concerns in EHR to review recent studies about the issue and to find the factors that influence the privacy concerns [19]. The study identified these following nine factors that affect patient data privacy concerns: (1) trust (may result from high-quality care), (2) demographic information (age group, employment status, etc.), (3) information dissemination (how data is processed, who has access), (4) computer literacy (how EHR system works, experience in IT), (5) sensitive data, (6) consent, (7) potential of privacy breach (ensure privacy of EHR), (8) legal and policy (design policies and privacy protection tools), (9) and training (how to manage and protect privacy).

5.3.2 End-to-End Communications in Healthcare

HRSA discussed three major ways for patients to access their medical records. These are the patient portals, partnering with a PHR provider, and giving electronic records directly to patients [18].

A patient portal is used by the patient to input data into the system. With the help of this portal, a patient can input and change his or her personal information, check status of the medication or the test reports, and so on. A patient would use different authentication methods to log into the system. However, if there is an access violation, the patient's information will no longer remain secure. The risk with PHR providers is that they can use the patient's data for their own purposes. Again, while transmitting the data to a PHR, the data can be intercepted and used for malpractice. A detailed discussion on how to ensure privacy in such cases is presented later in the chapter.

Similar cases of authentication and security violation may also occur while transmitting data between different healthcare providers. In any kind of communication, one must always ensure that the person accessing the information has the necessary authorization for it and the communication is occurring on a secure connection with encryption. These are the key components of a system and if they are compromised, the privacy of the patients will also be compromised.

5.3.3 mHealth Systems

In this subsection, a brief discussion of the privacy challenges in mHealth systems is presented.

5.3.3.1 Privacy Challenges in Cell Phone-Based mHealth Systems

Mobile health (mHealth) has become important in the field of healthcare information technology, as patients have already begun to use mobile phones and various medical sensors to record their daily activities and vital signs. Since such medical data are collected by sensors, transferred by a mobile phone application, and processed in a third-party server to provide a healthcare service, patients may wish to control data collection and distribution to protect their data and share only when the need arises.

To ensure this, patients must be able to grant or deny access to their data on the storage unit (cell phones or PHRs). Patients have certain legal rights to their health-data privacy, to protect their sensitive data, and to ensure that they are shared only where needed. Patients will not adopt mHealth technology unless they have confidence in the technology's infrastructure for supporting their privacy. On the other hand, patients will not trust, or use, the technology if the privacy support system is too complex. Therefore, it is essential to develop a user-friendly and efficient interface that can tackle all of the above challenges and ensure that privacy management is effortless.

We must note that once users share their health data with a third-party application, they typically have no control over retention periods for the data or associated metadata that will be maintained in perpetuity by the third party. The content produced by users may be revealed to both intended and unintended audiences. Therefore, in such a situation health data may be unintentionally exposed to various data recipients without users' knowledge. The accumulated health data existing in an application server can then be misused. Some mHealth applications are commercial companies that have a business model based on harvesting health data for business and proprietary purposes. They may release health data to different data recipients, including doctors, pharmaceutical and medical device companies, researchers, and non-profit organizations for their own personal gain. Aggregated health data is very valuable to commercial companies, such as drug and medical device manufacturers. Innovative data mining and health informatics technologies can link data produced from a variety of different sources to produce useful personal data aggregates or digital dossiers which can lead to privacy violation of the personnel. Last, but certainly not least, is another obvious issue in mHealth systems: the scale of the security risk.

5.3.3.2   Privacy Challenges in RFID Based mHealth Systems

With the deployment and use of RFID technology in the healthcare domain, there are increasing privacy concerns regarding the technical designs of RFID based mHealth systems.

There are different kinds of RFID applications used in mHealth systems. Usually, RFID-based sensing activities related to healthcare can be divided in two types:

- **Direct sensing activity**. These activities refer to various RFID-based identification and monitoring systems. Some of the most promising RFID-based direct sensing activity that are already being successfully tested (or deployed) in a number of hospitals are hospital personnel [20], patient and newborn identification and monitoring [20], patient drug usage monitoring [20], surgical instrument tracking and locating [20], and blood bag tracking [20].
- **Indirect inferred activity**. These activities basically refer to those systems that use direct sensing activity data to infer important information. For example, detecting pharmaceutical counterfeit, avoiding theft of medical equipment, the tagging of meal plateau to ensure that patients get proper diet according to their treatment, allergies, and tastes, and so on.

RFID-based mHealth systems have received considerable attention within the field of healthcare since early 2007. The technology's promise to efficiently track hospital supplies, medical equipment, medications, and patients is an attractive proposition to the healthcare industry. However, the prospect of wide-spread use of RFID in the healthcare area has also triggered discussions regarding privacy, particularly because RFID data in transit may easily be intercepted. Some major research challenges related to the development and deployment of RFID based healthcare are as follows:

- RFID tags can be read at a small distance, through materials or clothes. So, the owner of a tag can never be sure when it is being scanned. If the communication between tags and readers is performed in a wireless channel, adversary may try to infer personal information to track people remotely.
- Deployed ubiquitous healthcare systems may have both access permission and privacy invasion problems for the patient's individual medical data that may be overheard by unauthorized persons trying to access the system stealthily.
- The information sensed using RFID systems may need to be shared with various authorities to access healthcare services. The ID of the tag along with its EMR, collected over a period of time, may expose the user's private information.

The potential benefits of RFID technology-based mHealth services have been accompanied by threats of privacy violations [21]. These threats pertain to the potential risks of unauthorized data access, misuse of patient data, and the capabilities of permanently saving and linking information about individuals through temporal and spatial extension of data collection activities. For example, RFID tags can be read by an unauthorized reader without the user's knowledge since these tags can be read by a radio frequency signal. While RFID technology can improve the overall quality of various mHealth systems, the benefits must be carefully balanced with the prevention measures towards privacy and security threats. The use of RFID also introduces a new set of risks. These are security risks associated with the possible failure of the RFID system under various security attacks, that is, tracking, eavesdropping, denial of service, and attacks.

5.3.3.3 Privacy Challenges in Social Networking-Based mHealth Systems

Social networking and care coordination technologies allow community patients to connect, share knowledge, and provide support to other patients and their care providers. These social networks utilize a variety of means to facilitate communication among patients including discussion groups, chat, messaging, email, video, and file-sharing. While currently mostly web-based, these social networking and care coordination systems are becoming ever more accessible on mobile devices. For example, care coordination technologies utilize SMS (short message service) text or email messaging systems for health status monitoring, medical appointments reminders, chronic disease management, and health surveys. However, all of these services are highly prone to identity leakage of the users, thereby introducing challenges in maintaining user privacy.

From the perspective of social networks, privacy not only encompasses the protection of personal information, which users publish on their profiles, presumably accessible by their contacts only. Privacy is a fundamental human right and personal sensitive information is a key component of one's privacy. Privacy sensitive information includes personally identifiable information; that is, any information that could be used to identify or locate an individual, for example, name or address, or information that can be correlated with other information to identify an individual, for example, credit card number, zip code, and so on. It also includes sensitive information related to religion, race, health, sex, union membership, or other information that is considered private. This information additonally includes any kind of medical condition or medical diagnosis information. This type of detailed person specific data embedded in healthcare data stored and processed in a third-party application server presents a need for inclusion of highly effective information security measures so that sensitive information about individuals may not be easily revealed by analyzing the shared data. Research shows that patients could be simply identified by using identifiers or specific combined information (such as age, address, sex) in a certain healthcare dataset. Therefore, to provide better privacy facilities to cell phone-based mHealth service users, one needs to ensure that sensitive private information is not revealed to any third-party applications.

As part of integrity, the user's identity and data must be protected against unauthorized modification, tampering, and access. In addition to conventional modification detection and message authentication, integrity in the context of mobile application has to be extended. Parties in a social network structure are not arbitrary devices, but real, unambiguously identifiable persons. The creation of bogus accounts, cloned accounts, or other types of impersonation is easy to achieve in any social network. Identity checks do not necessarily have to be performed by a centralized service. However, all identification services have to be trusted by all participants involved.

Since some social networks are used as professional tools to aid their members' business or careers, data published by users has to be continuously available. In a social network, this availability specifically has to include robustness against censorship, and the seizure or hijacking of names and other key words. Aside from data access, availability has to be ensured along with message exchange among members.

5.3.4   Cloud-Based Healthcare Systems

The National Institute of Standards and Technology [22] defines "cloud computing" as "a model for enabling ubiquitous, convenient, on-demand network access to a shared pool of configurable computing resources (e.g., networks, servers, storage, applications, and services) that can be rapidly provisioned and released with minimal management effort or service provider interaction. Some of the key characteristics of cloud computing include massive scale, homogeneity, resilient computing, low cost software, virtualization, geographic distribution, service orientation, advanced security features [and] resource pooling" [23]. There is often a misconception among certain circles that cloud computing is simply a fad for the traditional datacenter hosting platform. This definition clarifies the distinction between the two digital hosting platforms. In terms of terminology, the cloud service vendor (e.g., Microsoft, Google, Amazon) is often referred to as a "cloud provider." The party that makes use of the services exposed by the *cloud provider* is often referred to as a "cloud consumer."

Undoubtedly, cloud computing presents exciting benefits for hosting digital solutions across various industries, including the ever so risk-averse healthcare industry. One of the main benefits of cloud-based applications includes the inherent cost savings associated with a typical *pay-as-you-go* public cloud model. Nonetheless, high performance, high-scalability, and high availability options offered by cloud providers or vendors make it more attractive for healthcare systems to consider this platform for hosting and processing digital content. While this attractive platform can be harnessed for incalculable benefits in the healthcare industry, there are a number of privacy issues that are unearthed by this new prodigy. Cloud infrastructure might be used for storing EHRs or for supporting a healthcare information systems solution. One notable healthcare solution hosted on cloud infrastructure in the United States is the Healthcare.gov web site. This web-based healthcare application is hosted on Verizon's Terremark Cloud [24].

Privacy remains a major inhibitor to the adoption of cloud solutions especially in geographic regions that enforce data protection legislation. In the United States, HIPAA compliance remains a major concern for adopting cloud solutions in healthcare circles. End-users often have qualms about having their data stored on a shared infrastructure solution. Beyond the innate shared model in public clouds, high availability and disaster recovery qualities of cloud computing often necessitate cross-datacenter replication of data by cloud vendors in an effort to provide the redundancy and scalability quality attributes, all of which remains a promise of the *cloud*. Because of the global nature of public cloud solutions, there is a potential for non-compliance against a host of country-specific regulations that may not be applicable beyond the boundaries of a given country [25]. Cross datacenter cloud solutions might employ the replication of data across country boundaries. From a regulatory standpoint, the compliance requirements for one country might differ from that of another country. This creates privacy and security concerns pertaining to loss of control, data integrity, data confidentiality, and the susceptibility of one's PII getting into the hands of governmental institutions based on the country in question's regulatory policies.

Susceptibilities in cloud computing are often related to cloud multi-tenancy, elasticity, information availability, secure information management, cloud secure federation, and information integrity and privacy [26]. Interestingly, privacy issues in cloud-based healthcare systems might take different forms depending on the cloud deployment and service models. Three notable cloud service delivery models [26, 27] include:

- **Infrastructure as a Service (IaaS)**. In this model, the cloud provider offers storage and computing power on-demand. The consumer does not manage or control the underlying virtual machines (VMs) or infrastructure, but has control of the operating system, firewall settings, and the load-balancing components. The cloud consumer has to handle security and privacy concerns at both the application and operating-system level.
- **Platform as a Service (PaaS)**. For this delivery model, the cloud provider provides a set of services and application protocol interfaces (APIs) for developers to host web sites and services without having to deal with the scalability issues of the application as the application usage grows. The cloud consumer will have minimal control over the security practices used at the operating system-level.
- **Software-as-a-Service (SaaS)**. In this scenario, the cloud provider exposes specific applications like Salesforce.com to consumers for use with a multi-tenancy approach that might use a subscription-based pay-per-use model. The cloud consumer will have even less control over the privacy and security implementation in the cloud-hosted solution.

Conversely, some of the cloud deployment models in use today include [28, 27]:

- **Public cloud**. The cloud is made available to the general public and it is owned by an organization that sells cloud services.

- **Private cloud**. It is usually operated or leased by a single organization and it is operated solely for that organization.
- **Community cloud**. It can be shared by multiple organizations and supports a specific community with shared concerns (e.g., security requirements, privacy compliance considerations, etc.).
- **Hybrid cloud**. A private cloud that can extend to use resources in public or community clouds even though both entities will remain unique.
- **Virtual private cloud (VPC)**. A combination of cloud computing resources with virtual private network (VPN) infrastructure to give users some form of abstraction of a private group of resources that are securely connected to the private or internal network.

It follows that the privacy concerns in each type of cloud delivery or cloud service model might be quite diverse.

5.4 Ensuring Privacy in Modern Healthcare

Despite the challenges mentioned, there are a number of approaches that can be used to improve patient privacy and ensure that medical information is only seen by a patient and those authorized by the patient. No one method can ensure total patient privacy. However, if care is taken in information storage and transmission and proper precautions are taken to guard against device theft and loss of data from the cloud, we can reduce the threat of the privacy challenges outlined in Chap. 7. The following are some methods that can be used to help ensure patient privacy.

5.4.1 Improving Privacy in Medical Information Storage

The Office of Civil Rights of The U.S. Department of Health & Human Services ensures the privacy of health information by enforcing the Privacy and Security Rules. It teaches health service workers about the privacy rights and confidentiality laws. It also investigates if there are any violations by any entities and takes measures. The rules are called HIPAA Privacy and Security Rules. HIPAA rules give the patients authority to define which data will be collected/used and how and who has access to that data.

Sufficient measures need to be taken into consideration while ensuring patient privacy. There must be policies and guidelines in place regarding privacy measures in health records. Different stakeholders should be trained. Access to the system should be monitored with different levels of access controls. For correct identification, secure passwords and other verification techniques should be implemented. Accessibility can also be controlled in workstations using a server. The server should have all the necessary access information on all the devices connected to it. A very important measure is to use encryption while storing the data.

A well-defined access control is highly critical in order to implement a secure storage system. Only the people with sufficient authorization level should secure access to the information. Another very important measure is to have encryption present in the system. The stored data needs to be encrypted and the key to the encryption and decryption should only be available to the appropriate individuals. Other entities should not have access to the encryption keys. In addition, there should be a saved list of entities that had access to a particular patient's information. The list should also have the information of any changes that any particular entity has made [29].

In addition to the previous security measures, the locality of the server is important as well. For example, if stored in a local physical location, the data are more prone to physical harms, that is, fire hazards, theft, and so on. To ensure integrity of the data different techniques of data backup can be established. The security of the location should be increased with access by authorization: otherwise the information will be prone to attackers. Using cloud servers is an alternative for storing data in a physical location. To secure the integrity and security of data, we need a server that is HIPAA compliant.

5.4.2 Improving Privacy in Medical Information Transmission

A discussion on different privacy concerns while storing information was presented in Sect. 5.4.2. This section discusses some security measures to ensure data privacy during transmission.

Like before, the most important and common method for privacy protection in transmission is also to use encryption. All communication should occur in an encrypted format on a secure connection. The patients should also have their login authorizations using secure passwords, pin codes, facial recognition, location-based authentication, or some multi-factor authentication. Patients should have assigned accounts for their activities. The software should be designed in a modular way so that different portions are secured under separate firewalls. For example, the system can consist of one or more databases, web-services, user-end applications, websites, and so on. These entities should be using their own authentication and firewalls to ensure data privacy. They can also exist in different physical or cloud locations. There should also be a damage control mechanism, so that a sudden security breach can be stopped instantaneously.

For PHR providers, it should be ensured that the system is HIPAA compliant. The provider should check for the integrity of the information and also be responsible for any violation of the data in their end. Encryption of the data is also very helpful on this end.

5.4.3 Improving Privacy in mHealth Systems

The mHealth-based application is currently one of the hottest topics in information technology. To maintain data privacy in an mHealth application it is essential for users to encrypt their sensitive private data before storing and processing them into the cloud or any other platform. Yet, there exist some shortcomings in the situation of traditional encryption. For example, when a secret key owner wants to look for some data that are stored in the cloud storage, the owner needs to download and decrypt all the data to perform any type of searching or processing with that information. If the amount of encrypted data is huge or the client is a mobile user, then this will be very inefficient and not feasible in some situations. Otherwise the user must send their key to the server, which performs the decryption and search procedures. In this section, a brief description of some existing methodologies that guarantee privacy is presented.

5.4.3.1 Encryption Methods

RuWei et al. [30] provide a privacy-preserving cloud storage framework supporting ciphertext retrieval. This framework is used to solve security and privacy problems while operating on encrypted data, to reduce the data owner's workload on management of data, and to support data sharing. Interaction protocol, key derivation algorithm, combination of symmetric and asymmetric encryption, and Bloom Filter are all used here [31]. The framework can operate on encrypted data, reduce data owner's workload on managing the data and storage space, and reduce communication, computation, and storage overhead. It can manage numerous keys, and is efficient, safe, and economic. However, it supports only owner-write-user-read and lacks in technique that support ciphertext-based computing. The main problem in using such an encryption based technique is that it limits the data usage, and adds an additional burden. Access control mechanisms are available to overcome the burden of the above overheads.

5.4.3.2 Access Control Mechanisms

Access control mechanisms that provide privacy protection have been discussed in articles presented in [32, 33]. A privacy preserving, access authenticated, access control scheme for securing data in clouds that verifies the authenticity of the user without knowing the user's identity before storing information has been proposed in [32]. Here only valid users are able to decrypt the stored information. This prevents reply attack, as well as achieving authenticity and privacy. It is decentralized and robust, which allows multiple read and write, distributed access control, and the protection of user identity. In [22], Fan et al. proposed that the access policy for each record stored in the cloud should be known, and should be based on assumption that the cloud administrator is honest. However, it does not support complex access control.

5.4.3.3   Remote Data Checking Using Provable Data Possession

Ateniese et al. introduce a model for provable data possession, which can be used for remote data checking in [34]. By having a sampling of a random set of blocks from the server, this model produces probabilistic proofs of possession, which will significantly reduce I/O costs. In order to minimize network communication, the challenge–response protocol transmits a small and constant amount of data. The model incorporates some mechanisms for mitigating arbitrary amounts of data corruption, and it is robust. It offers two efficient secure PDP schemes, and the overhead at the server is low. To add robustness to any remote data checking scheme based on spot checking, it proposes a generic transformation.

5.4.3.4   Privacy Preserving Data Integrity Checking

A privacy preserving remote data integrity checking protocol with data dynamics and public verifiability [35] make use of a remote data integrity checking protocol. The protocol provides public verifiability without the help of a third-party auditor. It doesn't leak any privacy information to the third party, which provides good performance without the support of that trusted third party and provides a method for independent arbitration of data retention contracts. But it adds unnecessary computation and communication cost.

5.4.3.5   Case Study: Improving Privacy in an mHealth System for Smoking Cessation

An mHealth system that was developed at Marquette University for smoking cessation among Native Americans is discussed in this section. In this system, the participants were enrolled via levels of surveys, and often sent motivational text messages to stop smoking. The following steps were taken to ensure patient privacy in the system.

The system has different levels of authentication for different roles. The participants, survey takers, and administrators can all log into the system, and are given a different view of the information according to their role. The system uses a HIPAA compliant server which has several components, such as database, web services, and so on. The server is surrounded with multiple levels of firewalls, and the communications from different workstations are limited to specific machines only.

The system ensures anonymity of the users and no personal details are stored in the database. All the participants are identified with a user ID. The text-messaging server that sends text messages to individual participants does not have local information about those participants. At a given time, the system does not hold the history of the previous communications. So, the behavior of the participants will be private in the main server.

5.4.4   Improving Privacy in Cloud-Based Healthcare Systems

It goes without saying that complete privacy or security protection is not achievable. However, this does not mean that privacy and security issues in healthcare cannot be significantly addressed. Therefore, solutions for minimizing an end-user's exposure to gaps in privacy protection might include policies, standards, guidelines, frameworks, awareness activities, and more. This chapter seeks to offer guidelines and best practices for minimizing the privacy vulnerabilities in cloud-based healthcare systems.

In the quest for privacy protection in cloud-hosted healthcare systems, it is imperative that the cloud customer perform a thorough trade-off analysis between the cost savings and privacy protection in using a public cloud solution. While the public cloud model is the most popular deployment model, a community cloud model that caters specifically to the privacy and security needs of healthcare solutions will offer more privacy protection options. Private clouds do not typically involve a shared physical infrastructure across multiple organizations, and therefore, offer a better option for insulating end-users from the privacy issues that are prevalent in a public cloud hosting model. However, a private cloud is likely to cost more than a public cloud because cloud cost saving draws heavily on the concept of economies of scale. Cloud consumers might also balance cost with security and privacy by leveraging public cloud resources to create their own secure private cloud, which is often referred to as a virtual private cloud (VPC) [22].

In some instances, a public cloud provider might offer HIPAA compliance. Microsoft Azure public cloud, for example, offers HIPAA compliance, though it is limited to some specific Azure cloud services. However, even in this setting, the cloud consumer has as much of a shared responsibility as the cloud provider to safeguard user data, and protect the privacy of patient information (often called protected health information or PHI). The cloud consumer has the principal responsibility for applying best practices for protecting private end-user data, while the cloud provider simply offers features to help enable consumer security and privacy compliance. In spite of this, the cloud provider might offer a Business Associate Agreement (BAA) to its consumers at a premium cost for the HIPAA compliance coverage. Penalties for violation of HIPAA Security Rules were strengthened through provisions in The Health Information Technology for Economic and Clinical Health (HITECH) Act in 2009 [36].

A more generic solution for improving data security and privacy in digital healthcare circles involves the encryption of electronic PHI (ePHI). ePHI data

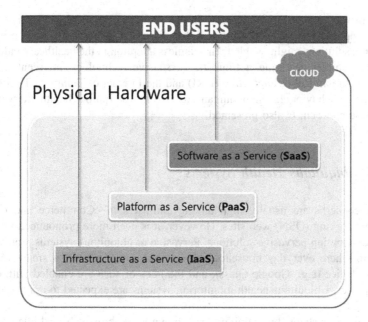

Fig. 5.1 Cloud service models

in-transit or at-rest must be encrypted to maximize the data protection scheme. In a cloud application, an abstraction layer of protection can be used to encrypt highly sensitive PHI information.

Considering the various cloud service models represented in Fig. 5.1, a cloud consumer might opt to use a Platform as a Service (PaaS) solution to minimize his or her responsibilities for ensuring privacy protection. A cloud consumer who opts to use an Infrastructure as a Service (IaaS) solution will need to take on more responsibility for end-user privacy, and security protection. In an IaaS model, the cloud consumer is responsible for installing the appropriate antivirus software, and software patches necessary to keep the application in compliance.

Other common approaches to addressing privacy concerns might include the use of regulatory frameworks, and the provision of redress within cloud environments, privacy enhancing techniques, anonymization, and more [37].

5.5 Future Challenges and Opportunities

There are more than a few opportunities for improving privacy in existing digital healthcare systems. Conversely, there are several forthcoming technologies that will see interesting applications in electronic healthcare (eHealth) applications soon. As some of these emerging technologies make their way into mainstream technology circles, the most critical deterrent to their adoption in healthcare systems will remain privacy and security concerns. In this section, some of the emerging technology applications in healthcare will be discussed along with how privacy-enhancing solutions might enable their seamless adoption in the healthcare industry. Two case studies featuring a futuristic persuasive technology intervention that draws on Human Robot Interaction (HRI) and the Internet of Things (IoT) concept to encourage behavior change in humans, as well as a ubiquitous health intervention for autistic children, is also presented.

5.5.1   Ubiquitous Health Systems

Privacy concerns are usually high among end-users of eCommerce and online social networking (OSN) web sites. However, it is even more pronounced when it comes to adopting pervasive solutions. Pervasive or ubiquitous systems represent a paradigm where everyday household objects like a refrigerator, a smart TV, an eyewear device (e.g., Google Glass), and the likes of such are enabled with computing power. Ubiquitous health monitoring systems are expected to only continue to grow [38].

Ubiquitous systems, by definition, are known to unobtrusively and intelligently collect large streams of data about our past, current, and future activities, in a bid to improve their ability to serve our needs [37]. However, this surreptitious approach to data collection might sometimes conflict with an end-user's privacy preferences. In most cases, concerns regarding user privacy also lead to reservations to adopting new technologies. While the Google Glass *wearable computing* solution is likely to have indescribable benefits in healthcare applications, privacy concerns regarding this wearable devices are likely to limit the adoption curve of this, otherwise innovative, invention.

5.5.1.1   Case Study: uHealth Intervention for Autistic Children

To unveil some of the challenges in ubiquitous health (uHealth) interventions, we consider an interesting uHealth application that might make use of a Microsoft Kinect for Windows sensor, with the goal of monitoring and interacting with autistic children. In most cases, young children suffering from autism can benefit from playing games that utilize a natural user interface as a form of intervention aimed at fostering facial expression learning. In this scenario, the Kinect Sensor acts as a natural user interface (NUI) for this gameplay healthcare intervention. However, the sensor collects information about the user's interaction with the game, and stores it in a cloud environment for further processing and analysis to determine the child's progress in the intervention program. A logical view of the interaction scenario is depicted in Fig. 5.2.

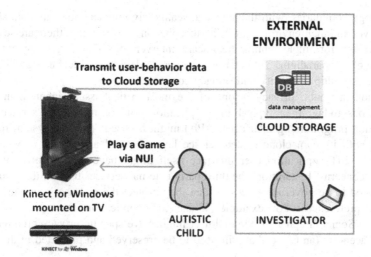

Fig. 5.2 Logical view of scenario interaction

Key Privacy Challenges
Some of the notable challenges that are inherent in this scenario include:

- **Parental consent**. In a setting where information about the children interacting in the smart environment is collected, parental consent will be critical. The Kinect-based game software vendor will need to implement some form of account verification and validation process to ensure that parents of the autistic participants have a certain level of trust and comfort with the approach, and consent to the use of this solution.
- **Child data usage**. The child's data as well as system-level data collected by the software should not be capable of being easily used to identify the participant.
- **Time to live for software dumps**. In addition, there should be a time to live (TTL) set to ensure that system-level data collected through the software is destroyed immediately after it has outlived its usefulness.
- **Opt out**. Parents may prefer to have an option to opt out of the program at any given point in time, with the expectation that the data that was previously collected about the child will be consequently destroyed.
- **Hardware vendor issues**. A standard protocol that is adhered to by all sensors and devices in the multimodal environment will be ideal.
- **Regulatory compliance**. In a uHealth environment, HIPAA compliance is a standard of interest, particularly in the United States.

5.5.2 The Internet of Things and Healthcare

The IoT can be described as a fusion of various heterogeneous digital devices, sensors, people, and services working collectively to solve a problem across technology boundaries, with the ability to seamlessly interact and share data about themselves and their environment. With this phenomenon in mind, there are several opportunities for implementing healthcare interventions that can draw out the promise of the paradigm. Yet, sharing data across devices and technology boundaries raises multiple security and privacy concerns.

Without a doubt, privacy is one of the most critical issues inherent in IoT applications today. In a typical IoT application, one or more web services or application programming interfaces (APIs) might be used. The IoT system might interact with its own cloud-hosted service layer, as well as external services or APIs. The IoT application user interface itself might have its own privacy and security concerns. In addition, the third party external services used in the solution might need to be governed to ensure that they protect the end-user's privacy and security preferences. For example, if the IoT application interacts with the Facebook Social Graph API, the end-user might have specific privacy preferences set on Facebook (an OSN) that will need to be preserved and protected in the IoT system.

5.5.2.1 A Case Study: An Internet of Things Healthcare Intervention Through Human Robot Interaction and Ubiquitous Computing

Addo et al. [39] described a futuristic health and wellness behavior change intervention for childhood obesity where a humanoid robot is employed to work collectively with a smart TV, smart refrigerator, a wearable activity monitoring wristband, and a smart phone device of choice. The IoT-based persuasive system interacts with the human subject (a child) throughout the day. The robot has routine dialogue with the child subject aimed at motivating him or her toward behavior change for weight loss and increased physical activity. The wearable wristband is used for recording the subject's physical activity throughout the day, and storing it to a cloud-hosted central database. The humanoid robot is able to tap into the collective intelligence gleaned by sensors in the smart phone and the wearable wristband to draw insightful conclusions about how the child can refine his or her behavior to meet the target physical activity goals.

A smart refrigerator tracks and records the subject's food selection choices. The child is able to interact with the smart TV to participate in a social virtual community where other like-minded children interact together to support each other on their competitive health and wellness goals. The smart TV features an application that affords the participating children interactive gameplay through a Kinect sensor device in a bid to motivate indoor physical activity as well. The smart TV game also has access to the child's profile and outdoor physical activity. Collectively, these devices interact together and share data solely for the purpose of supporting the participating child in his or her quest for weight loss. Figure 5.3 illustrates this scenario [39].

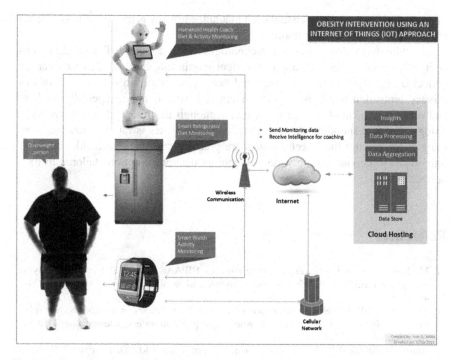

Fig. 5.3 HRI and IoT for childhood obesity intervention [39]

In this scenario several technology boundaries are crossed as multiple devices collaborate to share data across the environment. There are privacy concerns across the IoT system. Having a consistent privacy standard or policy that can be enforced across platforms and devices will prove to be very useful in this case. The cloud privacy guidelines presented in Sect. 5.4, are also likely to play a significant role in making the adoption of this type of IoT-based healthcare intervention solution viable.

5.6   Conclusions

Modern technology has provided a number of improvements to the existing healthcare field. Storage of patient documents can now be done cleanly and quickly, without the disorganization that can accompany paper records. These records can be transmitted across continents in the blink of an eye. Mobile healthcare technologies allow monitoring and management of health without requiring that patients be stationed in a hospital, and the use of cloud storage ensures that data can be shared and stored from multiple sources in one place. However, these systems have also brought great challenges to those who seek to ensure privacy across healthcare systems. Existing solutions cannot each guarantee privacy across these systems, but combined, they can greatly improve it.

In addition to this, emerging technologies such as the IoT and ubiquitous computing stand to greatly improve patient monitoring and the data that can be collected regarding various diseases and healthcare procedures. New methods of privacy protection will benefit practitioners and patients alike, especially as these and other new technologies grow in use. Although the future of healthcare technology and corresponding privacy protection approaches is rapidly changing, one thing is for certain: these technologies are greatly beneficial worldwide, allowing individuals to choose from a variety of prompt healthcare options tailored to their needs.

References

1. Moskop JC et al (2005) From Hippocrates to HIPAA: privacy and confidentiality in emergency medicine—Part I: conceptual, moral, and legal foundations. Ann Emerg Med 45:53–59
2. Ho K et al (2011) Telemedicine: opportunities and developments in Member States. WHO Press, Switzerland. http://www.who.int/goe/publications/goe_telemedicine_2010.pdf. Accessed 10 May 2014
3. Annas GJ (2003) HIPAA regulations—a new era of medical-RECORD privacy? N Engl J Med 348:1486–1490
4. File T (2013) Computer and internet use in the United States. Current Population Survey Reports, P20-568.U.S. Census Bureau, Washington, DC, USA
5. BBC News (2013) Mobiles "to outnumber people next year", says UN agency. http://www.bbc.co.uk/news/technology-22464368. Accessed 16 May 2014
6. United States Department of Labor, Safety and Health Topics. https://www.osha.gov/SLTC/healthcarefacilities/. Accessed 16 May 2014
7. Foreman J (2006) At risk of exposure. Los Angeles times. http://articles.latimes.com/2006/jun/26/health/he-privacy26. Accessed 16 May 2014
8. HealthIT.Gov, Definition and benefits of electronic medical records (EMR). http://www.healthit.gov/providers-professionals/electronic-medical-records-emr. Accessed 16 May 2014
9. Frequently Asked Questions (2014) HealthIT.Gov. http://www.healthit.gov/providers-professionals/frequently-asked-questions. Accessed 30 July 2014
10. Åstrand B et al (2009) Assessment of ePrescription quality: an observational study at three mail-order pharmacies. BMC Med Inform Decis Mak 9:8. doi:10.1186/1472-6947-9-8
11. Gunter TD, Terry NP (2005) The emergence of national electronic health record architectures in the United States and Australia: models, costs, and questions. J Med Internet Res 7(1). doi:10.2196/jmir.7.1.e3
12. Abidi SSR (2008) Healthcare knowledge management: the art of the possible. In: Riaño D (ed) Knowledge management for health care procedures. Springer, Berlin, pp 1–20
13. Or CKL, Karsh BT (2009) A systematic review of patient acceptance of consumer health information technology. J Am Med Inform Assoc 16(4):550–560
14. Eysenbach G (1999) Towards the millennium of cybermedicine. J Med Internet Res 1(Suppl 1):e2. doi:10.2196/jmir.1.suppl1.e2
15. Perera C (2012) The evolution of E-health—mobile technology and mHealth. J Mob Technol Med 1:1–2. doi:10.7309/jmtm

16. Millman, J (2014) What big data could do for healthcare. The Washington post. http://www. washingtonpost.com/blogs/wonkblog/wp/2014/07/09/what-big-data-could-do-for-health-care/. Accessed 30 July 2014
17. Kuo AM-H (2011) Opportunities and challenges of cloud computing to improve health care services. J Med Internet Res 13(3):e67. doi:10.2196/jmir.1867
18. U.S. Department of Health and human services, What are the privacy and security risks of electronic   v.   paper   health   records?   http://www.hrsa.gov/healthit/toolbox/ HealthITAdoptiontoolbox/PrivacyandSecurity/securityrisks.html. Accessed 16 May 2014
19. Rahim FA, Ismail Z, Samy GN (2013) Information privacy concerns in electronic healthcare records: a systematic literature review. In: 2013 international conference on research and innovation in Information system, pp 504, 509. doi: 10.1109/ICRIIS.2013.6716760
20. Wessel R (2005) RFID bands at the Jacobi Medical Center. http://www.rfidgazette.org/2005/ 12/rfid_bands_at_t.html. Accessed March 2012
21. Juban RL, Wyld DC (2004) Would you like chips with that?: consumer perspectives of RFID. Manage Res News 27(11/12):29–44
22. Mell P, Grance T (2009) A NIST definition of cloud computing, National Institute of Standards and Technology. http://csrc.nist.gov/publications/nistpubs/800-145/SP800-145.pdf. Accessed 16 May 2014
23. Mell P, Grance T (2009) Effectively using the cloud computing paradigm. NIST Information Technology, Gaithersburg
24. Addo ID, Ahamed SI, Chu W (2014) A reference architecture for high-availability automatic failover between PaaS cloud providers. To appear inTSA2014
25. Pearson (2012) Privacy, security and trust in cloud computing, HP Laboratories, 1–58. http:// www.hpl.hp.com/techreports/2012/HPL-2012-80R1.pdf. Accessed 25 Jan 2014
26. Behl A, Behl K (2012) An analysis of cloud computing security issues. Info Comm Technol 109–114
27. Mvelase P et al (2012) Custom-made cloud enterprise architecture for small and micro enterprises. Grid Cloud Comput 2:589–601
28. Yale University (2011)Health insurance portability and accountability act (HIPAA) policies, updates and reminders. Yale University. http://hipaa.yale.edu/guideance/policy.htm. Accessed 16 May 2014
29. Rodriguez L (2011) Privacy, security, and electronic health records. http://www.healthit.gov/ buzz-blog/privacy-and-security-of-ehrs/privacy-security-electronic-health-records/. Accessed 16 May 2014
30. Huang R et al (2010) Design of privacy-preserving cloud storage framework. In: 2010 9th international conference on grid and cooperative computing (GCC), pp. 128–132, 1–5 Nov 2010
31. Nojima R, Kadobayashi Y (2009) Cryptographically secure bloom-filters. Trans Data Privacy 2(2):131–139
32. Ruj S, Stojmenovic M, Nayak A (2012) Privacy preserving access control with authentication for securing data in clouds. In: 2012 12th IEEE/ACM international symposium on cluster, cloud and grid computing (CCGrid), pp 556, 563, 13–16 May 2012
33. Fan CI, Huang SY (2012) Controllable privacy preserving search based on symmetric predicate encryption in cloud storage. Future Gener Comput Syst 29(7):1716–1724. doi:10. 1016/j.future.2012.05.005
34. Ateniese G et al (2007) Provable data possession at untrusted stores. In: Proceedings of the 14th ACM conference on computer and communications security (CCS'07), ACM, New York
35. Hao Z, Zhong S, Yu N (2011) A privacy-preserving remote data integrity checking protocol with data dynamics and public verifiability. IEEE Trans Knowl Data Eng 23(9):1432–1437
36. HHS.gov. (n.d.) Health information privacy. U.S. Department of Health & Human Services. http://www.hhs.gov/ocr/privacy/hipaa/administrative/enforcementrule/hitechenforcementifr.html

37. Addo ID, Yang J, Ahamed SI (2014) SPTP: a trust management protocol for online and ubiquitous systems. To appear inCOMPSAC
38. Clifford G, Clifton D (2012) Wireless technology in disease management and medicine. Ann Rev Med 63:479–492
39. Addo ID, Ahamed SI, Chu WC (2013) Toward collective intelligence for fighting obesity. COMPSAC 690–695:2013

Chapter 6
Privacy in Peer-to-Peer Networks

Diego Suárez Touceda, José María Sierra Cámara
and Jesús Téllez Isaac

6.1 Introduction

In the client-server connectivity model participants' roles are clearly defined and are not interchangeable: one or more servers offer a range of services used by a group of clients. Although this model is a valid solution in most scenarios, there are environments in which the model is not feasible for technical, financial, social, or security reasons [1].

Conversely, P2P networks are designed to take advantage of dispersed network resources and enable participants to act as servers or clients (without the need for a fixed role); their main characteristics being the direct sharing of resources among users, their self-organization, stability, and autonomy. Based on this connectivity model, a multitude of applications have emerged, such as distributed computing systems Seti@home [2] or Genome@home [3], distributed database systems such as PIER [4] or Piazza [5], content distribution applications including Napster [6], Gnutella [7], or BitTorrent [8], and communications systems such as P2PSIP [9] or Skype [10].

D.S. Touceda (✉)
Evalues IT Evaluation Lab, Universidad Carlos III de Madrid,
Avda. Gregorio Peces Barba 1, 28918 Leganés Madrid, Spain
e-mail: diego.suarez@uc3m.es

J.M.S. Cámara
Computer Science Department, Universidad Carlos III de Madrid,
Avda. de la Universidad 30, 28911 Leganés Madrid, Spain
e-mail: sierra@inf.uc3m.es

J.T. Isaac
Computer Science Department, Universidad de Carabobo,
Avda. Universidad, Valencia, Venezuela
e-mail: jtellez@uc.edu.ve

© Springer International Publishing Switzerland 2015
S. Zeadally and M. Badra (eds.), *Privacy in a Digital, Networked World*,
Computer Communications and Networks,
DOI 10.1007/978-3-319-08470-1_6

However, despite their assets, P2P networks offer little privacy protection. Data, that can be sensitive, is no longer stored in trusted servers but in peers (potentially untrusted), and can be openly accessed and used (e.g., for advertising, users profiling and impersonation, etc.) [11]. Also, user accesses and publishing are no longer done through large companies, such as Google or Facebook, that have privacy policies protecting the users personal information from being public. These accesses are done through less-trustworthy entities that can disclose the users personal information or track its behavior [12]. Several P2P applications propose mechanisms to ensure privacy such as OceanStore [13] or Past [14]. However, these solutions remain insufficient. Managing privacy is not possible in current P2P networks without adding new privacy functionalities [11].

Therefore, users need to be concerned about privacy in P2P networks. They should know how to properly configure and use the software to restrict the information being shared. It is very common for a user to share the entire hard drive, including sensitive information, without knowing it. Hence, users have to be sure that they are not sharing personal information which could be exploited by malicious users [15].

With this problem in mind, in this chapter we analyze the existing privacy issues in P2P networks and the solutions that can be used to prevent them, aiming to help the reader to better understand privacy in P2P networks and applications.

The rest of the chapter is structured as follows. An overview of P2P networks is given in Sect. 6.2. Section 6.3 analyzes the privacy issues of P2P networks. The existing solutions that can be used to improve privacy in P2P networks are presented in Sect. 6.4. Section 6.5 discusses how the described solutions can be used to mitigate the existing issues and explore the challenges that must be addressed in the future. Finally, Sect. 6.6 outlines the conclusions of the contents presented in this chapter.

6.2 Background

In this section, we present some basic knowledge on P2P including its definition, classification, the layer architecture, and the applications.

6.2.1 P2P Definition

A review of the literature reveals that, due to the considerable number of different definitions of "peer-to-peer", there is no accurate definition of P2P today, mainly distinguished by the "broadness" they attach to the term. Many definitions are proposed trying to capture the main features of P2P systems. Some typical definitions include the following:

- A system to be P2P if the elements that form the system share their resources in order to provide the service the system has been designed to provide. The elements in the system both provide services to other elements and request services from other elements [16].
- Peer-to-peer systems are distributed systems consisting of interconnected nodes able to self-organize into network topologies with the purpose of sharing resources such as content, CPU cycles, storage and bandwidth, capable of adapting to failures and accommodating transient populations of nodes while maintaining acceptable connectivity and performance, without requiring the intermediation or support of a global centralized server or authority [17].
- A distributed network architecture may be called a Peer-to-Peer (P-to-P, P2P, ...) network, if the participants share a part of their own hardware resources (processing power, storage capacity, network link capacity, printers, ...). These shared resources are necessary to provide the Service and content offered by the network (e.g. file sharing or shared workspaces for collaboration). They are accessible by other peers directly, without passing intermediary entities. The participants of such a network are thus resource (Service and content) providers as well as resource (Service and content) requestors (Servent-concept) [18].

According to the above definitions, the following characteristics of P2P systems can be identified [19]:

- **Shared resources**. Peers in P2P systems are designed for sharing resources, by direct exchange, with each other in order to provide the services or content offered.
- **Self-organized**. Peers in P2P systems are self-organized into network topologies, respecting the autonomy of peers.
- **Dual role**. Peers in P2P systems act both as clients (requesting resources from others) and servers (providing resources to others) at the same time.
- **Stability**. P2P systems have the ability to adapt to peer failures (fault-tolerance) and to accommodate a large number of participating peers (scalability).
- **Autonomy**. Each peer maintains and controls, without the support of a central server or authority, its own content and resources.

Due to the absence of a centralized server, a P2P network is designed around the concept of each peer being client and server simultaneously. This model of network layout differs from the client-server model, which has a centralized server responsible for controlling the access of shared resources within the network, giving the clients limited privileges. Therefore, the P2P architecture is considered opposite of the client-server model.

Although the P2P model is perceived as an advantage, it introduces many management and security issues since there is no control over the content being shared within the network. Hence, the participating peers become prone to various threats and security violations [20]. Figure 6.1 illustrates the client-server architecture whilst Fig. 6.2 shows the P2P architecture.

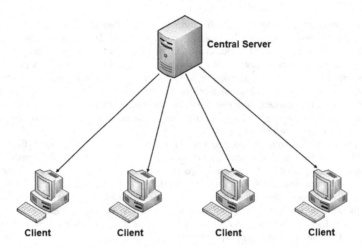

Fig. 6.1 Client-server architecture

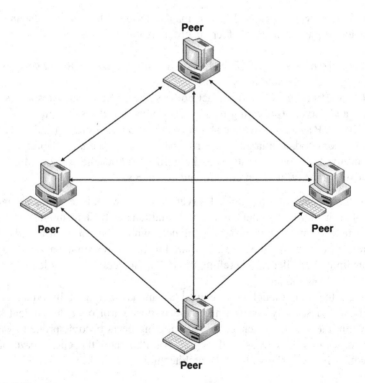

Fig. 6.2 P2P architecture

6.2.2 P2P Systems

A P2P system consists of three layers: underlying network, overlay network, and application. Figure 6.3 illustrates the model of a P2P system in a layered architecture [19].

- Underlying network is the communication network to which peers connect for routing packets.
- Overlay network is the network of peers that relies on the underlying network for routing packets to each other. It is responsible for providing P2P services for P2P applications built on top of it, performing many operations such as storing and retrieving data, management of nodes, management of resources, management of security, and so on.
- The Application-level layer is concerned with the content and service provided to users by P2P applications (such as P2P file-sharing applications, P2P instant messaging applications, P2P video streaming applications, and so on) using the P2P services provided by the overlay network.

In the following sections, we discuss the overlay network layer and the application layer of P2P systems.

6.2.3 P2P Overlays

In the last decade, several P2P overlay networks have emerged with diverse network structures, topologies, routing algorithms, and so on. Based on the network structure, P2P overlays can be classified in several types (see Fig. 6.4) that will be briefly discussed below.

Fig. 6.3 Layer architecture of P2P systems

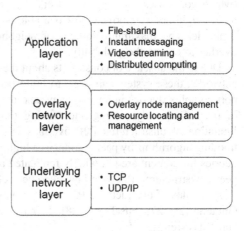

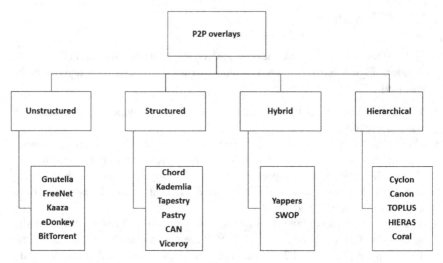

Fig. 6.4 Summary of overlay networks

6.2.4 Unstructured P2P Networks

In this category, peers are organized by the P2P overlay network into a random graph (in a flat or hierarchical manner), which means that it is not possible to establish a correlation among a peer and the content handled by it; owing to the arbitrary creation of the links between nodes. Therefore, in order to query content stored by overlay peers, an unstructured P2P network has to use flooding, random walks, or expanding-ring time to live (TTL) search, and so on on the graph. When a peer is visited, it will evaluate the query locally on its own content, and will support complex queries.

For the purpose of routing, a peer builds and maintains a local routing table (which contains some neighbor peers) by periodically checking the aliveness of these neighbors to remove the unavailable ones and to update them with new ones available. The maximum number of neighbors that a peer has is limited in an overlay to ensure the scalability.

Due to the absence of constraints about the topology of unstructured P2P overlay networks, these systems are easy to build and maintain [21]. Moreover, they support complex queries in an easy way, and they are highly robust against high rates of peers frequently joining and leaving the network (Churn) [19]. However, a limitation of unstructured P2P overlays is their scalability because the usage of flooding algorithms by peers produces a high network traffic [22, 23]. Also, because queries for content are not widely replicated and must be sent to a large fraction of peers, unstructured P2P overlays become inefficient [24].

Examples of unstructured P2P overlay networks are the following: Freenet [25] Gnutella [26, 27], FastTrack [28] /KaZaA [29], Overnet [30]/eDonkey2000 [31], and BitTorrent [32].

6.2.5 Structured P2P Networks

In this category, in contrast to unstructured P2P networks, structured P2P overlay networks provide a geometric topology that is tightly controlled and where contents are placed in specific locations and not in random peers.

A Distributed Hash Table (DHT) is implemented on most of the structured overlays based on an abstract key space. A unique key is assigned to each peer or data item which is taken from the key space using consistent hashing. To store a value in a node, a DHT must determine the node that has the minimal distance among the value's key and the node's identifier [19].

Two operations are provided by a DHT: a store operation (put(key,value)) and a retrieval operation (value = get(key)). The DHT will route the requested operation for a given key to the node responsible for the key. Each node maintains, for routing purposes, overlay links to a number of other nodes. Also, the IP address, the node's identifier, and other information of each of these nodes is stored in their routing tables. Using these routing tables, nodes forward the requests that receive to their closer link to the destination until these requests finally reach the destination node.

Structured P2P overlay networks provide a cooperative, stable, and robust mechanism for storing and retrieving content when their algorithms are executed correctly. Nevertheless, this class of systems does not support complex queries in its simple form, hence it is necessary to store a copy or a pointer to each data object (or value) at the peer responsible for the data object's key. Also, most of them deploy very minimalist security mechanisms that make them an attractive target for attackers [19, 24, 33].

Examples of structured P2P overlay networks are the following: Content Addressable Network (CAN) [34], Tapestry [35], Chord [36], Pastry [37], Viceroy [38], and Kademlia [39].

6.2.6 Hybrid P2P Networks

Hybrid P2P systems combine unstructured and structured topologies in their hierarchy with the intention of exploiting the advantages of kind of networks. These systems employ structured overlay topologies at their upper level whilst unstructured overlay topologies are used at their lower level, or vice versa.

6.2.7 Hierarchical Overlays

A hierarchical overlay is an overlay architecture that uses multiple overlays to organize its peers in a nested fashion (which are interconnected in a tree). Therefore, a message can be sent to a peer in a different overlay by forwarding the message to the nearest common parent overlay in the hierarchy with the destination peer. Examples of hierarchical overlays include: Cyclon [40], Hieras [41], Canon [42], and TOPLUS [43].

Hierarchical overlays can increase overall performance in P2P systems that exhibit locality in their operations.

6.2.8 P2P Applications

Nowadays, P2P systems have become one of the most common technologies used in the Internet. Although until 1999 the most common paradigm in the Internet was the client-server model, the emergence of Napster [44] (a P2P file-sharing application used to share music) has attracted attention and pushed P2P systems to become one of the most used (and controversial) technologies [45].

The P2P architecture has been widely used worldwide because of the following advantages [46]:

- **Scalability**. In P2P networks users contribute with resources, meaning that while the number of users increases, the ability of the network will also increase due to the additional resources brought by the new users.
- **Resilience**. P2P architecture prevents the single point of failure (inherent to client-server systems), hence, increasing the robustness and reliability of the system.
- **Cost-efficiency**. The installation and management cost are reduced in P2P networks by incorporating the resources of the users and not using dedicated servers.

Despite of the above advantages, P2P networks also have their limitations. One example are the new security threats that can emerge due to the direct exchange of resources among end-users without the participation of a secure server. Besides their most famous application, file-sharing, P2P systems have also been used for a variety of different application categories, including the following [17]:

- **Communication and collaboration**. Systems in this category provide the necessary infrastructure to allow the direct communication and collaboration between peer computers. Examples include instant messaging applications such as Aol, Yahoo, and MSN.
- **Distributed computation**. The goal of this category of systems is to take advantage of the available computer processing power (CPU cycles) of the peers of the network by decomposing a computer-intensive task into small work units which should be distributed among them. Every peer computer executes its corresponding work unit once it has been received before returning the results. Examples include projects such as Seti@home [47] and Genome@home [48].
- **Internet service support**: Many different applications have emerged based on P2P infrastructures to support a variety of Internet services, such as P2P

multicast systems [49], Internet indirection infrastructures [36], and security
applications, providing protection [50].

- **Content distribution**. In this category fall most of the current P2P systems that
  range from relatively simple direct file-sharing applications, to more sophisticated systems which create a distributed storage medium for securely and efficiently publishing, organizing, indexing, searching, updating, and retrieving
  data. Within the P2P content distribution domain, applications can be grouped
  as follows:

  - **P2P file-sharing**: P2P is one of the most successful architectures for
    file-sharing, both using structured and unstructured overlays. In this kind of
    networks, information about shared files (frequently stored locally at the
    owners machines) can be delivered to some specific peers or saved in a
    central server. In order to download a file, a peer has to perform the fol-
    lowing steps: searching and downloading. In the first step, a query is sent by
    the initiating peer to the network. Once received, this query is replied by the
    peers that keep files that match the search with the information about these
    files. However, there are also alternatives to this searching mechanism. For
    example, in BitTorrent [32] (a P2P system that uses a central location to
    manage users' downloads), contents are located using special types of files
    called "torrent files" (usually publicly accessible in web servers) which
    contain information about the content file, its length, name, hashing infor-
    mation, and the URL of a tracker (responsible for maintaining track of all the
    peers storing, both partially and completely, the content file) [19, 24, 32]. In
    the second step (downloading), the initiator peer reach directly the peers
    where the file is stored in order to complete the exchange of the file.
    In Fig. 6.5, the architecture and operation of BitTorrent are illustrated. A peer
    P1 which host a file and acts as the seed, is responsible for the following

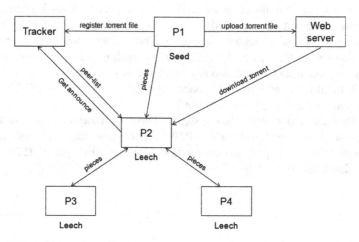

Fig. 6.5 BitTorrent architecture and operation

steps: upload the "torrent file" to a web server and register it to the tracker. The peer P2 could download the file by sending a Get message to the tracker whoever replies with a list of the peers that are hosting this file (P1, P2 and P3 in this case). Once the list is received by P2, it contacts peers P1, P3 and P4 to retrieve pieces of the file. Since P3 or P4 do not have the file completely, it can also retrieve the missing pieces from P2 (the ones P2 has retrieved from P1 and that P3 or P4 do not have) [19].

- **P2P streaming**: This category of P2P systems have been deployed recently to provide live and on-demand video streaming services on Internet at low cost. P2P streaming solutions create an overlay network topology for delivering content formed by the users of the network. These users can download or upload video assets, thus becoming active participants in the streaming process. rStream [51] is an example of this kind of application.

- **Video-on-Demand** (**VoD**): This is a technology that ensures the availability of a whole video at the time of the transfer. Since no content is generated/updated while data is transferred and rendered, users should be able to watch any point of the video at any time. In a P2P-based VoD (P2P-VoD) application, the entire stored media file needs to be retrieved at a rate that allows the recovered pieces of the file to be played in sequential order at the media playback rate. Therefore, if the retrieval rate is sufficient, the playback phase extends beyond the transfer phase. Examples include SplitStream [52] and pcVOD [53].

- **Live streaming**: In P2P live streaming applications, a root server generates video content in real time while peers connect to it as clients forming a tree. Content dissemination is acted upon by other peers (clients). The video playback is synchronized among all peers unlike peers in a VoD-like network, where each peer may be positioned in a different part of the video [45]. Anysee is an example of this kind of application [54].

- **P2PTV**: In a typical architecture of P2PTV, there are trackers that contains the information of the peers which distribute a specific channel. Therefore, to view a channel, a peer needs to query the tracker that is distributing the channel; to finally contact the peers of the trackers directly to receive the video stream from them. In these systems, each user is able to download a video stream and simultaneously upload it to other users in order to contribute to the overall available bandwidth. [19]. Examples of P2PTV application are Zattoo [55] and PPLive [56].

- **Other content distribution systems**: There are other content distribution applications developed using P2P technologies such as systems for pre-recorded TV program distribution (such as BBC-iplayer [57]), game updates, and so on [19].

6.3 Privacy Issues in P2P Networks

As noted in [58], the term privacy is an umbrella term, referring to a wide and disparate group of related things. The use of such a broad term is helpful in some contexts yet quite unhelpful in others. One of these contexts is security. In order to analyze the existing privacy issues in P2P Networks, we need to be more specific and not talk about privacy in general, but about specific users private attributes that may be under threat.

6.3.1 Privacy of User Identity

In order to connect to a P2P network users need to reveal some information about themselves (at least to the peers they are directly connected to), such as their IP address and port number. Also, if some kind of enrollment mechanism is in place, users may have to provide more information to satisfy the enrollment policy, for example, an ID, password, and so on. In some cases, a centralized mechanism, such as the offline certification authority (CA) used in RELOAD [9], can be used to control the enrollment to the network. In this way, users credentials are stored in a trusted third party (TTP) that can protect the privacy of the users attributes. However, to join the network, some information (credentials) must still be revealed to other peers (that may be malicious) to prove that the user is an authorized member of the network. Furthermore, when a user requests access to a resource stored in another peer it may need to reveal some information about itself to satisfy the resource access control policy. And, in the same way, the resource provider may need to reveal some information too, for example, for proving it is a valid content provider, to provide access to the resource.

Therefore, as privacy issues related to the users identity, we identify:

- Internet service provider (ISP) identification of peers through relating an IP address and port with the users subscription data.
- TTP identification of peers using the provided users attributes requested during the enrollment process.
- Directly connected peers identification of users through their IP address and port and (when used) the credentials needed to prove membership to the network.
- Resource owner identification of users through the credentials needed to satisfy the resources access control policy.
- User identification of resources providers through the credentials used while providing access.

The first two cases are common to most of the Internet applications: users have to reveal some private attributes to both their ISP, to contract a line to access the Internet, and to their service providers server (mail account, cloud storage, etc.), to be able to access their services. However, the last three threats are new. The first of these three cases appears due to the fact that in P2P networks users are directly connected to other (usually unknown) peers of the networks that may be malicious. The second and the third appear because users no longer access resources stored in a trusted server but in (usually unknown) peers that, again, may be malicious.

6.3.2 Privacy of User Location

As presented already, peers of a P2P network know the IP address and port of the peers they are directly connected to. Also, some applications need to make public these attributes of a user to all the participants of the network in order to allow them to communicate with each other. For example, in P2PSIP applications users IDs and locations (IP addresses and port numbers) are published in a DHT formed by all the peers of the network. This information can be used by other users of the network that wish to communicate with them to start VoIP phone calls or to send chat messages. However, as noted in [59], since this location information is stored in the DHT, the user cannot know which peers have requested it. Therefore, it is possible for malicious peers to lookup the user regularly and to map its IP addresses to geographic locations without the user being aware of it. This information can be used by those with malicious intent to make profiles of the users location. The same happens with other similar applications, such as Skype, as commented in [12].

Summarizing, the main location privacy issue for a P2P user is other peers having access to its location and being able to make a profile about its mobility.

6.3.3 Privacy of the User Access

In Sect. 6.3.1 we have already talked about the privacy of users identity when requesting access to a resource. Another related but different privacy issue appears during this access: the peer responsible for a resource also can monitor the accesses of the users of the network to it. In the same way, as noted in [15], the searched keywords and the downloaded files can be gathered. This information in conjunction with the users IP addresses can be used to create a database about the users accesses. One example of an application suffering this threat is P2PSIP. In response to this concern, the research [60] states that the P2P routing protocol opens the possibility for P2P users to record the activities of other users in the network. On the one hand, all the communications of a user are done through the fingers in its routing table that can monitor its activities. On the other hand, the peer responsible for storing a resource can monitor all the accesses over the resource it controls.

So, basically, the main threats here are users being monitored in the system by other peers; both when accessing and looking for a resource. This is also known as sender anonymity.

6.3.4 Privacy of User Publishing

Another privacy issue appears for a user publishing a resource: the party accessing or looking for a resource also learns which resources the user has published. This could be used, for example, for censorship governments to make a search for forbidden contents and ban or even prosecute the users of the network providing them. This is also known as recipient anonymity.

6.3.5 Privacy of Contents

In general, before reaching their final destination, Internet communications traverse several systems that may spy or even modify the exchanged data. This is even more notorious in P2P networks, where users rely on other peers to access the systems resources, providing the possibility for an intermediate peer to monitor the contents of a users communication.

Also, unlike the client-server model where data is centrally stored, in P2P contents are spread among all the peers of the network; being each peer responsible for a specific part of it. These contents can be public information, available for other users of the network, or non-public data, only available for the users private access. Due to the fact that the peer responsible for storing these contents may be malicious, a security mechanism should be implemented in order to prevent the storing peer or an attacker from accessing this data without authorization [60].

6.3.6 Application Misconfiguration and Misuse

In P2P networks computers act simultaneously as clients and servers. However, as noted in [15], to properly configure a server is not an easy task that typical end-users can do. To configure a secure Internet server requires professional experience. Therefore, despite configuring and using P2P software being easy, using it in a controlled way is much more complicated. As an example, in [61] a study about Kazaa usability is presented showing that it is very common for users to share private data: emails, text documents, configuration files, or even the whole disk without being aware of it. Since a user would not do this on purpose, it seems clear that we are facing an application misconfiguration problem.

Application misconfiguration therefore clearly represents another threat to privacy that should be taken into account.

6.3.7 Spyware and Malware

Spyware and Malware are further privacy threats for P2P applications. Spyware spies on the user by collecting information about its activities without the user's knowledge. For its part, malware goes a step further performing more harmful activities such as collecting more sensible information (credit card numbers, passwords, etc.) or giving remote control to an attacker over the users device.

Several P2P applications are bundled with spyware that gather and send information about the users activities to a third party. In turn, that third party uses the gathered data to gain information about their potential customers [15]. However, it is hard to check the spying activities and information leaked by these applications because most of them are closed-source. One example of such an application that includes spyware is Kazaa.

Other related threats to users privacy are the programs downloaded from P2P networks. Since the sources in a P2P network may not be trustworthy, these programs can contain spyware or malware that compromise the privacy of the user.

6.4 Solutions for Privacy Issues in P2P Networks

Most communications over the Internet lack privacy protection: the messages are not encrypted nor are the sender and the receivers identities protected. It is really difficult to achieve full protection against privacy threats on the Internet, either P2P based or not, just as normal people do not have the necessary means to be fully protected against professional thieves in the physical world [62]. However, average protection for the vast majority of scenarios is definitely possible. In the rest of this section, we analyze different solutions that could help a user to achieve a desirable level of privacy.

6.4.1 Anonymous Systems

Anonymity can enable censorship resistance and freedom of behavior without fear of persecution. Anonymity is mostly used to hide user identity. If anonymous communication channels are used, a channel listener is not able to understand the messages sent on the channel or who has sent them [11]. Since one of the first papers on anonymity was published [63] by D. Chaum in 1981 outlining an electronic mail system to hide who a participant communicates with through the use of mixes (nodes hiding the correspondences between their input and output messages in a cryptographically strong way), several protocols and applications to protect anonymity have emerged [60]. However, most of them follow a similar process: with the idea of preserving the privacy of the identity of the sender and the receiver of a message, as described in [64]: â€œWhen a sender Alice sends a message to a receiver Bob via a message router Rob, she first encrypts the message under Bob's public key and then encrypts the results together with Bob's name under Rob's public key. She then sends this final encryption to Rob who decrypts it, sees another encryption plus Bob's name and thus forwards this encryption to Bob. Upon receiving it, Bob decrypts and then can read the message from Alice. Thus, from the communication packets sent between Alice, Rob, and Bob one can only tell that Alice sent some message to Rob and that Rob sent some message to Bob".

Using this initial concept, several different approaches appear to improve anonymity: cache and mix messages before they are sent, use several routers in a row to increase the probability that at least one of them keeps the relation between the input and the output node secret, or randomly choose at each routing hop whether the message is sent to the final destination or to another intermediate routing hop. Examples of protocols to do so are Mix-networks, Mix-cascades, and Onion Routing.

What follows is a brief overview of the more relevant anonymous systems, focusing on those specifically designed for P2P networks:

- Tarzan [65] is an anonymous P2P network. A peer that wants to send a message through the network, instead of sending it directly, creates an encrypted tunnel to another peer and asks that peer to forward the message in its behalf. This process is repeated several times, creating an onion encrypted connection, that relays the message through a succession of intermediate peers.
- MorphMix [66] is very similar to Tarzan. The main difference between them is how the route a communication follows through the network is chosen. In Tarzan, the route is chosen by the source, while in MorphMix the intermediate nodes determine the next step.
- SwarmScreen [67] is a privacy preserving layer for P2P applications that tries to obfuscate the user's network behavior. Since a users behavior can be deduced by his or her interests, SwarmScreen connects the user to other users outside of their community of interest (by adding some percentage of extra random connections that are indistinguishable from the real ones), which can disguise the users interests and thus their behavior.
- Pr2-P2PSIP [59] has been created with the idea of providing P2PSIP user registration and session establishment, while preserving the privacy of the network participants. It is based on a central authentication server (AS). After the user authenticates with the AS, the AS provides the user with a certificate that binds the identity of the user with its public key. Besides its identity, each user has two pseudonyms fi and si (temporal identities that cannot be linked with the identity of the user). These pseudonyms allow the user to participate in two different overlays: one used to store the users contact information and another for forwarding messages.

All of the summarized systems have their advantages and drawbacks (this discussion is beyond the scope of this chapter). However, all of them have two main characteristics in common: they improve the anonymity of the user, but at a high performance cost.

6.4.2 Routing Modifications

Using an anonymous system, such as the ones presented in Sect. 6.4.1, may have an appreciable impact on the systems performance. In some cases, when performance is a key factor, another mechanism, such as routing modifications, can be used in order to improve the users privacy while maintaining a good performance. Router modifications can be carried out in two different ways: varying the routing algorithm and obfuscating routing headers. Both mechanisms help to improve a users privacy, mainly in structured P2P networks where routing is more deterministic and can reveal more information about the users behavior. The rest of this section is based on the authors previous research presented in [60].

6.4.2.1 Routing Variations

The study [68] analyzes the anonymity of the Chord protocol and concludes that the implemented recursive routing algorithm provides a high degree of sender anonymity against passive observers.

The proposal described in [69] goes a bit further and compares the anonymity of different alternatives with the original recursive routing algorithm:

- **Random recursive routing**. In this variation, peers forward the message at random to whatever finger is closer to the destination, instead of routing messages to the finger closest to its destination. Random recursive routing improves anonymity, but unfortunately it also increases the path length.
- **Weighted random routing**. Instead of picking the next forwarding hop at random from the closer fingers, fingers are weighted and picked with different probabilities: for example 1/2 for the closest, 1/4 for the second closest, and so on. In comparison to the random one, it reduces the average path length while maintaining a degree of anonymity that is nearly as good.
- **Indirect routing**. In this routing algorithm, when a peer wants to send a message, instead of routing it directly to its destination, it chooses at random an intermediary peer in the network to route the message on its behalf. Also, the query to the intermediary is secured using an m-of-n secret sharing scheme, that is, the message is split into n shares sent using independent routes and at least m shares (of n sent) need to be captured in order to reconstruct the message. This way, it is very difficult for an attacker to know the true destination of the query. Indirect routing improves the anonymity of the sender but it also increases the number of messages needed to route a query and its latency. A similar routing alternative is used in the AP3 system [70].

6.4.2.2   Headers Obfuscation

Besides the routing algorithm used, it could be also helpful, in order to improve users privacy, not to use header fields that may reveal information about the route followed by a message:

- Avoid setting fixed default values for TTL counters. Alternative methods, such as those implemented in Freenet [71], may be used.
- Methods such as the forwarding tables in AP3 [70] or the Truncated Via-Lists in RELOAD [9] should be used to obfuscate the information needed to route back the response of a query.

6.4.3   Protection of Contents in Transit

The most widely accepted measure to obfuscate the content of a message is encryption. However, as the authors presented in previous work [60], the special properties of routing in P2P networks suggest a clarification of how this mechanism should be implemented. In typical Internet routing, security is normally ensured end-to-end, that is, the sender encrypts and signs the message and delivers it to the recipient using some specific protocol for this task, such as TLS [72], DTLS [73], or IPsec [74]. Unfortunately, this approach is not valid in P2P networks, because the intermediate hops need access to some information of the message in order to route it properly. Therefore, the routing protocol needs to implement two features: it must separate the routing information (needed for the intermediate nodes to route the message) from the content of the message per se (that must be only accessed by the addressee). Also, it must permit use of both hop-by-hop and end-to-end security. First the sender encrypts and signs the content of the message with the public key of the ultimate receiver and the sender's private key respectively (end-to-end security at the application layer), then the sender appends to it the routing information and encrypts and signs the whole message for the first hop using TLS, DTLS, or IPsec (hop-by-hop security at the network/transport layer). This way, every hop can check and modify the routing information of the query in order to properly route it, but only the receiver can see its content. An example of a P2P protocol implementing both features is RELOAD [9].

6.4.4   Protection of Contents at Rest

Following the security analysis conducted in [60], there are mainly three mechanisms to protect the privacy of contents at rest in P2P networks: local control, cryptography, and dedicated security services.

6.4.4.1 Local Control

In this mechanism the node responsible for the resource is in charge of its access control and, therefore, of its privacy protection. Local control can be implemented in different ways. In the RELOAD protocol [9], for example, each resource identifier may contain multiple kinds of data identified by a Kind-ID. The definition of each data kind specifies rules for determining which certificates can access each Resource-ID and Kind-ID pair, controlling the data access. Another possibility is to use an access control list (ACL) to determine the privileges of each user over an object like in OceanStore [13] or Fairsite [75].

The main drawback of this approach is that, if the node responsible for the resource is malicious, it can access the resources content or allow unauthorized users to access it.

6.4.4.2 Cryptography

The more effective way to prevent malicious users from accessing the private data of other users within the network is to use cryptography. If a user wants to store a private resource for personal use, symmetric cryptography, such as the AES algorithm [76], could be used to encrypt the data before storing them in the network. On the other hand, if the private resource is intended to be accessed by other users, such as a voice-mail, it may be encrypted using the public key of the recipient, as described in [77]. If the publisher wants the resource to be accessible by a group of users, three possibilities arise: (1) to extend the scenario of a single recipient by storing one copy of the resource for each recipient encrypted with his or her corresponding public key; (2) to encrypt the symmetric key using the public key of all authorized readers and store the encrypted keys with the resource [75], or (3) to store only one copy of the resource encrypted with a symmetric key and send a private message to each recipient with the location of the resource in the network and the key needed to access it [13].

6.4.4.3 Dedicated Security Servers

Another solution is to add dedicated security servers to the architecture. The users rely on these servers for storing their private resources. Unfortunately, as noted in [78], these servers reduce the advantage of the P2P architecture by introducing an extra cost in its development, and issues such as load balancing and capacity problems.

6.4.5 Private and Split Credentials

Only a small number of elementary tasks can be carried out completely in an anonymous way. Usually, the user has to perform some kind of authentication, therefore revealing some private information [64]. As stated in [79], in P2P applications with anonymous authentication, if the privacy of peers is increased, the difficulties of ensuring authenticity and security are increased too. There is a clear trade-off between authentication and anonymity that is to be catered by P2P application developers.

A way to protect users access is to give users fake identities. Fake identities can be ensured by smartcard techniques where the real identity of the user is only known by the authority which distributes the smartcards. In this case, the authority must be considered as a TTP [11]. For example, in Past [14], smartcards are used to allow users to obtain necessary credentials to access resources in an anonymous fashion. However, the use of trusted party for authentication can be risky. Thus, there is a trade-off between accountability and trusted party for authentication. Users have to be able to manage their identities in order to reduce to the minimum the information about them disclosed during their operations in the network.

Private credentials [80] provide the same functionalities and security guarantees as the classical X.509 certificates, but give the user the possibility of controlling and separating its different identities. They are based on a very similar approach to the X.509 certificates, but with two particular features:

- **Single secret key, many public keys (cryptographic pseudonyms)**. Users can create several public keys related to their secret key, instead of having only one public key for each private key. Also, it is not possible to link these public keys to each other, being unfeasible to know if they are held by several different users or by the same user.
- **Transformable**. Credentials are linked to the users secret key not to their public key. In this way, a credential related to one public key of the user can be transformed into a credential related to another and different users public key. Furthermore, the new created credential may only include a chosen subset of the attributes includes in the original credential.

Private credentials "provide the same level of security (as classical certificates), but additionally guarantee privacy during the process", as stated in [62].

Another certificate variation that can be used together with private credentials is split certification, as presented in the authors previous work [81]. Split certification separates the identity of the user from the identity of the device the user is operating from. This way, overlay maintenance and routing communications are performed between nodes without the unnecessary knowledge of which users are connected to them. Likewise, user operations are not linked to its devices, so users perform actions in the network without having to explicitly announce the node they are operating from. Combining split certification with private credentials can reduce the users provided information when fulfilling an access control policy necessary to access a resource.

6.4.6   Hidden Services

We have already introduced (Sect. 6.4.2.1) the possibility of using an intermediate
peer to route messages on a users behalf in order to protect the senders anonymity.
A similar approach for P2P data sharing, presented in [82], uses buddies (community members the user has established trust relationships with) as "proxies"
during data requesting. The mechanism used to hide the identity of the requester is,
rather than sending the request by itself, the requester asks one or several of its
buddies to look up the data on its behalf. This process can be improved by having
the supplier respond to a request via its own buddies; protecting, therefore, not only
the identity of the requester but also the identity of the supplier.

In this vein, but using a more sophisticated and privacy preserving approach, are
the hidden services used in Tor [83]. Location hidden services allow a user to offer
a service without revealing its IP address. Using Tor "rendezvous points", other
users can connect to these hidden services, each without knowing the other's
identity. The steps to do so are:

1. The provider picks some introduction points (peers acting as intermediates) and
   builds circuits (hop-by-hop encrypted random path) to them.
2. The provider publishes the service using a hidden service descriptor (including a
   summary of each introduction point) in a distributed hash Table
3. The requester learns about the service from its hidden service descriptor and sets
   up a circuit with a rendezvous point (peer acting as intermediate for the
   requester).
4. The requester sends a message to one of the introduction points requesting
   access to the service and including its rendezvous point.
5. Finally, the provider creates a circuit to the requesters rendezvous point and
   provides the service.

6.4.7   Application Configuration

The default configuration of a P2P application should be as strict as possible, so that
the user willing to share a file had configured the application for doing so.
Unfortunately, as noted in [15], this is not desirable for P2P developers. They fear
that only a few users will change the configuration to allow sharing, if the default
settings of the application are no sharing, therefore, reducing the interesting content
available in the P2P network and forcing the users to use a different application with
more content.

With this in mind, one of the most simple and useful solutions a user can
implement in order to protect its privacy is to properly configuring a P2P application to only share the information the user wants before starting to use it.

6.4.8 Application Hardening

Users should use trusted applications, either open-source where the code can be checked for malicious behavior or, at least, downloaded from trusted sources, to prevent spyware or malware being installed on its computer. Also, P2P applications need to have some privileges in order to be able to carry out their activities [84]: network access, write and read permissions over the hard disk, and so on, that can be used maliciously to disclose private information or install malware on the users machine. To remedy this, [85] recommends to run the P2P application in a sandbox that isolates the portion of the hard disk the application has access to and restricts the operations it can perform. In the same way, the integrity and behavior of the whole users devices system should be checked using anti-virus and anti-malware solutions.

6.5 Recommendations, Challenges, and Opportunities

In Sect. 6.3 we presented P2P privacy issues and in Sect. 6.4 we discussed P2P privacy solutions. It is time now to see how the described solutions can be used to mitigate the existing issues and explore the challenges that must be addressed in the future, along with opportunities for new research directions. Table 6.1 presents a summary of the recommendations described during the rest of this section to protect privacy in P2P networks.

6.5.1 User Identity

As we have described already, there are five main issues related to the user identity privacy in P2P networks, two of them being common to any Internet-based system and the three others being unique to P2P networks due to the special conditions they present.

For the first issue, related to the ISP identification of peers, two possible solutions arise. The first one is to accept that in order to contract an Internet line the user should give some private information to the Internet provider and trust that it will not release it to third parties compromising the users privacy. When this solution is not acceptable, a second option is to use a public Internet access point, such as the free wireless access point provided in some public places like coffee shops, train stations, or airports.

For the second issue, related to the P2P application providers TTP identification of peers, three possible solutions arise. The first one is, again, to trust that the provider will not release the users identity information to other third parties. The second one, when possible (users are not requested to give personal identifiable

Table 6.1 P2P Privacy issues and possible solutions

P2P Privacy Issues and solutions	
Privacy issues	Solutions
User identity	Trust internet provider
	Use public access point
	Trust P2P application provider
	Use pseudonymous
	Use anonymous access applications
	Private and split credentials
User location	Privacy of user identity solutions
	Anonymous systems
	Hidden services
User access	Anonymous systems
	Routing modifications
	Protection of contents in transit
	Privacy of user identity solutions
	Private and split credentials
User publishing	Anonymous systems
	Hidden services
	Privacy of user identity solutions
	Protection of content at rest
Contents	Protection of contents in transit
	Protection of contents at rest
Application misconfiguration and misuse	Application configuration
Spyware and malware	Application hardening

information such as an account or credit card number but less identifiable information such as an e-mail that can be from an open provider), is to connect to the application using a pseudonym that cannot be related to the users real identity. Finally, the third solution is to only use P2P applications that accept anonymous users and that do not need the user to follow an enrollment process.

For the third issue, related to the directly connected peers identification of users, two possibilities arise. The first one is to trust that the Internet provider will not reveal to the other peers which user is behind the visible IP address used. The second is, again, to use public Internet access points so that the IP address can not be related to the users identity. Also, in both cases, when some kind of credential is needed in order to prove membership of the network, private and split credentials should be used.

For the fourth and fifth issues, related to the mutual identification of the resources requester and provider, the best solution is to use private and split credentials in order to hide their real identities.

6.5.2   User Location

It is impossible for a peer to hide its IP address, and therefore its location, from the peers it is directly connected to. It is, however, possible for a user to hide its location if the peers the user is directly connected to do not know the identity of the user behind the peer it is using. In order to do so, the user has to use one of the solutions presented in the previous point to hide its identity. But, what happens when the user necessarily has to make some attributes public (like an ID and IP address in P2PSIP) to allow the other users of the system to communicate with it. In this case, the best option for the user seems to be accessing the applications through an anonymous system and using a hidden service to hide its real location from the users trying to contact them. Unfortunately, the hops introduced in this communication may not be viable for a real-time communication such as P2PSIP needs. The challenge here would be to find a system that could hide the location of the user while providing it with viable connection for real-time communication. One possible approach would be to hide the real location of the user (through a hidden service) until it accepts the communication with the calling user and, once accepted, to reveal its real location to establish a direct communication valid for real-time applications. This would not hide the location of the user from an accepted caller but, at least, it would prevent a malicious user from building a profile of the user location without the user realizing it; since the real location of the user is not released until the call is accepted. However, this is still an open area of research.

6.5.3   User Access

The best way to keep private the resources accessed by a user is to use an anonymous system. This would prevent the peers directly connected to the user from knowing which resources the user requests and, also, it would prevent those responsible for a specific resource from knowing the origin of a request. Unfortunately, in some cases this solution may not be available or perhaps too costly. In such cases, a less secure option, but one that can provide some level of privacy, is to combine routing modifications with protection of the contents in transit. Another possible option is not trying to hide the access itself but the identity of the user that is behind. In this case, the user should use the solutions already described to retain the privacy of the user identity. In any case, if the access to the resource is protected by an access control policy the user should use private and split credentials in order keep the privacy of its access.

6.5.4   User Publishing

Protection against content censorship mechanism is best achieved using an anonymous system and publishing resources under a hidden service. Obtaining this protection when this solution is not possible is an ongoing problem. One possibility is to publish the content anonymously and hide the identity of the publisher using one of the solutions already described in order to protect the user identity privacy. Another possibility would be to try to implement the proxy solution, described in Sect. 6.4.6, for content distribution. One final option would be to use cryptography to protect the content of the resource at rest. Nevertheless, the last presented solution would only hide the contents of the publishing user from non authorized users. Furthermore, if one of the authorized users disclosed the content, it would be possible to prove that the user published it if the encryption for the disclosed content matched the published one.

6.5.5   Contents

In order to protect the privacy of content, both solutions for the protection of content in transit and at rest should be used. For the case of protection at rest, cryptography is the recommend solution, because it not only prevents an unauthorized user from seeing content, but it also prevents a malicious container from disclosing users private information stored in the P2P network.

6.5.6   Application Misconfiguration and Misuse

So far, we have seen how to protect the privacy of different users' attributes: its identity, location, accessed information, published resources, and private stored information. However, all these mechanisms are useless if the application used by the user to access the P2P network is not well configured and is sharing its personal private information. It is, therefore, crucial to do a proper and secure configuration of the application used before accessing a P2P network.

6.5.7   Spyware and Malware

Similarly to application misconfiguration and misuse, having spyware or malware that leaks the user's personal information can render all the privacy protecting mechanisms described before useless. So, it is very important to check that the user device is clean of spyware and malware using an application hardening solution before accessing a P2P network in order to protect the users privacy.

6.6 Conclusions

As we have seen, there are several privacy issues that must be taken into account when using P2P applications: privacy of user's identity, location, access, and publishing; privacy of contents; application misconfiguration and misuse; and spyware and malware. Also, several solutions exist that can be used to try to address these issues: anonymous systems, routing modifications, protection of contents in transit and at rest, private and split credentials, hidden services, and application configuration and hardening.

However, the choice of the one to be used in each case is a complicated task. Some solutions may be effective to protect the privacy of some attributes but ineffective in protecting others. Furthermore, implementing some of them (e.g., using an anonymous system) while neglecting others (e.g., application misconfiguration sharing documents with personal identifiable information) may render useless the solutions in place. It is, therefore, of great importance to have a holistic view of the existing issues and solutions in order to protect privacy in P2P networks.

References

1. Bryan DA, Lowekamp BB, Jennings C (2005) SOSIMPLE: A Serverless, Standards-based, P2P SIP Communication System. In: Proceedings of the First international workshop on advanced architectures and algorithms for internet delivery and applications, Washington, DC, USA. IEEE Computer Society, pp 42–49
2. The seti@home project website (1997) http://setiathome.berkeley.edu
3. The genome@home Project Website (2000) http://genomeathome.stanford.edu
4. HueBsch R, Hellerstein J, Lanham N, Thau Loo B (2003) Querying the internet with pier. In: Proceedings of the 29th VLDB conference
5. Halevy A, Ives Z, Mork P, Tatarinov I (2003) Piazza: data management infrastructure for semantic web applications. In: Proceedings of the 12th international conference on world wide web, pp 556–567
6. The Napster Website (2003) http://free.napster.com/
7. Gnutella A Protocol for a Revolution (2000) http://rfc-gnutella.sourceforge.net/index.html
8. Cohen B (2003) Incentives build robustness in BitTorrent. In: Proceedings of the 1st workshop on economics of peer-to-peer systems, P2PECON'03
9. Jennings C, Lowekamp B, Rescorla E, Baset S, Schulzrinne H (2011) Internet-draft: resource location and discovery (RELOAD) base protocol. draft-ietf-p2psip-base-13 (work in progress)
10. Skype Official Website (2003) http://www.skype.com, 2003
11. Jawad M, Serrano-Alvarado P, Valduriez P (2013) Supporting data privacy in p2p systems. In: Chbeir R, Al Bouna B (eds) Security and privacy preserving in social networks. Lecture notes in social networks, pp 195–244. Springer Vienna
12. Le Blond S, Zhang C, Legout A, Ross K, Dabbous W (2011) I know where you are and what you are sharing: Exploiting p2p communications to invade users' privacy. In: Proceedings of the 2011 ACM SIGCOMM conference on internet measurement conference, IMC '11, pp 45–60, New York, NY, USA. ACM
13. Kubiatowicz J, Bindel D, Chen Y, Czerwinski S, Eaton P, Geels D, Gummadi R, Rhea S, Weatherspoon H, Weimer W, Wells C, Zhao B (2000) OceanStore: an architecture for global-scale persistent storage. ACM SIGPLAN Notices 35(11):190–201

14. Druschel P, Rowstron A (2001) PAST: a large-scale, persistent peer-to-peer storage utility. In: Proceedings of the Eighth workshop on hot topics in operating systems, pp 75–80, Washington, DC, USA, 2001. IEEE Computer Society
15. Suvanto M (2005) Privacy in peer-to-peer networks. In: Helsinki University of Technology T-110.551 Seminar on Internetworking
16. Camarillo G (2009) Peer-to-peer (p2p) architecture: definition, taxonomies, examples, and applicability. Request for comments
17. Androutsellis-Theotokis S, Spinellis D (2004) A survey of peer-to-peer content distribution technologies. ACM Comput Surv (CSUR) 36(4):335–371
18. Schollmeier R (2001) Definition of peer-to-peer networking for the classification of peer-to-peer architectures and applications. In: Proceedings of the first international conference on peer-to-peer computing, pp 101–102
19. Ngo HG (2013) From Inter-connecting P2P overlays to co-operating P2P systems. PhD thesis, University of Nice—Sophia Antipolis
20. Bashir A (2012) Classifying p2p activities in netflow records: a case study (bittorrnet & skype). Master's thesis, Carleton University, Ottawa, Ontario
21. Chervenak A, Bharathi S (2008) Peer-to-peer approaches to grid resource discovery. In: Proceedings of the CoreGRID workshop on programming models grid and P2P system architecture grid systems, tools and environments, pp 59–76
22. Ripeanu M, Foster I, Iamnitchi A (2002) Mapping the gnutella network: properties of large-scale peer-to-peer systems and implications for system design. IEEE Internet Comput J 6
23. Markatos EP (2002) Tracing a large-scale peer to peer system: an hour in the life of gnutella. In: The second international symposium on cluster computing and the grid, pp 65–70
24. Lua EK, Crowcroft J, Pias M (2005) A survey and comparison of peer-to-peer overlay network schemes. IEEE Commun Surv Tutor 7(2):72–93
25. Clarke I, Miller SG, Hong TW, Sandberg O, Wiley B (2002) Protecting free expression online with freenet. IEEE Internet Comput 6(1):40–49
26. Ripeanu M (2001) Peer-to-peer architecture case study: Gnutella network. In: Proceedings of the first international conference on peer-to-peer computing (P2P 2001), pp 99–100
27. Klingberg T, Manfredi R (2002) Gnutella 0.6. http://rfc-gnutella.sourceforge.net/src/rfc-0_6-draft.html
28. Liang J, Kumar R, Ross KW (2006) The fasttrack overlay: a measurement study. Comput Netw 50(6):842–858
29. Liang J, Kumar R, Ross KW (2004) Understanding kazaa. http://infosec.pku.edu.cn/p2p/slides/2004
30. Bhagwan R, Savage S, Voelker GM (2003) Understanding availability. In: Peer-to-peer systems II. Springer, Berlin, pp 256–267
31. Heckmann O, Bock A (2002) The edonkey 2000 protocol, kom technical report 08/2002, ver. 0.8, dec. 2002. Technical report, Darmstadt University of Technology
32. Pouwelse J, Garbacki P, Epema D, Sips H (2005) The bittorrent p2p file-sharing system: measurements and analysis. In: 4th international workshop on peer-to-peer systems (IPTPS 2005), pp 205–216
33. Trifa Zied, Khemakhem Maher (2012) Taxonomy of structured p2p overlay networks security attacks. World Acad Sci Eng Technol 6(4):469–475
34. Ratnasamy S, Francis P, Handley M, Karp R, Shenker S (2001) A scalable content-addressable network. In: Proceedings of the 2001 conference on applications, technologies, architectures, and protocols for computer communications (SIGCOMM 2001), pp 161–172
35. Zhao BY, Kubiatowicz J, Joseph AD (2001) Tapestry: an infrastructure for fault-resilient wide-area location and routing. Technical Report UCB/CSD-01-1141, Computer Science Division (EECS), University of California, Berkeley
36. Stoica I, Morris R, Karger D, Kaashoek MF, Balakrishnan H (2001) Chord: a scalable peer-to-peer lookup protocol for internet applications. In: Proceedings of the 2001 conference

on applications, technologies, architectures, and protocols for computer communications (SIGCOMM 2001), pp 149–160

37. Rowstron A, Druschel P (2001) Pastry: scalable, distributed object location and routing for large-scale peer-to-peer systems. In: Proceedings of the IFIP/ACM international conference on distributed systems platforms, Heidelberg (Middleware 2001), pp 329–350

38. Malkhi D, Naor M, Ratajczak D (2002) Viceroy: A scalable and dynamic emulation of the butterfly. In: Proceedings of the twenty-first annual symposium on principles of distributed computing (PODC 2002), pp 183–192

39. Maymounkov P, Mazières D (2002) Kademlia: A peer-to-peer information system based on the xor metric. In: First international workshop peer-to-peer systems (IPTPS 2002), pp 53–65

40. Sanchez Artigas M, Garcia Lopez P, Pujol Ahullo J, Gomez Skarmeta AF (2005) Cyclone: a novel design schema for hierarchical dhts. In: Proceedings of the Fifth IEEE international conference on peer-to-peer computing (P2P 2005), pp 49–56

41. Xu Z, Min R, Hu Y (2003) Hieras: a dht based hierarchical p2p routing algorithm. In: Proceedings. 2003 international conference on parallel processing, pp 187–194

42. Ganesan P, Gummadi K, Garcia-Molina H (2004) Canon in g major: designing dhts with hierarchical structure. In: IEEE international conference on distributed computing systems (ICDCS 2004), pp 263–272

43. Garces-Erice L, Ross KW, Biersack E, Felber PA, Urvoy-Keller G (2003) Toplus: topology centric lookup service. In: Fifth international workshop on networked group communications (NGC 2003), pp 58–69

44. Saroiu S, Gummadi KP, Gribble SD (2003) Measuring and analyzing the characteristics of napster and gnutella hosts. J Multim Syst 9(2):170–184

45. Deaconescu R (2011) Protocol measurements and improvements in peer-to-peer systems. PhD thesis, University POLITEHNICA of Bucharest

46. Babaoglu Ö (2012) Introduction to peer-to-peer systems. Complex Syst Università 1/2 di Bologna 12:7

47. Anderson DP, Cobb J, Korpela E, Lebofsky M, Werthimer D (2002) Seti@home: an experiment in public-resource computing. Commun ACM 45(11):56–61

48. Larson SM, Snow CD, Shirts M, Pande VS (2002) Folding@home and genome@home: using distributed computing to tackle previously intractable problems in computational biology

49. van Renesse R, Birman K, Bozdog A, Dumitriu D, Singh M, Vogels W (2003) Heterogeneity-aware peer-to-peer multicast. In: Proceedings of the 17th international symposium on distributed computing (DISC2003)

50. Keromytis AD, Misra V, Rubenstein D (2002) Sos: secure overlay services. In: Proceedings of the 2002 conference on Applications, technologies, architectures, and protocols for computer communications (SIGCOMM 2002), pp 61–72

51. Wu C, Li B (2008) rstream: Resilient and optimal peer-to-peer streaming with rateless codes. IEEE Trans Parallel Distrib Syst 19(1):77–92

52. Castro M, Druschel P, Kermarrec A-M, Nandi A, Rowstron A, Singh A (2003) Splitstream: high-bandwidth multicast in cooperative environments. In: Proceedings of the nineteenth ACM symposium on operating systems principles (SOSP 2003), pp 298–313

53. Ying L, Basu A (2005) cvod: internet peer-to-peer video-on-demand with storage caching on peers. In: 11th international conference on distributed multimedia systems (DMS 2005), pp 218–223

54. Liao X, Jin H, Liu Y, Ni LM, Deng D (2006) Anysee: peer-to-peer live streaming. In: 25th IEEE international conference on computer communications (INFOCOM 2006)

55. Chang H, Jamin S, Wang W (2009) Live streaming performance of the zattoo network. In: Proceedings of the 9th ACM SIGCOMM conference on internet measurement conference (IMC 2009), pp 417–429

56. Hei X, Liang C, Liang J, Liu Y, Ross KW (2006) Insights into pplive: a measurement study of a large-scale p2p iptv system. In: Workshop on Internet Protocol TV (IPTV) services over World Wide Web in conjunction with WWW2006

57. Carlsson N, Eager DL, Mahanti A (2009) Peer-assisted on-demand video streaming with selfish peers. In: Proceedings of the 8th international IFIP-TC 6 networking conference (NETWORKING 2009), pp 586–599
58. Solove DJ (2006) A taxonomy of privacy. Technical report, 154 U Pa L Rev 477
59. Fessi A, Evans N, Niedermayer H, Holz R (2010) Pr2-P2PSIP: privacy preserving P2P signaling for VoIP and IM. In: Principles, systems and applications of IP telecommunications, IPTComm '10, New York, NY, USA. ACM, pp 134–145
60. Touceda D, Sierra JM, Izquierdo A, Schulzrinne H (2012) Survey of attacks and defenses on P2PSIP communications. IEEE Commun Surv Tutor 14(3):750–783
61. Good N, Krekelberg A (2003) Usability and privacy: a study of kazaa p2p file-sharing. In: Cockton G, Korhonen P (eds) CHI. pp 137–144. ACM
62. Camenisch Jan (2012) Information privacy?! Comput Netw 56(18):3834–3848
63. Chaum D (1981) Communications of the ACM. In: Rivest R, Chaum DL (eds) Untraceable electronic mail, return addresses, and digital pseudonyms. Commun ACM 24:84–90
64. Sandhu R, Zhang X (2005) Peer-to-peer access control architecture using trusted computing technology. In: Proceedings of the tenth ACM symposium on access control models and technologies, SACMAT '05, pp 147–158, New York, NY, USA. ACM
65. Freedman MJ, Morris R (2002) Tarzan: a peer-to-peer anonymizing network layer. In: Proceedings of the 9th ACM conference on computer and communications security, CCS '02, pp 193–206, New York, NY, USA. ACM
66. Rennhard M, Plattner B (2002) Introducing MorphMix: peer-to-peer based anonymous internet usage with collusion detection. In: De Capitani di Vimercati S, Samarati P (eds) Proceeding of the ACM workshop on privacy in the electronic society (WPES-02), New York. ACM Press, pp 91–102
67. Choffnes DR, Duch J, Malmgren D, Guierma R, Bustamante FE, Amaral L (2009) Swarmscreen: privacy through plausible deniability in P2P systems. Technical report, Northwestern EECS Technical Report
68. O'Donnell CW, Vaikuntanathan V (2004) Information leak in the chord lookup protocol. In: Proceedings of the fourth international conference on peer-to-peer computing, P2P '04, Washington, DC, USA. IEEE Computer Society, pp 28–35
69. Borisov N, Waddle J (2005) Anonymity in structured peer-to-peer networks. Technical Report UCB/CSD-05-1390, EECS Department, University of California, Berkeley
70. Mislove A, Oberoi G, Post A, Reis C, Druschel P, Wallach DS (2004) AP3: cooperative, decentralized anonymous communication. In: Proceedings of the 11th workshop on ACM SIGOPS European workshop, EW 11, New York, NY, USA. ACM
71. Clarke I, Sandberg O, Wiley B, Hong TW (2001) Freenet: a distributed anonymous information storage and retrieval system. In: international workshop on designing privacy enhancing technologies: design issues in anonymity and unobservability, New York, NY, USA. Springer, New York, Inc, pp 46–66
72. Dierks T, Rescorla E (2008) The transport layer security (TLS) protocol version 1.2. RFC 5246 (Proposed Standard)
73. Rescorla E, Modadugu N (2006) Datagram transport layer security. RFC 4347 (Proposed Standard)
74. Kent S, Seo K (2005) Security architecture for the internet protocol. RFC 4301 (Proposed Standard)
75. Adya A, Bolosky WJ, Castro M, Cermak G, Chaiken R, Douceur JR, Howell J, Lorch JR, Theimer M, Wattenhofer RP (2002) FARSITE: federated, available, and reliable storage for an incompletely trusted environment. In: Proceedings of the 5th symposium on operating systems design and implementation, OSDI '02, New York, NY, USA. ACM, pp 1–14
76. Information Technology Laboratory, NIST, Gaithersburg, USA. In: FIPS 197. Advanced Encryption Standard (AES)
77. Bryan DA, Lowekamp B (2006) Innovations in peer-to-peer communications. In: Proceedings of the 2006 Virginia Space Grant consortium research conference

78. Cao F, Bryan DA, Lowekamp BB (2006) Providing secure services in peer-to-peer communications networks with central security servers. In: AICT-ICIW '06: Proceedings of the advanced international conference on telecommunications and int'l conference on internet and web applications and services, p 105, Washington, DC, USA, 2006. IEEE Computer Society
79. Qureshi A, Rifa-Pous H, Megias D (2013) A survey on security, privacy and anonymity in legal distribution of copyrighted multimedia content over peer- to-peer networks. Technical report, IN3-Universitat Oberta de Catalunya
80. Brands SA (2000) Rethinking public key infrastructures and digital certificates: building in privacy. MIT Press
81. Touceda DS, Camara JMS, Villalba LJG, Marquez JT (2011) Advantages of identity certificate segregation in P2PSIP systems. IET Commun 5(6):879–889
82. Lu Y, Wang W, Bhargava B, Xu D (2006) Trust-based privacy preservation for peer-to-peer data sharing. IEEE Trans Syst Man Cybern Part A: Syst Hum 36(3):498–502
83. Dingledine R, Mathewson N, Syverson P (2004) TOR: the second-generation onion router. In: Proceedings of the 13th conference on USENIX security symposium, vol 13. SSYM'04, Berkeley, CA, USA. USENIX Association, pp 21–21
84. Wallach DS (2003) A survey of peer-to-peer security issues. In: Proceedings of the 2003 Mext-NSF-JSPS international conference on Software security: theories and systems, ISSS'03. Springer, Heidelberg, Germany, pages 42–57
85. Gheorghe G, Lo Cigno R, Montresor A (2010) Security and privacy issues in p2p streaming systems: a survey. In: Peer-to-peer network and applications

Chapter 7
Privacy in the Cloud

Ragib Hasan and Shams Zawoad

7.1 Introduction

Cloud computing is becoming popular among business and information technology (IT) organizations as it offers infinite infrastructure resources, very convenient pay-as-you-go services, and low cost computing. Small and medium scale industries find cloud computing highly cost effective as it replaces the need for expensive physical and administrative infrastructures, and offers the flexible pay-as-you-go structure for payment. An organization could save 37 % cost if they would migrate their IT infrastructures from an outsourced data center to the Amazon's Cloud [1]. The rapid adoption of cloud computing has effectively increased the current market value of clouds and it will continue to grow in the future. According to a report from Market Research Media, the global cloud computing market is expected to grow at a 30 % compound annual growth rate (CAGR) reaching $270 billion in 2020 [2]. As reported by Gartner Inc., the strong growth of cloud computing will bring $148.8 billion revenue by 2014 [3]. Cloud computing is getting popular not only in the private industry, but also in the government sector [4].

However, the privacy and trustworthiness of cloud infrastructures have become a rising concern as today's cloud infrastructures often suffer from security issues [5–9]. Cloud infrastructures use the multi-tenant usage model and virtualization to ensure better utilization of resources. Conversely, these fundamental characteristics of cloud infrastructures make it difficult to ensure confidentiality and privacy of users in the cloud. According to the International Data Corporation (IDC) IT cloud services user survey, 74 % of IT executives and

R. Hasan (✉) · S. Zawoad
Department of Computer and Information Sciences,
University of Alabama at Birmingham, Birmingham, USA
e-mail: ragib@cis.uab.edu

S. Zawoad
e-mail: zawoad@cis.uab.edu

© Springer International Publishing Switzerland 2015
S. Zeadally and M. Badra (eds.), *Privacy in a Digital, Networked World,*
Computer Communications and Networks,
DOI 10.1007/978-3-319-08470-1_7

CIOs referred to security as the main reason preventing their migration to the cloud services model [10]. Some real attacks on cloud computing platforms strengthen the security concern. For example, a botnet attack on Amazon's cloud infrastructure was reported in 2009 [11].

A typical information exchange in the cloud occurs when a user shares information with a cloud provider. When users send data to clouds for computation or store confidential files, they are unaware of the underlying technology of the cloud. Cloud infrastructures appear as a black-box to end-users. Without the knowledge of physical location of the server or of how the processing of personal data is configured, end-users use cloud computing for storing email, photographs, business documents, medical records, appointment calendar, address book, and many other purposes. The sensitive data stored in cloud infrastructures can reveal users' biographical, biological, historical, locational, relational, computational, and other information, which can reveal their identity. Data in clouds are easier to manipulate, but also easier to lose control of, and this is where the privacy issue arises.

In general, privacy is considered to be a fundamental human right that refers to end-users' control over the collection, use, and disclosure of their personal data by others [12], or more generally we can say that privacy is lost when personal data become public [13]. At consumer level, privacy is defined as the protection and appropriate use of the personal information of customers to meet their expectations about its usage. For business organizations, privacy refers to the application of laws, policies, standards, and processes by which personally identifiable information (PII) of individuals is managed. The aforementioned definitions of privacy suggest that users can lose privacy when they outsource data and computation to the cloud. Cloud service providers (CSP) can sell confidential data without users' consent and can use users' personal information for junk advertisement, or a malicious tenant virtual machine (VM) inside the cloud can steal data of other tenants. Hence, the usage of today's cloud computing relies on trusting the cloud providers.

In light of the above, it is important to examine and understand the critical privacy issues in cloud computing. The goal of this chapter is to motivate researchers about the various privacy threats in cloud computing, and provide them with a guideline towards solving the privacy challenges. In this chapter, we will discuss the major privacy issues related to cloud computing, and present existing state-of-the-art privacy, and provide an overview of future research opportunities that we need to explore before cloud computing can become mainstream.

7.1.1 Organization

The rest of this chapter is organized as follows. In Sect. 7.2, we present background information about various cloud models. In Sect. 7.3, we introduce the main issues that make ensuring privacy in the cloud paradigm challenging. Section 7.4 discusses existing solution approaches and analyzes the pros and cons of existing solutions. Next, in Sect. 7.5, we present a list of open problems, which provides the readers with a list of potential research questions that remain unsolved. Finally, we summarize the chapter and conclude in Sect. 7.6.

7.2 Background

To better understand the privacy challenges in cloud computing, we need to look into the unique operational and architectural models of cloud computing. In this section, we discuss the definition of cloud computing and various service models used in this computing paradigm.

7.2.1 Cloud Computing

Though cloud computing is a relatively new business model for outsourced services, the technology behind cloud computing is not entirely new. Over the last 40 years, we observed the development of virtualization, data outsourcing, and remote computation. The overarching concept of delivering computing resources through a global network is rooted in the 1960s. From the early 2000s, cloud computing has been providing a streamlined way of provisioning and delivering such services to customers. In this regard, cloud computing is best described as a business paradigm or computing model rather than any specific technology.

The US National Institute for Standards and Technology (NIST) has defined cloud computing as a computing model that provides a convenient way of on-demand network access to a shared pool of configurable computing resources, such as networks, servers, storage, applications, and services [14]. These computing resources can be rapidly provisioned and released with minimal management effort or service provider interaction. The Open Cloud Manifesto Consortium defines cloud computing as the ability to control the computing resources dynamically in a cost-efficient way and the ability of the end-user, organization, and IT staff to utilize the most of that resources without managing the underlying complexity of the technology [15].

According to the above definitions, a key characteristic of cloud computing is that, a cloud is by nature a shared resource. Therefore, the same physical hardware, such as storage device and memory, can be shared by multiple users. Another important characteristic of cloud computing is the rapid elasticity, which provides users with the facility of on-demand scaling up or down of computing resources. Cloud providers control and optimize the use of computing resources through automated resource allocation, load balancing, and metering tools.

7.2.2 Classification According to Service Model

Cloud computing can be divided into three main categories depending on the nature of services provided by CSPs: Software as a Service (SaaS), Platform as a Service (PaaS), and Infrastructure as a Service (IaaS) [14]. Figure 7.1 illustrates the three service models in cloud computing architecture.

- **Software as a Service (SaaS).** In the SaaS model, customers access software applications hosted on a cloud infrastructure. This approach is different from traditional software package distribution to individuals or organizations. Customers can access services, offered by CSPs from any Internet connected devices through web browsers or mobile applications; there is no need for software distribution. Usually, there is a monthly subscription fee to use the services provided by the SaaS application. This fee can sometimes vary according to the number of users of an organization. In this model, customers do not have any control over the network, servers, operating systems, storage, or even the application, except some access control management for multi-user

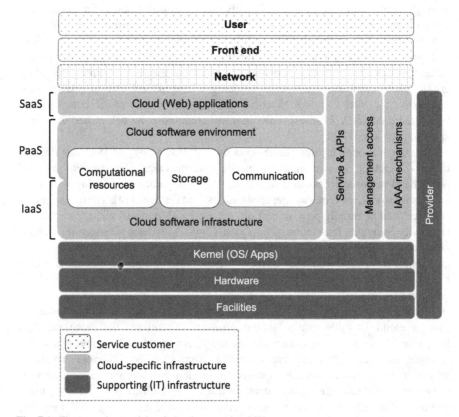

Fig. 7.1 Three service models of cloud computing [68]

applications. Hence, service providers are completely responsible for protecting the privacy and confidentiality of consumers' data. Some of the examples of SaaS are: Salesforce [16], Google Drive [17], and Google Calendar [18].

- **Platform as a Service (PaaS).** In the PaaS model, customers can build their own applications on top of a configurable software platform deployed in a cloud. Generally, customers pay according to the bandwidth usage and database usage. Using PaaS, a customer can deploy his own SaaS cloud and provide services to end-users. Customers do not manage or control the underlying cloud infrastructures including network, servers, operating systems, or storage, but have control over the deployed applications and some application hosting environment configurations. Hence, there lies a big responsibility for the customers to use best practices and privacy-friendly tools. However, customers can only use the application development environments, which are supported by the PaaS cloud provider. Therefore, customers have to trust that the platform is not compromised. Two examples of PaaS are: Google App Engine (GAE) [19] and Windows Azure [20].

- **Infrastructure as a Service (IaaS).** In the IaaS model, customers can rent processing power and storage to launch their own virtual machines and/or outsource data to a cloud. Using this model, customers can remove the costly process of maintaining their own data center. One of the most important features of IaaS is that customers can scale up or down the computing or storage resources according to their requirements. In this model, customers enjoy more flexibility than other cloud models in terms of configuring, running, and managing their own applications and software stack. Customers have full control over operating systems, storage, deployed applications, and possibly limited control of selecting networking components, such as, host firewalls. Therefore, customers have big responsibility to ensure privacy and to comply with some regulations, such as geographic restriction of data. Cloud service providers are responsible for securing the data centers, network, and systems. Two examples of IaaS are: Amazon EC2 [21] and Windows Azure VM [20]. EC2 and Azure VM provide users with access to VMs running on providers' servers. Customers can install any operating system, run any application, and deploy a SaaS cloud in the virtual machines rented from cloud providers.

7.2.2.1 Other Service Models

Motahari-Nezhad et al. proposed a more specific service model, which is Database as a Service (DaaS) [22]. This is a special type of storage service provided by cloud service providers. Most of the providers offer customers data storage in a key-value pair, rather than using a traditional relational database. Moreover, data of multiple users can be co-located in a shared physical table. Two of the examples of DaaS are: Amazon SimpleDB [23] and Google Bigtable [24]. The query language to store, retrieve, and manipulate the data depends on the implementation of a database system. There is a monthly fee depending on the incoming and outgoing volume of data and machine utilization. Hardware as a Service (HaaS) is another cloud service model, where the cloud provides access to dedicated firmware via the Internet, for example, XEN and VMWare [25]. Several other services are also proposed, for example, Security as a Service [26], and Logging as a Service [27].

7.2.3 Classification According to the Deployment Model

According to the deployment model, cloud computing can be categorized into four categories: private cloud, public cloud, community cloud, and hybrid cloud [28]. Figure 7.2 shows four different deployment models of cloud computing—private, community, public, and hybrid cloud.

- **Private cloud** In the private cloud model, the cloud infrastructure is fully operated by the owner organization. It is the internal data center of a business organization. Usually, the infrastructure is located at the organizations' premise. Private clouds can be found in large companies and for research purposes.
- **Community cloud** If several organizations with common concerns (e.g., mission, security requirements, policy, and compliance considerations) share cloud infrastructures, then this model is referred to as the community cloud. It is somewhat similar to a private cloud, but the infrastructure and computational

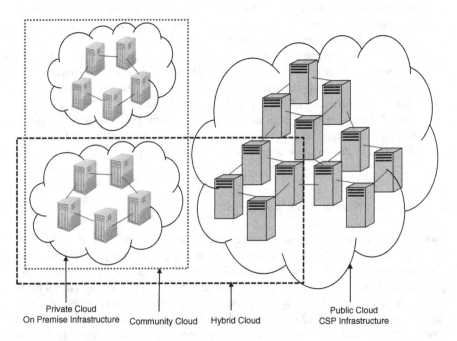

Fig. 7.2 Three different cloud deployment models

resources are shared between two or more organizations. Resource sharing can be done by communicating between different clouds, where each belongs to different organizations, or by building a common cloud infrastructure that can be used by different organizations in a shared manner.

- **Public cloud** In the public cloud model, cloud providers own and operate the cloud infrastructure to deliver cloud services to consumers and, by definition, this model is external to the consumers' organizations. All the examples given in the service-based cloud categorization are public clouds.
- **Hybrid cloud** As the name suggests, the hybrid cloud infrastructure is a composition of two or more clouds (private, community, or public; e.g., cloud bursting for load-balancing between clouds). A hybrid cloud architecture requires both on-premises resources and off-site (remote) server-based cloud infrastructures.

7.3 Privacy Issues

Researchers have studied privacy issues in distributed computing systems for a long time. However, there are several factors that make privacy in the cloud different from traditional distributed systems. We point out those factors to properly address the open problems of privacy in clouds; it is vital to understand what makes the cloud privacy different from traditional distributed systems.Section2 ID="Sec9">Multi-tenancy

One of the most critical issues that makes preserving privacy in cloud computing different from other distributed computing systems is the idea of multi-tenancy. Though there are some exceptions, such as OVH who provides dedicated cloud services [29], usually, the cloud infrastructure is based on the idea of multi-tenancy. Rather than using physical separation of resources as a control, cloud computing places greater dependence on logical separation at multiple layers of the application stack [28]. This means that, at any given time, multiple users will be sharing the same physical hardware and resources of a cloud infrastructure, where generally, the users have no relation between each other. However, this fundamental property of cloud computing has been manipulated by many attackers to attack the privacy of cloud users. Attackers can exploit multi-tenancy in several ways. Without violating any laws or bypassing any security measures, attackers can use the multi-tenancy feature to get inside a cloud infrastructure legitimately. Once inside the cloud infrastructure, attackers can then start gathering information about the cloud. Next, the attacker can gather information about other users who are sharing resources with the attacker. Finally, co-residency also exposes cloud users to active internal attacks launched by co-resident attackers.

Example: An example of the co-resident attack was presented by Ristenpart et al. in [30]. Here, the authors first reverse-engineered the internal IP address allocation map of Amazon EC2 to identify the location of a particular VM in the cloud. Then, they presented a network-based scheme to identify the co-resident.

Using the map and the co-residence checking technique, they showed how an attacker can achieve the co-residency with a targeted VM. After placing the VM in the same physical infrastructure, where a target-VM is located, attackers can launch some CPU cache-based side channel attacks, which can leak important information about the target-instance (e.g., password, number of visitors, etc.). A follow up work shows that the attackers can actually steal encryption keys using the side channel attack [31].

7.3.1 Trust Asymmetry

Preserving privacy in public clouds is more difficult than in other distributed systems because of the asymmetric trust relationship between cloud service providers and cloud users. Today's cloud computing models are designed to hide most of the inner workings of the cloud from users. Cloud infrastructures are like big black boxes and do not allow users to look into the inner structure or operation of the cloud. From the cloud provider's point of view, this is designed to protect the cloud infrastructure as well as the privacy of the users. However, the black-box nature of clouds prevents users from getting information beyond whatever is provided by the cloud service provider. In some cases, users can find it difficult to effectively check the data handling practices of the cloud provider and thus to be sure that the data is handled in a lawful way [32]. Users do not usually have control over the operation of their virtual machines or applications running on the cloud through the limited interface provided by the cloud service provider. In cloud computing, the control over data varies in different service models. Figure 7.3 shows the limited amount of control that customers have in different layers for the three service models—IaaS, PaaS, and SaaS. In IaaS, users have more control than in SaaS or PaaS. The lower level of control has made the privacy preservation in SaaS and PaaS more

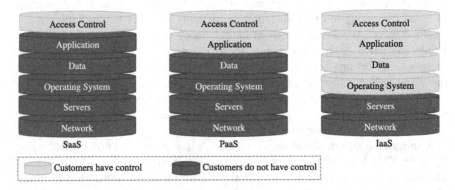

Fig. 7.3 Customers' control over different layers in different service model [64]

challenging than in IaaS. As a result, cloud users have to trust the cloud provider completely regarding the privacy and confidentiality of their data.

Example: Suppose a business organization, BO.CoLtd. uses a SaaS-based business management application to manage its business. The SaaS application needs to store all the business related information of BO.CoLtd. including information about the customers. Information about the customers should not be disclosed as it can violate customers' privacy. BO.CoLtd completely relies on the reputation and trustworthiness of the service provider to keep its customers' confidential information in the cloud storage. However, the cloud provider can sell the customers' information to other business organizations without the consent of BO. CoLtd., which definitely violates the privacy of the customers.

7.3.2 Legal Issues

A universal principle for the protection of personal data and privacy is the Madrid Resolution [33]. This resolution was approved in Madrid in 2009 by data protection authorities from 50 countries. It states the urgent need to protect privacy in the Internet world with no borders and presents a joint proposal for the establishment of international standards on privacy and data protection. The purpose of the Madrid Resolution was to define a set of principles and rights, which can guarantee the effectiveness and internationally uniform protection of privacy in respect of processing of personal data. Moreover, the Madrid Resolution encourages the implementation of proactive measures through privacy enhancing technologies (PETs), which can ensure better compliance with applicable privacy protection laws relating to the processing of personal data. Implementing PETs in cloud computing can reduce the risk of violating privacy principles and legislation, minimize the amount of data held about individuals, and allow individuals to take control of information about themselves at all times. However, standardization of PETs in cloud computing is challenging as we need to mitigate cloud-specific concerns on a case-by-case basis and in relation to the nature of the cloud services.

For business related data, disclosing the personal information of customers or employees, or electronic medical records (EMR) of patients to a cloud provider is often unrestricted by different regulation policies. The Privacy Act of 1974 imposes standards for the collection, maintenance, use, and disclosure of personal information [34]. If there is no contractual agreement between federal agency and the cloud service provider, storing personal information in clouds may violate the Privacy Act of 1974. The Gramm-Leach-Bliley Act does not allow financial institutions to disclose a consumer's personal financial information to a CSP [35].

According to the Health Insurance Portability and Accountability Act (HIPAA) [36], EMRs are private and confidential to a patient. HIPAA provides comprehensive policies to regulate the use and disclosure of individually identifiable health information by covered entities. By covered entities, HIPAA principally refers to healthcare and health plans providers. Using clouds for medical purposes may violate the HIPAA policies, as in this case, hospitals are giving the responsibility of storing or processing confidential EMRs to a cloud provider, which is not a covered entity.

The location of a cloud provider's data center may have a significant impact on the law that applies to data privacy. Data centers of cloud providers can be distributed worldwide and the same data can be stored in multiple locations at the same time. However, the privacy preservation or information sharing laws are not in harmony throughout the world, they may not even be the same in different states within one country. It may happen that a user is accessing the cloud computing service from one jurisdiction, whereas the data he or she is accessing reside in a different jurisdiction. Differences in laws between the two locations can affect the privacy preserving procedures of CSP. Because of the importance of location, the Privacy Level Agreement (PLA) guideline for cloud services operated in the European Union suggests that the locations of all data centers where personal data may be processed, stored, mirrored, backed-up, and recovered are specified [37].

Example: Let us assume that a hospital provides facilities to its patients for doctor appointments, accessing their health information, prescriptions management, bill payment to health insurance providers, and other services from a web-based application. If the hospital deploys the application in a privately owned infrastructure, then this will not violate the policies of HIPAA as the information is circulated among all the covered entities. However, to minimize the cost of maintaining a privately owned infrastructure, the hospital decided to move the application to a public cloud. Using a cloud for this application will violate the HIPAA policies since medical records are now stored or circulated through a third-party entity—the cloud service provider, which is not considered as a covered entity according to HIPAA.

Another example can be tax return preparation services through online facilities [34]. Generally customers of tax preparers enjoy some regulatory privacy protections. These customer protections in turn limit the ability of a tax preparer to deploy the online service in a cloud. It is difficult to see how an online tax preparation service, deployed in a cloud, can comply with the IRS rules and still disclose tax return information to the cloud provider. A tax preparer can not use a foreign cloud provider without taxpayer consent, moreover, disclosure of a Social Security Number (SSN) will be impossible.

7.3.3 Insider Threats

While designing the security of distributed systems, security experts mostly consider the threats from external attackers. Hence, significant efforts have been made by the experts to keep the malicious attackers outside the system perimeter. Unfortunately, in cloud paradigm, the attackers can legitimately be inside the system. Though the security experts are familiar with the concept of insider attacks, a malicious insider in a cloud might have access to a massive amount of information and on a much greater scale. The insider attackers only need to pay for the use of cloud resources. In most clouds, anyone possessing a valid credit card is given access to the cloud. Using this, attackers can get inside a cloud without actually violating any law or even the cloud provider's usage policy. Privacy threats to user data and applications in the cloud have been increased due to this insider access to cloud infrastructures. The global nature of cloud computing means that attackers from all over the world can target a victim just by accessing the cloud. Because of the shared resources in cloud computing, often there is the risk of collateral damage when other users sharing the same resources with a victim and may also face the effects of an attack.

Example: An example of an insider attack would be a curious employee of a cloud provider monitoring the network traffic flow by using a network monitoring tool from a cloud host machine. In this way, the employee can gather confidential information about cloud users, such as the websites that a user is interested in visiting often, or login credentials of a user for a website, which is not using the secured socket layer for communication. In [38], the authors provided some scenarios of insider attacks, such as cloning VMs, copying files from a cloud storage, and data redirection to an external nation state or criminal organization.

7.3.4 Data Outsourcing

Data outsourcing is a major usage of today's cloud computing. Managing very large-scale datasets, commonly referred to as "Big Data" is beyond the capacity of most local data storage systems. Therefore, people use clouds to store their Big Data. Another reason for using clouds is to ensure the reliability and survivability of data stored in an off-site cloud. However, in present times, cloud service providers do not provide any technical assurance for ensuring the privacy and integrity of outsourced data. As cloud providers do not allow users to examine or observe their inner workings, users have no idea where and how their data are being stored, and whether the integrity of the data is preserved.

For very large-scale datasets, often clients or one-time users of such data sets do not have the capability to download the data to their own systems and perform computation on that data. A very common technique is to divide the system into data providers (which has the data objects), computation providers (which provides the code), and a computational platform (such as a MapReduce framework where the code will be run on the data). But for datasets containing personal details, a big challenge is to prevent unauthorized leaks of private information. MapReduce is being used intensively for data mining applications on large-scale datasets. However, a malicious mapper node has access to the granular data and it can leak this data to violate the privacy of users.

Example: Let us assume that a researcher wants to perform an analysis on the medical records of 1 million patients of a hospital. The hospital cannot release the data to the researcher as patients' privacy depends on the medical records, but the hospital can make the data accessible to a trusted third-party computational platform, where the code supplied by the researcher (computation provider) is run on the data, with the results being sent back to the researcher. However, this model suffers from a vulnerability—if the researcher is malicious, he or she can write code that will leak private information from the medical records directly through the result data or via indirect means.

7.3.5 Access Control

Absence of proper access control mechanism in clouds can violate users' privacy because it will allow unauthorized users to access huge amount of sensitive information, stored in clouds. For medical and business records, a proper access control mechanism is mandatory so that only the designated persons can access their required information. Moreover, different kinds of data are stored in different layers of clouds, which need to be accessible to different stakeholders of the system, such as, users, system administrators, forensic investigators, and developers. System administrators need relevant information to troubleshoot the system. Developers need the required logs to fix bugs of an application. Forensic investigators need evidence that can help in their investigation. Hence, there should be a proper access control mechanism, so that everybody can get what they need exactly—nothing more, nothing less, and obviously, in a secure way.

Additionally, access control in online social networking is crucial, where users store personal information, such as photographs and videos. This information is stored in the cloud platform and it is very important that only the authorized users are given access to that information, because users often share the information with selected other users within their network. Without strong access control mechanisms, people outside the user's network or with whom the user is not interested in sharing his or her personal information can view and sell or distribute the confidential information. Access control is also necessary when documents are stored in clouds, for example, in Dropbox, and users want to share the documents with certain individuals.

Example: Suppose a business organization uses a cloud-based storage service to share and collaborate with the business documents between its employees. In the organization, not all employees have the privilege of accessing confidential documents. If the access control of the cloud storage system is not secured, attackers can exploit a vulnerability in the access control mechanism of the storage system to get unauthorized access. Thus, a dishonest employee of the organization can steal some confidential documents and sell those to a competitor organization.

7.3.6 Secure Identity

Accessing cloud-based services, such as sending emails, sharing documents and photographs, buying goods, and playing games require identity information to be given by users to cloud service providers. A typical Internet user has to provide some personal information to dozens of different websites and has left behind personally identifiable information everywhere he or she has been. Designing a privacy-aware identity system for cloud infrastructures is more challenging than for traditional distributed systems. In [12], several properties have been mentioned that are required for a privacy-aware identity service in clouds, such as: device independency, enabling single sign-on to thousands of different online services, allowing pseudonyms and multiple discrete but valid identities to protect user privacy, interoperability, transparency, and auditability.

Example: In [12], the authors presented several case studies, where we require a secure identity management system to protect the privacy of cloud users. People need privacy protected credentials in their online activities, such as blogs, collaborative wikis, social networks, and so on. Users have to expose personal information in online dating sites, hence users require strong assurances that their information will be treated with respect and will be used only for the agreed-upon purposes. Our cell phone preserves huge amounts of personal information, however, we frequently use cell phones for location-based services or as electronic wallets for payments. With electronic wallets, it is possible that the cellular network provider will know when, where, and how we are spending money. Additionally, by tracking others' electronic wallets, they could know who we are with.

7.3.7 Need for Accountability

Information accountability can ensure whether the data manipulation comply with the privacy rules and regulations of an organization. Hence, privacy risk in cloud computing can be reduced if cloud providers use a combination of privacy policies and contractual terms to create accountability for transparent data handling. While encryption can ensure confidentiality of outsourced data, ensuring accountability is difficult. Most likely, the clients do not have a copy of data, so comparing the stored version to the local copy is not a realistic assumption. A naive solution is to download the data completely to determine whether it was stored without any tampering. The naive solution might be suitable for small data, but for larger datasets this will not be feasible for the network bandwidth costs, and computing resources, available to clients. To resolve these challenges, researchers introduce the notion of public auditability, where cloud users can rely on an external entity—a trusted third-party auditor (TPA) to verify the integrity of the cloud content and to make sure that CSPs are abided by the privacy policies. Due to the limitation of computing resource and capability of users, they can assign a TPA to check the integrity of outsourced data when needed. However, introducing TPA brings new challenges in the verification phase. Introducing TPA in the loop brings new threats on the users' privacy. While verifying the data integrity, TPA can leak users' sensitive data.

Example: Provable Data Possession (PDP) first introduced public verifiability [39]. The proposed scheme splits large data into small chunks of data blocks and randomly verifies the blocks to prove data integrity. To verify the data stored in the cloud, users need to periodically send challenges to the cloud provider for a small and random set of blocks. After receiving a challenge request, the cloud provider needs to compute the response by reading the actual file blocks. PDP ensures that if the server has the actual file blocks, only then it will be able to respond correctly to the challenge. However, PDP requires the linear combination of sampled blocks exposed to external auditor, which may leak users' data to a TPA [40].

7.3.8   Cloud Forensics

Besides being used by legitimate users, clouds can be misused for malicious purposes. For example, an attacker can rent thousands of machines in a cloud for a relatively cheap price, and then send spam or host temporary phishing sites, or simply create a botnet to launch denial of service attacks. In [41], Chen et al. discussed the threat of using clouds for running brute force, spam, or botnets. Another malicious usage of clouds is password cracking. There are commercial password cracking services, such as WPACracker.com, which utilizes the computation power of cloud computing to crack WPA passwords in less than 20 min using a rainbow table approach.

To investigate these types of criminal activities involving clouds, we need to execute digital forensics procedures inside clouds, which is referred to as *cloud forensics*. Cloud forensics is the application of digital forensic principles and procedures in a cloud computing environment. Traditional digital forensics strategies and practices often fail when a suspect uses cloud computing to launch an attack. As an example, a suspect using a traditional file storage to store incriminating documents, would be easy to convict and prosecute—the law enforcement investigators can make an image of the suspect's hard drives and run forensic analysis tools there, which does not violate the privacy of any other persons. However, when the suspect stores the files in a cloud, many complications can occur. As resources are shared in clouds, gathering evidence from cloud infrastructures can violate the privacy of many other users, who are not related with the crime.

Example: Suppose a suspected terrorist stored attack plans or instructions for building a bomb in a cloud storage. Since the suspect did not have any files stored locally, seizing and imaging his drives did not reveal any information other than the suspect's use of the cloud storage service. The law enforcement agency issued a subpoena to the cloud provider and seized the storage devices from the data center of the cloud provider. However, this brings the privacy of other honest users into question, because many other unrelated people would have their confidential data stored in the same drives as the suspected user. Therefore, seizure or imaging of such drives will compromise the privacy of many users of the cloud.

7.4 Current Solutions

This section provides existing solution approaches, which can ensure privacy of cloud users from different perspectives.

7.4.1 Protection Against Exploiting Co-tenancy

The attacks from co-tenants described in [30] can be prevented by obfuscating the IP address allocation scheme in Amazon AWS, because attackers can exploit this knowledge to place their VM with targeted VMs. However, obfuscation cannot resolve the key features of the attack on co-resident users. Solution approaches suggested in [30] include using specially designed caches that will prevent cache-based side channels and cache wiping schemes. Unfortunately, the specialized nature of the cache hardware is not cost efficient to integrate with the existing cloud infrastructures.

7.4.2 Secure Architecture for the Cloud

One of the ways to ensure privacy is providing more control to users over their data. Therefore, we need to design cloud computing architectures that are transparent and provide clients with some accountability and control over privacy. To resolve this issue, researchers have proposed architectures that provide privacy guarantees to the users. There have been proposals in which part of the security decision and capabilities are extended to the client's domain [42]. In this approach, a virtual management infrastructure is used to control the cloud operations, and the clients are allowed to have control over their own applications and virtual machines.

Santos et al. designed a secure cloud infrastructure by leveraging trusted platform module or TPM chips to build a chain of trust [43]. They proposed a trusted cloud computing platform (TCCP), which can ensure that the VM is running inside a secured perimeter and protect the VM state against inspection or modification when it is in transit on the network. Two modules comprise the system: a trusted virtual machine monitor (TVMM), and a trusted coordinator (TC), which is hosted by a trusted third party. In the node management step, a mutual trust is established between nodes and the TC. Then before launching a VM or live VM migration, trust is established between a VM and a node through the cloud manager (CM).

There are several other research approaches for securing cloud architectures [44]. For example, Zhang et al. proposed hardening the hypervisor to enforce security [45]. Excalibur [46] is another system that uses remote attestations and leverages TPMs to ensure security of the cloud architecture.

By using hardware tokens, which are assumed to be trusted, cloud providers can provide users with the functionality of performing arbitrary confidential and verifiable computation in clouds. Function computation will be performed inside those tokens, where data are stored in encrypted form outside the tokens and decryption keys are stored in the tamper-proof tokens. Secure coprocessor is an example of such hardware token, which is a tamper-proof programmable device and can be attached to the cloud provider's computer to perform sensitive operations [47]. However, users need to trust the hardware token's manufacturer to keep the data shielded from cloud providers. Hence, cloud providers need to support hardware tokens from trusted third-party manufacturers or introduce the functionality of attaching tokens in their infrastructure, which are provided by users.

7.4.3 Confidentiality of Data

Many users need to store sensitive data items in cloud infrastructures. For example, healthcare and business data need extra protection mandated by many government regulations. However, storing sensitive and confidential data in untrusted third-party cloud providers exposes the data to malicious employees of cloud providers or malicious external attackers, who have compromised the cloud. The very basic approach to ensure data confidentiality is to encrypt data before sending them to a cloud. Unfortunately, encryption comes at a cost—searching and sorting encrypted data is expensive and reduces performance. A potential solution is to use homomorphic encryption for computation on encrypted data in a cloud [48, 49].

The fully homomorphic encryption scheme proposed in [48], allows one to compute arbitrary functions over encrypted data without the decryption key. A pure homomorphic encryption scheme enables private queries to a search engine, that is, the user submits an encrypted query and the search engine computes an encrypted answer without knowing the query in the plain-text format. It also enables searching on encrypted data. Therefore, homomorphic encryption will not allow a cloud provider to read the data while performing computations on the data. A cloud provider only receives ciphertext of the data and performs computations on the ciphertext without knowing what data it has operated on and returns the encoded value of the result to users. Only the user can decode the encrypted result. However, pure homomorphic encryption schemes are very inefficient due to high latency.

Sadeghi et al. propose a homomorphic encryption scheme to minimize the latency where the time between submitting a query and receiving response should be as small as possible [49]. The proposed solution combines the trusted hardware token with the secure function evaluation scheme to compute any functions on encrypted data without leaking any confidential information.

7.4.4   Privacy in Outsourced Computation

We need to perform outsourced computation using clouds while guaranteeing user privacy [50]. For outsourced computation using clouds, a developer can write malicious code to leak confidential data. To prevent such privacy violations, researchers have proposed techniques that use the notion of differential privacy (DP). A system is differentially private if every output is produced with similar probability whether any given input is included or not. The Airavat framework [50] modifies the MapReduce framework to incorporate DP, thereby preventing the leakage of private information. The system allows computation with sensitive data, for example, patient's medical record, shopping transactions, and so on in an untrusted cloud environment. There are three entities involved in the system: (1) the data provider, who stores data in the cloud with certain privacy parameters, (2) the computation provider, who writes data mining algorithm and can be malicious, and (3) the Airavat framework, which runs the computation and preserves the privacy of the data provider. The Airavat is comprised of modified MapReduce frameworks, DFS, JVM, and SELinux. The key idea is to confine the mappers to protect the privacy of data providers. It combines the mandatory access control (MAC) and DP. By using MAC, it prevents leaks through system resources and DP prevents leaks through the output of the computation. To achieve the DP, the system adds noise with the input to conceal the effect of an input on the output. The amount of noise depends on the sensitivity of the input, that is, how much a single input influences the output. However, the current state-of-the-art in this area is very inefficient in terms of performance, often causing more than 30% in overheads for privacy protection.

Sedic is another scheme that provides a privacy-aware computing facility for large-scale datasets in the hybrid cloud environment [51]. The system utilizes the special features of MapReduce to automatically split and schedule a data-intensive computing job across the public and private cloud according to the security levels of the data. The proposed system manages the MapReduce tasks in such a way that it outsources as much workload to the public cloud as possible, given sensitive data always stay on the private cloud. To preserve the data privacy, only the private nodes should be responsible for reduction tasks. Sedic accomplishes this goal by automatically transforming the reduction structure of a submitted job from the public cloud before sending the result back to the private cloud for final reduction.

7.4.5   Access Control Mechanisms

A strong access control mechanism is necessary to ensure data privacy. Access control mechanisms can be broadly classified into three categories: identity based access control (IBAC), role based access Control (RBAC), and attribute based access control (ABAC). However, IBAC is not feasible in clouds because the number of users in the cloud environment is too large to keep them in the access control list (ACL) that contains the identity of authorized users. In RBAC, roles are mapped to access permissions and users are mapped to appropriate roles. Therefore, in RBAC, data access policy is applied to a group of users rather than each individual person. Users are classified into different groups based on their individual roles and only the user, who has the sufficient role can access data. The roles and corresponding access policies are defined by the system administrator. In ABAC, users are tagged with certain attributes, and the data has attached access policies. Only the user with a valid set of attributes that satisfy the access policies, can access the data.

In [52], a role-based encryption (RBE) scheme is integrated with RBAC to ensure the privacy of the data, stored in a public cloud. In the RBE system, the owner of the data encrypts the data in such a way that only the users, who have appropriate roles according to a RBAC policy, can decrypt and view the data. Therefore, even though the cloud provider stores data, it will not be able to see the content of the data if the provider is not given the appropriate role. Based on the RBE scheme, a hybrid cloud storage architecture (composition of public and private cloud) is proposed. The hybrid architecture allows an organization to store the encrypted data in a public cloud, while maintaining the sensitive information, such as role hierarchy and user membership information in a private cloud.

Most of the existing works on ABAC-based access control mechanisms [53–55] use a cryptographic primitive—Attribute Based Encryption (ABE) [56]. Using ABE, the records are encrypted under some access policies and stored in a cloud. Users are given sets of attributes and corresponding keys. It is only when the users have a matching set of attributes that they can decrypt the information stored in the cloud. There are two classes of ABEs: Key-policy ABE (KP-ABE) [57] and Ciphertext-policy ABE (CP-ABE) [58].

HABE is an another access control mechanism for clouds, which is based on CP-ABE and hierarchical identity-based encryption. The proposed system provides high performance, fine-grained control policy, scalability, and full delegation of access controls [54]. In [55], a scheme for attribute revocation in an untrusted cloud environment has been presented, which can be applicable for both CP-ABE and KP-ABE. In the aforementioned works, the key distribution center (KDC) has been considered as a single, centralized entity, which is a single point of failure. Moreover, maintaining a centralized KDC is difficult in the cloud environment because of the large number of users that are supported in clouds. An access control scheme, which is based on decentralized KDC has been presented in [53]. This scheme facilitates cloud providers to have many KDCs in different locations. The scheme can also protect replay attacks, where a user can replace fresh data with the data from a previous write, even if the data no longer has a valid claim policy.

Sticky policy is another access control mechanism that can help to ensure accountable management and disclosure of confidential data in the cloud [59, 60]. This approach utilizes cryptographic mechanisms to strongly attach data access policies and conditions with the data. Sticky policies are passed between organizations to capture constraints about data access policy. The receiving parties must meet the attached conditions to access and use the associated personal data. In this way, users can be provided with fine-grained control over access and usage of their data within the cloud.

7.4.6   Privacy-Aware Identity Management

One of the major technologies that can enhance the privacy of cloud users is the anonymous credential system. Anonymous credential systems allow a user to obtain a credential from one organization and then later prove possession of this credential to another organization without revealing any other personal information. In this way, users do not need to provide their personal information on every new website that requires a login. Anonymous credential systems also allow selective disclosure of personal information by permitting the user to reveal some credential attributes or prove that they satisfy some properties, such as zip code, while hiding all the other credential attribute information. Idemix is an anonymous credentials management system, developed by IBM [61], based on group signatures. U-Prove is another system proposed by Microsoft, which is based on blind signatures and the work of Stefan Brands [62]. Using such services, cloud users can anonymously access various cloud services while revealing to the service provider only what is strictly needed to check his or her rights.

In order to facilitate privacy-aware identity service a free digital identity technology, OpenID was developed by an open community [63]. OpenID simplifies the online user experience by reducing the complexity of managing usernames and passwords for each website that the users need to sign in to. It also provides users with greater control over the personal information that they are required to share with websites when they log in. OpenID enables individuals to convert one of their already existing digital identifiers, such as their personal blog's URL, into an OpenID account, which can then be used as a log-in at any website supporting OpenID [12].

7.4.7   Privacy Preserving Evidence Collection

Forensics investigators should not violate the privacy of honest users, while collecting evidence from the cloud environment to prosecute a criminal case involving clouds. Analyzing various logs, such as process logs and network logs, plays a vital role in determining the guilt or innocence of a suspect. At the same time, logs can reveal confidential information about users' activity. To resolve this problem, SecLaaS stores virtual machines' logs and provides access to forensic investigators while ensuring the confidentiality of the cloud users [64]. For each running VM inside a cloud host, SecLaaS first extracts various kinds of logs from the host machine, then stores the data in a persistent log database. While storing the log data in a persistent storage, SecLaaS proposes to encrypt the sensitive information, for example, user ID, destination IP address for network logs, by using a common public key of all the investigation agencies. This will protect log information from malicious cloud employees who have access to the persistent storage. After saving a log entry in the log database, the system stores the proof of a log entry in a proof database. The proof of the logs, proposed here is generated using accumulator function, which ensures that adversaries cannot recover any log from the proof of logs.

Proof of past data possession (PPDP) is another scheme to provide evidence to forensics investigators while preserving users' privacy [65]. This is a continuous synchronization policy to prevent the loss of evidence after terminating the VMs running inside clouds. PPDP preserves the proof of data possession but without preserving the data itself. The proposed system preserves the proof of data possession using Bloom Filter [66]. Because of the one-way hash functions used in Bloom filter, it is not possible for an adversary to know about the data or to change history of data from the PPDP.

7.4.8 Privacy-Aware Public Verifiability

As we discussed in Sect. 7.3, introducing public verifiability by third-party auditor (TPA) can bring new threats to users' privacy. We need to make sure that introducing TPA should not bring new vulnerabilities in users' privacy.

Shah et al. proposed a solution that allows auditors to verify the integrity of outsourced data, while preserving users' privacy [67]. The proposed system encrypts data to hide it from the TPA, and stores both the encrypted data and key in the cloud storage. To check data integrity, the system uses a challenge-response protocol in which the cloud storage server can respond correctly only if both the encrypted data and keys are preserved without any alteration. Privacy is preserved by sending a number of pre-computed symmetric-keyed hashes over the encrypted data to the TPA. The auditor verifies both the integrity of the data file and the server's possession of a previously committed decryption key. However, this scheme only works for encrypted files, which may introduce burden to users when the keyed hashes are used up. Another method for a privacy-preserving TPA-based auditing system has been proposed in [40]. Similar to the previous approaches of auditability, the proposed system utilizes the public key-based homomorphic authenticator. However, by integrating the homomorphic authenticator with random masking, the system ensures that TPA cannot learn about the data content stored in the cloud server during the auditing process.

7.5 Challenges and Opportunities

Many open problems remain in the area cloud privacy. In this section, we discuss a few of these problems and the associated challenges.

7.5.1 Detachment from Reality

One of the major limitations of existing research on cloud privacy is the failure to look at reality. Many of the schemes that can ensure privacy in the cloud impose unrealistic overheads. In practice, users are not interested in using a system that has such an amount of overhead. Another issue facing current research efforts is the failure to consider economy. Many privacy schemes would cause significant changes to existing cloud infrastructures, which are not economically feasible. Finally, numerous attacks are based on flawed or impractical threat models and simply do not make any economic sense. For example, in most cases, a multi-billion dollar cloud service provider has little incentive to act dishonestly, but many solutions are designed with a cloud provider as the main adversary. Designing a realistic and practical threat model for privacy in cloud computing is vital for creating solutions to real-life problems.

7.5.2 Regulatory Compliance

We have observed a significant amount of research works, which have been conducted on many areas of cloud security involving data confidentiality, integrity, and privacy. However, very little research has been done in the area of regulatory compliance [6]. As we discussed previously, sensitive data such as patient medical records and business information are highly regulated through government regulations worldwide. For example, in the United States, the Sarbanes-Oxley Act regulates the confidentiality of financial data, whereas the HIPAA regulates the confidentiality of patients' medical information. Such regulations require strict integrity and confidentiality guarantees for sensitive information. Though there have been extensive research efforts for compliance with these regulations in local storage systems, it is not very clear whether any cloud-based system actually does comply with the regulations, given the fundamental nature and architecture of clouds. The proposed solutions, which ensure accountability and confidentiality in clouds, do not consider the regulatory policies while designing the solutions. Hence, there is a research opportunity for security experts to design a privacy preserving regulatory compliant cloud.

7.5.3 Legal Issues

Another major challenge of ensuring privacy in clouds is related to the jurisdiction of data, because in many cases, clouds span the whole world. For example, Amazon's clouds are located in North and South Americas, Europe, and Asia. It is not very clear whether a client's data should comply with the European Union privacy regulations if the subject is based in the United States, but those data are replicated in one of Amazon's data centers located in Europe. The existing Service Level Agreements (SLAs) between cloud providers and consumers do not clarify this issue. There is a need for global unity to overcome the challenges of the multi-jurisdictional issue.

7.6 Conclusion

Cloud computing has major implications for the privacy of personal information as well as for the confidentiality of business and governmental information. Cloud computing represents the massive changes occurring in our data processing and computational infrastructures. With their significant benefits in terms of greater flexibility, performance, and scalability, clouds are here to stay. However, as many of our everyday computing services have been moved to the cloud, we do need to ensure that the data and computation will be remain confidential and trustworthy. The global dimension of cloud computing requires appropriate methodologies and technical solutions to enable different stakeholders in clouds to assess privacy risks and establish adequate protection levels.

In this chapter, we have outlined the major research questions and challenges in cloud privacy to identify privacy and confidentiality issues that may be of interest or concern to cloud computing participants. The fundamental natures of clouds introduce new privacy challenges. Today's clouds are not secure, accountable, or trustworthy. Many open problems need to be resolved before major users will adopt cloud computing for sensitive data and computations. For wider adoption of cloud computing in critical areas, such as business and healthcare, it is vital to solve these problems. Solving the privacy issues will bring more cloud consumers, which in turn will lower costs and have a broader impact on our society as a whole.

Acknowledgments This research was supported by the National Science Foundation CAREER Award #CNS-1351038.

References

1. Khajeh-Hosseini A, Greenwood D, Sommerville I (2010) Cloud migration: a case study of migrating an enterprise it system to IaaS. In: Proceedings of the 3rd international conference on cloud computing (CLOUD). IEEE, pp 450–457
2. Market Research Media. Global cloud computing market forecast 2015–2020. http://www.marketresearchmedia.com/?p=839
3. Gartner (2010) Worldwide cloud services market to surpass $68 billion in 2010. http://www.gartner.com/it/page.jsp?id=1389313
4. INPUT (2009) Evolution of the cloud: the future of cloud computing in government. http://goo.gl/KrKexK

5. Balduzzi M, Zaddach J, Balzarotti D, Kirda E, Loureiro S (2012) A security analysis of amazon's elastic compute cloud service. In: Proceedings of the 27th annual ACM symposium on applied computing. ACM, pp 1427–1434
6. Brodkin J (2008) Gartner: seven cloud-computing security risks. Infoworld 1–3
7. Kandukuri BR, Paturi VR, Rakshit A (2009) Cloud security issues. In: Proceedings of IEEE international conference on services computing (SCC'09). IEEE, pp 517–520
8. Subashini S, Kavitha V (2011) A survey on security issues in service delivery models of cloud computing. J Netw Comput Appl 34(1):1–11
9. Zissis D, Lekkas D (2012) Addressing cloud computing security issues. Future Gener Comput Syst 28(3):583–592
10. Clavister. Security in the cloud. http://goo.gl/Hs4N0V
11. Amazon. Zeus botnet controller. http://aws.amazon.com/security/security-bulletins/zeus-botnet-controller/
12. Cavoukian A (2008) Privacy in the clouds. Identity in the Information Society 1(1):89–108
13. George Danezis and Seda Gürses (2010) A critical review of 10 years of privacy technology. In: Proceedings of surveillance cultures: a global surveillance society
14. Mell P, Grance T (2009) Draft NIST working definition of cloud computing-v15. Accessed 21 Aug 2009
15. Open Cloud (2009) Open cloud manifesto. The Open Cloud Manifesto Consortium
16. salesforce (2012) Social enterprise and crm in the cloud—salesforce.com. http://www.salesforce.com/
17. Google. Google drive. https://drive.google.com/start#home
18. Google. Google calendar. https://www.google.com/calendar/
19. GAE. Google app engine. http://appengine.google.com
20. Azure. Windows azure. http://www.windowsazure.com
21. Amazon EC2. Amazon elastic compute cloud (amazon ec2). http://aws.amazon.com/ec2/
22. Motahari-Nezhad HR, Stephenson B, Singhal S (2009) Outsourcing business to cloud computing services: opportunities and challenges. IEEE Internet Computing, Palo Alto, 10, 2009
23. Amazon. Amazon simpledb (2012) http://aws.amazon.com/simpledb/
24. Chang F, Dean J, Ghemawat S, Hsieh WC, Wallach DA, Burrows M, Chandra T, Fikes A, Gruber RE (2008) Bigtable: a distributed storage system for structured data. ACM Trans Comput Syst (TOCS) 26(2):1–26, article no. 4
25. Robinson N, Valeri L, Cave J, Starkey T, Graux H, Creese S, Hopkins PP (2010) The cloud: understanding the security, privacy and trust challenges. Privacy and Trust Challenges (November 30, 2010)
26. Alliance C (2011) Security guidance for critical areas of focus in cloud computing v3.0. Cloud Security Alliance
27. Ray I, Belyaev K, Strizhov M, Mulamba D, Rajaram M (2013) Secure logging as a service—delegating log management to the cloud. IEEE Syst J 7:323–334
28. Jansen W, Grance T et al (2011) Guidelines on security and privacy in public cloud computing. NIST Spec Publ 800:144
29. Dedicated Cloud. http://www.ovh.co.uk/dedicated-cloud/
30. Ristenpart T, Tromer E, Shacham H, Savage S (2009) Hey, you, get off of my cloud: exploring information leakage in third-party compute clouds. In: Proceedings of the 16th ACM conference on computer and communications security. ACM, pp 199–212
31. Zhang Y, Juels A, Reiter MK, Ristenpart T (2012) Cross-vm side channels and their use to extract private keys. In: ACM conference on computer and communications security, pp 305–316
32. Cloud computing security risk assessment (2009) Technical report, European Union Agency for Network and Information Security
33. Privacy in cloud computing (2012) Organized by ITU-T Technology Watch. http://goo.gl/NplPxC

34. Gellman R (2012) Privacy in the clouds: risks to privacy and confidentiality from cloud computing. In: Proceedings of the World privacy forum
35. Congress of the United States (1999) Gramm-leach-bliley financial services mod-ernization act. public law no. 106–102, 113 stat. 1338
36. www.hhs.gov. Health Information Privacy. http://goo.gl/NxgkMi
37. Privacy level agreement outline for the sale of cloud services in the european union (2013) http://goo.gl/fyKOmk
38. Duncan AJ, Creese S, Goldsmith M (2012) Insider attacks in cloud computing. In: Proceedings of the 11th international conference on trust, security and privacy in computing and communications (TrustCom). IEEE, pp 857–862
39. Ateniese G, Burns R, Curtmola R, Herring J, Kissner L, Peterson Z, Song D (2007) Provable data possession at untrusted stores. In: Proceedings of the 14th ACM conference on computer and communications security. ACM, pp 598–609
40. Wang C, Wang Q, Ren K, Lou W (2010) Privacy-preserving public auditing for data storage security in cloud computing. In: Proceedings of the 29th conference on computer communications (INFOCOM). IEEE, pp 1–9
41. Chen Y, Paxson V, Katz RH (2010) What's new about cloud computing security. University of California, Berkeley Report No. UCB/EECS-2010-5 January, 20(2010):2010–5
42. Krautheim FJ (2009) Private virtual infrastructure for cloud computing. In: Conference on hot topics in cloud computing. USENIX Association
43. Santos N, Gummadi KP, Rodrigues R (2009) Towards trusted cloud computing. In: Proceedings of the 2009 conference on Hot topics in cloud computing. USENIX Association, pp 3–7
44. Bouchenak S, Chockler G, Chockler H, Gheorghe G, Santos N, Shraer A (2013) Verifying cloud services: present and future. ACM SIGOPS operating systems review 47(2):6–19
45. Zhang F, Chen J, Chen H, Zang B (2011) Cloudvisor: retrofitting protection of virtual machines in multi-tenant cloud with nested virtualization. In: Proceedings of the 23rd ACM symposium on operating systems principles. ACM, pp 203–216
46. Santos N, Rodrigues R, Gummadi KP, Saroiu S (2012) Policy-sealed data: a new abstraction for building trusted cloud services. In: Proceedings of the USENIX security, pp 175–188
47. Sean W (1999) Smith and Steve Weingart. Building a high-performance, programmable secure coprocessor. Comput Netw 31(8):831–860
48. Gentry C (2009) A fully homomorphic encryption scheme. PhD Thesis, Stanford University
49. Sadeghi AR, Schneider T, Winandy M (2010) Token-based cloud computing. In: Trust and trustworthy computing. Springer, pp 417–429
50. Roy I, Setty STV, Kilzer A, Shmatikov V, Witchel E (2010) Airavat: security and privacy for mapreduce. In: Proceedings of the 7th USENIX conference on networked systems design and implementation. USENIX Association, pp 20–20
51. Zhang K, Zhou X, Chen Y, Wang XF, Ruan Y (2011) Sedic: privacy-aware data intensive computing on hybrid clouds. In: Proceedings of the 18th ACM conference on computer and communications security. ACM, pp 515–526
52. Zhou L, Varadharajan V, Hitchens M (2013) Achieving secure role-based access control on encrypted data in cloud storage. IEEE Trans Inf Forensics Secur 8(12):1947–1960
53. Ruj S, Stojmenovic M, Nayak A (2012) Privacy preserving access control with authentication for securing data in clouds. In: Proceedings of the 12th IEEE/ACM international symposium on cluster, cloud and grid computing (CCGrid). IEEE, pp 556–563
54. Wang G, Liu Q, Wu J (2010) Hierarchical attribute-based encryption for fine-grained access control in cloud storage services. In: Proceedings of the 17th ACM conference on computer and communications security. ACM, pp 735–737
55. Yu S, Wang C, Ren K, Lou W (2010) Attribute based data sharing with attribute revocation. In: Proceedings of the 5th ACM symposium on information, computer and communications security. ACM, pp 261–270
56. Amit Sahai and Brent Waters. Fuzzy identity-based encryption. In: Advances in cryptology–EUROCRYPT 2005. Springer, pp 457–473

57. Goyal V, Pandey O, Sahai A, Waters B (2006) Attribute-based encryption for fine-grained access control of encrypted data. In: Proceedings of the 13th ACM conference on computer and communications security. ACM, pp 89–98
58. Bethencourt J, Sahai A, Waters B (2007) Ciphertext-policy attribute-based encryption. In: Proceedings of IEEE symposium on security and privacy, (SP'07). IEEE, pp 321–334
59. Siani Pearson and Marco Casassa Mont (2011) Sticky policies: An approach for managing privacy across multiple parties. Computer 44(9):60–68
60. Pearson S, Mont MC, Chen L, Reed A (2011) End-to-end policy-based encryption and management of data in the cloud. In: 2011 IEEE third international conference on cloud computing technology and science (CloudCom). IEEE, pp 764–771
61. IBM. Identity Mixer. http://www.zurich.ibm.com/security/idemix/
62. Brands SA (2000) Rethinking public key infrastructures and digital certificates: building in privacy'mit press
63. OpenID. http://openid.net/
64. Zawoad S, Dutta AK, Hasan R (2013) SecLaaS: secure logging-as-a-service for cloud forensics. In: Proceedings of the 8th ACM symposium on information, computer and communications security (ASIACCS). ACM, pp 219–230
65. Zawoad S, Hasan R (2012) Towards building proofs of past data possession in cloud forensics. ASE Sci J 1(4):195–207
66. Bloom BH (1970) Space/time trade-offs in hash coding with allowable errors. Commun ACM 13(7):422–426
67. Shah MA, Baker M, Mogul JC, Swaminathan R et al (2007) Auditing to keep online storage services honest. In: Proceedings of the workshop on hot topics in operating systems (HotOS)
68. Grobauer B, Schreck T (2010) Towards incident handling in the cloud: challenges and approaches. In: Proceedings of the 2010 ACM workshop on cloud computing security workshop, CCSW '10, New York, NY, USA. ACM, pp 77–86

Chapter 8
Privacy in Vehicular Ad Hoc Networks

Jetzabel M. Serna-Olvera, Roberto A. Morales Pacheco,
Javier Parra-Arnau, David Rebollo-Monedero and Jordi Forné

8.1 Introduction

Road traffic injuries are currently the ninth leading cause of death in the world, killing nearly 1.3 million people annually. Unless effective actions are taken, road accidents are predicted to become the fifth leading cause of death by 2030 [1]. Intelligent transportation systems (ITS) [2] aim to provide innovative services that will potentially benefit traffic management. As the technical basis of ITS, Vehicular Ad hoc NETworks (VANETs) offer the possibility of significant improvements, and enable a wide range of safety and infotainment applications.

J.M. Serna-Olvera (✉)
Cyber-Security Research Group, Barcelona Digital Technology Centre,
Roc Boronat 117, 08018 Barcelona, Spain
e-mail: jserna@bdigital.org

R.A. Morales Pacheco
Computer Architecture Department, Universitat Politècnica de Catalunya (UPC),
Jordi Girona 1-3, 08034 Barcelona, Spain
e-mail: rmorales@ac.upc.edu

J. Parra-Arnau
Security Group, Barcelona Digital Technology Centre, Roc Boronat 117,
08018 Barcelona, Spain
e-mail: jparra@bdigital.org

D. Rebollo-Monedero · J. Forné
Department of Telematics Engineering, Universitat Politècnica de Catalunya (UPC),
C. Jordi Girona 1-3, 08034 Barcelona, Spain
e-mail: david.rebollo@entel.upc.edu

J. Forné
e-mail: jforne@entel.upc.edu

© Springer International Publishing Switzerland 2015
S. Zeadally and M. Badra (eds.), *Privacy in a Digital, Networked World*,
Computer Communications and Networks,
DOI 10.1007/978-3-319-08470-1_8

VANETs consist of communication vehicles equipped with on-board units (OBUs), and are able to communicate to the infrastructure, represented by road side units (RSUs). VANETs are intended not only to drastically reduce the number of road fatalities, but will also be capable of providing value added services in order to enhance drivers' comfort. Thus, in VANETs, the information exchanged plays an important role. In particular, for safety-related applications, where exchanged information is considered critical. If such information was manipulated by an attacker, this might endanger drivers' lives. Consequently, implementing security measures is of the utmost importance for VANETs to become a reality.

To be able to prevent a wide range of security attacks and establish secure communication channels, the adoption of public key infrastructure (PKI) technology has been considered [2]. Nevertheless, the sole use of PKI is insufficient to protect user privacy in vehicular networks.

Nowadays, people are increasingly concerned about their privacy. For the successful deployment of VANETs technology, communications within these networks should avoid any leakage of personal, sensitive data. Among the potential privacy risks of such networks are the linkage of an individual to an identifier, tracking a specific node, and profiling user behavior on the basis of location data. Especially in ad hoc networks, users may be reticent to place their trust in intermediaries such as anonymizing proxies [3] and mix networks [4, 5]. Privacy-enhancing technologies relying on user collaboration avoid the need for these trusted third parties (TTPs). On the other hand, it is fundamental that the anonymity-enforcing mechanisms implemented are aware of their impact on network performance that translates into quality of user experience.

This chapter is organized as follows. Section 8.2 introduces the main characteristics of VANETs. Fundamental privacy issues and requirements to be addressed for the successful deployment of VANETs are presented in Sect. 8.3. Section 8.4 gives an overview of promising approaches aimed at protecting users and vehicles privacy in VANETs' communications. Section 8.5 highlights that, despite the various promising privacy approaches, there remain important challenges that should be analyzed in future research. Finally, the main conclusions derived from this research are pointed out in Sect. 8.6.

8.2 VANETs

VANETs are a subgroup, and one of the most relevant representations of Mobile Ad hoc NETworks (MANETs). VANETs consist of two types of nodes: mobile and fixed nodes. The former are represented by vehicles and are equipped with OBUs. These vehicles communicate with the latter nodes, which constitute the VANET infrastructure and are represented mainly by RSUs located along the roads.

8.2.1 Communication Model

In the coming years it is envisioned that 40 % of all vehicular components will be equipped with processing, recording, and communication features [6]. This will make them capable of processing and storing a great amount of information (Fig. 8.1).

The communication between mobile nodes and fixed nodes is commonly classified as vehicle-to-vehicle (v2v) and vehicle-to-infrastructure (v2i) (Fig. 8.2). According to the dedicated short range communications (DSRC) standard [7], VANETs will be capable of communicating at data rates from 6 to 27 Mbps, and at a maximum transmission range of 1,000 m, thus, enabling nodes to exchange all kinds of application-related information.

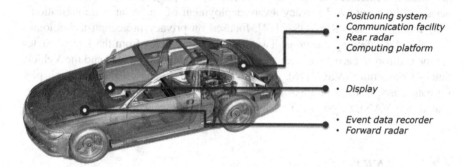

- Positioning system
- Communication facility
- Rear radar
- Computing platform

- Display

- Event data recorder
- Forward radar

Fig. 8.1 Smart vehicle

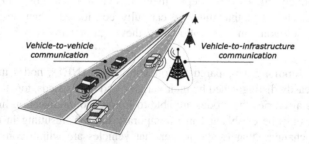

Vehicle-to-vehicle
communication

Vehicle-to-infrastructure
communication

Fig. 8.2 Vehicle-to-vehicle and vehicle-to-infrastructure communication

8.2.2 Projects and Organizations

At present, the networking community is putting significant effort into investigating inter-vehicle communications (IVC). The areas of current research range from the low layer protocols design, to the implementation of a wide range of applications and mechanisms for the effective deployment of VANETs. The development of these vehicular communication systems is driven by a number of national and international activities [8]. Examples include the Car-to-Car Communication Consortium (C2C-CC) [9] and the Cooperative Vehicles and Infrastructure Systems (CVIS) [10] sponsored by the European Union. Several research projects have been also developed in Europe during the last years. These projects include: SEVECOM [11], focused on providing a full definition and implementation of security requirements for vehicular communications; EVITA [12], aimed at designing security relevant components in order to protect sensitive data from being compromised in vehicular communications; PRESERVE [13], focused on providing the basis for the secure and privacy aware deployment of vehicular communications; and, among others, PRECIOSA [14], focused on privacy protection technologies for vehicular safety applications. Two important initiatives from the United States are the California Partners of Advanced Transit and Highways [15] and the Vehicle Safety Consortium (VSC) [16]. These organizations focus on building high performance architectures and extracting application specific functionality to be integrated into VANET systems (i.e., application specific packet routing).

8.2.3 VANETs' Features

As a subgroup of MANETs, VANETs share similar characteristics with other ad hoc networks [17]. These latter networks, however, have some distinctive features that can positively influence the deployment of several applications, and represent an interesting challenge that must be carefully considered when designing any architectural solution. In the following, these particularities will be briefly described.

- **Dynamic topology**. Compared to conventional MANETs, nodes in VANETs could be easily distinguished by their variable and high speeds, together with the different trajectories that nodes are able to follow; communication links among them can only be established in a temporary fashion, resulting in continuous topology changes, that is, the longer that vehicles are within communication range (e.g., vehicles following similar trajectories), the longer a particular topology is maintained.
- **Mobility models**. Despite the high mobility that is inherent to a VANET system, nodes' mobility is bounded in speed and space. The speed of vehicles is

usually constrained by (1) traffic lights, (2) routes intersections, (3) the speed of other vehicles, and (4) speed limits set in urban traffic areas (e.g., residential, educational, etc.). Meanwhile, the space is bounded due to the fact that vehicles travel along pre-established trajectories (roads).

- **Geolocalization capabilities**. Vehicles integrated with positioning devices such as Global Positioning System (GPS) receivers, along with other communication capabilities, enable a potential range of location-based applications.
- **Low latency requirements**. Due to the dynamicity of the environment, and the delay constraints introduced by safety applications, the information exchanged among vehicles in VANETs is extremely time-sensitive (e.g., warn vehicles of road conditions).
- **Energy supply**. In VANETs, resource constraints could be neglected, as a running vehicle is able to provide sufficient battery power and, consequently, it may have more computational power resources. This feature is quite an important advantage for certain computational intensive tasks related to security (i.e., cryptography).
- **Communication scenarios**. Communication in VANETs might be strongly dependent on the scenario [18]. Current research identifies two main scenarios: (1) highways, where vehicles travel at different speeds and unidirectional movement patterns can be observed and (2) urban scenarios, where environmental elements play a fundamental role, making v2v communications more complex.

The most challenging features inherent to a VANET system include the dynamic topology and the mobility models (vehicles moving at a variable and high speed and following different trajectories). On the other hand, thanks to the vehicle's geo-localization functionality and its "infinite" energy supply, VANETs are an enabler for a wide set of potential applications (further discussed in Sect. 8.2.4).

8.2.4 Applications

In VANET v2v and v2i communications, communicating nodes consist of vehicles equipped with OBUs communicating and fixed communication units along the road (either vehicles or RSUs). VANETs' communications are aimed at exchanging information about traffic issues, road conditions, and added value information. Thus, they allow the deployment of a wide range of applications. Potential applications for VANETs can be classified based on the scenario, the security objectives, and the target itself. However, for simplicity, in this chapter a common classification proposed by the authors in [19, 20], has been adopted:

- *Warning* refers to applications aimed to detect risky situations, such as, the propagation of alerts in case of accidents. Vehicles exchanging messages to inform each other about special events and dangers on the road, for example, alarm signals from emergency vehicles in action. This is done by sending current position, time, destination, and other related information, in order for other vehicles to understand that they could or must clear the way for the emergency vehicle.

- *Traffic management* is a safety-related application where messages are primarily exchanged to inform about traffic congestion and road conditions in a given region with the main purpose of optimizing traffic. Clearly, this may enhance road safety at the same time, preventing potential accidents due to congestion.
- *Added value* applies to applications aimed at providing a wide range of services, such as, payment services, location-based services (e.g., finding the closest hotel, restaurant, etc.), and infotainment (e.g., Internet access to offer e-mail, web browsing, video streaming, etc.).

As can be inferred by the aforementioned applications, VANETs will be capable of offering a wide range of valuable services. However, along with the rise of VANETs, some security issues have also emerged and will be discussed in Sect. 8.2.5.

8.2.5 Security Issues

Similar to other conventional MANETs, VANETs can also be vulnerable to a set of security attacks, which have been analyzed to a certain extent by [6, 20–22]. In the following subsections, security attacks, attackers, and their corresponding security requirements in VANETs [23] are described.

8.2.5.1 Types of Attacks

- **Identification and authentication**. An active, rational, and insider attacker pretending to be one or multiple different entities could achieve an imperson-ation attack by claiming to be an authorized entity such as an emergency vehicle and propagate wrong information in the network, for example, sending false information to alter traffic flow, slowing it down, or getting a vehicle-free road. Similarly, a vehicle could pretend to be multiple entities reporting a false bot-tleneck to achieve the same purpose. Finally, simple use of fictitious identities could lead to evasion of responsibility and legal obligation in case of an accident.
- **Confidentiality**. An attacker represented by a vehicle or by a false RSU could get illegal access to confidential information, or a passive attacker might eavesdrop on the communication and gather information on services requested by a vehicle.

- **Non-repudiation**. Achieved mainly by rational attackers colluding to share the same credentials.
- **Availability**. Denial of service attacks are commonly carried out by active malicious attackers willing to bring down the network. These attacks include channel jamming and aggressive injection of dummy messages.
- **Data trust**. Sending inaccurate data (malicious data attack) affects message reliability. This type of attack is usually performed by rational active attackers.

8.2.5.2 Types of Attackers

Attackers can be classified according to a wide range of aspects, including location, motivation, power, capabilities, and so on. Identifying a type of attacker facilitates considerably the study of their capacities, possible attacks, and, consequently, the damage that could be caused. The authors in [24] presented a general classification:

- *Insider* is an authenticated member of the network
- *Outsider* is considered by the other members of the network as an intruder.
- *Malicious* is an attacker that seeks no personal benefits from the attacks and aims to harm.
- *Rational* seeks personal profit and hence is more predictable.
- *Active* can generate packets or signals.
- *Passive* is content with eavesdropping on the wireless channel.

8.2.5.3 Security Requirements

The successful deployment and public acceptance of vehicular-network technologies will only become a reality if security systems can prevent any generic attack. On vehicular networks, the system should use a secure and trusted communication infrastructure able to satisfy the following set of requirements [8, 24, 25]:

- **Authentication**. The authentication of the sender's messages is needed to keep outsiders from injecting messages as well as misbehaving insiders.
- **Integrity**. All messages should be protected to prevent attackers from altering them, or, in the worst-case scenario, to detect its modification.
- **Confidentiality**. There are applications that require that only the sender and the intended receiver can access the content of a message.
- **Access control**. Vehicles and applications need fine-grained access rights. Sensitive information stored in vehicles should only be available to authorized parties.
- **Availability**. Transmitted messages must reach all necessary recipients despite the VANET's status.

- **Non-repudiation**. A vehicle sending a message should not be able to deny its transmission. In particular, in cases of liability or node's misbehavior, the system should be able to prosecute misuse.

In summary, since, in VANETs, access is granted by default, to be able to prevent any generic attack, the system should rely on a secure and trusted communication infrastructure. Such infrastructure must be able to satisfy the set of security requirements just introduced. An important challenge is to find the proper techniques, and architectural solutions capable of enforcing security, but, without disregarding the privacy requirements that are inherent to VANETs' users and applications. The importance of privacy implications, and the privacy requirements in VANETs, will be further discussed in Sect. 8.3.

8.3 Privacy in VANETs

A general and basic principle in VANETs and any communication network is that the information going through those networks should only be disclosed to authorized parties. The nature of vehicular networks facilitates the collection of a range of private data, especially location data, which may compromise user privacy [26]. Once privacy is lost it is very difficult to re-establish that state of personal rights and the trust that people had placed on this technology [25]. On one hand, strong security mechanisms are needed to protect applications and users from potential security attackers. On the other hand, the protection of user's private information (not limited to identity) should also be guaranteed. It is also worth mentioning that privacy protection is made mandatory by laws in many developed countries. A discussion of specific issues related to identity and privacy enhancing technologies for vehicular communications can be found in [26, 27]. Next, we classify privacy in VANETs according to different perspectives.

8.3.1 Identity Privacy

Identity privacy in VANETs refers to linking an identifier to a user/vehicle (ID disclosure). An attacker overhearing the communications, will be able to distinguish which identifier belongs to which vehicle, and consequently to which driver. Linking an ID to a user will afterwards allow an attacker to blackmail a driver if collected data contains compromising information. This attack could be achieved by an attacker RSU or a vehicle on a parking lot passively overhearing the communications.

8.3.2 Location Privacy

According to [28], location privacy refers to "the ability to prevent others from learning one's current or past location." In a VANET scenario, this includes current and past positions, speeds, and traveling routes, leading to the automatic monitoring of trajectories. An attacker able to identify vehicles' mobility patterns could also identify working and home addresses as well as points of interest (POIs).

8.3.3 Data Privacy

VANETs are expected to be able to store a lot of information including personal data; drivers should then be able to keep and control their personal and vehicle related information (e.g., license plate and driver's identifiable information). Such information should only be disclosed in cases of liability and to authorized parties.

Data privacy can also be considered by means of user/vehicle activities, including services being requested, which ultimately leads to user profiling. The frequent exchange of messages containing sensitive data [29], such as online activity, trip details, vehicle identification, and e-payment information among others pose serious privacy concerns, as attackers can potentially overhear messages and misuse the information they contain.

8.3.4 Privacy Requirements

The privacy of drivers should be protected, it should not be possible to automatically obtain private information about drivers or vehicle's behavior and activities, linking the activities (services requested and location) to and identifier and an identifier to a person. Thus, any privacy solution should consider the following requirements.

- **Anonymity**. In order to prevent the big brother scenario, linking an identifier to a user/vehicle should be avoided by providing anonymous communication. Anonymous communication is usually linked to the use of pseudonyms. Communicating nodes exchange messages using pseudo-identifiers instead of real identifiers (as shown in Fig. 8.3). Even though, from the driver's point of view, achieving perfect anonymity would be preferred. However, there are different cases where the system should be able to establish driver's liability. Therefore, a privacy requirement in VANETs would be conditional anonymity, meaning that the identity of a driver could only be disclosed by liability authorized parties.

Fig. 8.3 Anonymous
communications through
pseudonymity in VANETs

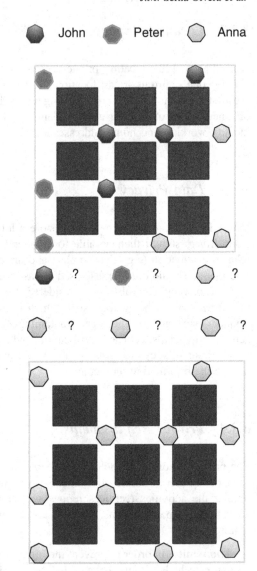

Fig. 8.4 Unlinkability in
VANETs communications

- **Unlinkability**. Another basic privacy requirement is that two different messages
  sent by the same vehicle cannot be linked. In other words, an observer should
  not be able to distinguish whether two different messages were originated by a
  same vehicle (as shown in Fig. 8.4). Similarly, the observer should not be able
  to link such messages to the vehicle and so to its driver. Note that this
  requirement is not fully compliant to the security requirements needed to prevent a sybil attack, where a single vehicle (malicious OBU) might impersonate
  multiple vehicles.

8.4 Privacy Approaches

The importance of privacy preservation in VANETs, related to the public acceptance of VANET's technology, has been highlighted by different authors in [26,
30]. Specifically, the authors of [26, 30] have presented an extensive study on the
privacy risks posed by vehicular networks. In particular, it has been stressed that the
sole use of PKI schemes is not enough to preserve user privacy. The fundamental
reason is that digital certificates include information regarding the node's identity.

An alternative approach is to hide the ID of the sending vehicles in order to
prevent eavesdroppers from linking a message to an identifier. However, most of
the potential applications require unique identifiers. Thus, different approaches
based on the use of pseudonyms have been proposed. This section first investigates
this particular approach and afterwards examines group-signature schemes,
identity-based cryptographic methods, approaches based on user collaboration, and
data-perturbative mechanisms.

8.4.1 Pseudonymity

Pseudonyms [31] are identifiers used by subjects to avoid the use of real information (e.g., no information about the vehicle of the driver such as name, driver
license, or vehicle identification numbers (VINs), it simply identifies the vehicular
node.

In VANETs, pseudonymity has been proposed to achieve privacy through
anonymity, and it refers to the use of digital pseudonyms as IDs, assuming that each
pseudonym refers to exactly one holder.

As aforementioned, communications in a VANET provide information about
location and each message has a timestamp associated. An attacker overhearing the
communications for long periods will be able to automatically collect the
exchanged messages and correlate pseudonyms with the corresponding locations
and timestamps. Having collected this information will enable the attacker to relate
pseudonyms to specific vehicles or individuals by identifying mobility patterns and
learn about working addresses or POIs. To address this issue, current
state-of-the-art solutions have proposed the use of multiple pseudonyms and the
corresponding algorithms to change them, in particular addressing a vehicle's
location privacy.

Location privacy in pervasive environments was first introduced by [28]. The
cited work defined the concept of mix-zones for a group of users connected in a
spatial region. The authors assumed that, within this region, users will change to a
new and unused pseudonym. In [26], the authors have explored the concept of
short-term certificates by proposing a centrally assigned pseudonym system. They
proposed a system where the nodes of the VANET changed their pseudonyms in a
certain region (mix-zone) pointed out by the system. Such a region is defined when

a large number of vehicles are within communication range. The main drawback of this approach is that it requires a large number of vehicles changing pseudonyms within the specified region.

Contrary to the centralized concept, in [32] the authors propose self-assigned digital pseudonyms. They suggest the use of the following measures while changing them: (1) synchronization of pseudonym change, (2) introduction of gaps (silent periods) and (3) the mix-zone concept, that is changing pseudonyms when several nodes are near (i.e., within the region or communication range). A similar approach has also been considered in [30]. Here, the authors combine the concept of mix-contexts with the change of pseudonyms, and find the appropriate context to replace them. In particular, they propose to protect the use of centralized mapping by means of laws and techniques such as a distributed mapping. Authors of CARAVAN project [33], also introduced a random silent period in order to hamper the linkability between pseudonyms. An improvement of mix-contexts has been proposed by the authors in [34], considering anonymity over randomly changing pseudonyms in certain intervals.

In [35], the authors proposed a system to balance auditability and privacy in VANETs based on symmetric cryptographic primitives and two different types of pseudonyms (short and long term). A study of practicability in pseudonymity deployment and implementation is done in [36]. The cited work concludes that potential solutions could be based on a hybrid approach, basically represented as the combination of the existing pseudonymity algorithms. Finally, [37] proposed a synchronous pseudonym change algorithm, this approach takes into account vehicular status information and, according to the authors, it is more effective than those based on the mix-zones concept.

8.4.2 Group Signature

The idea of group signatures emerged as an alternative to traditional PKI approaches, firstly to reduce the number of exchanged keys in VANETs, and secondly to provide anonymization.

In a basic group signature scheme [38] participants are identified as follows:

- **Group leader**. A trusted entity (vehicle or RSU) responsible for managing the group, that is, initializing and handling joins and leaves (revocations). In cases of liability, the group leader is also responsible for de-anonymizing a signature.
- **Group members**. Vehicle representing current set of authorized signers. Each vehicle has a unique private key allowing it to sign on behalf of the group and a group public key.

In [39] the authors proposed a solution based on group signature, which enabled vehicle OBUs to generate and certify their own pseudonyms. The group leader is the entity responsible for setting the group parameters, changing group public keys, and revoking anonymity in cases of liability. Generally, the group leader could be represented by a vehicle and not necessarily by a trusted third party.

Yet, a number of group signature schemes varying in assumptions, complexity, and features have been proposed. Authors in [40] introduced a group signature approach that also implemented role based access control (RBAC). In this approach, vehicles were able to sign messages on behalf of the group and, therefore, achieve conditional anonymity. Similar to [39], anonymization could only be reversed by the group leader.

Although an interesting proposal, the group establishment is still an open challenge. If it is handled in a static way, vehicles need to be pre-loaded with the corresponding group keys. Thus, for vehicles traveling to different domains (geographical regions), they must have in advance the keys of all the groups belonging to those regions, which in practice is unfeasible.

A similar concept was presented in [41], where the authors introduced a group-based approach in which vehicles owned group signing keys issued by a "trusted" group leader. Note that the election of group leader will sometimes encounter difficulties since a trusted entity cannot be found among communicating nodes.

A hybrid approach has been presented in [42], as an alternative to the aforementioned proposals. This proposal consists of a combination of group-based and identity-based signatures. The former has been proposed for authentication among private vehicles and the latter for public vehicles and RSUs.

To overcome the trust issues that originated due to the group leader being a regular vehicle, in [43] the authors present a new group-based certificate solution. The main difference among other group-based solutions is that group certificates are issued by the RSUs (assumed to be trusted by following a top authority approach). However, note that RSUs are also considered vulnerable to different security attacks and, therefore, can not be completely trusted.

Nevertheless, the main drawbacks of group-based approaches include: (1) vehicles must trust a group leader that is responsible for issuing the corresponding signing keys, (2) due to the speed and trajectories of vehicles, group members should be considered volatile rather than permanent and, therefore, using a regular vehicle as a group leader might compromise the communications availability, and finally, (3) a large number of members in a group could increase the computational complexity, the total number of exchanged messages, and thus severely impact the overall system performance.

8.4.3 Identity-Based Cryptography

Non-PKI approaches have mostly focused on identity-based cryptography (IBC). The concept of IBC was introduced by [44] to ease the deployment of the PKI by simplifying the management of a large number of public keys. However, IBC is based on an underlying public key cryptosystem and the issuance and utilization processes are very similar to those used in a traditional PKI domain.

In IBC systems the public key of an entity is derive from its identity information, avoiding the use of certificates for public key verification as in traditional PKI systems. For signature verification the identifier of the sender is needed.

In VANETs, this idea was first adopted by [41], which proposed IBC together with group-based signatures (as discussed earlier). In this line, other approaches such as [45, 46] aimed at enhancing privacy protection and improving computation and communication efficiency.

8.4.4   User Collaboration

In this subsection we examine those approaches where users collaborate to enhance their privacy.

An archetypical example of user collaboration is the Crowds protocol [47]. In the Crowds protocol, a group of users collaborate to submit their messages to a web server, from whose standpoint they wish to remain completely anonymous. In simple terms, the protocol works as follows. When sending a message, a user flips a biased coin to decide whether to submit it directly to the recipient or to send it to another user, who will then repeat the randomized decision.

Crowds provides anonymity from the perspective of not only the final recipient, but also the intermediate nodes. Consequently, trust assumptions are essentially limited to fulfillment of the protocol. The original proposal suggests adding an initial forwarding step, which substantially increases the uncertainty of the first sender from the point of view of the final receiver, at the cost of an additional hop. As in most anonymous communication systems, Crowds enhances user anonymity but at the expense of traffic overhead and delay.

Closely inspired by Crowds, [48] proposes a protocol that enables users to report traffic violations anonymously in VANETs. This protocol differs from the original Crowds in that, first, it does take into account transmission losses, and, secondly, it is specifically conceived for multi-hop vehicular networks, rather than for wired networks. Experimental results show the effectiveness of this probabilistic protocol in terms of anonymity, when users are disposed to sacrifice quality of service.

Another protocol for privacy enhancement, also relying on user collaboration and message forwarding, is [49]. The objective is to hide the relationship between user identities and query contents even from the intended recipient, an information provider. The main difference with respect to the Crowds protocol is that instead of resorting to probabilistic routing with uncertain path length, it proposes adding a few forged queries.

In location-based services, users submit queries along with the location to which these queries refer. An example would be the query "Where is the nearest car parking?", together with the geographic coordinates of the user's current location. In this scenario, [50] proposes a P2P spatial cloaking algorithm whereby users send their queries to an untrusted LBS provider without disclosing their precise location. The authors propose using the k-anonymity requirement [51, 52], a popular privacy criterion from the field of statistical disclosure control [53]. Accordingly, when a user wishes to submit a query to the provider, first they must find a group of $k - 1$ neighboring peers willing to collaborate. Once the group is formed, the originator of the query computes a geographical region including all users belonging to the group. After that, the user in question selects uniformly at random one of the members of the group. Ultimately, the originator sends both the query and the coordinates of that region to the selected user, which in turn is responsible for forwarding this information to the LBS provider on their behalf.

8.4.5 Data Perturbation

An approach to hinder an attacker in its efforts to compromise users' privacy consists in perturbing the information disclosed when communicating with the networking infrastructure or neighboring vehicles. The submission of false data, together with the user's genuine data, is an example of a data-perturbative mechanism. In these mechanisms, the perturbation takes place on the user's vehicle. This implies that users need not trust any external entity such as the communications infrastructure or RSUs. Data-perturbative techniques, however, come at the cost of system functionality and data utility, which poses a trade-off between these aspects and privacy protection.

An interesting approach to provide a distorted version of a user's profile of interests is query forgery. The underlying idea boils down to accompanying original queries or query keywords with bogus ones. By adopting this data-perturbative strategy, users prevent privacy attackers from profiling them accurately based on their queries. This is without having to trust neither the service provider nor the network operator, but clearly at the cost of traffic overhead. In other words, inherent to query forgery is the existence of a trade-off between privacy and additional traffic. Precisely, [54] studies how to optimize the introduction of forged queries in the setting of information retrieval.

Alternative solutions relying on the principle of query forgery are [55–60], which propose a system for private web browsing called PRAW. The purpose of this system is to preserve the privacy of a group of users sharing an access point to the Web while surfing the Internet. In order to enhance user privacy, the authors propose hiding the actual user profile by generating fake transactions, that is, accesses to a web page to hinder eavesdroppers in their efforts to profile the group. The PRAW system assumes that users are identified, that is, they are logged into a web site. However, the generation of false transactions prevents privacy attackers from the exact inference of user profiles.

Certainly, data perturbation may also be carried out by means of *suppression*. That is, users may be reluctant to disclose certain sensitive information such as location data and, consequently, they may wish not to send those data to the infrastructure or their neighboring peers. This suppression strategy has been investigated in the context of semantic web applications [61] and collaborative tagging systems [62]. Also, it has been studied in combination with the submission of false information for privacy enhancement in recommendation systems [63].

8.5   Challenges and Opportunities

Vehicular communications are aimed at reducing the number of traffic accidents by providing early emergency warnings. As long as the exchanged messages are trustworthy, they can greatly improve the overall road safety. A compromised VANET may disrupt the whole technology's applicability causing life-threatening situations (i.e., false warnings that could result in road accidents). Thus, any VANET solution must be designed to ensure that the transmission comes from a trusted source and has not been tampered with since it was transmitted. Furthermore, vehicular communications should not become a weak link in terms of privacy. Compromising the driver's privacy will limit the user acceptance of this technology.

In VANET's, many research efforts have introduced anonymity through the use of pseudonyms in order to protect privacy of vehicles and users. However, the use of a single pseudonym might lead an attacker to link users and vehicles' actions to a pseudonym, and a pseudonym to an ID. Consequently, most of the research proposals have focused on algorithms for pseudonym change.

Changing pseudonyms more frequently may provide a higher degree of privacy. However, the higher the frequency of pseudonym change, the larger the cost that the pseudonym-changing mechanism induces on the VANET. Just the management of cryptographic materials represents a real challenge, that is, the generation, delivery, storage, and verification of a wide number of keys and certificates related to the pseudonyms (private keys in the case of IBC solutions).

Certificate revocation has also been identified as one of these important issues for pseudonym implementations. Apart from the large number of certificates to be issued for a single vehicle, the need for "fresh" revocation information requires implementing additional mechanisms.

In summary, most of the proposed solutions are ineffective. Changing pseudonyms in a more efficient form is still needed. In addition, other privacy-related issues that pseudonym-based approaches do not address must be taken into consideration.

Pseudonym-based implementations cannot prevent the automatic collection of information, allowing an attacker to keep track of vehicles between pseudonym changes. As it has been extensively discussed in [64, 65], statistical models of the traffic in a given geographical area allow the tracking of vehicles despite frequent pseudonym changing and despite the potentially limited observational capabilities of an attacker. An example that illustrates why pseudonyms are insufficient to guarantee both anonymity and privacy is described next. Suppose that an observer has access to certain behavioral patterns of online activity associated with a vehicle/user, who occasionally discloses information that can be link to their ID, possibly during interactions not involving sensitive data, or in cases were there aren't many vehicles exchanging messages within the area. The same user/vehicle could attempt to hide under a different pseudonym ID^* to exchange confidential information. Nevertheless, if the user exhibited similar behavioral patterns, the unlinkability between ID and ID^* could be compromised through these similar patterns. In this case, any past profiling inferences carried out for the pseudonym ID^* would be linked to the actual user ID.

One promising approach is based on group signature; however, the efficiency of those signature schemes must be increased substantially before they can be deployed in practice. The dynamic management of groups in terms of trust and communication overhead remains an important challenge for these solutions.

In Sect. 8.4 we examined a broad range of privacy-enhancing technologies. Despite the great variety of approaches available in the literature, the fact is that their use is far from being widespread. One of the reasons is that there is certain ambiguity about these technologies and their effectiveness in terms of privacy protection. As we mentioned in that section, privacy-enhancing technologies normally come at the cost of system functionality and utility, and therefore it is challenging to evaluate whether the privacy gained outweighs the costs in utility. As a result, measuring the privacy level offered by a technology is fundamental to determine its overall benefit, to compare its effectiveness with other technologies, and eventually to optimize it in terms of the privacy utility trade-off posed.

Motivated by this, a great research effort has been devoted to the investigation of privacy metrics. However, most of these metrics are specific to concrete systems and adversary models, and often are not appropriately justified or fail to justify the choice. Some recent works in this regard have started to investigate quantifiable measures of privacy. For example, [66] provides a unified perspective of privacy metrics, drawing upon the principles of information theory and Bayesian estimation. One of the main contributions of this work is a framework where privacy is measured as an attacker's estimation error. Further, in the context of personalized information systems, [67] investigates Jaynes' rationale behind entropy-maximization methods to justify the Kullback-Leibler divergence and Shannon's entropy as metrics of profile privacy. The cited works represent helpful, illustrative steps towards the systematic modeling of privacy-preserving information systems, but the study of quantifiable measures of privacy is certainly an open problem.

8.6 Conclusions

Vehicular systems are currently an emerging and promising technology that may bring substantial benefits to road-safety applications. Communication standards such as DSRC broadcast users' private data in order to generate early emergency warnings. While this may contribute to overall road safety, vehicular networks prompt serious security and privacy concerns. The main objectives of this chapter have been to analyze the security and privacy risks arising from vehicular communications and to examine the most popular solutions in this field.

In this work, we have seen that many of the privacy issues are essentially addressed by resorting to pseudonym-based approaches. We have also shown, however, that the use of pseudonyms are insufficient to guarantee both anonymity and privacy. Because of the common belief that pseudonyms are important for VANETs' overall security, and are quite beneficial for protecting users' identity, a privacy compliant solution should be fully compatible with pseudonymity. Apart from pseudonyms, we have also explored other alternatives relying on group-signature schemes, identity-based cryptography, approaches based on user collaboration, and data-perturbative technologies.

While anonymity is primarily guaranteed with pseudonyms, very little attention has been devoted to other sensitive data going through vehicular communications. The passive collection of VANETs' communication information, especially regarding vehicles' activities, can lead to user profiling and ultimately to re-identification. As previously discussed, pseudonym-based approaches cannot prevent an attacker from collecting behavioral patterns, which can be obtained by observing the services that are being requested or by analyzing the contents of vehicle's queries.

Among the challenges that we have mentioned in this chapter, we consider it essential to quantify the level of privacy and security provided by the current solutions. Measuring the level of privacy and security offered is the only way to evaluate and compare the effectiveness of two or more technologies, and this will undoubtedly pave the way for the adoption of vehicular technologies.

References

1. WHO (2012) Global status report on road safety 2012. Technical report, World Health Organization
2. ITS Committee (2007) IEEE Std 1609.3—IEEE trial-use standard for wireless access in vehicular environments
3. Benjumea V, López j, Linero JMT (2006) Specification of a framework for the anonymous use of privileges. Telemat Informat 23(3):179–195
4. Chaum D (1981) Untraceable electronic mail, return addresses, and digital pseudonyms. Commun ACM 24(2):84–88
5. The Tor project, Tor: overview
6. Hubaux J-P, Capkun S, Luo J (2004) The security and privacy of smart vehicles. Secur Priv IEEE 02:49–55
7. European Telecommunications Standards Institute ETSI (2014). Dedicated short range communications (dsrc). http://www.etsi.org/index.php/technologies-clusters/technologies/intelligent-transport/dsrc
8. Zeadally S, Hunt R, Chen Y-S, Irwin A, Hassan Aamir (2012) Vehicular ad hoc networks (vanets): status, results, and challenges. Telecommun Syst 50(4):217–241
9. C2CCC (2014) Car to Car Communication Consortium. http://www.car-to-car.org/

10. Shulman M, Deering R (2010) Cooperative vehicles and infrastructure systems. www.cvisproject.org
11. SEVECOM (2014) SEcure VEhicular COMmunications. http://www.transport-research.info/web/projects/
12. EVITA (2014) E-safety vehicle intrusion protected applications. http://www.evita-project.org/
13. PRESERVE (2014) Preparing secure vehicle-to-x communication systems. http://www.preserve-project.eu/about
14. PRECIOSA (2014) Privacy enabled capability in co-operative systems and safety applications. http://www.preciosa-project.org/
15. PATH (2014) Partners for Advanced Transportation TecHnology. http://www.path.berkeley.edu/
16. Shulman M, Deering M (2007) Vehicle safety communications in the United States. US Department of Transportation, National Highway Traffic and Safety Administration (NHTSA). http://www-nrd.nhtsa.dot.gov/pdf/esv/esv20/07-0010-O.pdf
17. Zarki ME, Mehrotra S, Tsudik G, Venkatasubramanian N (2002) Security issues in a future vehicular network. In: European wireless, pp 270–274
18. Guerrero-Ibz A, Flores-Corts C, Damin-Reyes P (2012) Development of applications for vehicular communication network environments. Hershey IGI Global, USA, pp 183–204
19. Plossl K, Nowey T, Mletzko C (2006) Towards a security architecture for vehicular ad hoc networks. In: ARES '06, p 8
20. Raya M, Hubaux J-P (2005) The security of vehicular ad hoc networks. In: 3rd ACM workshop on security of ad hoc and sensor networks (SASN)
21. Aijaz A, Bochow B, Dötzer F, Festag A, Gerlach M, Kroh R, Leinmüller T (2006) Attacks on inter vehicle communication systems—an analysis. In: Proceedings of WIT, p 189–194
22. Parno B, Perrig A (2005) Challenges in securing vehicular networks. In: Proceedings of the workshop on hot topics in networks (HotNets-IV)
23. de Fuentes JM, Gonzàlez-Tablas AI, Ribagorda A (2010) Overview of security issues in vehicular ad-hoc networks. Handbook of research on mobility and computing. IGI global, pp 189–194
24. Raya M, Hubaux J-P (2007) Securing vehicular ad hoc networks. J Comput Secur 15(1):39–68
25. Kargl F, Ma Z, Schoch E (2006) Security engineering for vanets. In: ESCAR '06
26. Dötzer F (2005) Privacy issues in vehicular ad hoc networks. In: Proceedings of the 2nd ACM international workshop on vehicular ad hoc networks. ACM Press
27. Papadimitratos P, Kung A, Hubaux J-P, Kargl F (2006) Privacy and identity management for vehicular communication systems: a position paper. In: Workshop on standards for privacy in user-centric identity management. Zurich, Switzerland
28. Beresford AR, Stajano F (2003) Location privacy in pervasive computing. IEEE Pervasive Comput 2(1):46–55
29. Guerrero-Ibz JA, Flores-Corts C, Zeadally S (2013) Vehicular ad-hoc networks (vanets): architecture, protocols and applications. In: Chilamkurti N, Zeadally S, Chaouchi H (eds) Next-generation wireless technologies. Computer communications and networks. Springer, London, pp 49–70
30. Gerlach M (2006). Assessing and improving privacy in vanets. In: 4th workshop on embedded security in cars (ESCAR 2006)
31. Pfitzmann A, Hansen M (2005) Anonymity, unlinkability, unobservability, pseudonymity, and identity management—a consolidated proposal for terminology. Technical report, TU Dresden
32. Golle P, Greene D, Staddon J (2004) Detecting and correcting malicious data in vanets. In: VANET '04: proceedings of the 1st ACM international workshop on vehicular ad hoc networks, ACM. New York, NY, USA, pp 29–37
33. Sampigethaya K, Huangy L, Li M, Poovendran R, Matsuuray K, Sezaki K (2005) Caravan: providing location privacy for vanet. In: ESCAR '05
34. Gerlach M, Güttler F (2007) Privacy in vanets using changing pseudonyms—ideal and real. In: VTC spring. IEEE vehicular technology conference (VTC2007-Spring), pp 2521–2525

35. Choi JY, Jakobsson M, Wetzel S (2005) Balancing auditability and privacy in vehicular networks. In: Boukerche A, de Araujo RB (eds) Q2SWinet. ACM, New York, pp 79–87
36. Fonseca E, Festag A, Baldessari R, Aguiar RL (2007) Support of anonymity in vanets—putting pseudonymity into practice. In: WCNC, IEEE. pp 3400–3405
37. Liao J, Li J (2009) Effectively changing pseudonyms for privacy protection in vanets. In: Proceedings of the 2009 10th international symposium on pervasive systems, algorithms, and networks, ISPAN '09, IEEE Computer Society. Washington, DC, USA, pp 648–652
38. Chaum D, Van Heyst E (1991) Group signatures. In: Proceedings of the 10th annual international conference on theory and application of cryptographic techniques, EUROCRYPT'91. Springer, Berlin, pp 257–265
39. Calandriello G, Papadimitratos P, Hubaux J-P, Lioy A (2007) Efficient and robust pseudonymous authentication in vanet. In: Proceedings of the fourth ACM international workshop on vehicular ad hoc networks, VANET '07, ACM. New York, NY, USA, pp 19–28
40. Guo J, Baugh JP, Wang S (2007) A group signature based secure and privacy-preserving vehicular communication framework. Mobile Networking for Vehicular Environments
41. Lin X, Sun X, Ho PH, Shen X (2007) Gsis: a secure and privacy preserving protocol for vehicular communications. IEEE Trans Veh Technol 56(6):3442–3456
42. Liu H, Li H, Ma Z (2010) Efficient and secure authentication protocol for vanet. In: Proceedings of the 2010 international conference on computational intelligence and security, CIS '10, IEEE Computer Society. Washington, DC, USA, pp 523–527
43. Xue X, Ding J (2012) Lpa: a new location-based privacy-preserving authentication protocol in vanet. Secur Commun Netw 5(1):69–78
44. Boneh D, Franklin MK (2003) Identity-based encryption from the weil pairing. SIAM J Comput 32(3):586–615
45. Al-Hawi F, Al-Qutayri M, Yeun C (2010) Security and privacy of intelligent vanets. Computational intelligence and modern heuristics. In: Al-Dahoud Ali (ed) InTech. doi:10.5772/7815
46. Sun J, Zhang C, Zhang Y, Fang Y (Michael) (2010) An identity-based security system for user privacy in vehicular ad hoc networks. IEEE Trans Parallel Distrib Syst 21(9):1227–1239
47. Reiter MK, Rubin AD (1998) Crowds: anonymity for web transactions. ACM Trans Inform Syst Secur 1(1):66–92
48. Tripp-Barba C, Urquiza L, Aguilar M, Parra-Arnau J, Rebollo-Monedero D, Pallarès E, Forné J (2013) A collaborative protocol for anonymous reporting in vehicular ad hoc networks. Comput Stan Interfaces 36(1):188–197. ISSN 0920-5489
49. Rebollo-Monedero D, Forné J, Solanas A, Martïnez-Ballesté T (2010) Private location-based information retrieval through user collaboration. Comput Commun 33(6):762–774
50. Chow C, Mokbel MF, Liu X (2006) A peer-to-peer spatial cloaking algorithm for anonymous location-based services. In Proceedings of ACM international symposium on advances in geographic information systems (GIS). Arlington, VA, pp 171–178
51. Samarati P (2001) Protecting respondents' identities in microdata release. IEEE Trans Knowl Data Eng 13(6):1010–1027
52. Sweeney L (2002) k-anonymity: a model for protecting privacy. Int J Uncertain Fuzz Knowl-Based Syst 10(5):557–570
53. Willenborg L, DeWaal T (2001) Elements of statistical disclosure control. Springer, New York
54. Rebollo-Monedero D, Forné J (2010) Optimal query forgery for private information retrieval. IEEE Trans Inform Theory 56(9):4631–4642
55. Elovici Y, Shapira B, Maschiach A (2002) A new privacy model for hiding group interests while accessing the Web. In: Proceedings of workshop on privacy in the electronic society, ACM. Washington, DC, pp 63–70
56. Elovici Y, Shapira B, Maschiach A (2002) A new privacy model for web surfing. In: Proceedings of international workshop next-generation information technologies and systems (NGITS). Springer, pp 45–57

57. Kuflik T, Shapira B, Elovici Y, Maschiach A (2003) Privacy preservation improvement by learning optimal profile generation rate. In: User modeling. Lecture notes in computer science, vol 2702. Springer, Berlin, Heidelberg, pp 168–177

58. Shapira B, Elovici Y, Meshiach A, Kuflik T (2005) PRAW—the model for PRivAte Web. J Amer Soc Inform Sci Technol 56(2):159–172

59. Elovici Y, Glezer C, Shapira B (2005) Enhancing customer privacy while searching for products and services on the World Wide Web. Internet Res 15(4):378–399

60. Elovici Y, Shapira B, Meshiach A (2006) Cluster-analysis attack against a private web solution (PRAW). Online Inform Rev 30:624–643

61. Parra-Arnau J, Rebollo-Monedero D, Forné J, Muñoz JL, Esparza O (2012) Optimal tag suppression for privacy protection in the semantic web. Data Knowl Eng 81–82:46–66

62. Parra-Arnau J, Perego A, Ferrari E, Forné J, Rebollo-Monedero D (2014) Privacy-preserving enhanced collaborative tagging. IEEE Trans Knowl Data Eng 26(1):180–193

63. Parra-Arnau J, Rebollo-Monedero D, Forné J (2014) Optimal forgery and suppression of ratings for privacy enhancement in recommendation systems. Entropy 16(3):1586–1631

64. Buttyn L, Holczer T, Vajda I (2007) On the effectiveness of changing pseudonyms to provide location privacy in vanets. In: Stajano F, Meadows C, Capkun S, Moore T (eds) Security and privacy in ad-hoc and sensor networks. Lecture notes in computer science, vol 4572. Springer, Berlin, pp 129–141

65. Wiedersheim B, Ma Z, Kargl F, Papadimitratos P (2010) Privacy in inter-vehicular networks: why simple pseudonym change is not enough. In: Proceedings of the 7th international conference on wireless on-demand network systems and services, WONS'10, IEEE Press. Piscataway, NJ, USA, pp 176–183

66. Rebollo-Monedero D, Parra-Arnau J, Diaz C, Forné J (2012) On the measurement of privacy as an attacker's estimation error. Int J Inform Secur 12(2):129–149

67. Parra-Arnau J, Rebollo-Monedero D, Forné J (2014) Measuring the privacy of user profiles in personalized information systems. Future Gen Comput Syst, (Special Issue) Data Knowl Eng 33:53–63

Chapter 9
Privacy Law and Regulation: Technologies, Implications, and Solutions

Jasmine McNealy and Angelyn Flowers

9.1 Introduction

The early 21st century could easily be deemed the era of data collection and vulnerability. Governments collect rapidly increasing amounts of information, from voter registrations to driver license records to death certificates. Private corporations, too, compile databases of consumer information for marketing and advertising purposes. Of great assistance in the amassing of personal data, in both the public and private sectors, are new technologies able to track, retrieve, and decipher much of the information that individuals provide or leave behind while using networked services. Suffice it to say, on the Internet now, not only does everyone know that you are a dog, they may know your breed, where you were born, and the street where your dog house is located.

Of course some of the information collected could be considered benign, and many people subscribe to the "nothing-to-hide" perspective. This attitude asserts that the members of society should and would not care about the collection of their private information if they have nothing to hide. That is, if you are doing nothing wrong, privacy will not be a consideration. Professor Daniel Solove has identified the fallacies in this argument. The argument fails in that it reduces privacy to the hiding of things or information when privacy should be understood as "a plurality of related problems" [1]. Further, the argument deems the harms from possible privacy invasions as significant only if the outcome is tangible or sensationalistic. This ignores the harms that aggregated minor intrusions may cause [1].

J. McNealy (✉)
College of Journalism and Communications, University of Florida,
Gainesville, FL 32611, USA
e-mail: jemcnealy@jou.ufl.edu

A. Flowers
Department of Criminal Justice, Sociology, and Social Work,
University of the District of Columbia, Washington, DC 20008, USA

© Springer International Publishing Switzerland 2015   189
S. Zeadally and M. Badra (eds.), *Privacy in a Digital, Networked World*,
Computer Communications and Networks,
DOI 10.1007/978-3-319-08470-1_9

The failures of the nothing-to-hide argument may be best illustrated by detailing one of the major privacy outrages from the last few years. In 2013 Edward Snowden, an employee of defense contractor Booz Allen Hamilton, disclosed many top-secret documents to the public. The documents detailed a disturbing web of surveillance activities by government actors, particularly the National Security Agency (NSA), assisted by private communications providers [2; 3]. Of particular concern was the collection of metadata, or "data about data," as it is sometimes called. The NSA programs involved the collection of information about telephone calls, but not the contents of the calls, as well as collection of Internet data [2]. Far from benign, aggregated metadata enables the construction of inferences about private activities including medical issues, financial health, and intimate relations [2]. More importantly, the revelation of the surveillance programs demonstrated the global impact of one country's approach to privacy. Not only were US citizens targeted, but also the communications of citizens and political leaders in other countries, causing tension between the United States and other countries, as well as calls for inquiries and assurances about NSA activities [2].

Some of the strongest criticisms of US surveillance activities came from Brazil, which in 2014 passed the Marco Civil da Internet. The new law establishes rules with respect to many Internet-related issues. Of significance for the purposes of this chapter is its implementation of standards related to privacy and data retention. The law limits the amount of metadata that organizations can collect on Brazilian Internet users. As a whole, the law creates a framework for data protection similar to that of the European Union (discussed in Sect. 9.5) [4].

If nothing else, the Snowden anecdote demonstrates the immense range and complexities of government surveillance and information collection. Although US President Barack Obama has somewhat addressed the public and political concerns in connection to NSA activities, and privacy advocates and lawmakers are attempting to make changes by updating the various laws that allow law enforcement to access private information, what exists now in the United States is a hodgepodge of laws and regulations that affect personal information privacy either directly or indirectly. This chapter provides an overview of laws and regulations used to regulate privacy in the digital age, focusing on US law and how it interacts with other global privacy regulations.

First, this chapter considers the causes of increased data collection in this era. Following this, we examine the current state of law in the United States, including those laws directly and indirectly addressing privacy. Section 9.4 considers government surveillance and both the laws that allow it and those aimed at placing restraints on law enforcement activities. This is followed by an analysis of privacy regulation in the European Union. This chapter concludes with an examination of the opportunities for change with respect to privacy law and regulation.

9.2 Catalysts for Change

The late 20th century saw the rise in surveillance, sousveillance, and various privacy-limiting technologies. Yet even before the advent of these new technologies, both public and private organizations were collecting information about individuals in society. Governments have reason to collect some important private information. Censuses, for example, allow for a reasonable estimation of the population, as well as providing demographic information about the individuals within that population. These population counts also provide information integral to the administration of government.

Other forms of government information collection serve similar purposes. Driver license records provide the holder with a form of identification, while providing the state with a log of the holder's address, moving violations, and identifying characteristics. Birth, death, and marriage certificates similarly provide the state with records of human relationships and interactions that allow for the efficient administration of privileges, benefits, and mandates required under state law. Much of the information provided to, or collected by, the state has moved from paper copies to digital databases. On the federal level, the growth in government data collection mirrors the increase in government agencies and the growth in bureaucracy [5]. Government databases on both the state and federal levels provide ready fodder for private corporate databases used for advertising and marketing purposes.

By far the most significant cause of the increased collection of personal information is the war on terrorism. After the events of September 11, 2001, the US government and governments around the world expanded domestic and foreign surveillance and data collection activities. In the United States, prior to 9/11, there was a conscious effort to limit the amount of government use and collection of private information [6]. The barriers erected to prevent government sharing and possible abuse of private information were relaxed to allow collection of domestic and foreign intelligence thought to be useful in combating and preventing terrorism. Some of the anti-terrorism measures have come in the form of new laws that directly or indirectly affect personal privacy.

Anti-terrorism regulations have and continue to raise privacy concerns around the globe. As recent as July 2014 the United Kingdom passed the Data Retention and Investigatory Powers Act (Drip), which requires telecommunication providers to retain customer metadata for 12 months and to allow law enforcement and government agencies access to the information [7]. The law was met with criticism and concerns about the availability of personal data as well as claims that the government may have circumvented the democratic process by rapidly passing the law [8]. Of particular concern is that the law appears to conflict with privacy principles in both the European Convention on Human Rights and the European Charter of Fundamental Rights [8]. The passage of Drip and subsequent objections demonstrate continued tension between government regulations and legal principles with respect to privacy.

9.3 Current US Law

Privacy principles in the United States have their foundations in constitutional and common law, statutes, and the law of equity. In the United States the Constitution is the supreme law of the land. Under the system of federalism, each state or commonwealth has its own constitution as well. The federal Constitution provides, however, the foundation for the rights and privileges of individuals within the United States with respect to both state and federal governments. State constitutions may offer more rights or added protection, but may not encroach upon the rights of its citizens.

It is important to note that the word "privacy" is found nowhere within the Constitution. In fact, it was not until the 1965 case of *Griswold v. Connecticut* that the US Supreme Court ruled that individuals have a constitutional right to privacy that could be found in the "penumbras" of the guarantees enumerated within the Bill of Rights. *Griswold* was a case that involved the question of the legality of a Connecticut state law the criminalized contraceptive services for married couples. Writing for the majority, Justice William O. Douglas found that, although not specifically stated, the constitutional right to privacy could be formed from the "emanations" from the First, Third, Fourth, Fifth, and Ninth Amendments [9].

Within the First Amendment is found the right of association, that is, the right to freely meet and to have privacy in associations. The Third Amendment creates a zone of privacy in its prohibition against the government forcing the quartering of soldiers in any house during peacetime without the consent of the owner. The Fourth Amendment grants the "right of the people to be secure in their persons, houses, papers, and effects, against unreasonable searches and seizures." The Self-Incrimination Clause of the Fifth Amendment prohibits the government from forcing an individual to surrender, either the person or information, to his or her detriment. Finally, the Ninth Amendment states, "The enumeration in the Constitution, of certain rights, shall not be construed to deny or disparage others retained by the people" [10]. It should be noted that the US Supreme Court has ruled that most of the above named amendments, and some of those not mentioned, apply to the actions of state governments, as well, through the Incorporation Doctrine of the Fourteenth Amendment [11].

9.3.1 Laws Directly Affecting Privacy Rights

Of the aforementioned constitutional guarantees, perhaps, most connected to the right to privacy is the Fourth Amendment. It provides:

> The right of the people to be secure in their persons, houses, papers, and effects, against unreasonable searches and seizures, shall not be violated, and no warrants shall issue, but upon probable cause, supported by oath or affirmation, and particularly describing the place to be searched, and the persons or things to be seized [12].

The amendment has been used to "to protect personal privacy and dignity against unwarranted intrusion by the State" [13]. Early on the US Supreme Court interpreted the Fourth Amendment as invalidating laws and activities that invaded an individual's privacy with respect to the contents of domestic mail [14] and papers and other documents [15, 16]. These rulings have been restricted in the years since they were first announced.

The true nature of the Fourth Amendment controls the ability of government to conduct searches and seizures of objects. A seizure occurs when there is the physical taking of an object or an arrest [17]. Searches evoking the Fourth Amendment come in many different varieties including, dog sniffs outside of the home [18], examination of garbage within the curtilage of a home or building [19], as well as thermal imaging of a home [20]. Important for digital or electronic privacy are the cases that considered the constitutionality of electronic surveillance devices, discussed in Sect. 9.4.

Heretofore, the discussion has focused on constitutional privacy principles. It is important to note, however, that privacy protection has a basis in common law as well. In the United States, common law privacy has its foundations in an 1890 *Harvard Law Review* article by Samuel Warren and Louis Brandeis [21]. In it the two noted jurists argued that advances in new technology, at that time the handheld, instantaneous or "snap" camera, were allowing the press to invade the private lives of individuals [22]. The threat to privacy, therefore, required a legal solution.

Seventy years after Warren and Brandeis' article asserting the need for privacy, Professor William Prosser identified four separate actions that make up the tort of invasion of privacy:

1. Intrusion upon seclusion.
2. Public disclosure of private facts.
3. False light.
4. Appropriation [23].

The common law privacy tort most similar to the Fourth Amendment is intrusion. Intrusion, as defined by the Restatement (Second) of Torts, is the physical or other interference with the seclusion of another individual [24]. The intrusion must be highly offensive to a reasonable person to be actionable. As with the Fourth Amendment, this tort considers reasonableness with respect to what society is prepared to consider reasonable [25].

Intrusion is a claim about the behavior exhibited while gathering information, and whether an individual has a reasonable expectation in the sphere of privacy they claim was invaded. Similarly, the tort of public disclosure of private facts considers whether an individual has a reasonable expectation in the privacy of information that was disclosed. The courts have overwhelmingly ruled that once information is made public, a plaintiff no longer has a reasonable expectation of privacy in that information.

9.3.2 The Evolution of US Statutory Privacy Law

Most states have codified the torts of intrusion, public disclosure of private facts, and the other two privacy claims enumerated by Prosser. And, although there is no federal statute recognizing Prosser's privacy torts, a significant number of federal laws exist with direct and indirect implications for individual privacy. The underpinning for many of these laws was the 1973 Code of Fair Information Practices published by the US Department of Health, Education, and Welfare (HEW) [26]. The report established major principles enumerating the rights of individuals and the responsibility of government agencies with respect to private information:

- There must be no personal data record-keeping systems whose very existence is secret.
- There must be a way for an individual to find out what information about them is in a record and how it is used.
- There must be a way for an individual to prevent information about him or her obtained for one purpose from being used or made available for other purposes without their consent.
- There must be a way for an individual to correct or amend a record of identifiable information about him or her.
- Any organization creating, maintaining, using, or disseminating records of identifiable personal data must ensure the reliability of the data for their intended use and must take reasonable precautions to prevent misuse of the data [27].

Congress incorporated many of these principles into the laws directly and indirectly affecting privacy both during this era and after.

One of the first federal laws passed with privacy implications was the Wiretap Act, also called Title III. Passed in 1968, the Wiretap Act codified Fourth Amendment protections with respect to electronic surveillance by law enforcement [28]. The law applies to the use of electronic listening and recording devices and technologies. Congress amended the Wiretap Act 1984 with the passage of the Electronic Communications Privacy Act (ECPA). The ECPA extended some of the Wiretap Act's protections to, at the time, new communications technology such as email. The law also addresses law enforcement surveillance and acquisition of stored communications, under the Stored Communications Act [28, 29]. The third section of the ECPA regulates law enforcement use of technologies that record the number and delivery information for electronic communications [28, 30].

Congress passed the Fair Credit Reporting Act (FCRA) in 1970. The FCRA regulates consumer-reporting agencies, and provides citizens with rights with respect to how information is shared and collected [31]. Congress amended FCRA in 2003 with the Fair and Accurate Credit Transactions Act, which adds protections against identity theft. Although FCRA regulates private agency collection and sharing of consumer information, thereby offering a measure of privacy protection, the Bank Secrecy Act passed the same year requires banks to maintain records of consumers' financial transactions. These records are used to assist the government in criminal investigations [32].

Four years later, Congress passed the Privacy Act of 1974. The Privacy Act endows individuals with rights concerning the personal information about them stored by the federal government [33]. One of the most significant rights provided under the Privacy Act is that of the individual to inspect their personal records, and to have any inaccurate information corrected [33]. The same year brought the passage of the Family Educational Rights and Privacy Act (FERPA), also called the Buckley Amendment after its sponsor Rep. James L. Buckley. FERPA regulates the disclosure of personal information in the possession of a school [34].

Later laws reflected the major concerns of that specific era particularly with respect to new technology. Therefore, the expansion of media systems and computing in the 1980s brought the passage of laws with respect to those new systems with privacy implications. Along with the passage of the ECPA in 1986, Congress passed the Cable Communications Policy Act in 1984, mandating that cable companies protect the privacy of the consumer records [35]. The 1988 Computer Matching and Privacy Protection Act regulates government automated file comparison in investigations [36]. That same year, the Video Privacy Protection Act was passed to protect the privacy of videotape rental information [37].

The unifying theme of the laws passed in the 1990s was that of consumer protection. Therefore, Congress passed the Telephone Consumer Protection Act of 1991, allowing civil remedies against telemarketers [38], as well as the Driver's Privacy Protection Act of 1994, restricting the disclosure or sale of motor vehicle records [39], and the Identity Theft and Assumption Deterrence Act of 1998, criminalizing identity fraud [40]. This era also brought the passage of three important privacy-protecting laws. First is the 1996 passage of the Health Insurance Portability and Accountability Act (HIPAA). The law was supposed to make it easier for workers changing jobs to not be excluded from their new health plans because of pre-existing conditions [17]. This required the use of uniform transaction codes and the sharing of data by healthcare providers. The US Department of Health and Human Services promulgated rules to govern the privacy of medical records [17].

The second significant legislative enactment of the 1990s was the Children's Online Privacy Protection Act (COPPA) of 1998. COPPA restricts the collection and use of the personal information of children under the age of 13 by Internet service providers [41].

The Gramm-Leach-Bliley Act of 1999 is the third noteworthy piece of legislation enacted by Congress in the 1990s. The law requires financial institutions to provide consumers with privacy notices. Consumers must also be allowed to opt out of the disclosure of their personal information to other companies [42].

The 2000s saw the rise in anti-terrorism legislation following the attacks on the Pentagon and the World Trade Center on September 11, 2001. One of the most comprehensive laws enacted was the USA Patriot Act, which amended the ECPA, allowing for easier law enforcement acquisition of voicemail [28]. The Patriot Act also allows for the use of pen registers for the collection of metadata associated with electronic communications [28]. The Patriot Act is used in conjunction with ECPA and laws like the Communications Assistance for Law Enforcement Act (CALEA) to allow government and law enforcement access to electronic communications to facilitate anti-terrorism measures. CALEA, passed in 1994, requires that telecommunication service providers allow law enforcement wiretap access to their systems [43].

9.4 Government Surveillance

It is axiomatic that when the framers of the US Constitution wrote the Bill of Rights, electronic surveillance did not exist. Therefore, the Constitution provides no exact guidance on the legality of government use of advances in technology to invade privacy. The first case to examine electronic surveillance was *Olmstead v. United States*, in which the US Supreme Court had to decide whether law enforcement violated the Fourth Amendment when evidence against a bootlegging conspiracy was obtained from listening devices placed in telephone lines. The Court found that the telephone wires, though connected to the home or business, were not a part of the home and, therefore, were not within the protection of the Fourth Amendment [44].

Though the majority opinion in *Olmstead* found no constitutional violations from the law enforcement activities, Justice Louis Brandeis' dissent is of particular importance. In it the Justice asserts that the general language of the Constitution, and in particular the Fourth Amendment, should not be interpreted in such a way that would limit the ability to consider the changes in the world. The government could develop more ways and new means of invading privacy and the Court's interpretation of that Fourth Amendment had to expand to deal with the new technology. This would necessitate that the Court's decisions with respect to Fourth Amendment search cases go beyond the consideration of whether there was actual physical intrusion or trespass into an individual's home or office. The Court's opinion in *Katz v. United States* took a step in this direction. But, as in *Olmstead*, it is not the majority's opinion that offers the most important guidance about law enforcement activities and privacy.

The *Katz* case considered the constitutionality of FBI agents' use of an electronic listening device to monitor the phone calls of an alleged gambler. The agents attached the device to the outside of the phone booth Charlie Katz used, and used the recordings to convict him of multiple counts of violating federal laws by transmitting wagering information by telephone. In an express rejection of the *Olmstead* requirement of physical trespass by law enforcement, the US Supreme Court found that the Fourth Amendment "protects people, not places" [45]. This meant that the information or activities that a person sought to keep private could be constitutionally protected. This did not mean, however, that the Fourth Amendment created a constitutional right to privacy.

It is Justice Harlan's concurring opinion in *Katz* that has become of paramount importance in understanding privacy in nearly all contexts. The Justice recognized two requirements that result from the past precedents that considered privacy with respect to people. First, the person claiming an invasion of privacy has to have "exhibited an actual (subjective) expectation of privacy." Second, to be perceived as legitimate, that expectation has to be such that society is prepared to recognize it as "reasonable" [46]. With respect to the actual facts of *Katz*, Justice Harlan agreed that society recognized the expectation of privacy in the conversation using the services of a phone booth.

Important to note, however, are the limitations placed on the reasonable expectation of privacy. That is, the courts in the United States, have carved out exceptions to the reasonable expectations test that have major implications for privacy with respect to new forms of technology. The "third-party doctrine," the principle that an individual may no longer claim privacy over information provided to a third party, is one of the most significant of these exceptions. The majority opinion in *Smith v. Maryland* is from whence this principle comes. The *Smith* case examined whether the use of a pen register—technology that monitors the numbers dialed by a specific telephone when installed at the telephone provider—without a warrant, violated the Fourth Amendment guarantee against unreasonable searches [47]. The US Supreme Court expressed doubt as to whether there is an expectation of privacy in the numbers that people dial. According to the Court, people who use telephones know that they are, in essence, giving the phone number that they are dialing to the telephone company. Further, telephone companies commonly use pen register-like technologies to record phone numbers, and to check for illegitimate uses. The Court also rejected the idea that society would recognize the expectation of privacy in the telephone numbers dialed as reasonable, because the individual voluntarily exposes information to another party. Once given to another party, the originator of the information has no control over it.

The *Katz* reasonable expectation recently came under scrutiny with respect to new surveillance technology in the form of Global Positioning System (GPS). In *US v. Jones*, the US Supreme Court held that the law enforcement's placing of a GPS tracking device on a drug-trafficking suspect's vehicle constituted a search within the scope of the Fourth Amendment [48]. But, instead of using the *Katz* reasonable expectation of privacy test, the Court ruled that the government violated the Fourth Amendment because it had physically occupied the suspect's private property by attaching the GPS to his SUV [48]. In her concurring opinion, Justice Sotomayor wrote that in the future the Court would have to address the government use of new technologies that facilitate surveillance and what this means for privacy [49]. In his separate concurrence, Justice Alito wrote that society had an expectation that the government would not record every move made by its citizens [50]. According to Professor Christopher Slobogin, both concurring opinions expressed endorsement of what is called the "mosaic theory" of the Fourth Amendment [51]. The mosaic theory expresses the view that the aggregated information from certain kinds of government surveillance is a violation of constitutional privacy [51]. Of course this is not law, but there has been a call for mosaic theory to be codified [51].

9.5 European Privacy

The European approach to privacy stands in stark contrast to that of the United States. This contrast is illustrated in Table 9.1, which provides a brief comparison of underlying tenets of US approaches to privacy protection compared with their European counterparts.

This difference is a dichotomy in how privacy rights are viewed in the United States and in Europe. The privacy framework for the US approach is based on a negative right requiring the government to refrain from identified privacy violating activities. The European approach, on the other hand, places an affirmative duty on government to safeguard individual privacy [52]. As previously described in this chapter, there is no expressly stated right of privacy in the US Constitution. Instead it is derived from the penumbras of other Constitutional rights that are expressly stated. In Europe, privacy was expressly declared to be a human right and fundamental freedom in 1950 in the Convention for the Protection of Human Rights and Fundamental Freedoms adopted by 47 European nation-states. Article 8 of the European Convention on Human Rights (ECHR), titled "Right to respect for private and family life," provides that:

1. Everyone has the right to respect for his private and family life, his home and his correspondence.
2. There shall be no interference by a public authority with the exercise of this right except as such as in accordance with the law and is necessary in a democratic society in the interests of national security, public safety or the economic well-being of the country, for the prevention of disorder of crime, for the protection of health or morals, or for the protection of the rights and freedoms of others [53].

Fifty years later in 2000, with the promulgation of the Charter of Fundamental Rights, the European Union consolidated then existing rights that had previously been guaranteed by separate charters, treaties, or case law; as well as incorporated new rights emerging in the modern era [54]. The Charter of Fundamental Rights became legally binding on EU institutions and its member nation-states in 2009.

Table 9.1 Comparison of selected US–EU privacy principles

United States	Europe
Privacy is not expressly mentioned in the Constitution	Privacy right is guaranteed in the European Declaration of Human Rights and the European Union (EU) Charter of Fundamental Freedoms
The individual relinquishes control of personal information voluntarily given to third parties	The individual retains ownership of personal information
Individual privacy is protected from the government	Individual privacy is protected by government from the private sector

Among the new fundamental rights codified was a right to data protection. Article 8, titled "Protection of personal data," mandates that:

1. Everyone has the right to the protection of personal data concerning him or her.
2. Such data must be processed fairly for specified purposes and on the basis of the consent of the person concerned or some other legitimate basis laid down by law. Everyone has the right of access to data which has been collected concerning him or her, and the right to have it rectified.
3. Compliance with these rules shall be subject to control by an independent authority [55].

Article 8 of the EU Charter for Fundamental Freedoms reinforced the long-standing push in the EU for protection of personal data. Digital privacy has been a concern of the European Union almost since its formal inception in 1993. The EU Data Protection Directive (Directive 95/46/EC) was adopted in 1995. It was intended to set limits on the permissible collection and use of personal data of EU residents while simultaneously facilitating the free movement of that personnel data within the European Union [56]. The personal data of EU residents is protected even when they are using services and products of non-EU companies [57]. The Data Protection Directive required that each member state establish its own independent national body to ensure that this data was protected. As a result of the release of information on *PRISM*, the NSA project that included spying on European Diplomats among others, Europeans are also concerned about protecting their data from the US Government. This has led to increased calls for the establishment of European-based cloud services, relieving the need for EU members to rely on US cloud companies [58].

The guidelines established pursuant to the Data Protection Directive relate to the: quality, legitimacy, excluded categories, disclosure of information regarding the collector or controller of the information, individual's right of access to the information, right to object, specified exceptions and restrictions, confidentiality, and notification requirements when personal data is collected. For example, among the key requirements of the Data Protection Directive is a prohibition on processing personal demographic-type data related to items such as racial or ethnic origin, religious or philosophical beliefs, health, and sex life except within certain delineated instances [56]. Individuals also have a right to object on legitimate grounds to having data processed about them [56].

To consolidate enforcement and implementing regulations, in 2012, the European Union began work on a consolidated comprehensive reform of the 1995 Data Privacy Directive designed to strengthen online privacy rights as well as boost Europe's digital economy [59]. The General Data Protection Regulation (GDPR) was adopted in March 2014 by the European Parliament and sent to the Council of Ministers, the next stage in the reform process [60]. A brief summary of new and enhanced protections to be provided by the GDPR is presented in Table 9.2.

The most striking distinction between the United States and the European Union is a difference in the perceived need for privacy protections. Europeans appear to be more concerned about privacy encroachments by the private sector or corporations,

Table 9.2 GDPR selected individual empowerment provisions [64]

A Right to be Forgotten	In the absence of legitimate reasons for retention individual data must be deleted at the individual's request
A Right to Data Portability	Individuals can transfer their data among service providers
Consent requires an express affirmation	When consent it required it must be expressly stated, not inferred by a failure to say no
Privacy by design and default for all products and services	Default settings must be privacy friendly

while Americans seem more concerned with the likelihood of government encroachments [61, 62].

Reminiscent of the adoption of the Patriot ACT in the United States following the September 11, 2001 events, the European Union a few short years later also confronted a situation where goals of personal privacy and national security appeared to collide. In the aftermath of the Madrid train bombings in 2004 and the London bombings in 2005, the European Union attempted to address the conflicting nature of a strong right to privacy with the need of law enforcement to conduct criminal investigations. The EU Data Retention Directive (DPD) of 2006 identified a category of data, referred to as "covered data," that it was permissible to retain for a period of 6–24 months [63].

Citing the demonstrated importance of traffic and location data in the investigation, detection, and prosecution of criminal offenses, the DRD required member states to retain data that was necessary to identify the following [69]:

1. Source of a communication.
2. Destination of a communication.
3. Duration of a communication.
4. Type of communication.
5. Users' communication equipment or purported equipment.
6. Location of the mobile communications equipment.

While data about a specific communication is to be retained, the DRD specifically directs that no data about the content of that communication is to be retained [69]. Covered data is to be retained by the operator and provided only to the designated national authority [69].

In April 2014, however, the European Court of Justice (ECJ) declared the Data Retention Directive inconsistent with the EU Charter of Fundamental Rights asserting that it violated two basic rights, the right for private life and protection of personal data [64]. In its decision, the ECJ did recognize the legitimate law enforcement and anti-terrorism purposes for data retention, but determined that the DRD violated considerations of proportionality. Following the adoption of the DRD by the European Union, member states promulgated their own laws, regulations, and administrative provisions necessary for compliance with the DRD [69].

The subsequent decision of the ECJ left those member state directives in place but subject to judicial review. States responded to this challenge in different ways. For instance, the United Kingdom, after initially continuing to utilize the regulations it had developed for the DRD, in July 2014 passed the Drip Bill. As noted in Sect. 9.2, the passage of Drip proved controversial, and failed to abate the continuing tension between government regulations and legal principles in regards to privacy [70].

9.6   Challenges and Opportunities

Each time a bonus or savings card is used by someone in a grocery store, the individual's purchases are recorded. Targeted advertising appears on a computer monitor based on the tracking of the websites visited by the user or by their online purchases. "Do Not Track" prohibitions are the primary efforts used to protect individual privacy by restricting advertisers from tracking online behavior. But their activation often requires that the user take several affirmative steps.

Consider those insidious mechanisms such as the GPS locator on cell phones and the app that directs those phones to locate "friends" in the same geographic space. But what if the individual doesn't want to be located? Data mining of customer information is a lucrative enterprise. It has been estimated that in 2012 the value of the online data market was $62 billion [65]. This has led to complaints by US companies about the limitations placed by EU states on their ability to gather customers' personal information when doing business in the European Union, and it has been a continuing source of tensions between US companies and the European Union [61].

Traditional adherence in US privacy law to notions of the separate nature of government and the private sector is inconsistent with the operations of today's digital environment. Most users of many popular apps, for example, are unaware of the extent to which those apps "leak" personal information, which is then available for capture by government agencies, criminal enterprises, or other data mining companies [66]. An overarching challenge is to determine the appropriate levels of privacy protection that should be applicable.

The challenges and opportunities presented by the need to effectively shape personal privacy laws and regulations that meet the needs of the 21st century are myriad. The issues highlighted when comparing the two opposing approaches of the United States and the European Union raise several questions for consideration. For instance:

- What do we actually want to regulate to protect individual privacy—the government, the private sector, or both?
- How do we ensure that users are actually fully informed of the personal information that will be collected in a manner that is comprehensible to the user and offers them a viable choice?

- What is the feasibility of providing services in a way that is minimally intrusive on individual privacy by minimizing the personal information collected and the length of time it is held?

More importantly, it may be that the greatest challenge is recognizing that the nature of the questions makes a statement about the values that a society deems important with regard to personal privacy. The opportunity is in determining what those values should be.

As such, it may be instructive to look again at the guidelines aimed at strengthening privacy or information in the past. The five principles form the 1973 Code of Fair Information Practices noted in Sect. 9.3.2, for example, could prove, and has been, useful for constructing policy related to individual rights with respect to control over information [26]. An examination of these five principles, as well as the laws, policies, and court opinions detailed above, reveals the key themes of information access and control with respect to individual privacy.

The theme of access encompasses both the right of citizens to know that government collection of information exists, as well as the right to know what personal information is being collected. Government agencies, then, would be required to inform citizens about ongoing surveillance activities. This, of course, would not necessarily mean that specific individuals would be informed that they were being investigated. The citizenship, as a whole, should be informed, however, of ongoing government data collection, and what this may mean for their activities, digital or otherwise. In this way, there may not be a need for a repeat of the Edward Snowden saga.

Control of collected information would allow citizens the ability to correct the information collected. It also may include the right to force the deletion of information stored in government, or private, databases. This may be the most important and yet controversial principle to implement. By definition, this kind of right, as conceptualized in the right to be forgotten mentioned above, provides individuals with control over information in another's possession. This control would allow a person to force the erasure of that information.

In considering the ways to implement the principles of access and control, it may also be instructive to consider the privacy laws and policy frameworks from other parts of the globe. Japan, for instance, regulates the use of personal information contained in certain business databases, requiring data subjects to be provided with notice about the purpose of the use of their data [67]. The law also requires that businesses obtain consent from the data subject for any uses outside of the stated purpose, and before allowing third-party access to personal data [67].

Of particular note is that of Privacy by Design (PbD), a framework developed by Ann Cavoukian, the former information and privacy commissioner of Ontario, Canada. PbD is based on seven principles that incorporate both consumer control and access to information. The principles are:

1. Proactive not reactive (measures).
2. Privacy as the default.
3. Privacy embedded into design.

4. Full functionality.
5. End-to-end security.
6. Visibility and transparency.
7. Respect for user privacy [68].

Although the PbD framework appears to focus on business or organizations, the foundational principles evoking, again, the values of control, access, and, additionally, transparency would be beneficial for integration into government activities evoking personal privacy.

9.7 Conclusion

Privacy law is made up of a hodgepodge of statutory, constitutional, and common law ideas and principles that are adapting to developments in new technology. The United States has a long history of evolving its Constitutional interpretation and its laws to meet changing conditions. But technological changes are increasing rapidly. To keep pace, regulators must find ways to accelerate the amendments to laws implicating both government and private access and use of personal information.

The US approach to privacy is noticeably different from the EU model. The former has its basis in prohibitions against government activity, which have been applied to privacy, while the later focuses on privacy and data protection as express rights that protect the individual from corporate data-gathering efforts. To be effective, privacy laws and regulations must grow in tandem with the technology that is being regulated. Approaches to privacy that exclude information voluntarily disclosed to third parties from protection may be outdated in a world where digital technology is so intertwined in our lives that ordinary activities of daily living are predicated on some type of voluntary disclosure to access an essential service. It may be inevitable that as technology expands so too does its insidious creep into the private spaces of our lives. But there has to be an approach to maintaining some semblance of personal privacy without opting out of the benefits of the digital world.

References

1. Solove DJ (2007) I've got nothing to hide and other misunderstandings of privacy. San Diego Law Rev 44:745
2. G. U. interactive team, MacAskill E (2013) NSA files decoded: Edward Snowden's surveillance revelations explained. The Guardian
3. Gellman B, Blake A, Miller G (2013) Edward Snowden comes forward as source of NSA leaks. The Washington Post, 10-Jun-2013
4. Marco Civil da Internet (2014) vol. Lei No. 12.965
5. Solove DJ (2004) The Digital Person New York University Press, New York
6. De Rosa M (2003) Privacy in the age of terror. Wash Q 26(3):27–41

7. Fiveash K (2014) UK gov rushes through emergency law on data retention The Register, 10-Jul-2014
8. Travis A Drip (2013) surveillance law faces legal challenge by MPs. The Guardian, 22-Jul-2014
9. Griswold v. Connecticut (1965) US Reports vol 381, p 479
10. U.S. Const. am. 9
11. Lieberman JK, A practical companion to the constitution: how the Supreme Court has ruled on issues from abortion to Zoning. University of California Press, Oakland
12. U.S. Const. am. 4
13. Schmerber v. California (1966) US Reports vol 384, p 757
14. ex parte Jackson (1877) US Reports, vol 96, p 727
15. Boyd v. United States (1886) US Reports, vol 116, p 616
16. Gouled v. United States (1921) US Reports, vol 255, p 298
17. Solove DJ, Rotenberg M, Schwartz P (2008) Information privacy law
18. Florida v. Jardines (2013) US Reports, vol 133, p 1409
19. California v. Greenwood (1988) US Reports, vol 486, p 35
20. Kyllo v. United States (2001) US Reports, vol 533, p 27
21. Kalven H Jr (1966) Privacy in Tort law-were Warren and Brandeis wrong. Law Contemp Prob 31:326
22. Warren SD, Brandeis LD (1890) The right to privacy. Harv Law Rev 4(5):193
23. Prosser WL (1960) Privacy. Calif Law Rev 48(3):383–444
24. Restatement of the Law, Second, Torts, §652 (2014). http://cyber.law.harvard.edu/privacy/Privacy_R2d_Torts_Sections.htm. Accessed 13 April 2014
25. Solove DJ (2002) Conceptualizing privacy. Calif Law Rev 1087–1155
26. Rotenberg M (2001) Fair information practices and the architecture of privacy: (what Larry doesn't GET). Stan Tech Rev 2001:1–4
27. U.S. Dep't. of Health (1973) Education and Welfare, Secretary's Advisory Committee on automated personal data systems, records, computers, and the Rights of Citizens viii
28. Freiwald S, Metille S (2013) Reforming surveillance law: the swiss model. Berkeley Tech J 28
29. Stored wire and electronic communications and transactional records access, US Code, Title 18, sections 2701–2711
30. Pen registers and trap and trace devices, US Code, Title 18, sections 3121–3127
31. Fair Credit Reporting Act (1970) Public Law No. 90-32, US Code, Title 15, section 1681 et seq. 1970
32. Bank Secrecy Act (1970) Public Law No. 91-508
33. Privacy Act of 1974, US Code, Title 5, section 552a
34. Family Educational Rights and Privacy Act of 1974, US Code, Title 20, sections 1221 note, 1232 g
35. Computer Matching and Privacy Protection Act of 1988, US Code, Title 5, section 552a
36. Video Privacy Protection Act of 1988, US Code, Title 18, sections 2710–2711
37. Telephone Consumer Protection Act of 1994, US Code, Title 47, section 227
38. Driver's Privacy Protection Act of 1994, US Code, Title 18, sections 2721–2725
39. Health Insurance Portability and Accountability Act of 1996, Public Law No. 104–191
40. Identity Theft and Assumption Deterrence Act of 1998, US Code, Title 18, section 1028
41. Children's Online Privacy Protection Act of 1998, US Code, Title 15, sections 6501–6506
42. Gramm-Leach-Bliley Act of 1999, US Code, Title 15, sections 6801–6809
43. Communications Assistance for Law Enforcement Act of 1994, Public Law No. 103–414
44. Olmstead v. United States (1928) US Reports, vol 277, p 438
45. Katz v. United States, (1967) US Reports, vol 389 p 347
46. Katz v. United States (1967) US Reports, vol 389, p 361 (Justice Harlan concurring)
47. Smith v. Maryland (1979) US Reports, vol 442, p 735
48. US v. Jones (2012) Supreme Court reporter, vol 132, p 947
49. US v. Jones (2012) Supreme Court reporter, vol 132, p 954 (Justice Sotomayor concurring)
50. US v. Jones (2012) Supreme Court reporter, vol 132, p 957 (Justice Alito concurring)

51. Slobogin C (2012) Making the most of United States v. Jones in a Surveillance Society: A statory implementation of mosaic theory. Duke J Const Law Public Policy 8:1–37
52. Kuner C (2013) The transatlantic divide over data privacy rights 20 May 2013. https://www.privacyassociation.org/privacy_perspectives/post/the_transatlantic_divide_over_data_privacy_rights. Accessed 30 March 2014
53. Council of Europe (2014) European convention on human rights, 4 November 1950. www.echr.coe.int/Documents/Convention_ENG.pdf. Accessed 2 April 2014
54. Justice European Commission (2014) EU charter of fundamental rights, 25 July 2013. www.ec.europa.eu/justice/fundamental-rights/charter/index_en.htm. Accessed 5 April 2014
55. European Convention (2014) Charter of fundamental rights of the European Union, 7 December 2000. www.europarl.europa.eu/charter/pdf/text_en.pdf. Accessed 5 April 2014
56. Protection of personal data, 2 Jan 2011. http://europa.eu/legislation_summaries/information_society/data_protection/l14012_en.htm. Accessed 5 April 2014
57. Fromholz J (2014) The European Union data privacy directive. Berkeley Technol Law J 15 (1):461–484
58. PRISM Fuels Cries for EU Clouds (2013) Information Management, September/October, p 6
59. European Commission Justice (2014) Commission proposes a comprehensive reform of the data protection rules, 25 Jan 2012. http://ec.europa.eu/justice/newsroom/data-protection/news/120125_en.htm. Accessed 25 March 2014
60. European Commission (2014) Data protection: progress on EU reform now irreversible after European Parliament vote. European Commission, 12 March 2014. http://europa.eu/rapid/press-release_MEMO-14-186_en.htm. Accessed 25 March 2014
61. Sullivan B (2014) "La Difference" is Stark in EU, U.S. Privacy Laws, 19 Oct 2006 http://www.nbcnews.com/id/15221111/ns/technology_and_science-privacy_lost/t/la-difference-stark-eu-us-privacy-laws/#.U1CwB_mwJcQ. Accessed 10 April 2014
62. Fromholz J (2014) The European Union data privacy directive. Berkeley Technol Law J 15 (1):461–484 (note 2)
63. Taylor M (2006) The EU data retention directive. Comput Law Secur Rep 22:309–312
64. Digital Rights Ireland Ltd (C-293/12) v. Minterter for Com munications, Marine and Natural Resources, et al and KarnterLandesregierung (C-294/12) and others. European Court of Justice. Decided: 8 April 20
65. Dwoskin E (2014) Study: Digital Marketing Industry Worth $62 Billion. Blog: Wall Street Journal, 14 Oct 2013. http://blogs.wsj.com/digits/2013/10/14/study-digital-marketing-industry-worth-62-billion. Accessed 5 April 2014
66. Ball J (2014) NSA and GCHQ target 'Leaky' phone apps like Angry Birds to scoop user data. The Guardian, 27 Jan 2014. http://www.theguardian.com/world/2014/jan/27/nsa-gchq-smartphone-app-angry-birds-personal-data. Accessed 6 April 2014
67. Act on the Protection of Personal Information 2003
68. 7 Foundational principles. Privacy By Design. http://www.privacybydesign.ca/index.php/about-pbd/7-foundational-principles/. Accessed 28 Jul 2014
69. European Parliment and Council of the European Union, "Directive 2006/24/EC of the European Parliament and of the Council of 15 March 2006. Off J Eur Union L105:54–63. http://eur-lex.europa.eu/LexUriServ/LexUriServ.do?uri=OJ:L:2006:105:0054:0063:EN:PDF. Accessed 26 Jul 2014
70. Ermert M (2014) EU data retention directive finally before European Court of justice. Internet Policy Rev: J Internet Regul (05 Jul 2013). http://policyreview.info/articles/news/eu-data-retention-directive-finally-european-court-justice/162. Accessed 26 Jul 2014

Chapter 10
Privacy in Mobile Devices

Rinku Dewri and Ramakrishna Thurimella

10.1 Introduction

Personal computing has entered a new era with the wide adoption of mobile devices. Affordability of devices, reduction of implementation costs, and the possibility of novel business paradigms have driven the public acceptance of mobile technology at a scale much larger than desktop computing. The world's population is now close to having at least one mobile device per individual. Current generation mobile devices offer high-end computing platforms, connectivity to the Internet, and a range of applications, including but not limited to, local search, social networking, content sharing, entertainment, navigation, office suites, and games.

Consequently, this proliferation has also put the fundamental right to privacy of an individual at risk. Privacy is loosely defined as a "personally" assessed restriction on when and to whom an individual's data is deemed appropriate for disclosure. As user activities on a mobile device grow, so does the extent of personal information left behind in the device, and the inferences one can derive about the lifestyle, choices, and preferences of the user. Catering to privacy becomes difficult when the available data start to channel out to entities that are outside the trust boundaries of the user.

In the early days, privacy of mobile technology subscribers was regulated by federal legislations such as the Electronic Communications Privacy Act in the United States and the Data Protection Directive within the European Union. Network operators are bounded in terms of what data can be retained and how it can be used. The data itself involved records of calls and text messages. The same

R. Dewri (✉) · R. Thurimella
University of Denver, Denver, CO 80210, USA
e-mail: rdewri@cs.du.edu

R. Thurimella
e-mail: ramki@cs.du.edu

© Springer International Publishing Switzerland 2015
S. Zeadally and M. Badra (eds.), *Privacy in a Digital, Networked World*,
Computer Communications and Networks,
DOI 10.1007/978-3-319-08470-1_10

standards also applied when communication modes moved from the telephone network to the Internet. However, the rise of the Internet significantly increased the type and amount of data flowing through an internet service provider. Ideally, any user data flowing through the service providers are open to viewing, given that most is unencrypted. This is already concerning from a privacy standpoint; the only consolation is that the number of internet service providers are limited, and they can be monitored for illicit activities.

The use of mobile devices for personal communications, and subsequently for almost all types of data transactions, introduced the next level of privacy problems. Unfortunately, the adoption outpaced the law makers. Businesses and freelance developers flooded the market with applications never thought possible, and started engaging in massive data collection efforts about what users do on the mobile Internet, what they prefer, and what their tendencies are. The sheer number of service providers exploded, and innovative techniques came into light to use personal data collected at different sites to enhance the services. Data collection became more of a regular business practice. Explicit monitoring of what a provider is doing with the users data is no longer possible. Fair information practice principles had to be ruled out instead. These principles asked for a more transparent system where user consent should be obtained prior to data collection, and appropriate notices are given to the user about what is collected, how it will be put to use, who are the potential recipients, the method of collection, and how the data will be retained. The enforcement of these principles is mostly self-regulatory. This evolution of how personal data is handled has raised the question about who owns such data, and whether the individual is really in control any more.

The industry often does not view personal data collection as privacy breaching, as long as it is collected and used in a way such that the user cannot be identified from the data. This probably created the most common phrase one can read in a privacy policy—"data is collected and shared in an anonymized form." Perhaps this well-popularized practice prompted people to share more! The past decade saw a significant number of demonstrations to prove the loophole in this privacy blanket. Large fractions of the population can be identified by a combination of their gender, date of birth, and place of stay [15]. People may enter locations, interests, affiliations, in search queries, which make them unique in an anonymized web search database [3]. Knowing the ratings assigned to eight movies is sufficient to identify an individual, even when there is a two week error in obtaining the dates of the ratings [29]. Half of the individuals in the US population can be uniquely determined if their home and work locations are known at the level of a census block [16]. In GPS logs, people can be identified based on the last destination of the day and the most populated cluster of points [21, 25]. Individuals can also be identified by their social network structure [30], or their family tree [27].

New forms of inference possibilities are identified on a regular basis. This led to a significant push in educating the population about privacy in an electronic society, generating guidelines for the common application developer to be privacy sensitive, and a whole line of work in privacy-preserving design of application architectures. This chapter is a short review of the attempts that are under to retain the privacy of users constantly interacting with mobile devices for most daily activities. Given its breadth, we are not including the legal framework for privacy protection in this review. We begin with a background in mobile devices and their associated technologies in Sect. 10.2. In Sect. 10.3, we highlight the privacy issues surrounding the use of a mobile device. Section 10.4 discusses the solutions put forth to mitigate the emerging privacy concerns. We end the chapter in Sects. 10.5 and 10.6 with a discussion on the challenges we are faced with in making a mobile device a more privacy sensitive platform, and the opportunities they provide us.

10.2 Background

Mobile devices have been defined in multiple ways since their inception. The most basic of these is that of a small, handheld device capable of receiving and transmitting voice calls over a long range wireless medium. These basic wireless communication systems became well-known as "walkie-talkies," once more and more capabilities became a standard in generic mobile devices. Features such as the ability to perform rudimentary computing, user interactions through a display and a keyboard, and execute common business and entertainment applications, are extensions of what the device can do, but soon became synonymous with what a mobile device means. However, the features that are typical in current generation devices will change and be extended, thereby leaving us little room to succinctly lay down the defining characteristics of a mobile device.

10.2.1 Mobile Devices

Mobile device characteristics are constantly changing. Features become obsolete even before a large fraction of the population gets a chance to use them. Therefore, for the purpose of this chapter, we simply adopt characteristic hardware and software features that dominate the current mobile device market. These features have been outlined by National Institute of Standards and Technology of the United States Department of Commerce [36].

A mobile device is defined as a collection of the following hardware and software characteristics.

- A small form factor device with a display and a real/virtual keyboard.
- A microprocessor that executes instructions on data stored in memory, and has lower power requirements than a typical desktop processor.
- Access to a Wi-Fi and/or cellular network that provides connection to larger network infrastructures such as the Internet and the telephone network; modern device capabilities often include personal network interfaces such as Bluetooth and NFC (near-field communication), as well as interfaces to access satellite navigation systems such as the GPS.

- A local non-removable data storage medium, often in the form of EEPROM (electrically erasable programmable read-only memory) flash memory.
- An operating system similar to that of a desktop/laptop environment, however with a comparatively lower resource requirement.
- A system to deliver, manage and execute applications.

A cellular network is composed of roughly hexagonal cells, each covering a small area, a low power transceiver and a base station in each cell, and an underlying telephone network between the base stations. Each cell can serve a fixed number of users depending on the available number of channels. A control center, called the Mobile Telephone Switching Office (MTSO), keeps track of the cell where a user is located, and aids the transfer of a call from one cell's base station to that of another. The same mechanism helps connect a mobile device to other network infrastructures such as the Internet. Depending on the size of the cell and the number of base stations serving it, radio signal strengths can be weak or strong. Digital communication technology have made it possible to serve more users in a cell, have more reliable communication, higher data transmission rates, broader bandwidth, and provide more secure communication channels.

10.2.2 Device Types

Mobile devices started off as two-way communication devices. Compared to the bulky DynaTAC from Motorola in 1983, modern mobile devices weigh just over 100 grams, and are constantly being enhanced for portability. Early generation devices consisted of a basic dial-pad and LED display. As mobile devices became popular amongst the masses, major players like Nokia, Sony Ericsson and Motorola flooded the market with newer, smaller, and lighter versions of their devices. Nonetheless, for almost a decade, mobile devices were nothing but an embedded system designed for a very specific task, voice and text communication. With reductions in the cost of microprocessor technology, the modern notion of a smartphone was introduced by IBM in 1994, with capabilities such as fax and email, and employing x86-compatible microprocessors. Since then, the hardware in mobile devices have seen an exponential growth, and vendors frequently provide upgrades to the state-of-the-art computing power and possibilities of a mobile device. Current mobile devices boast of quad-core giga-hertz level microprocessors comparable to desktop systems 5 years ago, embedded graphics processors, high-definition touch screen displays, multi-sensor interfaces, extended battery life, and all of these wrapped in the thinnest and lightest possible casings.

The software applications available in a mobile device have seen equally impressive advances. Popularly known as a "personal digital assistant" (PDA), mobile devices stopped being simple voice communication devices and started offering other capabilities such as text messaging, email composition, personal information management, and audio/video playback and recording. Palm's Palm OS, Nokia's Symbian OS, and Microsoft's Windows CE were some of the forerunners in converting the mobile communication device to today's smartphone. These systems ported the notion of operating systems prevalent in desktop/laptop environments to the mobile environment, which were later replaced by more dominant players such as the Apple iOS and Google Android. Software applications that can run within these mobile operating systems are as diverse as office productivity suites, entertainment applications to watch streaming content, local search using GPS information, road navigation, networking with like-interest individuals, sharing content, playing games, and almost any other typical computing need we can satisfy using a desktop system. The combination of fast processor technology, wide adoption of mobile devices, and the surrounding business possibilities, have made it possible to develop an engaging computing device that has reached more individuals that any other technology.

10.2.3   Software Frameworks for Controlled Data Access

The complexity of the software system within a mobile device has seen tremendous growth in a short span of time. As our dependence on these systems grow, so does the necessity to carefully protect the personal data gathered during execution of the system. Almost all major mobile operating system vendors today realize this requirement, and employ one or more techniques to prevent software applications from arbitrarily accessing each others data and resources. Further, obtaining explicit user consent is crucial before any application is granted access to potentially private data.

10.2.3.1   Android

The Android platform is based on the Linux kernel, which is fundamentally based on separation of resources and data between different users. This user-based permissions model is also key to "sandboxing" an application's resources from that of others. Each application in Android is executed as if it is run by a different user. Since the user-based permission model, in the default form, does not allow interaction between processes originating from different users, an attempt by an application to read data belonging to another application will be prevented by the Android kernel. Applications under this model also have limited access to the operating system; in fact, operating system libraries, runtime environments, and application managers are also sandboxed in Android.

Every Android application has an associated manifest file (AndoridManifest.xml). An application developer uses the manifest file to inform Android about important application components, dependent libraries, and permissions required by the application to function, among others. As with any XML document, the manifest file is a collection of elements. For example, by using the uses − configuration element, an application can state its requirement for a certain type of keyboard, navigation device, or touch screen. An application can request for permissions such as access to the Internet, read location data, clear caches, read contacts data, send SMS, update security settings, and others, through the uses – permission element. Each permission has an associated protection level, and the Android system seeks user confirmation for higher-risk ones, during installation. Permissions given to installed applications can also be viewed by accessing the application's information in the system settings. However, the recent versions of Android are closed to any user manipulation of permissions already granted during installation. Also, all permissions requested by an application must be granted by the user for Android to install and execute the application.

10.2.3.2 iOS

The Apple iOS system provides application sandboxing by placing each application in its own home directory, and then allowing the application to read and write to files and subdirectories only under the home directory. Several key directories such as Documents , Library and tmp are created by the installer, and these standard directories form the view of the file system for the application. The iOS system uses access control lists (ACLs) to provide such a contained view to the applications.

Unlike in Android, permissions in the iOS system are granted as they are requested by the application. However, the set of features that require explicit user consent is limited to location services, contacts data, calendars, reminders, photos, bluetooth sharing and microphone. For these features, iOS provides a relatively straightforward control to enable and disable an application's access to the feature.

10.2.3.3 Windows Phone

Windows Phone applications run in a strictly isolated environment, with a structured method to communicate with other features. Data storage is also isolated for the applications. The executing environment also provides a minimal set of capabilities to the application. Similar to an Android manifest file, Windows Phone applications have a package manifest file containing details about the capabilities that the application requires to function. Software capabilities can include access to contacts data, to the camera, to location services, and to Wallet payment instruments, among others. Users are notified about the requested software capabilities during installation of the application from the Windows Phone Store.

10.3 Privacy Issues

Privacy, by definition, is a subjective matter. A technology that can potentially encroach on the privacy of individuals is often deployed with the argument that individual consumers have the option of rejecting the technology if they decide. It should be noted that the privacy issues surrounding a particular technology is not common knowledge, and without a detailed understanding, they can easily pass as minimal disclosures one must make for the technology to work. This specially holds true in software systems where interconnected components can transfer data between each other using highly technical methods, and vulnerabilities can help adversaries to evade securities protecting the data. Nonetheless, it is true that privacy is important only to the extent that an individual wishes to keep the right to control one's information. A 2013 consumer mobile data privacy study reveals that, while 76 % of users believe that they are ultimately responsible for their privacy, only 35 % read the privacy policy [38]. It is worth noting that less than 20 % of users are willing to share information such as date of birth, web surfing behavior, precise location, phone number, home address, photos/videos and list of contacts. Ironically, the most popular mobile applications constantly collect such forms of information.

In the following sections, we will elaborate upon the type of (personal) data that may be collected by a mobile application, and the methods by which this data may leak to third-parties. We will not attempt to highlight a certain form of data collection as a privacy issue, but will leave the inference of such a conclusion to the subjective discretion of the individual.

10.3.1 Private Surveillance

Public surveillance, specially using CCTV cameras, has always created privacy uproars in democratic societies. Such systems have been argued to be susceptible to abuse, and instruments for discrimination. Nonetheless, from a national security standpoint, they serve as a valuable tool to monitor high-traffic public places. Moreover, since only publicly visible activities are monitored in public surveillance, the threat to privacy is often viewed as minimal. On the other hand, constant surveillance of the private life of individuals is strongly opposed, and has till now been regulated by legislations. An enormous amount of resources will also be required to manually monitor the daily activities of even a small fraction of the population. Notably, the cost of privately surveilling large sections of the population has drastically come down due to the growing attachment between technology and the society.

Our daily activities in the physical world are getting more and more integrated with the digital world. We are constantly leaving a trail of digital breadcrumbs throughout the day, which if brought together, can produce a picture of our activities (public and private) with an alarmingly high accuracy. Further, the trails can be constructed on demand, for any period of time one seeks, and at a fraction of the cost of manual surveillance.

Let us explore what information may be left behind by an average technology-savvy individual on a typical day. We refer to this individual as Bob. All tracking activities stated here are very real, as has been evidenced in publications in academic journals, trade publications, news articles, and business privacy policies. From the smartphone in his pocket and the computer on his desk, to his job, to the purchases he makes and the food he eats, just about everything Bob does leaves some sort of digital trace behind. Bob's smartphone is monitoring his location at all times in order to improve the quality of his services. This data can potentially be shared with a wide variety of applications, websites, and advertisers. Like many people, Bob uses an online email provider, such as Gmail or Yahoo! Mail. All emails he sends and receives are stored by the email providers, along with other information such as the search queries he makes on his mail. As Bob drives to work, his car's GPS constantly triangulates his location. This data may be transmitted to a central host to allow the GPS to give directions. Bob also uses an electronic pass to make going through toll booths easier on him. However, geolocation data on these passes is read all through cities in order to assess traffic congestions. Speed cameras along his way also read his license plate, irrespective of whether he was speeding or not.

Like many modern professionals, Bob uses LinkedIn to make connections in the business world. It is likely that a quick perusal of his profile will reveal his entire work history, the people he works with and has worked with, his educational background, and more. Almost everything that Bob does at work is tracked, whether that be for tax purposes, payroll processing, to protect the company from illegal activities performed with company equipment, or simply to monitor behavior and assess the performance of employees. All Internet traffic is scanned, key strokes and mouse clicks are logged, calls are tapped, and email conversations are monitored by management and IT departments. Bob's employer is immune to privacy lawsuits in this regard, as long as it can be established that such monitoring is for the interest of the underlying business.

When it is time for lunch, Bob uses Grubhub, an online platform that lets him order food from any restaurant in the area. Such portals can indefinitely store almost every piece of information that passes through their system, including name, delivery address, phone number, food habits, and payment information. The information may not be disclosed to marketers and third-parties, but at the same time, is not proactively deleted. A restaurant's digital security may also not be a high priority. Physical eateries also record all reservations, orders, billing, and customer mannerisms and preferences. With the objective to enhance customer experience, this data can be quite comprehensive and accessible to most employees of the restaurant.

On his way back home, Bob stops by a store to replenish his supplies. His retailer membership card allows him to get discounts and coupons. The same card also lets the retailer profile Bob, his buying habits, and tendencies. The retailer can also track Bob inside the store through his smartphone, and later send out special coupons for items that Bob spend time looking but did not buy. Once back at home, Bob spends some time on the Internet. Most sites he visits use some form of user tracking, often in the form of beacons, cookies and browser fingerprinting. Bob's expenditure habits, on the Internet or in physical stores, are all well summarized in his credit report. Other businesses can also look at this data with little forewarning.

After a tiring day, Bob decides to play a few rounds of Madden on his XBox. Data on practically everything Bob does on the XBox Live service is collected, including the games he plays, the music and videos he purchases and listens/watches, and even samples of his voice if he uses the voice recognition service. Usage data is also collected when Bob interacts with other services such as iTunes, Amazon MP3, Spotify and the likes. Right before ending the day, Bob reads a book on his Kindle, which can monitor his reading habits, type of books he likes, and even offer special deals. Throughout the day, Bob also did some voluntary data sharing through status changes, comments, and posts in online social networks.

Clearly, an average individual is unlikely to be aware of all small data bits that is being tracked. A single technology, such as the mobile device, is also not responsible for making this possible; although, much of this has become possible due to the advances in one or another form of mobile technology, and the increasing usage of mobile devices. A full assimilation of the collected information is perhaps not feasible for a single commercial entity, but the push in Big Data mining activities do leave the possibility open.

10.3.2 Data Collection

Mobile devices have changed how people access information on the Internet. Typical desktop usages are interactions that a user initiates to find the desired information, often well in advance. With the vast proliferation of mobile devices, information access has become more reactive, where a user performs an action at the time when it is needed. Therefore, locality and usability of the served information has become an important feature of mobile applications. This also implies that many applications require metadata about the user in order to serve information that is relevant in the current context of the user. A mobile device being a personal companion, obtaining data corresponding to the specific user in question is also not difficult. This driving force has resulted in massive data collection exercises about users, and seems to have blurred the line between what is necessary for the application and what is simply extraneous.

10.3.2.1 Implicit Collection

Most of the basic voice and messaging features available in a mobile device are exclusive to mobile devices. It is only when a device is used to exchange information with an application server on the Internet, a mobile device's functionality is more like a portable computer. For a mobile device to be able to provide call, text/picture messaging, and Internet services, certain features such as call details, cell tower in use, text message details, and IP session and destination information are visible to the mobile carrier. Such data has huge marketing value. Since the phone number is a pseudo-identifier of the person/family, call records can reveal who we call, who calls us, as well as the locations from where the calls are made or received. They can also reveal the identities of our friends, the doctor we visit often, our vacation plans, the financial institutions we deal with, and even our favorite handyman. In the United States, voice, messaging and IP data can be retained from 3 days to 7 years depending on the carrier and type of information [39]. Long-term retention of such rich data poses one of the most severe threats to privacy.

10.3.2.2   Pertinent Collection

Mobile operating systems make it possible for an application to access software, hardware and user-specific features for proper functioning. For example, a typical social networking application in Android can specify the following elements in its manifest file.

```
<uses-permission   android.name="android.permission.ACCESS_FINE_LOCATION">
<uses-permission   android.name="android.permission.ACCESS_COARSE_LOCATION">
<uses-permission   android.name="android.permission.INTERNET">
<uses-permission   android.name="android.permission.CAMERA">
<uses-permission   android.name="android.permission.READ_PROFILE">
<uses-permission   android.name="android.permission.RECORD_AUDIO">
```

Once granted, the permissions enable the application to access the GPS module, location approximated based on the radio signal strength, the Internet, the camera, the user's profile stored in the device, and record audio. This data is also pertinent in the context of the application, without which the full potential of the application cannot be realized. However, once an application receives access to the requested data, the operating system loses control of how the data is used, and does not prevent the application from storing it or forwarding it to its servers.

When reviewing the pertinence of a data request, a question that we often fail to ask is whether the granularity of the requested information is critical for the application to offer its services. We exemplify this observation using the GPS access permission that a location-based application is likely to request. At first glance, it is unlikely that a location-based application can function without accessing the location feature. However, will the information generated by the application change substantially if accurate location data is not provided? For example, a weather application can retain its accuracy even by using an area code. For a non-trivial example, consider a local search application that helps the user find points of interest in the vicinity of the user's location. Although location is an important component in obtaining relevant results, local search services utilize a number of other factors (popularity, cost, references, etc.) to determine relevant results. Search results are also unlikely to change instantly due to movement of the user. Even in dense cities such as Los Angeles and New York, search results for the ten nearest Starbucks locations can stay invariant for areas as large as 87 km^2. [6].

Similar to the implicit data collected by network carriers, application specific data collected by application providers also have huge marketing value. Unlike the case of call records, whose sharing is heavily governed by federal legislations, data collected by application providers is very likely to be used for business gain. Potential (mis)uses of the data is invisible to the user, thereby opening up privacy concerns.

10.3.2.3   Extraneous Collection

Extraneous data collection refers to the activity where an application accesses information in the device that cannot be rationally attributed to the functioning of the application. A flashlight application accessing the user location, the contact list, the calendar, or media files is an example of extraneous collection. Clearly, the motivation here is not service quality, but creating a rich database of user data. While in some mobile operating systems, requests for such access can be denied at the time of access and still keep the application running, in others, the application must be granted all requested permissions prior to its execution. The latter design forces the user to comply with extraneous data collection requests, effectively foregoing privacy expectations.

Another potential issue arises when permission requests are added during the upgrade of an application. Early versions of an application are restricted to pertinent data collection; however, extraneous permissions may be added as upgrades are released. A user may be tempted to permit the extraneous collection simply to avoid the hassle of learning a new application. Such practices can lead to a user weighing down on privacy over time. Extraneous data collection can be performed by the mobile operating system vendors as well.

10.3.2.4   Web Tracking

In addition to data collection through mobile applications, user behavior tracking on the mobile web is an increasingly growing trend. Behavior tracking in the conventional Web is a well-known phenomena [24]. As web services grow in diversity, and vendors start offering entire product suites, the ability to monitor user viewing habits across the range of services is unquestionably an advantage. Various forms of web technologies are used for this purpose. The most common of these are cookies, which are small pieces of text data stored in the user device by a browser at the request of the web server. The data stored in a cookie can be a simple identifier (such as an IP address) of the user, along with details on the actions performed by the user at the web site. When the user visits the web site, or a companion site, at a later time, all previously created cookies can be retrieved from the user device and prior actions of the user can be extracted from them. Cookies can be disabled and deleted by the browser upon request by the user. An alternative is to use a web beacon, which can be a tiny (1 pixel by 1 pixel) image placed on web sites across different services. When a user visits the different web sites, the browser will request this particular image, and pass along metadata about the user as part of the request. Although not as flexible as cookies, web beacons can be used to track a user's browsing activity page by page, site by site.

All of the user-tracking technologies in the conventional Web can also be applied in the mobile Web. The mobile ecosystem is host to a number of applications that engage in data collection, often much personal than that is currently possible through a web page. When such data also become available to vendors of the web services, supposedly anonymous activities on the web can be linked with user profiles (and identities). A mobile browser can itself have access to multiple sensor data from the device (not possible in the conventional setting), including location, camera, microphone, and personal data such as calendars and contact lists. Efforts are ongoing (see Mozilla WebAPI[1]) to design Web APIs that allow web applications to access device hardware and other data stored in the device at a much granular level.

10.3.3 Data Leaks

Users of mobile devices are often made aware of the type of personal data collected by an application. The sandboxed model of data access in mobile operating systems makes it difficult for an application to bypass a user-consent dialog when accessing data that is deemed sensitive by the system designers. However, the data, once collected by an application, may be shared with (or leaked to) parties that are not directly authorized by the user.

10.3.3.1 Business Policy

The most common form of data leak is in fact a totally legal, user-authorized form of data sharing. A careful scrutiny of an application's privacy policy can reveal that the data collected from the device is not only used to improve the services of the application, but can also be shared with entities that support the execution of the different services pertaining to the application. For example, a section of the Facebook data use policy reads as follows.

> We give your information to the people and companies that help us provide, understand and improve the services we offer. For example, we may use outside vendors to help host our website, serve photos and videos, process payments, analyze data, conduct and publish research, measure the effectiveness of ads, or provide search results. In some cases we provide the service jointly with another company, such as the Facebook Marketplace. In all of these

---

[1]https://developer.mozilla.org/en-US/docs/WebAPI.

cases our partners must agree to only use your information consistent with the agreement we enter into with them, as well as this Data Use Policy.

Any user using an application agrees to its terms and conditions, in other words, grants permission to the application provider to share the collected data. In 2010, the *Wall Street Journal* published an article on the data being collected by some of the most popular applications and games in the iOS and Android platforms, and the subsequent automatic sharing of the data with other vendors [37]. The study used a *man-in-the-middle attack*[2] to observe which applications collected features such as username, password, contacts, age, gender, location, phone ID and phone number of the user, and to which other vendors this data is sent. A standard issue here is that details on the identity of the third-party service providers are often missing in the policy declaration. Hence, it is difficult to evaluate if the security infrastructure of a third-party provider is as good as that of the trusted application provider. It is argued that the anonymity of individuals is retained by sanitizing the shared data of personal identifiers such as names and addresses. However, quasi-identifiers such as age, gender and zip code are often sufficient to identify a person by cross-referencing with other databases [3, 15, 29, 30]. In addition, given that a mobile application can be developed and deployed by any developer, most of them do not have a privacy policy.

10.3.3.2 Permission Leaks

A second potential for data leak can originate from the functional design of the software application. An ill-designed application that has permission to access personal data content may erroneously leak the data to other applications. For example, an Android application can use the services of a map application to display the current location of the user. The application can request the service with two simple lines of code.

```
Intent intent = new Intent(Intent.ACTION_VIEW,
             Uri.parse(geo : 0, 0?q = 34.99, −106.61(Current Location)));
startActivity(intent);
```

While potentially harmless, this action can lead to a permissions leak, if the user only trusted this application with the precise location co-ordinates. The mobile operating system will not intervene in this case, since the map application is not attempting to obtain the data from the system. Mobile applications also implement handlers for many of the services they may provide to other applications. For example, an application with access to the contacts data in the device can serve it to

---

[2]An attack where an eavesdropper intercepts messages between two parties, and relays them either after simple observation or after modification, without detection by either party.

other applications. This can be a legitimate and useful action, but handlers that serve requests to such permission-protected data may have been left open for access by any application. Ideally, any interface that provides access to permission-protected data should be subjected to the same permissions as that of the data. In our example, if the user's permission is required to access the contacts list, then permissions should be set in the manifest file to protect access to any public method that accesses the contacts data.

10.3.3.3 Leaks via Embedded Content

Mobile applications can embed content of different types in their user interface. A free version of an application, for example, may embed advertisements from mobile marketers, or a mobile web page can be composed of elements collected from multiple sources. Consider a user interacting with an online shopping application. The user shares some personal information such as age, gender, and location, with the application in order to customize the search results. The shopping application returns useful results to the user, along with a pertinent advertisement from an ad-network. This observation is also typical in web browsing sessions. The HTML pages returned by such web servers often include embedded requests that encourage the browser to ask for advertisements and images from third parties.

Many of the current web-based applications expose web APIs that allow any other application to request content in the form of formatted objects by using standard HTTP protocols. Web APIs also make it easy for the calling application to pass parameter values to the web application. For example, once connected with the googleapis.com server, an application can request the translation of the word "Hello" to Spanish using the following request.

GET /language/translate/v2?q = Hello&target = spanish HTTP/1.1

A mobile application can use the web APIs exposed by an ad-network to retrieve advertisements (or other content) and in that process, leak private information, if user-specific data is included as parameter values in the request. When an online shopping application generates a request such as

GET /adj/...product; age = 30; gnd = 1; zip = 12345;... HTTP/1.1,

it leaks demographic information about the user to the ad-network, and potentially in unencrypted form. Request parameters can also include device identifiers, account preferences, and other forms of user data generated as part of the interaction process. While a single occurrence of such leaks is probably not concerning, if a single entity provides such services to a large and diverse set of applications, then tracking a user's activities across different types of applications becomes possible.

10.3.4   Data Interception

Signal interception, or eavesdropping in popular terms, is a threat to any form of private data exchange, and has raised concerns in technologies such as phone calls, text messaging, and emails. All data originating from a mobile device finally has to travel to the base station, from the base station to the MTSO, from one MTSO to another, and then from an MTSO to the public telephone network or the Internet infrastructure. All points in the flow are vulnerable to a man-in-the-middle attack, where an entity can intercept the signal, analyze it, block it, and in some cases modify it.

The 3G security specification (3GPP TS 33.102 V12.0.0 2014-03) requires that the mobile network and the device compare their ciphering capabilities to establish an encryption algorithm for use during communications. The specification gives the option to agree on unencrypted communications if the device and network agrees so. Because of the requirement to be backward compatible with the GSM security architecture (still predominantly in use), the ability to use unencrypted communications is still retained. With capabilities available for the network to choose an encryption algorithm, an adversary can set up a false base station in a localized area and force communications to be unencrypted. The false station can also continue to provide connections to the actual network by forwarding incoming content through a valid channel that it has established with a real base station. As a result, the adversary is able to observe all data originating from any device connected to the false base station. Also, since a mobile device automatically drops to a 2G network when a 3G network is unavailable, possibilities exist to force devices to use the 2G network by jamming the 3G frequencies. It does take considerable expertise to set up such a system; however, not outside the reach of law enforcement organizations and individuals with the required skills.

The most vulnerable portion in the communication path is when the data reaches the core network of the provider after the radio-based network. The internal infrastructure of telecommunication networks is often not encrypted. Starting from the cell base station site, to the telephone switching network, data flows through physical mediums such as wires, switches, servers and other mediums. Any raw data (basic voice/messaging and unencrypted application content) traveling through these nodes is susceptible to passive monitoring by an employee, a hacker who has compromised an intermediate server, or an agency who is lawfully allowed to intercept user communications.

10.4   Privacy Solutions

Multiple solutions to the potential privacy breaches that can emanate from data collection and tracking methods have been proposed. We will explore them under three headings (a) developer guidelines: best practices that an application developer should follow to respect and protect the user's personal data (b) user options: the tools available and proposed to enable self-regulation and (c) application architectures: novel technical solutions to execute common types of mobile applications, yet without requiring personal data disclosures. Solutions discussed under developer guidelines correspond to some of the issues mentioned in Sect. 10.3.2, and those under user options correspond to the issues in Sects. 10.3.3 and 10.3.4. The efficacy of all these techniques remains to be tested. Potential privacy issues in mobile devices are identified on a regular basis; although, solutions for their resolution are designed and enforced at a much slower pace. Given this widening gap, it is worth pondering whether personal privacy is indeed on its way to becoming a "thing of the past."

10.4.1 Developer Guidelines

Developers of mobile applications are the first party responsible for protection of user data. Every mobile operating system provides security features to restrict access to personal data, but their proper use can only be guaranteed by the developers. As such, vendors that provide the application development frameworks, such as Google[3] and Apple,[4] have guidelines for building trustworthy applications.

A privacy-sensitive application is transparent about the type of data collected from the device and how it is subsequently used. A clearly written privacy policy can go a long way in earning the trust of users, and getting the requisite access to make the application function. It has also become important to educate users why a certain piece of data is important for the application. Extraneous data collection should be avoided as they do not serve any useful purpose for the user. Collection of identifiers such as IP addresses and unique device identifiers also put the user at privacy risks. Similarly, if third-party sharing will be performed, a clear explanation should be provided about what will be shared, why is it necessary, and who it will be shared with. More details are better, but in a concise manner.

Whenever possible, applications should be developed assuming limited access to user data. Therefore, developers should include alternative control paths for cases when a user is not willing to share a certain piece of data. This enables the user to assess if the limited functionality of the application is still acceptable, and also enhances the user's trust in the application. Requesting access to sensitive data at the time when it is required also helps the user to understand the context in which it will be applied. On the other hand, asking for a set of permissions prior to usage only raises suspicion. It is common in open-source environments to reuse code written by other developers; it is critical to understand if the borrowed code follows the data access rules set forth by the developer.

---

[3]http://android-developers.blogspot.com/2010/08/best-practices-for-handling-android.html.
[4]https://developer.apple.com/library/ios/documentation/iphone/conceptual/iphoneosprogramming guide/AppDesignBasics/AppDesignBasics.html.

As far as possible, data logging and data storage on offsite servers should be avoided. Storage of data opens up possibilities for misuse later, some of which may directly impact the privacy expectations of the user. If data storage is crucial for the application, developers should determine the largest possible granularity of the information that the application requires–GPS location or postal code, phone number or area code, user details or username–and employ encryption techniques to ensure that the information is not visible on its route to the server.

Privacy oversight bodies also suggest that mobile application platforms (operating systems) should set requirements for developers to follow before their applications can be approved for distribution [10]. For example, dialog boxes used to obtain access permissions can be designed to obtain a one-time or a persistent consent. Platforms should also provide an informative dashboard where users can review existing permissions, logs of when applications accessed their data, and modify/revoke permissions if necessary. There should also be ample notification given to the user when personal data is being accessed, preferably through the use of icons in familiar locations of the user interface. Custom-built firmwares such as the TaintDroid [9] do make such notifications possible. However, these tools are mostly research prototypes, difficult to install for a novice user, and are not maintained by the mobile operating system vendors. As such, their availability and adoption in the long run are questionable.

10.4.2 User Options

User controls are available in most mobile platforms to help regulate what an application can learn about the user from the device. A platform such as Android requires a user to provide explicit permission to access all requested features before an application can be installed, while platforms such as the iOS ask for the permission when the application tries to access the sensitive data. The two models are different in terms of when they engage the user to make a decision, one giving the option to the user to review all information that the application will attempt to access, and the other allowing the user to potentially understand how the information will be used. Despite the differences, it must be noted that the user only controls access to data features that the platform designers have marked as sensitive. An application may be collecting other forms of personal data that do not require user permission. Some applications may assume that the user is always willing to share such data (default opt-in), while others assume that permissions are required for all kinds of access (default opt-out).

Besides the ability to review permissions during installation or just-in-time, users also have the option of changing permissions in certain platforms. The iOS platform provides a privacy dashboard that allows the user to enable or disable permissions of an application for features such as location, contacts, calendars, and microphone. Other systems may only allow viewing of permissions, with little or no option for the user to revoke single permissions. It is important for users to explore what privacy options are provided within the application itself. For example, a social networking application can provide controls to choose what category of other users (no one, friends, friends of friends, or everyone) can view the text, pictures, and videos posted by the user; a local search application can provide the option to use location approximations instead of precise GPS coordinates; in general, an application may require the user to tune the preferences so that it can perform within the privacy expectations of the user. By doing so, users may also be able to turn off extraneous data collection activities of the application, especially in platforms that do not allow permission modification. Research proposals also exist that analyze the application ecosystem in a mobile device to determine if permission leakage is possible during the execution of an application. Proof-of-concept tools such as the SCanDroid [13] can statically analyze if it is safe for an application to run with certain permissions, provided that data may flow in or out of other applications with different permission levels.

In order to prevent third-party tracking, a user may choose to disable cookies and scripts, or use the private browsing modes now provided in many browsers. However, disabling of cookies may also disable the functionality expected from certain web interactions, for example an online shopping experience. Technologies such as opt-out cookies and AdChoices notifications can help the user to proactively request a third-party to refrain from tracking, or reactively become aware of how a third-party may be tracking the user.

Opt-out cookies are similar to regular cookies, but they are placed by the user to be read by tracking websites. Trackers that honor such cookies always attempt to read opt-out cookies before storing and serving content corresponding to the users personal data. However, opt-out cookies have to be periodically renewed by the user, and may get removed while deleting other cookies. If an ad-network is instead enrolled in the AdChoices program, the user can learn more about the provider of an advertisement and also install opt-out cookies from provided links. Under such a program, the displayed ads embed a small text and graphical icon, clicking on which reveals details and opt-out links for the ad's source. Blocking tools are also available that consult public lists of third-party networks, and block content originating or addressed to such sites. Browser extensions are the most popular methods of executing such blocking tools.

Mobile operating systems have started deploying a unique user-specific identifier called an "advertising ID." An application can use it as a pseudonym for the user, although it is not as strongly tied to the user as a device identifier, and can be reset or disabled by the user. Both iOS and Android systems provide this feature so that developers can monetize their applications, and users have the control to protect their privacy by periodically breaking, or opting out of, tracking attempts carried by the application and associated third-parties. The World Wide Consortium (W3C) is also standardizing Do Not Track, which is a method that can be used by users to signal web sites about their tracking preferences. A simple implementation is by using an extra element in the HTTP header that browsers send while requesting web pages. For example, the presence of the header DNT : 1 can tell the web site that the user does not want to be tracked. However, it cannot be guaranteed that the web site will honor the request.

Protection against eavesdropping is possible using encrypted communications at various points of the communication channel. Users can choose to install end-to-end encryption solutions to prevent eavesdropping on their communications. Applications such as Cellcrypt can encrypt voice communications and text messages between two parties running the application. Such applications do not use the typical channels used during voice calls, but instead use the data channel to send communications as encrypted data, and then decrypt them at the other end. Therefore, depending on the data coverage, calls may be noisy. Incorporation of encryption technologies within the mobile network itself can free this dependence on data coverage, and provide protection against outsiders in basic services such voice calls and text messaging. Similarly, although proposals based on mix-networks and pseudonyms are available to hide the cell of a mobile device from the carrier [11, 23], they lack any real world deployment.

10.4.3   Application Architectures

Privacy solutions discussed so far rely on the adoption of best practices by the developer, and on the user being responsible about evaluating and regulating access to private data. A third method is to employ technical solutions such that private data is not directly available to an application, albeit the application can still provide the services. As such, methods in these categories are crafted to take advantage of an application's specific data requirements, and do not necessarily generalize to other applications. We will consider five prominent application types in this discussion, namely local search, friend finder, online social networking, navigation and web browsing. The solutions presented require significant modifications to existing application architectures; this can be one of the reasons why their adoption in practice is slow or non-existent.

10.4.3.1   Local Search

In a mobile local search application, the user specifies a search term signifying the type of objects (e.g. cafe, pizza, gas station, etc.) of interest, and the application, with access to the location of the user, retrieves the top few objects that match the user's query. The selection of these top objects is based on multiple factors. For example, selection of result objects in the Google Places [32] application is driven by two factors, namely the distance of the objects from the user's location and their prominence. The prominence of a POI is derived from multiple subfactors such as reference counts, highest score of objects that refer to this object, number of user reviews, and the extent of services offered, among others. The private data to be protected here is the location of the user.

An extensively explored method is to use the services of a trusted third party. In such a method, it is assumed that the users trust a third party with their location data, which in turn communicates with the application provider to retrieve results on behalf of the user. Since the trusted party will have access to the locations of different users, it can issue local search requests by specifying a region, instead of precise GPS coordinates. The region can be formed such that, at any given point in time, it includes multiple users [14, 18]. Such a "cloaking" region can also be formed to satisfy other properties: the number of still-object counts must also be above a user-specified threshold [2], the query terms corresponding to users in a region should be diverse [5], or the profile of users in a region should not be similar [35]. It is usually difficult to determine who the trusted party should be, and also introduces a single point of failure in the system. A compromise of the trusted party can compromise the location data of multiple users. Most of these techniques apply in the context of local search. Technical solutions for private local search assume that distance is the only factor used to determine the relevance of objects; unfortunately, it is only one of many factors, because of which the solutions are not easily applicable in a real application. A few recent proposals have appeared where it is treated more practically, but demands more exploration [7].

10.4.3.2   Friend Finder

Friend finder applications notify users when their friends (users included so in the application) are in close proximity. Applications such as Foursquare, Facebook's Nearby Friend, Find My Friends!, and other social networking applications provide such a feature. Finding nearby friends privately is referred to as "private proximity testing" in the literature, where the objective is to determine if two users are geographically close to each other without revealing the location of either user to the other. Such a problem can be reduced to a "private equality testing" problem where the task is to determine if two values are equal, and no user will know the value supplied by the other, unless they are equal. To perform such a reduction, the geographic area is divided into three overlapping hexagonal grids, and the size of cells in a grid is set subjective to a distance threshold [31]. Using a few encrypted data exchanges, a private equality testing protocol will allow two users to determine if they are in the same cell. The three grids help the users determine proximity even if they are on different, but nearby, cells.

An alternative to using location in proximity detection is to use transient signals from the environment. Referred to as "location tags," these signals can be derived from electromagnetic technologies such as Bluetooth, WiFi, GPS, and GSM, and are collectively specific to a certain area [33]. A location tag can be viewed as a vector of these signals, e.g. WiFi SSIDs visible to the device. An application can compute the number of elements common in the location tags of two users, and signal proximity when the number exceeds a certain threshold. To prevent inference of the location of the user from the tag itself, "private set intersection" protocols can be used [20, 22].

10.4.3.3 Online Social Networking

Users of online social networking applications entrust the application with their personal preferences and posts, and not simply the data that can be gleaned from the device. The tools provided by the applications to control who can view the voluntarily shared content is often limited. In addition, their sharing with unknown third-party affiliates is concerning. The use of public key cryptography to protect the data is not scalable. Since users may want to share different content with different users, they will be required to keep multiple copies of the encrypted content, will be unable to easily share content with a group of users, or must have already exchanged cryptographic keys prior to sharing. A solution to this problem is to encrypt the content with respect to an "access structure" [1]. An access structure is simply a logical expression of attributes that define a certain group of users, e.g. (neighbor OR football fan). Any user with access to a decryption key with respect to this structure, and has the attributes that satisfy the logical expression, can then view the content. This form of encryption is known as attribute-based encryption [17]. The encrypted content resides with an untrusted third-party. Removal of a user from a group will require that other users of the group are given new secret keys.

The privacy issues surrounding online social networking applications are primarily due to the centralized collection of user data. Decentralized architectures can diffuse such concerns. In a trivial implementation, the user's device can be the data storage location, and other users can view shared data by querying the device. Clearly, this method can have availability issues. As an extension, the data can be replicated across other locations, either in encrypted or in clear form. These locations are chosen based on a trust index assigned by a user to other users [4]. The solution does involve a third-party who can help manage pseudo-identifiers for the users, and connect and find them.

10.4.3.4 Navigation

Phone-based navigation has gained wide popularity in mobile devices with the introduction of GPS capabilities and the Internet in the devices. Services such as Google Maps, and applications such as Waze are typical examples. The ability to use real time traffic information in route determination has significant advantages. Privacy issues emanate because the routing service must know the origin and destination to compute the best route, as well as know intermediate locations to dynamically update the route. In essence, the routing service can track the places visited by the user. Privacy preserving navigation is a relatively new area of research, and techniques are rare.

Assuming that the user's device has the capability to store the topology of the road network (in the form of a graph), the route can be computed directly on the device. However, dynamic information such as traffic congestions, road constructions, and accidents cannot be stored on the device. The problem then is to compute the shortest route between the origin and destination nodes in the graph, using cost information from the service provider. However, the origin and destination nodes cannot be revealed to the service provider. The service provider can compute the shortest path for all pairs of possible origin and destination nodes, and store this data as a four column database–start node, end node, intermediate node, and a bit signifying if the intermediate node is in the shortest path from the start to the end node [40]. Private information retrieval methods will then allow the user to query the service provider if a certain neighboring node is in the shortest path. Such retrieval methods provide querying mechanisms such that the service provider will be oblivious to the row of data returned to the user [26]. Variants of the method include designing the database so that the user can privately retrieve the next hop with a lesser number of queries.

10.4.3.5 Web Browsing

Web-based services are becoming multi-party businesses, with advertisers, analytics services, social integration services, content providers, front-end services, and hosting platforms working together to create the ultimate customer experience [28]. Of course, data sharing can happen uncontrollably in such a model. Earlier, we discussed what options a user has to control this sharing. Several technical solutions have also been proposed to design third-party services that can benefit the user while preserving privacy. However, the coverage is mostly limited to online advertising.

Services such as online advertisement can be made private by employing anonymizing proxies [19]. The approach requires users to subscribe to advertisement networks via a proxy server. The proxy server collects non-sensitive broad demographics data from the users, assigns each user a unique identifier, and retrieves relevant ads from the advertisement network. The unique identifier can be used to track user activities. The proposal is similar to the concept of using advertising IDs in iOS and Android. The use of an anonymizing network such as TOR [8] is suitable in this context. User profiles are also created on the mobile device so that the ads retrieved from the proxy server can be further filtered in the device. Such profiles can also be released directly to the advertiser with permission from the user [12]. This model is similar to how browsers request permission to release the location (IP address) of the user when requested by a web site.

Ad auctions is another business paradigm that can be affected by Do Not Track compliant applications. In an ad auction, advertisers submit ads to an advertising network along with bids for their ad to be displayed to the user. The ad dealer (advertising network) attempts to serve ads (to users) that have higher bids on them, as well as a higher chance of being clicked. Calculation of the click chance requires information about the web page being browsed by the user, ad keywords, user search terms, and other characteristics describing the user's actions. If applications refrain from sharing such information with the advertisement network, ad auctions cannot be performed. More specifically, the ranking of ads is not possible for the ad network. However, assuming that the rank of an ad is a product of the bid and a score derived from user profile information, the ranking can still be performed through the exchange of a few encrypted messages [34]. Opportunities exist for the ranking to be done in the device, at the ad network site, or at a third party site.

The architectures discussed here are representative solutions for the application types. Readers should use the citations provided to explore more related proposals.

10.5   Challenges and Opportunities

It has become clear through the above discussions that the usage of mobile devices can potentially put a user at privacy risk. There have also been extensive attempts to mitigate this risk. Nonetheless, privacy worries continue to grow in the mobile arena, and technology and law has not been able to control the growth in collection of private data. We highlight below some of the challenges that lie ahead of us, and the opportunities they provide for new research directions.

Opinions on privacy. Enforcing any solution to a privacy problem in a mass scale is a challenge. There is hardly any consensus on whether a technology is privacy breaching or not. Businesses see value in the collection of user data as it allows them to create services highly customized to the requirements of the user. The individual users are divided in opinion–some do not mind sharing their information, while others are skeptical about sharing even broad demographics. Given this broad set of perspectives, neither a purely restrictive nor a discretionary solution will be adopted in practice.

Disclosure with consent. It is understood that data leakage is a concern. However, no simple solution exists to curb the leakage. Privacy policies tend to throw a big net to cover almost any form of data, although much of it may not be necessary or is not collected from the user. However, it is equally important to understand that an application that seeks consent for every small piece of data it records will undoubtedly create usability issues, and will not be accepted by users. Current methods to engage the user in the permission process are limited to a select few types of data. The question remains open as to when and how often the user should be asked for permission to access personal data.

Granularity in disclosures. Current mobile systems have adopted a binary method of controlling disclosure of information. An option is available either to disclose information in the least granular form, or not disclose at all. Similarly, applications are developed to operate with the most precise version of a piece of data, or not use it at all. This binary design forces the user to choose between using an application as it is or disregarding it. There exists opportunities to design fine-grained controls for data disclosures, and applications that can gracefully degrade in services based on a chosen disclosure level.

Mobile hardware. Research on privacy-preserving architectures for modern mobile applications started a decade ago. Many of these architectures try to preserve privacy by significantly augmenting the server-side functionalities, or engaging an intermediate party to perform computationally expensive operations.

The motivation for doing so is justified, given that mobile devices have only recently become powerful enough to be considered full fledged computing platforms. The state-of-the-art in the processing capabilities of mobile devices was around 400 MHz in 2007 (e.g. the 32-bit RISC ARM in the first iPhone), which has grown exponentially to support multicore systems with clock speeds of up to 2.5 GHz in 2014 (e.g. the Snapdragon 801 on the HTC OnePlus One). These advances in the computing power of mobile devices are yet to be availed in novel privacy preserving architectures. They may also prove to improve the performance of otherwise slow methods. Engaging the mobile device also allows for a more scalable architecture, since the computations will be highly distributed.

Using existing infrastructures. A number of technical solutions do exist to execute some of the prominent type of mobile applications and services in a privacy preserving manner. However, they involve complex architectures and data exchanges that are not typical in existing implementations. Heavy investments have already been made to deploy these implementations, and large user databases have already been created through such implementations. It is therefore unlikely that existing infrastructures will be discarded in favor of user privacy. Privacy-preserving solutions will have better chances of adoption if they can be executed using already existing server-side components. It is also important that solutions stay close to real world design trends and assumptions. For example, while local search trends continue to rise, the wide array of location privacy solutions seem unusable since most of them solve a nearest-neighbor problem, instead of a top-neighbor problem. Similarly, many solutions are based on using encryption to privately match two individuals in an online social network; albeit the sophisticated key management components necessary to achieve it in practice are missing in existing applications.

Providing data transparency. Application developers often do not implement each and every component in their design. In open-source environments, it is common for a developer to borrow code written by other developers. Many vendors also supply software development kits (SDK) that provide core libraries, debuggers, emulators, and sample code in order to make app-development easier. APIs are also available to interface one application with another. However, any code that executes as part of an application also inherits the access permissions granted to the application. Therefore, even if the developer's code is not actively collecting any data, the developer cannot assure that the library/API calls in the application are also not performing it. This prevents the application from being transparent about its data collection attempts.

Eco-system diversity. Current applications let users perform more than just a single task. For example, a news application pulls articles of interest from different sources. It also allows the user to share an article via one of many social networking platforms. It displays advertisements for trade magazines and periodicals based on the articles often explored by the user. It can help a group of readers in a locality to get together in person to discuss a story they all have been following closely. In other words, a news reader application also has components like a social networking application and a local search application, and is also an advertising platform. Given this diversity, will it be possible to enforce a privacy method that can cater to the requirements of all components? The technical solutions we discussed are in fact very specific to an application type! It is also unknown if different privacy solutions can work in conjunction to provide the necessary guarantees from all components of the application.

Privacy from carriers. Network operators routinely collect metadata on the traffic flowing through their networks. Ensuring the privacy of data collected at these operators is a difficult task, partly because the data must be visible to the carrier in order to route traffic, and partly because "lawful interception" rules require the operators to leave avenues open for interception. Interception technology has also become commonplace. Encrypted communications ought to be a standard in such environments, but lacks adoption in majority of applications.

Mobile privacy interface. Privacy disclosures often take the form of lengthy documents. Application vendors have shown effort in making them understandable by minimizing the amount of legal terminology. While this is certainly encouraging in desktop systems, it is not sufficient in a mobile interface. Mobile devices are not suitable for extensive reading, and the privacy policy should not become a long reading exercise for the user. Innovative designs are necessary to compress the most important parts of a mobile application's privacy policy, and present it using visualizations, instead of text. Standardizations for the format of a privacy policy are also required to facilitate fair comparisons. Besides the presentation of a privacy policy, interfaces are also required for users to review permissions, data access logs, and take actions accordingly.

Quasi-identifiers. Data collected from a user's mobile device do not pose a privacy threat to the user if it cannot be associated back to the user. The association is trivial if the collected data has personally identifiable information with unique identifiers (e.g. device ID). It is argued that without such unique identifiers the association is not possible, and hence privacy guarantees can be provided for any application that does not collect personally identifiable information. Such a perspective is flawed, since non-identifying information can sometimes uniquely identify an individual, especially when they are used in combination. This has been demonstrated many times, over different forms of data. Unfortunately, no technique exists to determine if a certain type of data can be used as a quasi-identifier, and if so, what contribution will it play in the identification. The challenge is in knowing how much sharing a user can do before becoming identifiable by the shared data.

Privacy by design. Mobile applications are developed by a wide spectrum of developers, ranging from novice programmers to dedicated teams of professional software developers. Most applications are designed with the objective of generating revenue, either directly from the user, or indirectly through advertisements or data sharing. Privacy is not an active part of the design of the application, and is added as a supplement at the end of the design cycle. This makes it difficult to restructure the data and control flow in the application once a privacy threat is identified. Privacy efforts in the application development cycle ought to be more proactive and user-centric. An application should have privacy settings enabled by default, and should attempt to accommodate all privacy expectations of the user. In fact, privacy should be a core functionality in the application, and be embedded in the design from the very beginning. However, application development can be prolonged if such requirements are to be met. An application developer may also not have the training necessary to accomplish such extensive design objectives.

10.6 Conclusion

Mobile devices will dominate the personal computing arena in the years to come. For businesses, this platform provides a rich environment to learn more about the user's intentions, likes, and dislikes, and use it to create custom experiences for every user. Mobile applications engage in the collection of varied types of user data, such as demographics, location, and behavior, and have been found to share it with multiple third-party service providers. This opens up a number of privacy concerns since users are no longer able to control who sees their data, and how it is used. Solutions based on best practice guidelines, public awareness, and novel privacy-preserving algorithms have been proposed to cater to such concerns. Unfortunately, their adoption has been slow, leaving behind a number of challenges to address. An effective solution will require application providers to consider privacy during design, users to be aware of available privacy options, and researchers to involve the existing infrastructure as much as possible in novel proposals.

Acknowledgments We thank the graduate and undergraduate students of Computer Science at the University of Denver who explored the privacy issues and solutions highlighted here, and helped bring it together in the form of this chapter.

References

1. Baden R, Bender A, Spring N, Bhattacharjee B, Starin B (2009) Persona: an online social network with user-defined privacy. In: Proceedings of the ACM SIGCOMM 2009 conference on data communication, pp 135–146
2. Bamba B, Liu L, Pesti P, Wang T (2008) Supporting anonymous location queries in mobile environments with privacy grid. In: Proceedings of the 17th international world wide web conference, pp 237–246
3. Barbaro M, Zeller T (2006) A face is exposed for AOL Searcher No. 4417749. New York Times
4. Cutillo LA, Molva R, Strufe T (2009) Safebook: a privacy-preserving online social network leveraging on real-life trust. IEEE Commun Mag 94–101
5. Dewri R, Ray I, Ray I, Whitley D (2010) Query m-invariance: preventing query disclosures in continuous location-based services. In: Proceedings of the 11th international conference on mobile data management, pp 95–104
6. Dewri R, Thurimella R (2013) Can a Phone's GPS lie intelligently? IEEE Comput Mag 46 (2):91–93

7. Dewri R, Thurimella R (2014) Exploiting service similarity for privacy in location based search queries. IEEE Trans Parallel Distrib Syst 25(2):374–383
8. Dingledine R, Mathewson N, Syverson P (2004) TOR: the second-generation onion router. In: Proceedings of the 13th USENIX security symposium, p 21
9. Enck W, Gilbert P, Chun BG, Cox L, Jung J, McDaniel P, Sheth A (2010) TaintDroid: an information-flow tracking system for realtime privacy monitoring on smartphones. In: Proceedings of the 9th USENIX symposium on operating systems design and implementation, pp 393–407
10. Federal Trade Commission: mobile privacy disclosures: building trust through transparency. Technical report. www.ftc.gov/os/2013/02/130201mobileprivacyreport.pdf
11. Federrath H, Jerichow A, Pfitzmann A: MIXes in mobile communication systems: location management with privacy. In: Proceedings of the 1st international workshop on information hiding, pp 121–135
12. Fredrikson M, Livshits B (2011) RePriv: re-imagining content personalization and in-browser privacy. In: Proceedings of the 2011 IEEE symposium on security and privacy, pp 131–146
13. Fuchs A, Chaudhuri A, Foster J (2009) SCanDroid: automated security certification of android applications. Technical report, University of Maryland (2009)
14. Gedik B, Liu L (2008) Protecting location privacy with personalized k-anonymity: architecture and algorithms. IEEE Trans Mob Comput 7(1):1–18
15. Golle P (2006) Revisiting the uniqueness of simple demographics in the US population. In: Proceedings of the 5th ACM workshop on privacy in electronic society, pp 77–80
16. Golle P, Partridge K (2009) On the anonymity of home/work location Pairs. In: Proceedings of the 7th international conference on pervasive computing, pp 390–397
17. Goyal V, Pandey O, Sahai A, Waters B (2006) Attribute-based encryption for fine-grained access control of encrypted data. In: Proceedings of the 13th conference on computer and communications security, pp 89–98
18. Gruteser M, Grunwald D (2003) Anonymous usage of location-based services through spatial and temporal cloaking. In: Proceedings of the 1st international conference on mobile systems, applications, and services, pp 31–42
19. Guha S, Cheng B, Francis P (2011) Privad: practical privacy in online advertising. In: Proceedings of the 8th USENIX conference on networked systems design and implementation, p 13
20. Hazay C, Lindell Y (2008) efficient protocols for set intersection and pattern matching with security against malicious and covert adversaries. Theory Cryptogr 155–175
21. Hoh B, Gruteser M, Xiong H, Alrabady A (2006) Enhancing security and privacy in traffic-monitoring systems. IEEE Pervasive Comput 5(4):38–46
22. Jarecki S, Liu X (2010) Fast secure computation of set intersection. In: Proceedings of the 7th conference on security and cryptography for networks, pp 418–435
23. Kesdogan D, Federrath H, Jerichow A, Pfitzmann A (1996) Location management strategies increasing privacy in mobile communication. In: Proceedings of the 12th IFIP international information security conference, pp 39–48
24. Krishnamurthy B, Wills CE (2009) Privacy diffusion on the web: a longitudinal perspective. In: Proceedings of the 18th international conference on world wide web, pp 541–550
25. Krumm J (2007) Inference attacks on location tracks. In: Proceedings of the 5th international conference on pervasive computing, pp 127–143
26. Kushilevitz E, Ostrovsky R (1997) Replication is not needed: single database, computationally-private information retrieval. In: Proceedings of the 38th annual symposium on foundations of computer science, p 364
27. Malin B (2006) Re-identification of familial database records. In: AMIA annual symposium proceedings, pp 524–528
28. Mayer JR, Mitchell JC (2012) Third-party web tracking: policy and technology. In: Proceedings of the 2012 IEEE symposium on security and privacy, pp 413–427
29. Narayanan A, Shmatikov V (2008) Robust de-anonymization of large sparse datasets. In: Proceedings of the 2008 IEEE Symposium on security and privacy, pp 111–125

30. Narayanan A, Shmatikov V (2009) De-Anonymizing social networks. In: Proceedings of the 2009 IEEE symposium on security and privacy, pp 173–187
31. Narayanan A, Thiagarajan N, Lakhani M, Hamburg M, Boneh D (2011) Location privacy via private proximity testing. In: Proceedings of the network and distributed system security symposium
32. O'Clair B, Egnor D, Greenfield LE (2011) Scoring local search results based on location prominence. US Patent 8046371 B2
33. Qiu D, Boneh D, Lo S, Enge P (2009) Robust location tag generation from noisy location data for security applications. In: The Institute of navigation international technical meeting
34. Reznichenko A, Guha S, Francis P (2011) Auctions in do-not-track compliant internet advertising. In: Proceedings of the 18th ACM conference on computer and communications security, pp 667–676
35. Shin H, Vaidya J, Atluri V (2011) A profile anonymization model for location based services. J Comput Secur 19(5):795–833
36. Souppaya M, Scarfone K (2013) Guidelines for managing the security of mobile devices in the enterprise. Technical report 800-124 Rev 1. National Institute of Standards and Technology
37. Thurm S, Kane YI (2010) Your apps are watching you. What They Know: The Wall Street J
38. Truste: US 2013 Consumer data privacy study—mobile edition. Technical report, Truste Inc
39. United States Department of Justice: Retention Periods of Major Cellular Service Providers. https://www.aclu.org/files/pdfs/freespeech/retention_periods_of_major_cellular_service_providers.pdf
40. Xi Y, Schwiebert L, Shi W (2013) Privacy preserving shortest path routing with an application to navigation. Pervasive Mobile Comput

Chapter 11
Privacy in Biometric Systems

Hisham Al-Assam, Torben Kuseler, Sabah Jassim and Sherali Zeadally

11.1 Introduction

Biometrics are physiological and/or behavioral characteristics of a person that have been used to provide an automatic proof of identity in a growing list of applications including crime and terrorism fighting, forensics, access and border control, securing e-/m-commerce transactions, and service entitlements. In recent years, a great deal of research into a variety of new and traditional biometrics has widened the scope of investigations beyond improving accuracy into mechanisms that deal with serious concerns raised about the potential misuse of collected biometric data. Despite the long list of biometrics' benefits, privacy concerns have become widely shared due to the fact that every time the biometric of a person is checked, a trace is left that could reveal personal and confidential information. In fact, biometric-based recognition has an inherent privacy problem as it relies on capturing, analyzing, and storing personal data about us as individuals. For example, biometric systems deal with data related to the way we look (face, iris), the way we walk (gait), the way we talk (speaker recognition), the way we write (handwriting), the way we type on a keyboard (keystroke), the way we read (eye movement), and many more. Privacy has become a serious concern for the public as biometric systems are increasingly deployed in many applications ranging from accessing our account on a smart phone or computer to border control and national biometric cards on a very large scale. For example, the Unique Identification Authority of India (UIDAI) has issued 56 million biometric cards as of January 2014 [1], where each biometric card holds templates of the ten fingers, the two irises, and the face. An essential factor behind

H. Al-Assam (✉) · T. Kuseler · S. Jassim
Applied Computing Department, University of Buckingham, Buckingham, UK
e-mail: hisham.al-assam@buckingham.ac.uk

S. Zeadally
College of Communication and Information, University of Kentucky,
Lexington, KY, USA

the growing popularity of biometrics in recent years is the fact that biometric sensors have become a lot cheaper as well as easier to install and handle. CCTV cameras are installed nearly everywhere and almost all smart phones are equipped with a camera, microphone, fingerprint scanner, and probably very soon an iris scanner.

Biometrics can be a very effective tool to keep us safe and secure, prevent individuals from applying for multiple passports or driving licenses, and keep the bad guys out or under control. However, the fact that we are surrounded by so many biometric sensors does limit our privacy in one way or another. The price we might have to pay for using many biometrics-reliant applications such as access control to a building, authorizing payments in supermarkets, and public transports is the loss of privacy as a result of being tracked in almost all of our daily life activities. Furthermore, recent research into biometrics shows that more and more personal information can be revealed from biometric data such as gender, age, ethnicity, and even some critical health problems such as diabetes, vision problems, Alzheimer's disease, and so on. Such confidential information might be used, for example, to discriminate between individuals when it comes to insurance, jobs, border entry enforcement, and so on.

This chapter is mainly concerned with privacy issues and solutions surrounding the use of biometrics as a means of recognizing individuals. As biometric security and biometric privacy are strongly related, it is useful to highlight the difference between these two topics first. *Biometric security* is concerned with protecting biometric data against theft for impersonation of the owner of the biometric data. *Biometric privacy* is concerned with preventing misuse of the biometric system for purposes of tracing and gaining information that may result in the person's loss of civil rights, discrimination against the person, victimization, and/or even denial of access to services.

The rest of this chapter is organized as follows: Sect. 11.2 provides essential background information on biometrics, while Sect. 11.3 discusses several privacy concerns about biometrics. In Sect. 11.4 privacy solutions proposed to address these concerns are explained. Outstanding challenges and opportunities for future research directions are discussed in Sect. 11.5.

11.2 Background on Biometrics

A reliable identity management system is a key component to preventing identity theft and satisfies the increased security requirements in a wide range of applications ranging from controlling international border crossings to accessing remotely stored personal information and assets. Establishing the identity of a person is a key task in any such identity management system. Typically, there are three ways to establish the identity of an individual, each of which has its own advantages and limitations [2]:

- **Knowledge-based authentication** or "something you know" that typically relies on a memorized password or PIN (personal identification number). A random and long password offers a strong security mechanism for user authentication. However, in practice, humans have difficulties in memorizing complex passwords, and passwords that they can easily remember are often short and, therefore, simple to guess or determined by a brute-force/dictionary attack.
- **Object-based authentication** or "something you have," which relies on the physical possession of an object, such as a token. The main drawback of a physical token is that, when lost or stolen, an impostor can gain unauthorized access.
- **Identity-based authentication** or "something you are," that is, *biometrics*. Biometric-based authentication offers an advantage over other authentication factors in that a legitimate user does not need to remember or carry anything. Furthermore, biometric-based authentication is known to be more reliable than traditional authentication due to the fact that it is directly linked with the identity of individuals. However, there exist several challenges, as we explain later in this chapter, which make biometric systems far from perfect. For example, unlike other credentials such as PINs, passwords, or smart cards, once biometric related information is compromised, it is impossible to make this information private again.

Biometric systems aim to identify or verify individuals' identity based on physical characteristics (e.g., face, iris, fingerprint, DNA, or hand geometry), and/or behavioral characteristics (e.g., speech, gait, or signature). A typical biometric system has two stages, enrolment and recognition. Figure 11.1 illustrates the process of the biometric enrolment stage (the face image was used from the Extended Yale Face Database B [3]), in which a user starts by presenting their biometric data to a biometric sensor (usually in a controlled environment). If the quality of the captured biometric sample is found to be adequate, the enrolment process proceeds to a pre-processing procedure to prepare the sample for the next step. A feature extraction technique is then used to extract a digital discriminating feature vector of the individual, called biometric template (BT), which will then be stored (often also called "enrolled") alongside the individual's identifier (ID) in a database.

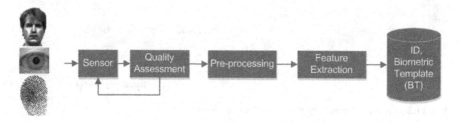

Fig. 11.1 A typical enrolment stage of a biometric system

At the recognition stage, biometric systems can function in two modes depending on the application context, namely authentication or identification mode.

11.2.1 Biometric-Based Authentication

Biometric-based authentication (also known as verification) is a one-to-one comparison of a freshly captured biometric sample(s), known as query, against an enrolled BT as illustrated in Fig. 11.2. In this mode, a user claims an identity and the biometric system aims to verify the authenticity of the claimed identity (e.g., the system answers the question: "Are you who you say you are?"). For example, authentication might be used when a user wants to access his or her bank account or computer. The matching process uses a distance or similarity function to calculate a score indicating the similarity between the stored BT and the fresh feature vector extracted from the query sample. If the matching score is high enough, that is, close enough to the enrolled template, the biometric system grants access to the user. Otherwise the requested access is rejected. The term "high enough" is determined by the administrator depending on the level of tolerance necessary for the specific application. This allows the system administrator to adjust the rates of false acceptance (i.e., wrongly accepted imposters as genuine users) and false rejection (i.e., wrongly rejected genuine users) to the desired levels. Typically, there is a trade-off between the false acceptance rate (FAR) and the false rejection rate (FRR), in which the reduction of one rate causes an increase in the other. Most biometric systems are configured to be highly secure by maintaining a very low (e.g., 1 in 10,000) FAR and an acceptable FRR. In an access control system, for example, it will generally be less problematic to have a false rejection by asking the genuine user to re-scan their biometric, rather than a false acceptance in which an unauthorized individual will be granted access.

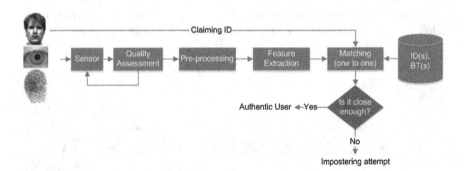

Fig. 11.2 Typical biometric system in authentication mode

11.2.2 Biometric-Based Identification

Biometric-based identification is a one-to-many comparison of the query against all templates in the database as illustrated in Fig. 11.3. In this mode, a biometric system aims to identify an individual by searching the set of available identities or the system returns "Not enrolled" if the matching module of the biometric system cannot find the identity. Identification functionality can be further classified into positive and negative identification. In positive identification, an individual attempts to positively identify themselves to the system without explicitly claiming an identity (i.e., the system answers the question: "Are you someone who is known to the system?"). Positive identification might be deployed, for example, to grant access to resources such as buildings or computers where the system knows the set of enrolled users. In contrast, in negative identification (also known as screening), an individual attempts to conceal their true identity and the system aims to answer the question: "Are you who you say you are not?" Screening might be used by national border agencies to check if a passenger's identity is on a watch-list or by authorities to prevent issuing multiple national ID cards, passports, or driving licenses to a single individual.

Biometric systems such as face recognition can be deployed in identification and authentication modes, depending on the application. For example, face-based authentication can be used to provide access control (i.e., letting the genuine person in), while face-based identification can also be applied as a "watch–list" system to find some particular individuals in a crowd, that is, keeping the targeted people out.

11.2.3 Challenges in Biometric Systems

Over the years, a large number of biometric modalities (also called biometric traits) together with a variety of feature extraction and matching schemes have been investigated. The suitability of any biometric modality for an application depends on several factors such as universality, uniqueness, invariance over time, measurability, usability, and cost [4]. The challenges in biometric research activities have expanded recently to include the maintenance of privacy and security of biometric systems beside the traditional work to improve accuracy, scalability, and usability.

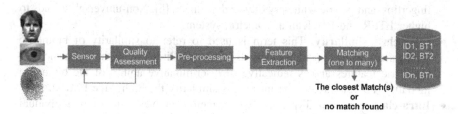

Fig. 11.3 Typical biometric system in identification mode

In other words, the challenge in biometrics is to design a system that is highly accurate, easily scalable to large datasets, convenient to use, and secure at the same time. In what follows, several challenges of biometric systems are briefly explained, leaving further detailed discussions on biometric privacy concerns to Sect. 11.3.

11.2.3.1 Biometric Accuracy

An ideal biometric system should have perfect accuracy, that is, it always recognizes genuine users and rejects imposters correctly. However, in practice, a biometric system can make four types of errors:

1. *False non-match rate* (FNMR), also known as false rejection rate (FRR), occurs when two samples, for example, collected at different times, of the same biometric modality of an individual are not recognized as a match.
2. *False match rate* (FMR), also known as false acceptance rate (FAR), occurs when two samples from different individuals are incorrectly recognized as a match.
3. *Failure to enroll rate* (FTER), occurs when an individual is unable to present the required biometric modalities (e.g., because of a finger or hand cut), is unable to interact correctly with the sensor, or the captured biometric samples quality is very poor.
4. *Failure to capture rate* (FTCR), occurs when a biometric sample provided by an individual during the recognition stage cannot be acquired or processed reliably.

In practice, these biometric errors can occur due to the following factors [5]:

- **Noisy sensor data**. Defective or improperly maintained sensors can lead to the capture of low quality and noisy biometric samples, which results in a significant reduction in the recognition accuracy by increasing the FRR of the biometric system.
- **Non-universality**. A biometric modality can be considered universal when every individual in a target population is able to present the biometric modality for recognition. Although universality is an essential requirement, not all biometric modalities are perfectly universal. The National Institute of Standards and Technology (NIST) has reported that it is not possible to obtain good quality fingerprint images from 2 % of the population, for example, people with hand-related disabilities, manual workers with many cuts and bruises on their fingertips, and people with very oily or dry fingers [6]. Non-universality leads to higher FTER and FTCR in a biometric system.
- **Inter-class similarity**. This term is used to refer to similarity of biometric samples from different individuals. It is strongly linked with the uniqueness of biometric features and is indicative of discriminative ability of the biometric modality (i.e., the greater the inter-class similarity the higher the FMRs).
- **Intra-class variation**. Typically, two biometric samples of the same individual are always different, which results in FNM errors explained earlier. These

intra-class variations may be due to improper interaction of the user with the sensor (e.g., changes in rotations or poses), changes in environmental conditions such as lighting conditions and inherent changes in the biometric modality such appearance changes due to ageing or facial hair.

- **Biometric scalability**. Ideally, the number of enrolled individuals should have no significant effect on the performance of the biometric systems in terms of both accuracy and speed. When a biometric system is set up to function in the authentication mode, scalability is not a problem because each authentication attempt involves one-to-one matching, that is, matching the query with the stored template of an individual. However, the number of enrolled individuals has crucial impact on the performance of biometric systems in the identification mode, where one-to-many matching is required to have a biometric sample identified. For example, if the size of a database is a million, and each matching requires 1 m, then the time required to identify one individual would be more than 16 min. Therefore, biometric identification systems that operate on large-scale databases involve some kind of filtering or indexing based on extrinsic (e.g., gender, ethnicity, age, etc.) or intrinsic (e.g., fingerprint pattern class) factors to prune the search procedure [7].

11.2.3.2 Security and Privacy of Biometric Systems

Public acceptance of biometric systems has a crucial impact on their success due to potential or perception of misuse of the collected biometric data. The growing deployment of biometric systems as a proof of identity tool for access control to physical facilities, entitlement to services, and in the fight against crime and terrorism has become a necessity in modern days, but it is also becoming a source of privacy and security concerns. Traditionally, the focus of biometrics research has been on accuracy, speed, cost, and robustness challenges, but gradually the scope widened to security and privacy issues of biometric systems. Questions such as: "What if my biometric data has been stolen or misused?" have recently attracted attention not only to reassure users about privacy intrusion but also to prevent misuse of stolen data.

Although a biometric-based authentication system is known to be more reliable than traditional authentication schemes, the system is subject to failure due to intrinsic factors mentioned earlier or adversary attacks. The security of biometric systems can be undermined in various ways. For example, a biometric template can be replaced by an impostor's template in a system database or be stolen and replayed [8]. As a result, the impostor can gain unauthorized access to whatever the owner has authorized access to. Moreover, it has been shown that it is possible to create a physical spoof starting from biometric templates [5]. For example, a "hill climbing attack" on a biometric system can be used to generate a good approximation of the target template in a finite number of iterations [9]. It is also possible to reconstruct fingerprint images from standard templates, which might then fool the fingerprint recognition system [10]. Furthermore, certain biometric data is not secret and can be easily acquired without the knowledge of the user. Individuals usually unintentionally leave (poor-quality) fingerprints everywhere such as on a glass, or a hidden camera can capture an image of a face or iris [11]. In fact, the level of secrecy and privacy varies greatly among different biometric modalities (e.g., the covert acquisition of face images or voice samples is much easier compared to collecting retina or palm vein samples). The effect of all these attacks on the security and acceptability of biometrics are not difficult to imagine and their consequences are far from limited to individuals. However, the related privacy concerns of such attacks and misuses of a system by insiders and/or secondary users are far from obvious. Section 11.3 discusses these biometric privacy concerns in more detail.

11.2.4 Multi-Modal and Multi-factor Biometric Recognition

Multi-modal and/or multi-factor biometric solutions have been proposed to overcome most of the aforementioned challenges that could degrade the performance of a biometric system. *Multi-modal systems* rely on combining two or more biometric modalities to establish the identity of an individual. For example, face, voice, and signature were combined together in the EU-funded SecurePhone FP6 Project [12] to provide a strong mean of authentication for mobile devices. Multi-modal biometrics have been deployed in a wide range of applications such as border entry and exit, access control, law enforcement, and network security. It has been demonstrated that using a combination of biometric modalities can significantly improve recognition accuracy by reducing FNMR and FMR. In addition, such an approach provides a secondary means of recognition if biometric samples of sufficient quality cannot be acquired from a particular individual. On the other hand, *multi-factor* biometric systems typically combine biometric data with knowledge-based and/or object-based authentication factors to produce a single representation of individuals. Multi-factor recognition can be very effective to improve recognition accuracy and is at the same time very easy to implement. For example, face biometric recognition can be combined with a four-digit PIN to significantly lower false acceptance rates. More details on exploiting multi-factor recognition as a means for generating cancellable or revocable templates to improve the privacy of biometric systems will be presented in Sect. 11.4.

11.3 Privacy Concerns with Biometrics

The growing number of applications that use biometrics coupled with the increased capabilities of biometric sensors in terms of resolution, accuracy, and capturing biometric data unobtrusively, introduces new challenging problems for maintaining privacy. In the past, fingerprints were only used to identify potential suspects at crime scenes, that is, the number of collected, analyzed, and stored fingerprints was relatively small. Nowadays, thousands of applications and devices use fingerprints to identify legitimate users. For example, Apple's latest iPhone generation, the iPhone 5 s, features "Touch ID," a fingerprint identity sensor that allows iPhone users to use their fingerprint instead of a PIN code to unlock their iPhones. Another smart phone example is the "Vital Signs Camera—Philips" app [13], already downloaded by hundreds of thousands of users. This app allows you to "Measure your heart rate and breathing rate from a distance, simply by using the camera of your iPad or iPhone!" Although the accuracy of the taken measurements might not be as good as measurements from dedicated heart rate monitors, these apps enable nearly everybody to easily and extensively collect sensitive biomedical data of any person in their proximity.

Improved sensor technology has also had an impact on maintaining and undermining privacy, in particular for biometric sensors that can work and collect data remotely (i.e., from a distance) without the individual's consent. Today, many of us (i.e., everybody living in an urban area) are monitored regularly. In 2011, it was estimated that on average a citizen of London in the United Kingdom, is caught approximately 100 times per day on a CCTV camera. This number is expected to increase due to continued reduction in the cost of CCTV camera production, installation, maintenance, and automatic data analyses.

The ease with which biometric data can be collected, processed, and stored has led to a large and fast growing number of huge biometric datasets on local (e.g., individual companies), national (e.g., US Visitor and Immigrant Status Indicator Technology (US-VISIT)) and international (e.g., European fingerprint database (EURODAC)) levels. This ever-increasing amount of information available about a human person was firstly named by Irma van der Ploeg as the "informatization of the body" [2]. This growing digitization of the human body away from its natural, very diverse form of physical existence into standardized digital code and information "may eventually affect embodiment and [human] identity as such" and finally offend human dignity [3]. Undoubtedly, recent advances in surveillance and sensors technologies will rapidly accelerate the speed by which this fully digitized and "informatized" body will become reality. It is questionable if fair information principles, and here in particular, the *principle of proportionality* stating "that identification systems should only be implemented if the benefits are worth the social costs, including the invasion of privacy, loss of autonomy, social discrimination, or imposition of conformity", are always respected [4]. It is more likely that technology advances will increase the risk of misuse of the available information as a result of unethical and/or illegal practices, if the users' sensitive data and privacy is not adequately protected.

However, it is important to note that it is the utilization of the biometric system that determines the impact on privacy, not the biometric modality itself [5]. For example, a company could legitimately use a face image recognition system to restrict access to sensitive and private company data. Also, face images from a

CCTV camera could be used to identify potential suspects at a crime scene. It is worth noting that the same biometric modality (face) is used in different applications; once to protect privacy, and once to infringe it.

The privacy concerns about biometrics emerge from four main biometric data misuses that are described below. It is important to highlight that the threat to privacy can either arise from the inside or from the outside of the involved systems and organizations. A threat coming from the inside can be, for example, a person (e.g., a system administrator), who works for one of the involved organizations. These people are often called secondary users. A threat from the outside can be, for example, an attacker, who has no further relation to the involved organizations or individuals and tries to attack the systems just for his or her benefit (e.g., to sell the stolen or collected private information).

11.3.1 Unnecessary and Unauthorized Collection

To preserve the individual's privacy as much as possible, the amount of data collected should be always minimized. Biometric systems should only be used in scenarios where the system or organization security will benefit from the installation. For example, if access to a specific area in a company does not need to be protected, no fingerprint or face recognition system should be installed at the entry points to that area. However, additional systems of that kind are often installed by companies, just to monitor and record employees' behavior. This is a typical example of a privacy threat coming from the inside.

Unauthorized and concealed collection of biometric data (e.g., via hidden cameras) is another privacy risk and often performed from the outside. As mentioned before, cameras are now widely used to monitor our everyday life. Very often, people benefit from this monitoring, for example, traffic jams or over-crowded underground stations can be easily and quickly detected and such information can be passed on to the other passengers to avoid these situations. However, this extensive data collection and analysis can also lead to privacy concerns. In 2012, politicians in Argentina announced that they will create a new centralized biometric database containing face images of Argentina's citizens. This announcement immediately raised resistance and critics pointed out that this new system could discourage political engagement and protests, because the database could also be used to help identify undesired demonstrators and suppress political activities. Another example of a biometric related privacy concern occurs in night clubs and bars in cities like Chicago and San Francisco in the United States. These bars use their security cameras now together with face detection software to broadcast real-time information on the number of male and female visitors in the club, together with their average age groups. This information can then be used by others to decide which bar to visit.

11.3.2 Unauthorized Use and Application of Cross-Matching

A further privacy concern arises from the fact that an individual's biometric data collected for different purposes and unrelated applications can be cross-referenced by comparing stored biometric templates. This allows, for example, the linking of bank datasets and financial records to medical related datasets, if both involved organizations (i.e., banks and medical agencies) hold the same biometric record or template of that individual. The actual sharing could either happen if an insider of one organization illegitimately shares the sensitive data with the other organization for his or her own financial benefits [14], or if both organizations agree to share the data within a strategic relationship benefitting both of them [15]. An example of a negative consequence of this type of information or application cross-matching and data sharing could be that a mortgage application of an individual is declined. The mortgage issuing bank has automatic access to the person's financial status via its own user records. If this bank has now also access to the applicant's medical records, a combined assessment could indicate that the mortgage risk is too high and the application is declined. Instead, an assessment of the financial status only could lead to an acceptance of the mortgage application.

11.3.3 Function or Purpose Creep

Function or purpose creep occurs when the biometric information collected by an application for one specific purpose (e.g., to give access to certain material or places) is also used in a completely different application scenario without the user's consent. One famous example of a large scale biometric function creep is the European Dactyloscopy (EURODAC) fingerprint database for identifying asylum seekers [16]. The original purpose of this database was to "help the effective application of the Dublin convention on handling claims for asylum." However, soon after the database was established, access to the data was also granted to other police and law enforcement agencies. This function creep then finally led to an official statement of the European Data Protection Supervisor (EDPS) saying that [17]:

> Just because the data has already been collected, it should not be used for another purpose which may have a far-reaching negative impact on the lives of individuals. To intrude upon the privacy of individuals and risk stigmatizing them requires strong justification and the Commission has simply not provided sufficient reason why asylum seekers should be singled out for such treatment.

Similar concerns were also raised in the United States where innocent UScitizens were imprisoned by mistake because of a large scale fingerprint sharing program called Secure Communities. This program administered by the Federal Bureau for Investigation (FBI) and the Department of Homeland Security wrongly identified

James Makowski as an illegal immigrant and he was placed in a maximum security prison for two months before the authorities realized their error and released him.

11.3.4 Disclosure of Medical Related Information

Biometric sensors may intentionally or unintentionally collect additional information (i.e., information beyond the data required to perform the intended task of biometric-based user identification and authentication, which may then reveal highly sensitive and personal information about the observed individuals). This contradicts the right of "informational privacy" that is, beside the physical and decisional privacy, one of the three elements of privacy every human should have [18]. "Informational privacy" refers here to the freedom of a person to decide who has access and is allowed to collect, process, and store personal information about him or her. One example where this right can be easily broken is biometrics based on motor skills. Data collected via a distant video camera for gait recognition, may also reveal physical handicaps of that individual. This surplus of collected data could then be used to discriminate or intimidate that person. This situation becomes even more of a problem when these actions are happening silently from a distance without the individual being aware of the ongoing process, or openly applied to vulnerable groups such as immigrants as well as the general public in the form of a biometric border [19].

The possible consequence that an individual will be discriminated against because of sensitive information revealed about him or her immediately raised the question within the research community of whether "privacy" really is at the center of the problem or if the "discrimination" following an information disclosure is the real problem [20]. People are not put at risk just because their ethical background, age, gender, or sexual orientation was revealed from the collected biometric data. The discrimination and the social actions against them based on the data expose them to real risks. However, addressing this general problem of mankind on the social and psychological level is extremely difficult. Researchers working in the field of biometrics continue to focus mainly on how to enhance the individual's biometric data privacy in the first place.

To protect the individual's privacy as much as possible, the following principles should be followed in order to address and minimize the above mentioned three privacy problems [21]:

- **Identity privacy**. Binding of the stored biometric data and the individual's additional identity information such as age, gender, and so on, should be minimized and protected. A close, unprotected link between the biometric data and the other stored identity information allows cross-referencing this information with data from other sources to generate, for example, more detailed user profiles.
- **Irreversibility and unlinkability**. Collected biometric data should be converted into a different, application specific, and non-reversible form before it is stored

in the database. This prevents application cross-matching and the use of bio-metric data outside its intended original application.

The following sections highlight examples of biometric modalities used today and what kind of potentially discriminating and privacy effecting—additional information can be extracted from the collected biometric sensor data. It is important to mention that the biometrics modalities and their corresponding bio-metrics sensors vary in terms of their actual usage in today's available applications, complexity of the involved biometric sensors, amount of additional information that can be revealed from the collected data, and the risk to which they expose the individual's privacy.

11.3.5 Fingerprints

One of the most widely used biometric modalities is the fingerprint. Fingerprint sensors are, for example, integrated in laptops to allow or deny access to the computer and used to identify individuals at border control or within company premises. Beside their original aim to reliably identify an individual in the afore-mentioned scenarios, research has showed that fingerprints or images of an entire finger can be used to reveal further information about the person (e.g., medical disorders like Down's or Turner syndromes).

Research further identified a correlation between fingerprints and the sexual orientation, that is, homosexuality [22]. These research results are highly contro-versial within the academic research community because they were identified as being far from conclusive [23] and human fingers are formed during prenatal development, which can be seen well before sexual orientations are developed. However, its publication in a well-known neuroscience journal clearly attracted attention within the general public [24] and may have persuaded the public to prejudge people.

11.3.6 Handwriting and Voice/Speech

The handwriting style and voice/speech are further biometric modalities that can be used to identify individuals as, for example, used in the "SecurePhone" project to sign contracts on smart phones. However, research showed that degradations in handwriting skills and changes in the writing style can also be a sign of Alzheimer's disease [25]. It was shown in particular that writing of cursive letters are chal-lenging for people suffering from Alzheimer's disease and that changes and anomalies in how they write cursive letters can be identified by a biometric system. This is in particular applicable to human signatures, which normally contain several cursive letters and paths. Similar findings were published on the detection of

Parkinson's disease [26]. The study showed that two simple writing tasks can differentiate healthy individuals from individuals suffering from Parkinson's disease. Signs of Parkinson's disease can also be detected by visible speech impairments [27] identified, for example, through regular voice/speech-based recognition, which has become increasingly popular. Technologies such as Apple's Siri are used now by millions of people on their iPhones and iPads [28] and could easily analyze and detect speech changes during normal operation.

However, not only medical disorders such as Alzheimer's and Parkinson's diseases can be identified by analyses of an individual's handwriting [29]. Research results have also suggested that more common and wide-spread social and health problems such as misuse of alcohol [30] or marijuana [31] can be detected via handwriting analyses too. This information about an individual can then, for example, be very interesting to an employer during a job interview or to monitor existing employees and their performance.

11.3.7   Retinal Vascular and Vein Pattern

Currently biometric modalities such as retinal or vein images are not widely used because these modalities are seen as more intrusive compared to fingerprints or handwriting. A retinal scanner illuminates the blood vessels in the eye using infrared light and then captures the reflected light for processing. This is seen as a potentially dangerous procedure to the eye and the eyesight by many people [32]. However, because of their high accuracy and advances in the scanner technology [33], it can be assumed that they will become more acceptable and popular in the near future. Nonetheless, today, available retinal scanners are already able to reveal medical conditions a person might have if the retinal image is examined by an automatic detection algorithm such as Automated Detection of Diabetic Retinopathy (ADDR) [34] or a human expert. Beside the given example of ADDR as one possible health condition revealed via retina scans, more than 100 genes have already been identified as contributing to human hereditary retinal degenerations [35]. This knowledge imposes a great privacy risk, as individuals might be rejected for certain jobs or have to pay higher health insurance premiums if the genes that are responsible for the retinal degeneration are also known to be contributing to other medical conditions. One such example is the USH2A gene, which is known to cause *retinitis pigmentosa* (a degenerative eye disease that causes severe vision impairment and often blindness), but also contributes to the Usher-Syndrome (genetic disorder resulting in hearing loss). This cross-reference could easily be made and negative implications could arise for the individual, regardless of whether this individual really develops a medical condition such as the Usher-Syndrome in his or her life or not.

Similar to the technology used to capture retinal pattern are vein pattern sensors. A Near-Infrared (NIR) sensor illuminates the region of interest (e.g., palm) and the reflected signals are then used to capture an image of the vein pattern structure.

An example of a commercial solution is the BASEmetric™ Finger vein authentication (VeinID) device, used in several hospitals in Ohio, United States, to help with returning patient identification. However, researchers showed that the captured vein structure can also reveal sensitive information about possible health conditions (e.g., palm veins can reveal the Hypothenar Hammer Syndrome (HHS) [36]). HHS is caused by repetitive use of the hand "as a hammer," as, for example, in contact sports such as boxing or fighting. This knowledge could persuade people to prejudge individuals as aggressive or violent if the privacy of this information is not adequately protected and becomes public.

The examples discussed in this section clearly show the importance of privacy within the biometric area and that sensitive and personal biometric data needs to be protected so that it cannot be used outside its original collected and designed purpose. Section 11.4 introduces several privacy-aware biometric solutions to address the aforementioned concerns.

11.4   Privacy-Aware Biometric Solutions

Over the last few years, several privacy-aware biometric solutions have been investigated to overcome some of the privacy concerns presented in Sect. 11.3. As stated earlier, a biometric template is a sensitive representation of its owner that can be exploited in different ways to compromise user privacy. This section reviews several privacy-aware template processing schemes and highlights their pros and cons. It also presents other effective solutions such as match-on-card and privacy-preserving multi-factor biometric for local and remote authentication.

Privacy-aware template processing schemes mostly transform biometric template feature vectors into other private (i.e., personalized) vectors and secure domains. Such transformations preserve the anonymity of their owners while maintaining the capability of distinguishing them from other individuals. Such processes protect privacy at the design stage rather than being an aftermath action adopted as an add-on service at later stages. Although privacy-aware template processing schemes have continued to mature in academia over the last decade, they have not yet been widely adopted by commercial and governmental organizations either due to the extra cost needed to incorporate these schemes or simply because user privacy is not a priority yet for such organizations. However, with increased public awareness of biometric privacy and security issues, biometric experts are expecting a growing deployment of such schemes in the near future.

An ideal privacy-aware biometric template processing scheme must satisfy four properties [8]:

1 **Diversity**: templates cannot be used for cross-matching across different databases in which users can be tracked without their permissions.
2 **Revocability**: templates can be revoked and new ones can be issued whenever needed.

3 **Security**: it is computationally infeasible to reconstruct the original template from the transformed one.
4 **Performance**: recognition accuracy must not degrade significantly when the protection scheme is applied.

The concepts of *revocability* or *cancellability* of biometric templates and *private biometric cryptosystems* have been developed as measures to improve user's privacy in biometric systems [37]. *Revocability* means that biometric templates are no longer fixed over time and could be revoked in the same way as lost or stolen credit cards are. The main approaches for privacy-aware revocable biometric templates are based on the use of a non-invertible (or infeasible to invert) secret personalized transformation of the biometric feature vectors. *Private biometric cryptosystems* work by generating anonymous biometric keys and hashes that can be used as a proof of identity. The main approaches are based on user-linked helper data (e.g., a secure sketch) extracted from the biometric feature vector. Existing helper schemes and secure sketches use a combination of quantization and error-correcting codes. The created or extracted helper data should not reveal much information about the biometric template itself or form a fresh biometric sample.

It can be argued that each of the above privacy-aware template schemes has its own advantages and limitations in terms of the level of privacy provided, computational cost, storage requirements, applicability to different kinds of biometric representations, and ability to handle inter-class variations in biometric data (i.e., maintaining the accuracy [5]). Therefore, the requirement of each system should be analyzed before recommending the right solution.

11.4.1 Parameterized Feature Transformations

The basic idea behind parameterized feature transformation is to use a function ꜰ to transform the original biometric template to a private and secure domain. The function ꜰ typically depends on a parameter or a key called a transformation key (TK). This TK is applied at the enrolment stage to transform the original template and generate a cancellable version of it. At the matching stage and for each recognition attempt, the same TK is applied on the freshly captured biometric samples to guarantee that the matching process takes place in a private and secure domain. Following this approach, revocation of a template simply requires a change of the TK.

Depending on the characteristics of ꜰ, feature transformations can be further categorized into salting and non-invertible transforms. In salting, ꜰ is invertible, that is, if the TK and the cancellable template are known, the original template or a good approximation of it should be recovered. However, it is assumed to be computationally infeasible to reconstruct the original template using the transformed template even if the TK is known in the non-invertible transform.

The TK can be user- or system-based depending on the usage scenarios and/or application, which enables privacy-aware feature transformations to be deployed in both authentication and identification mode. The following subsections describe two examples of feature transformations, namely random projections and secret-based shuffling, followed by an illustration to demonstrate how feature transformation can be used in authentication and identification modes.

11.4.1.1 Feature Transformation Using Random Orthonormal Projections

Several proposed schemes to produce cancellable biometrics involve the use of Random Orthonormal Projections (ROPs) to map biometric features onto private and personalized domains. ROP is a technique that uses random orthonormal matrices to project data points into other spaces where the distances among the data points before and after the transformation are preserved. The distance-preserving feature has made ROPs ideal for biometric systems to improve privacy and security whilst maintaining an acceptable level of accuracy. ROP has been proposed as a secure transform for biometric templates and it was used to meet the revocability property [38] and as a standalone template protection scheme in a salting approach to generate a cancellable template for fingerprint [39] and face image data [40, 41]. However, a quantization step might be added to make the transform more difficult to invert [42]. ROP has also been used as a building block for generating a private biometric-based key from biometric data [43, 44] to be used as a cancellable template in the recognition process as explained in Sect. 11.4.2. ROP-based transformations used to generate privacy-aware templates are typically created as follows:

1. Generate m pseudo random vectors or real values based on a secret key.
2. Apply Gram-Schmidt orthogonalization on the generated random vectors to produce an orthonormal matrix. A matrix A is called an orthonormal matrix if it is orthogonal and each column or row vector has a unit norm, equivalently $AA_t = I$, where A_t is the transpose of A and I is the identity matrix of the same size as A.
3. Transform the original template feature x to a secure domain using matrix product: $y = Ax$.

An efficient method of generating orthonormal matrices [45] exploits the fact that small size orthonormal matrices can be generated without a need for the Gram-Schmidt procedure, which is ill-conditioned for high dimensional spaces. Let x be the feature vector of size n, A be an $n \times n$ orthonormal random matrix, b a random vector of size n, and P a permutation matrix of size n. Then the transformation

$$Y = P(Ax + b) \tag{11.1}$$

defines a distance preserving mapping of the space of n-dimensional vector space R_n that enhances privacy while preserving the intra-class variation (i.e., while maintaining the same level of recognition accuracy) [45].

11.4.1.2   Feature Transformation Using Secret-Based Shuffling

Another example of a privacy-aware feature transformation is secret-based shuffling
to create revocable versions of iris templates [46]. A shuffling key of size k generated from a secret (e.g., password, PIN, or a random key) is used to shuffle an iris
code that is divided into k blocks. As illustrated in Fig. 11.4, if a bit in the key is 1,
the corresponding iris code block is moved to the beginning; otherwise it is moved
to the end.

11.4.1.3   User-Based Feature Transformations for Privacy-Aware
             Authentication

User-based feature transformations (UBFTs) are typically multi-factor biometric
recognition schemes that rely on applying user-based transformation keys on biometric features. These multi-factor biometric authentication schemes have been
proposed to enhance privacy and/or accuracy of biometric systems. Figure 11.5
illustrates the general operations of a multi-factor UBFT approach during enrolment
and authentication stages. Typically, UBFTs employ transformation keys generated
from passwords or PINs, or the keys are retrieved from a token. If a user is
subscribed to x different systems, there will be x different cancellable versions of
their biometric template by changing the user-based and/or system-based secret.
Arguably, this privacy-preserving approach improves authentication anonymity and
makes it infeasible to track users across different systems or databases.

11.4.1.4   Parameterized Feature Transformations for Privacy-Aware
             Identification

Clearly the above UBFTs cannot be applied in a biometric identification mode
where the system, for example, is supposed to identify individuals on the watch-list

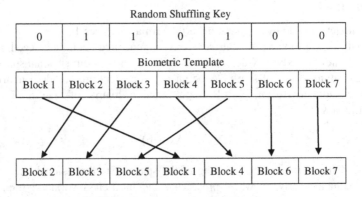

Fig. 11.4 Simple secret-based shuffling for iris codes [46]

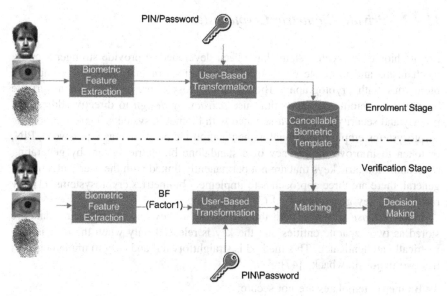

Fig. 11.5 General operations of a multi-factor biometric authentication system based on UBFTs approach during enrolment and authentication stages

without expecting them to declare their identity or presenting any additional information. Therefore, the transformation key in this scenario should be solely a system-based transformation. Figure 11.6 shows how a parameterized feature transformation can be used in privacy-preserving identification mode. It can be argued that such transformations can provide a good level of anonymity if the transformation is selected sensibly.

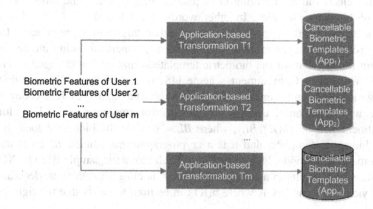

Fig. 11.6 Parameterized feature transformations for privacy-aware identification

11.4.2 Private Biometric Cryptosystems

Private biometric cryptosystems have been developed to provide stronger security mechanisms and to create revocable representations of individuals by combining biometrics with cryptography. Biometric cryptosystems, also known as private biometrics or biometric encryption, use *privacy by design* to directly address the privacy and security concerns associated with biometric systems. Typical biometric cryptosystems employ additional authentication factor(s) such as a password, PIN, or token to improve the privacy of a standalone biometric system by generating revocable biometric keys that are not permanently linked with the user's identity. In general, there are three approaches to implement biometrics cryptosystems: (1) key release, (2), key generation, and (3) key binding.

In *key release schemes*, both the cryptographic key and the biometric data are stored as two separate entities and the key is released only when the user is biometrically authenticated. This method is straightforward and easy to implement, but has two major drawbacks [47]:

1 Biometric templates are not secure.
2 The biometric matcher can be overridden.

In *key generation schemes*, a cryptographic key is directly derived from the biometric data without storing it anywhere. Such methods suffer from unacceptably high FRR [11].

In *key binding schemes*, the biometric template and the key are coupled to form a *biometric lock* [48] in a way that makes it computationally infeasible to retrieve the key without previous knowledge of the user's biometric data. While biometric data are fuzzy due to intra-class variations, cryptographic keys have to be repeatable every time. To bridge this gap, key-binding schemes typically rely on error correction techniques such as error correcting codes (ECC). The ECC algorithm is typically selected after analyzing error patterns of inter-class and intra-class variations of biometric samples. In other words, the selected ECC should tolerate (correct) up to a fixed number of bits (the so called threshold of the system). In key binding schemes, a cryptographic key is randomly generated during the enrolment stage but independent of the biometric template(s) and can be changed whenever needed. The Fuzzy Commitment scheme [48] is one of the earliest methods of binding biometrics and user keys. To commit (bind) a binary key K, a codeword C is generated based on K using a predefined error correcting code. The ultimate commitment will be $(h(K), BL)$, where $BL = B \oplus C$ is the biometric lock, B is a binary biometric template, and h is a cryptographic hash function. To remove a commitment, an individual has to provide a fresh biometric sample B' to be XORed with BL, which results in a codeword C'. If B' is close enough to B, decoding C' should yield the same key K where h(K) can be used to verify that the right key is released.

Figure 11.7 depicts a generalized version of such a system [11]. At the enrolment stage, biometric samples are captured and input into a feature extraction procedure

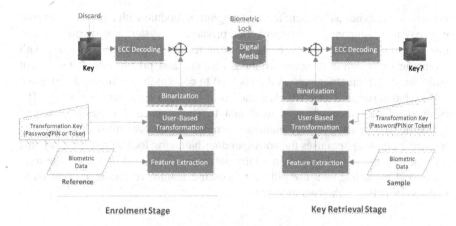

Fig. 11.7 General private biometric cryptosystem (key-binding scheme)

that outputs biometric template(s). Thereafter, a user-based transformation (e.g., personalized and private random orthonormal projection) is applied to transform the extracted biometric template into a private domain. Finally, a binary representation of the biometric sample is produced to be bound to the cryptographic key. To allow for the intra-class variations, error correcting techniques should be used whereby intra-class variations between biometrics samples at the enrolment and key retrieval stages can be considered as noise. The adopted error correction techniques should be capable of correcting up to a specific number of bits, which depends on the intended key size, biometric template size, and the amount of tolerated distortion in the biometric data to accommodate adequate variation in user samples.

The encoded cryptographic key is XORed with the binary representation of biometric data to yield the biometric lock or helper data. The key is then discarded and the biometric lock and the hash of the key are stored. At the authentication stage (key retrieval stage), the binary representation is calculated using a fresh biometric sample in the same way as described above and then XORed with the biometric lock. Next, the adopted error correcting technique in the decoding mode is used. The correction succeeds and the original cryptographic key is reproduced if the difference between the reference biometric sample(s) and the fresh biometric sample is within the predefined threshold (i.e., the fresh biometric sample belongs to the same individual). The predefined threshold is determined in the same way as before when defining a biometric authentication threshold through a training protocol that is application dependent, where appropriate tolerance of error rates is chosen in terms of FAR and FRR.

Private biometric cryptosystems can theoretically be extended to function under the identification mode in the same way as illustrated in Fig. 11.6. However, incorporating error-correcting techniques makes any identification process very slow. To improve the efficiency, a hybrid privacy-aware watch-list face recognition system [49] can be used, which was successfully deployed for Ontario Lottery and Gaming Corporation Self-Exclusion Program. The system is hybrid in nature because it combines a commercial face recognition module with a private biometric cryptosystem component. To improve the privacy, the system uses two databases; one contains biometric templates of the commercial face recognition along with biometric locks, while the other contains personal and private information about individuals. A biometric cryptosystem is used to conceal the relationship between a self-excluded person's face template and his or her other personal information. The commercial face recognition is used first to check whether a freshly captured biometric sample matches any biometric template on the watch-list. If it does, the biometric cryptosystem uses the corresponding biometric lock to release a key that will identify the record of personal information in the second database. The templates and biometric lock use different biometric feature vectors to prevent inter-operability between the two modules.

11.5   Challenges and Solutions—Current Trends

Security measures and technologies involve the collection of information about various people including their biometric data. This raises serious questions as to whether, and to what extent, the privacy of the biometric data owner (i.e., the individual) has been breached. A moderate level of invasion into an individual's privacy is sometimes considered to be an acceptable cost of enhanced personal safety and society security. However, the acceptable level of privacy invasion is not yet clearly defined in the trade-off between security and privacy. International efforts have been made to come up with a common understanding of the security–privacy trade-off at both state and citizen level to suggest best practices and guidelines to policymakers. For example, the SurPRISE (Surveillance, Privacy, and Security) project [50] is a three-year project (2012–2015) funded by the European Union under the Seventh Framework Programme (FP7) for Research and Technology Development. It aims to examine the trade-off between security and individual privacy and addresses questions such as: "Does more security justify less privacy?" and "What is the balance between these two?" It consults with citizens from several EU member and associated states on the question of the security–privacy trade-off as they evaluate different security technologies and measures.

The IRISS (Increasing Resilience in Surveillance Societies) project [51] (EU, FP7, 2012–2015) aims to investigate the development and deployment of surveillance technologies and their impact on citizens' privacy and democratic rights. Another example is the TURBINE (TrUsted Revocable Biometric IdeNtitiEs) project [52] (EU, FP7, 2007–2013), which investigates effective solutions on how to enable an individual to revoke an identity for a given application and create different "pseudo-identities" for different applications. The project suggested best practices for privacy-preserving biometric data processing. Another example is the 3DFace project [53] (EU, FP6, 2006–2009), in which the objective was to develop a prototype of an automated border control biometric system incorporating privacy-enhancing technology based on two- and three-dimensional face images.

Match-on-card technologies and other user-side matching devices are examples of solutions that have been proposed as effective privacy-preserving biometric solutions, because storage and matching of biometric samples are all done under the user's full control. However, more research needs to be carried out to come up with practical solutions on how to extend such technologies to be suitable for both identification and authentication modes. Other future research directions could investigate the feasibility of implementing privacy-preserving solutions at the hardware level. For example, is it possible to design a biometric sensor (e.g., camera, iris scanner, fingerprint scanner) to capture biometric data that serves the purpose of biometric recognition without revealing any extra piece of information to the outside?

11.5.1 Privacy-Aware Remote Biometric Recognition for Cloud Services

The increasing trend of many business organizations, government agencies, and customers to shift their services and data onto the cloud necessitates the need for secure and privacy-aware remote authentication schemes that are capable of preserving anonymity and are immune against fraud and identity theft at the same time [54]. However, the open nature of unattended remote authentication makes the privacy and security of biometric systems important issues. Hybrid challenge and response schemes that combine feature transformation and a private biometric cryptosystem can be used, for example, as a privacy-aware remote biometric authentication for cloud services [55]. Face modality was chosen for the implementation due to camera availability on almost all mobile devices and laptops.

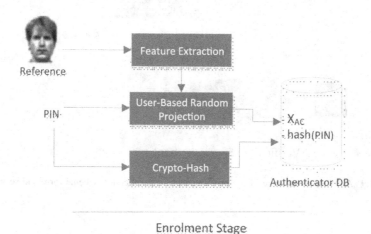

Fig. 11.8 Enrolment stage of the privacy-aware authentication scheme for cloud service

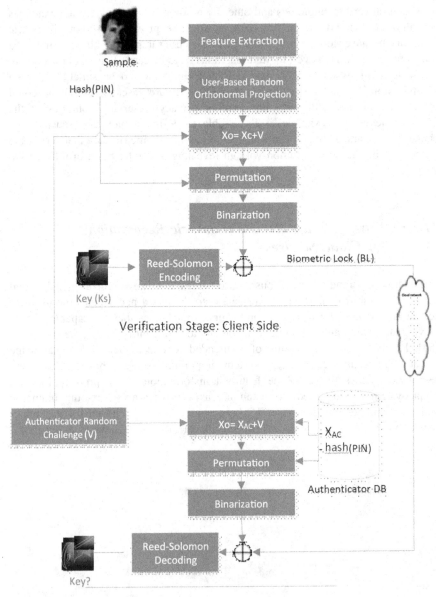

Fig. 11.9 Authentication stage of the privacy-aware authentication scheme for cloud service

At the enrolment stage, and to address some privacy concerns highlighted earlier, only a cancellable version of the user's biometric features X_{AC} and a hash of a PIN used to generate ROP are stored in the cloud authenticator's database as illustrated in Fig. 11.8.

As a case study, a user can use a smart phone or tablet PC that has a camera to capture face images along with a four-digit PIN to generate a user-based transformation key to be used for ROP. It is worth highlighting the fact that combining biometrics with the other authentication factors in this scheme enhances privacy while intra-class variations of biometric samples are preserved (i.e., it does not compromise accuracy) [55].

At the authentication stage and after extracting the biometric feature vector and applying ROP, the resulting cancellable feature vector X_C is combined with a one-time authenticator random challenge vector V by simple addition to produce a one-time privacy-aware cancellable feature vector X_O, which will be permuted based on a permutation key generated from the PIN as illustrated in Fig. 11.9. As mentioned earlier, due to the differences between the user's captured biometric sample and the enrolled biometric sample(s) stored by the authenticator, ECCs can be used to eliminate the effect of this noise. In this case study, a Reed-Solomon (RS) ECC is chosen to correct up to 30 % of the biometric feature vectors. This 30 % threshold is determined in a similar manner to define biometric authentication thresholds (i.e., a training protocol is used to determine appropriate tolerance error rates in terms of FAR and FRR). At the cloud authenticator side, if the correction succeeds, the process generates a key K' that matches the key bound to the user. This can only happen if the difference between the reference biometric sample(s) and the fresh biometric sample is within the predefined threshold (i.e., the fresh biometric sample belongs to the same individual).

11.6 Conclusion

The fact that biometric systems by their very nature collect more information than just the individual's fingerprints, retinal patterns, or other biometric data has precipitated an urgent need for new legislation to enforce privacy-preserving measures on biometric data collection, processing, and template storage. At a basic level, most biometric systems will record when and where a person is at the time of a scan, not to mention all the additional privacy concerns we have discussed earlier. Although data privacy and data protection acts exist in almost all countries, those related to biometric privacy and security are not mature enough yet, as they are still at very early stages.

The problem of privacy of biometric systems cannot be attributed solely to technology. No matter how secure the technology is, biometric systems insiders and secondary users, as well as third parties such as insurance companies, employers, and financial organizations, can become a source of attack or privacy concern. In other words, the problem is the combination of people and technology. Hence, technological solutions need to be complemented by a legal framework while educational-based and ethical-based tools are required to improve privacy for all of us.

References

1. The Unique Identification Authority of India. http://uidai.gov.in/. Accessed 08 Sept 2014
2. Ross A, Nandakumar K, Jain A (2011) Introduction to biometrics. Springer, New York
3. Georghiades AS, Belhumeur PN, Kriegman DJ (2001) From few to many: Generative models for recognition under variable pose and illumination. IEEE Trans Pattern Anal Mach Intell 23 (6):643–660
4. Li SZ, Jain AK (2009) Encyclopedia of biometrics. Springer, New York
5. Nandakumar K (2008) Multibiometric systems: fusion strategies and template security
6. NIST_Report NIST Report to the United States Congress. Summary of NIST Standards for biometric accuracy, tamper resistance, and interoperability, Nov 2002
7. Bhanu B, Tan X (2003) Fingerprint Indexing based on novel features of minutiae triplets. IEEE Trans Pattern Anal Mach Intell 25(5):616–622
8. Jain AK, Nandakumar K, Nagar A (2008) Biometric template security. EURASIP J Adv Signal Process 1–17
9. Adler A (2005) Vulnerabilities in biometric encryption systems. In: Proceedings of the 5th international conference on audio and video-based biometric person authentication, vol 3546, pp 1611–3349
10. Cappelli R, Lumini A, Maio D, Maltoni D (2007) Fingerprint image reconstruction from standard templates. IEEE Trans Pattern Anal Mach Intell 29(7):1489–1503
11. Hao F, Anderson R, Daugman J (2006) Combining cryptography with biometrics effectively. IEEE Trans Comput 1081–1088
12. The Secure Phone Project. http://www.secure-phone.info/. Accessed 08 Sept 2014
13. Philips Electronics Nederland B.V. (2013, July) Vital signs camera—Philips on the App Store on iTunes. https://itunes.apple.com/gb/app/vital-signs-camera-philips/id474433446?mt=8. Accessed 08 Sept 2014
14. Hoeksma J (2009, Oct) E-health insider: private medical records offered for sale, http://www.ehi.co.uk/news/ehi/5311. Accessed 08 Sept 2014
15. Hasson P (2009) The five country conference: joint enrollment and FCC information sharing project. US Department of Homeland Security
16. Védrine H (2000, Dec) council regulation (EC) No 2725/2000. Off J Eur Communities
17. European Data Protection Supervisor (EDPS) (2012, Sept) Peter Hustinx, EURODAC: erosion of fundamental rights creeps along
18. Woodward JD (2008) The law and the use of biometrics. In: Jain AK, Flynn P, Ross AA (eds) Handbook of biometrics. Springer, Chap. 18, pp 357–380
19. Amoore L (2006) Biometric borders: governing mobilities in the war on terror. Polit Geogr 25 (3):336–351
20. Bennett CJ (2011) In defense of privacy: the concept and the regime. Surv Soc 8(4):485–496
21. Nanavati R (2011, Dec) Biometric data safeguarding technologies analysis and best practices. Defence R&D Canada—Centre for Security Science, Technical report
22. Hal J, Kimura D (1994) Dermatoglyphic asymmetry and sexual orientation in men. Behav Neurosci 108(6):1203
23. Woodward J (1999) Biometrics: identifying law and policy concerns. In: Jain AK, Bolle R, Pankanti S (eds) Biometrics: personal identification in networked society. Springer, chap 19, pp 385–406

24. LeVay S (1996) Queer science: the use and abuse of research into homosexuality. The MIT Press, Cambridge
25. Forbes KE, Shanks MF, Venneri A (2004) The evolution of dysgraphia in Alzheimer's disease. Brain Res Bull 63(1):19–24
26. Rosenblum S, Samuel M, Zlotnik S, Erikh I, Schlesinger I (2013) Handwriting as an objective tool for Parkinson's disease diagnosis. J Neurol 260(9):2357–2361
27. Tsanas A, Little MA, McSharry P, Spielman J, Ramig L (2012) Novel speech signal processing algorithms for high-accuracy classification of Parkinson's disease. IEEE Trans Biomed Eng 59(5):1264–1271
28. Darell R (2014) Siri update: how, when & what we use her for. In: Bit Rebels. Accessed 08 Sept 2014
29. Faundez-Zanuy M (2013) Biometric applications related to human beings: there is life beyond security. Cognit Comput 5(1):136–151
30. Shin J, Okuyama T (2014) Detection of alcohol intoxication via online handwritten signature verification. Pattern Recognit Lett 35:101–104
31. Foley RG, Miller AL (1979) The effects of marijuana and alcohol usage on handwriting. Forensic Sci Int 14(3):159–164
32. Moody J (2004) public perceptions of biometric devices: the effect of misinformation on acceptance and use. Issues Inform Sci Inf Technol 1
33. Farzin H, Abrishami-Moghaddam H, Moin MS (2008) A novel retinal identification system. EURASIP J Adv Signal Process 2008(280635):1–10
34. Patton N (2006) Retinal image analysis: concepts, applications and potential. Progr Retinal Eye Res 25(1):99–127
35. Berson EL (2008) Retinal degenerations: planning for the future. In: Recent advances in retinal degeneration. Springer, Berlin, pp 21–35
36. Hartung D, Busch C (2009) Why vein recognition needs privacy protection. In: 5th international conference on Intelligent information hiding and multimedia signal processing 2009. IIH-MSP'09, pp 1090–1095
37. Ratha NK, Connell JH, Bolle RM (2004) Enhancing security and privacy in biometrics-based authentication systems. IBM Syst J 40(1):614–634
38. Goal N, Bebis G, Nefian A (2005) Face recognition experiments with random projection. Proc SPIE 5779:426–437
39. Teoh ABJ, Ngo DCL, Goh A (2004) BioHashing: two factor authentication featuring fingerprint data and tokenised random number. Pattern Recogn 37(11):2245–2255
40. Feng YC, Yuen PC, Jain AK (2008) A hybrid approach for face template protection, vol 6944, p 694408
41. Yongjin W, Plataniotis KN (2007) Face based biometric authentication with changeable and privacy preservable templates, pp 1–6
42. Al-Assam H, Jassim SA (2012) Security evaluation of biometric keys. J Comput Secur 31(2):151–163
43. Andrew B, Teoha D, Ngoa CL, Alwyn G (2004) Personalised cryptographic key generation based on FaceHashing. J Comput Secur 23(7):606–614
44. Goh A, Ngo DC (2003) Computation of cryptographic keys from face biometrics, pp 1–13
45. Al-Assam H, Sellahewa H, Jassim SA (2009) Lightweight approach for biometric template protection. Proc SPIE
46. Kanade S, Camara D, Dorizzi B (2008) Three factor scheme for biometric-based cryptographic key regeneration using iris. In: Biometrics symposium, pp 59–64
47. Nandakumar K, Jain AK, Pankanti S (2007) Fingerprint-based fuzzy vault: implementation and performance. IEEE Trans Inf Forensics Secur 2(4):744–757
48. Juels A, Wattenberg M (1999) A fuzzy commitment scheme. In: Proceedings of ACM conference on computer and communications security (CCS), Singapore, 1999, pp 28–36
49. Marinelli T, Stoianov A, Martin K, Plataniotis KN, Chibba M, DeSouza L, Cavoukian SA (2013) Biometric encryption: creating a privacy-preserving watch-list facial recognition system. Secur Priv Biometrics 215–238

50. Surveillance, privacy and security (SurPRISE), http://www.surprise-project.eu/. Accessed 08 Sept 2014
51. Increasing resilience in surveillance societies (IRISS) project, http://www.irissproject.eu/. Accessed 08 Sept 2014
52. Turbine project, http://www.turbine-project.eu/. Accessed 08 Sept 2014
53. 3Dface Project, http://www.3dface.org/. Accessed 08 Sept 2014
54. Kuseler T, Al-Assam H, Jassim SA, Lami IA (2011, April) Privacy preserving, real-time and location secured biometrics for mCommerce authentication. In: Mobile multimedia/image processing, security, and applications 2011, vol 8063, SPIE, Bellingham, WA
55. Al-Assam H, Jassim SA (2012) Robust biometric based key agreement and remote mutual authentication. In: The 11th international conference on trust, security and privacy in computing and communications (TrustCom), Liverpool, UK, 2012, pp 59–65

Chapter 12
Privacy in Social Networks

Traian Marius Truta, Michail Tsikerdekis and Sherali Zeadally

12.1 Introduction

12.1.1 A Brief History

The worldwide Web has radically changed the way we communicate and interact
with each other and how we manage our privacy. A good example of this is the
ability to take photos that automatically include geographical information (often
referred to as geotagging) and share them with a circle of friends. Traditional photos
did not contain any geographical information and so questions that usually followed
went along the lines of "where was this taken?" Such sentences are becoming
obsolete and this is just one of the myriads of changes in our 21st-century digital
lives. Of course change may not always be for the better. In the past decade we have
seen cases where social media made news as the dangers of exposing one's private
life where made apparent. Employees have been stalked online by employers [62]
and teenagers have been deceived by predators [6]. It seems that we are not yet fully
familiar with this new world that came into our lives, or are we familiar?

Long before the advent of the Web, in the early 1990 s there was a world of
social media used in organizations to enhance collaboration [31, 32]. The motivation behind social media at that time stemmed from the need to collectively create

T.M. Truta (✉)
Department of Computer Science, College of Informatics Northern Kentucky University,
Highland Heights, KY 41099, USA
e-mail: trutat1@nku.edu

M. Tsikerdekis · S. Zeadally
College of Communication and Information, University of Kentucky,
Lexington, KY 40516, USA
e-mail: tsikerdekis@uky.edu

S. Zeadally
e-mail: szeadally@uky.edu

© Springer International Publishing Switzerland 2015
S. Zeadally and M. Badra (eds.), *Privacy in a Digital, Networked World*,
Computer Communications and Networks,
DOI 10.1007/978-3-319-08470-1_12

and disseminate information and while early computer interfaces provided limited richness in people's communication, they were still effective enough to be adopted by organizations at the time. Bulletin board systems have been around since 1978 and have been used by people to make announcements, inform friends about meetings, and share other information through postings [65].

12.1.2   From Web 1.0 to Web 2.0

The revolutionary moment in history came with the advent of the Web or Web 1.0 in 1993 when it was released to the world [42]. While early web interface (e.g., gopher) provided the ability to view and edit pages (as it was the need of the early physicists at CERN (The European Organization for Nuclear Research) who needed to update and exchange results among them), it was, however, static and featured (technically) non-editable pages to individuals other than the owner of a server hosting those files. In fact, the Web remained this way for a while with people in 1999 describing web pages as "static screenfuls" [21]. There were various limitations as to the interactions provided by that early Web and so people who sought interactivity and exchange of content used software tools such as Internet Relay Chats (IRC) and MUD games [58]. Another prominent feature of Web 1.0 was the clear distinction between the user and the webmaster (the owner of a website). One-way communication between who contributes the content and to whom it is being delivered could clearly be identified. All of this was bound to change the moment new technologies allowed for an advanced level of interactivity online. Adoption of new technologies seems to be dependent on the age with the younger population being more receptive to new technologies [57]. During the period 1995–2000, we saw an under-representation for the older age groups [48] and the adoption of new technologies was becoming more ubiquitous. Bernal [5] has been one of the few people to articulate the shift between Web 1.0 and 2.0. He argued that while the focus of Web 1.0 was on delivering products, the focus for Web 2.0 has been toward the delivery of services and increasing interactivity among users. Bidirectional interaction was quickly achieved by combining and ensuring compatibility among multiple technologies along with expanding the processing and scalability capabilities of databases and web programming languages. Additional service-oriented architectures helped to promote these services further. There was tremendous potential for many user-driven businesses to thrive under a Web 2.0 model [70] but many have also advised caution and suggested that this change may not ensure commercial success for all businesses [38]. Today, many enterprises are enjoying the benefits of Web 2.0 technologies with the majority of top executives favoring such strategies [60]. Web 2.0 technologies provide flexible design and rich and responsive user interfaces. They allow for collaborative creation of content, developing new application and services that communicate across different platforms, and establishing social networks of people with common interests, as well as supporting collaboration and collective intelligence [60]. It is worth pointing out that people were collaborating online and forming communities well before Web 2.0 [39]. Howard [39] argued that the creation of online communities and collaboration could also happen with software (desktop applications or video games) that is not Web based. Gradually, a trend started appearing for Internet software that was providing more social tools to users. This is not surprising if one considers that users value personal interaction with the software as well as social interaction with other people [16]. The freedom provided by interactive social tools that allowed not only for two-way communication between users but also user contributions to content enabled Internet users to explore social interactions like never before. Networked communications have evolved to accommodate the needs of humans as social beings [40]. The idea of social media came to life.

12.2 Social Media

Social media and Web 2.0 are not the same. Social media refer to Internet-based applications that build on the foundations of Web 2.0 and allow for the creation and exchange of user-generated content [43]. Under the large umbrella of social media one can find applications which include, blogs, collaborative project (e.g., Wikipedia), social networking sites (e.g., Facebook), content communities (e.g., YouTube), virtual social worlds (e.g., Second Life), virtual game worlds (e.g., World of Warcraft), and micro-blogging (e.g., Twitter) [43, 44]. Social networks have had a great impact on our society and they are the most representative type of social media for their use of Web 2.0 technologies.

12.2.1 Social Networks

Social networks have gained a lot of interest and popularity over the last decade. Kaplan and Haenlein [43] defined them as applications that enable users to create personal profiles, invite friends to connect with them, and to have access to other people's profiles. These profiles can include various types of information such as photos, video, audio files, and even blogs. The basic ingredients of a social network are to allow for the construction of public or semi-public profile, to articulate a list of users that individuals share a connection with, and to view and share that list with others within a system [10]. There is also a distinction between a social network site and a social networking site. According to Boyd and Ellison [10], networking implies relationship initiation often between strangers. However, lines have been blurred with today's social networking services offering both networking with existing relationships as well as initiating new with strangers. Henceforth, we assume that by social networks we mean applications both for network as well as networking in terms of the goals of a social media service.

12.2.2 Social Networking Sites

The first social networking site according to many was SixDegrees.com and was launched in 1997 [10]. It was the first website to combine features that allowed profile creation, forming friend lists, and sharing those lists with others. The website managed to attract 3.5 million users until it finally closed down in 2000 after being bought off for $125 million [51]. Subsequently, several other services such as LiveJournal.com started offering social networking features [10], but it was really later on in 2003 when modern social networking sites were launched with the primary goal of providing a digital representation of user networks, initiating and managing relationships.

12.2.2.1 LinkedIn

Linkedin.com was launched in 2003 with the intent to connect professionals with their networks. In January 2009 the network had 32 million members and in March 2011 it had 100 million members.[1] At the time of writing, the website has 225 million users.[2] LinkedIn allows individuals to create professional networks, to view how they are linked with other members, and view what their degree of separation is (how many connections apart they have) from a target member [49]. This means that an individual's social network becomes tangible. As such, social capital has ceased to be an abstract concept but has become a visible structure that an individual can keep expanding and restructure.

12.2.2.2 Friendster

Another website that was launched in 2002 did not share the same success that LinkedIn did. Friendster is recognized as one of the best examples of early popular social networks [10]. The website started off as a dating website but encouraged users to join even if they were not looking for dates [8]. The idea behind Friendster was that friends of friends are good candidates for dates. The decision was made to arbitrarily allow people to connect with others as far as four degrees (connections between individuals) away in their network. Any individuals beyond four degrees from an individual could not be reached; a choice that is restrictive for a community according to the theory of six degrees of separation [75]. The website was launched in 2002 and by mid-August it had 1.5 million registered users [8]. Boyd [9] was one of the first researchers to study the popular website and suggested that the human–computer interaction community should consider the evolution of social community

---

[1]http://techcrunch.com/2013/01/09/linkedin-hits-200-million-users-worldwide-adding-new-users-at-rate-of-two-per-second/.

[2]http://www.linkedin.com/about-us.

along with the underlying technology. Her arguments made an accurate prediction of the technical and social difficulties that the website later experienced. Servers frequently failed because they could not sustain the increased traffic as premature web software of the time was not designed to handle the amount of interactive actions of millions of users. In turn, users became frustrated, leading to some of them switching their email addresses to Friendster's email service. Additional social issues (such as the influx of new users who were unfamiliar with community norms) also led to the decline of Friendster's online community. The balance of current social groups was shaken due to the influx of new users and users who wanted to connect with others beyond the four-degree limit [8]. The so-called fakester account was an early version of developing pages of special interests so that people can find others with common interests (e.g., fans of *Star Wars* movies). Many of these accounts had thousands of friends, which created computational loads for the ill-equipped servers at the time. The decision was made by Friendster to delete all of these accounts to resolve website issues. This resulted in a rejection of the website in the United States by early adopters due to several issues such as social collisions (e.g., employers being able to monitor their employees' work activities) and a loss of trust between users and the site as a result of the deletion of these accounts [25]. Many of these actions violated the hierarchy of needs for online users, which arguably if used could have put user needs first [50]. The website has made a comeback in recent years and in October 2008, according to a press release, it reached 85 million members worldwide.[3]

12.2.2.3 Myspace

Friendster was followed by Myspace, another popular social networking site that was launched in August 2003. Myspace grew rapidly as Friendster's popularity declined, because some of their adopters saw it as a safe haven to express their interests (something that was limited in Friendster due to its four-degree policy) [10]. Significant attention was given to bands and music, which helped to increase the number of users. Myspace expanded its features based on user demand and allowed for page personalization (e.g., adding HTML to alter the layout), which boosted its popularity further. Myspace also focused on developing policies to allow teenagers to join the service, which further increased its user base. At its peak, in 2008, the website had 75.9 million users[4] before the service started declining because of safety issues that plagued the service [10]. In June 2011, the service was down to 33 million users although after a recent redesign it has been picking up traffic once again.

---

[3]http://web.archive.org/web/20100522004359/ http://www.friendster.com/info/presscenter.php?A=pr48.

[4]http://mediadecoder.blogs.nytimes.com/2012/02/12/myspace-to-announce-one-million-new-users/?_r=0.

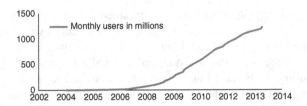

Fig. 12.1 Approximate growth of monthly users in millions for Facebook. *Source* https://newsroom.fb.com/

12.2.2.4 Facebook

One social networking service that perhaps gained from all the predecessor social networks that rose and fell was Facebook. It is the most popular social networking site currently and the longest to maintain such a title. The service has experienced a skyrocketing growth by designing its website to provide the best features by addressing several of the deficiencies of previous social networking services. Launched in 2004, Facebook has seen a dramatic increase of its user base worldwide (Fig. 12.1). In September 2013, the website had 1.19 billion users monthly with average daily unique users at 727 million.[5] Approximately 80 % of its daily user base is outside of the United States and Canada, with some countries reaching high penetration levels among their Internet users (higher than 90 %).[6]

12.2.2.5 Mobile Social Networking

Social network usage has increased by 64 % since 2005 [11]. Currently, Facebook and Twitter (a micro-blogging service) have reached 82 % of the world's Internet users [69]. In the last few recent years a dramatic shift has been observed in people accessing the Internet via mobile devices leading to the emergence of mobile social networking. Mobile social networking implies social networking services, which include social structures with entities (individuals or organizations) connected through various types of interdependency (e.g., common interest, friendship, etc.), that are used by individuals through their mobile devices [41]. Jabeur et al. [41] attribute the rise in popularity in the enabling of new ways for social interaction and collaboration by taking advantage of location-based services and data-sharing services (e.g., photos) provided by mobile devices in an immediate way. Mobile social networking services can be divided into two types, those with native support only for mobile devices (e.g., Instagram) and those offering mobile as well as web access to their services (e.g., Facebook).

---

[5]http://newsroom.fb.com/Key-Facts.
[6]http://www.internetworldstats.com/facebook.htm.

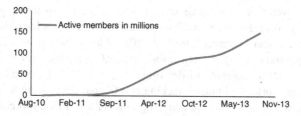

Fig. 12.2 Growth of active members in millions for Instagram. *Source* http://instagram.com/press/

Historically, early mobile social networking has been observed since 1999 [52]. These applications came usually pre-installed in mobile devices and some followed a subscription-based model. They are similar to primitive versions of early social networks with the ability to broadcast messages to many people at once, but focus less on profile creation and management. During the early 2000s, a transition was observed with the release of early wireless application protocols (WAP) third generation (3G) technologies when applications started being released with social networking features incorporated in them. These were still developed and maintained by the manufacturer, or in close association with the manufacturer or carrier of mobile services. By the late 2000s, applications developed by third parties (e.g., independent developers) were able to be installed in mobile devices, which radically altered the range of applications available for consumers.

One of the most popular examples of early native mobile social networking applications was Instagram, which was launched in October 2010. The application provided a photo and video sharing social networking service to mobile users in collaboration with other social networking services (through websites and mobile portals). The service was released for free through Apple's App Store and Google Play, which helped to increase its popularity. By April 2012 it had 100 million active users[7] when it was sold to Facebook for $1 billion.[8] Figure 12.2 depicts the growth of the service.

Many social networking sites also expanded their access to mobile devices. Facebook started offering mobile access to iPhone users in August 2007 and almost a year later it reached 1.5 million regular users. In 2008, a Facebook mobile application was offered to iPhone users. As of December 2013, 945 million users access Facebook monthly through mobile devices (approximately 77 % of its total monthly users).[9]

The increase in usage of mobile social networks has led to the emergence of geosocial networking. This is social networking that includes geographic services and features such as geocoding and geotagging, which alter the social dynamics of a mobile social networking service (e.g., recommendation systems that can help with

---

[7]http://instagram.com/press/.

[8]http://abcnews.go.com/blogs/technology/2012/04/facebook-buys-instagram-for-1-billion/.

[9]https://newsroom.fb.com/key-Facts.

attendance at events in close proximity based on past movement patterns and location history) [64]. For web-based social networks, a user's location is attached to content using their internet protocol (IP) address (which is tracked to an approximate position at city or area level) or wireless hotspot trilateration (which uses multiple wireless hotspots to determine the relative location of a user). For mobile social networks, cell phone tracking and Global Positioning System (GPS)-enabled services can be used to attach geographical information to content.

12.2.3 Impact of Social Networking on Society

The success of social networking sites can be attributed to their ability to satisfy social needs (e.g., the need to communicate with others and be a part of a social group) that online users have. Social networking sites have become an extension of an individual's real life, containing a detailed documentation of a person's social network along with aspects such as their experiences, thoughts, beliefs, and preferences. Social networking sites are helpful for people with low self-esteem and low life satisfaction and provide a tremendous advantage for managing social capital [25]. Social capital, defined loosely as the value of social relations that helps provide benefits to individuals or groups [17], became the term to define the well-being of groups and society. As the number of social networking users increases, a higher number of online relationships are expected to form, and, as a result, people connected to others are likely to receive more positive feedback from these relationships [76]. Positive feedback received by users' social networks enhances their social self-esteem as well as their well-being. People using social networking sites tend to have more virtual friends than real-life friends [78]. Corporations also exploit the benefits of using social networks for supporting brand promotion and marketing campaigns [12, 17]. Social networks can also be profitable business models [59].

Social networks have also been affected by various issues. One example is the differential adoption due to the digital inequality [35]. This digital divide has economic, sociological, and political drivers that affect not just the adoption of social networking sites but also the adoption of the Internet [30]. For users who end up using social networks, one of the most popular issues relates to privacy [3, 53, 68].

12.3 Privacy Issues in Social Networks

As discussed in the introduction to this chapter, there are a large number of privacy concerns in the field of social networks. These concerns have greatly increased in the past years due to the advent of online social networks. Facebook, LinkedIn, and Twitter are already well-known social networks that have a large audience in all age groups. Recently more trendy social sites such as Pinterest, Instagram, Vine, Tumblr, WhatsApp, and Snapchat are being preferred by the younger audience [63]. The amount of data that those social sites gather from their users is continually increasing and these data are very valuable for marketing, research, and various other purposes. At the same time, the data usually contain a significant amount of sensitive information, which should be protected against unauthorized disclosure. It is safe to say that any collection and storage of individual data regardless of intent, can lead to privacy implications that would not have existed otherwise [66]. One example of such a situation was in 2006 when, to stimulate research on real Internet data, AOL made available over 20 million search queries from over 650,000 users. Although the data was de-identified (in a poor way), individuals that conducted specific searches were identified in the data. The main reason why this was possible was that many users searched for their city, neighborhood, and even their first and/or last name. *The New York Times* published a story about one such re-identified individual, Thelma Arnold, from Liburn, Georgia in the United States, who was discovered through her queries terms [2]. Luckily, no significant harm was reported for any individual from the released data. However, the researcher responsible for de-anonymizing and releasing the data was dismissed and the AOL chief technology officer resigned.

For social network data, privacy can be seen from different angles. Imagine an online social network site (such as Facebook, Orkut, etc.). These sites gather data from a large number of users, and that data is published to other users based on privacy controls of the user that owns the data. For instance, Facebook has a series of privacy settings that allows a user to choose what to share and with whom. These controls go beyond these basic features, and a user can create various levels of friends, review any information that others post about them before it is posted, and so on. What is important to note at this point is that this view of privacy is user-centric or local. This type of privacy is commonly called *social privacy* [66]. A second view of privacy is when we look at the whole social network data. Any social network site will gather data and use this data for other purposes as specified in their data use policy. For instance, Facebook has a very detailed data use policy in which they describe how they use the information received from their users. Of particular interest for privacy is how this information is shared to other parties (companies):

"Your trust is important to us, which is why we don't share information we receive about you with others unless we have:

- received your permission;
- given you notice, such as by telling you about it in this policy; or
- removed your name and any other personally identifying information from it." [26]

As stated above, the social network data is de-anonymized prior to being shared to other companies. However, as seen from the AOL case, the de-anonymization process may not be fully successful and the privacy of certain individuals may still be at risk. This view of privacy is network-centric or global and it is commonly called *institutional privacy* [66]. The institutional privacy can also be seen from two distinct angles. First, the social network site, as the data collector (many times this is referred to in the literature as data owner, we chose to use this term since in many data use policies, such as Facebook's, the data owner is considered the user that provided the data), has unlimited access to all collected data, thus, protecting privacy from the data collector is an Herculean task. In general this situation is not considered a privacy concern because the data collector is trusted with the data directly by the user. The user has the option of not participating in that social network site and he or she remains unknown to the data collector. This is more difficult than it appears because in many cases the data is not voluntarily provided to a data collector. An example of such a situation is the data collection practices of NSA as revealed by the whistle-blower, Edward Snowden [24]. This type of privacy, when the social network data collector is not trusted or the data is gathered without the knowledge of the user, is known as *surveillance privacy* [66]. The second view of institutional privacy is when the social network data is shared by a trusted data collector to third parties. Due in major part to AOL anonymization failure, there are no recent attempts to publically provide anonymized data to researchers; however, this sharing of collected data happens when there is a significant benefit for the social network site. The data is anonymized (this is most likely specified in the data use policy, for instance, Facebook will anonymize their data before sharing it with others) and shared with companies that are in general trusted by the original data collector. However, the anonymization process must aim to protect the individual data from disclosure in case attempts to re-identification occur. In the context of social network data, we call this type of privacy *network privacy*. A variant to this scenario is when the data is not shared with other parties, but the data collector shares the result of various queries with third parties. While this approach seems to better protect the individual's privacy it still may lead to privacy breaches and it requires the data collector to be able to process the queries requested by other parties, anonymize the query result, and provide these results to requestors. We include this scenario in the context of network privacy. Figure 12.3 illustrates these privacy types.

We will present briefly the main privacy concerns related to each type of social network privacy (see Table 12.1 for a summary). A solution for each such problem

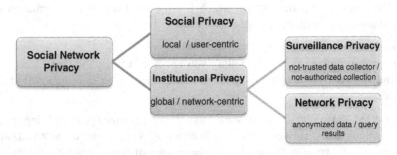

Fig. 12.3 Social network privacy types

Table 12.1 Social network privacy concerns

Social Privacy	User awareness Privacy controls complexity Privacy controls changes Privacy controls conflicts
Surveillance Privacy	Not-trusted social network provider Data collected without user permission No oblivion
Network Privacy	Data collected for profit Lack of proper anonymization Increase sharing of collected data

is presented in the next section. For *social privacy*, the main concern is whether or not the user understands the privacy risks he or she is taking when sharing information on a social network (*user awareness*). As recent as 2012, approximately 8 % of US Facebook users had never heard about Facebook privacy tools. What is more alarming is that even people that are aware of privacy risks do not take appropriate steps to protect their privacy. For instance 28 % of US Facebook users share their wall posts to a wider audience then their friends [18]. The positive news is that users have become more aware of their privacy. In a study that used public profiles from New York City, 52.6 % of the users hid their friends list from their public profile as of June 2011, whereas in March 2010, only a little bit more than a year earlier, 17.2 % of the users hid their friends list [19]. Related to the user awareness with respect to privacy, difficulty in setting privacy controls makes the users prone to giving up in selecting an appropriate privacy policy (*privacy controls complexity*). For example, Facebook privacy controls are spread in at least six different tabs: Privacy, Timeline and Tagging, Blocking, Followers, Apps, and Ads. An example of such a tab is shown in Fig. 12.4. To add to this complexity, the privacy controls are not easily accessible from the data use policy, and when there explanation is not clear or even provided [27].

Moreover, privacy controls may change and this can contribute to reducing the privacy (*privacy controls changes*). Again, we use Facebook as an example. As recent as late 2012, Facebook made significant changes to their privacy controls and policies. While these changes simplified the privacy control and policies, they create some additional privacy concerns. For instance, Facebook decided to remove the privacy setting that let users hide their Timeline from people who search for it [34]. In addition, some privacy shortcuts were disabled and made available only from the main privacy page. An example of such a privacy shortcut is the pop-up on the top of the News Feed that answered questions such as "Who can see my stuff?" [34]. Also, the data use policy does not offer direct links to privacy controls. To add to that, the Facebook privacy policy changed to allow more sharing of data to third-party companies. The new policy states:

> You give us permission to use your name, and profile picture, content, and information in connection with commercial, sponsored, or related content (such as a brand you like) served or enhanced by us.

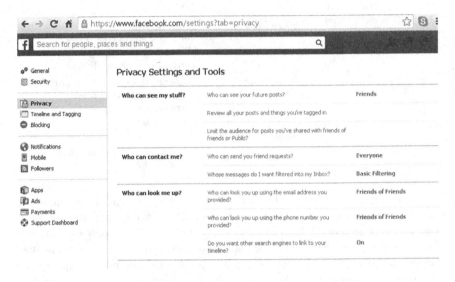

Fig. 12.4 Facebook privacy control—privacy tab

While the old policy was more user-friendly:

> You can use your privacy settings to limit how your name and profile picture may be associated with commercial, sponsored, or related content (such as a brand you like) served or enhanced by us. [27].

This new policy is more related to network privacy and it shows that some of the privacy concerns are applicable to more than one privacy type.

In some cases, the privacy controls may have conflicts and, when two controls specify the privacy setting for the same data item, it is difficult to know which privacy control takes precedence (*privacy controls conflicts*). Privacy policy conflicts exist in many common social networks such as Facebook, MySpace, Orkut, Twitter, and Google + [79]. For example, in Facebook, a user may choose to have his or her friends' list private. However, if some of that user's friends keep their corresponding friends list public, some friendship relations can be inferred by an authorized user. This type of conflict is common to other privacy settings as well [79].

With respect to *surveillance privacy*, an important concern is that the initially trusted social network becomes non-trusted (*not trusted social network provider*). Also, there are organizations that have the capability of collecting data without user approval and can use this data for their own purposes (*data collected without user permission*). In addition to these concerns, the fact that any published data may stay published or stored forever may increase the possibility of surveillance and constitute an important privacy concern. It is very difficult to enforce the right to be forgotten, also known as oblivion, on social networks (*no oblivion*). Different countries have opposing views with respect to oblivion and their regulations are contradictory to each other. For instance, in France, the law recognizes the right of oblivion, a convicted criminal can object to the publication of his criminal record after he or she has satisfied their punishment. In the United States, publication of criminal records is protected by the First Amendment.

Network privacy concerns are less known to the general user of a social network than the social and surveillance privacy concerns, but they are very important in any discussion of social network privacy. The main reason a social network site gathers user data is to be able to monetize that data. Gathering more personal data, which can be successfully analyzed, mined, and consequently used for target advertisement, is the main goal of a social network company. This ever increasing amount of personal data creates more and more potential privacy violations (*data collected for profit*). In the past few years, Facebook users disclosed less information publically, which shows increase in user awareness of social privacy concerns. However, during the same time, the average Facebook user seems willing to disclose more and more information privately to his or her friends. This contributes to more data collected by Facebook and third party apps, and this data can be used for advertisement or other purposes directly by the data collectors [73]. The collected data are usually released to other companies in an anonymized form; however, since the anonymization methods are not public, it is not clear if the anonymized data are able to avoid re-identification of individuals (*lack of proper anonymization*). For instance, Facebook can share user data if they "remove your name and any other personally identifying information from it." Currently, more and more companies are specialized in Big Data and data analytics. Developing efficient methods to analyze large amount of data will contribute to a need for social network data. A social network site will benefit from selling their anonymized data to such data analytics companies and potential privacy violations will increase (*increase sharing of collected data*).

The above classification is not completely disjointed; some of the privacy concerns are true for more than one privacy type. For instance, *user awareness* is also important for surveillance privacy and network privacy, and *no oblivion* privacy concerns exist in network privacy as well.

Section 12.4 will provide existing privacy solutions to the above concerns with a focus on technical solutions.

12.4 Privacy Solutions for Social Networks

Since there are many privacy concerns regarding social network data, there is not an easy solution to these problems. Moreover, to protect privacy of individuals the privacy solutions must be supported and provided by legislators, social network sites (social network service providers), and social networks users [67]. All these three entities have the ability to enhance the privacy protection for each type of entity. Figure 12.5 captures this interaction. Social network privacy is divided between social privacy, surveillance privacy, and network privacy (institutional privacy is not shown). The legislators, social network sites, and their users can provide privacy solutions for each type of privacy.

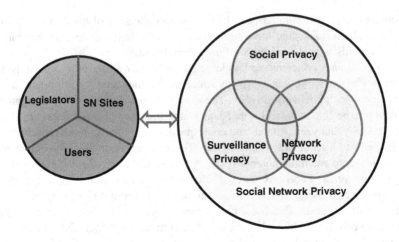

Fig. 12.5 Social networks privacy—a common effort

For *social privacy*, the legislators can require that social network sites have a privacy policy and a set of privacy controls that is appropriate for the type of data the site collects. The legislators can also require that the social network sites have a good education system of their users and the privacy implications of their data are disseminated to all their users. The social network sites also provide important solutions for social privacy concerns. Privacy friendly default settings, easy to use privacy controls that change infrequently or not at all, allowing creation of pseudonymous profiles as an option, and avoiding privacy conflicts are some of the solutions a social network site can employ to protect the privacy of their users. Last but not least, the users must be educated about the privacy implication of sharing their data. In the context of social privacy, the users should make sure who their friends are, and they should use appropriate privacy controls for the data they share. It is important to respect the privacy of others as well, and to also guard the privacy of one's children [67].

We provide an example regarding privacy policy conflict and we discuss how this problem can be solved.

In Fig. 12.6, the Celebrity user chose to make her list of friends private. Some of her friends (Friend 1 and Friend 2 are depicted) chose to make their list of friends

Fig. 12.6 Allow-take-precedence privacy policy

public. Due to their choice, the corresponding friendship relationships are public and this violates the choice of the Celebrity user. This privacy policy conflict, known as *allow-take-precedence policy*, is widely used in existing social networks such as Facebook and Orkut [79]. Solutions proposed for this privacy violation include [79]:

- **Redesign of privacy policy.** This is extremely difficult if the users can choose their own privacy policies. While it is easy to employ, it will set standard privacy policy for all users that can be viewed as either too restrictive or too permissive.
- **Deny-take-precedence policy.** The social network site may deny the Friend 1 and Friend 2 users the ability to publish their friendship relation with Celebrity user due to Celebrity user settings. This approach is known as deny-takes-precedence. Since it is based on both users' preferences, it requires more processing from the social network site software and it is not currently employed. This approach will give preference to privacy when there is a privacy policies conflict between users.
- **Avoid using bi-directional friendship relations.** This is possible in social networks that allow relations of type followers and following. In this case each user may choose their own preference for their corresponding lists. Still an adversary may infer entries of a private list from public lists of the victim's friends (followers or followings), and these solutions still have the original problem although in a limited scope.
- **Privacy policy negotiations.** In this scenario, privacy policies are dynamically updated based on given requirements of utility and privacy. Such policy negotiations are still in an early development stage and it is not clear how well they can satisfy all users. As an example, in a game theoretic approach used for those negotiations, users cannot protect their information if others sharing the information request to make it available [72].

For *surveillance privacy*, the most obvious solution is to avoid posting any sensitive information on online social networks. While this is an easy solution, it is difficult to enforce considering how pervasive the social networks are today. In this type of privacy, the social network site is not trusted and thus the private information should not be provided in clear form. The basic solution for enforcing this is the usage of cryptographic methods. There are several applications that use encryption to protect users' information on the social network sites. Some of them are listed below:

- **FlyByNight.** This application is implemented for Facebook and encrypts the user data before being stored on Facebook. Unfortunately, FlyByNight relies on Facebook servers for key management, so it fails to protect against the surveillance of the social network provider [55].
- **NOYB (none of your business).** NOYB is also used on Facebook and it uses encryption to protect personal details of users. It protects against the surveillance of the social network provider (Facebook in this case) but it is applicable only to

specific attribute data from the user profiles and it does not allow encryption of free text [29].

- **FaceCloack.** This application is a Firefox browser extension that uses a symmetric key to encrypt user personal information in Facebook. This method requires the use of dedicated FaceCloack servers that store part of the user profile in an encrypted form [56].
- **Scramble!** This application is designed as independent from a specific social network platform. The content is also encrypted prior to being shared in the OSN, and only friends can decrypt it [4].

Other solutions regarding surveillance privacy include implementation of a social network site as a distributed site, use of fake traffic to obscure user activity, and use of anonymous communication network such as Tor [20].

The main solution for *network privacy* is network anonymization. To define a network anonymization model it is important to understand what constitutes a privacy violation for a social network. A *privacy violation* (or breach) occurs when sensitive information about an individual is disclosed by an adversary. In the context of social networks the most common types of privacy violations are: *identity disclosure*, *attribute disclosure*, and *link disclosure* [80].

Identity disclosure refers to the correct re-identification of a node (such as a person or an institution) in an anonymized social network when the adversary uses the anonymized network and other available information about individuals from the network.

Attribute disclosure refers to an adversary finding out something new about the target individual, but in this case the adversary may not know which node in the network the individual represents.

Link disclosure occurs when an adversary discloses the existence of a sensitive relationship between two individuals from the social network. This type of disclosure assumes that some relationships are sensitive and their privacy must be protected.

In order to anonymize a social network it is also important to understand what types of data are sensitive and what types of data might be known from other sources. These assumptions lead to various *social networks models*. We present below an example of such a model.

We model a social network as a simple undirected graph $\mathcal{G} = (\mathcal{N}, \mathcal{E})$, where $\mathcal{N}$ is the set of nodes and $\mathcal{E} \subseteq (\mathcal{N} \times \mathcal{N})$ is the set of edges. Each node represents an individual entity. Each edge represents a relationship between two entities.

The set of nodes, $\mathcal{N}$, is described by a set of attributes that are classified into the following three categories: *identifier* attributes such as *Name* and *SSN* that can be used to identify an entity, *quasi-identifier* attributes such as *zip code* and *sex* that may be known by an adversary, and *sensitive* attributes such as *diagnosis* and *income* that are assumed to be unknown to an adversary.

For simplicity, only binary relationships are allowed in our model. Moreover, all relationships are of the same type and, as a result, they are represented via unlabeled undirected edges. Also, this type of relationship is considered to be of the same nature as all the other "traditional" quasi-identifier attributes. In other words, the graph structure may be known to an intruder and used by matching it with known external structural information; therefore, serving in privacy attacks that might lead to identity and/or attribute disclosure. In this model, link disclosures are not a privacy concern. An example of a social network is shown in Fig. 12.7. *Age* and *zip* are quasi-identifier attributes and *disease* is a sensitive attribute. The identifier attributes are not shown.

In addition to the privacy concerns that must be understand and captured in an anonymized network, of similar importance is the utility of the data. The anonymized network, while protecting the individual's privacy must also preserve much information to maximize the utility of the social network. Since it is difficult to know how the network is used, defining utility is not a trivial problem. Early work in social network anonymization uses the total number of edge additions and deletions to measure the utility loss [54]. Newer approaches focus on preserving the topological features of a network such as centrality measures, degree distributions, and clustering coefficients [1].

We present next some of the most common social network anonymization approaches.

The main two approaches to anonymize social networks are categorized as follows [80]:

- **Edge modification.** These techniques propose edge deletion and additions to help in anonymizing the network. The network structure will be altered by these changes, and the goal is to minimize the number of edge modifications while the privacy requirements are met and the data utility is maximized. The most used anonymization approaches in this category are: *k-degree anonymity* [54], *k-neighborhood anonymity* [81], and *k-automorphism* [82]. These approaches will

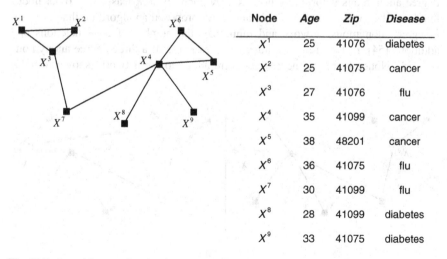

Node	Age	Zip	Disease
X^1	25	41076	diabetes
X^2	25	41075	cancer
X^3	27	41076	flu
X^4	35	41099	cancer
X^5	38	48201	cancer
X^6	36	41075	flu
X^7	30	41099	flu
X^8	28	41099	diabetes
X^9	33	41075	diabetes

Fig. 12.7 A social network example

be briefly introduced in this section. The above models focus on avoiding node re-identification. Other approaches such as *k-isomorphism* [15] and *l-opacity* [61] focus on preventing link disclosure, in which the adversary learn about a sensitive relationship between individuals.

- **Clustering or network generalization.** This technique proposes publication of aggregate information about the network structure. In this way attacks based on network structure are made very ineffective; however, the utility of the network may be too low. We will present the *k-anonymous clustered social network* [13, 74] in this section.

Two other approaches are as follows:

- **Randomization.** This is a special case of anonymization via edge modifications. The graph structure is modified by deleting and adding edges at random such that the total number of edges is unchanged. Unfortunately, this approach is altering significantly the utility of the data [36].
- **Differential privacy.** In this approach individual nodes are protected under the definition of differential privacy [23]. Usually in this approach the network is not anonymized and it is kept by the data owner, only releases of network measures such as degree distribution are allowed [37]. This constraint makes the differential privacy approach less flexible than the other anonymization approaches mentioned above. However, very recent developments allow non-interactive network data publication while differential privacy property is satisfied [14]. A high-level discussion about *differential privacy in social network data* is included in this section.

The *K-degree anonymity* model assumes that the degree sequence of nodes in a social network is potentially available to an adversary and the anonymization aims to create groups of nodes with similar degree values. A network $\mathcal{G} = (\mathcal{N}, \mathcal{E})$ is k-degree anonymous if for every node $X \in \mathcal{N}$ there exist at least $k - 1$ other nodes that have the same degree as X. Liu and Terzi proposed an algorithm that creates a k-degree anonymous network and minimizes the number of edge deletions and additions [54]. In Fig. 12.8 we illustrate an example of a three-degree anonymous network. Notice that three new edges were added to the network (shown in bold)

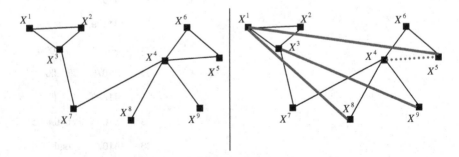

Fig. 12.8 A social network and a corresponding three-degree anonymous network

and one was deleted (dashed). In this example nodes X^1, X^3, and X^4 have the degree 4, and all other nodes have the degree 2.

The *k-neighborhood anonymity* model assumes that adversary knows the immediate subgraph of the target node. The immediate subgraph contains all neighbors and relationships between neighbors. A node X is k-neighborhood anonymous if there exist at least k-1 other nodes such that the subgraph constructed by the immediate neighbors of each such node is isomorphic (has the same structure) to the subgraph constructed by the neighbors of X. By immediate neighbors we mean the nodes that are directly connected to the starting node. A graph satisfies k-neighborhood anonymity if all the nodes are k-neighborhood anonymous. There are heuristic algorithms that construct k-neighborhood anonymous networks. Such algorithms start by identifying all different neighborhoods and then it creates groups of identical neighborhoods of size k using edge additions and deletions [81]. In Fig. 12.9 we show a three-neighborhood anonymous network. Notice that three new edges were added to the network (shown in bold) and two were deleted (dashed). In this example nodes X^3, X^4, and X^7 have isomorphic immediate neighborhoods. All the remaining six nodes have also isomorphic neighborhoods.

K-automorphism anonymity assumes that the adversary can know any subgraph around a certain node. A network is k-automorphic if the view of the network from any node is identical with the view of the network from at least k-1 other nodes. The complete mathematical definition for k-automorphism and a heuristic algorithm is presented in [82]. Note that in Fig. 12.9, the anonymous network is also k-automorphic.

Based on the above definitions, it is easy to notice that any k-automorphic network is also k-neighborhood anonymous network, and any k-neighborhood anonymous network is also k-degree anonymous network.

A *k-anonymous clustered social network* uses a different approach. Based on a grouping strategy that tries to maximize an objective function, the nodes from a network are partitioned into pair-wise disjoint clusters. These clusters will then be generalized to super-nodes, which may be connected by super-edges. The goal of

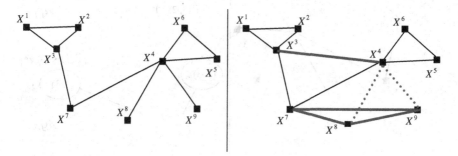

Fig. 12.9 A social network and a corresponding three-neighborhood anonymous network (which is also three-automorphic network)

this process is to make any two nodes coming from the same cluster indistinguishable based on their relationships. To achieve this objective, Campan and Truta developed intra-cluster and inter-cluster edge generalization techniques that were used for generating super-nodes and super-edges, and so generalizing the social network structure [13]. To satisfy the k-anonymous clustered model—derived from the well-known k-anonymity property for microdata—each cluster must have at least k nodes. The algorithm used in the anonymization process, called the SaNGreeA (Social Network Greedy Anonymization) algorithm, performs a greedy clustering processing of an initial social network in order to generate a k-anonymous clustered social network. In this algorithm the nodes that are more similar in terms of their neighborhood structure are clustered together using a greedy approach. To do so, a measure that quantifies the extent to which the neighborhoods of two nodes are similar to each other is used. Full descriptions of this measure and of the SaNGreeA algorithm are presented in [13]. Improving the SaNGreeA algorithm, Tassa and Cohen introduced a more efficient algorithm, namely sequential clustering algorithm, for creating k-anonymous clustered social network. Details about this new algorithm and a complete comparison in terms of both efficiency and utility with SaNGreeA can be found in [74]. Figure 12.10 shows two three-anonymous clustered networks.

Differential privacy in social networks is a new research direction that extends the differential privacy for tabular data to networks. Differential privacy is based on a mathematical guarantee of privacy which states that anything that is learnable from a table T can also be learned from a table T' which differs by only one record from table T [23]. Such a table T' is called a neighboring table for T. In case of networks, the notion of vicinity or neighboring can be defined in terms of both edges and nodes. Based on this, two models were created, edge differential privacy [33, 45, 46] that defines neighboring networks that differ by at most one edge, and nodes differential

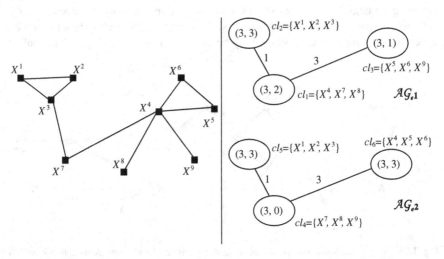

Fig. 12.10 A social network and two corresponding three-anonymous clustered social networks

privacy [7, 47] in which neighboring networks differ by one vertex and its corresponding edges. Until 2014, all of this work was based on an interactive setting, which means that a trusted curator that has access to the original network will receive queries from non-trusted users and will apply a differentially private algorithm to provide the answer to users. Each user will have a privacy budget that can be exhausted if too many queries are sent to the curator. Recently, one practical solution for non-interactive network data publication was introduced in [14]. This solution, called *density-based exploration and reconstruction (DER)* creates a sanitized network G_s from the original network G that satisfies ε-differential privacy for the privacy budget ε. In addition to differential privacy requirements, this models aims to provide privacy guarantee even for correlated data (the original differential privacy model assumes independent data) if the amount of correlation can be measured. Full details regarding this approach can be found in [14].

12.5 Challenges and Opportunities in Social Networks Privacy

As already presented in the previous sections, there is not a universal solution to social network privacy, and there are many reasons for this.

While in other domains such as healthcare or financial sectors there are privacy regulations that define an expectation of privacy, in the social networks privacy is not as well defined, being interpreted differently by various users and social network sites owners. *Common interpretations of privacy in social networks as well as regulations that protect individual's privacy* in this context are major challenges that need to be addressed in the future. There are users that do not expect privacy for any data they post on their social network; users that for minor financial benefits will voluntarily give up their private information; as well as users that are very privacy aware. To create a common view of privacy is a challenging task that needs to be solved from a sociological perspective. Related challenges include *users' awareness of privacy issues* and *difficulty to create useful privacy legislation in an online medium* where users "voluntarily" provide sensitive information.

To that end, privacy in social networks requires a clear and near universal definition that can be updated through time. We need a standard model (perhaps similar to the Open System Interconnection (OSI) Reference model) for privacy in social networks. This model will address questions regarding the minimum acceptable requirements for a social network to be considered safe. This will be in terms of privacy dealing with each layer that contains or transports private information. It will require research into what today's social media consumers want as well as legislative aspects associated with privacy. Research should also address which predefined relationships for users of social networks bearing various privacy settings (e.g., just like those currently in existence on Facebook) should be encouraged to exist in social networking services by default. In addition, another important research issue is:

should users have the power of customize relationships associations and their respective privacy settings and what is the degree of effectiveness for doing so? The literature indicates that people have a tendency to share private information even when they express privacy concerns [71]. Research needs to address whether user-based privacy customization is effective at protecting individual privacy.

There are also many technical challenges in social network privacy that provide opportunity for future research.

Balancing privacy and data utility remains an important challenge in this field. While much work has been done with respect to this problem, we still do not know how to share private data while protecting privacy and ensuring sufficient data utility in the shared data. The trade-off between utility and privacy was introduced in the form of the R–U confidentiality map [22]. Such a map is a set of values, R and U, of disclosure risk and data utility that correspond to various strategies for releasing the data. An example of such a map is shown in Fig. 12.11. Most of the work to release anonymized social networks is based on maximizing data utility while maintaining the disclosure risk under a given threshold. This technique, also known as privacy-based approach, corresponds to the RU map shown in Fig. 12.11.

Social network anonymization still provides an imperfect solution. The availability of data from various sources makes anonymization more and more challenging. Finding more secure anonymization approaches while preserving data utility remains a challenge in data privacy. The new paradigm of differential disclosure is promising but it requires better solutions that preserve network data utility to a satisfactory level. New solutions are needed for releasing data that are both confidential and preserve data utility.

Social networks are dynamic and protecting the individuals in this context is very challenging. Existing methods do not perform well with multiple releases of the data, because the data evolves in time and releasing just one version of the data is not acceptable in many practical problems. While there is some preliminary work in this area [77] more research is needed.

The advent of Big Data represents a privacy challenge as well. Businesses are able to use Big Data to learn more about their employees, increase productivity, and reduce cost. However, in these processes, the privacy of individuals is at high risk due to the high level of monitoring. Balancing how to use Big Data while preserving the privacy of individuals is a difficult problem that requires future research. Related to Big Data, the increasing use of technology generates more individual

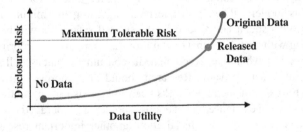

Fig. 12.11 An R–U confidentiality map

data. For instance, the use of wearable devices such as heart rate monitors or exercise devices and online activity (social networks, online searches, blogs) creates a continuous flux of data. To add to that, advances in Big Data analytics and other fields will likely reveal new trends and patterns about individuals. For instance, the likelihood of specific diseases such as Alzheimer may be computed in the near future based on genetic screening and other factors. Such developments will also create more privacy challenges.

The richness of information embedded in social networks creates major privacy challenges. A social network contains a variety of data in addition to its network structure. For instance geolocation data can be included as part of the profile, multimedia files may also contain sensitive information that is hard to detect without human intervention. How to protect individuals' privacy in this environment is extremely challenging and future research needs to address this problem.

An important opportunity that exists in this area is the creation of privacy software tools. We envision two types of software tools that have the potential to increase the awareness of privacy issues and to make privacy more user's friendly. In the first category of such tools, the social network users should automatically set their privacy preferences in a variety of social network sites. These tools have the potential to improve the social privacy component illustrated in Fig. 12.3. A second category of tools, used by social network owners, will aim to create anonymized social networks based on specified parameters. While prototypes of such tools exist for specific anonymization models, there are no tools that allow selection of the desired anonymity model and that are easy to use. Creating such privacy software tools will contribute to automating institutional privacy and in particular the network privacy component (see Fig. 12.3).

Finally, *privacy needs to be connected with deception literature and deception detection and prevention research.* Protecting one's privacy involves safeguarding software as much as safeguarding people from people. Social engineering has become prevalent through social networking sites [28], so privacy should not be examined disconnected from deception. Deception detection algorithms can contribute to helping maintain one's privacy by eliminating the potential for identity theft and consequences arising from that theft. Educating developers and designers as well as users about privacy also means educating them about deception. These two terms are linked. It is as necessary that we explore new research directions as that we update technical procedures that govern the development of social networking services.

References

1. Alufaisan Y, Campan A (2013) Preservation of centrality measures in anonymized social networks. In: Proceedings of the ASE/IEEE international conference on privacy, security, risk, and trust (PASSAT 2013), Washington D.C., USA
2. Barbaro M, Zeller T (2006) A face is exposed for AOL searcher no. 4417749. The New York Times, Published 9 Aug 2006

3. Barnes SB (2006) A privacy paradox: social networking in the United States. First Monday 11 (9):11–15
4. Beato F, Kohlweiss M, Wouters K (2011) Scramble! your social network data. In: Privacy enhancing technologies symposium (PETS), pp 211–225
5. Bernal J (2009) Web 2.0 and social networking for the enterprise: guidelines and examples for implementation and management within your organization. Pearson Education
6. Bhat CS (2008) Cyber bullying: overview and strategies for school counsellors, guidance officers, and all school personnel. Aust J Guid Couns 18(1):53–66
7. Blocki J, Blum A, Datta A, Sheffet O (2013) Differentially private data analysis of social networks via restricted sensitivity. In: Proceedings of the conference on innovations in theoretical computer science (ITCS), pp 87–96. doi:10.1145/2422436.2422449
8. Boyd DM (2003) Reflections on Friendster, trust and intimacy. In: Proceedings of the Fifth international conference on ubiquitous computing (Ubicomp 2003), Workshop application for the Intimate ubiquitous computing workshop, Seattle WA, USA
9. Boyd DM (2004) Friendster and publicly articulated social networking. In: Proceedings of the ACM CHI 2004 conference on human factors in computing systems, pp 1279–1282. ACM Press, New York NY, USA. doi:10.1145/985921.986043
10. Boyd DM, Ellison NB (2007) Social network sites: definition, history, scholarship. J Comput-Mediat Commun 13(1):1–19
11. Brenner J, Smith A (2013) 72 % of online adults are social networking site users. http://pewinternet.org/Reports/2013/social-networking-sites.aspx
12. Brown J, Broderick AJ, Lee NJ (2007) Word of mouth communication within online communities: conceptualizing the online social network. J Interact Mark 21(3):2–20. doi:10.1016/10.1002/dir.20082
13. Campan A, TrutaTM (2008) A clustering approach for data and structural anonymity in social networks. In: Proceedings of the 2nd ACM SIGKDD international workshop on privacy, security, and trust in KDD (PinKDD)
14. Chen R, Fung B, Yu PS, Desai B (2014) Correlated network publication via differential privacy. VLDB J 23(4):653–676. doi:10.1007/s00778-013-0344-8
15. Cheng J, Fu AWC, Liu J (2010) K-isomorphism: privacy preserving network publication against structural attacks. In: Proceedings of the ACM SIGMOD international conference on management of data (SIGMOD), pp 459–470
16. Choi D, Kim J (2004) Why people continue to play online games: in search of critical design factors to increase customer loyalty to online contents. Cyberpsychol Behav 7(1):11–24
17. Coleman JS (1988) Social capital in the creation of human capital. Am J Sociol 94:95–120. doi:10.1086/228943
18. Consumer Reports (2012) Facebook and your privacy. Who sees the data you share on the biggest social network? Consumer Rep Mag
19. Dey R, Jelveh Z, Ross KW (2012) Facebook users have become much more private: alarge-scale study. In: PerCom Workshops, pp 346–352
20. Dingledine R, Mathewson N, Syverson P (2004) Tor: the second generation onion router. In: USENIX security symposium, pp 303–320
21. DiNucci D (1999) Fragmented future. Print 53(4):32
22. Duncan GT, Keller-McNulty SA, Stokes SL (2001) Disclosure risk vs. data utility: the R-U confidentiality map. Technical Report Number 121. National Institute of Statistical Sciences
23. Dwork C (2006) Differential privacy. In: Proceedings of the international colloquium on automata, languages, and programming (ICALP)
24. Editorial Board (2014) Edward Snowden, whistle-blower. The New York Times. Accessed 2 Jan 2014
25. Ellison NB, Steinfield C, Lampe C (2007) The benefits of Facebook "friends:" social capital and college students' use of online social network sites. J Comput-Mediat Commun 12 (4):1143–1168. doi:10.1111/j.1083-6101.2007.00367.x
26. Facebook (2014) Data use policy. https://www.facebook.com/about/privacy/

27. Goel V (2013) Facebook to update privacy policy, but adjusting settings is no easier. The New York Times. 29 Aug 2012
28. Gross R, Acquisti A (2005) Information revelation and privacy in online social networks. In: Proceedings of the 2005 ACM workshop on Privacy in the electronic society, pp 71–80. doi:10.1145/1102199.1102214
29. Guha S, Tang K, Francis P (2008) Noyb: privacy in online social networks. In: Proceedings of the First workshop on online social networks, pp 49–54
30. Guillen MF, Suarez SL (2005) Explaining the global digital divide: economic, political and sociological drivers of cross-national internet use. Soc Forces 84(2):681–708. doi:10.1353/sof.2006.0015
31. Gundry J (1992) Understanding collaborative learning in networked organizations. In: Kaye AR (ed) Collaborative learning through computer conferencing. Springer, Berlin, pp 167–178
32. Gundry J (2006) Web 0.0 social media. Knowledge Ability Ltd. http://www.knowab.co.uk/socialmedia.html
33. Gupta A, Roth A, Ullman J (2012) Iterative constructions and private data release. In: Proceedings of the theory of cryptography conference (TCC), pp 339–356
34. Guynn J (2012) Facebook changes privacy controls again and takes a key one away. Los Angeles Times. Accessed 12 Dec 2012
35. Hargittai E (2008) Whose space? Differences among users and non-users of social network sites. J Comput-Mediat Commun 13(1):276–297. doi:10.1111/j.1083-6101.2007.00396.x
36. Hay M, Miklau G, Jensen D, Weis P, Srivastava S (2007) Anonymizing social networks. Technical report, University of Massachusetts, Amherst
37. Hay M, Li C, Miklau G, Jensen D (2009) Accurate estimation of the degree distribution of private networks. In: Proceedings of the international conference on data mining (ICDM)
38. Hoegg R, Martignoni R, Meckel M, Stanoevska K (2006) Overview of business models for Web 2.0 communities. In: Proceedings of the GeNeMe (Gemeinschaften in NeuenMedien), Dresden, Germany, pp 23–37
39. Howard TW (2010) Design to thrive: creating social networks and online communities that last. Morgan Kaufmann
40. Izquierdo E (2011) Social networked media: advances and trends. In: Proceedings of the 2011 ACM workshop on social and behavioural networked media access, pp 1–2. ACM, New York, NY, USA. doi:10.1145/2072627.2072629
41. Jabeur N, Zeadally S, Sayed B (2013) Mobile social networking applications. Commun ACM 56(3):71–79. doi:10.1145/2428556.2428573
42. Jones R (1994) Digital's world-wide web server: a case study. Comput Netw ISDN Syst 27 (2):297–306. doi:10.1016/0169-7552(94)90144-9
43. Kaplan AM, Haenlein M (2010) Users of the world, unite! The challenges and opportunities of social media. Bus Horiz 53(1):59–68. doi:10.1016/j.bushor.2009.09.003
44. Kaplan AM, Haenlein M (2011) The early bird catches the news: nine things you should know about micro-blogging. Bus Horiz 54(2):105–113. doi:10.1016/j.bushor.2010.09.004
45. Karwa V, Raskhodnikova S, Smith A, Yaroslavtsev G (2011) Private analysis of graph structure. Proc VLDB Endow 4(11):1146–1157
46. Karwa V, Slavkovic A (2012) Differentially private graphical degree sequences and synthetic graphs. In: Proceedings of the privacy on statistical databases conference. Lecture notes in computer science, vol 7556, pp 273–285
47. Kasiviswanathan S, Nissim K, Raskhodnikova S, Smith A (2013) Analyzing graphs with node differential privacy. In: Proceedings of the theory of cryptography conference (TCC), pp 457–476
48. Katz JE, Rice RE, Aspden P (2001) The Internet, 1995-2000: access, civic involvement, and social interaction. Am Behav Sci 45(3):405–419. doi:10.1177/0002764201045003004
49. Kietzmann JH, Hermkens K, McCarthy IP, Silvestre BS (2011) Social media? Get serious! Understanding the functional building blocks of social media. Bus Horiz 54(3):241–251. doi:10.1016/j.bushor.2011.01.005

50. Kim A. J. 2000. Community building on the Web. Peachpit Press
51. Kirkpatrick D. 2010. The facebook effect. Simon and Schuster
52. Lane N, Walton-Flynn N, Benlamlih F (2008) Mobile social networking. Informa UK Limited. http://www.telecoms.com/files/2009/05/buongiorno_final-fmt_nl-3110-f.pdf
53. Lenhart A, Madden M (2007) Teens, privacy and online social networks: How teens manage their online identities and personal information in the age of MySpace. Pew Internet and American Life Project. http://apo.org.au/?q=node/16750
54. Liu K, Terzi E (2008) Towards identity anonymization on graphs. In: Proceedings of the 2008 ACM SIGMOD international conference on management of data, pp 93–106
55. Lucas M, Borisov N (2008) Flybynight: mitigating the privacy risks of social networking. In: Proceedings of the 7th ACM workshop on privacy in the electronic society (WPES), pp 1–8
56. Luo W, Xie Q, Hengartner U (2009) FaceCloack: an architecture for user privacy on social networking sites. In: Proceedings of the international conference on Computational Science and Engineering (CSE), vol 3, pp 26–33
57. Morris MG, Venkatesh V (2000) Age differences in technology adoption decisions: implications for a changing work force. Pers Psychol 53(2):375–403. doi:10.1111/j.1744-6570.2000.tb00206.x
58. Muramatsu J, Ackerman M (1998) Computing, social activity, and entertainment: afield study of a game MUD. Comput Support Coop Work (CSCW) 7(1–2):87–122. doi:10.1023/A:1008636204963
59. Murchu IO, Breslin JG, Decker S (2004) Online social and business networking communities. In: Proceedings of the ECAI 2004 workshop on application of semantic web technologies to web communities, pp 241–267. doi:10.1007/978-1-4419-7142-5
60. Murugesan S (2007) Understanding Web 2.0. IT Professional 9(4):34–41. doi:10.1109/MITP.2007.78
61. Nobari S, Karras P, Pang H, Bressan S (2014) L-Opacity: Linkage-Aware Graph Anonymization. In: Proceedings of the international conference on extending database technology (EDBT), pp 583–594
62. O'Brien CN (2011) The first Facebook firing case under Section 7 of the National Labor Relations Act: exploring the limits of labor law protection for concerted communication on social media. Suffolk Univ Law Rev 45:29–66
63. Olson P (2013) Teenagers say goodbye to Facebook and hello to messenger apps. Obs J. http://www.theguardian.com/technology/2013/nov/10/teenagers-messenger-apps-facebook-exodus. Accessed 9 Nov 2013
64. Quercia D, Lathia N, Calabrese F, Di Lorenzo G, Crowcroft J (2010) Recommending social events from mobile phone location data. In: Proceedings of the IEEE 10th international conference on in data mining (ICDM), pp 971–976. doi:10.1109/ICDM.2010.152
65. Rafaeli S, Larose RJ (1993) Electronic Bulletin boards and "Public Goods" explanations of collaborative mass media. Commun Res 20(2):277–297. doi:10.1177/009365093020002005
66. Raynes-Goldie KS (2012) Privacy in the age of Facebook: discourse, architecture, consequences. PhD Thesis, Curtin University
67. Rome Memorandum (2008) Report and Guidance on Privacy in Social Networks Services —"Rome Memorandum". In: International working group on data protection in telecommunications, Rome, Italy
68. Rosenblum D (2007) What anyone can know: the privacy risks of social networking sites. IEEE Secur Privacy 5(3):40–49. doi:10.1109/MSP.2007.75
69. Shen X (Sherman) (2013) Security and privacy in mobile social network [Editor's Note]. IEEE Netw 27(5):2–3. doi:10.1109/MNET.2013.6616107
70. Shuen A (2008) Web 2.0: astrategy guide. O'Reilly Media, Inc
71. Squicciarini AC, Griffin C (2012) An informed model of personal information release in social networking sites. Proceedings of the 2012 International conference on privacy, security, risk and trust and 2012 International conference on social computing, pp 636–645. doi:10.1109/SocialCom-PASSAT.2012.137

72. Squicciarini A, Shehab M, Wede J (2010) Privacy policies for shared content in social network sites. VLDB J

73. Stutzman F, Gross R, Acquisti A (2012) Silent listeners: the evolution of privacy and disclosure on Facebook. J Privacy Confid 4(2):7–41

74. Tassa T, Cohen DJ (2013) Anonymization of centralized and distributed social networks by sequential clustering. IEE Trans Data Knowl Eng 25(2):311–324. doi:10.1109/TKDE.2011.232

75. Travers J, Milgram S (1969) An experimental study of the small world problem. Sociometry 32(4):425–443. doi:10.2307/2786545

76. Valkenburg PM, Peter J, Schouten AP (2006) Friend networking sites and their relationship to adolescents' well-being and social self-esteem. Cyber Psychol Behav 9(5):584–590. doi:10.1089/cpb.2006.9.584

77. Wang C-JL, Wang ET, Chen ALP (2013) Anonymization for multiple released social network graphs. Adv Knowl Discov Data Mining LNCS 7819:99–110. doi:10.1007/978-3-642-37456-2_9

78. West A, Lewis J, Currie P (2009) Students' Facebook "friends": public and private spheres. J Youth Stud 12(6):615–627. doi:10.1080/13676260902960752

79. Yamada A, Kim TH, Perrig A (2012) Exploiting privacy policy conflicts in online social networks. In: CMU-CyLab-12-005, Carnegie Mellon University

80. Zheleva E, Getoor L (2011) Privacy in social networks: a survey. Chapter in Social network data analytics. Springer Science and Business Media

81. Zhou B, Pei J (2008) Preserving privacy in social networks against neighborhood attacks. In: Proceedings of the IEEE international conference on data engineering (ICDE), pp 506–515

82. Zou L, Chen L, Ozsu TM (2009) K-automorphism: a general framework for privacy preserving network publication. In: Proceedings of the international conference on very large data bases (VLDB)

Chapter 13
The Right to Privacy in the Age of Digital Technology

Richard Spinello

13.1 Introduction

Computer technology has created enormous new opportunities for both suppliers and consumers of information. Every organization has at its disposal vast computerized resources for processing its many functional activities. Thanks to the revolutionary technology of digitization, information has become more permanent, mobile, and pliable. Pieces of information can be easily aggregated or recombined to create revealing profiles. At the same time, monitoring technologies and the Internet's open architecture allow for the careful tracking of a person's movements both in cyberspace and in the physical world. Technologies like mobile telephony also provide ample opportunities for such surveillance.

Digital networked technology, therefore, is systematically diminishing our actual privacy and lowering our expectations for the level of privacy to which we feel entitled. Public controversies sometimes slow down this irrevocable trend to make every person as transparent as possible, but strong privacy rights seem increasingly incompatible with these technologies. The threat to informational privacy, which involves a person's control over the flow of his or her personal information, is particularly pronounced [26].[1]

In certain situations, governments have pushed back with some alacrity to protect the privacy rights of their citizens. The European Union has been especially proactive in protecting personal information. It has recently focused attention on the activities and policies of search engines such as Google. It now requires the US company to remove the links to news articles or other documents associated with an

---

[1]Kang differentiates this form of privacy from privacy affecting our physical space.

R. Spinello (✉)
Management and Organization Department, Carroll School of Management, Boston College,
140 Commonwealth Avenue, Chestnut Hill 02467, MA, USA
e-mail: richard.spinello@bc.edu

© Springer International Publishing Switzerland 2015
S. Zeadally and M. Badra (eds.), *Privacy in a Digital, Networked World*,
Computer Communications and Networks,
DOI 10.1007/978-3-319-08470-1_13

individual's name if that individual so requests. Europeans claim that the "right to be forgotten" is an essential aspect of the right to privacy. Hence every individual should be allowed to insist upon the removal from the Internet of old or irrelevant information, especially if that information is incriminating in some way. Google has complied with this demand, and it now offers a web page where Europeans can request the search engine to remove undesirable links tied to their name [45].

As the Google case illustrates, the ethical issues involving privacy rights and information use are complex and intricate. This is partly because the value of privacy itself is contested and the concept of privacy still remains vague and mercurial. Should privacy be interpreted so broadly that it must include even this "right to forget"? If so, how do we determine the legitimate scope of such a right? Where do we draw the line in limiting a search engine's capabilities to make information more accessible?

A second problem arises because privacy is often confused with other rights such as freedom or self-determination, that is, the right to make decisions about one's life. Legal arguments that defend assisted suicide have been linked with privacy, referring to "ownership" over one's body and the liberty to determine the time and manner of one's death. As a result, definitions of privacy lack precision, and they are often conflated with normative justifications for a right to privacy. Therefore, before we set out to analyze privacy, we must precisely clarify the meaning of privacy, with special attention given to informational privacy, which is the primary axis of our discussion. Failure to understand the essential nature of privacy will interfere with any coherent ethical or policy analysis. Once we have set forth a workable definition of privacy, we can transition to a normative analysis. That analysis must come to terms with several questions of paramount importance. Is privacy an intrinsic human good or is it an instrumental one? Second, is the rights-based approach still a sound way of thinking about informational privacy, and is it a viable avenue for making prudent policy decisions? Or is privacy more constructively interpreted as a social value to be measured by its contribution to social welfare? If we conclude that privacy is a valid claim-right, how can that right be adequately secured? Should all countries adopt a regime of information law and policy that is similar to the EU model? That model relies on comprehensive regulations that safeguard personal privacy even in the vast realm of networked space. Or can privacy be protected through self-regulation and better technology design? Should the onus be on the state or the individual? Finally, we must consider the challenges ahead such as how to balance strong privacy rights with the need for information accessibility and the preservation of the Internet's open access structure.

Before we begin the task of conceptualizing privacy, however, it is instructive to review some important background on privacy problems created by digital information networks. Hence, we first turn to a brief overview of the threats posed to personal privacy, especially for vulnerable groups such as the consumer or users of social media. This discussion will help us to appreciate the nature and scope of the challenges posed by evolving information technologies such as social networking platforms.

13.2   Technology-Based Privacy Controversies

In past centuries, the primary threat to personal privacy was thought to originate from the state. As a consequence of the state's Orwellian tendencies, the US Constitution includes the Fourth Amendment, which protects citizens from unreasonable search and seizure by government authorities. In the 19th century US citizens were worried that the postal system, the national census, and even the nation's telegraphic network would somehow compromise their personal privacy. People were also troubled that photography would invade their personal space. The telephone caused even more concerns that were exacerbated in the troublesome *Olmstead* [36] case where the Supreme Court ruled that wiretapping or listening to conversations (without a warrant) was neither a search nor a seizure and so it did not violate the Fourth Amendment.[2]

None of these technologies, however, have posed the same sweeping threats as networked digital technology. Thanks in part to the rapid proliferation of computers and digital networks, arguably the new privacy adversary is the bureaucratic organization, whether it be in the private or public sector. Solove has argued that we need a new metaphor for capturing the current threat to privacy. He proposes that we turn to Kafka's novel, *The Trial*, a book which showcases the anonymous oppression of the legal system. According to Solove [51], "the growing use and dissemination of personal information creates a Kafkaesque world of bureaucracy, where we are increasingly powerless and vulnerable, where personal information is not only outside our control but also subjected to a bureaucratic process that is itself not adequately controlled."

Privacy is especially challenging for consumers who must provide certain data such as credit card information almost every time they make a purchase. Purchasing data is also typically collected at the point of sale. In addition, every move a consumer makes online leaves behind a digital imprint that can be captured, stored "forever" in a database, and easily recombined with other revealing data. The collection and assembly of all this information into comprehensive databases enables the creation of "digital dossiers," which include an expanding sequence of records on almost every facet of a person's life [51].

Perhaps the most subtle but ominous threat comes from the common process of data aggregation whereby information is collected from different sources and recombined into a single record. For example, information collected by a financial "supermarket" that sells banking or insurance products could be combined with information about spending habits, online purchases, or charitable contributions. The non-transparent aggregation from eclectic data sources by data brokers such as ChoicePoint and Acxiom poses a particularly severe problem for consumers who appreciate their privacy rights. Acxiom's enormous Infobase includes demographic

---

[2]In 1967 the Supreme Court reversed its decision on wiretapping in *Katz v. United States* [27]. See also [49].

and purchasing data that covers 115 million households and serves as an invaluable tool for direct marketing.

Consumers have a hard time evaluating the sensitivity of data they reveal because they cannot anticipate its future utilization nor how that data will be linked to other pieces of information in a completely different context. It might be that a discrete unit of information, such as a list of books and music purchased on amazon.com, is innocuous in itself but incriminating when combined with other data. As Nissenbaum [35] points out, it is an erroneous assumption that "an aggregate of information does not violate privacy if its parts, taken individually, do not."

As a result of collection, processing, and aggregation techniques, companies can engage in an unprecedented level of *data profiling*. This process is defined as "the collating of data about individuals in databases which can be used to identify, segregate, categorize and generally make decisions about individuals known to the decision maker only through their computerized profile" [3]. These profiles come in many different shapes and configurations. Some data brokers, for example, specialize in profiling financially at-risk consumers by gathering data from social media and other sources. This information is then sold to certain financial companies that target these individuals with products that often have punitively high interest rates. This information is collected and disseminated without a consumer's knowledge or consent [2].

Profiles of online activities have also multiplied exponentially. Consider what happens when consumers shop or browse online. Electronic commerce transactions often leave behind a revealing trail of *personally identifiable information*, including a consumer's name, address, e-mail address, and phone number. One way in which web site vendors can track the browsing activities of their customers is through the use of cookies, small data files that are written and stored on the user's hard disk drive by a web site such as amazon.com when the user visits that site with a browser. They contain information such as passwords, lists of pages within the web site that have been visited, and the dates when those pages were last examined. These cookies enable the monitoring of a user's movements when he or she visits the amazon web site. The cookie can reveal whether the user browses through history books or is more attracted to romantic novels. Amazon can use this information to send targeted ads or promotional emails.

Tracking tools are not confined to cookies. Marketers also rely on beacons, small pieces of software code installed on a user's hard drive (without their knowledge) that can track a web surfer's location and online activities. Both beacons and third-party cookies (installed by online ad agencies like DoubleClick) can track users from site to site. This enables the company that installed these devices to build a database of that user's online activities. Not only can this information be sold to advertisers, it can also be sold on a data exchange to data brokers that have the option of combining it with offline data.

Cookies and beacons, however, have a serious liability: they do not work with mobile devices and smart phones which are often used for online browsing. As a result, these technologies are being replaced by the assignment of unique ID numbers to each user that will do the tracking. Google, for example, might assign an ID number to a user and then track his or her activities across Gmail, their Android phone and its apps, and the Chrome browser on that user's PC. These unique ID numbers have the potential to monitor and record the user's movements on both his or her smart phone and PC. The end result is a more accurate and richer profile for advertisers [7].

Why do companies commit resources to all of this data collection, aggregation, and profiling? The principal objective is targeted marketing and advertising. Most corporations are convinced that the more detailed information they acquire about the consumer, the more ability they will have to tailor their marketing efforts and generate higher revenues. Targeted campaigns minimize risk and increase the likelihood of a positive reaction. It makes more sense to send someone ads for toys if he or she has recently made a purchase of toys on amazon.com or toysrus.com. Hence, it is probably safe to assume that this mature conviction about the predictive power of information has become a fixture of modern marketing techniques. According to Cohen [5], the "colonization of private spaces" by cookies, beacons, and other technologies is a foreseeable result of the "market-driven search for more and better information."

But where is the harm in this insatiable quest for consumer data? Why should consumers be so concerned about this loss of control over the information they provide online if the result is merely more targeted advertising? One problem is that this all goes on in a non-transparent way, without the consumer's knowledge or consent. As we have noted, financially troubled consumers can be surreptitiously profiled without any ability to correct or dispute the data collected about their financial affairs. Another concern is that these profiles create the potential for being "misdefined and judged out of context in a world with short attention spans" [46]. If someone judges John by the books he reads, his professional interests, and his civic associations they could easily come to the wrong conclusion about his political preferences.

A third problem stems from the fact that this collected data is subject to security breaches that have become all too common in recent years. In 2014, two large retailers, Target Corp. and Neiman Marcus, revealed that their computer systems were severely compromised. Those systems failed to block a powerful computer virus that allowed hackers to pilfer the credit card information of their customers. When this type of information falls into malicious hands, consumers are subject to financial harm.

In addition to consumers, users of social networks like Facebook are also at risk. Facebook often knows the most intimate details of a person's life. Social media users derive many benefits and pleasures from sharing personal information within their network of "friends" and associates. However, sometimes that information is shared too widely when users inadvertently make some Facebook settings public. In addition, there are obvious temptations for a company like Facebook to exploit information amassed about their users for the purposes of social research.

Facebook has had to contend with many privacy challenges in its brief history. In 2009, for example, Facebook suddenly modified its privacy settings. A person's "friends" could no longer be kept concealed from the public or from each other.

As a result, information that was once private such as one's profile picture, name, gender, address, professional networks, and so forth, became publicly available by default. According to MacKinnon [28], these changes were motivated by the company's need to monetize this "free" service, and were consistent with Zuckerberg's "strong personal conviction that people everywhere should be open about their lives and actions." Zuckerberg, among others, has clearly sought to lower privacy expectations. Facebook's decision to make previously confidential information "publicly available," was reversed thanks to public protest, and users now have the capability to control access to most of their personal information.

It is understandable that Facebook and other social networking platforms want to share some of this information with trusted advertisers for targeted ads, since this is the way the company generates revenue. But this must be done in a way that curtails the secondary use of this information or the aggregation of these data with information collected elsewhere. Otherwise, a social media user's privacy becomes easily jeopardized [4].

It should be evident from this brief discussion that the protection of privacy rights has become a daunting challenge when information can be so easily collected, processed, and disseminated. It can also amount to a great expense for governments that enforce privacy laws and corporations who must comply with those laws. Are the benefits worth these expanding costs? Is privacy still a value worth protecting? Before we address these questions we must provide a workable definition of privacy.

13.3 Common Theories of Privacy

Most consumers intuitively know that their privacy rights have been violated when companies obtain their personal information and use it without their permission. They are justifiably unsettled when web sites spy with impunity on their private lives. Nevertheless, they find it difficult to render a formal definition of privacy. Even philosophers and privacy theorists have struggled to define privacy with any real precision. According to Westin [56], "few values so fundamental to society as privacy have been left so undefined in social theory. . . ." This is because privacy itself is an ambiguous and fuzzy concept. We all have a strong sense that privacy is valuable and desirable. But our notions of privacy tend to be vague and our conception of what separates the "private" from "public" space tends to be amorphous.

Hence we must develop a cogent theory of privacy that will include and highlight a reasonable definition of privacy. We assume that privacy is a unitary concept that can be adequately differentiated from related concepts such as self-determination or property rights. Once we have a more precise idea of privacy we can objectively assess its normative value. Before we plunge into this theoretical reflection, however, it is instructive to review different conceptions of privacy and to point out their strengths and shortcomings. This cursory overview will also allow us to appreciate how the concept of privacy has evolved. To some extent all of these theories overlap but each one has a distinct nuance and accent.

One of the first and most widely cited theories of privacy was articulated by US Supreme Justices Warren and Brandeis [58]: "Recent inventions and business methods call attention to the next step which must be taken for the protection of the person and for securing the individual. . . . *the right 'to be let alone'*" (my emphasis). The notion of privacy as the fundamental "right to be let alone" resonated with many in the legal community, who saw the need to protect "private life," which includes things that "all men alike are entitled to keep from popular curiosity" [58]. Preserving this right, they argue, is especially critical in the face of encroaching new technologies (such as photography). The prescient Warren and Brandeis article, written in 1890, not only gave us a suggestive concept of privacy, but it also anticipated the link between the potential erosion of privacy and technological advancements.

This right to privacy, the right to prevent people from invading a person's private space, was cited and reaffirmed in many legal cases subsequent to the Warren and Brandeis article such as *Pavesich v. N.E. Insurance Co.* [38], which recognized a right to privacy in the common law that was "derived from natural law." However, in the infamous *Olmstead* case, the Court seemed to regress from its support of privacy rights when it ruled that wiretapping was not a violation of the Fourth Amendment. Brandeis dissented, however, arguing that this right to be let alone was "the most comprehensive of rights and the right most valued by civilized men" [36].

The Warren and Brandeis conception of privacy puts an emphasis on physical privacy or privacy as non-intrusion into a person's private physical space. Privacy is seen as necessary to block access to a person or to his or her physical possessions. This form of privacy is sometimes referred to as "accessibility privacy" because of its focus on the prevention of gaining access to another individual [6]. Privacy defined simply as the right to be let alone, however, is too broad and imprecise. Accordingly, it fails to provide adequate guidance for policymakers since there are clearly occasions when people cannot be left alone. There are times where the state must interfere in the lives of its citizens, but this theory does not specify valid exceptions to the right to be let alone nor does it provide any guidelines for determining what those exceptions might be.

Privacy has also been construed as secrecy. According to this simple model, privacy is violated when information that was previously concealed is disclosed [50]. Privacy is associated with the concealment of information or the right of an individual to conceal facts about himself or herself. According to proponents of this theory such as Posner [39], when people say they want privacy what they really want is "more power to conceal information about themselves that others might use to their disadvantage." This definition has some parallels in legal reasoning. In *Whalen v. Roe* [57] the Supreme Court stipulated that the right to privacy included "an individual interest in avoiding disclosure of personal matters" and "an interest in independence in making certain kinds of important decisions."[3] But this theory

---

[3]See also [50].

of privacy as secrecy is obviously unnuanced and it too needs more specification. How do we distinguish what sort of information people have the right to conceal?

A third theory conceptualizes privacy as a form of seclusion or inaccessibility. It includes the requirement of secrecy but is more comprehensive. Legal scholar, Ruth Gavison [20], defines privacy as the limitation of others' access to an individual with three irreducible elements: secrecy, anonymity, and solitude. Anonymity refers to the protection from undesired attention; solitude is the lack of physical proximity to others; and secrecy (or confidentiality) involves limiting the dissemination of knowledge about oneself. For Gavison, this inaccessibility is the common feature of all definitions of privacy. With Gavison's theory, the notion of privacy expands to emphasize more strongly psychological privacy, such as the ability to keep one's thoughts and feelings concealed from the prying eyes of others.

Despite its subtleties, Gavison's theory too has conspicuous shortcomings because it fails to adequately delineate morally justified conditions for the claim of limited access. The right to anonymity, secrecy, and solitude must be subject to certain limits for anyone who participates in civil society. Nonetheless, Gavison has laid the groundwork for a more refined understanding of what the right to privacy should entail.

A fourth theory sees privacy as control over one's personal information. According to Charles Fried [17], "privacy is not simply an absence of information in the minds of others, rather it is the control we have over information about ourselves." Similarly, Miller [32] argues that the right to privacy is constituted by "the individual's ability to control the circulation of information relating to him." Thus, one has privacy if one has some type of control over one's personal information or at least control over technologies that potentially threaten one's privacy. For example, thanks to the protest over cookies, web browsers were re-designed to give users more control over this intrusive technology.

The privacy through secrecy theory proposed that privacy must include suppression of certain information. The control theory follows this path as it continues to shift the focus away from physical privacy or non-intrusion to informational privacy, an obvious concern of this networked digital era. Whereas physical privacy is characterized by "seclusion and solitude," informational privacy is characterized by confidentiality, data protection, and control over one's personal information [34]. Floridi [19] defines this type of privacy as "freedom from epistemic interference" that is achieved by possession of the ability to control the facts about one's life or personal activities that are presently unknown to others. Since informational privacy is most at risk due to digital electronic technologies, it currently receives the lion's share of theoretical reflection and it is the primary focus of our analysis.

Unlike other frameworks, the control theory has the advantage of avoiding any confusion of privacy with related ideas such as self-determination. Also, as Tavani [54] points out, another benefit of this theory is its recognition of the roles that choice and discretion play in privacy protection. The notion of control, however, is still ambiguous because it is usually understood too broadly. Also it fails to answer an important question: how much control does one need over information in order to ensure privacy? It is virtually impossible to have absolute control, so the degree of control, usually left unspecified, is of considerable importance. Moreover, loss of control does not necessarily imply that there has been any infringement of privacy rights. It's very unlikely that I will be able to control all the ways in which an insurance company uses information about my various insurance policies. But if that information is not unnecessarily shared outside the company and if it is not being improperly used within the company, it is hard to argue that my privacy rights have been infringed.

Given the liabilities and limits of these notions of privacy, it should be apparent that a more synthetic approach is called for. All of these theories are suggestive, but none of them seems quite comprehensive or flexible enough. With this in mind we turn to a more nuanced way of framing the definition of privacy.

13.4   The Restricted Access-Limited Control Model

The extensive theoretical reflections of Tavani and Moor [55] on privacy build on the foundation provided by the theories we have explained.[4] They describe informational privacy in terms of "restricted access/limited control." The Tavani and Moor approach to privacy has the distinct advantage of distinguishing between the concept or definition of privacy as "restricted access" and the management of privacy as "limited control."

This theory prudently recognizes the critical importance of establishing a zone or sphere of privacy that restricts others from access to our personal affairs and information. It concedes, of course, that our information has to sometimes be shared with others so that the proper use of information must fall somewhere between total privacy (or secrecy) and complete disclosure.[5] The "restricted access" paradigm suggests the ability to shield personal data from some parties while sharing it with others. Thus, according to this perspective, an individual has privacy "in a situation with regard to others if and only if in that situation the individual is normatively protected from intrusion, interference, and information access by others" [33]. According to this definition, a "situation" can be a relationship, an activity of some sort, or any "state of affairs" where restricted access is reasonably expected. What constitutes a situation is left deliberately vague and open-ended so that it can encompass a broad range of contexts.

Moor also makes a critical distinction between situations that are naturally private (living on a secluded island or hiking in the mountains) versus normatively controlled private situations such as the doctor–patient relationship. In a situation where one is naturally protected from access by others, one has natural privacy or

---

[4]I have discussed this theory elsewhere (see [52]) and drawn from that material in this chapter. For a lucid and extended account of the Tavani and Moor model see [33, 55].

[5]Sometimes there are moral requirements for the sharing of information, so this zone is not beyond the rightful claims of other people.

natural secrecy. Normatively private situations can include a specific location (such as a person's home), an activity (casting a vote), or a relationship where information is exchanged between two parties (such as details of one's medical history) [55]. In a normatively private situation, norms such as laws or policies (based on ethical principles) are developed to create a protective zone of privacy because the situation requires such protection. Even a promise to protect someone's privacy or preserve confidentiality creates such a normatively private situation that binds the person who has made such a promise.

Natural privacy or secrecy can be lost. But when this occurs one's privacy rights have not been infringed. This is due to the absence of norms providing a privilege to or a right to a zone of privacy. Thus, if I am conversing with a close friend in a secluded place and someone accidentally discovers us and disrupts our conversation, we have undoubtedly lost our precious privacy. However, such an event does not warrant the claim that our privacy rights have been violated in any conceivable way.

As an illustration of this theory, consider a normatively private situation such as the relationship between a psychiatrist and his or her patient. A patient in this situation has every right to expect that his or her confidentiality will not be breached. This patient has privacy only if there is a condition of *restricted access* such that the patient's medical records are accessible only to his or her doctor, the mental health professionals who assist practitioner, and perhaps the patient's insurance company. The patient must be protected so that only the right people have *access* to his or her relevant information on an as-needed basis [33]. There will be privacy if a protective zone is created through norms, such as laws or ethical standards, which restrict the "wrong" people from accessing this delicate information.

The capacity to exercise "limited control" is also essential for protecting privacy. Individuals need as much control as realistically possible over their personal data in order to help ensure the reality of restricted access. That control will be exercised by mechanisms such as informed consent, which allows a user to opt-into the secondary use of the personal information he or she has provided to an organization for a specific purpose. It will also allow users to have some say over how and when their information is shared with third parties. Let's say that the psychiatrist wants to share his or her patient's information with their regular physician because the psychiatrist believes that this would be in the patient's best interests. The patient should have the right to control the flow of information in this situation by being informed and given the opportunity to override this decision. People also need to be able to dispute and correct inaccuracies in order to ensure the integrity of their data.

Arguably, the restricted access/limited control theory is the most feasible and practical one for understanding the nature of informational privacy. It captures the key idea that I cannot have privacy without some measure of control and without restrictions on information flows about myself when such restrictions are ethically warranted by a particular situation. By taking into account situations that deserve normative protection, this theory also gives emphasis to the neglected dimension of context. According to this paradigm, privacy can be best defined as a condition of limited accessibility. Invasions of privacy make an individual's information more accessible than it should be. Since limits to accessibility of information are contingent upon the moral agent's situation, this theory avoids the problems associated with other privacy theories that are overly broad such as those that interpret privacy simply as secrecy or the right to be let alone.

13.5 Normative Justifications for Privacy

We now understand that informational privacy, the main axis of our discussion, can be most accurately described or conceptualized in terms of "restricted access" and "limited control." This theory strongly conveys the need for privacy but we must go farther and offer a justification of that need from a purely ethical perspective.

While almost everyone agrees that privacy is important, there is far less consensus on whether to interpret privacy as an individual right or as a social value that makes the scope of privacy rights contingent on their contribution to society. Schwartz [47] argues for the latter view and claims that we should regard privacy as a constitutional value "that helps to form the society in which we live and to shape our individual identities." Along the same lines, Merton [31] contends that while privacy may be a "personal predilection," it should only be justified as "a requirement of social systems."

Correlative with this view is the argument that "normative individualism" or the traditional interpretation of privacy (and other rights) as belonging to the individual is simply outmoded. Just how are privacy rights "attached" to an individual? According to this line of reasoning, the narrow conception of privacy as a personal right provides an insufficient framework for formulating public policy. Critics of the classical notion of individual human rights argue that a rights-based approach is too dogmatic, inflexible, and individualistic [16].

Accordingly, some privacy scholars including Regan [42] and Solove [50] believe that far more attention must be focused on the social importance of privacy rather than an individual right to privacy. Privacy is primarily justified as a way of protecting those valuable activities that society deems worthy of protection. Privacy is a public value, and privacy rights are to be enforced only because of their value to the community. Thus, privacy rules or regulations should protect the individual only when it is in society's best interests to do so. As Solove [50] explains, "individual liberties should be justified in terms of their social contribution."

But who determines what's in the best interests of society or the community, and which personal activities deserve the legal protection provided by the state? The theories of Regan and Solove seem to give precedence to the collective welfare rather than the objective needs of the individual person. Many theories that stress this social nature of privacy are flawed by their inattention to the person and what is owed to that person in justice. In our view, privacy rules (or rights) should be justified not by social welfare concerns or by their larger value to the community, but by a consideration of their contribution to a person's well-being. The right to privacy, like all rights, is about fairness. This right, properly specified, supersedes competing concerns (including those about its "social contribution") because its infringement involves the damaging or impeding of goods essential for a person's flourishing. Thus, as we will demonstrate, we can best defend this individual right by proceeding from an understanding of the basic human goods that are constitutive aspects of personal well-being [12].

Many people refer to privacy as a "value," but it is more precise to describe privacy as a good. The term "good," when applied to human actions and principles, is understood as an object of interest or something wanted. Practical reason seeks satisfactory ways of acquiring this object or thing wanted [14]. As Aquinas [1] has explained, therefore, good has "the intelligibility (*ratio*) of an end," worthy of our pursuit. Privacy is certainly an end or objective that rational persons desire and pursue for the sake of their basic welfare. Privacy's benefits and intelligible desirability are the ultimate roots of its normativity.

But what kind of "good" is privacy? Some philosophers and computer ethicists have declared that privacy is a fundamental and intrinsic good, or they have advanced the equivalent thesis that privacy has intrinsic value. The argument has also been made that privacy has intrinsic value because it is linked so closely to our autonomy. According to Innes [25], for example, "privacy is intrinsically valuable because it acknowledges our respect for persons as autonomous beings...." Floridi [18], who claims that "a person ... is, after all, a packet of information," would also assign privacy intrinsic worth because any invasion of privacy is equivalent to a direct invasion of our personhood.[6]

In contrast to this viewpoint, it is more plausible to maintain that privacy is an instrumental good. To demonstrate the validity of this line of reasoning we need to present a viable theory of the good. This discussion will allow us to discern how the particular good of privacy should be properly categorized. Even many deontological ethical theories that emphasize duties or contract rights concede the need for some notion of the good. There are many "thin" theories of the good, found in the works of philosophers such as John Rawls. The list of primary goods proposed by Rawls [40] includes "rights and liberties, opportunities and powers, income and wealth ... and, above all, self- respect." However, Rawls conflates intrinsic goods with instrumental ones and does not offer a complete list of those basic goods that determine the opportunities for human flourishing.

Conversely, a more robust and viable theory of the good is elaborated in the new natural law framework, which takes its inspiration from the philosophy of Aquinas. The new natural law, which brackets the metaphysical suppositions of Thomistic philosophy, articulates a "thicker" conception of the good, which will give us a more complete understanding of the personal human goods that constitute our well-being and contribute to our flourishing. While people can desire many goods, some goods are more fundamental than others. These "basic human goods" are basic not because we need them to survive but because we cannot flourish as human

---

[6]Floridi has developed an ontological theory of informational privacy; a consideration of this unorthodox theory is beyond the scope of our analysis, but let it suffice to say that it shifts the focus of attention from the physical person to his or her digital personae, which Floridi describes as information entities. For a concise overview of his arguments see [18].

beings without them. Hence these irreducible goods, which are intrinsic aspects of human well-being and fulfillment, are the primary ends or reasons for action and the ultimate source of normativity. Our knowledge of these goods is self-evident, arrived at in non-inferential acts of understanding, in which we grasp a possible end as beneficial and worthwhile for its own sake [22].

What then are these basic human goods? Finnis [15] and George [21] both argue convincingly for the following list of basic irreducible human goods that are choice-worthy as ends-in-themselves: bodily life (and "component aspects of its fullness: health, vigor, and safety"); knowledge and aesthetic appreciation; religion or harmony with God; friendship or harmony between persons; marriage; skillful performance in work and play; and practical reasonableness, the good of harmony between one's judgments and behavior (authenticity) and between one's judgments and inner feelings (integrity). These goods "outline the worthwhile self" that a person constructs by his or her free choices [14].

If a good is not sought as an end in itself, it is not intrinsic to human fulfillment and, therefore, it cannot qualify as a basic human good. Instead, it must be classified as an instrumental good. Many material goods are quite important, but they are not basic for fulfillment. Life is more important than physical property. Even freedom or autonomy cannot be classified as a basic human good, because it is not an end in itself. Freedom is an extremely important good, but it's an instrumental one, since individuals are not ultimately fulfilled or perfected by freedom. Rather, they want freedom to pursue other goods such as knowledge of truth, relationships with friends of their choosing, or the worship of God in the way they deem proper.

Similarly, privacy cannot be considered as a basic good, since it is not intrinsically valuable, and it does not directly contribute to human flourishing. Privacy is not a basic good for two reasons. First, there is a strong cultural dimension to privacy. Privacy expectations can vary considerably from one culture to the next. People in simpler cultures, for example, might thrive and flourish in a milieu of almost complete transparency. Second, privacy is not intrinsic to the human person because it is always desired for the sake of some other good, that is, as an instrumental means to some further end such as health or friendship. Privacy is only intelligibly choice-worthy when seen in the light of these more fundamental goods.

Consider some of the reasons why a person demands or seeks privacy. One reason we require privacy is to ensure that certain personal relationships will adequately conserve a proper level of intimacy. According to Rachels [41], "there is a close connection between our ability to control who has access to us and to information about us, and our ability to create and maintain different sorts of social relationships with people." The intrinsic goods in jeopardy by the erosion of privacy are friendship and marriage. But privacy allows us to participate in these goods without self-consciousness and without the inhibition that comes from worrying about the prying eyes of a neighbor or some "peeping Tom."

People also desire privacy in order to maintain their security and safety, which is a "component aspect" of the fundamental good of life (and health). In the information age, informational privacy is absolutely essential for our security. As we pointed out, without privacy (understood as the condition of restricted access), we might be subject to identity theft or the pilfering of our credit card data. Or we might be judged out of context and presumed guilty even though our activities are purely innocent. In extreme cases, a person's life could be at stake, as illustrated in *Remsburg v. Docusearch* [44] where a data broker was hired by a stalker so that he could locate and murder a woman who was the target of his perverted obsessions.

We also require privacy for the sake of other instrumental goods such as autonomy. It is often difficult to properly exercise one's freedom without some degree of privacy. If someone openly monitors my actions or tracks my information, then he or she can force me to alter my activities or practices. For example, if a person knows that his or her employer is constantly watching them or monitoring their conversations, that individual is apt to be extremely cautious in his or her assertions so that they conform to the employer's expectations. According to Zuboff [59], it is not unusual to uncover reduced spontaneity and a high level of "anticipatory conformity" among those who are aware that they are being observed or having their information tracked through surveillance mechanisms.

Therefore, according to this analysis, we have sensible but ulterior reasons for seeking out privacy. We seek privacy as a means to other ends. Privacy's status as an instrumental good, however, does not diminish its importance. As we have intimated, the value of privacy assumes particular salience in a networked digital world so saturated with monitoring and data collection technologies. As Moor [33] points out, "in a highly computerized culture . . . it is almost inevitable that privacy will emerge as the expression of the core value, security."

What follows from this assessment? First, by conceiving privacy as a personal but instrumental good we dissipate some of the persistent confusion about privacy's ethical status. Vague language about privacy as a "social value" is not particularly illuminating. It is more helpful, however, to rely on basic human goods as the starting point of ethical reflection. This allows us to discern that privacy is an object of human desire, a good, that fosters human well-being, albeit indirectly. Also, because goods such as privacy and liberty are instrumental, we must resist tendencies to absolutize them and give them higher priority than intrinsic goods such as life and health. For example, Etzioni [9] makes the case that policymakers should not hide behind the cloak of privacy and prohibit HIV testing of infants, given the health issues at stake along with the benefits of early treatment.

Second, since privacy supports intrinsic objective goods that are constitutive aspects of human well-being, it is rightly interpreted as a critically important instrumental good that provides a foundation for moral judgments, especially judgments regarding justice and human rights [21].

13.6 The Right to Privacy

We have conceptualized privacy as an instrumental good that rational human beings strive for in order to participate properly in intrinsic human goods that contribute to their perfection and well-being. But we need to take this analysis a step further and consider whether people have a moral entitlement to pursue this good. Every moral entitlement or right implies a duty on the part of others to avoid depriving someone of this right and in some contexts to protect this right from deprivation [48].

Privacy's importance as a means to the end of human flourishing signals the validity of the rights-based approach with its emphasis on justice. Treating privacy as an inalienable right subject to limitations rather than a mere "interest" or social value highlights its proper worth and conveys the gravity of what's at stake when someone's privacy is breached in a situation where normative protection is called for. Moreover, our previous analysis strongly supports the notion that the right to privacy can be derived from its status as an instrumental good. As McCloskey [30] has pointed out, "any right to privacy will be a derivative one from other rights and other goods."

However, a right must not be understood in the Hobbesian sense as a liberty or as freedom to do something without interference. For Hobbes [23], a right is "inconsistent" with a duty or obligation, and hence in the state of nature "every man has a right to everything." Rather, a right in the strict sense must be regarded as that which ensures justice in a given situation or relationship between two or more persons. Rights provide a way of describing "what is just" from a specific perspective, that is, "from the viewpoint of the other to whom something is owed or due, and who would be wronged if denied that something" [15].

As we have intimated, the right to privacy is not justified on the ground that there is some sort of political or legal consensus that privacy is significant. This right is more firmly grounded in the fact that privacy is sometimes required as a pre-condition for the pursuit of intrinsic goods that are constitutive aspects of human flourishing. Since privacy is *necessary* to secure the benefits of these goods we can reason that there should be a right to privacy in order to ensure justice or fairness. Rights are based on need and since a person needs privacy (or the condition of restricted access) in certain situations, it follows that he or she has a rightful entitlement to make certain claims if that privacy is denied or threatened [16]. Recognition of this right to privacy directs us to act in certain ways out of respect for the welfare of our fellow-human beings who are affected by our actions.

In Hohfeld's [24] classic framework, privacy would be considered a claim-right such that one individual (the right-holder) has a claim on another (the duty-bearer). We can intelligibly postulate such a right where there is a positive or negative obligation (or requirement) imposed upon X not to interfere with Y's activity or Y's enjoyment of some form of the good. If a certain level of privacy is essential for Y to participate in certain intrinsic goods such as marriage and friendship, it follows that privacy is a critical factor for Y's flourishing and well-being. It also follows that Y is justly owed such privacy by others because Y would be wronged if denied it. Y, therefore, has a right to privacy and X has a correlative duty not to deprive Y of its privacy, lest X interferes with Y's well-being [15].

Thus, our basic argument is that in the various situations where normative protection of information is necessary and reasonably expected, a person has the claim-right to the condition of restricted access to his or her information. Individuals and organizations have a correlative duty to uphold and protect this right in these circumstances by respecting this person's desire to restrict access to his or her personal information and by giving that person the means to exercise limited control over that information.

This right to privacy, however, is not absolute. Those who argue that privacy should be interpreted as a social value worry about the potential unfairness of a unilateral claim to a privacy right that may unfairly affect others. But the solution is to adequately specify the right to privacy rather than eliminate such an individual right. Privacy rights must be limited by the comparable rights of others along with morally justified exceptions for the sake of the common good. For example, a privacy right to one's medical data could be circumscribed to protect intrinsic goods such as life and health in the case of a public health emergency. A doctor has every right to inform the state of his or her patient's infectious disease in order to protect the lives of others. However, purely utilitarian reasons do not provide a warrant for restrictions on privacy. Thus, while it may be necessary under some urgent circumstances to breach privacy in order to prevent an imminent terrorist attack, a corporation certainly cannot infringe on privacy rights merely for the sake of more efficient marketing practices and higher economic returns [13].

13.7 Protecting the Right to Privacy

If privacy is a basic right how can this right be properly secured? Is an expansive legal framework essential or can users protect their own privacy, at least under some circumstances? There are many tools available to protect privacy and so technology or software "code" may appear to be a promising approach. For example, users have the option of deleting cookies deposited by web sites or excluding them from their PC's. However, there is a growing skepticism that code and industry self-regulation are inadequate to deal with this magnifying problem of privacy erosion. Evidence of this is the long history of privacy transgressions by corporations and the most recent behavior of companies like Google and Facebook, which arguably have engaged in transgressive practices in order to monetize their user base. Digital information is a prime currency in the new economy and there is too much market incentive for corporations to commoditize information even when privacy may be compromised. As a result, strong laws seem necessary in order to deal with this market failure.

The comprehensive legal approach has been adopted by the European Union, which preemptively codified strict privacy protections for personal information. The primacy of a rights-based approach to policy issues is reflected in the jurisprudence of the European Court of Human Rights. Privacy in most European nations has long been regarded as a fundamental right that warrants the protection of the legal system. Europeans have preferred the suggestive term "data protection" instead of privacy, which is defined as "the right to control one's own data" [29]. Data protection laws in countries such as Sweden date back as far as 1973. Sweden's Data Protection Act, inspired by the Warren and Brandeis definition of privacy as the right to be let alone, was enacted to prevent "undue encroachment on personal privacy" [37]. It established a Data Inspection Board (DIB) responsible for monitoring and licensing those who maintained electronic data files. Most other European nations soon followed Sweden's bold precedent. Their stringent laws have consistently put more emphasis on "informational participation and self-determination" than the laws of other countries [29].

These heterogeneous statutes were eventually harmonized when the European Union adopted its elaborate Privacy Directive in 1995. This Directive, which requires member states to implement legislation incorporating its privacy standards, is unambiguous in its recognition of informational privacy as a basic right. The Directive's primary aim is quite clear: "to protect the fundamental rights and freedoms of natural persons, and in particular their right to privacy with respect to the processing of personal data" [10]. The EU model is consistent with our thesis that privacy is a principal instrumental good and hence a claim-right of some importance.

The EU Directive requires full data protection for all European citizens and the equitable treatment of their personal information. According to the Directive, every individual has the right to notice about the processing of his or her data beyond the purpose of the original data collection. Users have the right to opt out of data transfers to third parties for marketing purposes, along with the right to access their data and correct mistakes. There is also a quality provision requiring that personal data must be accurate and, where necessary, kept up to date. Finally, there are tighter restrictions on "sensitive information" such as a person's health or genetic data. The guiding principle is that personal data may not be processed without the user's consent unless "processing is necessary for the performance of a contract to which the data subject is party" [10]. The EU directive also mandates tight security safeguards.

By contrast, the United States has adopted a "market-dominated policy for the protection of personal information and only accords limited statutory and common law rights to information privacy" [43]. US policymakers have assigned more responsibility for privacy protection to the private sector rather than to the government itself. However, some notable privacy statutes have been enacted when vulnerable or particularly sensitive information is at stake, and the market cannot be trusted to protect such data. Those laws include the Children's Online Privacy Protection Act (COPPA), Health Insurance Portability and Accountability Act (HIPPA), which protects a patient's medical data, and the Gramm-Leach-Bliley Act, which protects financial data. Like their European counterpart, these laws also require security standards for personal information.

To understand the difference between the European and US approaches to privacy, consider how they differ in their treatment of the secondary use of information (using data unrelated to the purpose of its collection). The EU Directive provides strong regulation of secondary use. Personal data must be collected for a specific and legitimate purpose and cannot be "further processed in a way incompatible with [that] purpose" [10]. The United States, on the other hand, has some secondary use restrictions but does not provide the comprehensive protection of European law. In many cases, once a person provides his or her information there are few limits on how it can be reused [50]. Thus, a court found no problem with American Express when it sold personal information of its card holders to marketers without the consent those card holders [8].

In the absence of European-style legislation, the United States gives more weight to technology and industry self-regulation. Many companies that collect personal information, such as Google and Facebook, have adopted privacy policies in response to market pressures. Users are also encouraged to protect themselves by taking advantage of privacy settings and other technology tools. When companies step over the line regulatory agencies such as the Federal Trade Commission (FTC) usually intervene to protect consumers' interests.

While there is much to be admired with the thick legislative protection offered by the European approach, there are some drawbacks, such as the financial burdens that accompany an elaborate regulatory regime. The EU Directive, for example, requires an expensive bureaucratic infrastructure for its enforcement. In general, government intervention is not always welfare-enhancing, especially if self-interested policymakers are captured by industry interests. On the other hand, given the tepid success of industry self-regulation, many argue with some merit that the benefits of European style regulations far outweigh the costs.

However, current legal solutions are somewhat constrained because they are typically predicated on dichotomizing public and private information. In the US system, for example, some networked spaces such as online medical records are off limits while others—for example, the user profile on a Facebook page—are legally unprotected. Hence, it is not unlawful to harvest that data, link it to data captured by tracking a user's comings and goings on the Web, and sell the whole package to data brokers. Social media data and other forms of information in the public sphere lack normative protection.

This avenue for addressing privacy issues, therefore, often ignores the demands of "contextual integrity." Nissenbaum [34] argues that the criteria for what deserves normative protection must be based not only on the nature of the information in question but also its context. Thus, the effort to distinguish public from private information based on that information's presumed sensitivity has serious liabilities. First, it is difficult to determine what constitutes "sensitive" information in an age when information processing systems are so pervasive and possess such potent aggregative capabilities. Information that is not so revealing in one context may turn out to expose sensitive aspects about a person's life when linked to other data *in a different context*. In the latter case (but not the former), such data would quite probably deserve normative protection. Moreover, there is a tendency to presume that information shared with anyone is "up for grabs," giving latitude to data brokers to collect and assemble this information for commercial purposes. But the recipients of this information matter — it makes a big difference whether you share information with a neighbor, a group of friends, colleagues at work, or a data broker who can recombine that data with other information.

Finally, it should be underscored that law alone can never be the complete solution. Social media users often refuse to take advantage of the technological tools and privacy settings that can limit their exposure. However, social networking sites have not made it particularly easy for users to set the proper boundaries. Easier to use privacy tools embedded with defaults that protect privacy and more ethically informed policies could ameliorate this situation. Social networks such as Facebook need some capability to share certain non-identifiable personal information with trusted advertisers, but there should be no secondary uses of that information (beyond those advertisers), nor any sale of information to data brokers for combination with bits of data collected elsewhere [34]. This strict policy would respect the need for "contextual integrity." The social networking phenomenon suggests that self-regulation coupled with the use of responsibly coded privacy tools still has some role to play in the overall protection of personal privacy [53].

13.8   Challenges

We have argued that privacy is an important right and that no private or public organization can deprive people of that right either by overriding a valid restriction on information or by violating the strictures of contextual integrity. That might happen if a company engages in non-transparent data collection, processing, and aggregation in order to create a profile that exposes intimate details of someone's life. These profiles are mined by government agencies, but far more so by private entities seeking to exploit the predictive power of information. While laws are necessary, in some circumstances (such as social media) a partial solution is to let the user decide the proper access parameters and to give that user the necessary tools to execute his or her choices.

Protecting privacy in the age of digital information will always be difficult but several critical challenges stand out. First, how do we properly configure privacy rights in cyberspace so that this right does not become unnecessarily expansive? Does privacy include the "right to be forgotten" as recently declared by the European Court of Justice? If so, how broadly should this principle be applied? The danger is that if privacy rights are interpreted too broadly the free flow of information in cyberspace will be severely encumbered to the detriment of the common good.

Thus, a formidable challenge for regulators and jurists is how to strike the right balance between privacy rights and the free flow of information. The right to privacy must also be delicately balanced with other entitlements such as free expression. The implementation of this so-called "right to be forgotten" requires the removal of links to undesirable information, but isn't this a form of censorship? Should politicians be able to demand that Google remove links to negative but honest reviews of their tenure in office? It seems difficult to make a credible case that privacy rights should be so thick and extensive.

Second, the relentless progression of new technologies such as Google Glass will constantly menace efforts to preserve personal privacy. Glass is a tiny computer system worn like ordinary glasses and duplicating the functionality of a smart phone. Glass users can take photos, send messages, and search online. If Google Glass incorporated face recognition technologies it would be possible to quickly identity someone in the street by taking her photo and comparing it to online images. This combination of cameras everywhere, even on people's heads, along with the algorithms run by social media and other software systems that can process stored images is quite alarming. Such an encroachment of personal space would jeopardize anonymity and raise enormous new privacy concerns. Lawmakers must prudently weigh the benefits of these new technologies with these potentially high social costs [11].

But perhaps the most significant challenge is how to implement the sensible ideas of privacy theorists who insist that more attention be paid to the context rather than the nature of information. As we have discussed, public information about a person is usually unprotected by privacy norms, but aggregation techniques can result in profiles that reveal too much about that person and thereby infringe his or her privacy rights. Is it possible to formulate and mandate "just aggregation" principles that would preserve the "spatial disconnects" that separate one context from another? Such principles would surely impose more stringent limits on the collection, reuse, and transfer of personal information [4].

13.9   Conclusions

The threat to privacy seems exceptional in the age of digital information where vast amounts of information are collected about individuals and social groups. Some contend that privacy is an artifact and no longer important. But theoretical reflection on privacy sheds light on its continued relevance. Privacy has a spectrum of meanings, and so there are many theories of privacy ranging from the right to be let alone to secrecy. In our view privacy, particularly informational privacy, is best conceived in terms of restricted access by others to one's information and the exercise limited control over that information. The Tavani and Moor theory's emphasis on the need to assess normatively private *situations* takes into account the principle of conceptual integrity.

Some argue that privacy is not an individual right but is more productively construed as a social value. But what's missing in these novel accounts of privacy is a reflective awareness of privacy's role in protecting substantive human goods, especially in certain information-intensive cultures. Privacy is an important good (or value), but it cannot plausibly be categorized as an intrinsic good. Rather, privacy is an instrumental good that is necessary for participation in intrinsic goods such as friendship, health, and security. Since privacy is such an essential instrumental good, the logic of privacy as a rightful entitlement follows. That right is inalienable but limited by the moral requirements of the common good and the comparable rights of others.

Privacy rights should be promoted and protected by law, especially when sensitive information such as medical or financial data is at stake. However, more attention must also be given to context and to the reuse of "public" information that is not subject to regulatory controls. There is also a role for technological tools made available to the user. Giving the user some discretion, aided by education and proper technological design, will help to balance the preservation of privacy rights with an open access Internet.

References

1. Aquinas ST (1948) Summa theologiae, vol I–II. Leonine, Rome
2. Armour S (2014) Data brokers come under fresh scrutiny. The Wall Street Journal, February 13
3. Belgium K (1999) Who leads at half time? Three conflicting versions of Internet privacy policy. Richmond J Law Technol 6:8
4. Cohen J (2012) Configuring the networked self. Yale University Press, New Haven
5. Cohen J (2003) Privacy, ideology and technology. Georgetown Law J 89:53
6. DeCew J (1997) In pursuit of privacy. Cornell University Press, Ithaca
7. Dworkin E (2013) Web giants threaten end to cookie tracking. The Wall Street Journal, October 29
8. *Dwyer v. American Express Co.* (1995) 652 N.E. 2d 1351
9. Etzioni A (1999) The limits of privacy. Basic Books, New York
10. European Union Directive 95/46/EC of the European Parliament on the Protection of Individuals with regard to Processing of Personal Data (1995), article 1. http://europa.eu.int/eurlex/en/lif/dat/1995
11. The Economist (2013) Every Step you Take, *The Economist*, November 16
12. Finnis J (2011a) Reason in action. Oxford University Press, Oxford
13. Finnis J (2011b) Human rights and the common good. Oxford University Press, Oxford
14. Finnis J (1991) Fundamentals of ethics. Georgetown University Press, Washington, D.C
15. Finnis J (1980) Natural law and natural rights. Oxford University Press, Oxford
16. Freeman M (2011) Human rights. Polity, Cambridge, UK
17. Fried C (1990) Privacy: a rational context. In: David Ermann M, Williams M, Guitierrez C (eds) Computers, ethics, and society. Oxford University Press, New York, pp 50–63
18. Floridi L (1999) Information ethics: On the philosophical foundations of computer ethics. Ethics Inf Technol 1:37–56
19. Floridi L (2006) Informational privacy and its ontological interpretation. Computers and Society 36:45–51
20. Gavison R (1984) Privacy and the limits of the law. Yale Law J 89:421
21. George R (2007) Natural law. Am J Jurisprud 52:55
22. Grisez G (2001) A contemporary natural law ethic. In: McLean G (ed) Normative ethics and objective reason. http://216.255.45.103/book/Series01/111/chapter_xi.htm
23. Hobbes T (1962) Leviathan. Collier-MacMillan, New York
24. Hohfeld WN (1919) Fundamental legal conceptions. Yale University Press, New Haven
25. Innes J (1992) Privacy, intimacy, and isolation. Oxford University Press, Oxford
26. Kang J (1998). Information privacy in cyberspace transactions. Stanford Law Rev 50:1193
27. *Katz v. United states* (1967) 389 U.S. 347
28. MacKinnon R (2012) Consent of the networked. Basic Books, New York
29. Mayer-Schonberger, V (1997) Generational development of data protection in Europe. In: Agre P, Rotenberg M (eds) Technology and privacy: the new landscape. MIT Press, Cambridge, pp 219–242
30. McCloskey HJ (1980) Privacy and the right to privacy. Philosophy 55:37–52
31. Merton R (1996) On social structure and science. University of Chicago Press, Chicago

32. Miller A (1971) The assault on privacy. Harvard University Press, Cambridge
33. Moor J (2004) Towards a theory of privacy for the information age. In: Spinello R, Tavani H (eds) Readings in cyberethics. Jones & Bartlett, Sudbury, pp 407–417
34. Nissenbaum H (2010) Privacy in context. Stanford University Press, Stanford
35. Nissenbaum H (2004) Privacy as contextual integrity. Wash Law Rev 79:101
36. *Olmstead v. US* (1928) 277 U.S. 438
37. Paine L (1992) Note on data protection in Sweden. Harvard Business School, Boston
38. *Pavesich v. N.E. Life Insurance Co.* (1905) 122 Ga 190 (S.E. 68)
39. Posner R (1981) The economics of justice. University of Chicago Press, Chicago
40. Rawls J (1971) A theory of justice. Harvard University Press, Cambridge
41. Rachels J (1984) Why privacy is important. In: Schoeman F (ed) Philosophical dimensions of privacy. Cambridge University Press, New York, pp 272–309
42. Regan P (1995) Legislating privacy: technology, social values and public policy. UNC Press, Chapel Hill
43. Reidenberg J (2000) Resolving conflicting international data privacy rules in cyberspace. Stanford Law Rev 52:1315
44. *Remsburg v. Docusearch* (2003) 149 N.H. 152
45. Robinson F (2014) EU orders Google to let users erase past. The Wall Street Journal, May 14
46. Rosen J (2000) The unwanted gaze: the destruction of privacy in America. Random House, New York
47. Schwartz P (2000) Internet privacy and the state. Connecticut Law Review 32:815
48. Shue H (1980) Basic rights. Princeton University Press, Princeton
49. Smith R (2000) Ben Franklin's web site. Sheridan Books, Providence
50. Solove D (2008) Understanding privacy. Harvard University Press, Cambridge
51. Solove D (2004) The digital person. New York University Press, New York
52. Spinello R (2010) Informational privacy. In: Brenkert G, Beauchamp T (eds) Oxford handbook of business ethics. Oxford University Press, Oxford, pp 366–87
53. Spinello R (2014) Cyberethics: morality and law in cyberspace, 5th edn. Jones & Bartlett, Sudbury
54. Tavani H (2007) Philosophical theories of privacy. Metaphilosophy 38:7–19
55. Tavani H, Moor J (2001) Privacy protection, control of information, and privacy-enhancing technologies. Comput Soc 31:6–11
56. Westin A (1967) Privacy and freedom. Atheneum, New York
57. *Whalen v. Roe* (1977) 429 U.S. 589
58. Warren S, Brandeis L (1890) The right to privacy. Harvard Law Review 4:193
59. Zuboff S (1988) In the age of the smart machine. Basic Books, New York

Chapter 14
How to Explore Consumers' Privacy Choices with Behavioral Economics

Sören Preibusch

14.1 Introduction: The Economic Understanding of Online Privacy Beyond Data Protection

14.1.1 The Convenience of Online Consumption

The Web has enabled consumers to access and share an unprecedented amount of information, quickly, conveniently, and cheaply. Companies have embraced new information and communication technologies and moved offline phenomena such as shopping, entertainment, or social networking into the virtual realm. With the advent of the Web, services of a new kind have emerged, such as web search or blogging. In the United Kingdom, digital value creation accounted for 7.2 % of the gross domestic product in 2010 [1]; the share of the digital economy is predicted to continue growing rapidly to reach $4.2 trillion in the G-20 nations by 2016 [2].

Retailing is among the industries that have been fundamentally disrupted by the Internet. For products such as clothing and shoes, Internet sales in the United Kingdom now account for 11.3 % of total sales, with 17.6 % growth year-on-year [3]. Average weekly spending online in May 2014 was £727.5 million [3]. In parallel, the high street is expanding into multi-channel retailing to combine the benefits of an online and offline presence. Much of the reconfiguration of the value chain has happened behind the scenes, but there is a tangible impact for consumers as well. Being greeted by name and receiving personalized product recommendations used to be a distinction of up-market boutiques. Today, it is the sign of mass-personalized online shopping, and one of the ways in which a "data culture" is implemented. Harnessing the power of ubiquitous computing enables organizations to turn data into fuel for insight [4]. Given that they are a valuable resource that

S. Preibusch (✉)
Microsoft Research, Cambridge, UK
e-mail: mail@soeren-preibusch.de

© Springer International Publishing Switzerland 2015
S. Zeadally and M. Badra (eds.), *Privacy in a Digital, Networked World*,
Computer Communications and Networks,
DOI 10.1007/978-3-319-08470-1_14

touches all aspects of society and shapes new forms of production and consumption, personal data are said to be "the new oil of the Internet and the new currency of the digital world." [5].

Consumers enjoy the resulting personalization [6, 7: Sect. 21.3.1]. It reduces the time and effort they have to spend on finding and judging products. For companies, personalization is a powerful tool since it allows lock-in and efficient customer value extraction in fiercely competitive markets. Retailers create and satisfy needs their customers were not yet aware of. Amazon indicates that around 30 % of all purchases result from recommendations [8]; 27 % of European consumers indicate they have bought a product in the past twelve months because it was recommended by the retailer [9]. In short, data-driven personalization works, and benefits both consumers and companies.

14.1.2 Monetization of Personal Data and Mainstream Privacy Concerns

The monetization of personal data as a commodity, through targeted advertising or otherwise, also allows many expensive services to be offered free of charge [10]. It is estimated that UK consumers enjoy an annual surplus of £5 billion from free online content, or twice what they pay to access the Internet [2]. The World Economic Forum observes that "in practical terms, a person's data would be equivalent to their 'money'" [11], and foresees that consumers could control, manage, and exchange their data as they do with cash in their bank account. The European Data Protection Supervisor similarly observes that "personal information has become a form of currency to pay for so-called 'free' online services" [12]. From this follows a close interplay between data protection and consumer protection, and that privacy cannot be achieved through technical means alone.

Consumers experience invasions of privacy as the flip-side of data-powered high-value services, including personalization [13]. Their development and ongoing provision requires far-reaching collection of data and its long-term storage. Until recently, only a few privacy-aware consumers and data protection advocates were aware of the broad consent obtained by businesses through their privacy policies. Post-Snowden, privacy issues are now making headlines in mainstream media [14].

We live in a networked world where ubiquitous Web tracking of consumers and planet-scale government surveillance of citizens are not capabilities but realities. The resulting privacy challenges are calling for privacy-enhancing technologies (PETs), policies, and practices. As outlined above, advances in technical data protection are only part of the picture. The preferences and the incentives behind the choices of companies and their customers are equally important. Economics provide the tools for their study. Privacy failures have been caused at least as often by bad incentives as by bad system design. Ignoring potential users' privacy needs leads to PETs failing in the marketplace despite good engineering [15] (e.g., fully anonymous search engines). Economics provide tools and theories to reason about privacy failures, to suggest remedies, and to positively understand superior privacy practices as the source of competitive advantage.

14.1.3 Studying the Economics of Privacy

As a discipline, the consumer-centric economics of privacy study the value that consumers attach to items of personal information. The objects of analysis are exchanges of personal data. These happen in an environment where data protection is an unquestioned, constitutional, and human right, that provides minimum protection guarantees and remedies.

Other disciplines, beyond the scope of this chapter, challenge the assumption of guaranteed privacy. They discuss the welfare or political economy of information. Privacy as a right is questioned, by establishing its worth for society, or its impact on markets' efficiency. Recently, the blogosphere has restarted the debate under the concept of "post-privacy" [16].

The economics of privacy recognize that personal data have been commodified into a tradable asset. This empirical reality is embraced by studies of markets for personal information and of the behaviors of companies and consumers on such markets. Like many other markets, the market for personal information is far from perfect. It is a defining trait of behavioral economics to embrace these imperfections and make them the object of study: information asymmetries, barriers to entry and exit, externalities, monopolies, and oligopolies. With a focus on actual behavior observed in market players, research is descriptive rather that prescriptive. Experimental designs are inspired by theory, but the evidence need not be rationalized post hoc.

In the tradition of behavioral economics, consumers' reactions to systematically manipulated experiment conditions are observed. The experimental stimulus is an intervention and allows establishing causal relationships, for instance, between data-item sensitivity and consumers' propensity to protect those data. The influence of confounding factors (e.g., visual web site design, trust in companies and brands) can be abstracted away when held constant across treatments. These can be studied through research into human–computer interaction that complements economics experiments in deriving an overall successful user experience.

14.1.4 Supply and Demand for Privacy

On the supply side of data markets, barriers to entry are mostly immaterial: whereas up-front investments into data centers become dispensable when the cloud provides compute/storage infrastructure to new entrants without fixed costs, incumbents profit from previously collected data records. They can improve their offerings through 'learning by doing,' leading to economies of skill. The data records accumulated by a company are an intangible asset [17]. On the demand side, data subjects are typically unable to observe how their data is used and potentially shared and misused, creating an information asymmetry to their detriment. At the same time, poor data portability between alternative services and positive network effects create switching costs; the resulting lock-in makes contractual hazards more likely. Start-ups such as Mydex position themselves as intermediaries to profit from the market frictions by offering personal data vault services. The aim of regulation and enforcement is to create rules for the market of personal information that protect the consumer and increase efficiency and social welfare [18]. An example of such an initiative is the "midata" vision put forward by the UK government: consumers should be given access and insight into their personal data, including usage logs, to migrate these to an alternative supplier if desired [19].

14.1.5 Consumers' Choices for Price–Privacy Trade-Offs

Consumer empowerment relies on their effective ability to transact with a company that suits their preferences. Potential customers have the choice between alternative suppliers that compete on price and non-price attributes. This is true for electronic markets as well as traditional markets. In the grocery store, shoppers not only consider the price tag for a bag of apples, but also the quality of the produce, whether it is grown locally, and farmed according to ecological standards. In electronic retailing, the non-price attributes of a company's offering include its privacy practices.

When consumers engage in transactions that involve exchanges of goods or services, money, and their personal data, they may choose to withhold some of their details. The resulting decrease in service quality or an increase in price is the cost they have to bear to maintain their privacy. Behavioral studies allow measuring a lower bound for the value of privacy by observing consumers' willingness to pay for avoiding data collection or other invasions of privacy.

The issue that researchers and practitioners are facing today is the lack of studies that provide reliable and valid insight into consumers' privacy concerns and behaviors. Looking back, this lack can be explained by the relative recency of the field, even within the study of human–computer interaction. However, looking forward, the ability of new studies to deliver actionable insights hinges on a methodological reboot.

14.1.6 Structure of This Chapter

As a solution, this chapter aims at equipping researchers, practitioners, and poli-cymakers with the tools and the evidence to understand consumers' privacy behaviors. I begin by explaining why experiments rather than surveys or hypothetical choices are needed for delivering valid insights to decision makers. After an exhaustive review of the existing empirical evidence into the value that consumers attach to their privacy, I explain the methodological requirements of valid privacy experiments and offer practical advice for conducting privacy choice experiments. The research presented in this chapter will help in developing privacy-enhancing solutions and policies that meet consumers' needs.

14.2 Surveys Versus Experiments into Privacy Behaviors

14.2.1 Divergence of Privacy Attitudes and Behavior: A Fresh Look at the Privacy Paradox

When surveyed about data protection issues, consumers repeatedly report high concerns about their information privacy [20]. In the 2011 Eurobarometer on data protection, 70 % of respondents, representatively sampled from the EU population were concerned that their personal data held by companies may be used for a purpose other than that for which they were collected [13]. At the same time, the online population increasingly engages in online activities deemed privacy-threatening, namely online social networking [21]. Concern reported in surveys is higher than what can be inferred from observed real-life behaviors.

This discrepancy between attitudes and behaviors, called the *privacy paradox*, has mainly been described with regards to the interplay between privacy and online personalization: consumers want to enjoy the benefits from profiling, but they do not want to be profiled [7]. Disclosure on online social networking sites has also been described as a privacy paradox [22], although the combined horizontal and vertical relationships amongst users, and between users and the platform operator respectively, is harder to interpret.

Establishing the privacy paradox requires observing a divergence of privacy preferences and behaviors within the same population or between two representative samples thereof. Experimental studies provide such an opportunity to observe stated privacy attitudes and actual privacy-related behavior within subjects. In laboratory experiments, participants who reported high privacy concerns exhibited behavior that diminished their information privacy [23]. Looking at information-only transactions (Sect. 14.3.1), a similar discrepancy has been observed: they actually provided more information than they had previously stated to be willing to share [24].

However, other experiments do not necessarily support the notion of a paradox: individuals with stronger privacy concerns were found to place higher values on privacy in information-only transactions [25]. In a 2013 experiment on privacy in web search, participants' stated willingness to pay for privacy-enhancing features did not explain their behavior, but it also did not contradict their actual choices. Both variables were recorded as part of the same experiment [26].

It has also been argued that disclosure seemingly diverging from attitudes may be explained by strong beliefs in the confidentiality of the disclosed data. Divergence would originate in experimenter trust, framing effects, or deception used by the experimenter [27]. It seems that the supposed paradox would be an artefact, or mode effect, originating in measuring the varying behaviors and attitudes with experimental or survey methodologies respectively. A deeper understanding of privacy concerns and behaviors, therefore, requires valid survey instruments as well as behavioral studies.

14.2.2 When to Use Privacy Surveys and When not to

Even if existing empirical studies do not necessarily support the notion of a privacy paradox, they also show how behavioral intent or self-professed behavior from a survey has little predictive power for actual behavior. A recent study commissioned by Microsoft for Data Privacy Day 2014 serves as an example. The survey specifically recruited "technology elites," characterized, for instance, by self-identifying as influencers on technology and as early adopters of new technology. Amongst the 1,075 respondents in the United States and in the European Union, more than three quarters indicated that they read privacy policies before clicking "accept"; almost a quarter even indicated they read the terms in full [28]. However, web server logs of actual privacy policy visits suggest that this proportion is lower by several orders of magnitude, even amongst advanced users. Only a small minority of Web users actually read the privacy policies of sites they interact with.

The lack of commitment is a major reason why statements about behavior do not reflect real choices. In the absence of real-world transactions, a survey creates an artificial context, influenced by mode effects [29]. The incentives for respondents on how and what to reveal are different from real transactions, typically in a way that works against truthful revelation. One of the biases in a survey is respondents' tendency to give socially desirable answers. Furthermore, surveys have a "research appeal," which makes respondents disclose more information about themselves [30]. Yet, neither privacy nor money are ultimately at stake in a survey. In consequence, predictive power and ecological or external validity are largely reduced.

Despite the inability of surveys to be a reliable and valid predictor for consumer behavior, they do have their rightful place. In the early design stages of an experiment, low-cost surveys can help identify questions of interest an experiment should focus on. In the area of privacy economics, for instance, a pilot study could incorporate a Conjoint Analysis that helps researchers making a more substantiated decision about price differences in an experiment (Sect. 14.2.3). Once an experiment is about to be deployed, screening questionnaires can help in recruiting suitable participants, for instance when sampling a population with high privacy concerns. Survey elements are also crucial in complementing an experiment session as entry- and exit-questionnaires, and comprehension tests typically before the experiment. They deliver insights into the demographics of the sample, their attitudes and personality—in particular when well tested, validated instruments are used. A recent review of survey instruments to measure privacy concerns provides guidance on which methodology to use and how to deploy scales for privacy concern [31].

In summary, we acknowledge that privacy attitudes and privacy behaviors do not always agree. The methodological consequence is to measure both in their own right and with their dedicated procedures. Preference should be given to experimental procedures when studying privacy behavior; surveys lend themselves to assess attitudes. Both approaches must be subjected to the same scrutiny of reliability and validity [31]. In reviewing previous research into the behavioral economics of privacy, I therefore proceed by the methodology used, distinguishing between survey-like approaches (Sect. 14.2.3) and approaches relying on experiments (Sect. 14.3).

14.2.3   The Failure of Hypothetical Privacy Choices

The problems of privacy surveys also apply to survey-like methodologies when participants make hypothetical choices. Often, these works are erroneously labeled as experiments. In a typical survey-like procedure, participants are confronted with scenarios and asked whether they would be concerned about their privacy in such a scenario.

Sometimes a single scenario is used. For instance, participants are asked to imagine a university alumni association shares its members' names, contact, and other information with a car insurance company for a 30 % discount [32]. Other single-scenario work claimed to trial membership in an online bookstore, for which some personal information would be necessary, in exchange for some discount. The amounts of both varied by treatment [33]. In these two studies, the respondents had to report how happy, satisfied, or concerned they would be with the deal presented in the scenario. In a similar vein, participants have been presented with a simulated online shopping web site and asked whether they would intend to buy from that site [34]. Although this is a slight improvement, because the participants can experience the stimulus (i.e., the web site), it still remains a hypothetical choice.

Another strand of hypothetical choice studies presents participants with multiple scenarios: potential job-seeking university students were given four channels to advertise their talents and job interests, including three web sites [35]. All varied by privacy intrusion and chances of success. Participants indicated their preferred option amongst these four. There is, however, an undeniable framing bias: participants are given the impression they are supposed to have different preferences for different types of data collectors, even if the question of advertising their professional skills never occurred. The design is as flawed as asking a vegetarian whether they prefer their steak rare or well done.

Hypothetical choices are also the standard for studies using conjoint analysis. Conjoint analysis tries to decompose the joint influence of several factors on a respondent's preference for one option. There are several variables (e.g., price), each with multiple categorical levels (e.g., 1, 2, 5 euro). Several stimuli or scenarios are created by systematically combining different levels across the attributes. These can be aspects of privacy intrusion, monetary incentives, or prices. To keep the total number of stimuli manageable, an orthogonal design is often preferred over a full factorial design: one does not present all possible combinations of attribute values to the participants. Instead, multiple attributes are varied at once. Participants then rank the scenarios in decreasing appeal [36, 37]. Their rankings have no impact on payoff, but their responses were still interpreted as if they were valid.

An alternative to ranking multiple alternatives is to present scenarios in pairs; participants indicate the preferred one. When combined with an outside option ("neither"), the responses can be analyzed with choice-based conjoint analysis. Binary logistic regression can also be used. In one study, participants indicated the one preferred out of two web pages, in the absence of an outside option [38]. The stimulus was only the mock-up of a single page, not a full, interactive web site. Again, participants' payoff was independent of their choices.

14.3 Review of Privacy Choice Experiments

In contrast to surveys, choice experiments put participants in a decision-making context where their preference for one of the alternatives will have an impact on their lives. In privacy economics, decisions are made as part of a transaction between a consumer and a company (Fig. 14.1). A typical transactions involves the flow of money, personal information, and goods or services. Money may flow in either direction: customers pay a price; companies can offer vouchers. Composite transactions that include the exchange of money, personal data, and goods are common in online shopping. Money may be absent for services provided free of charge (e.g., web search) and goods are not provided when the information receiver collects data from the consumer in return for data (e.g., prize draws). Information-only transactions are observed when consumers volunteer data without compensation, such as in a poll.

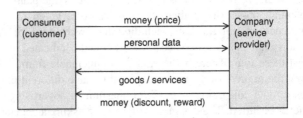

Fig. 14.1 Companies and their customers exchange personal information and goods or services when transacting online

In replicating composite transactions in a laboratory or in a field study, one can measure the monetary value that consumers attach to pieces of personal information. In this section, I review existing empirical studies, grouped by transaction type. Given the paucity of true experiments to date, this is an exhaustive review.

14.3.1 Experiments into Information–Money Exchanges

14.3.1.1 Experiment Design Varieties

In information–money exchanges, consumers receive payments in return for disclosing personal details. Three varieties of experiments have been conducted regarding *information–money exchanges*: incentivized disclosure for an unstated purpose [39], for actual or decoy research purposes [25, 40], and for a deceitfully stated and not implemented purpose [41, 42]. Only the most recent research on information-transactions, which is also the most robust in its design, did not involve deception, but told the participants up-front that the experiment was studying their privacy preferences when browsing the Web [43].

14.3.1.2 Measuring Willingness to Pay

Different mechanisms have been used to elicit willingness to pay. A reverse second-price auction is the most common [39, 41, 43]: participants put in their bids, stating how much they would want to be paid for releasing a specific item of personal information. The winner is determined by the lowest bid, and will be paid the second-lowest bid for disclosing his or her data. Participants have an incentive to bid their true valuation: winning with a bid below their true valuation will make them sell at a loss; asking for too much compensation puts them at risk of not being considered at all. It has also been noted that the auction mechanism is easy to implement and easy to explain to participants [43]—which are important practical considerations.

Amongst the auction mechanisms, the recent work into valuing the privacy of browsing behavior is most interesting and relevant by its design. Recruited though a survey on a major web portal in Spain, 168 participants installed a browser plugin, which invited them at intervals to place a bid for selling personal information relating to the web site they currently viewed [43]. In addition, bids were also solicited for various items of personal information detached from a browsing context. The median bid value across data categories was much higher for context-independent data (€25) than for context-dependent data (€7). A single piece of data was valued similarly to ten pieces of the same kind. A follow-up questionnaire further indicated that users approved of exchanging their data in return for improved service, but refused to have their data monetized by those same providers [43].

As an alternative to auctions, fixed amounts of money have been used, followed by observing whether and how many participants would accept the offer. Participants are asked whether they would disclose their data for a given compensation, such as $2 (in a field experiment, [40]) or for amounts varying between $0.25 and $1 (in a laboratory experiment by the same authors, [25]). The spreads can also be larger, varying between SG$1 and SG$9, equivalent to $0.60 and $5.40 (in a field experiment, [44]). In the latter experiment, participants were invited to a web form, disguised as a consumer research survey into mobile devices, which required items of personal information [44]. The number of data items, the compensation for completing the entire form, and the presence of privacy assurance through a statement or statement plus seal, were manipulated in the different treatments. Privacy assurances and monetary incentives both had a positive influence on disclosure [44], although disclosure was already very high without any of the two.

14.3.1.3 Volunteering of Personal Information

In one of my own studies, we explored the lower bound of what companies would need to pay their customers to stimulate data disclosure. Deployed as an online experiment, we recruited 1,500 web users to complete a form asking for ten items of personal data [30]. Items spanned identity and profile information of varying levels of sensitivity, such as first name and date of birth, as well as health and spending habits. The web form was chosen for its role as the primary mechanism to collect personal data from individuals on the Web. We manipulated the number of mandatory fields (none vs. two out of ten) and the compensation for participation ($0.25 vs. $0.50) to quantify the extent of over-disclosure, the motives behind it, the resulting costs and privacy invasion. A fully rational participant, eager to minimize her exposure and effort, would be expected to leave blank all fields but the mandatory. Quite the opposite, we observed a high prevalence of deliberate and unpaid over-disclosure of data. Participants regularly completed more form fields than required, or provided more details than requested. For instance, when asked when they had last spent $100, some not only provided the date, but also the purpose of the expenditure. We saw that more than two thirds of participants volunteered their date of birth and other personal details; disclosure rates, which were later confirmed in another study. Through careful experimental design, we verified that participants understood that additional data disclosure was voluntary, and the information provided was considered sensitive.

The experiment provides evidence that companies may be able to collect personal details without compulsion or offering incentives, but instead by leveraging consumers' psychological drivers towards completing optional web form fields. Through two manipulations, we benchmarked the efficiency of compulsion and incentives against volunteering. First, when two of the ten fields were marked as mandatory, disclosure rates for the remaining optional fields dropped. A company that forces its customers to complete certain fields reduces the amount of volunteered details. Second, monetary incentives for completing those same fields yielded positive spillover by increasing revelation ratios for other optional fields. Both effects are statistically highly significant [30]. The effects suggest that the transaction is not perceived as a market transaction but instead as a social exchange, that can be broken (through compulsion) or reinforced (through gifting).

14.3.1.4   Challenges for External Validity

In information–money exchanges, money compensates consumers for their loss of privacy. As with other setups, it is, therefore, important that participants incur a true loss of privacy, which is typically achieved through data verification and with the transaction having an impact beyond the protected realm of the study. However, some experiments have tried to create personal information artificially in a laboratory context: "the experimental instrument separated subjects from their natural identities and allowed information and privacy values to emerge endogenously in the laboratory" [27: 8]. These studies confound personal information with the economic notion of private information [45]. By design, the information to be disclosed is no longer personally identifiable. Such studies, therefore, do not measure an invasion of privacy, but participants' avoidance of embarrassing or socially undesirable disclosure.

As a more general critique, the absence of goods or service consumption in pure information transactions creates an incentive structure which resembles paid surveys. Although it may be interesting to estimate the minimum amount of money payable to consumers to reveal some personal or demographic information, this price tag does not implement the purpose-binding of personal information. This is a systematic flaw: if a purpose is unstated, participants are tempted make up a purpose in their mind in an uncontrolled manner. If instead a purpose is stated, but not implemented, participants are deceived. Even when researchers truthfully state and implement data usage, participants trust the researchers and they are biased towards helping research, resulting in personal data disclosure for low monetary values.

Information-only transactions are not happening at large on the Web today. One should be cautious not to generalize the results of information-only transactions to composite transactions. The incentive structures in an online shopping or social networking context are quite different.

14.3.2   Experiments into Information–Service Exchanges

In the early 2000s, laboratory experiments examined consumers' willingness to disclose items of personal information in return for a personalized shopping experience; in this section, I review two early studies. Personalized shopping is one scenario where the privacy paradox could be observed (Sect. 14.2.1).

The common design for *information–service exchanges* experiments is as follows: while participants proceed through an online shop, they can unlock personalization features by disclosing additional personal information. Importantly, participants who disclose more do not get higher monetary payoffs, but may enjoy personalization benefits. Payments are made to the participants, as show-up fees and subsidies to purchases, but these do not depend on the amount or kind of personal information revealed. Their aim is to increase overall participation and purchase ratios. Payments were unconditional [46] or—which is less preferable—distributed in a lottery amongst all buyers in the experiment [23]. Participants were also informed that the experiment studies a personalization scheme; this framing has been criticized for biasing participants towards voluntary disclosure in an attempt to help research [27].

In the experiment by Spiekermann et al. [23], 171 student participants visited a web site to shop for digital cameras or winter jackets, choosing from a broad assortment of 50 and 100 models respectively. While shopping, they could interact with an "anthropomorphic 3-D shopping bot that assisted participants" through a sales dialogue involving 56 questions relating to product attributes, usage, but also personal questions (e.g., "What is your motivation when taking photographs?" or "How important are trend models to you?") [23]. Responses to these questions allegedly served to compile a ranked list of the top ten products. The authors do not report whether this ranking was truly dependent on participants' responses.

In a later experiment by Kobsa and Teltzrow [46], 52 student participants could browse an online book store. A series of 32 questions spread over nine pages would help them navigate the assortment. Each page displayed a book counter, decreasing from 1 million to 50 matching books. However, the matching was an illusion, created by decreasing the counter. The participants ignored the fact that the final selection was predetermined by the authors based on assumed general appeal, and independent of participants' responses [46]. Although all personalization questions would seem plausible in a book store context, they were far more intrusive than in the shopping bot study [23]. For instance, participants were asked for political and religious interests, their preferences for erotic literature and interest in certain medical subareas [46]. All questions featured a "no answer" option. Interestingly, the authors implemented an ID check on the buyers: this may have been the first time truthful revelation of personal data was enforced in a laboratory context.

In another strand of research, observational studies and surveys have tried to measure social capital returns from disclosing personal data online, in particular on online social networking sites [47]. It has been argued that participation in a social networking site would indeed negatively impact on privacy; however, usage would also result in so strong a gratification for the users to the extent that it warrants self-disclosure [48]. Participating in a social network despite privacy concerns would not necessarily be a privacy paradox (Sect. 14.2.1). This stream of work opens up towards non-economic, but social exchanges.

14.3.3 Experiments into Information–Money–Goods Exchanges

The body of research into the value of personal information as part of goods transactions stands out by its paucity. Compared to the ever growing number of commercial opinion polls and academic surveys there are surprisingly few experimental studies into privacy economics. A recent literature review [8] only identified the work by Tsai et al. [49] and my own 2009 DVD experiment [50] as experimental studies; it also included an information-only experiment [44], which has already been discussed. Another comprehensive literature review into the behavioral privacy economics observed that such experimental designs were rare [51: Sect. 4.2.2]. Their comprehensive enumeration only included the works by Beresford et al. [52], Tsai et al. [49], Gideon et al. [53], and Jentzsch and Giannetti [54]. At the time, the latter was still in the design phase; in its current stage, it mixes the concepts of personal and private information [54]. Concordantly with the categorization used here, another featured experiment was classified as an information-only transaction [39].

Besides my own three experiments to date [50, 51, 55], detailed below, it therefore seems that the body of experimental works to study the privacy economics of composite transactions is limited to two studies: [49] and [53]. These works have shared authorship; their designs are similar and they build on one another. Both studies invited participants to a laboratory, where they shopped online and considered privacy issues on a competitive market. The experiments feature a field component in the form of external order fulfillment. The later, more sophisticated design is described first.

14.3.3.1 Experiment "Vibrators Versus Batteries"

Tsai et al. [49] consider consumers' trade-offs as they choose between competing sellers for the same good that differ by price and privacy. The authors have republished their findings several times. The following analysis is based on their initial report [49], which also gives the most detailed account of the experiment procedures.

The goal of the experiment "was to determine whether the prominent display of privacy information in search engine results causes privacy-concerned users to take privacy into account when making online purchasing decisions" [49]. The study was further aimed at determining "whether privacy-concerned users are willing to pay a premium to make their purchases from the more privacy-friendly merchants" [49]. As part of the study, 48 participants were invited to a laboratory session, spread across three treatments, followed by an exit-questionnaire. Participants were paid a show-up fee of $45.

The distinction between privacy-friendly and privacy-unfriendly was created and made salient in the laboratory through icon-annotated result listings in a product search engine. The privacy rating effectively took four levels, from missing to zero, two, and four out of four stars. Ratings of one or three stars were not encountered in the study.

Participants were instructed to perform searches for a series of products; the search terms were prescribed to match a single item sold by several retailers. Products included batteries and a vibrator, which can be considered as prototypical examples of office supplies and sex toys. In a preceding exploratory survey, these product categories were identified to engender low to medium concerns and high to medium purchase likelihood respectively.

The product search result was the main stimulus. The appearance of the first four results was controlled. It is reported that the order of the results was such, that lower rank was associated with a higher price and a better privacy rating [49: 12, 35]. The prices in the experiment were not controlled; the original, varying retail prices by the merchants were used.

The results were the following: guided by the visual four-star privacy rating, participants were willing to pay a premium of around $0.60 when shopping for vibrators and batteries respectively. The actual price differences between the different retailers varied. One cannot conclude that consumers paid $0.60 to shop with a well-rated merchant. In a control treatment, the rating was relabeled as "Handicap Accessibility" instead of "Privacy Report." Participants still preferred to pay higher prices to shop with a four-star merchant, although the difference in average prices was not significant in this case [49].

Although this study implemented real purchase transactions during which participants paid with their own money and released their personal credit card details to a commercial entity of their choice, they could provide a dummy shipping address instead of their own postal details. This resulted in a refund of the purchase price by the experimenters. The authors do not report the proportion of participants who placed orders with no intention to actually receive and use the purchased product [49].

The "vibrator vs. batteries" study improved upon an earlier study by Gideon et al. [53] from the same research group. Both studies used the same privacy-enhanced product search engine, and participants could choose amongst competing sellers. In the earlier study, 24 participants were recruited and paid a show-up fee of $10. Again, products varied by privacy sensitivity, with surge protectors and condoms as the extremes. Although prices differed amongst sellers, participants did not need to pay a premium for privacy, because all expenses were reimbursed by the experimenters. The main conclusion from this study would, therefore, be that consumers prefer privacy-friendly designs so long as they come for free.

14.3.3.2 Experiment "Gourmet Food"

In an earlier, unpublished experiment by Preibusch [55]—some material of which is depicted in Fig. 14.2—72 participants were invited to shop for gourmet food within

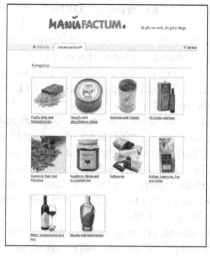

Fig. 14.2 Screenshots from a 2007 laboratory experiment, featuring an online store for gourmet food that could be browsed by product categories or through recipes by famed chefs

a single online store. Some 330 products were available along with 75 recipes by famous chefs to ease product selection. Participants were paid a €10 show-up fee and distributed evenly between two treatments. In one treatment, shoppers could twice receive an extra €5 for indicating their date of birth and their email address when making a purchase. Of all participants, 39 % placed an order, 15 of them in the incentivized treatment, 13 in the non-incentivized treatment. Through the incentives, the data disclosure ratio for date of birth could be increased from 75 % to 92 %; and from 81 % to 92 % for email. In the non-incentivized treatment, only 64 % provided their date of birth.

14.3.3.3   Experiment "DVDs"

In the 2009 DVD study, 225 participants had the choice between two DVD retailers that offered the same range of films. Thirty bestsellers were preselected and presented in a color-printed folder, but buyers had access to the entire Amazon product range through a real-time search API, offering around 100 thousand titles. In fact, almost half of the buyers (47 %, 35 in 74) made their purchase after having requested titles not in the original catalogue. We partnered with an existing bricks-and-mortar retailer of new and used CDs and DVDs [50].

Buyers had the choice between two competing branches, Cologne and Frankfurt. The order forms listed the movie titles with their prices side-by-side to the personal details required for the checkout, so that neither the prices nor the privacy aspects where given priority. Frankfurt was the privacy-invasive retailer, always asking for income and phone number when Cologne only required favorite color. In one treatment, prices were the same; in the other treatment, Frankfurt was €1 cheaper. When prices were the same, buyers seemed to pick an online store at random. They did not systematically prefer the privacy-friendly branch. When prices differed, very few were willing to pay an extra euro for not revealing their mobile phone number and income. However, they were retrospectively less satisfied with the seller's privacy practices—as found in the exit-questionnaire [52]. We also saw that the discount was overriding participants' privacy preferences: for Frankfurt buyers, there was a significant negative association between their willingness to provide the data items required by the privacy-invasive retailer, and their actual data disclosing behavior.

14.3.3.4   Experiment "Cinema Tickets"

The most thorough experiment into privacy economics to date is the 2012 cinema ticket study. It builds on the earlier DVD study, described in Sect. 14.3.3.3. The cinema ticket experiment took into consideration the lessons learnt from the DVD study. In the face of an overhaul of the EU legislation on data protection, the study on "monetizing privacy" was commissioned and funded by the European Network and Information Security Agency (ENISA) and done in collaboration with researchers at the German Institute for Economic Research. The over-arching research questions were:

- Do some customers of online services pay for privacy?
- Do some individuals value their privacy enough to pay a mark-up to an online service provider who protects their information better? [51]

To answer these questions, we created an online shopping experience where consumers faced a trade-off between privacy and price. Ultimately more than 500 laboratory participants were invited to buy up to two cinema tickets. Purchase ratios were high (43 %) and most of the buyers bought two tickets. The report published by ENISA [51] gives the results for the first 443 participants, who purchased a total of 344 tickets—here I am reporting the results for loyal buyers, who purchased two tickets from the same firm. Upon checkout, buyers had a choice between two different retailers, shown side-by-side (Fig. 14.3). One of them asked for their mobile phone number in addition to the basic data of name, email, and date of birth. More than 80 % of buyers chose the privacy-friendly seller when prices were the same. The privacy-friendly retailer continued to attract a demand when its prices were higher. Around a third of the loyal buyers paid €1 extra for keeping their phone number private. These results are statistically highly significant. We also fielded this experiment nationwide and the results were corroborated, providing strong evidence that the results from the laboratory do generalize.

The design of the cinema ticket study closely followed the earlier DVD experiment, with some improvements. Again, a laboratory experiment was

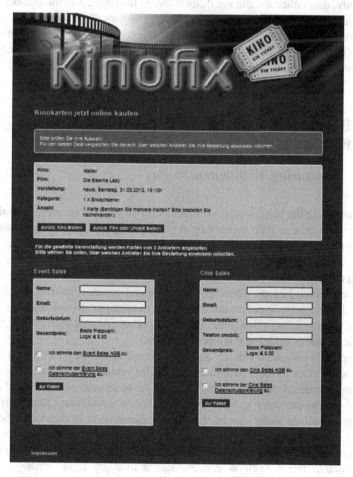

Fig. 14.3 Public-facing web site deployed for the cinema ticket study, featuring the price and privacy points of two alternative sellers side-by-side

implemented, but complemented with a hybrid and a field deployment. In the field experiment, all interactions took place on a public web site. Participants ignored the fact that they were partaking in an experiment. In the hybrid, participants interacted with the same public web site, but were explicitly invited to participate, using university mailing lists. Consequently, the hybrid and the laboratory experiments build on a student-dominated participant pool, whereas the field experiment samples from the general online population.

The experiment was framed as a study into how consumers make purchase decisions. Online sales of cinema tickets was taken as an example; cinema going is a broad social phenomenon [56], and ticket purchases and the consumption of culture are widespread activities on the Web [57: Table 10]. The advantages of DVDs, including low price and homogeneity, also apply to cinema tickets. The main difference in the experimental setup is a more pronounced privacy gradient. For the DVD study, data collection did not differ between the retailers in the number of data items required, and participants needed to inspect the two order forms closely to spot the difference. In contrast, the cinema ticket sellers differed in the number of data items collected and, with four versus three items, the variation is relatively high. Furthermore, the side-by-side display on-screen made comparisons easy.

14.4 How to Run Experiments in Behavioral Privacy Economics

14.4.1 Measuring Willingness to Pay

Experiments into the behavioral economics of privacy aim to measure the value that consumers attribute to their privacy or to privacy-enhancing features. Examples of privacy-enhancing features can be found easily in digital goods and services: a web browser with enabled tracking protection, a webmail provider that refrains from scanning messages, or a search engine that offers its users the ability to disable or to curate their search history. There is a research and business interest in measuring how much these privacy enhancements appeal to users, in absolute monetary terms (e.g., for pricing subscriptions) and relative to other features such as search result quality (e.g., for prioritizing engineering efforts).

Examples of enhanced privacy are often found in the way companies provide goods and services to their customers. An online retailer may refrain from asking sensitive personal information, or may not use the order confirmation email address provided by the customer to send them unsolicited newsletters. Better privacy is thus operationalized along one of the privacy dimensions of data collection, use, retention, and sharing. Research and business are interested in two ways in which consumers articulate their value of privacy. First, would they pay money or give up other desirable things such as personalization to enjoy more privacy? Second, framed inversely, would they give up privacy to receive discounts, higher payoffs, or to enjoy more functionality and convenience? Whereas the first question examines a willingness to pay for privacy, the second question looks at the willingness to accept incentives towards increased data disclosure. It has been speculated that the willingness to pay and to accept differ; however, available evidence is inconclusive [40, 58].

An economic experiment into the value of privacy places consumers into a decision-making situation where they have to trade off privacy against money/convenience/functionality. Their choices are observed in a laboratory or field study. Willingness to pay for privacy is revealed through controlled variation of the stimulus across treatments, such as the discount an online shop grants the customer for revealing his or her mobile phone number.

As a discipline, experimental economics have developed principles on how to conduct such experiments. In some aspects, these differ from other disciplines that are also looking at decision making, including psychology [59]. First, experiments in economics are scripted: participants' progress through the experiment, their possible choices and payoffs are set forth in a detailed protocol. Second, the payoffs are variable and depend on the choices participants have made and their performance. Third, deception is avoided throughout the experiment [59].

The methodological differences between economists and psychology researchers can be a practical challenge. The design of an experiment may face opposition when reviewed by an ethics committee that subscribes to the respectively other research standard. Especially performance-dependent payoffs may face resistance amongst psychology scholars.

14.4.2 Essential Stages of the Experiment

14.4.2.1 Sign-up and Participation

An experiment that measures consumers' value of privacy usually progresses through several stages, some of which happen before and some after the session (Fig. 14.4). Potential participants sign up beforehand, at which a screening questionnaire may be deployed to sample a specific population. At the time of the session, identity checks are carried out; only registered participants are admitted, without walk-in participation. Although a single session is attended by multiple participants, they progress at their own pace and must not communicate with each other, unless the procedures explicitly foresee teaming.

14.4.2.2 Instructions and Consent

The session starts by explaining the procedures to the participants, the choices they will have during the session and how their choices will impact their payoffs.

Fig. 14.4 Stages of an experiment session into the behavioral economics of privacy

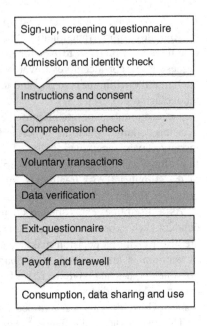

Sign-up, screening questionnaire

Admission and identity check

Instructions and consent

Comprehension check

Voluntary transactions

Data verification

Exit-questionnaire

Payoff and farewell

Consumption, data sharing and use

The instructions, succinct yet complete, are distributed as hard-copies to the participants, so that they can refer to them easily later on. Experimenters may also read them out loud; and arising questions are answered. As an ethical obligation, participants are also informed about potential harms and about what will happen with their data. Participants may still withdraw at this stage without being sanctioned, as participation is voluntary and requires consent. It is important that participants understand the procedures, because otherwise the nexus between the stimulus and their actions is broken.

14.4.2.3 Voluntary Transactions and Data Verification

Voluntary transactions are at the core of the session. They bring a real-world scenario into the laboratory and at best replicate every aspect of the consumption scenario. The creation of a realistic environment is resource-intensive; further details are provided below. The interaction is typically fully computerized although ancillary non-digital materials may be used. Computer-mediated delivery allows high levels of instrumentation so that participants' actions are logged precisely to be analyzed later on. It also makes data verification possible, which is crucial in privacy experiments: if participants provide fake data, they can avoid privacy risks and thereby contravene the experimental protocol. Contact details including mailing addresses, email addresses, and mobile phone numbers can be verified through delivery checks, when a sent confirmation code has to be rekeyed into a web site.

Personal details including name, date of birth, and nationality can be verified using ground truth such as identity cards, leveraging the face-to-face interaction the laboratory offers. Biometrics can be checked in place, through observation (e.g., gender) or by measurement (e.g., body height and weight).

14.4.2.4   Payment Collection

If the transaction involves payment by the participant, such as for an online purchase, payment collection should happen as part of the transaction. This includes electronic payment, where PayPal can be offered as long as the extra third party does not subvert the experiment design. Preference should otherwise be given to a white-label credit card acquirer—however, this leads to substantial overhead. Offering card payments contributes to a realistic shopping environment and makes sure that those without cash at hand can engage. Cash payments may be settled as part of the final payoff.

14.4.3   Creating Real-World Shopping Scenarios

14.4.3.1   Purchase Ratios and Product Selection

True choices require voluntary transactions. This can be challenging when studying privacy economics in electronic retailing as only buyers contribute observations into price–privacy trade-offs. Researchers must, therefore, achieve high purchase ratios to make the most of the recruited sample. At the same time, participants' decisions to make a purchase should not be systematically associated with their privacy attitudes or demographics, which can be checked through the exit-questionnaire. Purchase ratios between 40 % and 60 % can be achieved. Product selection is key and there are five guiding principles. First, the product should appeal universally, regardless of age, gender, or education. Second, the product should be affordable, especially for cash-strapped student samples. Third, the product should lend itself to impulse purchases, without requiring much thought or outside information seeking. Fourth, the product must be homogenous: its quality should be unaffected by whoever sells it. Finally, regulation rules out certain products: in most countries, age restrictions apply to alcohol, tobacco, or pornography; licenses may also be required. Train tickets, although an otherwise suitable product, may only be sold by authorized persons in the United Kingdom. A fixed subsidy can be offered to stimulate purchases; but Germany, for instance, forbids discounts on books. The research design guides whether multiple products or quantities can be bought or whether unit demand is enforced.

14.4.3.2 Real and Fulfilled Transactions

The laboratory is the gold standard for human subject experiments: it allows rich data collection in a controlled environment that rules out confounds beyond the stimuli of the experiment. All the same, results established in the laboratory are sometimes criticized for low generalizability beyond this protected realm. In economics, behaviors observed in the laboratory have been found repeatedly to be a good predictor for the outside world, even when student volunteers are recruited [60]. Having a realistic decision-making environment is key in delivering valid results that generalize beyond the laboratory.

It is, however, not sufficient for transactions in a laboratory experiment to be realistic; they need to be real. This mandate follows from the proscription of deception. Deception pollutes the shared resource of a participant pool by creating distrust [61]. This ethical argument against deception is complemented by an argument of scientific validity. Deception has been found to have an impact on participants' behavior [62]: their actions become inconsistent, a sign that they stop taking the experiment seriously. It also has a negative effect on return rates and may yield self-selection biases. Deception, therefore, is a serious threat to the validity of the findings.

In an experiment into privacy behaviors, all aspects of the transaction must be real. Taking the example of online shopping, participants who make a purchase will have to pay for it with their own money, and they need to be provided with the good they bought. Researchers must be able to fulfill orders, although this will typically be easier for products that also improve purchase ratios, as discussed above. The exchange of personal information must be real and any uses or third-party sharing that were communicated to the participant have to be executed. For instance, if allergies are collected to filter products in an online grocer, this functionality must be implemented. If participants were told that their data would be shared with a company, this data transfer needs to happen, because a deflected privacy threat also counts as deception. It is intended that participants' choices during the experiment have an impact on their lives after the session [62].

14.4.3.3 Partnering with External Companies

One of the challenges in creating a real transaction is to bring a commercial service provider or retailer into the laboratory. When studying exchanges of money and personal data between companies and their data, one cannot achieve valid results when making participants interact with a trusted institution like a university. In the instructions, participants must be told truthfully that they transact with an existing company. Researchers, therefore, have to collaborate with established firms: the setup of a working relationship with a retailer requires negotiation talent and an understanding of business requirements. For a company, it is typically a cost to support a research study. Practical hurdles are the use of branding and the licensing of intellectual property such as designs and product images or descriptions. When granted permission, these elements will be used to re-create a real web shop in the laboratory (Fig. 14.2).

14.4.4 Maintaining the Institutional Separation Between University and Corporate Representation in the Laboratory

Participants must be supported in understanding that an experiment features two separate institutions, a university by members of which and on the premises of which the session is administered, and a company that is their transaction partner. This separation is crucial as participants will react differently to their information requests. The university benefits from a positive trust bias when collecting and using personal information that should not spill over to the company, or the validity of the results would suffer. The two institutions (university versus company) can be separated by experiment phases (Fig. 14.4). Whilst the company collects personal details during a voluntary transaction, university researchers ask participants to complete an exit-questionnaire. Truthful responses in the latter hinge on confidentiality towards the company. For instance, buyers may be asked how they rate the shopping experience. Without institutional separation, this question would be subject to a social desirability bias.

The logical separation between the university and the company corresponds to an administrative separation of the inner and outer phases of the experiment session (Fig. 14.4). A visual break can help participants: parts of the experiment related to the university may feature a different visual language, different fonts, or colors, or it might address the participant differently (e.g., John vs. Mr. Doe, "participant" vs. "dear customer").

An exit-questionnaire records socio-demographic key indicators, such as age, gender, income, and education level. All participants take this questionnaire, whether or not they decided to transact. It allows controlling for potential decision drivers such as computer literacy and past experiences with the chosen company or with cyber-crime. Personality traits such as materialism, reciprocity, risk-aversion, and indeed privacy concerns are measured using instruments with pre-established reliability [31].

14.4.5 Deploying the Experiment: The Relative Merits of the Laboratory, the Field, and Online Platforms

Researchers have the choice between three channels for deploying their experiments: the laboratory, the field, and online platforms (e.g., Amazon Mechanical

Turk—mTurk). Each of these platforms has their own advantages and disadvantages. Dual deployment or hybrids between the channels promise more robust findings.

Laboratory sessions are the traditional way of running experiments in behavioral economics. Their main advantage is the full control that researchers have over the experimental design and the deployment. The lab creates an isolated realm, which allows controlled manipulation of the stimulus under investigation. Possible confounds can be minimized or ruled out entirely. The laboratory also features synchronized face-to-face administration of the experiment, allowing the pairing of participants without them having to wait for one another. Rich apparatus such as eye-tracking or biometric sensors can be used. In privacy experiments, tracking the gaze of participants allows the experimenter to check whether the subjects have actually read a web site's privacy policy, seen any available discounts, or all the potentially sensitive data items requested on the checkout form. Experimenters are also able to verify personal information on site, for instance, through direct observation or with an identity check; verifying someone's name over the Internet is often prohibitively difficult. The drawback of lab experimentation is their over-reliance on student participants and on educated subjects from rich Western societies [63], which may come at the expense of generalizability. Furthermore, it is difficult to scale laboratory experiments beyond a few hundred participants, as subject pools deplete.

Field experiments give access to a potentially unlimited population, although one typically restricts recruiting to a single country for practical reasons, such as language localization or compliance with national regulation. In a field study, researchers create a public facing web site or team up with an existing company to bring the interaction from the laboratory into the wild. Often, it is no longer obvious that the web site is part of a research study. The main advantage is that the experiment is no longer pushed onto participants; instead customers come to the web site self-motivated and task-driven. Pull engagement has the advantage of capturing the consumers when and how they want to transact online. This brings new challenges for recruitment: laboratory subject pools may be invited to join the field study, although it bears the risk of contaminating the natural interaction, which has otherwise no connection to a university or research institution. To recruit for field studies, advertising campaigns may be necessary, resulting in recruiting costs that might be higher than for the laboratory. Logging referrers to the fielded web site is essential. The main cost driver for field experiments remains the requirement to create an instrumentation that survives in the wild. There is a higher bar for design and visual appeal, for security, and any fielded materials face regulatory exposure, as the web site created for research purposes now enters the competitive market. A mentality shift is required for researchers, from administering an experiment session to delivering customer support. Exit-questionnaires and follow-ups are more difficult to administer in a field study; the diversity of the sampled population may go unnoticed. Researchers should be prepared that the field gives noisier data than the laboratory.

Crowdsourcing platforms have started a new wave of studies with human participants. They allow researchers to collect data more quickly and cheaply than through laboratory studies. For many computer scientists, the first experiment with human participants they ever run will be online. Amazon Mechanical Turk (mTurk) is the best-known platform, although numerous crowdsourcing platforms are now available. Started as a labor market for large numbers of small, tedious tasks such as transcribing business cards, mTurk has been seized by researchers who need to conduct experiments and deploy surveys. Comprehensive guidance is available to researchers to on-board with the platform [64]. Cost savings and timely turnaround are the two main advantages of online experiments. Payments to participants can be lower by one order of magnitude and experiments can be run around the clock with minimal supervision. The major difficulty is the introduction of a new sampling bias towards a population that goes after pennies and is recruited in a task-focused mind-set. Cheaters and spammers are common on mTurk; many of them have previously participated in psychology experiments involving deception, so their behavior may be distorted [61]. Finally, platform operators such as Amazon impose strict guidelines on what is allowed on the platform. The main hindrance for privacy researchers is the proscription to collect personal information [65], and the resulting inability to create a real invasion of privacy. Whilst crowdsourcing lends itself to many experiment procedures, researchers should refrain from retrofitting their research question or experiment design. Despite their pragmatic appeal, platforms such as mTurk are often unable to accommodate for the requirements of research into privacy economics.

14.5 Conclusions and Future Challenges

14.5.1 Principles for Empirically Studying Privacy Behaviors

Privacy is top of mind for corporate executives, regulators, and policymakers. Since the Web has brought mass-personalization to every aspect of online consumption, privacy advocates have argued how ubiquitous web tracking poses a threat to users' informational self-determination. Today, we know the reality of planet-scale government surveillance, and Big Data companies demonstrate how personal information can be monetized. This revived interest in improving the protection of consumers' personal information suffers from a serious knowledge gap into consumers' privacy concerns and behaviors. When public opinion polls repeatedly diagnose high levels of privacy concern, it seems paradoxical that consumers keep enjoying privacy-invasive services. There is surprisingly little knowledge on how consumers make privacy/price/convenience trade-offs and about the value they attach to their personal information. Reliable and valid evidence is needed to develop privacy-enhancing technologies that meet the consumers' needs.

Behavioral economics provide the methodological toolkit to explore consumers' privacy choices.

Well-crafted experiments in the laboratory or in the field put participants in real-world decision-making scenarios that allow observation of their privacy choices with predictive power. Applied to the study of privacy in electronic retailing, for instance, this means offering participants the ability to voluntarily purchase goods or services; the transaction is fulfilled with exchanges of real products, money, and personal data. Conversely, the lack of commitment and incentive-compatibility makes surveys, hypothetical choice scenarios, or studies involving deception fail to deliver actionable insight.

14.5.2 *Future Challenges*

In this chapter, I have outlined the principles of conducting empirical research into consumers' privacy consumption behaviors. For researchers, practitioners, and policymakers more challenges lie ahead.

Challenges for researchers include the development of new measurement instruments for privacy concerns and behaviors. On the one hand, we witness the emergence of new kinds of personal information, collected through the proliferation of sensors in mobile devices and public spaces: real-time location data, biometrics collected from eye-tracking, video surveillance, and health sensors. Big Data is not just more of the same, but introduces challenges of a new type [66, 67]. On the other hand, well-conducted experiments are time and resource consuming to a point where knowledge production has difficulties keeping up. This calls for an experiment infrastructure to conduct empirical studies at a faster pace and with lower investments, and it also calls for reliable and valid low-cost survey instruments.

Challenges for companies lie in the diversity of consumers' privacy preferences. How can a company implement superior privacy practices, when customers are diverse in how they balance the trade-off between convenience and data minimization? How can business models succeed beyond the monetization of personal data when the majority of buyers choose cheap prices over good privacy? Privacy negotiations allow companies to offer their customers the choice between different privacy regimes where the current one-size-fits-all approach of inflexible privacy statements fails [68].

Challenges for regulators include the unification of consumer protection and data protection. Two different enforcement regimes need to be combined as market power is redefined in the digital economy. Barriers to entry are no longer capital investments but access to large quantities of historical data; the demand-side network effects in data-intensive products can quickly turn a successful firm into a dominant firm. A mark-up on prices is the traditional symptom of monopolies, but how does market concentration manifest when products and services are offered free of charge. Ultimately, regulators aim to create an environment where privacy-friendly products and companies will thrive.

For companies making sense of big personal data without alienating their customers, for regulators upholding privacy norms, and for researchers envisioning new data protection technologies, it is key to understand consumers' privacy concerns and behaviors. In this chapter, I have shown how laboratory experiments and field studies can observe consumers making real-world privacy choices and thereby provide decision makers with the reliable and valid empirical evidence they need.

Acknowldgements Kat Krol (University College London) provided helpful comments on earlier versions of the chapter.

References

1. The Boston Consulting Group (2012) The digital manifesto. How companies and countries can win in the digital economy
2. The Boston Consulting Group (2010) The connected kingdom. How the internet is transforming the U.K. Economy
3. Office for National Statistics (2014) Retail Sales, May 2014
4. Nadella S (2014) A data culture for everyone. http://blogs.technet.com/b/microsoft_blog/archive/2014/04/15/a-data-culture-for-everyone.aspx
5. Kuneva M (2009) Keynote Speech: roundtable on online data collection, targeting and profiling. In: European Commission
6. Personalization consortium, personalization & privacy survey, 2000, 2005, via Internet Archive, 2014
7. Kobsa A (2007) Privacy-enhanced web personalization. In: Brusilovsky P, Kobsa A, Nejdl W (eds) Privacy-enhanced web personalization, vol 4321. Springer, Berlin, pp 628–670
8. Hess T, Schreiner M (2012) Ökonomie der Privatsphäre. Datenschutz und Datensicherheit—DuD 36:105–109
9. Consumer Commerce Barometer, February 2012. http://www.consumerbarometer.eu/chartlink?id=T1332485008
10. Hamilton Consultants, Inc. (2009) Economic value of the advertising-supported internet ecosystem. IAB
11. World Economic Forum (2011) Personal data: the emergence of a new asset class
12. European Data Protection Supervisor (2014) Privacy and competitiveness in the age of big data. European Data Protection Supervisor
13. European Commission/TNS Opinion & Social (2011) Attitudes on data protection and electronic identity in the European Union
14. Preibusch S (2015) Privacy behaviours after Snowden: the brief impact of exposed state surveillance. Commun ACM 58(5):48–55
15. Anderson R, Moore T (2006) The economics of information security. Science 314(5799):610–613
16. Heller C (2011) Post-Privacy. C.H. Beck, Prima leben ohne Privatsphäre
17. Feijóo C, Gómez-Barroso JL, Voigt P (2014) Exploring the economic value of personal information from firms' financial statements. Int J Inf Manage 34(2):248–256
18. Novotny A, Spiekermann S (2013) Personal information markets and privacy: a new model to solve the controversy. In: 11 Internationale Tagung Wirtschaftsinformatik, Leipzig
19. Department for Business, Innovation & Skills, The midata vision of consumer empowerment
20. The Gallup Organization (2008) Data protection in the European Union. Citizens' perceptions (analytical report). In: European Commission

21. Acquisti A, Gross R (2006) Imagined communities: awareness, information sharing, and privacy on the Facebook. In: Privacy enhancing technologies
22. Barnes SB (2006) A privacy paradox: social networking in the United States. First Monday 11(9)
23. Spiekermann S, Grossklags J, Berendt B (2001) E-privacy in 2nd generation e-commerce: privacy preferences versus actual behavior. In: Proceedings of the 3rd ACM conference on electronic commerce, EC '01, New York, NY, USA
24. Norberg P, Horne D, Horne D (2007) The privacy paradox: personal information disclosure intentions versus behaviors. J Consum Affairs 41(1):100–126
25. Grossklags J, Acquisti A (2007) When 25 cents is too much: an experiment on willingness-to-sell and willingness-to-protect personal information. In: Workshop on the economics of information security (WEIS)
26. Preibusch S (2013) The value of privacy in Web search. In: Workshop on the economics of information security (WEIS)
27. Rivenbark DR (2010) Experimentally elicited beliefs explain privacy behavior. University of Central Florida—College of Business Administration
28. Microsoft, Trustworthy computing—data privacy day. http://www.microsoft.com/en-us/twc/privacy/data-privacy-day.aspx
29. Connelly K, Khalil A, Liu Y (2007) Do I do what I say?: Observed versus stated privacy preferences. In: Proceedings of the 11th IFIP TC 13 international conference on human-computer interaction, INTERACT'07
30. Preibusch S, Krol K, Beresford AR (2012) The privacy economics of voluntary over-disclosure in Web forms. In: Workshop on the economics of information security (WEIS)
31. Preibusch S (2013) Guide to measuring privacy concern: Review of survey and observational instruments. Int J Hum Comput Stud 71(12):1133–1143
32. Wathieu L, Friedman A (2005) An empirical approach to understanding privacy valuation. In: Workshop on the economics of information security (WEIS)
33. Ward S, Bridges K, Chitty B (2005) Do incentives matter? an examination of online privacy concerns and willingness to provide personal and financial information. J Mark Commun 11(1):21–40
34. Castañeda JA, Montoro F (2007) The effect of Internet general privacy concern on customer behavior. Electr Comm Res 7:117–141
35. Baumer DL, Poindexter JC, Earp JB (2006) An experimental economics approach toward quantifying online privacy choices. Inf Syst Front 8:363–374
36. Hann I-H, Hui K-L, Lee S-YT, Png IP (2007) Analyzing online information privacy concerns: An information processing theory approach. In: 40th Annual Hawaii international conference on system sciences (HICSS 2007)
37. Hann I-H, Hui K-L, Lee S-YT, Png IP (2002) Online information privacy: measuring the cost-benefit trade-off. In: 23rd international conference on information systems (ICIS)
38. Jensen C, Potts C, Jensen C (2005) Privacy practices of internet users: self-reports versus observed behavior. Int J Hum Comput Stud 63(1–2):203–227
39. Huberman B, Adar E, Fine L (2005) Valuating privacy. IEEE Secur Priv 3(5):22–25
40. Acquisti A, John LK, Loewenstein G (2013) What is privacy worth? J Legal Stud 42(2):249–274
41. Cvrcek D, Kumpost M, Matyas V, Danezis G (2006) A study on the value of location privacy. In: Proceedings of the 5th ACM workshop on privacy in electronic society, WPES '06, New York, NY, USA
42. Kai-Lung H, Hai TH, Tom LS-Y (2007) The value of privacy assurance: an exploratory field experiment. MIS Q 31(1):19–33
43. Carrascal J, Riederer C, Erramilli V, Cherubini M, de Oliveira R (2011) Your browsing behavior for a big mac: economics of personal information online. In: Proceedings of the 22nd international conference on World Wide Web
44. K-L Hui, Lee SYT, Teo HH (2007) The value of privacy assurance: an exploratory field experiment. MIS Q 31(1):19–33

45. White TB (2004) Consumer disclosure and disclosure avoidance: a motivational framework. J Consum Psychol 14(1/2):41–51
46. Kobsa A, Teltzrow M (2005) Impacts of contextualized communication of privacy practices and personalization benefits on purchase behavior and perceived quality of recommendation
47. Ellison NB, Steinfield C, Lampe C (2007) The benefits of Facebook "friends:" social capital and college students' use of online social network sites. J Comput-Mediat Commun 12 (4):1143–1168
48. Taddicken M, Jers C (2011) "The uses of privacy online: trading a loss of privacy for social web gratifications? In: Privacy Online. Springer, Berlin, pp 143–156
49. Tsai J, Egelman S, Cranor L, Acquisti A (2009) The impact of privacy indicators on search engine browsing patterns. In: Symposium on usable privacy and security (SOUPS), New York, NY, USA
50. Preibusch S, Kübler D, Beresford AR (2013) Price versus privacy: an experiment into the competitive advantage of collecting less personal information. Electron Comm Res 13(4):423–455
51. Jentzsch N, Preibusch S, Harasser A (2012) Study on monetising privacy. An economic model for pricing personal information. ENISA
52. Beresford A, Kübler D, Preibusch S (2012) Unwillingness to pay for privacy. Econ Lett 117 (1):25–27
53. Gideon J, Cranor L, Egelman S, Acquisti A (2006) Power strips, prophylactics, and privacy, oh my!. In: Symposium on usable privacy and security (SOUPS), New York, NY
54. Jentzsch N, Giannetti C (2011) Disclosure of personal information under risk of privacy shocks. SSRN
55. Preibusch S (2008) Economic aspects of privacy negotiations., Berlin, Germany: Technische Universität Berlin/Fachgebiet Volkswirtschaftslehre [Technical University Berlin/Institute of Economics]
56. Eurostat (2006/2011) Percentage of persons who have attended the cinema at least once in the last 12 months by gender and age group
57. van Eimeren B, Frees B (2012) 76 Prozent der Deutschen online—neue Nutzungssituationen durch mobile Endgeräte. MEDIA PERSPEKTIVEN, pp 362–379
58. Plott CR, Zeiler K (2005) The willingness to pay-willingness to accept gap, the "Endowment Effect", subject misconceptions, and experimental procedures for eliciting valuations. Am Econ Rev 95(3):530–545
59. Hertwig R, Ortmann A (2001) Experimental practices in economics: a methodological challenge for psychologists? Behav Brain Sci 24(3):383–403
60. Exadaktylos F, Espín AM, Brañas-Garza P (2013) Experimental subjects are not different. Sci Rep 3(1213)
61. Horton JJ, Rand DG, Zeckhauser RJ (2011) The online laboratory: conducting experiments in a real labor market. Exp Econ 14(3):399–425
62. Jamison J, Karlan D, Schechter L (2008) To deceive or not to deceive: the effect of deception on behavior in future laboratory experiments. J Econ Behav Organ 68(3–4):477–488
63. Henrich J, Heine SJ, Norenzayan A (2010) The weirdest people in the world? Behav Brain Sci 33(2–3):61–83
64. Mason W, Suri S (2012) Conducting behavioral research on Amazon's mechanical Turk. Behav Res Methods 44(1):1–23
65. Amazon.com, Inc. (2013) FAQs | Help | Requester | Amazon Mechanical Turk. https://requester.mturk.com/help/faq#restrictions_use_mturk
66. Executive Office of the President (2014) Big data: seizing opportunities, preserving values
67. Crawford K, Schultz J (2014) Big data and due process: toward a framework to redress predictive privacy harms. Boston Coll Law Rev 55(93)
68. Preibusch S (2006) Implementing privacy negotiations in E-commerce. In: Frontiers of WWW research and development—APWeb 2006, Berlin Heidelberg

Chapter 15
Techniques, Taxonomy, and Challenges of Privacy Protection in the Smart Grid

Suleyman Uludag, Sherali Zeadally and Mohamad Badra

15.1 Introduction

The scope of the rights of individuals has been constantly evolving. It has long been established that the full protection of life and property falls within the individual rights coverage for most cultures throughout the human history. While the early boundaries of the "right to property" have only incorporated the tangible dimension, the intangible portion has been expanding [1] rapidly since the industrial revolution. One important component of the intangible part is defined by the right to privacy, coined by Warren and Brandeis in 1890 [1].

A strong positive correlation between technological development and privacy concerns is almost universally agreed [2]. In Warren and Brandeis' terminology, "the right to be left alone" has expanded to include other personally associable phenomena such as audio, photographs, video, data, and more recently biometric identification and genetic data) rather than mere physical property. Computerization, automation, transmission, and storage of data, enabled by recent advances in tele-communications, Internet technologies, and mobile and cloud computing services, have increased the importance and relevance of the term "privacy".

S. Uludag (✉)
The University of Michigan—Flint, Michigan, USA
e-mail: uludag@umich.edu

S. Zeadally
College of Communication and Information, University of Kentucky,
Lexington, KY, USA
e-mail: szeadally@uky.edu

M. Badra
Zayed University, Dubai 19282, UAE
e-mail: mohamad.badra@zu.ac.ae

© Springer International Publishing Switzerland 2015
S. Zeadally and M. Badra (eds.), *Privacy in a Digital, Networked World*,
Computer Communications and Networks,
DOI 10.1007/978-3-319-08470-1_15

343

In spite of its wide usage, the term privacy does not have a universally-agreed-upon definition [3].[1] It is quite remarkable that such an important concept has evaded a formal definition. The concept of privacy has a long history of discussions of importance, from Greek philosophers including Aristotle (public sphere of political activity versus private sphere [3]) and Socrates, to Biblical and Quranic passages [5]. Allen West in his landmark work [2] defines privacy in terms of self-determination as follows:

> Privacy, now, is the claim of individuals, groups, or institutions to determine for themselves when, how, and to what extent information about them is communicated to others.

Another important document about the principles of privacy protection was developed in 1981 by the Organization for Economic Co-operation and Development (OECD) [6][2] and was later updated in 2013 [7]. Yet, even these guidelines are not observed by many countries. For example, while the European Union seems to be following them, the United States does not.

Widespread adoption of privacy protection mechanisms depends on the political will, which seems to be prioritizing other concerns such as public safety, especially since September 11, 2001. However, the awareness and demand of the public for a stronger adoption and enforcement of the privacy regulations has been increasing unabated. Many recent developments and news such as Wikileaks, US NSA leaks by Edward Snowden, Facebook's recent disclosure of Emotion Experiment, EU's recent ruling on "right to be forgotten," have been keeping the topic of privacy discussions current and fresh in the public sphere, thereby increasing demand for more action.

In line with technological developments, the ever-changing field of ubiquitous applications, and high-level penetration of mobile and other electronic devices, the potential for privacy violation has been increasing in scope. While there is a perceived clash between the technology and privacy protection, there are also many efforts to put the use of technology in its defense. One pioneering work that has spawned quite a lot of attention, interest, and follow-up studies is Chaum's paper [8] in 1985 on providing privacy to individuals and organizations bi-directionally in a secure fashion. He argues for embedding privacy-providing mechanisms in the design and development of the technology by means of cryptography. Chaum's ideas are further developed and formalized under the term of privacy-enhancing technologies (PET) in 1995 [9] and then in 2003 [10]. PET is defined in [10]:

> PET stands for a coherent system of ICT measures that protects privacy by eliminating or reducing personal data or by preventing unnecessary and/or undesired processing of personal data, all without losing the functionality of the information system.

Our work in this chapter is line with the notion of PET, which we use to provide an understanding and awareness of privacy issues, challenges, and threats in the

---

[1]Some technology company executives have gone so far to declare privacy irrelevant, dead, or even defunct. A more elaborate debunking of these myths can be found in [4].

[2]http://www.oecd.org/internet/ieconomy/oecdguidelinesontheprotectionofprivacyandtransborder flowsofpersonaldata.htm.

Smart Grid (SG), the next generation of the traditional Power Grid enhanced with state-of-the-art computing and communications technologies. Just as is the case with many engineering and technical decisions, the touted benefits of the SG initiative comes with many risks and trade-offs. The deployment and adoption of Smart Grid technologies have opened up several security issues at the levels of the consumer, the communication, and the energy provider. Security aspects such as confidentiality, authentication, authorization, integrity, and non-repudiation have been extensively investigated and various innovative solutions have been proposed in the literature. There are many publications on SG security, including survey style articles and books, such as [11–36]. While some of these address privacy, explicitly or implicitly, there is a need for an up-to-date coverage of SG privacy techniques. In contrast to most previous works with the SG security focus, our main motivation in this chapter is to review, classify, discuss, and analyze recent SG privacy solutions that have been proposed in the literature. In addition, we also provide a comprehensive treatment of the approaches, mechanisms, and cryptographic tools used in the SG to support the use and design of privacy enforcing techniques.

15.1.1 Contributions

In this chapter, we provide a novel taxonomy of privacy provisioning and protection techniques in the SG. The comprehensive survey, explanations, and discussions of the various privacy schemes are expected to serve as a good reference for those interested in working on privacy issues in the SG environment. The rest of the chapter is organized as follows. Section 15.2 presents a brief SG overview. Section 15.3 discusses the privacy-related problems within the SG environment and explains why privacy is crucial in the overall success of the SG paradigm. Section 15.4 presents a novel taxonomy of recently proposed privacy-preserving solutions for the SG. Section 15.5 explores outstanding challenges that must be addressed in the future and opportunities for new research directions. Section 15.6 concludes the chapter.

15.2 Background on Smart Grid

In this section, we present the main features of the traditional Power Grid followed by the SG vision.

15.2.1 Traditional Power Grid

The current traditional electric Power Grid is considered to be the largest man-made machine in the world. Its infrastructure and operations have not changed

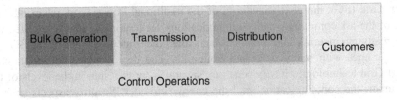

Fig. 15.1 Architecture of the traditional electric power grid

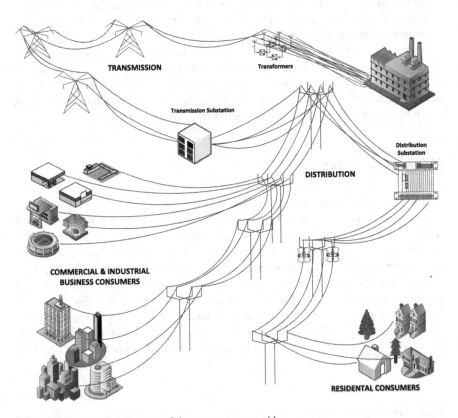

Fig. 15.2 A high-level structure of the current power grid

significantly over the past century. Its architecture mainly consists of four sections, as shown in Fig. 15.1: generation,[3] transmission, distribution, and consumption. A high-level structure of its topology and its components are displayed in Fig. 15.2. The generation of energy is highly centralized and is carried out in bulk mode, such as nuclear systems, hydroelectric systems, wind farms, and others. The high-voltage

---

[3]We use the terms *generation* and *production* interchangeably.

electricity is relayed in the transmission subsystem over long distances. When handed off to the distribution subsystem, the energy is converted into medium voltage. Through the distribution subsystem substations, the voltage is reduced to lower values and then distributed to a variety of end-users, from commercial, industrial, business, to residential areas. The energy production and distribution schema are supervised by a centralized control system, known as Supervisory Control and Data Acquisition (SCADA) systems, in charge of mapping and visualizing any operational activity in the field as well as controlling the storage and demand of power. In fact, SCADA systems can remotely and locally control the power transmission and distribution based on the current demand and peak loads thereby minimizing unnecessary power generation.

15.2.2 The Smart Grid Vision

SG is a term generally used to refer to an enhancement of the traditional Power Grid, especially, in terms of the computing and communications technologies. SG can be defined as follows [37, 38]:

> The SG can be regarded as an electric system that uses information, two-way, cyber-secure communication technologies, and computational intelligence in an integrated fashion across electricity generation, transmission, substations, distribution and consumption to achieve a system that is clean, safe, secure, reliable, resilient, efficient, and sustainable.

"System of Systems" is a term generally used to qualify the SG in the literature to emphasize its heterogeneity.

Economic development and its sustainability are closely coupled with the effective, efficient, and robust use of the energy. The energy sector, and especially the grid infrastructure, has traditionally focused on the reliable provisioning. Until recently, communications and flow of information have been considered only with extraneous significance. Under an aging and ineffective energy distribution system, unprecedented initiatives have recently been instituted in many countries to improve the Power Grid with the SG. The key facilitators of the SG are two-way energy and information flows between the suppliers and consumers. The conventional supply chain of the energy is being expanded to include alternative sources of energy, such as solar, wind, tidal, biomass, and so on. from a variety of distributed small and large energy producers. The consumers are becoming more active participants by means of such devices as smart meters, smart thermostats, smart appliances. The grand vision of an autonomic, self-healing SG with a dynamic demand response model with pricing still has many challenges, not the very least from the perspective of the networking infrastructure and distributed computing. Demand Response (DR) is defined by the US Department of Energy as follows [39]:

> Changes in electric usage by end-use customers from their normal consumption patterns in response to changes in the price of electricity over time, or to incentive payments designed

to induce lower electricity use at times of high wholesale market prices or when system reliability is jeopardized.

The sheer size of the contemplated SG of the future is to rival the Internet in the number of participants. Smarter generation, transmission, distribution, and consumption of electricity are essential to achieve a reliable, clean, safe, resilient, secure, efficient, and sustainable power system [37].

Some of the noteworthy standardization efforts, high-level conceptual reference models, and roadmaps for the SG are given by the NIST Framework and Roadmap for SG Interoperability Standards [40], IEC SG Standardization Roadmap [41], CEN/CENELEC/ETSI Joint Working Group on Standards for SGs [42], and IEEE P2030 [43]. A conceptual view of the NIST's SG reference model is depicted in Fig. 15.3 with seven domains: customers, markets, service providers, operations, generation, transmission, and distribution. As compared to Fig. 15.2, the generation is no longer in bulk; it also includes the distributed and renewable energy sources as well. It is also worth noting from Fig. 15.3 the bi-directional electricity and information flows and the integration of the renewables. Another important conceptualization is the addition of third-party services to enhance the energy consumption experience of the end-users by means of open markets. The financial gears are also in place: global investment on SG had exceeded $15 billion as of 2013, more than a four-fold increase from 2008 levels [44].

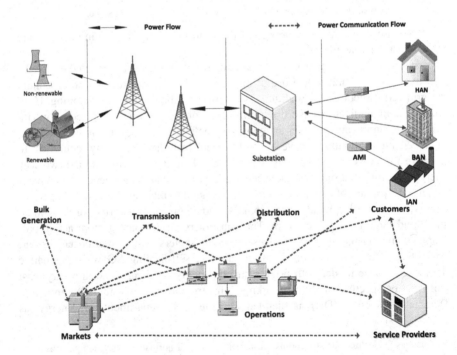

Fig. 15.3 NIST's 7-domain smart grid conceptual model

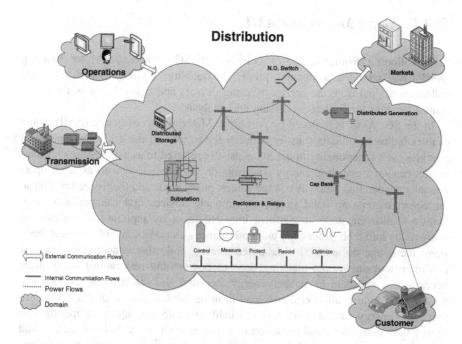

Fig. 15.4 Distribution domain of NIST's smart grid conceptual model

The most relevant domain of the NIST Conceptual Model for this chapter is the Distribution Domain (as depicted in Fig. 15.4), because it is the main physical interface between the end-user and the SG and it is the center of almost all of the potential privacy violations. Note that it is also the Distribution Domain that is responsible for achieving the most widely-cited benefits of the SG which include control, measurement, sensing, data collection and storage, and optimization of operations that take place in or for it.

The anticipated benefits [40] of the SG include:

- Increased power reliability and quality.
- Optimized resources to smoothen the power demand to avoid using expensive peaker capacity.
- Improved resilience to disruption by natural disasters and attacks.
- Automated systems to enable self-healing responses to system disturbances.
- Incorporation of distributed and/or renewable energy sources.
- Reduction of greenhouse emissions.
- Actionable and timely energy usage information to customers.
- Facilitation of plug-in electric vehicles and new energy storage options.

15.2.3 Smart Meters and AMI

In transitioning from the Power Grid to the SG, Automatic Meter Reading (AMR) has provided a stepping stone functionality. AMR provides automatic collection of data from the energy metering devices and transmission of them to a central location for further processing and analysis.

In the SG, AMR is replaced by Advanced Metering Infrastructure (AMI) which enables bidirectional data transfer between the meter and the grid. The meter that provides such functionality in the SG is usually referred to as a *Smart meter*. Smart meters can read real-time energy consumption information as well as other operationally needed data, such as voltage values, phase angle and the frequency, and so on. Smart meters are solid state programmable devices that can perform many functions allowing users to perform intended tasks by inputting a sequence of instructions into their processing unit and memory. Among some of the tasks that a smart meter can do are [45]: time-based pricing, collecting consumption data for consumer and utility, net metering, loss of power (and restoration) notification, better access and data to manage energy, decision and selection of rate options, remote turn on/turn off operations, load limiting for *bad pay* or demand response purposes, energy prepayment, power quality monitoring, meter tampering and energy theft detection, costs reduction in wrong estimations of billings, service and operational reduction in traditional tasks of metering reading, or communications with other intelligent devices or appliance devices in the home. Although all these tasks may not be supported by a particular meter and there might be other tasks that it can do, the overall idea is that smart meters make it possible to add some kind of intelligence to the network and individual features of each residential consumer.

There are several technologies and applications that have been integrated to perform as one in an AMI system [45] including: smart meters, wide-area communications infrastructure, Home (local) Area Networks (HANs), Meter Data Management Systems (MDMS), and operational gateways working as main collectors. Figure 15.5 shows a model of AMI system as envisioned by NIST from the perspective of computer networking terminology by means of interconnected nodes and clouds to emphasize the bidirectional nature of the communication enabled by AMI.

Another abstraction of the AMI network is presented in Figs. 15.6 and 15.7 that show the concepts of HAN, Building Area Network (BAN), Industrial Area Network (IAN), Neighborhood Area Network (NAN), and Field Area Network (FAN).

There is some notion of hierarchy in AMI when data are collected, processed, and analyzed to optimize the energy use and bring about the benefits of the SG. Such a hierarchy of the communications architecture is depicted in Fig. 15.8. Smart meters span out from feeders, which may also serve as natural data aggregation points. Feeders are controlled by the distribution substations, which are in turn connected to the transmission substations. NIST domains interact with this hierarchy to provide a new level of experience and service as part of the SG.

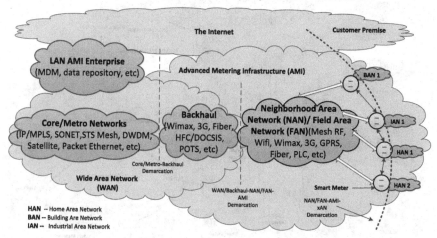

Fig. 15.5 Smart grid advanced metering infrastructure reference architecture

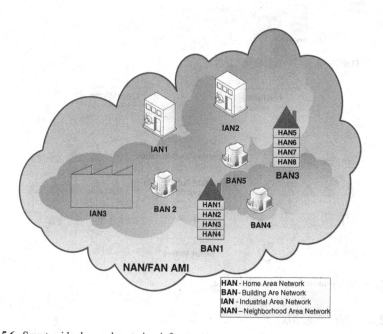

Fig. 15.6 Smart grid advanced metering infrastructure

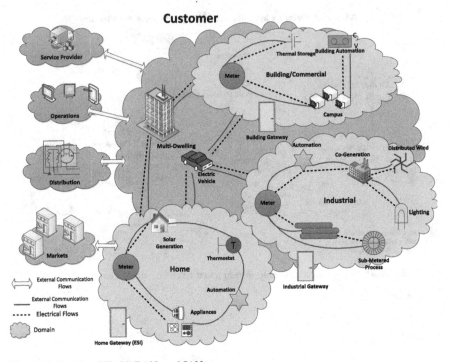

Fig. 15.7 Details of HAN, BAN, and IAN

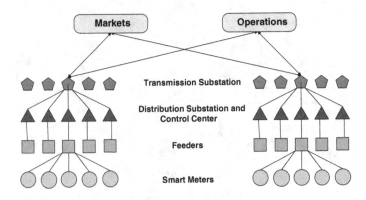

Fig. 15.8 SG communications architecture

15.2.4 Microgrids

One of the many new mechanisms of the SG for power delivery is *microgrids* [46–48]. As a low voltage distribution network, microgrids[4] are autonomous energy

---

[4]Microgrids are referred to as Distributed Resource Island Systems in IEEE 1547 terminology.

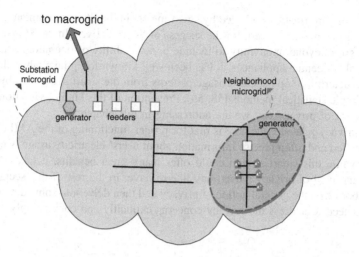

Fig. 15.9 A microgrid model

management systems under the control of a single administrative authority that is capable of operating in parallel to or in intentional or accidental islanded mode from the existing Power Grid. They usually include distributed and renewable energy sources as well as some level of energy storage subsystems. A representation of a microgrid model is shown in Fig. 15.9.

15.3 Smart Grid Privacy Issues

Demand Side Management (DSM) is one of the most important components of the grid of the future [49]. The overarching goal of DSM is to improve the efficiency and effectiveness through energy consumption scheduling. DSM tries to shift and/or reduce the load to achieve its objective by reducing the Peak-to-Average Ratio (PAR), cost, and so on. In [50], energy-cost and PAR minimization are performed with the help of an energy consumption scheduler and a Linear Programming (LP) formulation. Joint energy payment and waiting time minimization are studied in [51]. A game theoretic approach is proposed to maximize the utility function in [52]. In [53], a consumption scheduling algorithm based on Integer Linear Programming (ILP) and game theory is applied to minimize load. In contrast to the current grid, one of the key features of the future grid is to adjust loads dynamically, turning them on or off as needed. This is called *load shedding*. In [54], an optimization framework is proposed to find the minimum amount of load to shed while satisfying load-balancing and shedding constraints. Dynamic load-shedding schemes have been studied in the presence of large disturbances accounting system dynamics [55, 56]. Du and Nelson [57] presents a two-step algorithm for the optimal load shedding in an intentional island.

Given the information collected by smart meters in the SG environment, privacy issues become a vital concern for the success of SG initiatives. In the SG AMI, the privacy goes beyond anonymity to include undetectability of operational status of individual residential appliances. It has been well-known for quite a while that it is trivial to determine sophisticated usage patterns from the smart meter data by using rather simple statistical methods [58, 59]. Prevention of this kind of violation is the main aspect of privacy that we are addressing in this chapter.

The privacy-related issue here is that for proper functioning of the AMI system, very detailed and often precise information about users' electricity usage is needed. Hence, while this smart system could offer many great benefits, it takes away a significant level of privacy a user may like to have. In the rest of this section, we first elaborate on the general notion of privacy and then delve into some details as to why we need to address the privacy concerns explicitly and convincingly.

15.3.1 Basic Privacy Concepts

Privacy may be defined as the claim of individuals, groups, or institutions to determine when, how, and to what extent information about themselves is communicated to others [2]. The notion of privacy may vary from person to person, and from culture to culture. It could also be defined as the right to informational self-determination, that is, individuals must be able to determine for themselves when, how, to what extent, and for what purpose information about them is communicated to others [60]. This term is often related to an entity's (individual, group, or institution) identity or anonymity. As human beings, each of us likes to keep certain information about ourselves confidential while we like to express some information to draw a distinct line with others or to make a presence in the society that we live in. Similarly, a group or institution may have some information for disclosure to the public while sensitive information must be protected from being disclosed to unwanted parties. The unwanted parties may include individuals who are not members of the group or institution, other groups or institutions, a person with short-term membership, or a deliberate intruder (attacker) attempting to retrieve information illegitimately.

The definition and boundaries of privacy tend to vary among different societies and cultures and as such, there is no clear list of categories of privacy that can be applicable for all. However, four major types of privacy are generally recognized:

- **Personal privacy**. This includes mainly body privacy and territorial privacy. Body privacy varies among individuals in terms of the types of clothing one wears to protect the body. Territorial privacy means making a boundary or to create a barrier between the person and others. This can be implemented by erecting walls, fences, or screens, by using cathedral glass/partitions, by maintaining a distance, among other things.

- **Information privacy**. This kind of privacy is mainly related to passing of information over various media and could also be called communications privacy. Some of the notable information privacies are:

  - *Internet privacy*. The ability to determine the kind of information one reveals or withholds about oneself over the Internet, who has access to such information, and for what purposes one's information may or may not be used.
  - *Financial information privacy*: information about own bank account, amount of money, transaction details, debt, and so on.
  - *Medical privacy*: information about a persons health conditions.
  - *Political privacy*: political stance such as who a person may have voted for.
  Information privacy also means how someone expresses matters about him- or herself in any field. People are sometimes willing to give up information about themselves not because they are ignorant or because they are being tricked by evil corporations, but because it can sometimes be in their best interests to do so [61, 62]. Such information can be posted on the Internet or via social networks or other channels the person is involved with. So, in such a case, a person may judge the benefit of exposing such information, which he or she may like others to know but not through him- or herself directly, to be avoiding the accountability or responsibility of such apparent "leak" of information.

- **Organization privacy**. this includes the confidential information about an organization such as business strategies, loss and profit statistics, current trend in the market, future products, potential customers, transaction details, and similar information. An organization may put some information in the public arena for transparency (which will show the ethical standard of the organization, commonly accessible by anybody) and declares certain information as classified, which is a categorization applied to information that a government or a group claims as sensitive. Prominent examples of organizational security could be often associated with trade secrets and national security.

- **Spiritual and intellectual privacy**. This kind of privacy includes a person's spiritual nature, of his or her feelings and intellect. A person may have certain religious beliefs but may not like to express these to others. It may be because of the adverse or hostile environment. Also, a highly intelligent person may act as dumb or may not like to show his or her intelligence in all gatherings. For example, a person working in a research group may restrain from showing all his or her talents to others so that others may not take his or her ideas away without giving proper credit, or it may be that the person is selfish or may like not to actually get involved in intellectual contribution in the group for some personal reasons.

As the meanings of privacy are different in various scenarios, there are other ways of looking at it. [63, 64] described six types of privacies related to a mans personality: (1) solitude, (2) isolation, (3) anonymity, (4) reserve, (5) intimacy with friends, and (vi) intimacy with family. Solitude is the most complete state of privacy that individuals can achieve. It is a type of privacy in which the individual is alone and unobserved. Pedersen [63] differentiates between isolation termed as alone and away from others and solitude defined as alone by oneself and free from observation by others. Anonymity is a type of privacy that occurs when it is possible to move around in public or, for example, browsing through the Internet without being recognized or being the subject of attention. Reserved behavior includes examples of low self-disclosure. Finally, any kind of intimacy is a type of privacy that relates to an individual's or group's desire to promote close personal relationships. All of these personal traits of human beings need to be studied and thoroughly understood while making any policy related to privacy in any sector, because the same human beings are the beneficiaries or users of these systems.

15.3.2 The Need for Privacy in the Smart Grid

In a SG network, key questions regarding setting the policies on user data privacy are [65]:

- Who owns the data of the customer?
- How is the access to and use of customer data regulated?
- Who guarantees privacy and security of customer data (e.g., against risk of surveillance or criminal activity)?
- Will sale or transfer of customer data be allowed, and under what terms and to whose benefit?
- In jurisdictions with retail choice, are measures needed to ensure competing electricity providers have access to customer data on the same terms as the incumbent utility?

In fact, rival electricity providers may compete to dominate the market, and their access to users electricity usage patterns and behavioral information could be very crucial. The electricity providers or provider agents may use the user data to determine their business strategies and special packages or offers. In an open market environment, such data could be partially collected after the offers are made public and some information is available for all, but if privacy is breached beforehand and specific user data is available to some parties, then these electricity providers may have unfair gains. Appropriate privacy policies may restrict, mitigate, or resolve such use of unfair means in setting business strategies. All these issues explain why the privacy of data of SG users is a very critical issue both for users and the electricity providers.

The privacy of SG users is a very important issue. The strong integration of Information and Communication Technologies (ICTs) for the SGs operation introduces different types of privacy concerns. Depending on how the consumer (or user) uses electricity and recharges it, the privacy of the user can be affected by two usage scenarios namely:

- **The user recharges electricity balance via personal interaction (private mode)**. For instance, the user goes in person to the electricity providers agent and recharges his "smart electricity card" similar to a credit or debit card that can be reloaded and placed into the electricity meter. The other personal interaction may happen via the phone or in person by going to the agent and getting a new recharge or reload number, similar to that used in many places for pre-paid mobile phone balance or validity extension. The customer can also obtain a recharging number obtained from a pre-paid card. This method does not reveal the identity of the person who has purchased the card, which is later used in the electrical meter to do the reloading task. It is worth pointing out that the authorization number will need to be validated and authenticated before electricity consumption. When this number is entered from any home or building (connected to the SG), it passes through an authentication process during which information could be stored by the utility company or one of its designated agents. This information needs privacy protection measures in place.

- **The users recharge their electricity balance via the Internet (public mode)**. If any website or online system is used and the balances are adjusted via payment through some bank account or other payment methods, then all the cybersecurity-related privacy issues must be considered. When a web interface is used and there is a back-end database, web attacks (such as Structured Query Language (SQL) injection [66]) could affect the privacy of the user by disclosing not-to-be-exposed data from the back-end database. The web-based (i.e., online) form to recharge the user's electricity balance could be made as simple as requiring a single identification number from the user. The privacy issue in this process is whether the user wants to be known at the time of recharging a balance for future electricity usage. In fact, user's information can be used by different departments or branches of the electricity provider. The user may choose who can access the information and who can not. An instance of personal preference can be the option of receiving company related news, updates, or offers of newly introduced packages or benefits from the electricity supplier company to the user's email address. For managing user's own preferences, agent technology [67] could be used, in which each subscriber or user is assigned an agent representing the user's interests. Each service can also be assigned an agent to reap the most benefit. A service agent could negotiate with subscriber agents about information and authorizations versus the quality of the offered service.

The level of personal information involved and used will dramatically increase with the modernization of the grid. Smart meters and smart appliances could lead to a data explosion of intimate details of daily life. However, at this point, it is quite unclear as to who will gain access to this information, besides the customer's utility provider, and control utilities. With the deployment of the SG, energy measurements can take place at much shorter intervals (unlike at the end of the billing cycle as in conventional methods).

Currently, there are several types of concerns related to the privacy and security of data associated with the SG. In this chapter, we focus on the issue of privacy linked with consumer information. Potential privacy concerns of SG consumers include: how the required information is going to be collected, used, and disclosed; how customer information is expected to be safeguarded and how it may be used for or against the consumers; how permissions will be granted for the collected data to be shared with multiple agencies; and the liabilities related to any breaches of consumer information. It is also worthwhile exploring how the SG will know about individuals. For example, the energy fluctuation pattern of home appliances is so unique that it may be possible to infer, for example, the model applied for a user's refrigerator. It is also worth noting that many times data that is harmless when collected in isolation may become a privacy threat when combined with other types of data, or examined by a third party for a pattern.

Even when the data about electricity consumption is not collected at regular intervals, information can still be collected at a slower rate through the persistent monitoring of energy consumption. As a result, private information such as how many people live in a household, their presence and absence at home, their schedules for taking showers, watching TV, frequency of microwave use, and their sleeping patterns can be collected or deduced. For many individuals, the collection of this type of information represents an invasion of the "sanctity of the home", and one may argue that such intimate details of someone's daily life should not be accessible. The user's data could disclose their usage pattern of electric devices, and very intimate details of household equipment, even their possible locations (e.g. if the SG concept also is combined with the smart home concept where, when a person leaves a room the lights and electric equipment are automatically turned on or off). In such a case, even the movement pattern of the user within his or her own home could be deduced!

The privacy concerns discussed here are further confirmed by a study called Privacy Impact Assessment (PIA) [12] conducted in September 2009 by the Privacy Sub-Group of the Cyber Security Working Group. The report has identified the following issues and concerns related to consumer-to-utility information exchanges in the US SG:

- There is no clear understanding of the privacy issues on the SG.
- There are a lack of standards, privacy policies, or procedures by the entities involved in the SG and the collection of information.
- Definitions of personally identifiable information are inconsistent in the utility industry.
- Smart meters and distributed energy systems may reveal information about residential consumers and activities within the house.
- Roaming SG devices (e.g., electrical vehicle recharging at other charging stations such as a friend's house) may generate more personal information.
- Even though the National Association of Regulatory Utility Commissioners adopted the 2000 resolution[5] urging the adoption of privacy principles, only a few state utility level commissions have begun to assess privacy issues associated with the SG. This is the case with the state of California through its eight

[5]http://www.naruc.org/Resolutions/privacy_principles.pdf.

Fair Information Practice (FIP) principles[6] such as transparency, right to access information collected (individual participation), individual access to see and copy information stored on an individual, limited types of information that may be collected on an individual (collection limitation), limited internal use of information about an individual, data quality and integrity, data security, accountability, and auditing.

15.3.3 Load-Monitoring Techniques

As we mentioned previously, the possibility of learning information about individuals' behaviors, personal habits, and lifestyle raises concerns. This becomes an important issue when this information can be used for other purposes besides delivering electricity. Electric utilities and other providers may have access to information about the in-house activities of customers, the times when they are using various devices and appliances, as well as the type of devices being used. The initial goal of collecting electricity usage information to generate an electricity profile has now become a source of behavioral information with an immense potential. The most serious threats related to the privacy deterioration of SG consumers include: cyber-attack and intrusion, identity theft, tracking and observing the behavioral patterns of the consumers and the appliances being used, and real-time spying and surveillance. In intrusive load monitoring (ILM), there is an individual monitor for each appliance to acquire the aggregate energy consumption of household electric devices. An alternative technique for deducing the appliance usage characteristics is called non-intrusive load monitoring (NILM), or non-intrusive appliance load monitoring (NIALM), where only one individual monitor is enough to decide the energy usage from the aggregate data. NILM was first reported in 1992 [68]. Since then, various other techniques have been developed for NILM that separate individual appliance power consumption levels from from single, aggregated measurements. Recent surveys about NILM can be found in [59, 69]. An illustration of the concept is presented in [70], where a behavior extraction algorithm implemented in Matlab is used. DSM and Demand response systems provide sufficient power usage information to reveal in-home activities that might be disturbing for the privacy of the households. It is worth noting that NILM can be easily implemented using off-the-shelf hardware and software without much technical expertise.

---

[6]Senate Bill 1476 was passed in 2010 to protect the privacy and security of customer data generated by advanced meters. The California Public Utilities Commission (CPUC) subsequently issued Decision (D.)11-07-056 on July 28, 2011 to implement SB 1476. See http://www.cpuc.ca. gov/NR/rdonlyres/D77BA276-E88A-4C82-AFD2-FC3D3C76A9FC/0/TheEvolvingRoleofState RegulationinCybersecurity9252012FINAL.pdf for more details.

As a result, privacy concerns, coupled with a degree of security related issues, may lead to any of the following unintended consequences [31, 71, 72], or some other vulnerabilities not currently identified:

- Hackers could manipulate power consumption and billing.
- Cyber-terrorists might fake power consumption data on a large scale to attack the power system.
- Attackers may take control of the smart meters for manipulation at will.
- Direct marketers, criminals, law enforcement agencies may use the energy consumption data without prior approval or notification.
- Energy consumption patterns of individual appliances can be identified with high accuracy.

Thus, privacy is the Achilles' heel for the success of the SG and needs to be carefully investigated and addressed.

15.4   Privacy Solutions

In this section, we present a novel taxonomy of the privacy techniques proposed for the SG domain, and we provide a synopsis of each category with references, and compare and contrast them.

15.4.1   Taxonomy of Privacy Techniques

A comprehensive and novel taxonomy of the SG privacy-protection mechanisms and approaches is given in Fig. 15.10. We divide the SG approaches into *spatial*

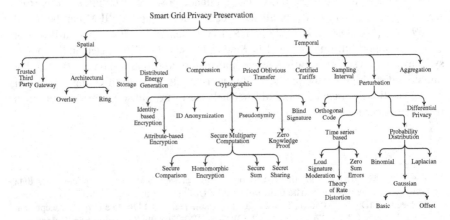

Fig. 15.10 Privacy-preservation techniques used in the SG

and *temporal* broad categories. The former include those that devise privacy into the system by means of a physical device or entity while the latter incorporates privacy into the system by means of logical extensions. We note that the individual categories identified in Fig. 15.10 do not necessarily indicate an exclusive technique. In fact, a privacy preservation proposal reported in the literature may, and usually does, implement a combination of them. The categorization of Fig. 15.10 is to provide a delineation of identifiably distinguishable techniques to provide a smoother and clear explanation in what follows. A different approach has been taken in [73] where privacy preservation techniques are presented with a combination of methods from parts of Fig. 15.10 on a per paper basis.

Next, we provide a discussion of the spatial and temporal categories along with their subclasses.

15.4.2 Spatial Privacy Techniques

There are five main categories of spatial privacy-protection mechanisms proposed in the literature for the SG, as shown in Fig. 15.11, together with the cited references.

15.4.2.1 Trusted Third Party

A trusted third party (TTP) in cryptography is an independent entity that acts as a liaison between two or more collaborating organizations; which, in our case, is between the end-user and the power utility [74–76]. The TTP has to be completely trusted by all participants with respect to its intentions, technical competence, and so on, so mutual trust can be achieved. In the literature, TTP is also referred to as the third party escrow service [75].

In what follows, we elaborate on the approach in [75] as one example in this category: [75] provides a mechanism for anonymizing high-frequency energy

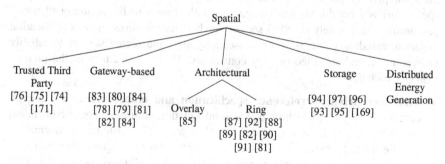

Fig. 15.11 Spatial privacy-provisioning techniques for the smart grid

measurement data (such as usage patterns of specific electrical appliances) through the use of a Pseudonymous Identity (PID). The anonymous meter readings are difficult to associate with a particular smart meter or customer, thus offering a higher level of privacy to the SG user.

The distinguishing feature of the Escrow smart meter is that it has two separate IDs, rather than a single ID as is the case with standard smart meters. The two IDs are the high-frequency ID (HFID) which is anonymous, and the low-requency ID (LFID) [77], which can be related to a specific customer or smart meter. The main idea of the scheme is to provide anonymity of the HFID messages. The anonymity is implemented by not disclosing the HFID to the utility or the smart meter installer. The HFID is 'hidden' inside the smart meter, or hard-coded to be used for all HFID-related messages. In order for the utility to verify the legitimacy of the HFID, a third party Escrow mechanism is implemented. The third-party can be the manufacturer of the smart meter itself or some other trusted third-party, which has been given access to this information. The manufacturer can assign two unique IDs to each smart meter that is produced, only one of which (LFID) is visible to the utility, both during the procurement and deployment procedures. Essentially, the manufacturer (or the Escrow service) is the only party that is aware (and has a record) of the connection between a valid HFID or LFID pair. The Escrow is required to comply with a strong data privacy policy. For example, the Escrow may not be expected to access, process, or store smart metering data—it will only know about the relationship between a valid HFID and LFID.

15.4.2.2 Gateway-Based Approaches

In the gateway-based approach, an external entity outside of the customer premises acts on behalf of the end-users to obfuscate the relationship between the data and the owner [78–84].

The Smart Energy Gateway (SEG) architecture [83] is deployed at users' premises and uses a privacy manager, which is designed as a software component running on SEG, deployed at users' premises. The idea behind the architecture is to provide user-centric privacy, which means that the user could be in control of his or her own privacy parameters. The proposed privacy manager has the ability to specify privacy conditions and obligations with respect to the handling of users' private data, and to rely on SEG security architecture features such as application isolation, mandatory access control, pseudonymity, and secure storage to reliably enforce the users' specified privacy constraints. The main features of the privacy manager include:

- **Customer privacy preference specification and enforcement**. The energy customer would express how personal information disclosed should be handled and the utility or service provider would express how customer's information will be treated. Privacy policies enforcement: each SEG application policy is bound to a smart software agent and has to be validated against the SEG platform integrity policy both during the installation and at runtime. This ensures that SEG only hosts and runs smart software agents that meet pre-defined gateway security requirements (e.g., that the former will not access locally-stored energy usage data collected at this particular premise).

- **Secure storage and data masking.** The secure storage will guarantee the confidentiality and accuracy of locally-stored energy usage data. Only trusted and legitimate applications (e.g., billing provider software agent) can access the metered data repository.
- **Pseudonymity.** Enables the customer to use SG resources or related services without revealing their respective identities but remaining accountable for their transactions.
- **Privacy feedback.** Allows the display of feedbacks to the energy customer regarding the handling of its personally identifiable information.

15.4.2.3 Architectural Schemes

Architectural schemes arrange the topology of the smart meters in order to implement privacy protection. Two distinct categories are considered:

1. **Overlay.** Randomly organized smart meters form peer-to-peer groups in [85] using Chord algorithm [86]. Peer anonymization algorithm together with in-network aggregation enhance the privacy protection capabilities of the proposed approach.
2. **Ring topology.** A few proposed approaches [81, 82, 87–92] take advantage of imposing some form of a ring architecture for the SG meters. For example, a virtual ring architecture is proposed in [87] to provide a privacy protection solution using symmetric or asymmetric encryption of customers' requests belonging to the same group.

15.4.2.4 Storage-Based Mechanisms

As the name implies, a type of energy storage infrastructure is employed for the privacy protection in this category [93–97]. For example, the authors in [94, 95] assume that future smart homes will contain several energy storage and energy generation devices, and thus *electrical power routing* will be feasible. More details of this are given in Sect. 15.4.3.6, under Time series-based privacy.

15.4.2.5 Privacy with Distributed Energy Generation

The main idea behind privacy protection using Distributed Energy Generation (DEG or a.k.a. Distributed Energy Resources or DER) relies on the intermittent and stochastic energy values provided by DEG to mask the actual energy consumption from the disclosed values assuming that DEG is private to the end-user.

15.4.3 Temporal Privacy Techniques

A second major category of privacy preservation techniques we consider includes those that implement techniques over time without relying on an external tangible entity. We describe some of these techniques in this category.

15.4.3.1 Compression-Based Approach

As the name implies, the energy consumption data is transformed using compression techniques to protect the privacy [98, 99]. Compression alone may not be strong enough and thus [99] uses it in combination with other techniques.

Li et al. [98] makes use of the technique of *compressed sensing* from signal processing to provide privacy protection. Compressed sensing [100–102], also known as sparse sampling, assumes the smart meter data is sparse with uniform delay and uses a secret random sequence so that the original data can be reconstructed at the receiving end.

15.4.3.2 Cryptographic

There are various cryptographic techniques reported in the literature that are used to provide privacy in the SG as shown in Fig. 15.12. We divide the cryptographic temporal privacy-protection techniques into seven categories and discuss them here.

Privacy Through Identity-Based Encryption

An identity-based encryption (IdBE) scheme is a public-key cryptosystem where the key may be selected to be any string, such as email addresses, dates, and so on. It was first introduced as a problem in [103] with solutions in [103–105]. IdBE may be used for privacy in the SG as discussed in [106].

Privacy Through Attribute-Based Encryption

In the attribute-based encryption (AbE) [107], ciphertexts are associated with sets of attributes. Private keys are coupled with access structures to control which ciphertexts can be used to decrypt them. AMI is an important component of the

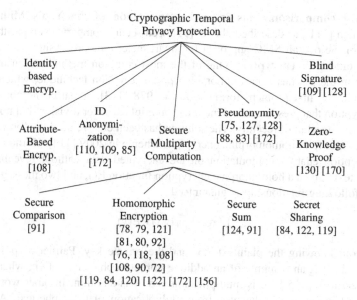

Fig. 15.12 Cryptographic temporal privacy-protection techniques for the smart grid

overall DR system, as defined before in Sect. 15.2.2. In [108], the authors propose to protect multicast communications involving crucial DR messages from the control center to the smart meters by means of an AbE implementation.

Privacy Through ID Anonymization

Anonymization is a general term that decouples a message from its originator. Several proposals in the literature take advantage of the anonymization techniques for the SG privacy [15, 85, 109, 110].

Secure Multiparty Computation

Secure multiparty computation (SMC) has been developed as an alternative to the TTP approach. SMC is a set of techniques to compute a function collectively with the assurance that at the end of the multiparty computation, no participant can learn anything except its own input and the result. Then intended information should be inferable only from these two pieces of information. Historically, SMC was initiated to address Yao's Millionaire Problem [111] where two parties can know which of them is richer without disclosing their actual wealth. Yao's two-party solution was extended to multiple parties in [112].

1. **Secure comparison**. This is an implementation of the Yao's Millionaire Problem [111], as described above. [91] used secure comparisons algorithms as part of the overall SMC approach for smart meter data processing.

2. **Homomorphic encryption**. One of the most common methods to ensure privacy in the SG has been the homomorphic encryption technique, which dates back to the first problem formulation in 1978 [113]. A partial homomorphic encryption that preserves the structure of multiplication or division, but not both, has been used until recently. The solution has been elusive until the formulation of the first fully homomorphic encryption scheme in 2009 [114]. Homomorphic encryption enables computation on the encrypted data without revealing the plaintext. Given a homomorphic encryption function E(), and two messages x, y, the following relationship is guaranteed:

$$E(x \odot y) = E(x) \star E(y), \tag{15.1}$$

without knowing the plaintext x, y, and the private key. Paillier cryptosystem [115, 116] is an example of an additive homomorphic encryption, where with respect to Eq. 15.1, $\odot$ is multiplication and $\star$ is addition. In other words, the sum of plaintext is calculated from multiplication of the ciphertext. Another commonly used additive homomorphic encryption is the Boneh-Goh-Nissim (BGN) cryptosystem [117], which is based on Paillier but with bilinear groups.

   Implementation of homomorphic encryption techniques for privacy preservation in the Smart grid are given in [72, 76, 78, 79–81, 84, 90, 92, 108, 118–120, 121, 122]. For example, the authors of [121] propose an Energy Privacy Preserving Aggregation (EPPA) scheme for secure SG communications. EPPA uses a multi-dimensional data aggregation approach based on the homomorphic Paillier cryptosystem [116], which is composed of three algorithms namely, key generation, encryption, and decryption. The proposed technique is based on composite residuosity classes, whose computation is believed to be computationally difficult. It is a probabilistic asymmetric algorithm for public key cryptography and inherits additive homomorphic properties [113]. Homomorphic encryption allows specific types of computations to be carried out on ciphertext and obtain an encrypted result. For example, one user could add two encrypted numbers and then another user could decrypt the result, without either of them being able to find the value of the individual numbers. Homomorphic encryption schemes are malleable by design. Another homomorphic encryption system for the privacy-preserving data collection and aggregation is proposed in [84, 122] based on the Lite Cramer-Shoup Scheme [123].

3. **Secure sum**. One way to implement the secure sum is by means of Paillier cryptosystem, as proposed in [91]. Another secure sum technique is used in [124] based on the algorithm in [125]. The basic idea of this algorithm is shown in Figs. 15.13, 15.14, 15.15, 15.16, 15.17 and 15.18. Bob, Alice, and Charlie have their own secrets, as shown in Fig. 15.13, and they would each like to compute the sum without revealing their own secret values. Any arbitrary

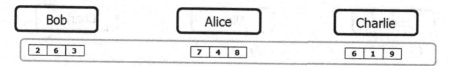

Fig. 15.13 Secrets of Bob, Alice, and Charlie

initiator may start the process. Let Bob initiate it in our example by generating a random profile, as shown in Fig. 15.14. Bob adds the random secret profile to its secret profile, shown in Fig. 15.15.

Bob sends its secret plus random secret to Alice. Note that Alice cannot break up the totals to find out Bob's secret. Alice adds her own secrets to the values received from Bob, as shown in Fig. 15.16. Figure 15.17 show that Charlie gets Alice's transmission and adds his values. Bob receives the profile from Charlie,

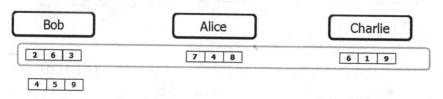

Fig. 15.14 Bob's secret random values

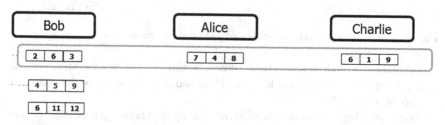

Fig. 15.15 Bob's secret random values added to his own secret

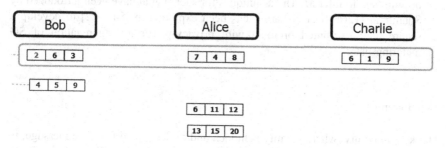

Fig. 15.16 Alice receives Bob's transmission

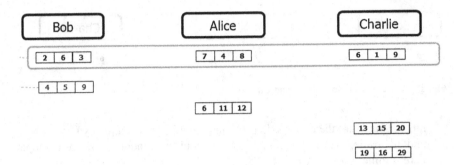

Fig. 15.17 Charlie receives Alice's transmission

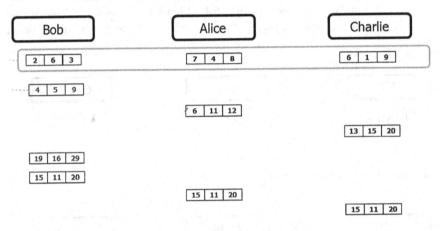

Fig. 15.18 Bob receives Charlie's transmission and computes the sum

subtracts the random secret only known to him and reaches the sum, without knowing either Alice's or Charlie's values and disseminates it to the others, as shown in Fig. 15.18.

4. **Secret sharing**. The basic idea of secret sharing is to break up a message M into k parts before transmission in such a division that the original message M can be assembled together from these n pieces while even access to $n - 1$ parts will not be sufficient to infer M. The techniques for such a goal have been introduced by Shamir in [126]. Secret sharing has been exploited in [84, 122] to develop a secure and distributed protocol with privacy-preserving aggregation of SG metering data.

Pseudonymity

Unlike anonymity, where identity is hidden and/or decoupled from the message, in pseudonymity, fictitious names are used to represent messages. The real identity to the fictitious mapping must be kept secret. Examples of this approach are proposed in [75, 88, 83, 127, 128]. We provide some details of one these here.

The privacy-preserving authentication scheme for an SG network (PASS) [127] involves the use of a smart appliance (located at customers homes) attached to a tamper-resistant device for generating pseudo identities and signatures on messages. A customer is given this device when he or she opens an account or registers a newly purchased smart appliance. The characteristic features of the PASS architecture are as follows:

- Message authentication: before a smart appliance transmits a request message to the control center, it has to include a hash-based message authentication code (HMAC) signature on the message using the regional system key. This regional system key is only known by the control center, the substation, and all tamper-resistant devices within the region. Hence, an outside attacker (who does not belong to the region or is not a registered smart appliance) does not know how to generate a valid HMAC signature. Thus, the PASS scheme protects from outsider attacks.
- Identity privacy: in all request messages sent by a smart appliance, real identities are used instead of pseudo identities.
- Request message confidentiality: the amount of electricity required by a smart appliance is encrypted using the public key of the control center. Thus, except for the control center, no one can decrypt the value representing the electricity amount. On the other hand, the encryption feature in the PASS architecture allows a substation to aggregate request messages sent by smart appliances within its region but the substation does not need to know about those individual amount values.

Zero-Knowledge Proof

Zero-knowledge proofs are those convincing assertions that yield nothing but their validity [129]. In other words, one party proves to another without revealing any information besides a statement of affirmation or decline. The authors of [130] deal with preserving the privacy of metered data. The authors propose a set of privacy-preserving protocols amongst a provider, a user agent, and a simple tamper-evident meter by taking advantage of a zero-knowledge proof. This work considers a scenario where the privacy of the metered data is preserved by employing encryption mechanisms along with certification techniques. Within the boundary of a home environment, plaintext is used, but when sending or communicating with entities outside the home boundary, certification, and encryption techniques are used. The authors argue that their scheme can be applied to all types of smart metering including electricity, waters and gas metering, and can be extended for other future smart meter-based systems. The main contribution of this work can be summarized as follows: the meter produces certified readings of measurements and transmits them to the user via a secure communication channel.

For billing, the user combines those readings with a certified tariff policy to produce a final bill. The bill is then transmitted to the provider alongside a zero-knowledge proof that ensures the calculation to be correct and leaks no additional information. A zero-knowledge proof of knowledge [131] is a two-party protocol between a prover and a verifier. The prover demonstrates to the verifier its knowledge of some secret input (witness) that fulfills some statements without disclosing this input to the verifier. The protocol should meet two properties: (1) it should be a proof of knowledge, which means that a prover without knowledge of the secret input convinces the verifier with negligible probability, and (2) it should be zero-knowledge, that is, the verifier learns nothing but the truth of the statement. The fact that a witness is not distinguishable from active participants is a weaker property which requires that the proof does not reveal the witness (among all possible witnesses) used by the prover.

Blind Signature

In [109], the authors consider an SG network as three basic layers: at the highest layer, there is a control center maintained by the power operator, the second layer has substations inside the distribution network and each substation is responsible for the power supply of an area, and the lowest layer has the smart meters which are placed at the users' premises as shown in Fig. 15.19.

The proposed anonymous credential architecture [109] preserves users' privacy information, including their daily electricity usage pattern from third parties as well as from the power operator. The scheme is based on *blind signatures* [132]. Blind signature is a method that allows the first party (Party 1) to sign a message generated by a second party (Party 2), without knowing its actual content. When a third party (Party 3) receives the signed message, it can verify that the message is signed by Party 1. The anonymous credential scheme uses the blind signature technique to allow the control center (Party 1) to sign a credential generated by a customer (Party 2) without knowing its actual content. At a later time, the control center itself

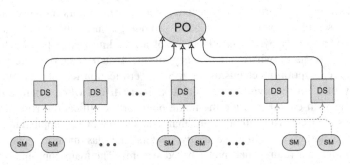

Fig. 15.19 A three-layer smart grid architecture. *PO* power operator, *DS* distribution substation, *SM* smart meter

(Party 3) can verify that the credential is indeed signed by Party 1 without knowing who requested the signature or when the signature was generated. The use of the blind signature technique in this scheme is as follows: the customers prepare a set of credentials, each stating the amount of electricity requested, and request the control center to sign them blindly so that the customer can submit any of these credentials for the request of electricity. Since Party 1 does not know the actual content of the message sent by Party 2, the message is verified using a special technique which is widely adopted in e-cash schemes. Party 2 generates n messages using different blinding factors. It then blinds the n messages and sends them to Party 1. Next, Party 1 randomly chooses m messages ($m < n$) and challenges Party 2 to reveal them by providing the m blinding factors. If the m blinding factors are correct, Party 1 accepts the signature request and signs the remaining ($m - n$) messages. The scheme assumes that any smart meter can communicate with the control center via a secure communication channel (such as one using the advanced encryption standard (AES) and third parties cannot read the contents without the key concerned).

When a customer presents a credential anonymously, the control center cannot tell which customer is making the request, yet it can verify the signature to confirm that it is from a valid customer (since only valid customers can request blind signatures). The four phases involved in the Anonymous Credential scheme are as follows:

- **Setup phase**. The control center assigns a Ron Rivest, Adi Shamir and Leonard Adleman (RSA) public and private key pair for signing credentials.
- **Registration phase**. Carried out at the beginning of each month. This phase is not anonymous. Customers need to be authenticated using their real identities via an authenticated channel.
- **Power requesting phase**. Can be executed at any time during the month when the smart meter of a customer finds that it needs more power to support all the electric appliances. This phase is anonymous. Customers are validated via anonymous credentials.
- **Reconciliation phase**. Carried out at the end of each month. This phase is not anonymous. The smart meter sends the unused credentials back to the control center to evaluate the amount of power requested so far.

Another approach based on the fair blind signature [133] method is reported in [128] for the vehicle-to-grid (V2G) system, involving both charging and discharging of battery vehicles (BVs). Fair blind signature is an extension of the basic blind signature scheme where misuse of the system against black-mailing and money laundering is prevented by means of an embedded property to remove anonymity via a trusted entity. In our case, it is used to ensure proper billing.

15.4.3.3 Priced Oblivious Transfer

Oblivious transfer, introduced in 1981 in [134], is a protocol in which the sender remains unaware of what has been transmitted out of the potentially transferable many pieces. Using oblivious transfer protocol, a protocol is developed in [135], called priced oblivious transfer, to enable buyers purchase digital goods from vendors without letting the seller learn *what*, and to the extent possible, *when* and *how much*. Priced Oblivious protocol is used in [136] to propose a privacy preserving billing protocol which guarantees the power operator gets the correct amount of money without learning the current energy consumption of each customer.

15.4.3.4 Certified Tariffs

As explained in Sect. 15.4.3.2 (the subsection on Zero-knowledge proof) from [130], the energy provider cannot gather any fine-grained readings. The provider is guaranteed that the correct fee is calculated based on the actual readings and time-of-use tariffs without learning.

15.4.3.5 Sampling Interval

Smart meters in the AMI system provide sampling of measurements and potentially other useful information and report them back to the power operator or other third parties. The sampling process is the center of privacy concerns as it transmits potentially sensitive information. The authors in [137] consider sampling as a design parameter in the performance of DR schemes to explore some trade-offs between performance and privacy. An optimization problem is considered to find the right sampling interval given a set of performance goals and desired privacy level.

15.4.3.6 Perturbation

Another technique for privacy preservation that has gained a considerable attention is a set of techniques collectively known under the term *perturbation*. A taxonomy with the cited work is depicted in Fig. 15.20. A common theme in these techniques is the transformation of the energy consumption data from what gets disclosed out of the customer premises. We provide details of this category with its subclasses in what follows.

Privacy Using Orthogonal Code

The work in [138] analyzes security and privacy in the SG and specifically emphasizes the privacy aspects. The authors propose a secure and efficient in-network data aggregation and dispatch scheme for AMI in home area networks for the SG. In-network aggregation is the process of collecting content from multiple sources or devices in a network. With this mechanism, the authors propose the use of Walsh function [139] based on Hadamard code [140] to generate mutual orthogonal chip codes to be used in the secure in-network data aggregation and

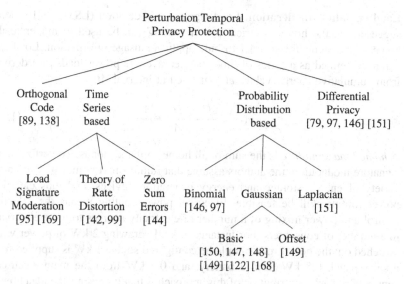

Fig. 15.20 Perturbation-based temporal privacy-provisioning techniques for the smart grid

dispatch scheme. The use of orthogonal code allows multiple users to communicate simultaneously over a single frequency. This is achieved by the use of spreading codes whereby a single data bit is "spread" over a longer sequence of transmitted bits. These codes, also known as chip sequences, must be carefully chosen so that the data may be correctly "de-spread" at the receiver. Such codes are known as orthogonal codes. The Hadamard code [140] is an error-correcting code that is usually used for error detection and correction when transmitting messages over very noisy or unreliable channels. In their work, the authors apply these techniques envisioning that the smart meter works as an authentication server that is connected with multiple smart devices and each smart device contributes to the formation of confidential data, which can be regenerated at the smart meter. This work describes the coding techniques and the steps on how the original data readings are spread and then mixed up with the spreading code of other smart devices. The smart meter can reconstruct the original reading data from the mixed data using the chip code established with smart devices during their initialization procedure through mutual authentications.

Another work that encrypts measured data by orthogonal codes by using Walsh code is reported in [89], which uses a ring communication architecture.

Time Series-Based Privacy

One way to look at the measurements coming out of the smart meters is a series of data giving way to a wealth of methods that can be invoked from the field of time series. We present a survey of some of these methods here.

1. **Load signature moderation**: Load signature moderation (LSM) [95] scheme
   suggests that the home electrical power routing can be used to moderate the
   home's load signature in order to hide appliance usage information. Load signature is defined as a series of time-stamped average power loads $p(t)$ derived
   from cumulative energy values $e(t)$ metered at interval Δt:

$$p(t) = \frac{e(t) - e(t - \Delta t)}{\Delta t} \qquad (15.2)$$

A *home load signature* is the sum of all home appliance loads. To perform load
signature moderation, the authors assume that future smart homes will contain a
variety of energy storage and energy generation devices, and thus electrical
power routing will be feasible. Electrical power routing means the selective
control and power mixing of a number of electricity sources to route electricity
to a number of consumers. For instance, a kettle drawing 2 kW of power when
switched on; the power router could be configured so that 1 kW is supplied from
a solar panel, 0.5 kW from a battery, and 0.5 kW from the main electricity
supply. The basic contribution of this approach is that it presents the idea how to
provide sufficient privacy for the user by including privacy mechanisms for the
smart meters which is supposed to record the usage. The authors also propose a
power management model using a rechargeable battery, a power mixing algorithm, and evaluate its protection level by proposing three different privacy
metrics: an information theoretic (relative entropy), a clustering classification,
and a correlation/regression one. We will briefly review these metrics:

- *Relative entropy*: the relative entropy or Kullback Leibler distance [141] is a
  well-known information theoretic quantity which can be used to compare
  two sources of information. The distance here is not the mathematical
  meaning of distance but rather it quantifies the relation between probability
  densities. If p_0 and p_1 are two probability densities, the Kullback-Leibler
  distance is defined to be,

$$D(p_0 \| p_1) = \int_{xmin}^{xmax} p_1(x) log \frac{p_1(x)}{p_0(x)} dx \qquad (15.3)$$

  where p_0 and p_1 are the probability density functions of p_0 and p_1,
  respectively.
  Relative entropy is always positive, and for identical p_0 and p_1, it is zero.
  Hence, the authors in [95] state that the level of privacy protection offered by
  a mapping $\emptyset$ can be measured by the relative entropy, $D_\emptyset(p_0 \| p_1)$ such that
  the higher the level of protection offered by $\emptyset$, the larger the relative entropy.
- *Clustering classification*: the authors propose using any of the available
  clustering classification mechanisms which takes a set of data with a distance
  metric and groups them into n clusters that minimize the distance between
  points. The distance metric here is the difference between power consumption

values. They propose to use a simple method of trace analysis that aims to recover information about device power usage from a small amount of information sent via the signals.

- *Regression analysis*: as a third metric, the work described in [132] quantifies privacy by combining cross correlation and regression procedures, which can be termed as regression analysis. In statistics, regression analysis includes many techniques for modeling and analyzing several variables, when the focus is on the relationship between a dependent variable and one or more independent variables. A dependent variable is what is measured in an experiment and what is affected during the experiment. This kind of variable responds to the independent variable. It is termed so because it depends on the independent variable. In a scientific experiment, there cannot be a dependent variable without an independent variable. Just as an example, if someone is interested to find out how time spent on studying changes "test score", then it is understood that the test score does not change the time spent, as that had happened earlier. In this case, "studying time" is the independent variable and "test score" is the dependent variable. Based on these foundations and ideas, the authors in this work apply regression analysis on the received signals to recover information by comparing them over time.

This work can be extended to include other types of privacy metrics, such as mutual entropy or equivocation. In addition, smarter battery privacy algorithms may be designed, which the authors have left as future works.

2. **Theory of rate distortion**: Rate-distortion theory is a subfield of information theory that addresses the problems of lossy compression. It analyzes the theoretical fundamentals of determining the bit rate to be communicated over a communications channel in order for the original data to be reconstructed at the receiver subject to a distortion level.

Information theoretic approaches to SG privacy have been proposed in a few studies [99, 142, 143] by means of the rate-distortion theory. Rate-distortion theory has been used to provide SG privacy in a few recent studies [99, 142, 143]. Rajagopalan et al. [99] and Sankar et al. [143] attempt to quantify privacy in order to gain insight into the tradeoff between sharing information (utility) and hiding it (privacy). The utility is represented by means of square error (distortion D)

$$D = \frac{1}{n} \sum_{k=1}^{n} \mathbb{E}[(X_k - \hat{X}_k)^2] \tag{15.4}$$

where X_k is the actual measurement, $\hat{X}_k$ is the exposed value; while privacy is represented by information leakage:

$$L = \frac{1}{n} \mathscr{I}(Y_n; \hat{X}_n) \tag{15.5}$$

where Y_n represents the inferred data as a random variable correlated with the measurement variable X. Some examples of interference sequence Y_n include the known appliance signatures that are provided by NILM techniques discussed earlier in Sect. 15.3.3. The proposed algorithm, interference-aware reverse waterfilling solution, exposes high power but less private appliance information and filters out components with lower power to a distortion threshold. However, this proposal is only limited to a framework proposal and an algorithmic approach is not detailed enough to implement it.

Another rate-distortion theory based approach is given in [142]. However, similar to the previous ones, it also suffers from unrealistic assumptions and the approach is complex. For instance, the assumption about binary input and output loads are unrealistic.

3. **Zero-Sum Errors**. The authors of [144] propose a cooperative state vector estimation technique that preserves the privacy of the personal behavior of the user. Unlike most other privacy preservation techniques for the SG where energy consumption information is the focus, the authors here provide privacy protection for phase angle measurements. Thus, they take advantage of the state estimation methodology [145]. The key objectives are to ensure mainly two things: (1) the power measurement is well obfuscated such that users do not fully disclose their private behavioral information, and (2) the obfuscated data retains the necessary or basic information such that the state vector (a column vector whose components are the state variables of the system) can be accurately estimated from the perturbed data. "Perturbed data" are the original measurement data that are modified to conceal the information and to make it difficult to infer the original data. Another significant contribution of this work is that the authors evaluated the performance of the proposed data obfuscation scheme with 1,349 measurement data sets. For this, they used the data sets as if they are connected to five different IEEE test systems that are portions of the Middlewestern US Electric Power Grids. They also evaluated the illegibility to human inspectors, resilience to automated data mining attackers, and communication overhead.

Privacy with Probability Distribution Functions

Another method of transforming the exposed measurement data is by means of adding noise from probability distribution functions.

1. **Binomail**. Binomial distribution is proposed in [97, 146].
2. **Gaussian**.

   a. Basic: straight Gaussian distribution is used to determine the magnitude of the noise in [147–150].
   b. Offset: [149] proposed a noise canceling mechanism by using a technique which is based on the Central Limit Theorem. In the offset method, the

margin caused by noises in previous time slots is compensated to achieve zero error in billing computation.

3. **Laplacian**. Laplace distribution is the basis for computing the noise in [151]. Chen et al. [79] employs symmetric geometric distribution, which can be regarded as a discrete approximation of Laplace distribution. The use of geometric distribution for the noise was pioneered by [152].

Differential Privacy

The notion of differential privacy is coined in [153, 154]. Differential privacy has emerged from the field of database queries where the goal is to answer queries in an accurate way while preserving the privacy of individuals. Differential privacy yields plausible deniability to blur the data hidden behind. It is about an information-releasing algorithm with a mathematical underlying model. Differential privacy boils down to distorting the answers to the database queries by means of adding a predefined noise so that the intended receiver filters it out to reach an almost accurate answer. As can be seen from the problem definition, this is applicable to the SG privacy case as well. Differential privacy-based mechanisms have been proposed in [79, 97, 146, 151].

15.4.3.7 Aggregation

To secure the data-collection task, there are two major approaches: one is to ensure the protection of the data content directly without regard to the data semantics. The approach presented in [60] is based on symmetric cryptography to provide data confidentiality and authentication between sensors and the base station. [155] describes a protocol for data collector (DC) to collect data from a measurement device (MD), but direct communication between the DC and the MD is assumed. Another category for providing security exploits the *aggregate* statistics of the sensed data, such as summation, average, minimum, maximum, and so on. These approaches take advantage of in-network data processing (also referred to as *aggregation*) to apply some obfuscating operations on the transmitted data [72, 122, 138, 156–162]. A few common examples in this category include cluster-based private data aggregation [159] and its integrity enhanced version [160], secret perturbation [157], k-indistinguishable privacy-preserving data aggregation [158], a centralized authentication server based in-network aggregation for AMI [138, 161], homomorphic encryption-based aggregation [72, 78, 80], a secure architecture for distributed secure hierarchical data collection aggregation of additive data [84, 122], a secure and scalable data collection protocol for smart meter data [163, 164], multifunctional, privacy-protecting aggregation [79], and a network coding-based encryption between smart meters and aggregators [162]. Another one is reported in [121]. Many of the existing data aggregation schemes collect information as one-dimensional information. However, smart meter data could be considered as multi-dimensional in nature, because, these include including various aspects of the information such as the amount of energy consumed, the time it was consumed, the purpose of the consumption, and so on. Considering the high data collection frequency, multi-dimensional information and the large number of users, current data aggregation schemes generate not only huge communication costs but also impose overwhelming processing load on local gateways. In contrast to traditional one-dimensional data aggregation methods, Energy Privacy Preserving Aggregation (EPPA), as discussed earlier in "Secure Multiparty Computation", is shown to greatly reduce computational cost and significantly improve communication efficiency while satisfying the real-time high-frequency data collection requirements in SG communications. The main drawback of the work is that it is highly theoretical and it does not really provide enough details on how such an approach can be deployed in practice.

15.5 Challenges and Opportunities

The preservation of privacy in the SG environment has many fundamental open challenges that still need to be solved. As our literature survey shows, several research projects have been investigating privacy-preserving techniques for the SG environment in the last few years. We found that there is need for privacy to be comprehensively regulated through legal and regulatory frameworks for enhancing users' confidence and for reinforcing individual's privacy rights. These frameworks should provide a comprehensive view of both the challenges and limitations related to personal data protection rights as they pertain to the SG technology.

In recent years, a lot of work has been undertaken on designing privacy-preserving methods using various technical approaches, which vary according to the context and the architecture in use. Throughout this chapter, various SG privacy solutions aimed at preserving smart meters' privacy have been discussed. As we have pointed out earlier, most of the recently proposed SG solutions have limitations and they do not always follow the recommendations being made by standardizations entities and governmental agencies [40]. Although it is not mandatory to follow the recommended guidelines made by standardization bodies, for future interoperability and scalability, SG privacy solutions should nevertheless take these recommendations into consideration. We discuss here some of the challenges that still need to be addressed in the future by researchers and designers working in the area of SG privacy.

- **Third party issue**
  The privacy issues in the SG are particularly magnified by the large-scale infrastructures, the diversity of communication technologies, the number data sources, and the high volume of data generated. In the past, most of the SG services were basically limited to governments or large enterprises, which have

traditionally built by proprietary and isolated infrastructures (e.g., electrical power network) to provide services to customers. However, third parties can actually offer their infrastructures and services with limited control from governments and, hence, concerns have arisen about third-party access to the customer's personal information.

- **Privacy and authentication**

  Privacy is often closely linked with authentication. The issue of trade-off between privacy rights of entities and the need to authenticate them needs to be explored further. Unfortunately, authentication leads to personal information becoming available. However, authentication is a very important security service that may help to eliminate some of the cyber attack classes such as man-in-the-middle attacks and false data injection attacks. The latter consists of forging and manipulating the quantities of energy supply and requests. It is worth noting that authenticated nodes may also inject false data without being detected as is the case with recently proposed homomorphic encryption-based solutions [87, 165].

- **Privacy and forensics**

  Privacy solutions are also closely linked with verifiability requirements [166] and with tractability as well as forensic techniques. We should formulate threat models to detect cyber attacks and data leakage scenarios [166] such as infrastructure attacks and rogue nodes. In particular, a privacy-preserving solution should provide a well-maintained log that may help in preventing fraud and in resolving disputes. Traceability and forensic techniques should be taken into consideration during service design and the development of service architectures [167]. In the context of the SG and real-time ecosystems, we should not only cover the effectiveness of privacy-preserving methods, but also have the ability to monitor and detect anomalies in real-time and analyze the data collected and aggregated from the different sources. The challenge here is to define an effective method to identify legitimate traffic, to enable forensic investigation on subversive and illegal activities, and to mitigate any possible insider attacks against the infrastructure. In fact, security and forensics techniques are fundamental, especially when an adversary tampers with a device from which data are collected or aggregated or when the same adversary successfully performs cloning attacks.

Multi-disciplinary research approaches which consider training, legal, and technological aspects should be developed to address the privacy issues that arise with the SG environment. Future SG privacy solutions should include the design and development of architectures that prevent unnecessary linking between the user identity and the SG services, while guaranteeing traceability and accountability in the presence of an important set of interconnected engineering resources and nodes. We argue that a holistic approach is needed to identify and address privacy challenges throughout the engineering phase of the SG in order to ensure SG solutions that maintain privacy and are also secure, scalable, and cost-effective.

15.6 Conclusion

Over the past several years we have witnessed huge investments and interests from industry and governments in SG technologies. Various stakeholders (residential/commercial customers, local government, utility operators, etc.) are expected to reap several benefits associated with the SG including improved energy efficiency, increased reliability, reduced energy costs, greater flexibility in energy consumption, better safety and security, and an improved environment (through renewable, renewable non-variable, non-renewable/non-variable energy sources). The deployment of SG technologies has also raised considerable concerns in data privacy issues of SG users, as we have discussed in this chapter. The privacy concerns are mostly related to the collection and use of energy consumption data. In this context, we have discussed various SG privacy issues and we have presented SG privacy architectures and approaches that have been recently proposed in the literature. A unique taxonomy of the various privacy protection mechanisms proposed in the literature has been developed. We also identified the various strengths and weaknesses of these privacy solutions. The success of SG technology and its wide acceptance rely on gaining the trust and confidence of customers, which in turn depends on assurances regarding the protection of their privacy.

References

1. Warren SD, Brandeis LD (1890) The right to privacy. Harv Law Rev 4(5):193–220. doi:10. 2307/1321160, url:http://www.jstor.org/stable/1321160
2. Westin AF (1967) Privacy and freedom. Atheneum
3. DeCew J (2013) Privacy. In: Zalta EN (ed) The Stanford encyclopedia of philosophy, fall 2013 edn, url:http://plato.stanford.edu/entries/privacy/
4. Richards NM (2014) Four myths of privacy. In: Sarat A (ed) A world without privacy?, April 2014 edn, url:http://papers.ssrn.com/sol3/papers.cfm?abstract_id=2427808
5. Holvast J (2007) 27—history of privacy. In: Leeuw KD, Bergstra J (eds) The history of information security. Elsevier Science B.V., Amsterdam, pp 737–769. doi:http://dx.doi.org/10.1016/B978-044451608-4/50028-6, url:http://www.sciencedirect.com/science/article/pii/B9780444516084500286
6. OECD, for Economic Co-operation, O., Development (1981) Guidelines on the protection of privacy and transborder flows of personal data. Organisation for Economic Co-operation and Development; OECD Publications and Information Center Paris, Washington, D.C, url: http://oe.cd/privacy, http://www.oecd.org/internet/ieconomy/oecdguidelinesontheprotectionofprivacyandtransborderflowsofpersonaldata.htm
7. OECD (2013) Guidelines on the protection of privacy and transborder flows of personal data. Organisation for Economic Co-operation and Development; OECD Publications and Information Center Paris, Washington, D.C, url:http://www.oecd.org/sti/ieconomy/oecd_privacy_framework.pdf
8. Chaum D (1985) Security without identification: transaction systems to make big brother obsolete. Commun ACM 28(10):1030–1044. doi:10.1145/4372.4373, url:http://dl.acm.org/citation.cfm?id=4372.4373

9. van Rossum H, Gardeniers H, Borking J, Cavoukian A, Brans J, Muttupulle N, Magistrale N (1995) Privacy-enhancing technologies: the path to anonymity. Information and Privacy Commissioner/Ontario, Canada & Registratiekamer, Den Haag, The Netherlands

10. Blarkom GV, Borking J, Olk J (2003) Handbook of privacy and privacy-enhancing technologies. Privacy incorporated software, pp 42–50, url:http://www.andrewpatrick.ca/pisa/handbook/Handbook_Privacy_and_PET_final.pdf

11. DRAFT NISTIR 7628 Revision 1 (2013) Guidelines for smart grid cyber security. Supportive analyses and references, vol 3. Smart Grid Interoperability Panel (SGIP), Smart Grid Cybersecurity Committee, url:http://csrc.nist.gov/publications/drafts/nistir-7628-r1/draft_nistir_7628_r1_vol3.pdf

12. DRAFT NISTIR 7628 Revision 1 (2013) Guidelines for smart grid cybersecurity. Privacy and the smart grid, vol 2. Smart Grid Interoperability Panel (SGIP), Smart Grid Cybersecurity Committee, url:http://csrc.nist.gov/publications/drafts/nistir-7628-r1/draft_nistir_7628_r1_vol2.pdf

13. DRAFT NISTIR 7628 Revision 1 (2013) Guidelines for smart grid cybersecurity: smart grid cybersecurity strategy, architecture, and high-level requirements, vol 1. Smart Grid Interoperability Panel (SGIP), Smart Grid Cybersecurity Committee, url: http://csrc.nist.gov/publications/drafts/nistir-7628-r1/draft_nistir_7628_r1_vol1.pdf

14. Asghar M, Miorandi D (2013) A holistic view of security and privacy issues in smart grids. In: Cuellar J (ed) Smart grid security. Lecture notes in computer science, vol 7823. Springer, Berlin, pp 58–71, url:http://dx.doi.org/10.1007/978-3-642-38030-3_4

15. Barenghi A, Pelosi G (2011) Security and privacy in smart grid infrastructures. In: Proceedings—international workshop on database and expert systems applications, DEXA, pp 102–108. doi:10.1109/DEXA.2011.74

16. Hauser CH, Bakken DE, Dionysiou I, Gjermudød KK, Irava VS, Helkey J, Bose A (2007) Security, trust and QoS in next-generation control and communication for large power systems. Int J Crit Infrastruct 4:3–16

17. Chen TM (2010) Survey of cyber security issues in smart grids. doi:10.1117/12.862698, url: http://dx.doi.org/10.1117/12.862698

18. Cleveland FM (2008) Cyber security issues for advanced metering infrastructure (AMI). In: Power and energy society general meeting—conversion and delivery of electrical energy in the 21st century, 2008 IEEE, pp 1–5. doi:10.1109/PES.2008.4596535

19. Das SK, Kant K, Zhang N (2012) Handbook on securing cyber-physical critical infrastructure. Elsevier Science, url:http://books.google.com/books?id=MftTeQivgA0C

20. Fleury T, Khurana H, Welch V (2009) Towards a taxonomy of attacks against energy control systems, pp 71–85. Springer. doi:10.1007/978-0-387-88523-0_6, url:http://www.springerlink.com/content/d38w8553g6211838/

21. For E, Chan AC, Zhou J (2013) On smart grid cybersecurity standardization: Issues of designing with NISTIR 7628. Commun Mag, IEEE 51(1):58–65. doi:10.1109/MCOM.2013.6400439

22. Fries S, Falk R, Sutor A (2013) Smart grid information exchange securing the smart grid from the ground. In: Cuellar J (ed) Smart grid security. Lecture notes in computer science, vol 7823. Springer, Berlin, pp 26–44, url:http://dx.doi.org/10.1007/978-3-642-38030-3_2

23. Hahn A, Govindarasu M (2011) Cyber attack exposure evaluation framework for the smart grid. IEEE Trans Smart Grid 2(4):835–843. doi:10.1109/TSG.2011.2163829

24. Hull J, Khurana H, Markham T, Staggs K (2012) Staying in control: cybersecurity and the modern electric grid. Power Energy Mag, IEEE 10(1):41–48. doi:10.1109/MPE.2011.943251

25. Jokar P, Arianpoo N, Leung VCM (2012) A survey on security issues in smart grids. Secur Commun Netw. doi:10.1002/sec.559, url:http://dx.doi.org/10.1002/sec.559

26. Li X, Liang X, Lu R, Shen X, Lin X, Zhu H (2012) Securing smart grid: cyber attacks, countermeasures, and challenges. Commun Mag IEEE 50(8):38–45. doi:10.1109/MCOM.2012.6257525

27. Liu J, Xiao Y, Li S, Liang W, Chen CLP (2012) Cyber security and privacy issues in smart grids. Commun Surv Tutor IEEE 14(4):981–997. doi:10.1109/SURV.2011.122111.00145
28. McBride AJ, McGee AR (2012) Assessing smart grid security. Bell Labs Tech J 17(3):87–103. doi:10.1002/bltj.21560, url:http://dx.doi.org/10.1002/bltj.21560
29. Mo Y, Kim TH, Brancik K, Dickinson D, Lee H, Perrig A, Sinopoli B (2012) Cyber-physical security of a smart grid infrastructure. Proc IEEE 100(1):195–209. doi:10.1109/JPROC.2011.2161428
30. Nordell DE (2012) Terms of protection: the Many faces of smart grid security. Power Energy Mag IEEE 10(1):18–23. doi:10.1109/MPE.2011.943194
31. Systems S, McDaniel P, McLaughlin S (2009) Security and privacy challenges in the smart grid. Secur Priv IEEE 7(3):75–77. doi:10.1109/MSP.2009.76
32. Wang W, Lu Z (2013) Cyber security in the smart grid: survey and challenges. Comput Netw 57(5):1344–1371. doi:http://dx.doi.org/10.1016/j.comnet.2012.12.017 , url:http://www.sciencedirect.com/science/article/pii/S1389128613000042
33. Wang Y, Ruan D, Gu D, Gao J, Liu D, Xu J, Chen F, Dai F, Yang J (2011) Analysis of smart grid security standards. In: 2011 IEEE international conference on computer science and automation engineering (CSAE), vol 4, pp 697–701. doi:10.1109/CSAE.2011.5952941
34. Xiao Y (2013) Security and privacy in smart grids. Taylor & Francis, url:http://books.google.com/books?id=QQ2oY0IrRM8C
35. Yan Y, Qian Y, Sharif H, Tipper D (2012) A survey on cyber security for smart grid communications. Commun Surv Tutor IEEE 14(4):998–1010. doi:10.1109/SURV.2012.010912.00035
36. Zhou L, Chen S (2012) A survey of research on smart grid security. In: Lei J, Wang F, Li M, Luo Y (eds) Network computing and information security. Commun Comput Inf Sci 345:395–405 (Springer, Berlin, url:http://dx.doi.org/10.1007/978-3-642-35211-9_52
37. Fang X, Misra S, Xue G, Yang D (2012) Smart grid the new and improved power grid: a survey. IEEE Commun Surv Tutor 14(4):944–980. doi:10.1109/SURV.2011.101911.00087, url:http://ieeexplore.ieee.org/lpdocs/epic03/wrapper.htm?arnumber=6099519
38. Gharavi H, Ghafurian R (2011) {Smart grid}: the electric energy system of the future. Proc IEEE 99(6):917–921. doi:10.1109/jproc.2011.2124210, url:http://dx.doi.org/10.1109/jproc.2011.2124210
39. US Department of Energy (2006) Benefits of demand response in electricity markets and recommendations for achieving them—a report to the United States Congress Pursant to Section 1252 of the Energy Policy Act of 2005, pp 122
40. National Institute of Standards and Technology (2013: NIST framework and roadmap for smart grid interoperability standards, Release 2.0. smart grid interoperability panel (SGIP), url:http://j.mp/1rs1tKs http://collaborate.nist.gov/twiki-sggrid/pub/SmartGrid/IKBFramework/NIST_Framework_Release_2-0_corr.pdf
41. International Electrotechnical Commission (2010) IEC Strategic Group 3, Smart grid standardization roadmap, url:http://www.iec.ch/smartgrid/downloads/sg3_roadmap.pdf
42. European Committee for Electrotechnical Standardization (2011) Final report of the CEN/CENELEC/ETSI Joint Working Group on Standards for Smart Grids
43. IEEE guide for smart grid interoperability of energy technology and information technology operation with the electric power system (EPS) (2011) End-use applications, and loads. IEEE Std 2030-2011, pp 1–126. doi:10.1109/IEEESTD.2011.6018239
44. International Energy Agency (2013) Tracking clean energy progress 2013. IEA input to the clean energy ministerial, url:http://www.iea.org/publications/TCEP_web.pdf
45. National Energy Technology Laboratory, the U.S. Department of Energy, D.O.E., Office of Electricity Delivery and Energy Reliability (2008) Advanced metering infrastructure. White Paper
46. Kroposki B, Pink C, Basso T, DeBlasio R (2007) Microgrid standards and technology development. In: Power engineering society general meeting, 2007, pp 1–4. IEEE. doi:10.1109/PES.2007.386053

47. Lasseter RH (2002) MicroGrids. In: Power engineering society winter meeting, vol 1, pp 305–308. IEEE. doi:10.1109/PESW.2002.985003
48. Vaccaro A, Popov M, Villacci D, Terzija V (2011) An integrated framework for smart microgrids modeling, monitoring, control, communication, and verification. Proc IEEE 99 (1):119–132. doi:10.1109/JPROC.2010.2081651
49. Masters GM (2004) Renewable and efficient electric power systems. Wiley, New York)
50. Mohsenian-Rad AH, Wong VWS, Jatskevich J, Schober R, Leon-Garcia A (2010) Autonomous demand-side management based on game-theoretic energy consumption scheduling for the future smart grid. IEEE Trans Smart Grid 1(3):320–331. doi:10.1109/TSG.2010.2089069
51. Mohsenian-Rad AH, Leon-Garcia A (2010) Optimal residential load control with price prediction in real-time electricity pricing environments. IEEE Trans Smart Grid 1(2):120–133. doi:10.1109/TSG.2010.2055903
52. Samadi P, Mohsenian-Rad AH, Schober R, Wong VWS, Jatskevich J (2010) Optimal real-time pricing algorithm based on utility maximization for smart grid. In: IEEE SmartGridComm, pp 415–420). doi:10.1109/SMARTGRID.2010.5622077
53. Zhu Z, Tang J, Lambotharan S, Chin WH, Fan Z (2011) An integer linear programming and game theory based optimization for demand-side management in smart grid. In: GLOBECOM workshops (GC Wkshps), 2011 IEEE, pp 1205–1210. doi:10.1109/GLOCOMW.2011.6162372
54. Hajdu LP, Peschon J, Tinney WF, Piercy DS (1968) Optimum load-shedding policy for power systems. IEEE Trans Power Apparatus Syst PAS-87(3):784–795. doi:10.1109/TPAS.1968.292194
55. Aponte EE, Nelson JK (2006) Time optimal load shedding for distributed power systems. IEEE Trans Power Syst 21(1):269–277. doi:10.1109/TPWRS.2005.857826
56. De Tuglie E, Dicorato M, La Scala M, Scarpellini P (2000) A corrective control for angle and voltage stability enhancement on the transient time-scale. IEEE Trans Power Syst 15 (4):1345–1353. doi:10.1109/59.898111
57. Du P, Nelson JK (2009) Two-step solution to optimal load shedding in a micro-grid. In: Power systems conference and exposition, 2009. PSCE '09. IEEE/PES, pp 1–9. doi:10.1109/PSCE.2009.4840112
58. Molina-Markham A, Shenoy P, Fu K, Cecchet E, Irwin D (2010) Private memoirs of a smart meter. In: Proceedings of the 2nd ACM workshop on embedded sensing systems for energy-efficiency in building, BuildSys '10. ACM, New York, NY, USA, pp 61–66. doi:10.1145/1878431.1878446
59. Wang Z, Zheng G, Member S (2012) Residential appliances identification and monitoring by a nonintrusive method. IEEE Trans Smart Grid 3(1):80–92. doi:10.1109/TSG.2011.2163950
60. Perrig A, Szewczyk R, Tygar JD, Wen V, Culler DE (2002) SPINS: security protocols for sensor networks. Wirel Netw 8(5):521–534. doi:10.1023/A:1016598314198
61. Miller J (2008) Who are you, Part II: more on the trade-off between information utility and privacy. IEEE Internet Comput 12(6):91–93. doi:10.1109/MIC.2008.135, url:http://ieeexplore.ieee.org/lpdocs/epic03/wrapper.htm?arnumber=4670125
62. Miller J (2008) Who are you? The trade-off between information utility and privacy. IEEE Internet Comput 12(4):93–96. doi:10.1109/MIC.2008.91, url:http://ieeexplore.ieee.org/lpdocs/epic03/wrapper.htm?arnumber=4557986
63. Pedersen DM (1982) Personality correlates of privacy. J Psychol 112(1):11–14. doi:10.1080/00223980.1982.9923528, url:http://www.tandfonline.com/doi/abs/10.1080/00223980.1982.9923528
64. Brierley N (1992) The meaning and use of privacy: a study of young adults. Ph.D. thesis, The University of Arizona
65. International Energy Agency (2011) Technology roadmap: smart grids, url:http://www.iea.org/papers/2011/
66. Kindy DA, Pathan ASK (2011) A survey on SQL injection: vulnerabilities, attacks, and prevention techniques. In: 2011 IEEE 15th international symposium on consumer electronics

(ISCE), pp 468–471. IEEE. doi:10.1109/ISCE.2011.5973873, url:http://ieeexplore.ieee.org/lpdocs/epic03/wrapper.htm?arnumber=5973873

67. Singh M (2002) Privacy for telecom services. IEEE Internet Comput 6(1):4–5. doi:10.1109/MIC.2002.978364, url:http://ieeexplore.ieee.org/lpdocs/epic03/wrapper.htm?arnumber=978364

68. Hart GWG (1992) Nonintrusive appliance load monitoring. In: Proc IEEE **80**(12):1870–1891. doi:10.1109/5.192069, url:http://ieeexplore.ieee.org/lpdocs/epic03/wrapper.htm?arnumber=192069

69. Zeifman M, Roth K (2011) Nonintrusive appliance load monitoring: review and outlook. IEEE Trans Consum Electron 57(1):76–84. doi:10.1109/TCE.2011.5735484, url:http://ieeexplore.ieee.org/lpdocs/epic03/wrapper.htm?arnumber=5735484

70. Lisovich MA, Mulligan DK, Wicker SB (2010) Inferring personal information from demand-response systems. IEEE Secur Priv Mag 8(1):11–20. doi:10.1109/MSP.2010.40, url:http://ieeexplore.ieee.org/lpdocs/epic03/wrapper.htm?arnumber=5403146

71. Khurana H, Hadley M, Lu N, Frincke DA (2010) Smart-grid security issues. IEEE Secur Priv 8:81–85. doi:10.1109/MSP.2010.49

72. Li FF, Luo B, Liu P (2010) Secure information aggregation for smart grids using homomorphic encryption. In: IEEE SmartGridComm, pp 327–332. IEEE. doi:10.1109/SMARTGRID.2010.5622064, url:http://ieeexplore.ieee.org/lpdocs/epic03/wrapper.htm?arnumber=5622064

73. Zeadally S, Pathan AS, Alcaraz C, Badra M (2013) Towards privacy protection in smart grid. Wirel Pers Commun 73(1):23–50. doi:10.1007/s11277-012-0939-1, url:http://dx.doi.org/10.1007/s11277-012-0939-1

74. Budka K, Deshpande J, Hobby J, Kim YJKYJ, Kolesnikov V, Lee WLW, Reddington T, Thottan M, White CCA, Choi JICJI, Hong JHJ, Kim JKJ, Ko WKW, Nam YWNYW, Sohn SYSSY (2010) GERI—Bell labs smart grid research focus: economic modeling, networking, and security & privacy. In: 2010 first IEEE international conference on smart grid communications (SmartGridComm), pp 208–213. IEEE. doi:10.1109/SMARTGRID.2010.5622043, url:http://ieeexplore.ieee.org/lpdocs/epic03/wrapper.htm?arnumber=5622043

75. Efthymiou C, Kalogridis G (2010) Smart grid privacy via anonymization of smart metering data. In: SmartGridComm, pp 238–243. doi:10.1109/SMARTGRID.2010.5622050

76. Vetter B, Ugus O, Westhoff D, Sorge C (2012) Homomorphic primitives for a privacy-friendly smart metering architecture. In: SECRYPT 2012—proceedings of the international conference on security and cryptography, pp 102–112, url http://www.scopus.com/inward/record.url?eid=2-s2.0-84867646415&partnerID=tZOtx3y1

77. Cardenas A, Safavi-Naini R (2012) Security and privacy in the smart grid. In: Das SK, Kant K, Zhang N (eds) Handbook on securing cyber-physical critical infrastructure

78. Chen L, Lu R, Cao, Z (2014) PDAFT: a privacy-preserving data aggregation scheme with fault tolerance for smart grid communications. Peer-to-peer networking and applications, pp 1–11. doi:10.1007/s12083-014-0255-5, url:http://dx.doi.org/10.1007/s12083-014-0255-5

79. Chen L, Lu R, Cao Z, AlHarbi K, Lin X (2014) MuDA: multifunctional data aggregation in privacy-preserving smart grid communications. Peer-to-peer networking and applications, pp 1–16. doi:10.1007/s12083-014-0292-0, url:http://dx.doi.org/10.1007/s12083-014-0292-0

80. Chim T, Yiu S, Li V, Hui C, Zhong J (2014) PRGA: privacy-preserving recording amp; Gateway-assisted authentication of power usage information for smart grid. IEEE Trans Dependable Secure Comput PP(99):1. doi:10.1109/TDSC.2014.2313861

81. Gómez Mármol F, Sorge C, Petrlic R, Ugus O, Westhoff D, Martnez Pérez G (2013) Privacy-enhanced architecture for smart metering. Int J Inf Secur 12(2):67–82. doi:10.1007/s10207-012-0181-6, url:http://dx.doi.org/10.1007/s10207-012-0181-6, http://link.springer.com/10.1007/s10207-012-0181-6

82. Liang X, Li X, Lu R, Lin X, Shen X (2013) UDP: usage-based dynamic pricing with privacy preservation for smart grid. IEEE Trans Smart Grid 4(1):141–150. doi:10.1109/TSG.2012.2228240

83. Phom HS, Kuntze N, Rudolph C, Cupelli M, Liu J, Monti A, Simo Fhom H (2010) A user-centric privacy manager for future energy systems. Power System, pp 1–7. doi:10.1109/POWERCON.2010.5666447, url:http://ieeexplore.ieee.org/xpls/abs_all.jsp?arnumber=5666447, http://ieeexplore.ieee.org/lpdocs/epic03/wrapper.htm?arnumber=5666447

84. Rottondi C, Verticale G, Capone A (2013) Privacy-preserving smart metering with multiple data consumers. Comput Netw 57(7):1699–1713. doi:http://dx.doi.org/10.1016/j.comnet.2013.02.018, url:http://www.sciencedirect.com/science/article/pii/S1389128613000364

85. Finster S, Baumgart I (2013) Elderberry: a peer-to-peer, privacy-aware smart metering protocol. In: Proceedings—IEEE INFOCOM, pp 3411–3416. doi:10.1109/INFCOM.2013.6567173

86. Stoica I, Morris R, Liben-Nowell D, Karger DR, Kaashoek MF, Dabek F, Balakrishnan H (2003) Chord: A scalable peer-to-peer lookup protocol for Internet applications. IEEE/ACM Trans Netw 11:17–32. doi:10.1109/TNET.2002.808407

87. Badra M, Zeadally S (2014) Design and Performance analysis of a virtual ring architecture for smart grid privacy. IEEE Trans Forensics Secur 9(2):321–329. doi:10.1109/TIFS.2013.2296441

88. Finster S, Baumgart I (2013) Pseudonymous smart metering without a trusted third party. In: Proceedings—12th IEEE international conference on trust, security and privacy in computing and communications, TrustCom 2013, pp 1723–1728. doi:10.1109/TrustCom.2013.234

89. Li S, Choi K, Chae K (2014) OCPM: ortho code privacy mechanism in smart grid using ring communication architecture. Ad Hoc Netw. doi:http://dx.doi.org/10.1016/j.adhoc.2014.05.007, url:http://www.sciencedirect.com/science/article/pii/S1570870514001024

90. Mármol F, Sorge C, Ugus O, Pérez G., Mármol FG, Pérez GM (2012) Do not snoop my habits: preserving privacy in the smart grid. IEEE Commun Mag 50(5):166–172. doi:10.1109/MCOM.2012.6194398, url:http://ieeexplore.ieee.org/lpdocs/epic03/wrapper.htm?arnumber=6194398

91. Thoma C, Cui T, Franchetti F (2012) Secure multiparty computation based privacy preserving smart metering system. In: 2012 North American power symposium (NAPS), pp 1–6. IEEE. doi:10.1109/NAPS.2012.6336415, url:http://ieeexplore.ieee.org/lpdocs/epic03/wrapper.htm?arnumber=6336415

92. Yu C, Chen C, Kuo S, Chao H (2014) Privacy-preserving power request in smart grid networks. Syst J IEEE 8(2):441–449. doi:10.1109/JSYST.2013.2260680

93. Ge B, Zhu WTW (2013) Preserving user privacy in the smart grid by hiding appliance load characteristics. In: Wang G, Ray I, Feng D, Rajarajan M (eds) Cyberspace safety and security. Lecture notes in computer science, vol 8300. Springer International Publishing, pp 67–80 (2013), url:http://link.springer.com/chapter/10.1007/978-3-319-03584-0_6

94. Kalogridis G, Cepeda R, Denic SZ, Lewis T, Efthymiou C (2011) ElecPrivacy: evaluating the privacy protection of electricity management algorithms. IEEE Trans Smart Grid 2(4):750–758. doi:10.1109/TSG.2011.2160975, url:http://ieeexplore.ieee.org/lpdocs/epic03/wrapper.htm?arnumber=6003811

95. Kalogridis G, Efthymiou C, Denic SZ, Lewis TA, Cepeda R (2010) Privacy for smart meters: towards undetectable appliance load signatures. In: 2010 first IEEE international conference on smart grid communications (SmartGridComm), pp 232–237. doi:10.1109/SMARTGRID.2010.5622047

96. Kalogridis GG, Denic SZ (2011) Data mining and privacy of personal behaviour types in smart grid. In: Proceedings—IEEE international conference on data mining, ICDM, pp 636–642. IEEE. doi:10.1109/ICDMW.2011.58, url:http://ieeexplore.ieee.org/lpdocs/epic03/wrapper.htm?arnumber=6137440

97. Zhao J, Jung T, Wang Y, Li XY (2014) Achieving differential privacy of data disclosure in the smart grid. In: IEEE INFOCOM 2014

98. Li H, Mao R, Lai L, Qiu RC (2010) Compressed meter reading for delay-sensitive and secure load report in smart grid. In: 2010 first IEEE international conference on smart grid communications (SmartGridComm), pp 114–119. IEEE. doi:10.1109/SMARTGRID.2010.5622027, url:http://ieeexplore.ieee.org/lpdocs/epic03/wrapper.htm?arnumber=5622027

99. Rajagopalan SR, Sankar L, Mohajer S, Poor HV Smart meter privacy: a utility-privacy framework. In: 2011 IEEE international conference on smart grid communications, SmartGridComm 2011, pp 190–195. doi:10.1109/SmartGridComm.2011.6102315

100. Candes E, Romberg J, Tao T (2006) Robust uncertainty principles: exact signal reconstruction from highly incomplete frequency information. IEEE Trans Inf Theory 52 (2):489–509. doi:10.1109/TIT.2005.862083, url:http://ieeexplore.ieee.org/lpdocs/epic03/wrapper.htm?arnumber=1580791

101. Candes EJ, Tao T (2006) Near-optimal signal recovery from random projections: universal encoding strategies? IEEE Trans Inf Theory 52(12):5406–5425. doi:10.1109/TIT.2006.885507, url:http://ieeexplore.ieee.org/lpdocs/epic03/wrapper.htm?arnumber=4016283

102. Donoho DL (2006) Compressed sensing. IEEE Trans Inf Theory 52(4):1289–1306. doi:10.1109/Tit.2006.871582, url:http://ieeexplore.ieee.org/lpdocs/epic03/wrapper.htm?arnumber=1614066

103. Shamir A (1985) Identity-based cryptosystems and signature schemes. In: Proceedings of CRYPTO 84 on advances in cryptology, pp 47–53. doi:10.1007/3-540-39568-7_5, url:http://dl.acm.org/citation.cfm?id=19478.19483

104. Boneh D, Franklin M (2003) Identity-based encryption from the weil pairing. doi:10.1137/S0097539701398521

105. Cocks C (2001) An identity based encryption scheme based on quadratic residues. Cryptogr Coding, pp 360–363. doi:10.1007/3-540-45325-3_32, url:http://link.springer.com/chapter/10.1007/3-540-45325-3_32

106. Kalogridis G, Sooriyabandara M, Fan Z, Mustafa MA (2014) Toward unified security and privacy protection for smart meter networks. Syst J IEEE 8(2):641–654. doi:10.1109/JSYST.2013.2260940

107. Goyal V, Pandey O, Sahai A, Waters B (2006) Attribute-based encryption for fine-grained access control of encrypted data. In: Proceedings of the 13th ACM conference on computer and communications security—CCS '06. ACM Press, New York, p 89. doi:10.1145/1180405.1180418, url:http://dl.acm.org/citation.cfm?id=1180405.1180418

108. Li D, Aung Z, Williams J, Sanchez A (2014) P2DR: privacy-preserving demand response system in smart grids. In: 2014 international conference on computing, networking and communications (ICNC), pp 41–47. doi:10.1109/ICCNC.2014.6785302

109. Cheung JCL, Chim TW, Yiu SM, Hui LCK, Li VOK (2011) Credential-based privacy-preserving power request scheme for smart grid network. In: 2011 IEEE global telecommunications conference—GLOBECOM 2011, pp 1–5. IEEE. doi:10.1109/GLOCOM.2011.6134566, url:http://ieeexplore.ieee.org/lpdocs/epic03/wrapper.htm?arnumber=6134566

110. Chim T, Yiu S, Hui L, Li V, Mui T, Tsang Y, Kwok C, Yu K (2012) Selling power back to the grid in a secure and privacy-preserving manner. In: Chim T, Yuen T (eds) Information and communications security, vol 7618., Lecture notes in computer scienceSpringer, Berlin, pp 445–452

111. Yao AC (1982) Protocols for secure computations. 23rd annual symposium on foundations of computer science (sfcs 1982), pp 160–164. doi:10.1109/SFCS.1982.38, url:http://ieeexplore.ieee.org/lpdocs/epic03/wrapper.htm?arnumber=4568388

112. Goldreich O, Micali S, Wigderson A (1987) How to play any mental game. In: ACM symposium on theory of computing, STOC '87, pp 218–229. ACM. doi:10.1145/28395.28420

113. Rivest RL, Adleman L, Dertouzos ML (1978) On data banks and privacy homomorphisms. In: Foundations of secure computation, pp 169–179

114. Gentry C (2009) A fully homomorphic encryption scheme. Ph.D. thesis. doi:10.1145/1536414.1536440, url:http://cs.au.dk/stm/local-cache/gentry-thesis.pdf

115. Paillier P, Pointcheval D (1999) Efficient public-key cryptosystems provably secure against active adversaries. In: ASIACRYPT'99, vol 99, pp 1–13. doi:10.1007/978-3-540-48000-6_14, url:http://link.springer.com/chapter/10.1007/978-3-540-48000-6_14

116. Paillier P, Stern PJ, Eurocrypt C (1999) Public-key cryptosystems based on composite degree residuosity classes. Advances in cryptology EUROCRYPT 99, vol 1592, pp 223–238. doi:10.1007/3-540-48910-X_16
117. Boneh D, Goh E, Nissim K (2005) Evaluating 2-DNF formulas on ciphertexts. Theory of cryptography, pp 325–341. doi:10.1007/978-3-540-30576-7_18
118. Erkin Z, Tsudik G (2012) Private computation of Spatial and temporal power consumption with smart meters. In: Applied cryptography and network security. Lecture notes in computer science, vol 7341, pp 561–577, url:http://link.springer.com/chapter/10.1007/978-3-642-31284-7_33
119. Garcia FF, Jacobs B (2011) Privacy-friendly energy-metering via homomorphic encryption. Secur Trust Manage 6710:226–238, url:http://link.springer.com/chapter/10.1007/978-3-642-22444-7_15
120. Kirschbaum M, Plos T, Schmidt JM (2013) On secure multi-party computation in bandwidth-limited smart-meter systems. In: 2013 international conference on availability, reliability and security, pp 230–235. IEEE. doi:10.1109/ARES.2013.137, url:http://ieeexplore.ieee.org/lpdocs/epic03/wrapper.htm?arnumber=6657245
121. Lu R, Liang X, Li X, Lin X, Shen X (2012) EPPA: an efficient and privacy-preserving aggregation scheme for secure smart grid communications. IEEE Trans Parallel Distrib Syst 23:1621–1632. doi:10.1109/TPDS.2012.86
122. Rottondi C, Verticale G, Krauss C (2013) Distributed privacy-preserving aggregation of metering data in smart grids. IEEE JSAC 31(7):1342–1354. doi:10.1109/JSAC.2013.130716
123. Cramer R, Shoup V (1998) A practical public key cryptosystem provably secure against adaptive chosen ciphertext attack. In: EUROCRYPT '98: advances in cryptology, pp 13–25. doi:10.1007/BFb0055715, url:http://www.springerlink.com/content/bejnetn8v8n5vkc3/
124. Baharlouei Z, Hashemi M (2014) Efficiency-fairness trade-off in privacy-preserving autonomous demand side management. IEEE Trans Smart Grid 5(2):799–808. doi:10.1109/TSG.2013.2296714, url http://ieeexplore.ieee.org/lpdocs/epic03/wrapper.htm?arnumber=6740907
125. Clifton C, Kantarcioglu M, Vaidya J, Lin X, Zhu MY (2002) Tools for privacy preserving distributed data mining. SIGKDD Explor Newsl 4(2):28–34. doi:10.1145/772862.772867
126. Shamir A (1979) How to share a secret. Commun ACM 22(11):612–613. doi:http://doi.acm.org/10.1145/359168.359176, url:http://doi.acm.org/10.1145/359168.359176
127. Chim TW, Yiu SM, Hui LCK, Li VOK (2011) PASS: privacy-preserving authentication scheme for smart grid network. In: 2011 IEEE international conference on smart grid communications, SmartGridComm 2011, pp 196–201. IEEE. doi:10.1109/SmartGridComm.2011.6102316, url:http://ieeexplore.ieee.org/lpdocs/epic03/wrapper.htm?arnumber=6102316
128. Liu H, Ning H, Zhang Y, Xiong Q, Yang LT (2014) Role-dependent privacy preservation for secure V2G networks in the smart grid. IEEE Trans Inf Forensics Secur 9(2):208–220. doi:10.1109/TIFS.2013.2295032
129. Goldreich O, Micali S, Wigderson A (1991) Proofs that yield nothing but their validity or all languages in NP have zero-knowledge proof systems. J ACM 38(3):690–728. doi:10.1145/116825.116852, url:http://dl.acm.org/citation.cfm?id=116825.116852
130. Rial A, Danezis G (2011) Privacy-preserving smart metering. In: Proceedings of the 10th annual ACM workshop on privacy in the electronic society—WPES '11. ACM Press, New York, p 49. doi:10.1145/2046556.2046564, url:http://dl.acm.org.proxy2.library.illinois.edu/citation.cfm?id=2046556.2046564
131. Bellare M, Goldreich O (1993) Advances in cryptology CRYPTO 92. In: Brickell EF (ed) Advances in cryptology CRYPTO 92. Lecture notes in computer science, vol 740. Springer, Berlin, pp 390–420. doi:10.1007/3-540-48071-4, url:http://www.springerlink.com/index/10.1007/3-540-48071-4
132. Chaum D (1983) Blind signatures for untraceable payments. In: Chaum D, Rivest RL, Sherman AT (eds) Advances in cryptology 1983. Springer, Boston, pp 199–203. doi:10.1007/978-1-4757-0602-4, url:http://link.springer.com/10.1007/978-1-4757-0602-4

133. Stadler M, Piveteau JMJJM, Camenisch J (1995) Fair blind signatures. In: Advances in Cryptology Eurocrypt 95, pp 209–219. doi:10.1007/3-540-49264-X_17, url:http://link.springer.com/chapter/10.1007/3-540-49264-X_17
134. Rabin MO (1981) How to exchange secrets by oblivious transfer
135. Aiello B, Ishai Y, Reingold O (2001) Priced oblivious transfer: how to sell digital goods. In: Advances in cryptology EUROCRYPT 2001. Lecture notes in computer science, vol 2045. Springer, Berlin, pp 119–135. doi:10.1007/3-540-44987-6_8, url:http://www.springerlink.com/index/557e8bykh3vbf0kc.pdf
136. Fan CI, Huang SY, Artan W (2013) Design and implementation of privacy preserving billing protocol for smart grid. J Supercomput 66(2):841–862. doi:10.1007/s11227-013-0905-z, url: http://dx.doi.org/10.1007/s11227-013-0905-z
137. Cárdenas A, Amin S, Schwartz G (2012) Privacy-aware sampling for residential demand response programs. In: Proceedings of 1st international ACM, url:http://www.eecs.berkeley.edu/schwartz/HiCons2012ASG.pdf
138. Yan Y, Qian Y, Sharif H (2011) A secure and reliable in-network collaborative communication scheme for advanced metering infrastructure in smart grid. In: IEEE WCNC, pp 909–914. doi:10.1109/WCNC.2011.5779257
139. Chrestenson HE (1955) A class of generalized Walsh functions. Pac J Math 5(1):17–31, url: http://projecteuclid.org/euclid.pjm/1103044605
140. Wallis JS (1975) On Hadamard matrices. J Comb Theory Ser A 18(2):149–164. doi:10.1016/0097-3165(75)90003-5, url:http://www.sciencedirect.com/science/article/pii/0097316575900035
141. Berrar DD, Dubitzky W (2013) Information gain (KullbackLeibler divergence). In: Dubitzky W, Wolkenhauer O, Cho KH, Yokota H (eds) Encyclopedia of systems biology 2013. Springer, New York, pp 1022–1023. doi:10.1007/978-1-4419-9863-7, url:http://link.springer.com/10.1007/978-1-4419-9863-7
142. Gunduz D, Gomez-Vilardebo J, Poor HV, Tan O (2013) Information theoretic privacy for smart meters. In: 2013 information theory and applications workshop (ITA), pp 1–7. IEEE. doi:10.1109/ITA.2013.6503006, url:http://ieeexplore.ieee.org/lpdocs/epic03/wrapper.htm?arnumber=6503006
143. Sankar L, Rajagopalan SR, Mohajer S, Poor HV (2013) Smart meter privacy: a theoretical framework. IEEE Trans Smart Grid 4(2):837–846. doi:10.1109/TSG.2012.2211046
144. Kim Y, Ngai ECH, Srivastava MB (2011) Cooperative state estimation for preserving privacy of user behaviors in smart grid. In: 2011 IEEE international conference on smart grid communications, SmartGridComm 2011, pp 178–183. doi:10.1109/SmartGridComm.2011.6102313
145. Huang YF, Werner S, Huang J, Kashyap N, Gupta V (2012) State estimation in electric power grids: meeting new challenges presented by the requirements of the future grid. IEEE Signal Process Mag 29(5):33–43. doi:10.1109/MSP.2012.2187037, url:http://ieeexplore.ieee.org/lpdocs/epic03/wrapper.htm?arnumber=6279588
146. Jia W, Zhu H, Cao Z, Dong X, Xiao C, Member S (2014) Human-factor-aware privacy-preserving aggregation in smart grid. Syst J IEEE 8(2):598–607. doi:10.1109/JSYST.2013.2260937
147. Bohli JM, Sorge C, Ugus O (2010) A privacy model for smart metering. In: IEEE ICC, pp 1–5. doi:10.1109/ICCW.2010.5503916
148. Lin HY, Tzeng WG, Shen ST, Lin BSP (2012) A practical smart metering system supporting privacy preserving billing and load monitoring. In: Feng B, Samarati P, and Zhou J (ed) Applied cryptography and network security. Springer, Berlin, pp 544–560, url:http://link.springer.com/chapter/10.1007%2F978-3-642-31284-7_32#
149. Ren X, Yang X, Lin J, Yang Q, Yu W (2013) On scaling perturbation based privacy-preserving schemes in smart metering systems. In: 2013 22nd international conference on computer communication and networks (ICCCN), pp 1–7. IEEE. doi:10.1109/ICCCN.2013.6614162, url:http://ieeexplore.ieee.org/lpdocs/epic03/wrapper.htm?arnumber=6614162

150. Zhang H, Yu N, Wen Y, Zhang W (2014) Toward optimal noise distribution for privacy preserving in data aggregation. Comput Secur. doi:http://dx.doi.org/10.1016/j.cose.2014.05. 009, url:http://linkinghub.elsevier.com/retrieve/pii/S016740481400090X, http://www.sciencedirect.com/science/article/pii/S016740481400090X

151. Acs G, Castelluccia C, Gergely Acs G (2011) I have a DREAM! (DiffeRentially privatE smArt Metering). In Filler T, Pevný T, Craver S, Ker A (eds) Information hiding. Lecture notes in computer science, vol 6958. Springer, Berlin, pp. 118–132. doi:10.1007/978-3-642-24178-9, url:http://www.springerlink.com/index/10.1007/978-3-642-24178-9, http://link.springer.com/10.1007/978-3-642-24178-9, http://link.springer.com/chapter/10.1007/978-3-642-24178-9_9

152. Ghosh A, Roughgarden T, Sundararajan M (2009) Universally utility-maximizing privacy mechanisms. In: Proceedings of the 41st annual ACM symposium on theory of computing—STOC '09. ACM Press, New York, p 351. doi:10.1145/1536414.1536464, url:http://dl.acm.org/citation.cfm?id=1536414.1536464

153. Dwork C (2008) Differential privacy: a survey of results. Theory Appl Models Comput 4978:1–19. doi:10.1007/978-3-540-79228-4_1, url:http://www.springerlink.com/index/u963k75981004046.pdf

154. Dwork C, Kenthapadi K, McSherry F, Mironov I, Naor M (2006) Our data, ourselves: privacy via distributed noise generation. Lecture notes in computer science (including subseries Lecture notes in artificial intelligence and Lecture notes in bioinformatics), vol 4004. LNCS, pp 486–503. doi:10.1007/11761679_29

155. Dan G, Lui KSKS, Tabassum R, Zhu Q, Nahrstedt K (2013) SELINDA: a secure, scalable and light-weight data collection protocol for smart grids. In: 2013 IEEE international conference on smart grid communications (SmartGridComm), pp 480–485. IEEE. doi:10. 1109/SmartGridComm.2013.6688004, url:http://ieeexplore.ieee.org/lpdocs/epic03/wrapper.htm?arnumber=6688004

156. Cho S, Li H, Choi BJ (2014) PALDA: efficient privacy-preserving authentication for lossless data aggregation in smart grids. In: 2014 IEEE international conference on smart grid communications (SmartGridComm). Venice, Italy

157. Feng T, Wang C, Zhang W, Ruan L (2008) Confidentiality protection for distributed sensor data aggregation. In: IEEE INFOCOM. doi:10.1109/INFOCOM.2008.20

158. Groat MM, He W, Forrest S (2011) KIPDA: k-indistinguishable privacy-preserving data aggregation in wireless sensor networks. In: IEEE INFOCOM, pp 2024–2032. doi:10.1109/INFCOM.2011.5935010

159. He W, Liu X, Nguyen H, Nahrstedt K, Abdelzaher T (2007) PDA: privacy-preserving data aggregation in wireless sensor networks. In: IEEE INFOCOM 2007, pp 2045–2053). doi:10. 1109/INFCOM.2007.237

160. He W, Nguyen H, Liu X, Nahrstedt K, Abdelzaher T (2008) iPDA: an integrity-protecting private data aggregation scheme for wireless sensor networks. In: IEEE MILCOM 2008, pp 1–7. doi:10.1109/MILCOM.2008.4753645

161. Kursawe K, Danezis G, Kohlweiss M (2011) Privacy-friendly aggregation for the smart-grid. Privacy enhancing technologies, vol 6794. Springer, pp 175–191. doi:10.1007/978-3-642-22263-4_10

162. Nicanfar H, Alasaad A, Talebifard P, Leung VCM (2013) Network coding based encryption system for advanced metering infrastructure. In: IEEE ICCCN, pp 1–7. doi:10.1109/ICCCN.2013.6614158

163. Jin H, Uludag S, Lui KS, Nahrstedt K (2014) Secure data collection in constrained tree-based smart grid environments. In: 2014 IEEE international conference on smart grid communications (SmartGridComm): communications and networks to enable the smart grid (IEEE SmartGridComm'14 symposium—communications and networks). Venice, Italy (2014)

164. Uludag S, Lui KS, Ren W, Nahrstedt K (2014) Practical and secure machine-to-machine data collection protocol in smart grid. In: Workshop on security and privacy in machine-to-machine communications (M2MSec'14) in conjunction with IEEE conference on communications and network security (CNS). San Francisco, USA

165. Badra M, Zeadally S (2013) An improved Privacy Solution for the Smart Grid. Int J Netw Secur 17(1):225–232
166. Cloud Security Alliance (CSA), B.D.W.G. (2013) Expanded top ten big data security and privacy challenges. White Paper
167. Castelluccia C, Druschel P, Hübner SF, Gorniak S, Ikonomou D, Pasic A, Preneel B, Tschofenig H, Tirtea R (2011) Privacy, accountability and trust challenges and opportunities (The European Network and Information Security Agency (ENISA)). White Paper, url: https://www.enisa.europa.eu/activities/identity-and-trust/library/deliverables/pat-study
168. Rottondi C, Barbato A, Verticale G (2014) A privacy-friendly game-theoretic distributed scheduling system for domestic appliances. In: 2014 IEEE international conference on smart grid communications (SmartGridComm). Venice, Italy
169. Egarter D, Prokop C, Elmenreich W (2014) Load hiding of household's power demand. In: 2014 IEEE international conference on smart grid Communications (SmartGridComm): communications and networks to enable the smart grid (IEEE SmartGridComm'14 symposium—communications and networks). Venice, Italy
170. Mashima D, Roy A (2014) Privacy preserving disclosure of authenticated energy usage data. In: 2014 IEEE international conference on smart grid communications (SmartGridComm). Venice, Italy (2014)
171. Paverd A, Martin A, Brown I (2014) Privacy-enhanced bi-directional communication in the smart grid using trusted computing. In: 2014 IEEE international conference on smart grid communications (SmartGridComm). Venice, Italy
172. Yang L, Xue H, Li F (2014) Privacy-preserving data sharing in smart grid systems. In: 2014 IEEE international conference on smart grid communications (SmartGridComm). Venice, Italy

Chapter 16
Location-Based Privacy, Protection, Safety, and Security

Roba Abbas, Katina Michael and M.G. Michael

16.1 Introduction

Privacy is often expressed as the most complex issue facing location-based services (LBS) adoption and usage [44, p. 82, 61, p. 5, 66, pp. 250–254, 69, pp. 414–415]. This is due to numerous factors such as the significance of the term in relation to human rights [65, p. 9]. According to a report by the Australian Law Reform Commission (ALRC), "privacy protection generally should take precedence over a range of other countervailing interests, such as cost and convenience" [3, p. 104]. The intricate nature of privacy is also a result of the challenges associated with accurately defining the term [13, p. 4, 74, p. 68]. That is, privacy is a difficult concept to articulate [65, p. 13], as the term is liberally and subjectively applied, and the boundaries constituting privacy protection are unclear. Additionally, privacy literature is dense, and contains varying interpretations, theories and discrepancies as to what constitutes privacy. However, as maintained by [65, p. 67], "[o]ne point on which there seems to be near-unanimous agreement is that privacy is a messy and complex subject." Nonetheless, as asserted by [89, p. 196], privacy is fundamental to the individual due to various factors:

> The intensity and complexity of life, attendant upon advancing civilization, have rendered necessary some retreat from the world, and man, under the refining influence of culture, has become more sensitive to publicity, so that solitude and privacy have become more essential to the individual.

R. Abbas (✉) · K. Michael · M.G. Michael
School of Computing and Information Technology, University of Wollongong,
Wollongong, NSW, Australia
e-mail: roba@uow.edu.au

K. Michael
e-mail: katina@uow.edu.au

M.G. Michael
e-mail: mgm@uow.edu.au

© Springer International Publishing Switzerland 2015
S. Zeadally and M. Badra (eds.), *Privacy in a Digital, Networked World*,
Computer Communications and Networks,
DOI 10.1007/978-3-319-08470-1_16

The *Oxford English Dictionary* definition of security is the "state of being free from danger or threat." A designation of security applicable to this research is "a condition in which harm does not arise, despite the occurrence of threatening events; and as a set of safeguards designed to achieve that condition" [92, pp. 390–391]. Security and privacy are often confused in LBS scholarship. Elliot and Phillips [40, p. 463] warn that "[p]rivacy is not the same as security," although the two themes are related [70, p. 14]. Similarly, Clarke [21] states that the term privacy is often used by information and communication technology professionals to describe data and data transmission security. The importance of security is substantiated by the fact that it is considered "a precondition for privacy and anonymity" [93, p. 2], and as such the two themes are intimately connected. In developing this chapter and surveying security literature relevant to LBS, it became apparent that existing scholarship is varied, but nonetheless entails exploration of three key areas. These include: (1) security of data or information, (2) personal safety and physical security, and (3) security of a nation or homeland/national security, interrelated categories adapted from [70, p. 12].

This chapter will discuss the interrelated concepts of privacy and security with reference to LBS, with a specific focus on the notion of location privacy protection. The latter can be defined as the extent and level of control an individual possesses over the gathering, use, and dissemination of personal information relevant to their location [38, p. 1, 39, p. 2, 53, p. 233], whilst managing multiple interests (as described in Sect. 16.1.1). Location privacy in the context of wireless technologies and LBS is a significant and complex concept given the dual and opposing uses of a single LBS solution. That is, an application designed or intended for constructive uses can simultaneously be employed in contexts that violate the (location) privacy of an individual. For example, a child or employee monitoring LBS solution may offer safety and productivity gains (respectively) in one scenario, but when employed in secondary contexts may be regarded as a privacy-invasive solution. Regardless of the situation, it is valuable to initially define and examine the significance of "privacy" and "privacy protection," prior to exploring the complexities involved.

16.1.1 Privacy: A Right or an Interest?

According to Clarke [26, pp. 123–129], the notions of privacy and privacy protection emerged as important social issues since the 1960s. An enduring definition of privacy is the "right to be let alone" [89, p. 193]. This definition requires further consideration as it is quite simplistic in nature and does not encompass diverse dimensions of privacy. For further reading on the development of privacy and the varying concepts including that of Warren and Brandeis, see [76]. Numerous scholars have attempted to provide a more workable definition of privacy than that offered by Warren and Brandeis.

For instance, [21] maintains that perceiving privacy simply as a *right* is problematic and narrow, and that privacy should rather be viewed as an *interest* or *collection of interests*, which encompasses a number of facets or categories. As such, privacy is defined as "the interest that individuals have in sustaining a 'personal space', free from interference by other people and organisations" [21, 26]. In viewing privacy as an interest, the challenge is in balancing multiple interests in the name of privacy protection. This, as Clarke [21] maintains, includes opposing interests in the form of one's own interests, the interests of other people, and/or the interests of other people, organizations, or society. As such Clarke refers to privacy protection as "a process of finding appropriate balances between privacy and multiple competing interests."

16.1.2 Alternative Perspectives on Privacy

Solove's [80] taxonomy of privacy offers a unique, legal perspective on privacy by grouping privacy challenges under the categories of information collection, information processing, information dissemination, and invasion. Refer to [80, pp. 483–558] for an in depth overview of the taxonomy which includes subcategories of the privacy challenges. Nissenbaum [65, pp. 1–2], on the other hand, maintains that existing scholarship generally expresses privacy in view of restricting access to, and maintaining control over, personal information. For example, Quinn [73, p. 213] insists that the central theme in privacy debates is that of access, including physical access to an individual, in addition to information access. With respect to LBS and location privacy, Küpper and Treu [53, pp. 233–234] agree with the latter, distinguishing three categories of access: (1) third-party access by intruders and law enforcement personnel/authorities, (2) unauthorized access by providers within the supply chain for malicious purposes, and (3) access by other LBS users. Nissenbaum [65, pp. 1–2] disputes the interpretation focused on access and control, noting that individuals are not interested in "simply *restricting* the flow of information but ensuring that it flows *appropriately*." As such, Nissenbaum offers the framework of contextual integrity, as a means of determining when certain systems and practices violate privacy, and transform existing information flows inappropriately [65, p. 150]. The framework serves as a possible tool that can assist in justifying the need for LBS regulation.

A primary contribution from Nissenbaum is her emphasis on the importance of context in determining the privacy-violating nature of a specific technology-based system or practice. In addition to an appreciation of context, Nissenbaum recognizes the value of perceiving technology with respect to social, economic, and political factors and interdependencies. That is, devices and systems should be considered as *socio-technical* units [65, pp. 5–6].

In relation to privacy, and given the importance of socio-technical systems, the complexities embedded within privacy may, therefore, arise from the fact that the term can be examined from a number of perspectives. For instance, it can be understood in terms of its philosophical, psychological, sociological, economical, and political significance [21, 26]. Alternatively, privacy theory can provide varying means of interpretation, given that available approaches draw on inspiration from multiple disciplines such as computer science and engineering, amongst others [65, p. 67]. It is also common to explore privacy through its complex dimensions.

According to Privacy International, for instance, the term comprises the aspects of information privacy, bodily privacy, privacy of communications, and territorial privacy [72]. Similarly, in providing a contemporary definition of privacy, Clarke [26] uses Maslow's hierarchy of needs to define the various categories of privacy; that is, "privacy of the person," "privacy of personal behavior," "privacy of personal communications," and "privacy of personal data." Clarke argues that since the late 1960s the term has been confined, in a legal sense, to the last two categories. That is, privacy laws have been restricted in their focus in that they are predominantly based on the OECD fair information principles, and lack coverage of other significant categories of privacy. Therefore, the label of *information privacy*, typically interchangeable with *data privacy*, is utilized in reference to the combination of communications and data privacy [21], and is cited by [58, pp. 5–7] as a significant challenge in the information age.

16.2 Background

16.2.1 Defining Information Privacy

In Alan Westin's prominent book *Privacy and Freedom*, information privacy is defined as "the right of individuals, groups and institutions to determine for themselves, when, how and to what extent information about them is communicated to others" [90, p. 7]. Information in this instance is *personal information* that can be linked to or identify a particular individual [33, p. 326]. For a summary of information privacy literature and theoretical frameworks, presented in tabular form, refer to [8, pp. 15–17].

16.2.2 Information Privacy Through the Privacy Calculus Perspective

For the purpose of this chapter, it is noteworthy that information privacy can be studied through differing lenses, one of which is the *privacy calculus* theoretical perspective. Xu et al. [95, p. 138] explain that "the calculus perspective of information privacy interprets the individual's privacy interests as an exchange where individuals disclose their personal information in return for certain benefits." It can be regarded a form of "cost–benefit analysis" conducted by the individual, where privacy is likely to be (somewhat) relinquished if there is a perceived net benefit resulting from information disclosure [33, p. 327]. This perspective acknowledges the claim that privacy-related issues and concerns are not constant, but rather depend on perceptions, motivations, and conditions that are context or situation dependent [78, p. 353]. A related notion is the *personalization–privacy* paradox, which is based on the interplay between an individual's willingness to reap the benefits of personalized services at the expense of divulging personal information, which may potentially threaten or invade their privacy. An article by Awad and Krishnan [8] examines this paradox, with specific reference to online customer profiling to deliver personalized services. The authors recommend that organizations work on increasing the perceived benefit and value of personalized services to ensure "the potential benefit of the service outweighs the potential risk of a privacy invasion" [8, p. 26].

In the LBS context, more specifically, Xu et al. [94] build on the privacy calculus framework to investigate the personalization–privacy paradox as it pertains to overt and covert personalization in location-aware marketing. The results of the study suggest that the personalization approaches (overt and covert) impact on the perceived privacy risks and values. A complete overview of results can be found in [94, pp. 49–50]. For further information regarding the privacy calculus and the personalization–privacy paradox in the context of ubiquitous commerce applications including LBS, refer to [78]. These privacy-related frameworks and the concepts presented in this section are intended to be introductory in nature, enabling an appreciation of the varied perspectives on privacy and information privacy, in addition to the importance of context, rather than providing thoroughness in the treatment of privacy and information privacy. Such notions are particularly pertinent when reflecting on privacy and the role of emerging information and communication technologies (ICTs) in greater detail.

16.2.3 Emerging Technologies, m-Commerce and the Related Privacy Challenges

It has been suggested that privacy concerns have been amplified (but not driven) by the emergence and increased use of ICTs, with the driving force being the manner in which these technologies are implemented by organizations [21, 26]. In the m-commerce domain, mobile technologies are believed to boost the threat to consumer privacy. That is, the intensity of marketing activities can potentially be increased with the availability of timely location details and, more significantly, tracking information; thus enabling the influencing of consumer behaviors to a greater extent [25]. The threat, however, is not solely derived from usage by organizations. Specifically, the technologies originally introduced for use by government and organizational entities are presently available for consumer adoption by members of the community. For further elaboration, refer to Abbas et al. [1] and chapter 8 of Andrejevic [4]. Thus, location (information) privacy protection emerges as a substantial challenge for the government, business, and consumer sectors.

16.2.4 Defining Location (Information) Privacy

Location privacy, regarded a subset of information privacy, has been defined and presented in various ways. Duckham [38, p. 1] believes that location privacy is "the right of individuals to control the collection, use, and communication of personal information about their location." Küpper and Treu [53, p. 233] define location privacy as "the capability of the target person to exercise control about *who* may access her location information in *which situation* and in *which level of detail*." Both definitions focus on the aspect of control, cited as a focal matter regarding location privacy [39, p. 2]. With specific reference to LBS, location privacy and related challenges are considered to be of utmost importance. For example, Perusco and Michael [70, pp. 414–415], in providing an overview of studies relating to the social implications of LBS, claim that the principal challenge is privacy.

In [61, p. 5] Michael et al. also state, with respect to GPS tracking, that privacy is the "greatest concern," resulting in the authors proposing a number of questions relating to the type of location information that should be revealed to other parties, the acceptability of child tracking and employee monitoring, and the requirement for a warrant in the tracking of criminals and terrorists. Similarly, Bennett and Crowe [12, pp. 9–32] reveal the privacy threats to various individuals, for instance those in emergency situations, mobile employees/workers, vulnerable groups (e.g., elderly), family members (notably children and teenagers), telematics application users, rental car clients, recreational users, prisoners, and offenders. In several of these circumstances, location privacy must often be weighed against other conflicting interests, an example of which is the emergency management situation. For instance, Aloudat [2, p. 54] refers to the potential "deadlock" between privacy and security in the emergency context, noting public concerns associated with the move towards a "total surveillance society."

16.2.5 Data or Information Security

It has been suggested that data or information security in the LBS domain involves prohibiting unauthorized access to location-based information, which is considered a prerequisite for privacy [88, p. 121]. This form of security is concerned with "implementing security measures to ensure that collected data is only accessed for the agreed-upon purpose" [46, p. 1]. It is not, however, limited to access but is also related to "unwanted tracking" and the protection of data and information from manipulation and distortion [10, p. 185]. The techniques and approaches available to prevent unauthorized access and minimize chances of manipulation include the use of "spatially aware access control systems" [34, p. 28] and security- and privacy-preserving functionality [9, p. 568]. The intricacies of these techniques are beyond the scope of this investigation. Rather, this section is restricted to coverage of the broad data and information security challenges and the resultant impact on LBS usage and adoption.

16.2.6   Impact of Data or Information Security on LBS Market Adoption

It has been suggested that data and information security is a fundamental concern influencing LBS market adoption. From a legal standpoint, security is an imperative concept, particularly in cases where location information is linked to an individual [41, p. 22]. In such situations, safeguarding location data or information has often been described as a decisive aspect impacting on user acceptance. These claims are supported in [85, p. 1], noting that user acceptance of location and context-aware m-business applications are closely linked to security challenges. Hence, from the perspective of organizations wishing to be "socially-responsive," Chen et al. [19, p. 7] advise that security breaches must be avoided in the interest of economic stability:

> Firms must reassure customers about how location data are used...A security lapse, with accompanying publicity in the media and possible 'negligence' lawsuits, may prove harmful to both sales and the financial stability of the firm.

Achieving satisfactory levels of security in location- and context-aware services, however, is a tricky task given the general issues associated with the development of security solutions; inevitable conflicts between protection and functionality; mobile-specific security challenges; inadequacy of standards to account for complex security features; and privacy and control-related issues [85, pp. 1–2]. Furthermore, developing secure LBS involves consideration of multiple factors; specifically those related to data or information accuracy, loss, abuse, unauthorized access, modification, storage, and transfer [83, p. 10]. There is the additional need to consider security issues from multiple stakeholder perspectives, in order to identify shared challenges and accurately assess their implications and the manner in which suitable security features can be integrated into LBS solutions. Numerous m-business security challenges relevant to LBS from various perspectives are listed in [85]. Data security challenges relevant to LBS are also discussed in [57, pp. 44–46].

16.3 Privacy and Security Issues

16.3.1 Access to Location Information Versus Privacy Protection

The issue of privacy in emergency situations, in particular, is delicate. For instance, Quinn [73, p. 225] remarks on the benefits of LBS in safety-related situations, with particular reference to the enhanced 911 Directive in the US, which stipulates that the location of mobile phones be provided in emergency situations, aiding in emergency response efforts. The author continues to identify "loss of privacy" as a consequence of this service, specifically in cases where location details are provided to third parties [73, p. 226]. Such claims imply that there may be conflicting aims in developing and utilizing LBS. Duckham [38, p. 1] explains this point, stating that the major challenge in the LBS realm is managing the competing aims of enabling improved access to location information versus allowing individuals to maintain a sufficient amount of control over such information. The latter is achieved through the deployment of techniques for location privacy protection.

16.3.2 Location Privacy Protection

It is valid at this point to discuss approaches to location privacy protection. Bennett and Grant [13, p. 7] claim that general approaches to privacy protection in the digital age may come in varied forms, including, but not limited to, privacy-enhancing technologies, self-regulation approaches, and advocacy. In terms of LBS, substantial literature is available proposing techniques for location privacy protection, at both the theoretical and practical levels. A number of these techniques are best summarized in [39, p. 13] as "regulation, privacy policies, anonymity, and obfuscation." A review of complementary research on the topic of privacy and LBS indicate that location privacy has predominantly been examined in terms of the *social challenges and trade-offs* from theoretical and practical perspectives; the *technological solutions* available to maintain location privacy; and the *need for other regulatory response(s)* to address location privacy concerns. The respective streams of literature are now inspected further in this chapter.

16.3.3 Social Challenges and Trade-Offs

In reviewing existing literature, the social implications of LBS with respect to privacy tend to be centered on the concepts of invasion, trade-off, and interrelatedness and complexity. The first refers primarily to the perceived and actual intrusion or invasion of privacy resulting from LBS development, deployment, usage, and other aspects. Alternatively, the trade-off notion signifies the weighing of privacy interest against other competing factors, notably privacy versus convenience (including personalization) and privacy versus national security. On the other hand, the factors of interrelatedness and complexity refer to the complicated relationship between privacy and other ethical dilemmas or themes such as control, trust, and security.

With respect to the invasion concept, Westin notes that concerns regarding invasion of privacy were amplified during the 1990s in both the social and political spheres [91, p. 444]. Concentrating specifically on LBS, [62, p. 6] provides a summary of the manner in which LBS can be perceived as privacy-invasive, claiming that GPS tracking activities can threaten or invade the privacy of the individual. According to the authors, such privacy concerns can be attributed to a number of issues regarding the process of GPS tracking. These include: (1) questionable levels of accuracy and reliability of GPS data, (2) potential to falsify the data post-collection, (3) capacity for behavioral profiling, (4) ability to reveal spatial information at varying levels of detail depending on the GIS software used, and (5) potential for tracking efforts to become futile upon extended use as an individual may become nonchalant about the exercise [62, pp. 4–5]. Other scholars examine the invasion concept in various contexts. Varied examples include [55] in relation to mobile advertising, [51] in view of monitoring employee locations, and [79] regarding privacy invasion and legislation in the United States concerning personal location information.

Current studies declare that privacy interests must often be weighed against other, possibly competing, factors, notably the need for convenience and national security. That is, various strands of LBS literature are fixed on addressing the trade-off between convenience and privacy protection. For instance, in a field study of mobile guide services, Kaasinen [50, p. 49] supports the need for resolving such a trade-off, arguing that "effortless use" often results in lower levels of user control and, therefore, privacy. Other scholars reflect on the trade-off between privacy and national security. In an examination of the legal, ethical, social, and technological issues associated with the widespread use of LBS, Perusco et al. [71] propose the LBS privacy–security dichotomy. The dichotomy is a means of representing the relationship between the privacy of the individual and national security concerns at the broader social level [71, pp. 91–97]. The authors claim that a balance must be achieved between both factors. They also identify the elements contributing to privacy risk and security risk, expressing the privacy risks associated with LBS to be omniscience, exposure, and corruption, claiming that the degree of danger is reduced with the removal of a specific risk [71, pp. 95–96]. The lingering question proposed by the authors is "how much privacy are we willing to trade in order to increase security?" [71, p. 96]. Whether in the interest of convenience or national security, existing studies focus on the theoretical notion of the privacy calculus. This refers to a situation in which an individual attempts to balance perceived value or benefits arising from personalized services against loss of privacy in determining whether to disclose information (refer to [8, 33, 78, 94, 95]).

The relationship between privacy and other themes is a common topic of discussion in existing literature. That is, privacy, control, security, and trust are key and interrelated themes concerning the social implications of LBS [71, pp. 97–98]. It is, therefore, suggested that privacy and the remaining social considerations be studied in light of these associations rather than as independent themes or silos of information. In particular, privacy and control literature are closely correlated, and as such the fields of surveillance and dataveillance must be flagged as crucial in discussions surrounding privacy. Additionally, there are studies which suggest that privacy issues are closely linked to notions of trust and perceived risk in the minds of users [44, 48, 49], thereby affecting a user's decision to engage with LBS providers and technologies. It is commonly acknowledged in LBS privacy literature that resolutions will seek consensus between issues of privacy, security, control, risk, and trust—all of which must be technologically supported.

16.3.4 Personal Safety and Physical Security

LBS applications are often justified as valid means of maintaining personal safety, ensuring physical security and generally avoiding dangerous circumstances, through solutions that can be utilized for managing emergencies, tracking children, monitoring individuals suffering from illness or disability, and preserving security in employment situations. Researchers have noted that safety and security efforts may be enhanced merely through knowledge of an individual's whereabouts [71, p. 94], offering *care* applications with notable advantages [61, p. 4].

16.3.5 Applications in the Marketplace

Devices and solutions that capitalize on these facilities have thus been developed, and are now commercially available for public use. They include GPS-enabled wristwatches, bracelets, and other wearable items [59, pp. 425–426], in addition to their supportive applications that enable remote viewing or monitoring of location (and other) information. Assistive applications are one such example, such as those technologies and solutions suited to the navigation requirements of vision impaired or blind individuals [75, p. 104 (example applications are described on pp. 104–105)].

Alternative applications deliver tracking capabilities as their primary function; an example is the Australian-owned Fleetfinder PT2 Personal Tracker, which is advertised as a device capable of safeguarding children, teenagers, and the elderly [64]. These devices and applications promise "live on-demand" tracking and "a solid sense of reassurance" [15], which may be appealing for parents, carers, and individuals interested in protecting others. Advertisements and product descriptions are often emotionally charged, taking advantage of an individual's (parent or carer) desire to maintain the safety and security of loved ones:

> Your child going missing is every parent's worst nightmare. Even if they've just wandered off to another part of the park the fear and panic is instant… [It] will help give you peace of mind and act as an extra set of eyes to look out for your child. It will also give them a little more freedom to play and explore safely [56].

16.3.6 Risks Versus Benefits of LBS Security and Safety Solutions

Despite such promotion and endorsement, numerous studies point to the dangers of LBS safety and security applications. Since their inception, individuals and users have voiced privacy concerns, which have been largely disregarded by proponents of the technology, chiefly vendors, given the (seemingly) voluntary nature of technology and device usage [6, p. 7]. The argument claiming technology adoption to be optional thereby placing the onus on the user is certainly weak and flawed, particularly given situations where an individual is incapable of making an informed decision regarding monitoring activities, supplementary to covert deployment options that may render monitoring activities obligatory. The consequences arising from covert monitoring are explored in [59] (refer to pp. 430–432 for implications of covert versus overt tracking of familiy member) and [1]. Covert and/or mandatory overt monitoring of minors and individuals suffering from illness is particularly problematic, raising doubt and questions in relation to the necessity of consent processes in addition to the suitability of tracking and what constitutes appropriate use.

In [59, p. 426] Mayer claims that there is a fine line between using tracking technologies, such as GPS, for safety purposes within the family context and improper use. Child tracking, for instance, has been described as a controversial area centered on the safety versus trust and privacy debate [77, p. 7]. However, the argument is not limited to issues of trust and privacy. Patel discusses the dynamics in the parent–child relationship and conveys a number of critical points in relation to wearable and embedded tracking technologies. In particular, Patel provides the legal perspective on child (*teenager*) monitoring [68, pp. 430–435] and other emergent issues or risks (notably linked to embedded monitoring solutions), which may be related to medical complications, psychological repercussions, and unintended or secondary use [68, pp. 444–455]. In Patel's article, these issues are offset by an explanation of the manner in which parental fears regarding child safety, some of which are unfounded, and the role of the media in publicizing cases of this nature, fuel parents' need for monitoring teenagers, whereas ultimately the decision to be monitored (according to the author), particularly using embedded devices, should ultimately lie with the teenager [68, pp. 437–442].

16.3.7   Safety of "Vulnerable" Individuals

Similarly, monitoring individuals with an illness or intellectual disability, such as a person with dementia wandering, raises a unique set of challenges in addition to the aforementioned concerns associated with consent, psychological issues, and misuse in the child or teenager tracking scenario. For instance, while dementia wandering and other similar applications are designed to facilitate the protection and security of individuals, they can concurrently be unethical in situations where reliability and responsiveness, amongst other factors, are in question [61, p. 7]. Based on a recent qualitative, focus group study seeking the attitudes of varied stakeholders in relation to the use of GPS for individuals with cognitive disabilities [54, p. 360], it was clear that this is an area fraught with indecisiveness as to the suitability of assistive technologies [54, p. 358]. The recommendations emerging from [54, pp. 361–364] indicate the need to "balance" safety with independence and privacy, to ensure that the individual suffering from dementia is involved in the decision to utilize tracking technologies, and that a consent process is in place, among other suggestions that are technical and devices related.

While much can be written about LBS applications in the personal safety and physical security categories, including their advantages and disadvantages, this discussion is limited to introductory material. Relevant to this chapter is the portrayal of the tensions arising from the use of solutions originally intended for protection and the resultant consequences, some of which are indeed inadvertent. That is, while the benefits of LBS are evident in their ability to maintain safety and security, they can indeed result in risks, such as the use of LBS for *cyber stalking* others. In establishing the need for LBS regulation, it is, therefore, necessary to appreciate that there will always be a struggle between benefits and risks relating to LBS implementation and adoption.

16.3.8   National Security

Safety and security debates are not restricted to family situations but may also incorporate, as [59, p. 437] indicates, *public safety* initiatives and considerations, amongst others, that can contribute to the decline in privacy. These schemes include national security, which has been regarded a priority area by various governments for over a decade. The Australian government affirms that the nation's security can be compromised or threatened through various acts of "espionage, foreign interference, terrorism, politically motivated violence, border violations, cyber attack, organised crime, natural disasters and biosecurity events" [7]. Accordingly, technological approaches and solutions have been proposed and implemented to support national security efforts in Australia, and globally. Positioning technologies, specifically, have been adopted as part of government defense and security strategies, a detailed examination of which can be found in [60], thus facilitating increased surveillance. Surveillance schemes have, therefore, emerged as a result of the perceived and real threats to national security promoted by governments [92, p. 389], and according to [63, p. 2] have been legitimized as a means of ensuring national security, thereby granting governments "extraordinary powers that never could have been justified previously" [71, p. 94]. In [20, p. 216], Cho maintains that the fundamental question is "which is the greater sin—to invade privacy or to maintain surveillance for security purposes?"

16.3.9 Proportionality: National Security Versus Individual Privacy

The central theme surfacing in relevant LBS scholarship is that of proportionality; that is, measuring the prospective security benefits against the impending privacy- and freedom-related concerns. For example, [71, pp. 95–96] proposes the privacy– security dichotomy, as means of illustrating the need for balance between an individual's privacy and a nation's security, where the privacy and security elements within the model contain subcomponents that collectively contribute to amplify risk in a given context. A key point to note in view of this discussion is that while the implementation of LBS may enhance security levels, this will inevitably come at the cost of privacy [71, pp. 95–96] and freedom [61, p. 9].

Furthermore, forsaking privacy corresponds to relinquishing personal freedom, a consequential cost of heightened security in threatening situations. Such circumstances weaken the effects of invasive techniques and increase, to some degree, individuals' tolerance to them [41, p. 12]. In particular, they "tilt the balance in favor of sacrificing personal freedom for the sake of public safety and security" [36, p. 50]. For example, Davis and Silver [35] report that the trade-off between civil liberties and privacy is often correlated with an individual's sense of threat. In reporting on a survey of Americans post the events of September 11, 2011, the authors conclude that civil liberties are often relinquished in favor of security in high-threat circumstances [35, p. 35], in that citizens are "willing to tolerate greater limits on civil liberties" [35, p. 74]. Similarly, in a dissertation centered on the social implications of auto-ID and LBS technologies, Tootell [86] presents the Privacy, Security, and Liberty Trichotomy, as a means of understanding the interaction between the three values [86: chapter 6]. Tootell concludes that a dominant value will always exist that is unique to each individual [86, pp. 162–163].

Furthermore, researchers such as Gould [45, p. 75] have found that while people are generally approving of enhanced surveillance, they simultaneously have uncertainties regarding government monitoring. From a government standpoint, there is a commonly held and weak view that if an individual has nothing to hide, then privacy is insignificant, an argument particularly popular in relation to state-based surveillance [81, p. 746]. However, this perspective has inherent flaws, as the right to privacy should not be narrowly perceived in terms of concealment of what would be considered unfavorable activities, discussed further by [81, pp. 764–772]. Furthermore, the "civil liberties vs. security trade-off has mainly been framed as one of protecting individual rights or civil liberties from the government as the government seeks to defend the country against a largely external enemy" [35, p. 29].

Wigan and Clarke state, in relation to national security, that "surveillance systems are being developed without any guiding philosophy that balances human rights against security concerns, and without standards or guidance in relation to social impact assessment, and privacy design features" [92, p. 400]. Solove [82, p. 362] agrees that a balance can be achieved between security and liberty, through oversight and control processes that restrict prospective uses of personal data. In the current climate, given the absence of such techniques, fears of an Orwellian society dominated by intense and excessive forms of surveillance materialize. However, Clarke [27, p. 39] proposes a set of "counterveillance" principles in response to extreme forms of surveillance introduced in the name of national security, which include:

> independent evaluation of technology; a moratorium on technology deployments; open information flows; justification of proposed measures; consultation and participation; evaluation; design principles; balance; independent controls; nymity and multiple identity; and rollback.

The absence of such principles creates a situation in which extremism reigns, producing a flow-on effect with potentially dire consequences in view of privacy, but also trust and control.

16.4 Solutions

16.4.1 Technological Solutions

In discussing technology and privacy in general, Krumm [52, p. 391] notes that computation-based mechanisms can be employed both to safeguard and to invade privacy. It is, therefore, valuable to distinguish between privacy-invasive technologies (PITs) and privacy-enhancing technologies (PETs). Clarke [23] examines the conflict between PITs and PETs, which are tools that can be employed to invade and protect privacy interests respectively. Technologies can invade privacy either deliberately as part of their primary purpose, or alternatively their invasive nature may emerge in secondary uses [23, 24, p. 209]. The aspects contributing to the privacy-invasive nature of location and tracking technologies or transactions include the awareness level of the individual, whether an individual has a choice, and the capability of performing an anonymous transaction amongst others [22]. In relation to LBS, [23] cites person-location and person-tracking systems as potential

PITs that require the implementation of countermeasures, which to-date have come in the form of PETs or "counter-PITs."

Existing studies suggest that the technological solutions (i.e., counter-PITs) available to address the LBS privacy challenge are chiefly concerned with degrading the ability to pinpoint location, or alternatively masking the identity of the user. For example, [62, p. 7] suggests that "[l]evels of privacy can be controlled by incorporating intelligent systems and customizing the amount of detail in a given geographic information system", thus enabling the ethical use of GPS tracking systems. Similarly, other authors present models that anonymize user identity through the use of pseudonyms [14], architectures and algorithms that decrease location resolution [46], and systems that introduce degrees of obfuscation [37]. Notably, scholars such as Duckham [37, p. 7] consider location privacy protection as involving multiple strategies, citing regulatory techniques and privacy policies as supplementary strategies to techniques that are more technological in nature, such as obfuscation.

16.4.2   Need for Additional Regulatory Responses

Clarke and Wigan [31] examine the threats posed by location and tracking technologies, particularly those relating to privacy, stating that "[t]hose technologies are now well-established, yet they lack a regulatory framework." A suitable regulatory framework for LBS (that addresses privacy amongst other social and ethical challenges) may be built on numerous approaches, including the technical approaches described in Sect. 16.4.1. Other approaches are explored by Xu et al. [95] in their quasi-experimental survey of privacy challenges relevant to push versus pull LBS. The approaches include compensation (incentives), industry self-regulation, and government regulation strategies [95, p. 143]. According to Xu et al., these "intervention strategies," may have an impact on the privacy calculus in LBS [95, pp. 136–137]. Notably, their survey of 528 participants found that self-regulation has a considerable bearing on perceived risk for both push and pull services, whereas perceived risks for compensation and government regulation strategies vary depending on types of services. That is, compensation increases perceived benefit in the push but not the pull model and, similarly, government regulation reduces perceived privacy risk in the push-based model [95, p. 158].

It should be acknowledged that a preliminary step in seeking a solution to the privacy dilemma, addressing the identified social concerns, and proposing appropriate regulatory responses is to clearly identify and assess the privacy-invasive elements of LBS in a given context- we have used Australia as an example in this instance. Possible techniques that can be employed to identify risks and implications, and consequently possible mitigation strategies, are a Privacy Impact

Assessment (PIA) or employing other novel models such as the framework of contextual integrity.

16.4.3 Privacy Impact Assessment (PIA)

A PIA can be defined as "a systematic process that identifies and evaluates, from the perspectives of all stakeholders, the potential effects on privacy of a project, initiative or proposed system or scheme, and includes a search for ways to avoid or mitigate negative privacy impacts" [29, 30]. The PIA tool, originally linked to technology and impact assessments [28, p. 125], is effectively a "risk management" technique that involves addressing both positive and negative impacts of a project or proposal, but with a greater focus on the latter [67, pp. 4–5].

PIAs were established and developed from 1995 to 2005, and possess a number of distinct qualities, some of which are that a PIA is focused on a particular initiative, takes a forward-looking and preventative as opposed to retrospective approach, broadly considers the various aspects of privacy (i.e., privacy of person, personal behavior, personal communication, and personal data), and is inclusive in that it accounts for the interests of relevant entities [28, pp. 124–125]. Regarding the Australian context, the development of PIAs in Australia can be observed in the work of Clarke [30] who provides an account of PIA maturity pre-2000, post-2000, and the situation in 2010.

16.4.4 Framework of Contextual Integrity

The framework of contextual integrity, introduced by [65], is an alternative approach that can be employed to assess whether LBS, as a socio-technical system, violates privacy and thus contextual integrity. An overview of the framework is provided in [65, p. 14]:

> The central claim is that contextual integrity captures the meaning of privacy in relation to personal information; predicts people's reactions to new technologies because it captures what we care about when we question, protest, and resist them; and finally, offers a way to carefully evaluate these disruptive technologies. In addition, the framework yields practical, step-by-step guidelines for evaluating systems in question, which it calls the CI Decision Heuristic and the Augmented CI Decision Heuristic.

According to Nissenbaum [65], the primary phases within the framework are: (1) *explanation*, which entails assessing a new system or practice in view of "context-relative informational norms" [65, p. 190], (2) *evaluation*, which involves "comparing altered flows in relation to those that were previously entrenched" [65, p. 190], and (3) *prescription*, a process based on evaluation, whereby if a system or practice is deemed "morally or politically problematic," it has grounds for resistance, redesign or being discarded [65, p. 191]. Within these phases are distinct stages: establish the prevailing context, determine key actors, ascertain what attributes are affected, establish changes in principles of transmission, and red flag, if there are modifications in actors, attributes, or principles of transmission [65, pp. 149–150].

The framework of contextual integrity and, similarly, PIAs are relevant to this study, and may be considered as valid tools for assessing the privacy-invasive or violating nature of LBS and justifying the need for some form of regulation. This is particularly pertinent as LBS present unique privacy challenges, given their reliance on knowing the location of the target. That is, the difficulty in maintaining location privacy is amplified due to the fact that m-commerce services and mobility in general, by nature, imply knowledge of the user's location and preferences [40, p. 463]. Therefore, it is likely that there will always be a trade-off ranging in severity. Namely, one end of the privacy continuum will demand that stringent privacy mechanisms be implemented, while the opposing end will support and justify increased surveillance practices.

16.5 Challenges

16.5.1 Relationship Between Privacy, Security, Control and Trust

A common thread in discussions relating to privacy and security implications of LBS throughout this chapter has been the interrelatedness of themes; notably, the manner in which a particular consideration is often at odds with other concerns. The trade-off between privacy/freedom and safety/security is a particularly prevalent exchange that must be considered in the use of many ICTs [36, p. 47]. In the case of LBS, it has been observed that the need for safety and security conflicts with privacy concerns, potentially resulting in contradictory outcomes depending on the nature of implementation. For example, while LBS facilitate security and timely assistance in emergency situations, they simultaneously have the potential to threaten privacy based on the ability for LBS to be employed in tracking and profiling situations [18, p. 105]. According to Casal [18, p. 109], the conflict between privacy and security, and lack of adequate regulatory frameworks, has a flow-on effect in that trust in ICTs is diminished. Trust is also affected in the family context, where tracking or monitoring activities result in lack of privacy between family members [59, p. 436]. The underlying question, according to Mayer [59, p. 435] is in relation to the power struggle between those seeking privacy versus those seeking information:

> What will be the impact within families as new technologies shift the balance of power between those looking for privacy and those seeking surveillance and information?

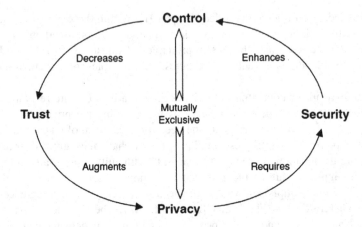

Fig. 16.1 Relationship between control, trust, privacy, and security, after [70, p. 14]

Mayer's [59] question alludes to the relevance of the theme of control, in that surveillance can be perceived as a form of control and influence. Therefore, it can be observed that inextricable linkages exist between several themes presented or alluded to throughout this chapter; notably privacy and security, but also the themes of control and trust. In summary, privacy protection requires security to be maintained, which in turn results in enhanced levels of control, leading to decreased levels of trust, which is a supplement to privacy [70, pp. 13–14]. The interrelatedness of themes is illustrated in Fig. 16.1.

It is thus evident that the idea of *balance* resurfaces, with the requirement to weigh multiple and competing themes and interests. This notion is not new with respect to location monitoring and tracking. For instance, Mayer [59, p. 437] notes, in the child tracking context, that there is the requirement to resolve numerous questions and challenges in a legal or regulatory sense, noting that "[t]he key is balancing one person's need for privacy with another person's need to know, but who will define this balancing point?" Issues of age, consent, and reciprocal monitoring are also significant. Existing studies on location disclosure amongst social relations afford the foundations for exploring the *social* and ethical challenges for LBS, whilst simultaneously appreciating *technical* considerations or factors. Refer to [5, 16, 32, 42, 43, 47, 62, 84, 87].

16.6 Conclusion

This chapter has provided an examination of privacy and security with respect to location-based services. There is a pressing need to ensure LBS privacy threats are not dismissed from a regulatory perspective. Doing so will introduce genuine dangers, such as psychological, social, cultural, scientific, economic, political, and democratic harm; dangers associated with profiling; increased visibility; publically damaging revelations; and oppression [31]. Additionally, the privacy considerations unique to the "locational or mobile dimension" require educating the general public regarding disclosure and increased transparency on the part of providers in relation to collection and use of location information [11, p. 15]. Thus, in response to the privacy challenges associated with LBS, and based on current scholarship, this research recognizes the need for technological solutions, in addition to commitment and adequate assessment or consideration at the social and regulatory levels. Specifically, the privacy debate involves contemplation of privacy policies and regulatory frameworks, in addition to technical approaches such as obfuscation and maintaining anonymity [37, p. 7]. That is, privacy-related technical solutions must also be allied with supportive public policy and socially acceptable regulatory structures.

For additional readings relevant to LBS and privacy, which include an adequate list of general references for further investigation, refer to [17] on privacy challenges relevant to privacy invasive geo-mash-ups, the inadequacy of information privacy laws and potential solutions in the form of technological solutions, social standards and legal frameworks; [12] report submitted to the Office of the Privacy Commissioner of Canada, focused on mobile surveillance, the privacy dangers, and legal consequences; and [57] report to the Canadian Privacy Commissioner dealing with complementary issues associated with mobility, location technologies, and privacy.

Table 16.1 Summary of solutions and techniques

Solution/Technique	Merits	Limitations
Technological mechanisms	• Provide location obfuscation and anonymity in required situations • Myriad of solutions available depending on level of privacy required • In-built mechanisms requiring limited user involvement • Unlike regulatory solutions, technological solutions encourage industry development	• Result in degradation in location quality/resolution
Regulatory mechanisms	• Variety of techniques available, such as industry self-regulation and government legislation • Can offer legal protection to individuals in defined situations/scenarios	• Can be limiting in terms of advancement of LBS industry
Impact assessments, contextual frameworks, and internal policies	• Provide proactive approach in identifying privacy (and related) risks • Used to develop suitable mitigation strategies • Preventative and inclusive in nature	• Tend to be skewed in focus, focusing primarily on negative implications • Can be limiting in terms of advancement of LBS industry

Based on the literature presented throughout this chapter, a valid starting point in determining the privacy-invasive nature of specific LBS applications is to review and employ the available solution(s). These solutions or techniques are summarized in Table 16.1, in terms of the merits and benefits of each approach and the extent to which they offer means of overcoming or mitigating privacy-related risks. The selection of a particular technique is dependent on the context or situation in question. Once the risks are identified it is then possible to develop and select an appropriate mitigation strategy to reduce or prevent the negative implications of utilizing certain LBS applications. This chapter is intended to provide a review of scholarship in relation to LBS privacy and security, and should be used as the basis for future research into the LBS privacy dilemma, and related regulatory debate.

References

1. Abbas R, Michael K, Michael MG, Aloudat A (2011) Emerging forms of covert surveillance using GPS-enabled devices. J Cases Inf Technol (JCIT) 13(2):19–33
2. Aloudat A (2012) 'Privacy Vs Security in national emergencies. IEEE Technol Soc Mag Spring 2012:50–55
3. ALRC 2008 (2012) For your information: Australian privacy law and practice (Alrc Report 108). http://www.alrc.gov.au/publications/report-108. Accessed 12 Jan 2012
4. Andrejevic M (2007) Ispy: Surveillance and Power in the Interactive Era. University Press of Kansas, Lawrence
5. Anthony D, Kotz D, Henderson T (2007) Privacy in location-aware computing environments. Pervas Comput 6(4):64–72
6. Applewhite A (2002) What knows where you are? Personal safety in the early days of wireless. Pervas Comput 3(12):4–8
7. Attorney General's Department (2012) Telecommunications interception and surveillance. http://www.ag.gov.au/Telecommunicationsinterceptionandsurveillance/Pages/default.aspx. Accessed 20 Jan 2012
8. Awad NF, Krishnan MS (2006) The personalization privacy paradox: an empirical evaluation of information transparency and the willingness to be profiled online for personalization. MIS Q 30(1):13–28
9. Ayres G, Mehmood R (2010) Locpris: a security and privacy preserving location based services development framework. In: Setchi R, Jordanov I, Howlett R, Jain L (eds) Knowledge-based and intelligent information and engineering systems, vol 6279, pp 566–575
10. Bauer HH, Barnes SJ, Reichardt T, Neumann MM (2005) Driving the consumer acceptance of mobile marketing: a theoretical framework and empirical study. J Electron Commer Res 6 (3):181–192
11. Bennett CJ (2006) The mobility of surveillance: challenges for the theory and practice of privacy protection. In: Paper prepared for the 2006 Meeting of the international communications association, Dresden Germany, June 2006, pp 1–20
12. Bennett CJ, Crowe L (2005) Location-based services and the surveillance of mobility: an analysis of privacy risks in Canada. A report to the Office of the Privacy Commissioner of Canada, under the 200405 Contributions Program, June 2005. http://www.colinbennett.ca/recent-publications/reports-2/
13. Bennett CJ, Grant R (1999) Introduction. In: Bennett CJ, Grant R (eds) Visions of privacy: policy choices for the digital age. University of Toronto Press, Toronto, pp 3–16

14. Beresford AR, Stajano F (2004) Mix zones: user privacy in location-aware services. In: Proceedings of the Second IEEE Annual conference on pervasive computing and communications workshops (PERCOMW'04) pp 127–131
15. Brickhouse Security (2012) Lok8u GPS Child Locator. http://www.brickhousesecurity.com/child-locator.html. Accessed 9 Feb 2012
16. Brown B, Taylor AS, Izadi S, Sellen A, Kaye J, Eardley R (2007) Locating family values: a field trial of the whereabouts clock. In: UbiComp '07 Proceedings of the 9th international conference on Ubiquitous computing, pp 354–371
17. Burdon M (2010) Privacy invasive geo-mashups : Privacy 2.0 and the limits of first generation information privacy laws. Univ Illinois J Law Technol Policy (1):1–50
18. Casal CR (2004) Impact of location-aware services on the privacy/security balance. Info: J Policy Regul Strategy Telecommun Inf Media 6(2):105–111
19. Chen JV, Ross W, Huang SF (2008) Privacy, trust, and justice considerations for location-based mobile telecommunication services. Info 10(4):30–45
20. Cho G (2005) Geographic information science: mastering the legal issues. Wiley, Hoboken
21. Clarke R (1997) Introduction to dataveillance and information privacy, and definitions of terms. http://www.anu.edu.au/people/Roger.Clarke/DV/Intro.html
22. Clarke R (1999) Relevant characteristics of person-location and person-tracking technologies. http://www.rogerclarke.com/DV/PLTApp.html
23. Clarke R (2001a) Introducing PITs and PETs: technologies affecting privacy. http://www.rogerclarke.com/DV/PITsPETs.html
24. Clarke R (2001) Person location and person tracking—technologies, risks and policy implications. Inf Technol People 14(2):206–231
25. Clarke R (2003b) Privacy on the move: the impacts of mobile technologies on consumers and citizens. http://www.anu.edu.au/people/Roger.Clarke/DV/MPrivacy.html
26. Clarke R (2006) What's 'Privacy'? http://www.rogerclarke.com/DV/Privacy.html
27. Clarke R (2007a) Chapter 3. What 'Uberveillance' is and what to do about it. In: Michael K, Michael MG (eds) The Second workshop on the social implications of national security (from Dataveillance to Uberveillance and the Realpolitik of the Transparent Society). University of Wollongong, IP Location-Based Services Research Program (Faculty of Informatics) and Centre for Transnational Crime Prevention (Faculty of Law), Wollongong, Australia, pp 27–46
28. Clarke R (2009) Privacy impact assessment: its origins and development. Comput Law Secur Rev 25(2):123–135
29. Clarke R (2010a) An evaluation of privacy impact assessment guidance documents. http://www.rogerclarke.com/DV/PIAG-Eval.html
30. Clarke R (2010b) Pias in Australia—A work-in-progress report. http://www.rogerclarke.com/DV/PIAsAust-11.html
31. Clarke R, Wigan M (2011) You are where you've been: the privacy implications of location and tracking technologies. http://www.rogerclarke.com/DV/YAWYB-CWP.html
32. Consolvo S, Smith IE, Matthews T, LaMarca A, Tabert J, Powledge P (2005) Location disclosure to social relations: why, when, & what people want to share. In: CHI 2005(April), pp 2–7, Portland, Oregon, USA, pp. 81–90
33. Culnan MJ, Bies RJ (2003) Consumer privacy: balancing economic and justice considerations. J Soc Issues 59(2):323–342
34. Damiani ML, Bertino E, Perlasca P (2007) Data security in location-aware applications: an approach based on Rbac. Int. J. Inf Comput Secur 1(1/2):5–38
35. Davis DW, Silver BD (2004) Civil Liberties Vs. Security: public opinion in the context of the terrorist attacks on America. Am J Polit Sci 48(1):28–46
36. Dobson JE, Fisher PF (2003) Geoslavery. IEEE Technol Soc Mag 22(1):47–52
37. Duckham M (2008) Location privacy protection through spatial information hiding. http://www.privacy.vic.gov.au/privacy/web2.nsf/files/20th-meeting-16-july-2008-duckham-presentation/$file/pvn_07_08_duckham.pdf

38. Duckham M (2010) Moving forward: location privacy and location awareness. In: SPRINGL'10 November 2, 2010, San Jose, CA, USA, pp 1–3
39. Duckham M, Kulik L (2006) Chapter 3. location privacy and location-aware computing. In: Drummond J, Billen R, Forrest D, Joao E (eds) Dynamic and Mobile Gis: investigating change in space and time. CRC Press, Boca Raton, pp 1–20. http://www.geosensor.net/papers/duckham06.IGIS.pdf
40. Elliot G, Phillips N (2004) Mobile commerce and wireless computing systems. Pearson Education Limited, Great Britain 532 pp
41. FIDIS 2007, D11.5: The legal framework for location-based services in Europe. http://www.fidis.net/
42. Fusco SJ, Michael K, Aloudat A, Abbas R (2011) Monitoring people using location-based social networking and its negative impact on trust: an exploratory contextual analysis of five types of "Friend" Relationships. In: IEEE symposium on technology and society (ISTAS11), Illinois, Chicago, IEEE 2011
43. Fusco SJ, Michael K, Michael MG, Abbas R (2010) Exploring the social implications of location based social networking: an inquiry into the perceived positive and negative impacts of using LBSN between friends. In: 9th international conference on mobile business (ICMB2010), Athens, Greece, IEEE, pp 230–237
44. Giaglis GM, Kourouthanassis P, Tsamakos A (2003) Chapter IV. Towards a classification framework for mobile location-based services. In: Mennecke BE, Strader TJ (eds) Mobile commerce: technology, theory and applications. Idea Group Publishing, Hershey, US, pp 67–85
45. Gould JB (2002) Playing with fire: the civil liberties implications of September 11th. In: Public Administration Review, 62 (Special Issue: Democratic Governance in the Aftermath of September 11, 2001), pp 74–79
46. Gruteser M, Grunwald D (2003) Anonymous usage of location-based services through spatial and temporal cloaking. In: ACM/USENIX international conference on mobile systems, applications and services (MobiSys), pp 31–42
47. Iqbal MU, Lim S (2007) Chapter 16. Privacy implications of automated GPS tracking and profiling. In: Michael K, Michael MG (eds) From Dataveillance to Überveillance and the Realpolitik of the Transparent Society (Workshop on the Social Implications of National Security, 2007) University of Wollongong, IP Location-Based Services Research Program (Faculty of Informatics) and Centre for Transnational Crime Prevention (Faculty of Law), Wollongong, pp 225–240
48. Jorns O, Quirchmayr G (2010) Trust and privacy in location-based services. Elektrotechnik & Informationstechnik 127(5):151–155
49. Junglas I, Spitzmüller C (2005) A research model for studying privacy concerns pertaining to location-based services. In: Proceedings of the 38th Hawaii international conference on system sciences, pp 1–10
50. Kaasinen E (2003) User acceptance of location-aware mobile guides based on seven field studies. Behav Inf Technol 24(1):37–49
51. Kaupins G, Minch R (2005) Legal and ethical implications of employee location monitoring. In: Proceedings of the 38th Hawaii international conference on system sciences, pp 1–10
52. Krumm J (2008) A survey of computational location privacy. Pers Ubiquit Comput 13 (6):391–399
53. Küpper A, Treu G (2010) Next generation location-based services: merging positioning and web 2.0. In: Yang LT, Waluyo AB, Ma J, Tan L, Srinivasan B (eds) Mobile intelligence. Wiley Inc, Hoboken, pp 213–236
54. Landau R, Werner S (2012) Ethical aspects of using GPS for tracking people with dementia: recommendations for practice. Int Psychogeriatr 24(3):358–366
55. Leppäniemi M, Karjaluoto H (2005) Factors influencing consumers' willingness to accept mobile advertising: a conceptual model. Int. J Mobile Commun 3(3):197–213
56. Loc8tor Ltd. 2011 (2012), Loc8tor Plus. http://www.loc8tor.com/childcare/. Accessed 9 Feb 2012

57. Lyon D, Marmura S, Peroff P (2005) Location technologies: mobility, surveillance and privacy (a Report to the Office of the Privacy Commissioner of Canada under the Contributions Program). The Surveillance Project, Queens Univeristy, Canada. www.sscqueens.org/sites/default/files/loctech.pdf

58. Mason RO (1986) Four ethcial challenges in the information age. MIS Q 10(1):4–12

59. Mayer RN (2003) Technology, families, and privacy: can we know too much about our loved ones? J Consum Policy 26:419–439

60. Michael K, Masters A (2006) The advancement of positioning technologies in defense intelligence. In: Abbass H, Essam D (eds) Applications of information systems to homeland security and defense. Idea Publishing Group, United States, pp 196–220

61. Michael K, McNamee A, Michael MG (2006) The emerging ethics of humancentric GPS tracking and monitoring. International conference on mobile business. IEEE Computer Society, Copenhagen, Denmark, pp 1–10

62. Michael K, McNamee A, Michael MG, Tootell H (2006) Location-based intelligence—modeling behavior in humans using GPS. IEEE international symposium on technology and society. IEEE, New York, United States, pp 1–8

63. Michael K, Clarke R (2012) Location privacy under dire threat as Uberveillance stalks the streets. In: Precedent (Focus on Privacy/FOI), vol 108, pp 1–8 (online version) & 24–29 (original article). http://works.bepress.com/kmichael/245/

64. Neltronics 2012 (2012) Fleetfinder Pt2 Personal Tracker. http://www.fleetminder.com.au/gps-systems/fleetfinder+PT2. Accessed 9 Feb 2012

65. Nissenbaum H (2010) Privacy in context: technology, policy, and the integrity of social life. Stanford Law Books, Stanford 288 pp

66. O'Connor PJ, Godar SH (2003) Chapter XIII. We know where you are: the ethics of LBS advertising. In: Mennecke BE, Strader TJ (eds) Mobile commerce: technology, theory and applications. Idea Group Publishing, Hershey, pp 245–261

67. Office of the Victorian Privacy Commissioner 2009 (2010) Privacy impact assessments: a single guide for the victorian public sector. www.privacy.vic.gov.au/privacy/web.nsf/content/guidelines. Accessed 3 March 2010

68. Patel DP (2004) Should teenagers get Lojackedt against their will? An argument for the ratification of the United Nations convention on the rights of the child. Howard L J 47(2):429–470

69. Perusco L, Michael K (2005) Humancentric applications of precise location based services. IEEE international conference on e-business engineering. IEEE Computer Society, Beijing, China, pp 409–418

70. Perusco L, Michael K (2007) Control, trust, privacy, and security: evaluating location-based services. IEEE Technol Soc Mag 26(1):4–16

71. Perusco L, Michael K, Michael MG (2006) Location-based services and the privacy-security dichotomy. In: Proceedings of the 3rd international conference on mobile computing and ubiquitous networking, London, UK. Information Processing Society of Japan, pp. 91–98

72. Privacy International 2007, Overview of Privacy. www.privacyinternational.org/article.shtml?cmd[347]=x-347-559062. Accessed 3 Dec 2009

73. Quinn MJ (2006) Ethics for the information age, 2nd edn. Pearson/Addison-Wesley, Boston 484 pp

74. Raab CD (1999) Chapter 3. From balancing to steering: new directions for data protection. In: Bennett CJ, Grant R (eds) Visions of privacy: policy choices for the digital age. University of Toronto Press, Toronto, pp 68–93

75. Raper J, Gartner G, Karimi HA, Rizos C (2007) Applications of location-based services: a selected review. J Locat Based Serv 1(2):89–111

76. Richards NM, Solove DJ (2007) Privacy's other path: recovering the law of confidentiality. Georgetown Law J 96:123–182

77. Schreiner K (2007) Where We At? Mobile phones bring GPS to the masses. IEEE Comput Graph Appl 2007:6–11

78. Sheng H, Fui-Hoon Nah F, Siau K (2008) An experimental study on ubiquitous commerce adoption: impact of personalization and privacy concerns. J Assoc Inf Syst 9(6):344–376

79. Smith GD (2006) Private eyes are watching you: with the implementation of the E-911 Mandate, Who will watch every move you make? Federal Commun Law J 58:705–726

80. Solove DJ (2006) A taxonomy of privacy. Univ Pennsylvania Law Rev 154(3):477–557

81. Solove DJ (2007) I've Got Nothing to Hide' and other misunderstandings of privacy. San Diego Law Rev 44:745–772

82. Solove DJ (2008) Data mining and the security-liberty debate. Univ Chicago Law Rev 74:343–362

83. Steinfield C (2004) The development of location based services in mobile commerce. In: Priessl B, Bouwman H, Steinfield C (eds) Elife after the Dot.Com Bust. www.msu.edu/~steinfie/elifelbschap.pdf, pp 1–15

84. Tang KO, Lin J, Hong J, Siewiorek DP, Sadeh N (2010) Rethinking location sharing: exploring the implications of social-driven vs. purpose-driven location sharing. In: UbiComp 2010, Sep 26–Sep 29, Copenhagen, Denmark, pp 1–10

85. Tatli EI, Stegemann D, Lucks S (2005) Security challenges of location-aware mobile business. In: The Second IEEE international workshop on mobile commerce and services, 2005. WMCS '05, pp 1–10

86. Tootell H (2007) The social impact of using automatic identification technologies and location-based services in national security. PhD Thesis, School of Information Systems and Technology, Informatics, University of Wollongong

87. Tsai JY, Kelley PG, Drielsma PH, Cranor LF, Hong J, Sadeh N (2009) Who's Viewed You? the impact of feedback in a mobile location-sharing application. In: CHI 2009, April 3–9, 2009, Boston, Massachusetts, USA, pp 1–10

88. Wang S, Min J, Yi BK (2008) Location based services for mobiles: technologies and standards (Presentation). In: IEEE ICC 2008, Beijing, pp 1–123

89. Warren S, Brandeis L (1890) The right to privacy. Harvard Law Rev 4:193–220

90. Westin AF (1967) Privacy and freedom. Atheneum, New York 487 pp

91. Westin AF (2003) Social and political dimensions of privacy. J Social Issues 59(2):431–453

92. Wigan M, Clarke R (2006) Social impacts of transport surveillance. Prometheus 24(4):389–403

93. Wright T (2004) 'Security. Privacy and Anonymity', crossroads 11:1–8

94. Xu H, Luo X, Carroll JM, Rosson MB (2011) The personalization privacy paradox: an exploratory study of decision making process for location-aware marketing. Decis Support Syst 51(2011):42–52

95. Xu H, Teo HH, Tan BYC, Agarwal R (2009) The role of push-pull technology in privacy calculus: the case of location-based services. J Manage Inf Syst 26(3):135–173

Index

© Springer International Publishing Switzerland 2015
S. Zeadally and M. Badra (eds.), *Privacy in a Digital, Networked World*,
Computer Communications and Networks,
DOI 10.1007/978-3-319-08470-1

Printed in the United States
By Bookmasters